A Companion to the
VICTORIAN NOVEL

A Companion to the
VICTORIAN NOVEL

Edited by
William Baker and
Kenneth Womack

GREENWOOD PRESS
Westport, Connecticut • London

Library of Congress Cataloging-in-Publication Data

A companion to the Victorian novel / edited by William Baker and Kenneth Womack.
    p.   cm.
    Includes bibliographical references and index.
    ISBN 0–313–31407–1 (alk. paper)
    1. English fiction—19th century—History and criticism—Handbooks, manuals, etc.
    I. Baker, William, 1944–   II. Womack, Kenneth.
    PR871.C64   2002
    823′.809—dc21   2001042326

British Library Cataloguing in Publication Data is available.

Library of Congress Catalog Card Number: 2001042326
ISBN: 0–313–31407–1

First published in 2002

Greenwood Press, 88 Post Road West, Westport, CT 06881
An imprint of Greenwood Publishing Group, Inc.
www.greenwood.com

Printed in the United States of America

The paper used in this book complies with the
Permanent Paper Standard issued by the National
Information Standards Organization (Z39.48–1984).

10 9 8 7 6 5 4 3 2 1

Contents

Acknowledgments

Compiling a work of this nature requires the generous contributions of a variety of individuals. We are particularly grateful to Carole Bookhamer and Matt Masucci for their assistance in seeing our manuscript through its various stages of production. We would like to extend our warmest thanks to Kate Latterell's Spring 2001 seminar on the "Editorial Process" for their efforts on behalf of this volume. As always, we would like to thank George Butler, Senior Editor of Academic and Trade Publishing, Lori Ewen, Production Editor, and the editorial staff of Greenwood Press for their encouragement and guidance on behalf of our project.

William Baker would like to thank his colleagues in the Department of English and University Libraries at Northern Illinois University for granting him release time from teaching and other duties. Kenneth Womack would like to extend thanks to Kjell Meling, Associate Dean and Director of Academic Affairs, and the Altoona College Advisory Board for their assistance in the form of a course-load reduction.

Preface

In this reference work, a number of distinguished international scholars representing eclectic perspectives and different generations collaborate on an introductory guide to the Victorian novel, particularly in terms of the genre's historical and cultural implications. The chapters in *A Companion to the Victorian Novel* offer fresh accounts of past, current, and new directions in our understanding of nineteenth-century fiction and its prodigious literary and cultural influence.

Deliberately flexible and self-consciously protean, *A Companion to the Victorian Novel* is divided into five sections. The first section, "Victorian Literary Contexts," focuses upon the emergence of the Victorian novel and its literary precursors, with particular emphasis upon the growth of serialization and the development of novel syndication. In addition to addressing the evolution of the Victorian literary marketplace, the chapters in this section discuss the role of illustration in nineteenth-century fiction and the nature and scope of Victorian literacy.

The second section, "Victorian Cultural Contexts," features chapters that explore a host of significant sociological and cultural facets of nineteenth-century British literature. Particular attention is devoted to the ways in which these cultural nuances ultimately shaped the course of Victorian fiction. The chapters in this section also investigate various political, religious, philosophical, and scientific aspects of the Victorian novel.

The third section, "Victorian Genres," includes chapters that examine the principal features of each genre, in addition to offering representative examples of each literary discipline. This section provides general introductions to Victorian ghost stories, the Gothic novel, detective fiction, the social problem novel, the sensation novel, juvenilia, and the contemporary film adaptation of nineteenth-century fiction.

The chapters in the fourth section, "Major Authors of the Victorian Era," provide a valuable introduction to many of the period's most significant voices. Each chapter affords attention to the author's biographical and literary life, with special emphasis upon the author's critical reception and his or her major works. This section features chapters devoted to the Brontës, Charles Dickens, George Eliot, Thomas Hardy, William Makepeace Thackeray, Anthony Trollope, George Meredith, Elizabeth Gaskell, and Wilkie Collins.

The chapters in the fifth section, "Contemporary Critical Approaches to the Victorian Novel," offer an overview of various aspects of critical theory and discuss their application to the study of nineteenth-century fiction. In addition to chapters that examine the significance of postcolonialism and feminist criticism to the study of the Victorian novel, this section includes chapters that explore such issues as multiculturalism, aesthetic criticism, mythology, Biblical criticism, and psychological criticism. Each chapter in *A Companion to the Victorian Novel* is followed by a listing of selected works for further reading.

I
Victorian Literary Contexts

The Victorian Novel Emerges, 1800–1840

Ian Duncan

Looking back from the brink of World War I, the great critic George Saintsbury viewed the Victorian novel as one of the splendors of English literature, comparable with the Elizabethan-Jacobean drama or Romantic poetry. Yet more admirable than the Victorians themselves, Saintsbury implies, are the novelists of an earlier generation:

> Scott, like Miss Austen, at once opened an immense new field to the novelist, and showed how that field was to be cultivated. The complement-contrast of the pair can need emphasizing only to those on whom no emphasis would be likely to impress it: but it may not be quite so evident at once that between them they cover almost the entire possible ground of prose fiction. (210)

"Scott and Miss Austen" constitute a virtual, archetypal totality, larger than their individual achievements in domestic realism or historical romance—larger, perhaps, than the achievement of anyone who came later. Together they form the "complementary antithesis" that was needed to bring the novel to its dialectical completion. They won the empire that the Victorians merely colonized.

Most modern histories of British fiction, from F. R. Leavis to Nancy Armstrong, have collapsed Saintsbury's "complementary antithesis" in favor of a main tradition of Austenian domestic realism, leaving Scott and historical romance to wilt on the side. The account that finds Austen defining an authentically modern kind of narrative belongs to the twentieth century, however, and is somewhat at odds with Victorian reception history. Although individual titles were reprinted in Bentley's *Standard Novels* series in the 1830s, Austen's works did not achieve wide popularity until after the publication of J. E. Austen-Leigh's memoir of his aunt in 1870, and a collected edition did not appear until 1882. Long before the *fin-de-siècle* phenomenon of the "Janeites," Austen had been admired by discerning readers, especially other authors (beginning with Scott himself). Even there the record is mixed: Urged to read Austen by G. H. Lewes, Charlotte Brontë complained of a lack of passion or feeling for nature. In contrast, Mary Russell Mitford paid homage to "Miss Austen's delicious novels" at the beginning of *Our Village* (1824), a work that remained popular throughout the century. But Mitford softens Austen's irony to cozy sentiment, converts her "three or four families in a country village" into a bourgeois idyll, and in general anticipates the later Victorian and Modern cult of "Jane." It is Mitford's example, rather than Austen's, that Elizabeth Gaskell transfigures in *Cranford* (1853), the first of the notable mid-Victorian fictions of "provincial life."

Austen's incomparably subtle technique was not lost, all the same, on a range of Victorian writers, including the exponents of provincial life. They learned much from her: the ironical control of narrative via free indirect discourse, the discrimination of character through speech and manners, the lucid assumption of a social habitus from the inside. Margaret Oliphant (author of an 1870 *Blackwood's* essay comparing "Miss Austen and Miss Mitford") brilliantly rewrites *Emma* in *Miss Marjoribanks*, one of her "Chronicles of Carlingford" (1866); George Eliot undertakes a philosophical enlargement of the Austenian theme of "moral stupidity" in her great study of provincial life, *Middlemarch* (1872), and pits updated versions of the Austen domestic novel and the Scott historical romance against one another (installing the opposition Saintsbury will take for granted) in *Daniel Deronda* (1876). Leavis's "Great Tradition" is not entirely a critic's fabrication—or only so in what it excludes. Meanwhile, novelists up to the present day have continued to find in Austen a rich technical and moral resource.

The temporal structure of this influence clarifies Austen's achievement in the history of the novel: Rather than originate a new kind, she refined a prior tradition, realizing the potential for perfection in any genre. The tradition in question was the female *Bildungsroman*, or narrative of "a young lady's entry into the world," developed in the eighteenth century by Samuel Richardson and Frances Burney. The satiric comedy of gentry and bourgeois manners mediates the heroine's recognition of a proper marriage partner as well as, in some cases, her self-reformation; and Richardson's *Sir Charles Grandison* (1754) pioneered what would become a central moral topic of Victorian fiction, the middle-class reconstruction of the gentleman. Austen's contribution was to insist on the disciplinary extension of the heroine's insight to her own folly or blindness: a significant turn, since heroines elsewhere had tended to be paragons, providing, for example, George Eliot with the ethical structure of her later fiction.

Meanwhile the persistence of the female *Bildungsroman*, the renovation of its basic plot and tropes throughout the nineteenth century, testifies to its cultural force as well as to the variety of practitioners. Nancy Armstrong credits the domestic novel with nothing less than the invention of modern, middle-class subjectivity: private, self-regulating, committed to literacy-based modes of cognition and discrimination. The genre had been flexible enough to be taken up by writers of all parties in the French Revolution controversy, for whom it posed the vexed foundation of politics upon private life and relations within the family. Sentiment, duty, women's rights, and the authority of fathers were its contentious themes. Austen's refusal of an overt didacticism for a subtler pedagogy of manners expresses, at the time, her conservatism, although the critical reading she initiates can serve radical ends. Elsewhere the genre's conduct-book origins remain (or become newly) conspicuous, as it is infused with new ideological currents such as evangelical Presbyterianism (Mary Brunton, Susan Ferrier) or liberal reformism (Maria Edgeworth).

The didactic version of domestic fiction would remain a strong tradition well into the Victorian period, especially in association with the dissenting and radical journalism that flourished after the 1832 Reform Act. New periodicals, aimed at middle-class and even working-class readers, carried fiction in aid of social-reformist causes, and they proved especially hospitable to women writers, who were able to engage in public debate under the cloak of journalistic anonymity. A number of notable Victorian careers began in this milieu. Harriet Martineau wrote for *Tait's Edinburgh Magazine* (effectively edited by a woman novelist, Christian Isobel Johnstone) in the early 1830s. Best known for her social criticism, Martineau made an unconvincing attempt at the domestic novel in *Deerbrook* (1839) and achieved considerable success with *Illustrations of Political Economy* (1832–35), a series of exemplary fables aimed at juvenile and working-class readers. *Illustrations of Political Economy* developed a genre pioneered earlier in the century by Maria Edgeworth (*The Parent's Assistant* [1796]; *Moral Tales for Young People* [1801]; *Popular Tales* [1804]) and by the conservative and evangelical Hannah More, who published homiletic tales in cheap tracts and chapbooks so as to reach a working-class public. This kind of explicitly didactic fiction—written for children, the poor, and colonial subjects—and distributed by mainstream publishers as well as evangelical and missionary societies, would constitute a substantial part of the nineteenth-century publishing industry.

The huge international popularity of Scott's Waverley novels and the fame of their author, lasting from his lifetime through the early twentieth century, inaugurated a recognizably "Victorian" profile of the successful novelist: voluminous output, vast but unstable profits, the dignity of a civic monument. Any account of the nineteenth-century novel (and not only in Great Britain) must recognize Scott's overwhelming ubiquity and influence, from the cultural constitution of "literature," including the social status of the novel and the author, through epochal innovations in subject matter and technique, to the material conditions of publishing and marketing.

From the start Scott's success mobilized a horde of imitators and rivals. Literal imitations constitute the least interesting of consequences, although historical fiction, the genre defined by Scott, would retain its prestige throughout the century. The historical novelists who flooded the market in the 1830s, G.P.R. James and Harrison Ainsworth among them, took after Scott's more fantastic romances with medieval or Tudor settings *(Ivanhoe, Kenilworth)*, exaggerating their Gothic sensationalism, rather than the Scottish novels with their greater social realism. The more ambitious novelists defined themselves against Scott, as rivals rather than followers, both in his lifetime and afterwards. Indeed, all the major Victorian novelists felt obliged to reckon with Scott in one way or another, whether they rejected Scott's example (as Emily Brontë subverts Scott's regional dynastic romance in *Wuthering Heights* [1847] and Charlotte Brontë rewrites the mad-wife scenario of *The Bride of Lammermoor* in *Jane Eyre* [1847]) or absorbed and transmuted it (George Eliot, relocating history upon a Wordsworthian as well as Austenian ground of the domestic affections in *Middlemarch*).

Scott's influence was as decisive for historiography as for historical fiction, again with important consequences for the novel. If Macaulay cheerfully acknowledged a debt to Scott, Thomas Carlyle's early masterpieces enact a strenuous refusal of Scott's cultural authority, amounting to a rejection of the novel (and what Clifford Siskin calls "novelism") as such, in the decade when popular imitations thronged the market. *Sartor Resartus* (1834) dismantles the narrative complex of history, fiction, *Bildung*, and national character set in place by Scott; *The French Revolution* (1837) reconstructs a radically antinovelistic, anti-Enlightenment, epic, and romantic mode of history. After Carlyle, the novelists could no longer take history for granted. When they turned to historical fiction, it was with deliberation, as to a virtuoso performance, a show of prowess, in the genre Scott had raised to classical status. Charles Dickens, jealous of Scott's achievement but temperamentally closer to Carlyle, contracted to write a three-volume historical romance at the very beginning of his career (1836); when *Barnaby Rudge* finally appeared in weekly parts (1841), it drew on Carlyle to stage an apocalyptic quarrel with Scott. Two decades later Dickens addressed Carlyle's revolutionary theme in *A Tale of Two Cities* (1859), only to produce a work more thoroughly compromised by the novelistic conventions defined by Scott. Thackeray marked his essay in the three-volume historical novel as a pastiche, down to a facsimile of period typeface, in the consummate "tale of the eighteenth century" *Henry Esmond* (1852); this followed his more original "Novel Without a Hero" (the very phrase extending a Scott topos) *Vanity Fair* (1848), a historical novel of domestic life set in Scott's own period. George Eliot embarked on the "epic" phase of her career, in the manner of Virgil or Milton, by laboriously researching Renaissance Florence in order to write *Romola* (1863).

The end of the century brought a revival of the Scottish historical fiction associated with Scott's earlier career, in the tales of Robert Louis Stevenson and a generation of followers (S. R. Crockett, Neil Munro, Violet Jacob, John Buchan). The serialization of Stevenson's *Kidnapped* in *Young Folks* (1886) points to the late-century descent of the Waverley novels (in Leslie Stephen's phrase) "from the library to the school-room" and the proliferation of genres besides historical fiction that flowed out of Scott. The imperial romance or adventure story, designated for "big and little boys" in H. Rider Haggard's *King Solomon's Mines* (1885), adapted Scott's fable of the young Englishman's journey to a wild colonial frontier by replacing the Highlands of Scotland with a far remoter, more primitive and dangerous hinterland—central Africa, Tibet, the Amazon. The genealogy of imperial adventure also comprises the naval romances and serials of Frederick Marryat and Michael Scott (no relation) in the late 1820s and 1830s, which harked back to the heroic era of the Napoleonic wars through the revived medium of eighteenth-century picaresque.

Fiction with Scottish settings also flourished thanks largely to Scott, although the ironical Ayrshire chronicles of John Galt—written to contest Scott's example—inspired a more sentimental tradition of Scottish idylls at the end of the century in the so-called "Kailyard" school. (Gaskell's *Cranford* owes much to Galt's *Annals of the Parish* [1821], including the depiction of an encroaching modern economy.) Even where he was not their originator, Scott's popularity was such that genres and conventions were transformed through his practice or reshaped by other writers in response to his gravitational pull. Edgeworth had pioneered regional and national fiction in her Irish tales—inventing, in *Castle Rackrent* (1800), not just the regional comedy of manners but the ironically naïve narrator, in this case the family retainer, imitated by Wilkie Collins in *The Moonstone* (1868) and Stevenson in *The Master of Ballantrae* (1889). Sydney Owenson romanticized the genre in *The Wild Irish Girl*

(1806), introducing the plot of a jaded English hero who travels to the Irish hinterland and falls in love with a dispossessed local heiress; their marriage allegorizes a cultural renewal of the nation through the enlightened union between metropolitan center and Celtic fringe. Edgeworth took up the plot in her later Irish tales, and Scott adapted it in *Waverley* (1814), for a decisively historical narrative of the production of modernity as a complex set of sociological and psychological transformations. Subsequent Irish authors would respond to Scott's Scottish reworking, as well as to the Irish originals, with Gothic disruptions of the plot of historical emergence, from C. R. Maturin through Sheridan LeFanu.

The influence of *Waverley* and its successors was epochal beyond particular genres, including the historical novel, which, as Lukács argues, receded to the status of a "special genre" under the ascendancy of the Victorian social novel. The great achievements of the late 1840s can be read as successful renovations of Scott's historical romance, addressing its representation of modernity to a modern setting. *Vanity Fair* and the Brontës have already been mentioned; turning away from the past, Dickens assimilated Scott's romance techniques in *Dombey and Son* (1848); and reviewers hailed Gaskell's *Mary Barton: A Tale of Manchester Life* (1848) as a polemical adaptation of the regional historical novel to the social conflicts of the present. These examples show the profound reach of Scott's historicism, beyond the accumulation of antiquarian detail and beyond any particular ideological agenda. That historicism comprehends the formation of social and psychological identities in time as well as space, as it links both categories in a newly specified, contingent historical geography of "uneven development." Modernization, for Scott, is a complex process involving loss as well as gain, elegiac regret with fulfillment, in a melancholy and skeptical as well as comic affirmation of the present.

Scott's technique appears at its most ambitious in *The Heart of Mid-Lothian* (1818), a strong candidate for the prototypical "Victorian novel," and not only because a series of later works will develop its critique of a social order through trials of female virtue and fallen motherhood: Gaskell's *Ruth* (1853), Eliot's *Adam Bede* (1859), Hardy's *Tess of the d'Urbervilles* (1891). *The Heart of Mid-Lothian* combines different narratives into an expansive, complex, and variegated structure that projects schemes of analogy and metaphor across drastic mutations and discontinuities of form and theme. This narrative structure, amplified in the great "multiplot" novels of Dickens, Thackeray, Trollope, and Eliot, is able to articulate the relations among a bewildering diversity of classes, cultures, regions, and epochs. No less crucially, it brings together (as it specifies) separate domains of public and private life, exploring the relations between collective and individual, social and psychosexual processes of conflict and development. Scott's narrative opens up a dynamic heterogeneity of language: releasing, rather than containing, a polyphonic babble of styles, dialects, discourses, literary forms, and genres. The novel attends as it has never before to a social and regional variety of speech, especially popular speech, rendered with an unprecedented vividness as well as moral dignity. No less influential, if more problematical, was Scott's adaptation of the stock types of genteel hero and heroine—especially the hero, a male version of the sensitive heroine of Ann Radcliffe's Gothic romances of the 1790s. Scott's "passive hero," borne along by obscure historical forces, enacts a critical revision of traditional styles of masculinity for modern civil society; his heirs populate much of Victorian fiction. Last, and not least, Scott's novels are consequential through their dynamic interplay of different literary styles and genres, as the novel reflects on its historic absorption of a host of other discourses, from history, travelogue, memoir, and law-case through popular ballad, chapbook, and folktale. The apparent simplicity of a modernizing scheme in which archaic "romance" must give way to "real history" accompanies a simultaneous insistence on the condition of the novel *as* a novel, a work of fiction, exposing the provisional, "romantic" character of the historical reality it sets in place. Scott's novels bequeathed to the Victorians the powerful affirmation of fiction as such, a specific discourse bearing its own cognitive authority, not in the end reducible to other didactic or ideological registers of meaning.

In 1913, Saintsbury could declare the novel a canonical genre, along with tragedy and lyric poetry, yet 100 years earlier it had scarcely even been considered as "literature." By 1850 Dickens was claiming a high social and moral purpose for fiction (although many regarded him as a mere entertainer), and in the 1870s George Eliot would personify the novelist as Victorian sage, a public intellectual in the manner of Ruskin or Carlyle. Once again it was Scott's example, more than any other, that raised prose fiction from the condition of an ephemeral, disreputable amusement to the dignity of a national form. A few years earlier, Maria Edgeworth had won critical respect for the seriousness of her tales, becoming in 1804 the first novelist to be noticed by the *Edinburgh Review*, and Anna Barbauld edited the first canon of "British Novelists" in 1810. But Scott's example was decisive; in adopting the prestigious discourse of history, the Waverley novels were acclaimed for their elevation of fiction from the degraded, feminine abyss of "romance" to the masculine domain that Ina Ferris has called "literary authority." The domain was marked by the new quarterly reviews, above all the *Edinburgh Review*, established at the beginning of the century for the critical regulation of literary culture. Scott followed the reviewers' practice of assuming authorial anonymity, so as not to compromise his gentility. Nevertheless it was widely known that "the Author of *Waverley*" was Sir Walter Scott, whose novels brought him fortune, celebrity, and honors, including a baronetcy. Scott's ruin in 1825–26 meant the end of his anonymity, and a further, still more influential turn: the emergence of the novelist as a kind of national monument, enshrined in biography and a collected works. The so-called "Magnum Opus" edition of the Waverley Novels (1829–33), for which Scott supplied textual revisions, additional notes and introductions, incorporating biographical as well as historical information, established a new cultural formation: the novelist as Author, presiding over and informing his *oeuvre*, in an organic unity of life and works. Scott had prepared such a formation by editing a canon of British fiction with biographical and critical prefaces (*Ballantyne's Novelist's Library* [1821–24]), and it would be sealed with a full-scale biography, *Memoirs of the Life of Sir Walter Scott, Bart.* (1837–38) by his son-in-law John Gibson Lockhart. As well as learning their technique from Scott, the Victorian novelists were haunted by the narrative of a career of superhuman industrial production issuing in wealth, fame, ruin, and an honorable but fatal toil of reparation.

Scott's success helped determine the material conditions of novel-publishing throughout the nineteenth century. The popularity of the Waverley novels encouraged publishers to sustain high wartime book prices, with *Kenilworth* (1821) setting the format for polite fiction that would remain in place until 1894: the so-called "three decker," or novel in three volumes, post octavo, retailing at a guinea and a half (31s. 6d.). Too expensive for all but the wealthiest of private readers, new novels were almost entirely bought up by the circulating libraries, which exerted increasing control over the market. At the same time, the continued popularity of Scott's novels drove his publishers to exploit the copyrights with reprint editions, at first in relatively fancy octavo and then in progressively cheaper and smaller formats (12mo, 18mo). Archibald Constable, publisher of Scott and the *Edinburgh Review*, is credited with foreseeing the revolutionary potential of a cheap reprint series that would target the new markets of the industrial age, although Constable's ruin (and Scott's) in the financial crash of 1825–26 left the idea for others to exploit. *Constable's Miscellany* (1826–35; published by Robert Cadell) pioneered the serial part-issue in monthly numbers, consisting at first of history, biography, and travel-writing, that would dominate the depressed literary marketplace of the 1830s. Fiction assumed the new format in 1829 with the Scott "Magnum Opus" edition, issued in monthly volumes (with 1½ or 2 volumes per title) at 5 shillings each; new technologies such as the steam press and steel engraving enabled the relatively cheap but high-quality mass production. Colburn and Bentley's *Standard Novels* (1831–55), an avowed supplement to "Magnum Opus," reprinted selected novels in single volumes at 6 shillings each, setting the pattern for second-issue fiction publishing for most of the century.

The 1825–26 crash had devastated Edinburgh publishing, and the national trade continued in a state of depression throughout the following decade. Cautious publishers invested in reprints and "useful knowledge," with new novels regarded as high-risk ventures. The situation encouraged the appearance of fiction in serial form: whether in a magazine or miscellany, juxtaposed with other contents, or in monthly parts devoted wholly to the new work. However the runaway success of *Pickwick Papers* (1836–37), commissioned as the accompaniment to a series of sporting illustrations before it mutated into a "novel," can give a misleading impression of the popularity of the monthly part-issue as a vehicle for fiction; only Dickens was able to sustain the format with continuous success. Serialization in magazines proved more reliable. *Blackwood's Edinburgh Magazine* had featured fiction (mostly short stories and sketches) from 1817; the serialization of novel-length narratives began in earnest in Marryat's *Metropolitan Magazine* (from 1832) and was taken up in *Bentley's Miscellany* (1837), initially edited by Dickens. Meanwhile *Chambers's Edinburgh Journal* (1832) pioneered newspaper serialization, which Dickens (again) would adopt in *Household Words* (1850).

Dickens's early career provides a vivid sense of the conditions of literary production in the 1830s and, especially, the metropolitan genres that constituted the major innovations in fiction between Scott's death and the appearance of the "Victorian novel" proper. Writing at first for newspapers and magazines, Dickens drew on the vogue for sketches of high and low life in London practiced in essays by Leigh Hunt and in fiction by Pierce Egan and Theodore Hook. The picaresque adventures of Jerry Hawthorn and "Corinthian Tom" in Egan's *Life in London* (1820–21) established what would become the standard Victorian representation of the capital as "two cities," the fashionable West End and raffish City, each rendered as a distinctive habitus with its own customs, manners, and languages. The two cities polarize into the most popular genres of the 1830s besides historical fiction, the "silver-fork" novel depicting aristocratic manners and intrigue and the "Newgate novel" plumbing the criminal underworld. Both genres exploit a middle-class voyeurism—the reader's fascination with arcane, morally alien subcultures, both high and low—as well as the intimation of a radically divided society. Silver-fork fiction drew on the earlier genre of "tales of fashionable life" (the title of a series by Edgeworth, 1809–12), which articulated a middle-class critique of aristocratic values, often through the vehicle of female *Bildungsroman*. The new genre, exemplified in works by Catherine Gore, the Countess of Blessington, Theodore Hook, and the early fiction of Edward Bulwer Lytton and Benjamin Disraeli, tended toward sensational plotting for its own sake and an obsessive attention to styles of taste and dress.

Bulwer, along with Ainsworth, was also a leading exponent of Newgate fiction, a genre that provoked fierce controversy even as it attracted tens of thousands of readers. These novels, worked up from criminal biographies compiled in *The Newgate Calendar*, competed with the post-Scott historical novel to revive the settings and tropes of late-eighteenth-century Gothic fiction—with frequent overlapping between genres, as in Ainsworth's historical-Newgate hybrid *Rookwood* (1834). *Oliver Twist* (1838) was associated with the Newgate novel, and Dickens (despite disclaimers) would amplify the genre's vision of a criminal abyss shadowing metropolitan life throughout his mature work. The Newgate novel's adaptation of the Gothic to modern conditions, revitalized by the French urban-mysteries fiction of Eugène Sue and Victor Hugo, would remain fertile throughout the century, mutating via Dickens's serials into 1860s "sensation fiction" and the *fin-de-siècle* detective tale.

The example of Newgate fiction shows us what is missing from Saintsbury's account of the novel, and from the "entire possible ground" of a normative, middle-class kind of novel represented by Scott and Austen: radical, demotic, disruptive, even pathological styles and energies of narration, surfacing in these new, unrespectable genres from urban popular culture. It is no reflection on the intrinsic quality of a genre or individual work, meanwhile, that it did not perpetuate itself in a tradition. Some of the most original and accomplished works of pre-Victorian fiction would leave no progeny; others would cast intermittent and distorted shadows. "The imaginary student pursued by the misshapen creature he had impiously made, was not more wretched than I, pursued by the creature who had made me," writes the narrator of *Great Expectations* (1861), referring to Mary Shelley's *Frankenstein* (1818). Dickens might also have been referring to a kind of literary haunting, the discontinuous recurrence of earlier styles and forms in a rhythm quite different from the developmental continuity implied in the term "tradition." The late-Gothic mode of a fragmented and intercalated narration—perfected by Shelley, by Maturin in *Melmoth the Wanderer* (1820), and by James Hogg in *The Private Memoirs and Confessions of a Justified Sinner* (1824)—performs a disturbance of the narrative conventions of organic unity, historical continuity, and evolutionary progression. It is fitting that later authors attempting a similar disturbance would resort to the practice, in Collins's sensation novels (*The Woman in White* [1860]), and in horror tales by Stevenson and Bram Stoker (*Dr. Jekyll and Mr. Hyde* [1886]; *Dracula* [1897]).

WORKS CITED AND SELECTED WORKS FOR FURTHER READING

Armstrong, Nancy. *Desire and Domestic Fiction: A Political History of the Novel.* New York: Oxford UP, 1987.

Butler, Marilyn. *Jane Austen and the War of Ideas.* Oxford: Clarendon, 1975.

Chittick, Kathryn. *Dickens and the 1830s.* Cambridge: Cambridge UP, 1990.

Duncan, Ian. *Modern Romance and Transformations of the Novel: The Gothic, Scott, Dickens.* Cambridge: Cambridge UP, 1992.

Easley, Alexis. "The Periodical Press: The Case of Harriet Martineau." *Nineteenth-Century Prose* 24.1 (1997): 39–50.

Erickson, Lee. *The Economy of Literary Form: English Literature and the Industrialization of Publishing, 1800–1850.* Baltimore: Johns Hopkins UP, 1996.

Ferris, Ina. *The Achievement of Literary Authority: Gender, History and the Waverley Novels.* Ithaca: Cornell UP, 1991.

Kelly, Gary. *English Fiction of the Romantic Period, 1789–1830.* London: Longman, 1989.

Leavis, F. R. *The Great Tradition: George Eliot, Henry James, Joseph Conrad.* New York: Chatto and Windus, 1963.

Lukács, Georg. *The Historical Novel.* 1937. London: Merlin, 1962.

Lynch, Deidre Shauna. *The Economy of Character: Novels, Market Culture, and the Business of Inner Meaning.* Chicago: U of Chicago P, 1998.

Millgate, Jane. *Scott's Last Edition: A Study in Publishing History.* Edinburgh: Edinburgh UP, 1987.

Poovey, Mary. *The Proper Lady and the Woman Writer: Ideology as Style in the Works of Mary Wollstonecraft, Jane Austen and Mary Shelley.* Chicago: U of Chicago P, 1984.

Saintsbury, George. *The English Novel.* London: J. M. Dent, 1913.

Siskin, Clifford. *The Work of Writing: Literature and Social Change in Britain, 1700–1830.* Baltimore: Johns Hopkins UP, 1998.

Southam, B. C., ed. *Jane Austen: The Critical Heritage.* New York: Barnes and Noble, 1968.

Trumpener, Katie. *Bardic Nationalism: The Romantic Novel and the British Empire.* Princeton: Princeton UP, 1997.

Periodicals and Syndication

Graham Law

Serial fiction was not a Victorian invention. The practice of issuing narrative at intervals in "fascicles"—independent numbers bound in paper covers—can be traced back to the late seventeenth century (Wiles, *Serial*); the second quarter of the eighteenth century saw a boom in printing fiction by installments in cheaper newspapers both metropolitan and provincial (Wiles, *Freshest*); and by the 1770s, serial stories were a leading attraction in many "common miscellanies"—magazines aiming less to inform than to amuse (Mayo). In these ways, publishers of fiction material could spread the production costs, and subscribers the purchase price, painlessly over a lengthy period. Moreover, the distribution network for periodical publications was already more highly developed than that for books. Nevertheless, in contrast to the typical Victorian serial novel, continuous stories in the eighteenth century tended to be reprinted, abridged, or translated works, or, if original, by undistinguished authors; to be broken into incomplete units and indifferent to the art of serialization; and to be unillustrated as well as shorter than novel-length. Although there were many exceptions to these tendencies individually, there was perhaps only one on all counts: Smollett's *Sir Lancelot Greaves*, which ran originally in the author's *British Magazine* (1760–61), and which in many ways prefigured the art of the Victorian serial.

By the mid-Victorian decades, when the reading public was expanding rapidly, the novel in parts had become far more pervasive and its motivation was no longer simply a matter of economy. It seems likely that, for almost the whole of the Victorian era, a significant majority of "original" novels published as books had appeared previously in installments—as independent numbers, in magazines, or in the columns of the newspapers. There were even cases throughout the period where novels were issued simultaneously in more than one serial format. Benjamin Disraeli and Charlotte Brontë were among the few major novelists to have no novels serialized; significantly, both wrote mainly before the mid-century and were less than prolific. Particularly in the earlier Victorian decades, however, there was also undoubtedly a vast, and still largely uncharted, sea of stories, published serially in popular periodicals but never reprinted as books. Later, editors turned increasingly to serial fiction to attract readers not only to general miscellanies but also to journals targeting specific interest groups. As Hughes and Lund argue (Chapter 1), Victorian culture seems to have been especially receptive to the narrative rhythm of the serial, its expansive, episodic, cumulative development perhaps reflecting prevailing socioeconomic values.

In the first half of the nineteenth century, as for almost a century before, periodical publication was distorted by fiscal constraints on paper consumption, news publication, and advertisements, known collectively as the "taxes on knowledge." From their introduction in 1712, up to a peak in 1815, until their final abolition by 1861, these onerous charges were designed less to collect revenue than to control dissent by limiting popular access to the print medium. They also had side effects on the market for serial fiction. In the decades following their abolition, however, the new enterprise apparent in the periodical market should also be seen as a response to the conservatism of the book trade in original fiction. This was dominated by lavish multivolume editions, still sold at the inflationary prices scaled after the Napoleonic Wars, and aimed mainly at the circulating libraries with their respectable middle-class clientele. The general trend was thus from a predominance of monthly serialization in expensive, low-circulation formats, produced as petty commodities for the bourgeoisie by book publishers, to that of weekly serialization in cheap, high-circulation formats, produced as commodities for the masses by newspaper proprietors. Thus emerged the first fully capitalist mode of production in the British fiction industry. The shift from "fat" monthly to "thin" weekly installments, in Coolidge's terms, also undoubtedly influenced the form of Victorian fiction in the long term, favoring "climax and curtain" endings to installments and the mechanics of enigma and suspense. In order to chart this shift, it is useful to divide the era into three overlapping periods: early (1830s–1850s), middle (1850s–1870s), and late (1870s–1890s).

EARLY PERIOD

In the earlier Victorian decades the dominant forms of serial transmission of bourgeois fiction were publication in monthly literary magazines and in independent monthly parts. Though some common miscellanies with their secondhand serials survived into the following century, it was not until after 1819, when legislation removed the threat of the imposition of stamp duty on monthly periodicals, that there began to appear a generation of magazines featuring full-length original serials by established writers. These new monthlies were of two types. First, there were the salty Tory review magazines led by *Blackwood's Edinburgh Magazine* (1817–1980), which as early as 1820 began to include serials of Scottish provincial life. Also noteworthy in this category were *Fraser's* (1830–82), which carried Thackeray's early fiction, and the *Dublin University Magazine* (1833–77), which serialized novels by Charles Lever, its editor from 1842. All three journals were long-lived and remained important vehicles of imaginative writing. *Blackwood's*, for example, was later to carry sequences of "chronicles" by Edward Bulwer-Lytton, Anthony Trollope, and Margaret Oliphant. The second group comprised the lighter, frothier miscellaneous magazines, which tended to be liberal in sentiment and to have shorter effective lives. Captain Marryat's *Metropolitan Magazine* (1831–50) was perhaps the first to carry serial fiction, beginning with his own *Peter Simple* from 1832. The most successful was *Bentley's Miscellany* (1837–68), an illustrated magazine initially edited by Dickens and featuring *Oliver Twist*. Colburn's *New Monthly* (1814–84) was an established review journal that shifted to the miscellany format in imitation of *Bentley's*, carrying serials by Marryat, G.P.R. James, and Harrison Ainsworth. Ainsworth had succeeded Dickens as editor of *Bentley's* as early as 1839, but soon left to found *Ainsworth's Magazine* (1842–54), which led off with his own *The Miser's Daughter*. Thus, by the mid-1840s, original serial fiction by best-selling writers was a firmly established feature of the monthly magazines, which tended to be owned by established book publishers, priced at half-a-crown or more, and with sales under 10,000 even at their peak.

By this time there was also a boom in the publication of new novels in independent monthly parts, generally comprising thirty-two octavo pages with a couple of illustrations inside a colored paper wrapper, and sold at a shilling. This fashion was started, famously, by the unanticipated runaway success of Dickens's *Pickwick Papers* (Patten, Chapter 3). *Pickwick* started out in early 1836 as a series of humorous plates to which the young writer was asked to attach a loose narrative. A healthy 1,000 copies of the first number were issued in April 1836, but sales were disappointing. However, they began to pick up from the fourth part with the appearance of Sam Weller and had reached close to

40,000 before the final double installment appeared in November 1837. Dickens had quickly established personal control of the project, and the twenty monthly parts in their duck-green wrappers remained his preferred mode of initial publication throughout his career. His last complete novel, *Our Mutual Friend* (1864–65), appeared in identical format. However, this fact has tended to encourage exaggeration of the prevalence of the practice. In reality, new novels in monthly numbers flourished only in the 1840s and were thereafter only a safe option for writers at the peak of their popularity (Sutherland, *Victorian Fiction* Chapter 4). Lever, Ainsworth and Marryat, plus Frances Trollope—perhaps the only female writer to exploit this format profitably—were among the first to cash in on Dickens's success. Minor authors gaining fame through monthly installments included Henry Cockton with *Valentine Fox* (1840) and Frank Smedley with *Frank Fairleigh* (1849–50). Bradbury and Evans issued Trackeray's *Vanity Fair* and *Pendennis* almost back-to-back in numbers from January 1847, in bright yellow covers and illustrated by the author, though neither seems to have achieved sales much above 10,000. Chapman and Hall similarly brought out a number of Trollope's works at the height of this fame, beginning with *Orley Farm* from 1861. But the flow of monthly installment novels had virtually dried up by the following decade, with Trollope's *The Way We Live Now* (1874–75) being one of the last.

Exceptions soon emerged to the norm that fiction with pretensions to respectability was serialized in monthly portions. Although, as at the end of the eighteenth century, there were still many cheaper weekly periodicals carrying reprint fiction, Chapman and Hall's experiment with *Master Humphrey's Clock* (1840–41), an illustrated 3d. weekly miscellany written entirely by Dickens, was probably unique. This journal was originally planned to feature only shorter pieces, both fiction and nonfiction, but poor sales soon forced Dickens to turn to the serial novel (Patten, Chapter 6). *The Old Curiosity Shop* and *Barnaby Rudge* thus appeared first in this format. However, Dickens found the constraints of weekly composition not to his liking, so the trial was soon abandoned. Similarly, the appearance of Ainsworth's *Jack Sheppard* in weekly numbers at 3d. in 1840, concurrently with its monthly appearance in *Bentley's Miscellany*, was unusual. Other and more significant exceptions are to be found in the metropolitan weekly press, following significant reductions in the taxes on knowledge.

With the 1832 Reform Bill, the campaign to abolish the taxes on knowledge gained strength, but the result was a series of unsatisfactory compromises. By 1836 the advertisement tax and paper duty had been halved, and the newspaper stamp itself was reduced from 4d. to 1d. per copy. At the same time, however, the new legislation increased the value of the security bonds to be posted against the issuing of criminal libel, and thus did little to ease the fiscal burdens on the small-scale publisher seeking an audience among the masses (Collet, Chapter 21). The main stimulus was thus to the metropolitan weekly newspaper. Soon there were attempts to serialize original fiction in weekly papers experimenting with illustration, most notably the well-established *Sunday Times* (established in 1822) and the new *Illustrated London News* (established in 1842). The *Sunday Times* began to publish novels in fifty-two weekly parts accompanied by large-scale illustrations from January 1840, and its circulation jumped immediately by over a third to 20,000 an issue. Ainsworth and G.P.R. James were among the featured authors. The *Illustrated London News* published rather shorter serials less regularly, beginning with Cockton's *The Sisters* in 1843. However, priced at sixpence or more, these weeklies were still well beyond the reach of the masses, and the experiments ceased by the early 1850s as the proprietors sought to establish a more sober reputation.

One reason was that the weekly melodramatic serial was becoming increasingly associated with the lower depths of the proletarian market. Literature aimed at the working class was then written by a distinct set of hack writers, published by a group of dubious "Salisbury Square" publishers, and distributed by street hawkers or in tobacconist's shops rather than through established book sellers. Yet the urban "penny blood," which was then rapidly superseding the traditional rural popular forms of the ballad, broadside, and chapbook, is best understood as a miniaturized, plagiarized version of the bourgeois monthly serial (Louis James, Chapter 1). The dominant subgenres of the novel of the 1830s—whether the Gothic romance, silver-fork novel, domestic melodrama, or Newgate novel—all soon had their reduced counterparts in the slum market. Indeed, the prefix "penny" itself then not only denoted the price but also connoted this process of diminution. From the second half of the 1830s, serial novels in penny weekly parts, in penny Sunday papers, and in penny weekly miscellanies began to appear in turn, often from the same writers and publishers.

Melodrama in penny weekly installments, generally leaflets of eight double-column large octavo pages with fierce woodcuts at the head, began as early as 1835 with Gothic tales like *The Calendar of Horrors*. Blatant imitations of bourgeois best-sellers by Dickens or G.P.R. James were common—beginning with *The Penny Pickwick* from 1838—as were tales of criminal heroes like Jack Sheppard, already celebrated by Ainsworth. *Ada the Betrayed* (1841–42) and *Varney the Vampire* (1845–47) both probably by Malcolm Rymer (1804–82), were typical popular titles. The *Mysteries of London* (1845–50), principally by the republican G.W.M. Reynolds (1814–79), was among the longest running. Many were published by Edward Lloyd (1815–90), who moved to premises in Salisbury Square, off Fleet Street, in 1842, thus producing the sobriquet used to designate the penny publishers. Among the Salisbury Square hacks,

Reynolds was probably the most sophisticated in stylistic terms as well as the most challenging to conventional morality (Dalziel, Chapter 4). However, in the bourgeois world, the penny bloods had a blanket reputation for scurrility they hardly deserved.

From the early 1840s Salisbury Square began to mimic the bourgeois periodical as well as the novel in parts. This can be seen initially in unstamped penny Sunday papers that imitated the names and formats of established journals like the *Weekly Dispatch* or the *Sunday Times*. The penny imitations were generally four-page folios with a garish woodcut under the heading banner. They seem to have narrowly escaped breaching the tax laws, because their main appeal was lurid crime reporting that was largely fictional, but they also tended to follow the *Sunday Times* in offering melodramatic serial stories. A typical short-lived example was *Clark's Weekly Dispatch* (1841), but the most persistent and significant was Lloyd's *Penny Sunday Times*, which seems to have survived virtually throughout the 1840s. However, the nature of the stamp legislation made this a hazardous enterprise, and it was soon apparent that the safer course was to divide news and fiction into separate periodicals. Thus were started a series of penny weekly miscellanies, *Bentley's* in miniature, that, in addition to a generous helping of serial and complete fiction, featured a variety of instructive and entertainment matter. The commonest format emerged as sixteen quarto pages in two or three columns, once more with a dramatic woodcut on the front page. From the start, these journals attempted to appeal to a family audience by cultivating a more respectable image than the penny installment novels. The first and most austere was John Biggs's *Family Herald* (1843–1940); rather more daring were those associated with George Reynolds, who was the first editor of the *London Journal* (1845–1912) before leaving to run his own *Reynolds' Miscellany* (1846–69). At around the same time, the more stable Salisbury Square publishers began to issue their own legitimate Sunday papers—notably *Lloyd's •Weekly News* (1842–1931) and *Reynold's Weekly* (1850–1967)—still strong on violent crime and radical in opinion, but with no serials and duly and legally stamped.

The Salisbury Square publishers obviously at first learned something from the mass production methods used for bourgeois best-sellers like *Pickwick Papers*. There Chapman and Hall had been forced to resort to stereotyping—printing with a solid plate cast from a mold taken from the surface of a form of type—once sales exceeded 10,000 per month and back numbers were in demand. But Edward Lloyd and his like were producing many different serials on a weekly basis, and it has been estimated that a minimum run of 20,000 copies of each issue of the penny bloods was necessary to clear costs—indeed, Reynolds' *Mysteries of London* was rumored to have approached sales of 500,000 per issue. This was probably an exaggeration, but there seems little doubt that by the mid-1850s the most popular penny miscellanies were selling well over 250,000 copies, and the new radical Sunday papers cleared close to 100,000. It is thus not surprising that in 1843 the *Family Herald* claimed to be the first journal ever to be typeset, printed, and bound entirely by machine, and in 1855 Lloyd was the first English publisher to import the new Hoe rotary printing press from America.

MIDDLE PERIOD

In the middle stage of fiction serialization centering on the decade from 1860, the first trend to be noted is the simultaneous erosion of the autonomy of the proletarian market and of bourgeois prejudice against the weekly number. By the end of the decade, the typical penny installment novel had shifted noticeably from the "penny blood" sold in the slums to the "penny dreadful" aimed at the emerging juvenile market, while the penny miscellanies were increasingly reorienting themselves towards an expanding female market. *Reynolds' Miscellany*, with the lowest circulation among the three journals, was terminated in 1869 when its position had already been overtaken by *Bow Bells* from the same publishing house. By supplementing its serial fiction—notably by the aging Ainsworth—with music, needlework, and dress patterns, *Bow Bells* seems to have appealed especially to young female servants. Another sign of this crossing of borders in the alarm caused by the fashion for what were soon being called "sensation novels"—serials like Wilkie Collins's *The Woman in White* (1859–60) or Mary Braddon's *Lady Audley's Secret* (1862)—that set improper and mysterious events within respectable domestic environments. The outrage was due largely to the fact that sensation fiction transgressed accepted social boundaries. It did this not only by inserting what had hitherto been seen as the plebeian themes of violence, infidelity, and insanity into bourgeois settings but also by encouraging the middle classes to participate in the proletarian mode of weekly serialization.

The underlying point is that, during this period, the dominance of the monthly serial underwent a serious and finally successful challenge from the weekly serial, in the form both of cheap family miscellanies issued in the metropolis, and of the news miscellanies that sprang up like mushrooms in the provincial cites on the abolition of the taxes on knowledge. However, this development has often been obscured in conventional accounts of the Victorian periodical, which tend rather to emphasize the brief boom in new shilling monthly literary magazines in the 1860s. These journals were generally illustrated, ran to at least 120 pages, and carried more than one original serial novel, as well as a wealth of miscellaneous prose and verse. They offered good value to circulating library subscribers, and quickly dented the market both for the older generation of miscellanies like *Blackwood's*, and for the novel in monthly parts. Smith, Elder's *Cornhill* (1860–1975), begun with a fanfare in early 1860, attracted the most attention. With Thackeray as editor, serials by both him and Trollope, and illustrations by Millais, the magazine went all out for quality. Nearly 110,000 copies of the first issue were sold, and the circulation remained above 70,000 for the first two years, allowing the proprietors to bid extravagant sums for serials, like the £10,000 initially offered for George Eliot's *Romola* (1862–63). But within three years sales had fallen to below 50,000 and to little more than half of that by the end of 1868. This was not entirely due to the boom in competing monthlies.

The most distinguished of the other house magazines was *Macmillan's* (1859–1907), where serial fiction was intended initially to be only a minor attraction. In this it shared common ground with Chapman and Hall's new review, the *Fortnightly* (1865–1954), which, despite the title, became a monthly from 1866, and carried superior serials. Lesser publishing houses soon followed suit with their own magazines, including Bentley's *Temple Bar* (1860–1906), *Tinsley's* (1867–92), and *Broadway Magazine* from Routledge (1867–72). Other shilling monthlies of second rank were vehicles for the work of their popular editors: Braddon's *Belgravia* (1866–99), Mrs. Henry (Ellen) Wood's *Argosy* (1865–1901), and Anthony Trollope's *St. Paul's* (1867–74). Like the *Cornhill*, a few started spectacularly with circulations approaching six figures, though many soon had to be satisfied with an audience below 10,000. *Belgravia* was typical with a peak of over 18,000 in 1868 falling to around 13,000 in 1876, when it was sold. By the early 1870s the boom in the shilling monthlies was over, and a couple of the weakest expired at this point, although most struggled on with declining circulations until toward or even beyond the end of the century. But by the 1880s the menu of fiction offered by, say, *Belgravia, Temple Bar*, or even the *Cornhill*, often seemed second-rate compared with that of the liveliest weekly journals.

By the mid-1860s there was also a wide variety of cheap weeklies combining installment fiction with other instructive and entertainment matter, aimed at a broad family audience, ranging from the solid middle classes down to the servants and skilled artisans of the "respectable" working class. The origins of these journals were twofold. Some obviously evolved from the proletarian penny miscellanies. Others were influenced by the cheap weekly papers started up in the 1830s by bourgeois philanthropic bodies aiming to bring the gospel, either of Christ or of political economy, to the benighted poor. Of these, the most prominent were the utilitarian *Penny Magazine* (1832–46) and its evangelical rival the *Saturday Magazine* (1832–45). Both eschewed fiction material, whereas *Chambers's Journal* (1832–1956), produced commercially in Edinburgh, but with a similar program, included "wholesome" complete tales from the start and was soon achieving a rather wider circulation. In the later 1850s James Payn took over the editorship, and production switched to London. Serial fiction from established names became a major attraction, including Payn's own fashionable mystery, *Lost Sir Massingberd* (1864). *Chambers's* by then faced a host of competitors. Notable evangelically inclined weeklies included the Religious Tract Society's *Leisure Hour* (1852–1905), and *Cassell's Family Paper* (1853–74) was best-known among those in the "useful knowledge" tradition. By the mid-1860s, however, there was little difference in form or content between *Cassell's* and the original proletarian miscellanies like the *Family Herald.*

Nevertheless, it is difficult to underestimate the role of Dickens's family journals in making the weekly miscellany acceptable to the solid middle class. Both *Household Words* and its successor *All the Year Round,* published as well as conducted by Dickens following the row with Bradbury and Evans over his marital difficulties, were unillustrated, sixteen-page, double-column octavo miscellanies, selling at 2d. a week. *Household Words* was more instructive and reformist. It sold a healthy average of about 40,000 copies a week, but only carried shorter serial fiction occasionally. *All the Year Round* seems regularly to have sold over 100,000 copies during Dickens's lifetime, was less agitative in tone, and led off each issue with an installment of a full-length serial, including many of the best-selling sensation novels, among them *Great Expectations.* A competitor at the upper end of the weekly market was the illustrated threepenny *Once a Week,* launched by Bradbury and Evans on Dickens's departure, which featured George Meredith's *Evan Harrington* among its early serials. In sum, by around 1870 the weekly miscellanies offered a serious challenge to the dominance of the monthly magazines, which had already passed their peak of popularity. The weeklies were issued not only by established novel publishers like Bradbury and Evans but also by a wide range of periodical specialists, philanthropic bodies, and newspaper companies with the capital and technology to produce *en masse.* They had penetrated the circles of circulating-library readers, but also extended much further down the social scale. This is made clear by a comparative study of the sales of the principal periodicals at this time (Ellegard, 13–22).

The success of the weekly literary miscellanies seems to have militated against the reintroduction of serial fiction into metropolitan weekly newspapers for a considerable period after the removal of the taxes on knowledge. The continuing campaign against these eventually achieved adequate parliamentary support. The advertisement tax, newspaper stamp (except as an optional postal charge), and paper duty were all finally removed, in 1853, 1855, and 1861 respectively, though the security system persisted until 1869. The immediate results for existing papers were a rapid decrease in price and an increase in both circulation and advertising revenue, with the last by no means of lesser importance. Magazines were designed from the first to be bound up into volumes for preservation, and thus the monthly miscellanies, like novels issued in parts, tended to carry ephemeral advertising material only on their disposable wrappers. However, from their beginnings cheap newspapers were considered ephemeral and thus were not designed for binding into volumes, so that they were free to include advertising material within the body of the publication. Thus, after the mid-century, for newspapers with any pretensions to commercial success the proportion of revenue deriving from advertising would have been well over half.

These fiscal changes clearly had long-term effects on the metropolitan daily press. Nevertheless, the impact of the repeal of the taxes on knowledge was more immediately visible in the provinces, where there was an explosion of new newspapers. Between 1854 and 1856, while only a dozen new journals appeared in London, the number of English provincial newspapers jumped suddenly from 264 to 379, with a similar growth in Scotland and Wales. Most urban areas of any importance soon had at least two competing newspaper proprietors. Among this profusion of new provincial organs, there were soon both penny morning and halfpenny evening papers, but perhaps the most prevalent and distinctive were the weekly news miscellanies. These normally appeared on a Saturday, contained a variety of entertainment matters as well as a summary of the week's news, plus advertisement in quantity. Priced generally at only a penny, they tended to reach a wide geographical and social readership. These weekly papers gradually began to feature fiction material: at first in Scotland, where fewer magazines circulated, and then in northern and western England and Wales; at first local or reprinted material, but gradually original work by established authors. The need for steady sources of supply encouraged the development of various modes of fiction syndication, initially small-scale and carried out informally by editors or authors themselves, but soon widespread and requiring independent syndication agencies operating systematically. Though this process was already a growing force in the 1860s, it did not reach its full potential for at least another decade.

LATE PERIOD

By the later 1870s, however, the dominant mode of installment publication (whether measured in terms of the number of works issued, size of audience reached, or remuneration offered to authors) had shifted unmistakably from serialization in single metropolitan magazines—whether monthlies like *Belgravia* or weeklies like *Chambers's*—to syndication in groups of provincial weekly papers with complementary circulations. The firm of Tillotsons, proprietors of the *Bolton Weekly Journal* (1871–   ), were the pioneers in this development. Their "Fiction Bureau," a newspaper syndication agency specializing in serial novels founded in 1873, had a nationwide clientele from the start and an international one within a decade. Braddon was Tillotsons's first major client and their most faithful. Other well-known sensation novelists like Collins and Charles Reade signed up during the 1870s, though respected regional novelists like Thomas Hardy, Margaret Oliphant, or William Black also served the Bolton firm frequently in later decades.

Tillotsons's system involved two distinct stages, concerning the sale of first and subsequent serial rights. Initially, for each serial purchased, Tillotsons worked to create a "coterie" of up to a dozen major British provincial weeklies, which would pay substantial sums—up to £100 for the biggest names—to serialize new novels simultaneously. In addition, Tillotsons began to maintain backlists of fiction already published in volume, but for which the firm retained serial rights. These works were sold to lesser journals for as little as a shilling per column in the case of little-known writers. Text was available from Bolton in the form of proofs to be reset by the local publisher or, from around 1876, as stereotype columns to be locked into the form. The major city journals joining the coteries were often content to receive material in reprint, whereas the country papers generally preferred stereo. From the late 1880s, however, the stereo plates often included illustrations, and thereafter tended to appeal even to the major papers. By the mid-1880s the Bolton firm also had many client newspapers not only in the colonies and continental Europe but also in the United States, thus helping to kick-start the American fiction syndication industry (Johanningsmeier, Chapter 2).

Tillotsons's striking success quickly attracted competition, and almost immediately there were other British organizations syndicating fiction to local newspapers nationwide, whether based in the provinces, like the rival firms of Lengs and Leaders in Sheffield, or operating out of London like Cassell's or the National Press Agency. But these direct competitors served rather to expand the market for syndicated fiction and were thus less of a threat to the Bolton firm than a variety of indirect rivals who emerged from the early 1880s. In combination, these new entities succeeded in undermining the brief dominance of the provincial newspaper as a vehicle for serial fiction and returning the initiative to the London press. The period of transition, however, led to many cases of "belt-and-braces" serialization, when novels appeared simultaneously in a metropolitan periodical and a syndicate of local papers (Law, Chapter 4). One new metropolitan force was the professional literary agent, most notably A. P. Watt, who by the early 1890s wielded enormous influence in the periodical market. Another was a new generation of metropolitan weekly newspapers targeting a nationwide audience, which also began to carry novels in installments. These included both "class" and "mass" journals—that is, papers aimed at either the distinct professional classes or the undifferentiated masses. Among the more expensive and respectable class weeklies featuring installment novels in the 1870s were society journals like the *World* or pictorial papers like the *Graphic*. The mass penny weeklies, which began to include serial fiction during the 1880s, included new populist Tory Sunday papers like the *People*, old radical journals like *Lloyd's*, and fragmentary entertainment miscellanies led by George Newnes's *Tit-Bits*, the latter two achieving sales of well over 500,000.

This shift of commercial power back to the metropolitan publishers heralded an even more rapid process of commodification of fiction—most obviously represented by the new mass-market formulae of adventure, mystery, and romance—than had occurred under the provincial syndicators. In the 1890s there also emerged a new generation of illustrated monthlies, produced not by established book publishers but by the new press barons. The most successful was George Newnes's *Strand Magazine* (1891–1950), followed by *Pearson's Magazine* (1896–1939). Both were populist and imperialist, sold at only sixpence, and claimed circulations of over 250,000 by the end of the century. But these new miscellanies tended to eschew long articles or serials, and sequences of short stories gradually emerged as the dominant periodical narrative form. By then, of course, the average length of the novel had shrunk significantly following the demise of the multivolume format. Though pioneering modernists like Joseph Conrad and H. G. Wells still often issued their novels in various serial formats after the turn of the century, as Henry James lamented (19–21), the Golden Age of the large-scale installment novel was by then long past.

WORKS CITED AND SELECTED WORKS FOR FURTHER READING

Altick, Richard. *The English Common Reader: A Social History of the Mass Reading Public*, 1800–1900. Chicago: U of Chicago P, 1957.

Collet, Collet Dobson. *History of the Taxes on Knowledge*. 2 vols. London: T. Fisher Unwin, 1899.

Coolidge, Archibald Cary. *Charles Dickens as Serial Novelist*. Ames: Iowa State UP, 1967.

Dalziel, Margaret. *Popular Fiction 100 Years Ago: An Unexplored Tract of Literary History*. London: Cohen and West, 1957.

Donaldson, William. *Popular Literature in Victorian Scotland: Language, Fiction, and the Press*. Aberdeen: Aberdeen UP, 1986.

Ellegard, Alvar. "The Readership of the Periodical Press in Mid-Victorian Britain." *Victorian Periodicals Newsletter* 13 (1971): 5–22.

Feltes, N. N. *Modes of Production of Victorian Novels.* Chicago: U of Chicago P, 1986.

Haining, Peter, ed. *The Penny Dreadful: Or, Strange, Horrid and Sensational Tales!* London: Victor Gollancz, 1975.

Hamer, Mary. *Writing by Numbers: Trollope's Serial Fiction.* Cambridge: Cambridge UP, 1987.

Harden, Edgar F. *The Emergence of Thackeray's Serial Fiction.* London: Prior, 1979.

Hepburn, James. *The Author's Empty Purse and the Rise of the Literary Agent.* Oxford: Oxford UP, 1968.

Houghton, Walter E., ed. *The Wellesley Index to Victorian Periodicals.* 5 vols. Toronto: U of Toronto P, 1966–89.

Hughes, Linda K., and Michael Lund. *The Victorian Serial.* Charlottesville: UP of Virginia, 1991.

James, Henry. *Notes of a Son and Brother.* New York: Scribner's, 1914.

James, Louis. *Fiction for the Working Man, 1830–1850.* Oxford: Oxford UP, 1963.

Johanningsmeier, Charles. *Fiction and the American Literary Marketplace: The Role of Newspaper Syndicates in America, 1860–1900.* Cambridge: Cambridge UP, 1997.

Keating, P. J. *The Haunted Study: A Social History of the English Novel, 1875–1914.* London: Secker and Warburg, 1989.

Law, Graham. *Serializing Fiction in the Victorian Press.* Basingstoke, Hampshire: Palgrave, 2000.

Lee, Alan J. *The Origins of the Popular Press in England, 1855–1914.* London: Croom Helm, 1976.

Martin, Carol A. *George Eliot's Serial Fiction.* Columbus: Ohio State UP, 1994.

Mayo, Robert Donald. *The English Novel in the Magazines, 1749–1815.* Evanston: Northwestern UP, 1962.

Mitchell's *Newspaper Press Directory* (1846– ; *Benn's* from 1978).

Myers, Robin, and Michael Harris, eds. *Serials and Their Readers, 1620–1914.* Winchester: St. Paul's Bibliographies, 1993.

New Cambridge Bibliography of English Literature: Vol. 3, 1800–1900, ed. George Watson. Cambridge: Cambridge UP, 1969.

Patten, Robert L. *Charles Dickens and His Publishers.* Oxford: Clarendon, 1978.

Sullivan, Alvin. *British Literary Magazines.* 4 vols. Westport: Greenwood, 1984.

Sutherland, J. A. *Victorian Fiction: Writers, Publishers, Readers.* London: Macmillan, 1995.

———. *Victorian Novelists and Publishers.* London: Athlone, 1976.

Sutherland, John. *The Stanford Companion to Victorian Fiction.* Stanford: Stanford UP, 1989.

Vann, J. Don. *Victorian Novels in Serial.* New York: MLA, 1985.

Vann, J. Don, and Rosemary T. VanArsdel, eds. *Periodicals of Queen Victoria's Empire: An Exploration.* Toronto: U of Toronto P, 1996.

———. *Victorian Periodicals and Victorian Society.* Aldershot: Scolar, 1994.

Victorian Fiction Research Guides. Vols. 1–28. St. Lucia, Queensland: Victorian Fiction Research Unit, University of Queensland, 1979–99.

Wiles, R. M. *Freshest Advices: Early Provincial Newspapers in England.* Columbus: Ohio State UP, 1965.

———. *Serial Publication in England before 1750.* Cambridge: Cambridge UP, 1957.

Wolff, Michael, et al., eds. *The Waterloo Directory of Victorian Periodicals, 1824–1900.* Waterloo, Ontario: Wilfred Laurier UP for the University of Waterloo, 1977.

Book Publishing and the Victorian Literary Marketplace

Peter L. Shillingsburg

The Victorian period is famously the Age of the Novel. Educated estimates suggest that 40,000 to 50,000 novels by some 3,500 different authors were written and published in England between 1830 and 1900 (Altick, *English*; Eliot; Ray; and Sutherland, "Victorian Novelists"). That figures out at an average of 714 novels a year, but statistics suggest that in fact fewer than 100 were published each year in the 1830s and 2,000 to 3,000 per year by the end of the century. Primary factors in the growth of novel writing and publishing, which considerably surpassed the rate of population growth, were an increase in education and literacy that accompanied advances in economic growth and democratic tendencies, improvements in the machinery of printing and book production, and changes in taxation on paper and print that became more favorable to the dissemination of cheap reading materials. John Sutherland, in what at first seems a very comprehensive survey, provides individual notes on just under 900 novelists in his *Stanford Companion to Victorian Fiction*. There is no comprehensive account of the genre, but large and excellent listings of special collections of Victorian fiction are offered by Sadlier and by Wolff. It has been argued that the majority of novels in the early period were written by women, but that as mechanization facilitated production and reduced costs, and as the reading population increased in number—thus making the profession of authorship more profitable—the proportion of authors who were male grew to dominance (Tuchman and Fortin).

During the Victorian period, sharper differentiations developed between the trades of stationers (sellers of paper supplies), booksellers, and magazine sellers, who were retail tradesmen; and compositors, printers, and bookbinders, who were mechanics or industrial tradesmen; and publishers, who were the directors and bankrollers of all these operations and were at worst the merchants of ideas and at best the purveyors of culture. Bradbury and Evans and Company, publishers of Charles Dickens, William M. Thackeray, and Robert Smith Surtees, for example, was a prominent printer and stationer until the early 1840s when the company launched *Punch*, which quickly became very popular and lasted over 130 years. The move led Bradbury and Evans a step up to the level of publisher, albeit of what many considered to be a low comic magazine. From this start, however, B & E developed in time into a respectable publishing business, providing serial novels and books in a variety of other forms. Given its history, B & E naturally did its own printing and binding. Publishers such as Eyre and Spottiswoode, Bentley's, Colburn's, and Chapman and Hall had similar trajectories of development at about the same time. In a highly class-conscious society, in which the word "trade" had lowering connotations, one consequence of these trade histories was a hesitation among authors aspiring to reach the highest levels of respectability to submit their work to printers-cum-publishers. W. M. Thackeray, who as a journalist was a steady contributor to *Punch*, is said to have tried five or more other publishers with his first major novel, *Vanity Fair*, before submitting it in 1846 to the publishers of *Punch* because he hoped to publish his ambitious book with a more prestigious press. Bradbury and Evans were known as stationers, printers, and the publishers of a low-toned magazine rather than as publishers of serious or legitimate fiction. However, times were changing. Charles Dickens, whose own social standing was still on the rise, also chose Bradbury and Evans as his book publisher in 1846, and Dickens's and Thackeray's works did as much as anything to raise the respectability and reputation of Bradbury and Evans as publishers.

The more familiar names in Victorian publishing such as John Murray Ltd., Macmillan and Company, and Longman, Brown, Green, and Longman's had developed in the same way, from stationers and printers to book publishers, but they had longer traditions and higher pretensions as publishers. For example, Longman's, replying in the late 1850s to Anthony Trollope's complaint that he could get a higher price for his novel *The Three Clerks* from another publisher, answered that Trollope should consider whether "our names on your title-page are not worth more to you than the increased payment" (Trollope, 99). He declined Longman's £100 plus half profits in favor of Bentley's outright purchase of the copyright for £250 (Shillingsburg). Smith, Elder and

Company, a well-established banking and international trading company, began a publishing subsidiary in the 1830s, starting with books of science and travel and later condescending to publish fiction. Although Smith, Elder's early history in publishing was clouded by embezzlement (by Elder, who was eased out of the company), its connection with the trading and banking company gave it a solid financial base; and the energy of its founder, George Smith, soon established this company as one of the most profitable and best paying of publishers. Smith, Elder did not acquire its own composing operation and printing presses until the late 1850s. In the end it was George Smith, by then already known as "the prince of publishers," who engineered Anthony Trollope's rise into fame, recognition, and relative wealth by publishing, in 1860 in his new *Cornhill Magazine* and then in book form, Trollope's first best selling novel, *Framley Parsonage*. It is not clearly established whether Trollope's book ensured the success of the *Cornhill Magazine* or whether the magazine established Trollope's success.

The number of printers and publishers in London, Edinburgh, Glasgow, and Dublin that published fiction in the Victorian period grew substantially by the end of the century. They represented the full range of size, financial stability, and competence from the small and shoddy to the great engines of Victorian high culture. Near the bottom rung were publishers such as Thomas C. Newby, the printer who undertook to produce first books by Anne and Emily Brontë, managing the business without correcting proof or paying the authors. Newby may not even have read the books that he published, for he was the long-standing purveyor of sappy romances by Henriette Maria Smithies and published her *Warning to Wives* in the same year that he produced the radically contrary *Wuthering Heights*. Newby also published Anthony Trollope's first work. In the middle register were publishers such as Bentley's, which became one of the most prolific though not the most respectable publisher in London, and William Tinsley, which in the final quarter of the century published many wildly best-selling sensational novels. In the early Victorian period William Harrison Ainsworth, the novelist, became publisher of a magazine and of novels, and was briefly a rival of Bentley's.

A like differentiation in readership propelled publishers to specialize in fiction that appealed to certain classes of readers: silver-fork novels, that is, novels of high life said to have appeal as etiquette books to the rising middle class as well as being escapist romances; Newgate fiction, consisting of sensational tales of crime; gothic novels, continuing the tradition of eighteenth-century gothic tales in spite of the satiric send-ups of the genre such as Jane Austen's *Northanger Abbey* and Thomas Love Peacock's *Nightmare Abbey* in 1817 and 1818; morally edifying tales, perhaps most famously represented by the popular works of Maria Edgworth, Mrs. Opie Reade, Ouida, and Jane Porter; historical romances in imitation of Sir Walter Scott, by such writers as Dickens, Thackeray, Bulwer-Lytton, Ainsworth, and G.P.R. James; social protest novels, of which Charles Dickens's *Oliver Twist* is probably the best known; and a range of working-class fiction by writers such as J. M. Reynolds (James, *Fiction, English*; Hollingsworth; R. Colby; V. Colby; Mews; and Kennard). The "class" of fiction was reflected to some extent in the prices and forms in which the books were printed.

A democratic tendency in education, politics, and economics resulted in a growing range of readers in the Victorian period. This growth, both in number of readers and in range of social, educational, and economic backgrounds they represented, propelled the variety of forms and prices for fiction as much as did developing technology and reforms in taxation on paper and print. With education reforms, increases in population, better and cheaper forms of printing, and economies of scale came an increase in the amount of printed fiction that became available (the number of titles, the number of copies, and the range of literary quality) and in the variety of forms and prices that fiction took.

Previous to 1825, producers and users of paper avoided large sizes because taxes increased sharply with the size of sheets (Pollard). The repeal of taxation on paper, and a few years later reductions and then elimination of taxes on newspapers and periodicals from 1829 to 1831 (Cross), made possible and profitable the invention of wove (as opposed to laid) paper that could feed off of a giant roll and the development of steam-driven machine presses that could accept paper in that form (Gaskell). The reduction in taxation on newspapers led to cheaper and greater newspaper distribution.

Varieties in book sizes, both in number of pages and in the size of pages, have been available to printers and publishers since the fifteenth century, but the art of determining the best form in which to package and sell books has been in constant development. The two most famous forms in Victorian England for fiction were three-volume duodecimo (twelve leaves to each gathering) and monthly serialized octavo formats (eight leaves to each gathering). Many other sizes and a variety of approaches to the quality of paper and the amount of white space left on the page makes it impossible in a short span to describe them all or to describe the presses and other machinery developed in the nineteenth century to mechanize book production (Dooley; Shillingsburg; Gaskell). The most noted developments in the formats of Victorian fiction have been installment publications of the sort made famous by Charles Dickens's *Pickwick Papers* and the three-volume novel or three-decker associated with Mudie's Circulating Library. Fiction had been serialized for over 100 years in newspapers, magazines, separate installments, and multiple volumes before the commencement, in 1837, of Dickens's *Pickwick*; but the great success of that novel signaled a form of publication that Dickens and many others would use for the next thirty years (Butt and Tillotson).

The standard Victorian serial novel installment consisted of two octavo sheets of text wrapped in a paper cover on which were printed not only an elegant decorated title page but, on the back and inside covers, a variety of advertisements of the sort one could also find in newspapers and magazines of the time. The installment, wrappers, and advertisements were sewn together through three "stab holes" in the side of the spine. The thirty-two pages of text were otherwise separate from this additional material, so that when the novel was completed, unsold installments, stripped of the advertisements and paper covers, along with remaining and, when warranted by expected sales, newly printed sheets of the text could be made up into bound copies of the first book edition.

Many bound copies of books made up from the originally issued installments have visible stab holes in the gutter margins, evidence of their earlier format. Installments sold for a shilling monthly and, so, fell within the purchasing power of many working-class readers. Great publishing successes, like Dickens's *Pickwick*, which sold 40,000 copies each month, or *Dombey and Son*, which sold 32,000 copies, made large profits for both authors and publishers, but many novels selling as few as 3,500 to 5,000 copies a month, such as Robert Smith Surtees's *Mr. Sponge's Sporting Tour* (4,000) and W. M. Thackeray's *Vanity Fair* (5,000), were also considered successes (Shillingsburg).

The standard length of these installment novels was twenty installments of 32 pages each or about 640 pages, though some were as short as twelve or sixteen and many extended to twenty-four installments. In this form, typically, each page consisted of forty-eight lines of 10 to 12 words per line. Allowances being made for chapters beginning and ending on separate pages and for the inclusion of illustrations and allowing for variations in the density of type, these novels in general ranged from 240,000 words for novels in sixteen parts to 345,000 words for one in twenty-four parts. Because most of these novels were written as they were being published, authors and publishers could react to readers' responses by adjusting plots and characterizations and by reducing or increasing the number of installments. Thackeray's *Pendennis*, for example, was intended to be twenty numbers but was extended midstream to twenty-four. Most of these novels were illustrated, at least with one or two full-page engravings added to each installment and many times with woodcuts incorporated into the texts. Novels in sixteen to twenty installments were usually marketed upon completion as one-volume works; those extending to twenty-four numbers usually were bound and sold as two-volume works. The resulting books in octavo format measured approximately 8.5 by 5.75 inches.

The great rival to this form of publishing for new fiction was the three-decker or three-volume novel, a form encouraged and sustained by the mutual interests of publishers and circulating libraries, especially by the giant of the industry, Mudie's Circulating Library (Griest). By common agreements that now would probably be challenged in the courts as price fixing, three-decker novels cost 31 to 36 shillings, placing them well out of purchasing range of most working families. However, for one guinea, readers could subscribe to Mudie's and gain borrowing privileges for a year (Griest). With thousands of readers subscribing for his services, Mudie's had enormous buying power with the publishers who supplied the library with tens and hundreds of copies of each title at a 40 to 50 percent discount, agreeing all the while not to sell copies to individuals at under the retail price. C. E. Mudie's personal taste in literature and his sense of the market for his services led him to insist on a strict moral code for the novels available through his subscription library. He acted, then, as a substantial and stable customer for relatively bland and safe if not always morally uplifting fiction. By insisting on the three-volume format, Mudie's could lend each copy of each novel to three subscribers at once. From the publisher's point of view, any novel that passed Mudie's muster was a potentially profitable venture even with print runs of 350 or fewer copies. The publisher would make a little profit on every novel, but would seldom make very much money off of any single novel. Thus, in order to make money, publishers had to publish many different titles. Relatively short runs ensured that few if any copies would be left unsold but also ensured that no fortunes would be made. From the authors' point of view, there was an almost sure sale for "Mudie quality manuscripts" but little hope of making much money. Many authors sold their copyrights for 20 pounds or agreed to a half share of the profits, which frequently did not amount to much or was reported as nonexistent. Few three-decker novels commanded the £1,200 fee George Smith paid to Thackeray for *Henry Esmond*, which sold about 3,500 copies because it had a broad appeal among wealthy individual buyers, over and above the copies sold to Mudie's. Although the length of three-deckers in number of pages usually fell between 850 to 950 in all, there was great variety in the number of words, ranging from the relatively short 180,000 words of Mary Elizabeth Braddon's *Lady Audley's Secret* (1862) to the relatively long 280,000 words of George Eliot's *Mill on the Floss* (1860). Such variations were achieved by adding or subtracting 30 or so pages for each volume and by increasing or decreasing the number of lines per page and the number of words on a line. Volumes in both sets measured approximately 7.75 by 5.5 inches. Colonial editions of three-decker novels were sometimes produced by reprinting the same typesetting but with the spacing removed between the lines, thus reducing three volumes to one without recomposing the work (Nowell-Smith).

Less often discussed, but perhaps more important for what Nigel Cross called "the common writer," were other forms of publication. Many works of fiction appeared (and disappeared) as serials in newspapers, many of them provincial papers that have not survived. Others appeared in magazines, of which the Victorian period boasts well over 5,000 (see Poole's *Index*), many of them short-lived. Pamphlets with paper wrappers and single-volume novels were frequently produced either in single columns or double columns of print. These formats imitated the formats of literary magazines and ranged in price from 1 to 6 shillings. Publishers in the mid-century believed that new fiction did not sell well except in the two major formats previously discussed, serial installments and three volumes. They used the single-volume format primarily for reprints. Successful series of reprints were developed in English by the continental publisher Bohn (Bohn's Standard Novels) who established a company in England. Other series begun in the late 1840s and 1850s, such as Bentley's Standard Novels, Simms and McIntyre's Parlour Novelists (later the Parlour Library), Routledge's Railway Library, and Blackwood's London Library, combined the issuing of reprints with publication of new fiction at 1 or 2 shillings a volume. These forms of publication provided a steady income for the publishers, who drew small sums from the works of many writers, and a meager pittance for most of the novelists involved who usually sold their copyrights for well under 100 pounds and who could produce no more than one or at most two books per year (Cross).

The idea of a series of cheap novels, which worked for fiction in general, worked also for certain of the more successful novelists. Dickens and Thackeray were able to reissue their serial and three-decker novels (originally costing 20 to 36 shillings each) in so-called "cheap editions" without illustrations and with smaller type and smaller margins at 6 shillings. Thackeray's *Vanity Fair*, which during his lifetime sold a grand total of 6,000 copies in its original format, sold 20,000 copies in the "cheap edition."

In the last quarter of the century the concept of "best seller" changed radically. Whereas in 1850 sales of 30,000 copies of a novel were rare and wonderful, by the 1860s novels published in *Macmillan's Magazine* or *The Cornhill Magazine* sold 80,000 to 120,000 copies and by the 1870s the 1 shilling reprints of Braddon's *Lady Audley's Secret* and Mrs. Henry Wood's *East Lynne* sold in the millions. But for each novel of this sort there were many that lost money or barely succeeded. The arrangement between the circulating libraries and publishers, which kept the price of three-volume novels artificially high and ensured at least a marginal profitability for all three-deckers published, began to fall apart in the early 1890s. For many years the arrangement had supported the publication of a plethora of mediocre and bland novels, but changes in the demographics and increases in the number of readers and increased competition from shorter, cheaper, more sensational, or popularized fiction led to the demise of the three-volume format. It has been argued that economics of the newer forms, sustained not by publishers' and circulating library moguls' agreements but supported only by the will of the book-buying public, was much more cruel to the ordinary mediocre author who had enjoyed a certain stable comfortableness with Mudie's (Cross), but it has also frequently been lamented that the new forces in publishing were driving the common run of fiction downward into popular entertainments at the expense of moral, intellectual, and artistic standards.

Though the Victorian period is not famous for its short stories, there were, nevertheless, a number of venues for short fiction, ranging from broadsides (single sheets) with fictionalized accounts of crime and scandal to highly decorated and often expensive annuals and Christmas books containing both poetry and short fiction. The broadsides were more prevalent at the beginning of the period, when other forms of disseminating fiction were still relatively expensive. Moral tales were also printed in the form of tracts for distribution by religious societies. Most of this sort of fiction has been lost and gone unrecorded aside from references to their existence in other forms of literature, such as Thackeray's comments in *Vanity Fair* on tracts with titles like "The Applewoman of Finchley Common" and "The Sailor's True Binnacle." And periodicals from the whole period are laced with moral, comic, and historical short fiction. For authors of great popularity, it was profitable for their publishers to gather the scattered periodical short pieces, including essays, poems, sketches, and short fiction into collections called Miscellanies. And at Christmas, many writers, Charles Dickens most famously, wrote short Christmas tales of about the length of Dickens's *A Christmas Carol* to be given as gifts and stocking stuffers. These and the annuals, which were designed to sit out on coffee tables, were often quite elaborately decorated, not only but especially on their covers. Many annuals and Christmas books also had illustrations and would be available in copies both watercolored by hand or left in black and white.

Beginning in 1847 and developing through the century as an increasingly important mode of publication and source of income to British authors were the continental editions in English published for the tourist trade (see Todd and Bowden). Of the continental publishers, the most important was Bernhard Tauchnitz of Leipzig. Although British laws prohibited the importation from the Continent of English books that had British copyrights, there was no international agreement that protected English books on the Continent. Tauchnitz, however, by paying for and thus securing advanced sheets from British authors and by his efficiency and a very wide distribution system, managed to forestall most of the competition on the Continent from other publishers. For the books he had purchased for publication, Tauchnitz's contracts with the British authors stood in place of the nonexistent copyright laws to prevent the authors and British publishers from selling any advanced sheets or other rights to other European publishers. Thus many Tauchnitz editions, set in some cases from manuscripts and in others from proofs of the English editions, contain some draft readings that were corrected or revised in England before original publication.

Most Victorian novels were published but once; but successful novels were reprinted, either in second, third, or more printings of the same edition or, more interestingly, in a variety of different formats. Charles Dickens's *Great Expectations* first appeared as a three-volume novel, then simultaneously as a weekly and a monthly serial in periodicals. Later, of course, it was issued again in a "cheap" one-volume form, and then it was incorporated into each of the many collected editions of Dickens's works. Multiple appearances of novels in this way reached many more readers than they would otherwise, for it was few readers that would have access to or would or could purchase more than one form of the work. Different formats at different prices reached different audiences or "markets." Not enough research has been conducted in Victorian target marketing of books.

WORKS CITED AND SELECTED WORKS FOR FURTHER READING

Altick, Richard. *The English Common Reader: A Social History of the Mass Reading Public, 1800–1900.* Chicago: U of Chicago P, 1957.
———. *The Presence of the Present: Topics of the Day in the Victorian Novel.* Columbus: Ohio State UP, 1991.
Butt, John, and Kathleen Tillotson. *Dickens at Work.* London: Methuen, 1957.
Colby, Robert A. *Fiction with a Purpose: Major and Minor Nineteenth-Century Novels.* Bloomington: Indiana UP, 1967.
Colby, Vineta. *The Singular Anomaly: Women Novelists of the Nineteenth Century.* New York: New York UP, 1970.
Cross, Nigel. *The Common Writer: Life in Nineteenth-Century Grub Street.* Cambridge: Cambridge UP, 1985.
Dooley, Allan C. *Author and Printer in Victorian England.* Charlottesville: UP of Virginia, 1992.
Eliot, Simon. *Some Patterns and Trends in British Publishing, 1800–1919.* London: Bibliographical Society, 1994.
Gaskell, Philip. *A New Introduction to Bibliography.* Oxford: Oxford UP, 1972.
Griest, Guinevere. *Mudie's Circulating Library and the Victorian Novel.* Bloomington: Indiana UP, 1970.

Harvey, John. *Victorian Novelists and Their Illustrators.* New York: New York UP, 1971.

Hollingsworth, Keith. *The Newgate Novel, 1830–1847: Bulwer, Ainsworth, Dickens, and Thackeray.* Detroit: Wayne State UP, 1963.

James, Louis. *English Popular Literature, 1819–1851.* New York: Columbia UP, 1976.

———. *Fiction for the Working Man, 1830–1850.* Oxford: Oxford UP, 1963.

Kennard, Jean E. *Victims of Convention.* Hamden: Archon, 1978.

Mews, Hazel. *Frail Vessels: Woman's Role in Women's Novels from Fanny Burney to George Eliot.* London: Athlone, 1969.

Nowell-Smith, Simon. *International Copyright Law and the Publisher in the Reign of Queen Victoria.* Oxford: Clarendon, 1968.

Pollard, Graham. "Notes on the Size of the Sheet." *Library* (Fall 1941): 105–37.

Poole, William Frederick, and William Isaac Fletcher, eds. *Poole's Index to Periodical Literature.* 6 vols. Gloucester: Peter Smith, 1958.

Ray, Gordon N. *Bibliographical Resources for the Study of Nineteenth-Century Fiction.* Los Angeles: Clark Library, 1964; Norwood: Norwood Editions, 1978.

Sadleir, Michael. *Nineteenth-Century Fiction: A Bibliographical Record Based on His Own Collections.* 2 vols. Berkeley: U of California P, 1951.

Shillingsburg, Peter. *Pegasus in Harness: Victorian Publishing and W. M. Thackeray.* Charlottesville: UP of Virginia, 1992.

Sutherland, John. *The Stanford Companion to Victorian Fiction.* Stanford: Stanford UP, 1989.

———. "Victorian Novelists: Who Were They?" In *Victorian Writers, Publishers, Readers,* pp. 151–152. New York: St. Martin's, 1995.

Todd, William, and Ann Bowden. *Tauchnitz International Editions in English, 1841–1935.* New York: Bibliographical Society of America, 1988.

Tuchman, Gaye, and Nina Fortin. *Edging Women Out: Victorian Novelists, Publishers, and Social Change.* New Haven: Yale UP, 1989.

Trollope, Anthony. *Autobiography.* New York, 1883.

Wolff, Robert Lee. *Nineteenth-Century Fiction: A Bibliographical Catalogue Based on the Collection Formed by Robert Lee Wolff.* 5 vols. New York: Garland, 1981–86.

Victorian Illustrators and Illustration

Lynn Alexander

A large number of books were published during the Victorian era: in the late 1850s about 2,600 volumes were published annually, by 1874 the number increased to 4,500, and by the end of the 1890s the number was around 6,000 (Wakeman, 11). A majority of these books were illustrated, often with the writer and illustrator working in collaboration. Early in the nineteenth century, book illustrations consisted mainly of a frontispiece, drawn to establish the setting or highlight a particular character. Because they were not tied to specific lines from the text, such illustrations were often executed for their visual appeal rather than their relevance to the text.

Later in the century, the serialization of novels in monthly or weekly parts offered more opportunities for illustration. Each monthly part of a Dickens or Thackeray novel began with an illustrated cover and two full-page illustrations inspired by the thirty-two pages of text. Used to attract attention and draw readers, these drawings were often sensational and highlighted particularly dramatic events. As a novel progressed, the illustrations were also sometimes used as mnemonic devices as well as a means of heightening reader involvement. But the illustrations of serialized novels are not confined to the vivid instances of character or mood; rather, they can develop a novel's themes subtly, delicately, and powerfully. As critics such as J. R. Harvey, Joan Stevens, and Martin Meisel have noted, illustrations often extended the story line, supplied visual frameworks for characters, alerted the reader to significant patterns, or added metaphorical comment. Often a collaboration between writer and artist, Victorian novel illustrations extend the preoccupations of the novelist while retaining their integrity as visual art.

In many cases the relation between text and illustration is clearly reciprocal. Each refers to the other, in a back and forth movement mimicking the experience of the reader in which his eye moves back and forth between illustration and text. By incorporating two different kinds of signs, linguistic and graphic, the illustrated novel created an apparent bridge between the fictive and real worlds. In successful novel illustration the connection is such that neither element can be said to have priority: The pictures are about the text; the text is about the pictures. For example, in describing his reaction to Cruikshank's portrait of Fagin in his cell, G. K. Chesterton noted,

There was about Cruikshank's art a kind of cramped energy which is almost the definition of the criminal mind. His drawings have a dark strength: yet he does not only draw morbidly, he draws meanly. In the doubled-up figure and frightful eyes of Fagin in the condemned cell there is not only a baseness of subject, but there is a kind of baseness in the very technique of it. It is not drawn with the free lines of a free man; it has the half-witted secrecies of a hunted thief. It does not look merely like a picture of Fagin; it looks like a picture by Fagin. (112)

Interestingly, it is not the cell that is cramped and claustrophobic; on the contrary, a soaring ceiling and open floor space suggest an unexpected roominess. Rather, it is Fagin, doubled up and huddling on his bunk, who is cramped, and his wild eyes suggest the hysteria of claustrophobia. But regardless of the cause, the illustration does not merely mirror Dickens's text; it expands it through visualization.

Early Victorian illustrators used wood engraving for their illustrations. In making wood engravings, the illustrator first drew or transferred the picture onto a prepared wood block. If any areas were to print less heavily than the rest, their surfaces were worked over with a mezzotint rocker to lower them. The picture was then redrawn and the engraver cut away the wood with a steel engraver. Another method used early in the Victorian era was etching. To make an etching, the surface of the plate, usually copper or steel, was first covered with an etching ground, heated, and then blackened. The picture was then copied on tracing paper with a pencil, and the tracing placed face down on the plate. Then both were passed through a rolling press, with the image appearing reversed on the plate in fine silvery lines. The etcher then drew through the ground with a series of steel etching needles. Finally the bared lies were bitten away with acid. Although never a major illustration process, some of the most respected illustrators used etching, the greatest probably being George

Cruikshank. He is perhaps best known in this field for his illustrations for Charles Dickens's *Oliver Twist* (1837–39), Harrison Ainsworth's *The Tower of London* (1840), and *The Ingoldsby Legends* (1840–47).

Cruikshank began etching before the turn of the eighteenth century, and his early work owes a considerable debt to Hogarth. Cruikshank's lifelong gift for play-acting, mimicry, and storytelling also shaped all his illustrations. In 1820 he began working with his brother, Robert, and Pierce Egan on *Life in London* (1820–21), which was published in monthly parts with thirty-six hand-colored aquatints. The widely read publication marked the beginning of Cruikshank's move from political caricature to social observation and book illustration. Cruikshank's book illustrations brought him recognition as the leading exponent of the arts in Europe. Among the works he illustrated are the first edition in English of *Kinder und Hausmärchen* (1812–15) by Jacob Ludwig Carl Grimm and Wilhelm Carl Grimm, the plates for which Ruskin thought the best etchings since those of Rembrandt. He also illustrated Walter Scott's Waverly novels (1836–38) and Daniel Defoe's *Robinson Crusoe* (1831), as well as works for Tobias George Smollett, Henry Fielding, and Miguel de Cervantes.

But Cruikshank's best known illustrations are those done for the works of Charles Dickens. He illustrated Dickens's first book, *Sketches by Boz* (1836), and his third, *Oliver Twist* (1838). The twenty-four etchings for *Oliver Twist*, including the famous "Fagin in the Condemned Cell," are considered the finest illustrations ever made for Dickens. But they are also the last illustrations he did for Dickens, as Dickens objected to the increasingly grim visualization of characters in the final plates. Also Cruikshank desired a greater control over the illustrations and the text than Dickens was willing to allow.

Most of Cruikshank's work was on copper, etched by himself, but the illustrations on wood were engraved by others. In his illustrations, Cruikshank never attempted to follow changing tastes, although he modified his style to accommodate the tone of the text and the medium of reproduction. There are over 6,000 published graphic works and thousands of pencil sketches, scribbles, and watercolors in various collections over the world. The most important collection can be found in the British Museum.

Dickens worked closely with several illustrators, including George Cattermole, John Leech, Daniel Maclise, Marcus Stone, Luke Fildes, and his son-in-law Charles Allston Collins. His closest association, however, was with Hablot Knight Browne ("Phiz"). Their association began when he illustrated *Sunday under Three Heads* (1836), an anti-Sabbatarian pamphlet published pseudonymously by Dickens. Later Dickens preferred Browne to Thackeray as collaborator in the production of *The Posthumous Papers of the Pickwick Club* (1836–37), and it is from this work that the signature "Phiz" derives: Browne first signed his work "Nemo" then "Phiz," a depicter of physiognomies, to parallel Dickens's "Boz." Browne illustrated ten of Dickens's fifteen serialized novels, including *Nicolas Nickleby* (1838–39), *David Copperfield* (1849–50), and *Bleak House* (1853). As he continued to work for Dickens, he refined his style, often focusing on domestic interiors whose details, often pictures, are in ironical counterpoint to the main actions. The dark-plate etchings for *Bleak House* are considered to be among his finest, providing not only narrative interest but also a visual drama unprecedented in his earlier work.

Browne also illustrated texts by Charles Lever, William Ainsworth, and Anthony Trollope, but none with the comedic or narrative impact of his work with Dickens. Partially paralyzed in 1867, he worked very little in his later life, but his earlier achievements as an illustrator were recognized with the award of a Royal Academy pension.

Unusual is the work of William Thackeray, better known as a novelist than an illustrator. When Dickens needed an illustrator for the *Pickwick Papers*, Thackeray applied for the post and later claimed that if his application had been successful, he might have made his living as an illustrator rather than a novelist. From 1842 to 1851 Thackeray was employed as a writer and artist by *Punch* magazine. He illustrated all his early novels, including *Vanity Fair* (1848) and *Pendennis* (1850). As an author and illustrator, Thackeray saw the relationship between work and image as a kind of dialogue, as emphasized in the subtitle of *Vanity Fair*: "Pen and Pencil Sketches of English Society."

Thackeray follows the tradition of graphic satire, but lacked the technical expertise of his mentor, George Cruikshank. Only the very best of his published drawings retain the spontaneity of his private sketches, and many critics argue that rather than adding to the reader's understanding of the text, the illustrations rely on the text to have an effect. Although he continued to illustrate some of his minor works such as *The Rose and the Ring* (1854), Thackeray chose to have his later novels, with the exception of *The Virginian* (1859), illustrated by other artists, particularly Richard Doyle. Nevertheless, Thackeray's novels and essays demonstrate his lifelong love of painting: *The Newcomes* (1853) has a section on an artist's life in Rome, and the historical novels all allude to the art of the period.

Thackeray drew three kinds of illustrations: pictorial capitals at the beginning of a chapter, usually metaphoric; intratextual illustrations, placed to affect the reading of the text; and full-page illustrations, with titles suggesting basic presentation of the text. Martin Meisel notes that the full-page illustrations often follow the conventions of straightforward "realization," although there are exceptions, including the familiar "Second Appearance of Clytemnestra" (335). It is in the small vignette or initial letter, however, where Thackeray's gift for illustration is best seen, his wit and exuberance flourishing within a compressed space. Although a pictorial capital letter is generally considered a more modest field for an artist than the full-page etchings or the large wood-engravings that appear mid-text, for Thackeray the capitals allowed an imaginative use of visual irony and analogy unhindered by the need to depict a "real" scene. In Thackeray's works, the capitals are often surprisingly large, increasing in size from novel to novel as his interest in the form grows.

A survey of the early chapters of *Vanity Fair* reveals how quickly Thackeray came to understand the possibilities of the illuminated letter. The early chapters are relatively straightforward in their depictions: Chapter 1 is neatly defined by the picture of a coach coming towards and by an ending vignette of a coach driving away. The chapter begins with the two heroines awaiting the coach that will transport them from the routine of school to the turmoil of Vanity Fair, and concludes with Miss Jemima watching the coach depart. The illustration for Chapter 2 is primarily decorative: a rococo decoration of a W resting on the shoulders of a satyr. Chapter 3 illustrates Jos's character, framing a sketch of whim with a large capital A, suggesting his physique. But by Chapter 4, Thackeray seems to have grasped the ironic subtleties of indirect allusion: A little girl holds a fishing rod for a large, round fish, referring to Becky's angling for Jos.

As the series of pictorial capitals advances, Thackeray begins to create a series of men in fool's costume; interspersed among the more representative initials, they come to function as a chorus. Further, each monthly part of *Vanity Fair* opened with a cover picture of a Fool preaching to Fools, and Thackeray warns the reader in Chapter 8: "And while the moralist, who is holding forth on the cover (an accurate portrait of your humble servant), professes to wear neither gown nor bands, but only the same long-eared livery in which his congregation is arrayed: yet, look you, one is bound to speak the truth as far as one knows it, whether one mounts a cap and bells or a shovel-hat." The direct reference to the capital illustration here and elsewhere in the novel is significant, as John Harvey notes, because "by referring to this picture in the text Thackeray was able to project it over the action of the novel like a lantern-slide" (88). Over the course of the novel the interspersing of the Fools with other satiric pictorial capitals reinforces the unifying theme of the novel—"vanitas vanitatum"— without becoming monotonous or intrusive.

But book illustration was not without drawbacks. An example is the "'sixties" book, verse or prose with illustrations by a Victorian artist reproduced by competent if often unexciting wood engraving, which briefly dominated the publishing market. Artists such as Arthur Boyd Houghton, G. J. Pinwell, John Everett Millais, and John Tenniel illustrated books during this period. Millais illustrated a number of books, including several novels by Anthony Trollope, the most notable being *Orley Farm* (1862). But many of the great illustrated books of this period were a by-product of magazines, and the engravings were made to stand on their own. In most cases any accompanying text was written afterwards, explaining why so many of the illustrations are squared up and so few are vignettes. This is also why many collectors think they appear at an advantage away from the books they were designed to illustrate and in the collections that were often made of them years later. Many of the most famous illustrated books of the period are collections of poetry or short stories, allowing for a series of static impressions. The first major book was William Allingham's poetry volume *The Music Master* (1855), containing eight engravings by Arthur Hughes, one by D. G. Rossetti, and one by Millais. Similarly Moxon's Tennyson (1857) showcased the works of the Pre-Raphaelites but did little to balance text and illustration. When the book was reissued in 1901, photographs of the original drawings were included for comparison with the illustrations, indicating that the illustrations of the sixties were legendary by the end of the century. The most remarkable illustrations of the period are John Tenniel's illustrations to the *Alice* books, where the text and illustrations harmonize remarkably well for their period. It is perhaps significant that these are the only noteworthy illustrations Tenniel ever made.

Tenniel began his career as a fresco artist, but following a fencing accident in which he was blinded in his right eye, he relied on what he called "a wonderful memory of observation" and concentrated on book illustration. He first achieved success with *Hall's Book of British Ballads* (1842) and *Aesop's Fables* (1848). The *Times* lauded his work for Thomas Moore's *Lalla Rookh* (1861) as "the greatest illustrative achievement of any single hand." A notable success, the overlay of Anglican virtues in Moore's "Persian" poems with the naïvely simple facial expressions in Tenniel's illustrations creates a vehicle of high imperialism. In contrast, in *Aesop's Fables,* Tenniel exaggerated the animals' features, producing a critique of High Anglican bourgeois manners.

But it is in his illustrations for Lewis Carroll's *Alice's Adventures in Wonderland* (1865) and *Through the Looking Glass* (1872) that Tenniel's ability to match illustration with subtext clearly shows. Tenniel's illustrations draw to the forefront Alice's ability to remain unperturbed while meeting and interpreting the extraordinary. And even though Carroll's fame has overshadowed that of his illustrator, Tenniel's drawings continue to dominate and shape readers' memories of the *Alice* stories. By creating interesting characters and farcical humor appealing to children while providing a second, more sophisticated, level of visual irony appealing to adults, in his drawings Alice transcends the borders of nursery and drawing room. And unlike the narrative, the illustrations do not require a linear unfolding but are instantly set in memory. Yet the collaboration between Tenniel and Carroll was troubled: Initially they could agree only on the picture of Humpty-Dumpty, and Tenniel refused to use any of Carroll's models, either photographical or life. The final products, however, endure as two of the greatest examples of illustrated books.

One other notable book with wood-engraved illustrations that have been fitted into the text is Charles Kingsley's *The Water Babies* (1885), with illustrations by Linley Sambourne. This has been called "the only distinguished woodcut book of the eighties" (Balston). During the last third of the century, color wood-engraving, a more attractive process than the reproductive black-and-white method, was developed. In this process the drawings were actually photographed onto the wood, an indication of the direction in which illustration reproduction was moving. Some of the most famous examples are the Kate Greenaway books published by Edmund Evans. Hugh Thomson, one of the first pen draughtsmen in England to benefit from process reproduction, illustrated works such as Oliver Goldsmith's *The Vicar of Wakefield* (1891) and Elizabeth Gaskell's *Cranford* (1892).

One of the most famous producers of illustrated books at the end of the century is William Morris's Kelmscott Press. Just as photoengraving began to make inroads in book illustration, Morris revived wood engraving in a primitive woodcut manner. Using fifteenth-century methods, Morris used hand presses, heavy paper, and lavish designs; however, only a few are illustrated, and even these depend to a surprising extent on their surrounding decorations for effect. One of the most remarkable books is *The Canterbury Tales* (1896) with designs by Edward Burne-Jones. But as with earlier books illustrated by Pre-Raphaelite artists, the illustrations tend to stand alone, often seeming removed from the text they are to illustrate. As Bruce Rogers, a distinguished American typographer, remarked, Morris's books "are some of them very beautiful but they are rather curiosities of book-making than real books" (quoted in Bland, 275). Morris labeled himself a decorator rather than an illustrator, saying illustration was first of all decoration and storytelling second.

The only great book illustrator of the 1890s was Beardsley, who stands out from the lush romanticism typical of the period. He was the first artist to see the possibilities of the process-line block in his use of single, fine lines, white space, and solid blacks, as in his drawings for Oscar Wilde's *Salome* (1894). Later, in works such as the illustrations for Alexander Pope's *The Rape of the Lock* (1896), he also incorporated textured patterns and stippled effects. While working on illustrations for *Salome* and *Morte Darthur*, Beardsley began work for what became a series of books and that made him better known at the time than the limited-audience work he had been doing. He did the title page and cover for George Egerton's (Mary Chavelity Dunne) *Keynotes* (1893), and for the back cover devised an ornamental "key" combining the author's initials. The novel became the first of a series of thirty-four works published by Elkin Mathews and John Lane under the *Keynotes* colophon. Beardsley designed the covers and title pages for twenty-two novels in the series, and the monogram "keys" for fifteen. The series, which included then-scandalous works such as Grant Allen's *The Woman Who Did*, and fiction by Arthur Machen, Kenneth Grahame, and Florence Farr, was among the most popular of the decade and for years afterward Beardsley's work was seen through it when it was otherwise unavailable.

During his lifetime many people who admired Beardsley's talent deplored how he used it. In his introduction to R.E.D. Sketchley's *English Book Illustration of To-day*, A. W. Pollard, for example, could not praise Beardsley's superb use of line for process blocks without the added commentary, "degenerate and despicable as was almost every figure he drew" (quoted in Ray, 194). It should be kept in mind, however, that Beardsley only lived to be twenty-five and his excesses could be an aspect of his youth. Near the end of his life, he told his sister Mabel, "The more society relaxes the less charm and point there is in Bohemianism" (*Letters*, 424). Despite his abbreviated life, Beardsley was quite prolific, especially between 1892 and 1896, and virtually all of his work found its way into publication. His designs were a potent force in establishing the vogue of Art Nouveau, not only in England but throughout Europe and America, and influenced several of the leaders of the Modernist movement in painting.

WORKS CITED AND SELECTED WORKS FOR FURTHER READING

Balston, T. "English Book Illustration, 1880–1900." *New Paths in Book Collecting: Essays*. Ed. John Carter. New York: Scribner's, 1934.

Beardsley, Aubrey. *The Letters*. Ed. Henry Maas, J. L. Duncan, and W. G. Good. New York: Associated UP, 1975.

Bland, David. *A History of Book Illustration: The Illuminated Manuscript and the Printed Book*. Berkeley: U of California P, 1958.

Chesterton, G. K. *Charles Dickens: A Critical Study*. New York: Dodd, Mead, 1935.

Harvey, John R. *Victorian Novelists and Their Illustrators*. New York: New York UP, 1971.

Meisel, Martin. *Realizations: Narrative, Pictorial, and Theatrical Arts in Nineteenth-Century England*. Princeton: Princeton UP, 1983.

Ray, Gordon N. *The Illustrator and the Book in England from 1790 to 1914*. Oxford: Oxford UP, 1976.

Stevens, Joan. "Thackeray's *Vanity Fair*." *Review of English Literature* 6 (1965): 19–38.

Wakeman, Geoffrey. *Victorian Book Illustration: The Technical Revolution*. Detroit: Gale Research, 1973.

II
Victorian Cultural Contexts

The Nineteenth-Century Political Novel

Julian Wolfreys

INTRODUCTION

Is it possible to talk about the "political novel" in the nineteenth century? Can we be certain that we can distinguish between novels that are political (supposing, for the moment, that the meaning of this term is self-evident) as opposed to those that are not? How, in speaking of a century which saw the enlargement of the franchise, Catholic Emancipation, the rise of women's suffrage, union and other forms of collective organization, revolution throughout Europe if not in Britain, and the suspicion, by the end of the century, of anarchy virtually everywhere (at least in the imagination of governments, the police, and popular journalism), is it possible to begin to address the discourse of politics or—an even more difficult task—to separate the very notion of politics from itself, as multiple and fissured, rather than as a single object of inquiry, concept, or practice? Is it possible, or even desirable, on the one hand, to address politics narrowly conceived as the social, institutionally organized representation of the nation by its elected representatives and the laws that these representatives enact, regardless of political party, while, on the other, to speak of "politics," defined more widely as those social movements and phenomena just alluded to? And, to return to the instituting question of this chapter, is it possible to speak of novels that are political, whether narrowly or broadly, as distinct from those that appear to speak neither of governments and politicians (as, for example, in the case of certain of the novels of Anthony Trollope or Benjamin Disraeli) nor of union agitation (*North and South*, *Mary Barton*, *Hard Times*) or the rights of women?

Given the fraught condition of definition with which one is faced, it may equally be tempting to suggest that all novels are political, though all are not equally so. It might be said that some novels are born political, some become political, others have the political thrust upon them. There is something of a minefield in this approach, in that if everything is political (including the novels being read, the culture in which they are produced, their reception in subsequent periods, and the critical reading of them), it would seem that the political is in danger of being depoliticized, or, at least, mystified to some extent. Of course, we have to run this risk, attending all the while not to simple imaginary divisions between the political and nonpolitical but seeking to read difference within the idea of the political as well as the politics of difference. However problematic, this is doubtless a gesture in the right direction at least, inasmuch as we admit that the political—which, we feel it necessary to interject, is never simply a single identity—is as much discursive and ideological as *it* is institutional and a matter of lived, often contradictory, if not actively paradoxical and ambivalent practices. Such contradictoriness and ambivalence in turn serves however indirectly to produce narrative discourse in the form of fiction that is, itself, not simply consonant or harmonious within itself, but, always already, fractured, dissonant, and heterogeneous. In that novels of the nineteenth century mediate and are mediated by a heterogeneous range of discourses outside the immediate scope of the literary, and, furthermore, inasmuch as most novels configure through a play of rhetorical, mimetic devices a perceptibly "real" world within which they come into print (even dystopian fictions such as Samuel Butler's *Erewhon* or Anthony Trollope's *The Fixed Period*), their language (what we conventionally, and, perhaps, mistakenly refer to, for the sake of convenience as "narrative voice") is as complex—and therefore *political*—as the social and cultural environment out of which they are produced.

The question of the "political novel" is, then, transformed, for it has become a question of how we choose to read and, in so doing, rather than distinguishing between the political, whether narrow or broad and the non- or apolitical, choosing instead to learn how to read in different and diverse manners, in order that, as we read, we comprehend that what we define as the political changes according to the text with which we are concerned. In this, there seems to be something of a tacit acknowledgment of how the novel itself appears to address contemporary concerns in the nineteenth century, as, in all its various, highly individual guises, it accommodates itself to, even as it interprets, that most semantically flexible of discursive categories, which always and in some fashion signifies and is brought to bear on material, cultural, and social conditions: politics.

FROM SOCIAL PROBLEMS TO THE POLITICAL

The novels conventionally defined as "social-problem novels" are *Hard Times* (Dickens), *Mary Barton* and *North and South* (Elizabeth Gaskell), *Alton Locke* (Charles Kingsley, whose *Yeast* might also be added to this list), *Sybil* (Benjamin Disraeli), and Eliot's *Felix Holt* (Guy, 3; see also Ingham [*Language*], who discusses Gaskell, Dickens, and Eliot; and Childers, who discusses Kingsley and Gaskell). What distinguishes the novels here is their interest in representations of class and labor relations, even though, as Josephine Guy points out, the novels were not thought of as a "group by their nineteenth-century readers or critics" (Guy, 3). The labels "social-problem novel" or "industrial novel" have been affixed in the second half of the twentieth century as a typical phenomenon of the role of institutionalized literary criticism (as Guy's study makes plain, 3–63). The definition or identification of such a subgenre goes hand in hand with the interest in the related questions of literature and culture, literature and history, and what is all too broadly defined as literature's context. As Josephine Guy, again, clarifies, the rise in interest in the "industrial novel" is, itself, a historical phenomenon that occurs in critical discourse, as the debate around the importance of the historicized study of literature and literary production is taken up, insisted on, for example, by Oxford critic F. W. Bateson on the one hand and dismissed on the other by Cambridge critic F. R. Leavis. (There is, in this, a politics of interpretation and a political history of literary criticism, which would be useful to read with regard to the question of canonization.)

However, as Guy goes on to show, the modern critical perception has, until recently, been at odds with the Victorian reception of the novels in question, not least for the variance between the mid-nineteenth and late-twentieth century comprehension of problems as, on the one hand, individual and, on the other, social (9–10). This disjunction calls to account the very role of historical knowledge for Guy in the interpretation of literary texts, so that, whether from what she describes as Marxist, contextualist, or New Historicist perspectives, there is a shared "attempt to explain social-problem novels in terms of the historical circumstances which produce them" (5). Ironically, the three analytical modes share for Guy a lack of awareness of the "political and social topicality" of the texts in question (8). This occurs, at least in part because, in the words of Patricia Ingham (citing Mary Poovey), "literary critics . . . seem readily to overlook the possibility that the representation of social class and that of industrial society were similarly 'in the making' and 'open . . . to dispute'" (Ingham, *Language*, 2). Moreover, critical tendencies assuming similarity rather than difference have, to some degree, tended to overlook the complex mediations of competing and frequently contradictory discourses that come together in the novel, as Elizabeth Deeds Ermath has been at pains to stress (84–93). In relation to the politics of gender in the Victorian novel, Poovey shows how any narrative account of gender is "both contested and always under construction; because it was always in the making, it was always open to revision, dispute and the emergence of oppositional formulations." What may appear today about Victorian representations of politics, class and gender as coherent and organically of a piece, was, in the nineteenth century "actually fissured by competing emphases and interests" (Poovey, 3).

Change is a keyword in the nineteenth century, and was, furthermore, according to Joseph Childers, "lived at 'such a depth' and so saturated society that it attained hegemonic status" for the Victorians (23). One aspect of change was the "new language of class," first critically identified by Asa Briggs (1967), but subsequently given further development as a subject of critical inquiry in relation to the political novel by Patricia Ingham (6). The language of class—itself a signifier of modernity that separates the Victorians discursively and politically from their ancestors—dependent on a perception of the relation between economic and social status, transforms Victorian self-awareness, as it replaces the more static, hierarchically fixed and organic language of rank and station (Ingham, *Language*, 4–5). That the emphasis is on language, that is to say on signifying systems, rather than on some simply assumed reality and its unproblematic representation is telling. Both Ingham and Childers in their studies of political discourse in the Victorian text bring out with great subtlety the complex interanimation through the medium of language between the areas of politics and literature, in order to demonstrate the constant process of change taking place both socially and linguistically during the 1830s, '40s, and '50s, a period in which political, economic, and social crisis was matched and mediated by "linguistic crisis or conflict of discourses" (Ingham, *Language*, 3). There is thus not available to us a "univocal totality without contradictions," as Childers suggests (23), whether one analyzes political discourse as a language of progress emanating from Parliament or other political sources, or via its manifestations in literary texts. Moreover, "politics and the novel are two major systems that often overlap each sharing certain aspects of its language and interpretations with the other" (Childers, 35). It is such interweaving for which we should read, and which, in turn can give us to comprehend the novel in the nineteenth century as political in the broadest sense imaginable, thereby allowing our critical acts to move beyond the restrictive categorization of the "social-problem," "industrial," or "condition of England" novel.

CONINGSBY: ENGLAND IN TRANSITION

Coningsby, like George Eliot's *Felix Holt, The Radical*, is set in the period of the 1832 Reform Act (a narrative strategy used again by Eliot in *Middlemarch* [1871–72]), by which the franchise was extended in Great Britain. In doing so, Disraeli (and, arguably Eliot) relies for the cogency of his various narratives and ideological perspectives on a reading of founding political moment for both the modern era to which he belongs, and for the construction of a narrative that implies politics as that which offers to the Victorian reader what Eliot is to refer to in *Daniel Deronda* as "the make-believe of a beginning" (35). As Joseph Childers puts it, *Coningsby*, "besides being arguably the first English political novel, [it] combines and examines two major interpretive systems of nineteenth-century Britain: the novel and parliamentary politics":

In doing so, it maintains not only that political representations of the world may be "factitious" but that the truth claims of fiction often may carry more weight than their political counterparts. This is particularly momentous for the status of the novel in Victorian England. For, in spite of Disraeli's often paradoxical explications of social and political change, *Coningsby*'s assertion that novels can offer workable . . . explanations of the rapidly changing world helps establish the genre as an instrument of social criticism and an interpretive discourse that actively informs Victorian culture. (12)

I quote Childers at some length, for the argument he puts forward, drawing on the exemplary status of the text of Disraeli is precisely the argument presented in this chapter concerning the necessity of reading the political differently: not simply as a critical-theoretical gesture of the late-twentieth century but also as a (political) response and understanding of the work of the novel in the nineteenth. The status of the novel is, itself, political, and that status changes as the discourses comprising literary and fictional prose actively take on the facticity, as Childers puts it, of political discourse and event. To write from the make-believe of a beginning, which is the First Reform Act, is not only to "ground" the play of fiction on a historical fact, it is also to acknowledge the sense in which the world and its representations are actively textual.

The First Reform Act is not, of course, the only political event of the first third of the nineteenth century, even though its significance was undeniable inasmuch as it doubled the number of those who could vote, from approximately 500,000 to 1,000,000. In the years following the Act of 1832, up to the coronation of Victoria, other equally significant Acts of Parliament were passed, along with other events, which today, can be read as both determining what we understand as the narrative of the Victorian period and providing for the Victorians themselves a variety of narrative details which are, themselves, political, and by which the Victorians can define a self-aware narrative of modernity separating them from their Hanoverian predecessors (with the death of William IV all ties to Hanover were finally broken, and the English Monarchy became, arguably, for the first time, English).

Amongst the political changes that took place were the 1834 Poor Law Amendment Act. This decreed that no able-bodied person was eligible for poor relief unless he or she entered the workhouse. The fear of the workhouse was so public and so long-lasting that if one takes the works of Dickens, one will find ambivalent reference to its horrors and abuses from *Oliver Twist* (1838), through Scrooge's Malthusian allusion in *A Christmas Carol* (1843), again in *Bleak House* (1853) and *Little Dorrit* (1857) in the figure of Nandy, the workhouse occupant, and, finally his last completed novel, *Our Mutual Friend* (1865), with the character of Betty Higden, who would rather kill herself and baby Johnny than be taken to the workhouse (324). If we pause at Dickens before returning to Disraeli, taking our cue from the work of deconstruction and the ways in which it has taught critics to read questions such as those of politics differently, we can suggest that the Dickensian text gives us the possibility of reading the complex and persistent, encrypted manifestation of, and response to, politics, to which, if we are not attendant, then we are liable to make assumptions that certain novels are political while others are not. In the case of Dickens, it is very much a question of reading a different appearance of politics and reading politics differently. The text of Dickens persistently manifests the trace and discursive effect of the Poor Law Amendment Act. In fact, we can suggest that the Act, though hardly, if ever, named as such nonetheless returns in a reiterative fashion as the spectral trace of political discourse and institutional practice, haunting the Dickensian text. At the same time, thinking the question of the political novel differently, and paying attention to such "incidental" traces, allows us to read Dickens's novels as political novels, albeit different in degree rather than kind from more apparently obviously politically engaged novels, such as *North and South*.

The year following the Poor Law Amendment Act saw the 1835 Factory Act, which ensured, in principle at least, inspection of working conditions in factories, while, in the same year there came about the abolition of slavery in those states belonging to the British Empire. During this year, closer to home, but with profound political ramifications, was the Municipal Corporation Act, which transformed the political management and government of local boroughs and the towns therein, in ways that have lasted piecemeal to the present day. In 1836, the working-class movement known as the People's Charter, or Chartism, as it is more commonly called, came to be established, demanding universal suffrage; in 1838, the Anti-Corn Law League was also established (lasting eight years) in order to combat the political fixing of corn prices in favor of domestic product, which led directly to artificially high bread prices (Hobsbawm, 41).

These, then, are some of the overtly political domestic events taking place between the moment in which *Coningsby* is set and the year in which it is published. If we recall the complications of the idea of the political novel put in place earlier, the following comment from Thom Braun, the editor of the Penguin edition of Disraeli's novel, is instructive: "His novels of the 1840s were political, not just in being about politics, but in being themselves manipulative, and in attempting to present disparate, paradoxical, and often contradictory views within an artificially created organic whole" (8). To an extent I agree with Braun's assessment, but where we part company is over the aesthetic inflection of the editor's remark, where *political*, in being equated obliquely with conscious effort, becomes a sign of awkward, dishonest construction. As is implied throughout this chapter (and recalling the remarks of Guy, Ingham, Ermath, and particularly Childers's description of "Disraeli's often paradoxical explications of social and political change"), contradiction and paradox are the conditions of discursive flow and mediation, particularly that so obviously in the throes of cultural transition, and infected so clearly with the signs of its historicity. Disraeli's novel *is* political certainly, but not simply in the double sense afforded it by Braun.

With Disraeli's *Sybil* (1845) and *Tancred* (1847), *Coningsby* was part of what became referred to as the "Young England" trilogy. The trilogy mediates the politics of early Victorian England in interesting ways, conceiving "of history as structured like a spiral, permitting progress or displacement forward provided it is conceptualized in terms that evoke a hallowed past" (Bivona, 3). The collective term for the trilogy is instructive, sounding as it does like a slogan for the current Labour Party under the leadership of Tony Blair. It points to the youthful modernity that mid-Victorian England was already constructing for itself as the narrative of its own progress and change, as well as signaling an attempted divorce from its regency parents. This is caught in the narrative concerns of *Coningsby* itself, and summarized succinctly in political and ideological terms by Daniel Bivona. Coningsby, "the aristocratic hero of the novel," regains his lost inheritance from his grandfather; this

and his eventual marriage to Edith Millbank are intended to mark the metaphorical passage of landed wealth from a decadent Regency aristocracy to a youthful, but serious and reform-minded, Victorian one, and, more importantly, a symbolic merger of the manufacturing class with the landed aristocracy: a fantasy empowerment which is presented here as a taming process which softens and civilizes the unpolished manners of the middle classes as it appropriates their world-historical energies. (Bivona, 5–6)

Thus, the novel is not simply political because it addresses more or less directly political characters and events, or the "agitation which for a year and a half had shaken England to its very center" as Disraeli chooses to put it (36), nor because it works its fictions against a discernibly "true" historical narrative (however manipulated). It is also political—and this having to do with the politics of national identity and the question of a somewhat self-reflexive narrative mediating the desires of a reading public eager to have presented to it a progressive, yet essentially English vision of itself—in that it tells a "historicized" tale whereby the new and the old commingle in the name of nation and as an articulation of national discourse. And what perhaps is most telling is that Disraeli's text, and the two subsequent novels of the trilogy, actively mediate the political, social, and economic transactions between classes in the instance of national transition, can be read as justifying politically its entire trajectory from that one line, just cited here. The rhetoric of agitation and solicitation, touching the very core of Englishness (wherever that core or center may chance to be located; Disraeli is silent on this point), is so forceful, not to say violent, in condition, that the political necessity, not to say inevitability, for political transformation is all but assured.

LITTLE DORRIT

Like *Coningsby, Little Dorrit* is a novel that constructs an historical narrative of the Victorian Era and Victorian political discourse and institutions by turning back to earlier times, although in Dickens's case the moment is the late 1820s, and not the moment of the Reform Act of 1832. His novel is therefore less directly political (as has been said of his other novels) and yet has more to do with a certain political, or, rather, ideological flow that serves in turn to define the attitudes and perspectives of particular sections of the British public. Moreover, there is something decidedly readable, in the historical work of the text, a doubling of political commentary, requiring an equally double focus on the part of the reader. Thus, the novel is imbued with a certain strategic historicized anachronism, whereby "time is out of joint," so to speak.

On the one hand, one possible reading of the novel's political condition would turn its attention to the political situations of the 1820s, to the transformations and transitions underway, culturally and ideologically, in the Britain of William IV, particularly as these are given a somewhat oblique focus through the estranged cultural figure of Arthur Clennam. Clennam, already in his early 40s upon his return to Britain, belongs to another age, and moves, with an "other" perception or perspective on the Britain that he encounters. He is therefore written by Dickens so as to afford the reader of the 1850s a different vantage point from within English culture from which to view the national, cultural self. On the other hand, Dickens's representation of the Office of Circumlocution (itself a composite) as a figure for the practice, institution, discourse, and ideological self-interest of British politics and its close relations with economic matters affecting the lives of all Britons is readable as a somewhat transgenerational, if not transhistorical, figure.

It may be addressed, therefore, as speaking to the question of, as well as encrypting and analyzing in what Diane Elam describes as an "alienating" manner (168), the political configuration in both moments, the 1820s and 1850s. Elam's analysis addresses particularly the question of time—the several times of the novel (as she puts it, clock, psychic, organic), which seem anachronistically untimely, and all the more modern for that. Time for Elam is particularly related to matters of debt (168–71), itself a literal and figural, and, indeed, political concern of *Little Dorrit*, wherein one may say that it is debt rather than money that circulates, and that comes back, within time, across time, and from time to time (as if there were a manifestation of Nietzschean eternal recurrence haunting the structure of the Dickensian text or, as Elam herself suggests, a somewhat uncanny encounter with Heideggerian concepts of temporality *avant la lettre* [168ff]).

What Elam's reading of time does not specifically address are the related matters of facticity, historicity, and the narratives of temporality that these invoke, and to which the question of the novel qua political is yoked. From this vantage point, and in order to read politically the very political question of national identity, the reader may come to understand that a persistent characteristic of Englishness in the nineteenth century is a certain mystification and obfuscation with regard to the perpetration and perpetuation of political power. In this political reading of the novel, we may also wish to read the Dickensian construction of the convolutions of political machinery as, itself, a political response, albeit one that as a number of critics of the novel have argued, is partially recuperated into the very same political aspects of Englishness that are manifested through the Circumlocution Office. What returns is not only Arthur Clennam; what returns is what is always already in operation, the recurring politics of the political system, a certain historical revenance and recirculation that both defines and maintains the politics of Englishness and the Englishness of (these) politics.

To take the political reading further, thereby opening the politics of the novel in another fashion: There is also, very much, and very much encrypted in the text, a question of colonial political relations, not least in the references to Arthur Clennam's having worked in his father's business in China for many years and Flora Casby's inane questions concerning received English (narrative) wisdom about Mandarins and pigtails. Jeremy Tambling's Foucauldian inflected reading of the text (98–128) takes full account of the various histories that inform *Little Dorrit*, looking at how both historical past and political present come to inform the novel as an anachronistic and political site. The background of the novel's composition is the Crimean War (99), while the Opium War of 1840–42 led to another war (1856–60), in the name of Free Trade (116–17). Yet the Clennam firm's interest in China belongs very firmly to the period between the 1780s and 1820s (the period of Arthur's youth) of the East India Company, colonial trade, and imperial expansion (see Tambling, 116). Clennam's return to Britain occurs, arguably, at a point in British history where foreign trade begins to be superseded by domestic economic enterprise.

So, whereas from one perspective, Clennam may, as Patricia Ingham correctly suggests, draw together the various strands of the narrative by his "itinerant" activity (Ingham, "Nobody's Fault," 101), temporally, historically, Clennam's mobility, we might say his *motivation* (or at least the motivation behind his agency) is to thread a discontinuous weave between periods and moments of English political and economic endeavor, between the various presents, pasts, and futures of the text, so as to open to view the persistence of the national political interest. If, from one perspective, "change" is a Victorian word, in the text of *Little Dorrit*, maintenance (alongside change) also, equally, has a cogent political valence. As Disraeli had sought to bring together the aristocracy and productive middle-classes, so Dickens, through the figure of Clennam, observes the economic and political and economical transformations *and* inheritances. Clennam tries to adapt, leaving the parental firm because it is no longer of the times, and eventually turns to the economic potential and industry (in more than one sense) of Daniel Doyce. (Although this also is somewhat anachronistic, Doyce's workshop in Bleeding Heart Yard having more of artisanal endeavor about it than the mass productivity of the industrial revolution.) Yet this fails also, because Clennam is always figured as hopelessly out of date and out of time.

Thus, there is, in *Little Dorrit*'s reading of the condition of England, a sense of political ambivalence: Arthur Clennam, perhaps a typical English businessman, no different except in degree from either the modern entrepreneur Mr. Merdle or the aging remnant of the late eighteenth century, Mr. Dorrit, fails (despite the projected romantic happiness of the novel's conclusion). For, we read *Little Dorrit* suggesting, without radical political transformation, that the English imprison themselves and will continue to do so. Mr. Meagles's brass weighing scales may well be a sign of the times, but which times we're not exactly sure. "Do Not Forget," the phrase inherited from Arthur's father (ironically, appropriately) suggests that, whether one is located in the 1780s, the 1820s, or the 1850s, in not forgetting, the English can never move on. Given the imminent political and economic rise of the United States particularly, and

Germany shortly thereafter, in the period following the publication of *Little Dorrit*, the novel becomes available as all too prescient.

KINGSLEY, DICKENS, AND THE INDIVIDUAL

Although Charles Kingsley arguably "embodied the contradictions in the critique of industrial capitalism more fully than any other Victorian writer" (Gallagher, 88), and although his writing is marked by an "ambivalence about the relationship between character and circumstances" (89), he began his career as a novelist in an avowedly polemical manner, with two novels, *Yeast* (1848) and *Alton Locke* (1850), that, undeniably address contemporary political concerns and issues. Published in the year of European revolutions, *Yeast* addresses two different, yet prevalent concerns of the mid-Victorian period: the impoverished conditions of the rural working class and their exploitation by the landed gentry, and the abandonment of the Church of England by a number of the younger generation in favor of Catholicism. The two narratives are not kept separate, but the discourses of Christianity and politics are shown to commingle, in the figure of the responsible individual, in this novel, Lancelot Smith who embodies the mid-Victorian concept of Christian manliness. (On the subject of Christian manliness and for a reading of Kingsley's *Alton Locke*, see David Alderson, 43–61; on the subject of muscular Christianity in the nineteenth century in general, see also Donald E. Hall and Norman Vance).

A novel in which Kingsley "illustrates the interconnectedness he finds among sexual repression, dirt and disease" (Fasick, 95), *Yeast* is unusual, if not unique, among overtly political novels in that it deals with the rural rather than the urban poor, unlike the novels of Gaskell, Disraeli, and Dickens. Causing something of a stir at the time of its serial publication (it had to be ended abruptly, so many complaints did *Fraser's Magazine* receive), *Yeast* was derived from three principal sources of which Kingsley had firsthand knowledge: his own encounters with the conditions of rural workers; the philanthropic work of his brother-in-law Sidney Godolphin Osborne, a Dorset rector who sought to establish better living conditions for farmhands; and the 1843 *Reports of Special Assistant Poor Law Commissioners on the Employment of Women and Children in Agriculture*, which provided harsh detail of the abject state of rural working conditions. However, it is a sign of the contradictory, if not contestatory, tussle of political discourse that marks this, and other novels, as historically rather than personally determined, that, while Kingsley's reformist tendencies manifest themselves in full sympathy for workers' conditions, there is also the sign of political conservatism in the novel's distrust of radical and systematic Christian doctrine, while, simultaneously, there is a conservative moral judgment at work in response to the middle-class, land-owning heroine, Argemone Lavington, whose desire to reject a conventional gender role and sexual life is read, in the text, as "unnatural and . . . unhealthy in its consequences" (Fasick, 96).

Like its predecessor, *Alton Locke*, a novel inspired by the Chartist movement, brings together the reformist concern over working conditions—this time those of the novel's titular character, an East End London tailor and poet—and the particular ideological currents of Victorian Christianity in transition. Kingsley, typical of Victorian novelists of whatever political orientation, focuses on the individual as a means of humanizing political struggle, and thereby both mystifying and depoliticizing the rights of the proletariat from certain perspectives. (As Josephine Guy puts it, "mid-Victorian writers (of whatever political persuasion) tended to understand problems in society in individual, rather than social terms" [*Language*, 9].) As if to argue against any form of system that does not have as its center or origin the idea of the individual, the novel is, as David Alderson puts it, "a significant text in the representation of the demise of Chartism as being a result of the movement's own ineptitude" (44).

To turn to Dickens momentarily, in relation to the Victorian politics of individuality as opposed to the systematic: Consider, for example, the relatively crude polarization in Dickens's *Hard Times* between the all-too-human and pathetic figure of Stephen Blackpool, who is cast against not only the impersonal systems of the employers but also, disingenuously and ideologically on Dickens's part, the equally impersonal and therefore inhuman union movement. The labor movement is read in the text as monstrous because it has no room to comprehend or allow for Stephen's personal domestic dilemmas. However to read the politics of this narrative differently, it is important to understand how the novelist's act of humanization is itself political in that it insists on the primacy of personal, individual emotional experience, over collective political need and class-based rights. Structurally this forms an extended narrative gesture that, undoubtedly, found political resonance of the most conservative kind in the reading of F. R. Leavis, who, with a disingenuous gesture surpassing Dickens's own, described the novel as a "moral fable."

Reception aside, however, what can be read is that, although variously outraged at politically charged and engendered conditions, novelists such as Dickens and Kingsley were responding out of personal moral and ethical understandings rather than consciously political ones, and that this is so may be seen in that both men, despite reformist sympathies and polemical literary activities, evince repeatedly in their writing a distrust of institution, abstract intellectualism, and all manifestations of systematicity at the supposed expense of the individual (whether one is speaking of the Tractarian or union movement). The individualism of Victorian political economists, the discursive-ideological focus on the individual, is the inevitable humanist focal point of political democracy in the nineteenth century (Alderson, 45), and, discursively, this interest is translated by the novel (consider how many Victorian novels take individuals' names for their titles), which, in turn, is readable as part of a broad ideological focus, regardless of narrow political or philosophical affiliation. In this we come to read what Josephine Guy calls the Victorian "emphasis on the individual as the basic unit of inquiry" (10).

Comprehending, then, the importance of the representation of the individual at the center of political turmoil (and all too often the victim of impersonal political forces) is key to any understanding of both the political novel and the politics of the novel in the Victorian era. What is all the more complex, and which therefore requires our more patient focus (for which there is not the space here), is the paradoxical, if not ambivalent nature of Victorian narrative when comprehended politically. It is not a question of hurrying to judge Dickens, Kingsley, or any other writer for that matter, simply as politically "right" or "wrong," but instead, to seek to read the various political traces within texts in all their contradictoriness as signs of the times, so to speak (and from there to begin to come to terms with the ways in which our acts of reading the political novel in the nineteenth century is similarly positioned within the historical limits of our thought).

The Water-Babies takes a somewhat different track, constructing not a single perspective but what Elizabeth Deeds Ermath describes as a "perspective system" (93). Such systems are, argues Ermath, prevalent in the Victorian novel; they are the ways in which a "historical continuum" (85) is forged in the form of a narrative out of a range of different discourses, demanding of the reader that she attend "not to events and characters but to the perception of events and characters—in short to the act of historical attention" (93). Such narrative ordering offers a positive response to political and philosophical dilemmas faced by the Victorians as it mediates its discursive, ideological, and philosophical strands in the face of the "upheaval in the very basis of social order" (84), which generates such anxiety amongst so many Victorian writers.

Kingsley's personal response is to adapt social and political narrative through the mediation of the discursive modes of fantasy and satire in *The Water-Babies*. Though it is possible to read this novel as a retreat from overtly political narrative, this is still to read within a limited conception of what the political novel might look like. Equally, this fantasy of Tom, the chimney sweep who dies and becomes a water-baby, is readable as a series of oblique commentaries on contemporary political and social matters, not least the exploitation of children as sweeps. When published, "it was immediately striking as a fresh endeavor by the Reverend Kingsley to express through fiction some of the social and spiritual—and even scientific—dilemmas that were his constant preoccupation" (xiv). Thus, we would argue, the novel develops a strategy that is itself political in that it seeks to disturb its reception through the estranging mediation of political issues, in order to push the reader into thinking differently about contemporary social matters. And it is a sign of its political effectiveness that, a year later, the 1864 Chimney Sweepers' Act was passed in Parliament, as an attempt to alleviate the plight of exploited children.

ANTHONY TROLLOPE

While the "social-problem novel," retrospectively constructed as a subgenre, is very much discernible as a product of the 1840s and 1850s, there are still to be found social problems that are also, at least for certain facets of the Victorian readership, political problems. In many ways Anthony Trollope's novels of the 1870s and early 1880s expose not only the author's anxieties concerning political questions defined both narrowly and broadly but also the circulation of political and ideological issues, having to do with the matter of Englishness, the ability to discern one's—and others'—positions and roles in a society where cultural identities are in a condition of rapid flux, and the ever-more persistent questioning of issues of class and gender. Though Trollope never wrote an industrial novel, and though his fictions restrict their representation of the working classes to quasi-comical figures such as the Bunces in *Phineas Finn* or otherwise to dimly perceived, often anxious if not ambivalent depictions of "mobs" and "masses" (usually in the act of agitating, as though this were a defining characteristic of the proletariat *en masse*), nonetheless, there is a very real sense in which Trollope's novels are readable as political novels, specifically in their attention to problems of identity.

Identity-as-problem, it must be stressed, is not that of the individual in the mixed social milieu of the Trollopian text. Rather, identity is the mediated, and mediating, flow of conceptual markers, keywords, attitudes, and beliefs (for example, the nebulous ways in which the idea of the "gentleman" is defined within English middle- and upper-middle-class culture; see Wolfreys 151–176) by which one defines one's cultural subjectivity within the social flow. Such cultural traces are also those marks by which Trollope's narratological strategies seek to identify the authenticity (or otherwise) of the various subjects who inhabit the political demi-monde of Trollope's England. Frequently there is a readable anxiety, as a general diffuse register, in the text of Trollope, in the face of a certain undecidability concerning authentication. This anxiety or, as previously suggested, ambivalence, becomes further amplified by the interanimation between seemingly radical discourses and intergenerational antagonisms (where conservatism is usually, though by no means exclusively, the provenance of the older generation) given a political and social contextualization. This can be seen in the confrontation between the question of women's rights and the suffragist movement and the Victorian cult of Girlhood (begun in the late 1860s and lasting for over a decade) in Trollope's *Is He Popenjoy?* (1878).

Indebted to the then-popular subgenre of the sensation novel, Trollope's novel addresses simultaneously the precarious navigation of Mary Germain through the politics of suffragism and the claims of the "Popenjoy" of the title to the title of Marquis of Brotherton. It is around this latter plot strand that Trollope constructs a narrative that nags at matters of cultural authenticity, signaled by the question that is the title, although taken as a whole, the double plots chart the complexity of political and ideological issues that achieve a certain dominance in the third quarter of the nineteenth century. And it is, perhaps, precisely because Trollope draws on the sensation novel, as if to direct our attention away from the politics of the narrative, thereby attempting to turn "it all into a romp" as James Kincaid puts it (*Child-Loving*, 287), that we should give our scrutiny all the more seriously to the question of the encoding of politics in various more or less subterranean manners in the Victorian novel, rather than simply seek it out in the more obvious textual places. Indeed, if Trollope is anxious about matters of identity, there is a sense, citing Kincaid once more, in which this novel is politically deceptive, involving as it does a certain recurring and "duplicitous shift" from the comic and the superficial to the dark and the ambivalent (*Child-Loving*, 240–244). Nothing, suggests Trollope, is quite what it seems, and nothing, it seems, is less apparently like itself than this late novel, where the politics are duplicitous, and to be duplicitous (recalling Disraeli) in narrative strategy is to be political.

But, of course, this is *The Way We Live Now*. Or, at least, this is the political reading of contemporary society that the novel of this title would like, somewhat cynically, to lay open before its readers. This novel interweaves the story of the avaricious and unscrupulous novelist Lady Carbury and her circle, and that of the financier Augustus Melmotte, whose background is suitably uncertain, as the text circulates through the City of London's financial institutions, the aristocratic homes of London's West End, and the various gentlemen's clubs, in which the practice of *realpolitik* takes place as much as in any bank or parliamentary chamber. As with Trollope's other political novels, the flow of power circulates in words, interpretations, and anticipations rather than in actual political acts such as parliamentary reform or working-class activity, while "actual deeds have been reduced to appearances, [and] men to shirt-fronts" (Kincaid, *Novels*, 166). Trollope's conservative response to contemporary society is to depict a world of simulacra and undecidability, where financial "solidity" comes to be "embodied," as it were, in the figure of Melmotte. The

financier and speculator's authenticity as a peculiarly English figure and product is at odds constantly with the cultural perception of his inauthenticity as an
English gentleman. England—or, at the very least, those who wield its political
and economic power—make Melmotte, even as he destabilizes the very conceptual frameworks of the categories by which his access to English society is
made possible. And it is not, we should add, that this is a question of any deliberate act of destabilization on Melmotte's part, even though that too is arguably
readable. Rather, it is through the ambiguity of satire, by which Trollope's text
manifests a range of heterogeneous, and, therefore, always already destabilized
and self-destabilizing discourses, that the troubling constitution of Melmotte's
undecidability serves, itself, as a political performance of identity. This is an
identity that subverts, even as it plays with, reflecting back upon, those markers
of a liberal-conservative identity that Trollope's novel is so worried about preserving, while inscribing them as being caught up in the very possibility of their
erasure.

Thus, in attempting to express a range of politically, or, at the very least,
ideologically oriented fears concerning British society, Trollope's text is available to another political reading, one that reads the politics of Victorian identity, as well as the identity of a particular strand of Victorian politics in the face
of social transformation. And Trollope's novels *are* political, from narrow to
broad senses of that word, inasmuch as they are woven from, even as they depict and seek to analyze, the various flows and concatenations of heterogeneous modes of power that constitute the system we name society. Yet, what is
perhaps more interesting, in coming to terms with the text of Trollope as a political text, is the recognition of it as an exemplary manifestation of that very
same politics: a politics of self-reflection and surfaces (much as is the case with
the society of the Veneerings in Dickens's *Our Mutual Friend*), where political
power depends upon identifying its own defining features in some other form,
without ever fully coming to the realization that those features are not, themselves, essential to any particular identity but are themselves reflected fragments in an endless circulation.

CONCLUSION

It has been the aim of this chapter to reintroduce, rather than simply introduce, the "political novel," distinct from conventional wisdom concerning
particular subgenres that have persisted critically for the last fifty years or so.
Implicit in this attempt has been the understanding that Victorian novelists
cannot be gathered together and labeled, without respect for the different ways
in which contemporary discourses of the political and ideological come to inform the writing of individual texts. It has also been my, at times implicit, argu-

ment that each novelist responds to the trace of the political in ways that he or she cannot always control, and that the narrative or literary discourse on the political in English society of the nineteenth century will inevitably assume myriad and heterogeneous forms, often becoming readable after the event as fractured, dissonant within a single narrative, contradictory and often marked by a limit to which "thinking the political" can extend within the era in question. In this, it is equally important that we come to terms with the fact that "the 'solutions' which Victorian writers prescribe are solutions to problems in society which they perceived and defined quite differently from the ways in which a modern social commentator would" (Guy, 10).

An important step in recognizing the Victorian novel qua political is to see to what extent it is internally fissured in its political articulations, riven by the paradoxes and blind spots that attend any age, and to see furthermore that there emerges "a new kind of relationship between the novel and the social and political worlds which produced it" (Guy, 3). Such a relationship is itself political in that "in social narratives, novelists by the hundreds *experiment* across a whole range of social circumstance with [the] new relationship between individual voice and collective identity. What is at stake here is nothing less than a shift in the way an entire culture constructs identity" (Ermath, 119–120; emphasis added). Such experiment involves the strategic narrative use in the novel of different, though recognizably familiar historical moments, or the employment of fantasy and satire, and thus literary discourse adapts in a broadly political manner to the transformation of political and social change, thereby implicating itself into the political weave from out of which transitions in literary language take place. What is of special interest today, I would argue, after the insights made available to critics by what we loosely term literary theory, is that experiment and inquiry, engagement and response are readable. Also available is a perception of the different, differing ways the trace of the political is readable, in those very narrative situations that, on the surface at least, seem from conventional perspectives not to treat of politics, narrowly defined: in children's fantasy, in a love story, in social comedy, as well as in those most obvious novels that address the question of political activity.

The Victorian political novel provides fictions of the political; which is not to say that such novels are not necessarily "true" in any sense, but rather to recognize the extent to which realist narrative of whatever ostensible narrowly defined political position (liberal, conservative, radical) in the nineteenth century is implicated in the political discourse that it seeks to represent, as though "literary" modes could be so easily separated from "political" ones. Rather, inasmuch as the Victorian age was a self-aware age, concerned actively in the production and dissemination of necessary fictions concerning itself, and the possibilities that representation afforded society for telling itself about itself, then every narrative, every novel, is, in some manner, as we suggested at the outset, political, though all not equally so, nor in any measure in the same fashion. Every text will necessarily differ from the next, and the political novel as such cannot, therefore, by definition be defined.

In the face of such a recognition, what is needed is that readers of Victorian novels learn to read the signs of politics as they hide themselves, as they write themselves otherwise, as they display themselves in full view, apparently as though the question were not one of politics at all, but of common sense, historical inevitability, cultural contingency, and so forth. In coming to terms with such diversity, then we might begin to read, if not the political novel, as distinct, say, from some mythical text that is allegedly not political, then the trace of the political in the novel, in each and every novel, and as the partially submerged trace of that text's exemplarity that, when read as such, is also the trace that allows us to move beyond text and context and to recognize the movement of the political across the wide, diverse body of nineteenth-century textuality.

WORKS CITED AND SELECTED WORKS FOR FURTHER READING

Alderson, David. "An Anatomy of the British Polity: *Alton Locke* and Christian Manliness." In *Victorian Identities: Social and Cultural Formations in Nineteenth-Century Literature*, pp. 43–61. Ed. Ruth Robbins and Julian Wolfreys. London: Macmillan, 1996.

Bivona, Daniel. "Disraeli's Political Trilogy and the Antinomic Structure of Imperial Desire." In *Desire and Contradiction: Imperial Visions and Domestic Debates in Victorian Literature,* pp. 1–31. Manchester: Manchester UP, 1990.

Briggs, Asa. "The Language of 'Class' in Early Nineteenth-Century England." *Essays in Labour History.* Ed. Asa Briggs and J. Saville. London: Macmillan, 1967.

Childers, Joseph W. *Novel Possibilities: Fiction and the Formation of Early Victorian Culture.* Philadelphia: U of Pennsylvania P, 1995.

Connor, Steven. *Charles Dickens.* Oxford: Basil Blackwell, 1985.

Cottom, Daniel. *Social Figures: George Eliot, Social History, and Literary Representation.* Minneapolis: U of Minnesota P, 1987.

Dickens, Charles. *Little Dorrit.* 1857. Ed. Stephen Wall and Helen Small. London: Penguin, 1998.

———. *Our Mutual Friend.* 1865. Ed. Adrian Poole. London: Penguin, 1997.

Disraeli, Benjamin. *Coningsby.* 1844. Ed. Thom Braun. London: Penguin, 1989.

Elam, Diane. "'Another day done and I'm deeper in debt': *Little Dorrit* and the Debt of the Everyday." In *Dickens Refigured: Bodies, Desires and Other Histories,* pp. 157–177. Ed. John Schad. Manchester: Manchester UP, 1996.

Eliot, George. *Daniel Deronda.* 1876. Ed. Barbara Hardy. London: Penguin, 1986.

————. *Middlemarch: A Study of Provincial Life.* 1871–72. Ed. David Carroll. Oxford: Oxford UP, 1988.

Ermath, Elizabeth Deeds. *The English Novel in History, 1840–1895.* London: Routledge, 1997.

Fasick, Laura. "Charles Kingsley's Scientific Treatment of Gender." In *Muscular Christianity: Embodying the Victorian Age,* pp. 91–113. Ed. Donald E. Hall. Cambridge: Cambridge UP, 1994.

Francis, Mark, and John Morrow. *A History of English Political Thought in the Nineteenth Century.* London: Duckworth, 1994.

Gallagher, Catherine. *The Industrial Reformation of English Fiction: Social Discourse and Narrative Form, 1832–1867.* Chicago: U of Chicago P, 1985.

Guy, Josephine M. *The Victorian Social-Problem Novel: The Market, the Individual, and Communal Life.* London: Macmillan, 1996.

Hall, Donald E., ed. *Muscular Christianity: Embodying the Victorian Age.* Cambridge: Cambridge UP, 1994.

Hobsbawm, Eric. *The Age of Revolution, 1789–1848.* 1962. New York: Vintage, 1996.

Ingham, Patricia. *The Language of Gender and Class: Transformation in the Victorian Novel.* London: Routledge, 1996.

————. "Nobody's Fault: The Scope of the Negative in *Little Dorrit.*" In *Dickens Refigured: Bodies, Desires and Other Histories,* pp. 98–116. Ed. John Schad. Manchester: Manchester UP, 1996.

Kincaid, James R. *Child-Loving: The Erotic Child and Victorian Culture.* New York: Routledge, 1992.

————. *The Novels of Anthony Trollope.* Oxford: Oxford UP, 1977.

Kingsley, Charles. *Alton Locke.* 1850. Ed. Elizabeth A. Cripps. Oxford: Oxford UP, 1987.

————. *The Water-Babies.* 1863. Ed. Brian Alderson. Oxford: Oxford UP, 1995.

————. *Yeast.* 1848. Introd. Julian Wolfreys. Stroud: Alan Sutton, 1994.

Poovey, Mary. *Uneven Developments: The Ideological Work of Gender in Mid-Victorian England.* Chicago: U of Chicago P, 1988.

Tambling, Jeremy. *Dickens, Violence, and the Modern State.* London: Macmillan, 1995.

Trollope, Anthony. *Is He Popenjoy?* 1878. Ed. John Sutherland. Oxford: Oxford UP, 1991.

————. *The Way We Live Now.* 1875. Ed. Frank Kermode. London: Penguin, 1994.

Vance, Norman. *The Sinews of the Spirit: The Ideal of Christian Manliness in Victorian Literature and Religious Thought.* Cambridge: Cambridge UP, 1985.

Wolfreys, Julian. *Being English: Narratives, Idioms, and Performances of National Identity from Coleridge to Trollope.* Albany: State U of New York P, 1994.

The Sociological Contexts of Victorian Fiction

M. Clare Loughlin-Chow

At last I came to a wood—the first real wood that I had ever seen; not a mere party of stately park trees growing out of smooth turf, but a real wild copse. . . . As I stood looking wistfully over the gate, alternately at the inviting vista of the green embroidered path, and then at the grim notice over my head, "All trespassers prosecuted," a young man came up the ride, dressed in velveteen jacket and leather gaiters, sufficiently bedrabbled with mud. A fishing-rod and basket bespoke him some sort of destroyer, and I saw in a moment that he was "a gentleman." . . .

"May I go into your wood?" asked I at a venture, curiosity conquering pride.

"Well! What do you want there, my good fellow?"

"To see what a wood is like—I never was in one in my life."

"Humph! Well—you may go in for that, and welcome. Never was in a wood in his life!—poor devil! . . . I say—I forgot—don't go far in, or ramble up and down, or you'll disturb the pheasants."

I thanked him again for what license he had given me—went in, and lay down by the path-side. . . .

I recollect lying on my face and fingering over the delicately cut leaves of the weeds, and wondering whether the people who lived in the country thought them as wonderful and beautiful as I did:—and then I recollected the thousands whom I had left behind, who, like me, had never seen the green face of God's earth; and the answer of the poor gamin in St. Giles's, who, when he was asked what the country was, answered, "*the yard where the gentlemen live when they go out of town*"—significant that, and pathetic;—then I wondered whether the time would ever come when society would be far enough advanced to open to even such as he a glimpse, if it were only once a year, of the fresh, clean face of God's earth. (116–118)

Charles Kingsley's description of his cockney protagonist's first encounter with the countryside in the novel *Alton Locke* (1850) is expressive of the nature and extent of one of the most significant changes to English society between 1800 and 1900, that of massive and widespread urbanization, and the growth and redistribution of the population of the country. That Kingsley has his character present the totality of his urban experience as representative of a significant portion of the metropolis rather than as a startling anomaly is significant. It marks Alton Locke as one of the new urban working-class dwellers, city-born and bred, and marks Kingsley as one of the many writers of the period to use the increasingly complex genre of the novel in an attempt to analyze and make sense of the new sociological constructs of nineteenth-century Britain, constructs largely dominated by this movement to a primarily urban mode of living.

At the beginning of the nineteenth century, England was still a predominantly agricultural and rural society, with a population of roughly 12 million. It was ruled by a landed elite, transportation between regions was slow and difficult, and the majority of the population had little experience of travel beyond their own locality. In 1800, London was the only city in Britain with a population of over 100,000; when Victoria came to the throne in 1837, there were five such cities; and in 1891 there were twenty-three. Over 1 million people lived within ten miles of Westminster in 1800; at mid-century this figure had grown to 2.6 million, and by the end of the century 6.5 million people (approximately 20 percent of the population of England and Wales) lived in the same area. By the end of the nineteenth century the population had more than trebled, and the large majority of these people lived in cities or towns. Large urban centers had expanded, with economics based on cotton, coal, and iron. Changes to the rural environment were also significant during the Victorian age: The traditional countryside was being transformed (in spite of the attempts of many writers throughout the century to render it an eighteenth-century pastoral ideal); the demands of profit-seeking and consequent modernization of farming methods were felt keenly. The process of enclosure reached its climax in the early years of the century, and the coming of the railways impacted upon life in the country still further. The enclosures changed social relations of the countryside as customary social and economic relations were replaced by monetary ties—the "cash-payment nexus" isolated and criticized by Thomas Carlyle as the basis for industrial relations, found its way into rural society as well. The changes claimed many victims, as one pattern of social relations involving certain expectations of one's neighbors and social superiors was replaced with another. The landless laborers newly and increasingly subject to the landlord and tenant farmer largely paid the price of change, many migrating to the cities in search of employment, which further swelled the numbers of the urban population, already developing in response to the patterns of industrialism (Dentith; Dyos and Wolff; Morris and Rodger, 1–39).

So the nineteenth century was set off from earlier eras by the complex of social changes associated with the Industrial Revolution: the unprecedented urban development, the transformation of the English economy from a rural to an industrial base, and the breakdown of old relationships between employer and employee. Altered terminology at this time reflected these changes: "working class" (as distinct from "lower class") first appeared around 1815, and by the mid-1820s, "class" was established as a social label, distinct from eighteenth-century terms such as "degree," "estate," or "order." The writers of the period grappled throughout the century, not only with the concrete problems of urban living such as overcrowding, the appearance of slums, pollution, inadequate sanitation, disease, and crime, but also with attempts to analyze and describe the larger nature of this changed mode of existence and social relations, to give shape and meaning to a completely unprecedented way of life. And, looking back over the cultural production of the nineteenth century, we can see that the dominant mode in which to engage in such explorations became the novel, primarily because of its capacity to integrate imaginative accounts of many diverse characters and events, to create an imagined community that spanned the dividing constructs of class in a manner relatively accessible to an ever-increasing literate audience.

Those novels retrospectively given variously the labels of "social-problem," "industrial," or "condition-of-England" novels were among the starkest examples of an attempt to address the problems inherent to the urban products of the new industrial enterprise. Largely appearing from the pens of middle-class writers such as Elizabeth Gaskell, Charles Kingsley, and Benjamin Disraeli, these works described conditions in the cities of the industrial midland and the North, and suggested various solutions to the social "muddle" (as described by the millworker Stephen Blackpool in Dickens's *Hard Times* [1854]); mid-century tension between workers and masters was a particular concern of these novels. Sheila Smith has shown how the works of several industrial novelists, but those of Disraeli in particular, are indebted to the selective use and presentation of material from the "Blue Books," or reports of various government-sponsored commissions sent to investigate the conditions of the industrial cities. Disraeli crystallized his view of the new and flawed shape of society in his novel *Sybil* (1845), when his highly intelligent working-class radical, Walter Gerard, instructs the aristocratic hero, Egremont, as to its divided composition. Victoria, Gerard maintains in Disraeli's *Sybil*, rules over:

"Two nations; between whom there is no intercourse and no sympathy; who are as ignorant of each other's habits, thoughts, and feelings, as if they were dwellers in different zones, or inhabitants of different planets; who are formed by a different breeding, are fed by a different food, are ordered by different manners, and are not governed by the same laws."

"You speak of———" said Egremont, hesitatingly.

"THE RICH AND THE POOR." (96)

A similar perception of a gulf or divide between classes is a central preoccupation of Elizabeth Gaskell's *Mary Barton* (1845), with its key portrayal of the desperation of John Barton, a Chartist worker driven by an aggregate of socioeconomic factors to the politically motivated assassination of his employer's son. Less inclined to rhetorical flourishes than Disraeli, Gaskell's fiction derives its particular power from a quality admitted by even the fiercest of her critics: "She has evidently lived much among the people she describes, made herself intimate at their firesides, and feels a sincere, though sometimes too exclusive and indiscriminating, sympathy with them" (Greg, 402). It was, however, precisely this level of sympathy perceived as suspect by W. R. Greg that was central to Gaskell's novelistic project—through graphic and detailed descriptions of the appalling living conditions of many of the Manchester workers, and through the essential humanity of their characterization, Gaskell hoped to engender in her middle-class readers some sympathy for their plight, and through that sympathy, a working basis for amelioration of the then-current social disunity. Where Disraeli's solution to the skewed nature of industrial society in the 1840s proposed the renewal of an idealized medieval model of social relations in the tenets of "Young England," Gaskell, the wife of a Unitarian minister, based her hopes for sociological improvement on Christian belief:

[T]he wish which lay nearest to his heart was that . . . a perfect understanding, and complete confidence and love, might exist between masters and men; that the truth might be recognized that the interests of one were the interests of all; and as such, required the consideration and deliberation of all . . . in short, to acknowledge the Spirit of Christ as the regulating law between both parties. (*Mary Barton*, 460)

North and South (1855), which Gaskell wrote partially in response to criticisms that her first industrial novel was too one-sided, revises this hope into a somewhat more realistically grounded vision, where the "utmost expectation" of the sympathetically rendered factory owner at the end of the novel "only goes so far as this—that they [his innovations] may render strikes not the bitter, venomous sources of hatred they have hitherto been. A more hopeful man might imagine that a closer and more genial intercourse between classes might do away with strikes. But I am not a hopeful man" (526).

Unsurprisingly, the proposed solutions of Gaskell and Disraeli, however divergent in detail, share with other "condition-of-England" novels, such as Brontë's *Shirley* (1849), Dickens's *Hard Times* (1854), and Kingsley's *Alton Locke*, an inability and unwillingness to consider any fundamental or radical change of the social order of the kind proposed by Friedrich Engels in his contemporaneous study of Manchester and other industrial cities: *The Condition of the Working Class in England* (1845). Rather than issue a fundamental challenge to the status quo, these middle-class novelists, writing for a largely middle-class audience, content themselves to appeal for a renewed sense of responsibility among the classes, for a recognition of the interdependence of worker and master in the industrial project. There is no Romantic appreciation of the ideals of the French Revolution here—the Chartist activity of the late 1830s and the 1840s was too close to home for this, and where the fictionalized workers are presented as organizing against the established sources of social power and government, all of these novels display a descent into violence and riot, which serve only to operate as a warning to their readers of the potential disastrous outcomes if the conditions in which the working class were forced to live and work continued unchecked by responsible reform from above.

The cities of the industrial midlands were not the only sites of urban investigation by novelists—London held an obvious attraction for the writer interested in the depiction of nineteenth-century society, and creative works were produced alongside and in dialogue with more strictly sociological investigations such as the highly influential work by Henry Mayhew, *London Labour and the London Poor* (1849). Dickens was acknowledged as the supreme novelist of London, one contemporary describing his ability to evoke the conditions of life in the city as that of "a special correspondent for posterity" (Bagehot 140). He recognized, and throughout his writing career depicted, the complications and contradictions of urban living, especially the particular isolating power of the metropolis, where, in the midst of hundreds of thousands of people, an individual tragic figure such as the "shabby-genteel" man struggled for lonely respectability and survival (Dickens, *Sketches by Boz*, 260–264), and where an insomniac Uncommercial Traveller understands and surrenders to the impulse of crossing Waterloo Bridge solely "to have a halfpenny worth of excuse for saying 'Good night' to the toll-keeper, and catching a glimpse of his fire" (Dickens, *Uncommercial Traveller*, 128). It may well have been this awareness of London's power to divide and isolate, often expressed most cogently in his sketches, essays, and journalism, which reinforced Dickens's desire to make connections among the inhabitants of this urban society across the complicated texture of his multiplot novels.

Bleak House (1853), is, of course, Dickens's most clearly envisioned attempt to negotiate the divisions of the mid-Victorian metropolis. From his use of the image of the all-enveloping fog of the opening chapters, to his conscious employment of coincidence to establish links among the multivarious cast of characters, *Bleak House* emphasizes the still-existent bonds between members of society, and appeals to those members not to give in to the very real possibility of individual and class isolation. This appeal is most clearly made through the direct addresses of the apocalyptic third person narrator, who, for instance, asks of the reader:

What connexion can there be, between the place in Lincolnshire, the house in town, the Mercury in powder, and the whereabouts of Jo the outlaw with the broom, who had that distant ray of light upon him when he swept the churchyard-step? What connexion can there have been between many people in the innumerable histories of this world, who, from opposite sides of great gulfs, have, nevertheless, been very curiously brought together! (272)

Dickens goes on to further establish the principle of connection that he has evoked to call for reform of social problems specific to urban society, in answering his own question: Jo, one of the "maggot numbers" inhabiting "Tom-all-Alone's," a London slum, and who is a victim of a society more interested in foreign missions than the children of its own streets, inadvertently infects the blameless middle-class heroine (and first-person narrator) with a life-threatening and disfiguring disease. Like the typhus-ridden and destitute widow of Carlyle's *Past and Present* (1843), Jo asserts his cross-class brotherhood through the transmission of infection—Dickens effects at the level of plot the warning of the narrator concerning the ultimate "revenge" of Tom-all-Alone's if the slum is left to continue its existence unchecked:

Even the winds are his messengers, and they serve him in these hours of darkness. There is not a drop of Tom's corrupted blood but propagates infection and contagion somewhere. It shall pollute, this very night, the choice stream (in which chemists on analysis would find the genuine nobility) of a Norman house, and his Grace shall not be able to say Nay to the infamous alliance. (683)

The complex interweaving of the "web of very different lives" (703) in this, Dickens's masterpiece, is characteristic of the long nineteenth-century novels that Henry James was later famously to criticize as "loose baggy monsters"—novels that used complex multiple plotlines, a vast number of characters, and often the voices of two or more distinct narrators in order to present their view of the complex nature of nineteenth-century social existence. The image of the web, however, is one that is more usually associated with George Eliot's finest achievement, *Middlemarch* (1866), as she uses it to contrast her own novelistic techniques with those of Henry Fielding in the previous century:

A great historian, as he insisted on calling himself, who had the happiness to be dead a hundred and twenty years ago, and so to take his place among the colossi whose huge legs our living pettiness is observed to walk under, glories in his copious remarks and digressions as the least imitable part of his work, and especially in those initial chapters to the successive books of his history, where he seems to bring his arm-chair to the proscenium and chat with us in all the lusty ease of his fine English. But Fielding lived when the days were longer (for time, like money, is measured by our needs), when summer afternoons were spacious, and the clock ticked slowly in the winter evenings. We belated historians must not linger after his example; and if we did so, it is probable that our chat would be thin and eager, as if delivered from a camp-stool in a parrot-house. I at least have so much to do in unravelling certain human lots, and seeing how they were woven and interwoven, that all the light I can command must be concentrated on this particular web, and not dispersed over that tempting range of relevancies called the universe. (116)

Eliot's "Study of Provincial Life" does indeed focus closely upon the inner lives of her characters, and the ways in which their decisions and choices impact upon their relationships with others in the relatively compact society of the town of Middlemarch—compact, that is, when compared to the metropolitan setting of *Bleak House,* or the panoramic view of society presented in Thackeray's *Vanity Fair* (1848), or Trollope's *The Way We Live Now* (1875). *Middlemarch* is in many ways the finest example of Eliot's developing realist aesthetic, a set of principles and techniques with which she and other novelists of the period experimented, in order to render both psychological and social experience as truthfully as possible. Eliot's own development can be traced from a relatively straightforward attempt to render her "simple story" of rural England using the image of a mirror in *Adam Bede* (1859), acknowledging even then, however, that this is problematic, as "[t]he mirror is doubtless defective; the outlines will sometimes be disturbed; the reflection faint or confused," but continuing to assert the worth of the attempt, maintaining that "I feel as much bound to tell you, as precisely as I can, what that reflection is, as if I were in the witness-box narrating my experience on oath" (221). By the time of *Middlemarch,* she has moved to a more expanded conception of form, an organic model based on relations, a theory perhaps best described in her essay "Notes on Form in Art" (1868). In this essay, doubtless influenced by Darwinian theory, she maintains that we view an object first as a whole—for example, a flower. We then observe that it is composed of parts (petals, stem, leaves), and that it is also part of a larger whole (a meadow). Form is found only in a larger perception of the thing, in a comprehension of its interrelations with other things: "Form . . . as distinguished from merely massive impression, must first depend on the discrimination of wholes and then on the discrimination of parts." The highest example of form is that which displays the most "varied

group of relations bound together in a wholeness which again has the most varied relations with all other phenomena" (232). For Eliot, reality, and in particular social reality as it is portrayed in *Middlemarch*, is a complex interweaving of
relations among discrete elements in an organic whole.

I have focused here upon Eliot's commitment to realism, as it is representative of a larger nineteenth-century concern about the means and ends of artistic representation, a concern that can be linked to deeper anxieties in the
period. As George Levine puts it:

Despite its appearance of solidity, realism implies a fundamental uneasiness about self,
society, and art. . . . Such intensity of commitment to speaking the truth suggests difficulties where before none had been perceived. . . . Realists take upon themselves a special role as mediator, and assume self-consciously a moral burden. . . . [T]heir
responsibility is to a reality that increasingly seems "unnameble" . . . but it is also to an
audience that requires to be . . . freed from the misnaming literatures. (12)

It is an unease that is also demonstrated thematically in the religious novels of
the period, which, rather than focus upon doctrinal abstracts contingent upon
the surety of undisturbed faith, instead center around difficulties of faith and
doubt posed by the increasing scientific and technological advances of the
nineteenth century. From Samuel Butler's *The Way of All Flesh* (1903), to J. H.
Newman's *Loss and Gain* (1848), to J. A. Froude's *The Nemesis of Faith* (1849),
to Mrs. Humphry Ward's *Robert Elsmere* (1888), the continued popularity of
this new kind of religious novel demonstrated a real audience for studies of the
impact of religious doubt upon one's life and social relations. Eliot herself had
struggled with the loss of her Christian faith, had ultimately come to a positivist view on the purpose of her own life and place within the complicated soci-
etal structures of Victorian England, and felt that she had a duty to use her
talents to propound a greater sense of connection amongst her readers. Like the
earlier industrial novelists, Eliot's novelistic project involves an extension of
our sympathies, hence the shifting perspectives insisted upon in *Middlemarch*,
where the narrator demands, for instance, "But why always Dorothea? Was her
point of view the only possible one with regard to this marriage?" (229), and
where the multitudinous scratches of the pier-glass are likened to events, illuminated into a pattern of concentric circles by the flame of a candle representative of any one individual's ego. As Eliot had earlier stated: "It is not enough
simply to teach truth . . . we want it to be so taught as to compel men's attention
and sympathy" (*Selected Essays*, 368–369). The consciously philosophical nature of her work is more sophisticated than the earlier novelists of the 1840s,
and yet this premise of the extension of sympathies, and recognition of the
bonds that unite members of nineteenth-century society remains constant.

The later urban novelists of the nineteenth century, however, are less confident of their ability to link the disparate levels of their society in this way, and certainly in the novels of George Gissing and Arthur Morrison, for example, there is presented a darker and bleaker vision of irreparable social division. It is more akin to the emphases of the later Victorian urban explorers and sociologists, writers whose own perceptions of the urban landscapes investigated are revealed in the titles they choose to attach to their works, such as Andrew Mearns's *The Bitter Cry of Outcast London* (1883) and William Booth's *In Darkest England and the Way Out* (1888). Both Morrison and Gissing were influenced by the social and aesthetic theories of the naturalist school of French novelists such as Zola; naturalism, broadly speaking, being the application of the principles of scientific determinism to literature.

Gissing had firsthand experience of working-class life, having dissociated himself from his middle-class background through his marriage to a prostitute whom he hoped to help reform from alcoholism. He was forced to live for a time in the slums (at least partly from real poverty) and supplemented this personal experience with meticulously documented research for his fictional treatment of the late-century urban working classes. Throughout the course of his career he vacillated between pity and loathing for the downtrodden urban workers; this tension is apparent in his fiction, particularly in *Demos* (1886). One of the main attractions that naturalism held for Gissing was the greater freedom that it gave the novelist to approach certain subjects normally avoided or approached obliquely in English fiction, and he exploited this to the best of his ability and the constraints of his time.

A certain development is traced by P. J. Keating in Gissing's approach to his subject. His was originally a radical spirit of social reform (akin to the purpose of the mid-Victorian "condition of England" authors); in the period of *Workers in the Dawn* (1880) he was determined to "bring home to people the ghastly condition (material, mental and moral) of our poor classes, to show the hideous injustice of our whole system of society, to give light upon the plan of altering it, and, above all, to preach an enthusiasm for just and high *ideals* in this age of unmitigated egotism and 'shop.'" But he soon after reversed this opinion, and rejected all concern with social reform, taking on the position (akin to that of the naturalists) of the disinterested artist:

My attitude henceforth is that of the artist pure and simple. The world is for me a collection of phenomena, which are to be studied and reproduced artistically. In the midst of the most serious complications of life, I find myself suddenly possessed with a great calm, withdrawn as it were from the immediate interests of the moment, and able to regard everything as a picture. . . . Brutal and egotistic it would be called by most people. What has that to do with me if it is a fact? (quoted in Keating, *Working*, 54)

A movement can be traced in Gissing's fiction to a combination of these two positions, where the dispassionate tone of *The Nether World* (1889) is used as a newly conceived method of encouraging reform.

Demos is imbued with a tension between Gissing's conflicting views of the working classes, and the treatment is consequently less coherent than the more artistically perfect *The Nether World*. *Demos* is actually the most snobbish and didactic of his works. Gissing depicts Richard Mutimer, an ardent working-class socialist enticed by capitalist attitudes upon the inheritance of money, and the implication throughout is that the working-class man can never really rise above his environment; his nature has already been determined by his heredity and milieu. Thus, although Richard is initially presented as superior to others of his class, in moments of pressure the worst aspects of his personality come to the fore, and this can be seen in the jealousy of his relations with his wife, and his constant feeling of inferiority to her. For instance, in an important quarrel:

The thin crust of refinement was shattered; the very man came to light, coarse, violent, whipped into fury by his passions. . . . Whether he believed his wife guilty or not he could not have said; enough that she had kept things secret from him, and that he could not overawe her. Whensoever he had shown anger in conversation with her, she had made him sensible of her superiority; at length he fell back upon his brute force and resolved to bring her to his feet, if need be by outrage. Even his accent deteriorated as he flung out his passionate words; he spoke like any London mechanic, with defect and excess of aspirates, with neglect of g's at the end of words, and so on. Adela could not bear it; she moved to the door. But he caught her and thrust her back; it was all but a blow. (367)

Gissing's techniques in *Demos* remain strikingly Victorian. He retains the omniscient author convention, and unhesitatingly uses such traditional narrative tropes as sudden inheritance, the unexpected discovery of a will causing a reversal of fortunes, the element of coincidence involved in Emma Vine's brief salvation of Richard, and the extremely conventional remarriage of Adela to Eldon, forming a union of the type that will not be permitted in *The Nether World*.

With *The Nether World*, a crucial change was marked in Gissing's technique, that of presenting the working classes in their own terms, regarding their behavior as relative to their habits and capabilities, in general, displaying more understanding and tolerance than that which falls to Richard Mutimer in *Demos*. The very title of the later novel emphasizes Gissing's view of the essential nature of late nineteenth-century working-class society. Its infernal connotations are clear, but in a purely sociological sense, it is also a world apart, cut off from the middle and upper classes. Unlike other working-class novelists who use the motif of the exploration of an unknown world to awaken the conscience and class fears of their audience, Gissing merely displays the depressing reality of slum life, from which there can be no possibility of escape. The characters move within an extremely restricted set of surroundings, impressing upon the reader the depressing reality of the slum. Jane Snowdon is surely trapped within her environment, and the romantic trope of inheritance, even inheritance to be used for philanthropic purposes, cannot save her. Indeed, even a character like Clara Hewett, who attempts an escape from the slum, only reinforces the impossibility of escape, as she returns, maimed and disfigured by her contact with a world to which she cannot possibly belong. The Dickensian use of the slum as a connection between the different levels of society is rejected: "Really, we shall soon be coming to the conclusion that the differences between the nether and the upper world are purely superficial."

This sense of division is further emphasized in Arthur Morrison's *A Child of the Jago* (1896), where "the Jago" is a specific section of East End slum from which any avenue of escape for Dicky Perrott, the child of the title, is brutally restricted. Morrison too had some experience of working-class life, having been brought up in the East End (his early history, however, remains incompletely accounted for, as he went to great lengths later in life to conceal his origins). Morrison is the first of the late-century English slum writers to abandon the omniscient narrator and present the conditions of life in poverty in a stark, frank, and unbiased manner. His novel is to some extent a naturalistic reworking of Dickens's *Oliver Twist*, and, in contrast to this earlier fairy-talelike vision of a child's escape from a life of urban crime, the existence of a child in the Jago is certainly nasty, brutish, and short. Unlike the mid-Victorian social-problem novelists, Morrison was not inhibited in presenting drunkenness, brutality, swearing, and other behavior in an impassive manner, where previous authors had felt it necessary to either implicitly or explicitly condemn the fictional representation of such behavior by displaying it only in depraved or criminal characters. The reader of *A Child of the Jago*, by contrast, is enveloped in this alien world of violence and poverty with little guidance from the author as to methods of coping with it.

Late-century solutions involving eugenics are hinted at, particularly in the conversation between an East End missionary priest and a doctor who has just delivered a baby in the slum:

Father Sturt met the surgeon as he came away in the later evening, and asked if all were well. The surgeon shrugged his shoulders. "People would call it so," he said. "The boy's alive, and so is the mother. But you and I may say the truth. You know the Jago far better than I. Is there a child in all this place that wouldn't be better dead—still better unborn? But does a day pass without bringing you just such a parishioner? Here lies the Jago, a nest of rats, breeding, breeding, as only rats can; and we say it is well. On high moral grounds we uphold the right of rats to multiply their thousands. Sometimes we catch a rat. And we keep it a little while, nourish it carefully, and put it back into the nest to propagate its kind."

Father Sturt walked a little way in silence.

Then he said: "You are right of course." (Morrison, 157)

The novel culminates in one final outpouring of violence, and the prospect of the tearing down of the slum is offered only as another futile example of moving the problem on, in much the same way, although on a greater scale, as the "moving on" of Jo throughout *Bleak House*.

I have throughout this chapter focused on the attempts of novelists to comprehend and express the nature of the sociological constructs of the developing urban environments of nineteenth-century Britain. The late-century versions of pastoral and counterpastoral found in the novels of Thomas Hardy could be juxtaposed against this account, as could consideration of the apocalyptic envisionings found in the science fiction of H. G. Wells, or the negotiation of the mysteries of the city performed by Sherlock Holmes, or the strange vision of a metropolis ultimately reclaimed by nature found in Richard Jefferies's *After London* (1885). The attempts of the Victorian novelist to represent the new social relations that existed among individuals and classes took many forms throughout the century, forming both attempts to integrate and more pessimistic accounts of essential separation. The question as to whether or not Lazarus and Dives could ever ultimately be reconciled depended upon the vision of the individual author, and his or her view of the sociological contexts of Victorian Britain.

WORKS CITED AND SELECTED WORKS FOR FURTHER READING

Altick, Richard D. *The English Common Reader: A Social History of the Mass Reading Public, 1800–1900.* Chicago: U of Chicago P, 1957.

Bagehot, Walter. *Literary Studies.* 2 vols. Ed. R. H. Hutton. London: Longman and Green, 1879.

Dentith, Simon. *Society and Cultural Forms in Nineteenth-Century England.* London: Macmillan, 1998.

Dickens, Charles. *Bleak House.* 1854. Ed. Norman Page. London: Penguin, 1971.

———. *Sketches by Boz and Other Early Papers, 1833–1839.* Vol. I of *The Dent Uniform Edition of Dickens's Journalism.* Ed. Michael Slater. London: Dent, 1993.

———. *The Uncommercial Traveller.* 1860. Oxford: Oxford UP, 1958.

Disraeli, Benjamin. *Sybil; or, the Two Nations*. 1845. Ed. Thom Braun. London: Penguin, 1980.

Dutton, H. I., and J. E. King. *"Ten Per Cent and No Surrender": The Preston Strike, 1853–1854*. Cambridge: Cambridge UP, 1981.

Dyos, H. J., and Michael Wolff, eds. *The Victorian City*. 2 vols. London: Routledge and Kegan Paul, 1973.

Eliot, George. *Adam Bede*. 1859. Ed. Stephen Gill. London: Penguin, 1980.

———. *Middlemarch*. 1866. Ed. David Carroll. Oxford: Oxford UP, 1986.

———. *Selected Essays, Poems, and Other Writings*. Ed. A. S. Byatt and Nicolas Warren. London: Penguin, 1990.

Flint, Kate. *The Victorian Novelist: Social Problems and Social Change*. London: Croom Helm, 1987.

Gallagher, Catherine. *The Industrial Reformation of English Fiction: Social Discourse and Narrative Form, 1832–1867*. Chicago: U of Chicago P, 1985.

Gaskell, Elizabeth. *Mary Barton: A Tale of Manchester Life*. 1848. Ed. Stephen Gill. London: Penguin, 1970.

———. *North and South*. 1855. Ed. Dorothy Collin. London: Penguin, 1970.

Gissing, George. *Demos*. 1886. Ed. Pierre Coustillias. Brighton: Harvester Press, 1972.

Greg, W. R. "[Review of *Mary Barton*]." *Edinburgh Review* 89 (April 1849): 402–35.

Guy, Josephine M. *The Victorian Social-Problem Novel: The Market, the Individual, and Communal Life*. London: Macmillan, 1996.

Hollis, Patricia. *The Pauper Press: A Study in Working-Class Radicalism of the 1830s*. Oxford: Oxford UP, 1970.

Hughes, Linda K., and Michael Lund. *The Victorian Serial*. Charlottesville: UP of Virginia, 1991.

James, Louis. *Fiction for the Working Man, 1830–1850*. Oxford: Oxford UP, 1963.

Keating, P. J. *Into Unknown England, 1866–1913: Selections from the Social Explorers*. Manchester: Manchester UP, 1976.

———. *The Working Classes in Victorian Fiction*. London: Routledge and Kegan Paul, 1971.

Kingsley, Charles. *Alton Locke, Tailor and Poet: An Autobiography*. Ed. Elizabeth A. Cripps. Oxford: Oxford UP, 1983.

Levine, George. *The Realistic Imagination: English Fiction from Frankenstein to Lady Chatterley*. Chicago: U of Chicago P, 1981.

Matthew, Colin, ed. *The Nineteenth Century. The British Isles: 1815–1901*. Oxford: Oxford UP, 2000.

Morris, R. J., and Richard Rodger, eds. *The Victorian City: A Reader in British Urban History, 1820–1914*. London: Longman, 1993.

Morrison, Arthur. *A Child of the Jago*. 1896. Ed. P. J. Keating. London: MacGibbon and Kee, 1969.

Patten, Robert L. *Dickens and His Publishers*. Oxford: Clarendon, 1978.

Schwarzbach, F. S. *Dickens and the City*. London: Athlone, 1979.

Smith, Sheila M. *The Other Nation: The Poor in English Novels of the 1840s and 1850s.* Oxford: Clarendon, 1980.

Stedman Jones, Gareth. *Outcast London: A Study in the Relationship between Classes in Victorian Society.* Oxford: Clarendon, 1971.

Sutherland, John. *The Longman Companion to Victorian Fiction.* London: Longman, 1988.

———. *Victorian Fiction: Writers, Publishers, Readers.* London: Macmillan, 1995.

———. *Victorian Novelists and Publishers.* Chicago: U of Chicago P, 1976.

Webb, Robert K. *The British Working-Class Reader, 1790–1848: Literacy and Social Tension.* London: George Allen and Unwin, 1955.

Faith, Religion, and the Nineteenth-Century Novel

Nancy Cervetti

INTRODUCTION

Whether in the form of Shelley's atheism, Martineau's infidelity, or Huxley's agnosticism, many Victorians turned away from the security and constraints of orthodox religion. Nineteenth-century work in embryology, comparative anatomy, geology, and evolutionary theory nourished a new focus on the material and concrete, and both George Eliot and Karl Marx referred to religion as the opiate of the people (Haight 3, 366; Marx, 54). Well before the publication of *The Origin of Species* in 1859, theories of descent with modification had taken hold. Through the work of Lamarck, Charles Lyell, Herbert Spencer, and others, new ideas regarding adaptation, geological time, species, and "survival of the fittest" (Spencer's term) emerged in scientific and literary circles.

For some, abandoning the Genesis story meant the loss of special status, a fall from grace and a second coming out of the garden to face the harsh reality of waste, struggle, and purposelessness. Others, feeling less at the mercy of an incomprehensible universe, found a "new faith" in human authority and responsibility to understand and even control nature. Once awake, once out of the cave, there were new tools such as sociology, psychology, and chemistry to investigate natural laws and develop this new faith, and Swinburne proclaimed, "Glory to man in the highest!" Literature, too, grasped the significance of the upheaval. George Eliot, Charles Dickens, Samuel Butler, and Thomas Hardy were major participants in the discussions, rendering in narrative their analyses of the relation of divine, natural, and human agency and supernatural versus material existence.

ADAM BEDE

George Eliot's novels, beginning with her first literary publication *Scenes of Clerical Life*, serve as an especially fine gallery of Anglican and nonconformist clergy. From Amos Barton to Irwine, Stelling, and Farebrother, Eliot realistically conveys their particularities and foibles in a variety of settings.

Eliot's break with the fervent religion of her youth represented a transition that many nineteenth-century intellectuals experienced. In addition to her extensive reading in theology, Romanticism, and Comte's positivism, Eliot translated David Strauss's *Life of Jesus, Critically Examined* and Ludwig Feuerbach's *The Essence of Christianity*, principal texts of German higher criticism that were viewed as subversive and heretical. Eliot's orthodox Christianity became a "religion of Humanity," a secular faith in the potential of science combined with social responsibility to cure disease, improve living standards, and preserve culture. In *Adam Bede*, set in the rural village of Hayslope in 1799, Eliot begins to process the implications of what had become a much more complex world.

The Methodism of Dinah and Seth, attracting working-class laborers and the rural poor, is a religion preoccupied with prayer and resignation. Dinah, a cotton-mill worker, moves "among the sick and the mourning, among minds hardened and shriveled through poverty and ignorance" (114). "Reared on oat-cake and lived coarse," they believed in "present miracles, in instantaneous conversions, in revelations by dreams and visions; they drew lots, and sought for Divine guidance by opening the Bible at hazard" (40). Seth tells his mother, "Thee mustna undervally prayer. Prayer mayna bring money, but it brings us what no money can buy—a power to keep from sin, and be content with God's will, whatever He may please to send" (47). Seth also calls attention to the relation between religion and labor: "It's the preacher as empties th' alehouse; and if a man gets religion, he'll do his work none the worse for that" (12).

Yet, enthusiastically espousing religion and church attendance as the right and decent thing to do maintains the economic interests of the upper classes. Frank M. Turner writes, "As Britain assumed the leadership of the counter-revolutionary coalition against France the protection of religion in turn became increasingly associated with the preservation of the existing social and political structures. For all the propertied classes religion came to have a new importance and became something that required fostering" (12). In contrast to Seth's naïve view, Eliot expands on the relation between religion and labor in *The*

Mill on the Floss, pointing out that only in the institutionalized space of the Anglican Church do the two classes meet: the workers to take their opium and the bourgeoisie to valorize the taking (254–255).

Met in only the best of houses, *Adam Bede*'s Anglican Rector Irwine illustrates the great divide between laborers and bourgeoisie. Eliot's affection for Irwine is matched by her keen insight into the problematic nature of his position as a spiritual leader. Anglicanism, more cultural than spiritual, produces such "large-hearted, sweet-blooded natures that never know a narrow or a grudging thought; Epicurean, if you will, with no enthusiasm, no self-scourging sense of duty . . . no lofty aims, no theological enthusiasm" (69). With powdered hair tied with a black ribbon, Irwine is playing chess with his mother when we first meet him. He enjoys his dogs and horses and the revenues of more than one church living (a situation finally prohibited by an Act of Parliament in 1838), and his personal charms contrast with a more historical view. Will Maskery calls him an "idle shepherd," and Irwine himself says, "I *am* a lazy fellow" (4, 65).

With a "pagan mental palate," a "lax theology," and a seeming indifference to the poverty and ignorance of Dinah's Methodist followers, Irwine fails to help even those closest to him, a defect clearly demonstrated in his relationship with Arthur Donnithorne. Irwine is Arthur's mentor and father figure, but when Arthur seeks guidance, Irwine cannot take the attraction to Hetty seriously enough. He tells Arthur, "When I've made up my mind that I can't afford to buy a tempting dog, I take no notice of him, because if he took a strong fancy to me, and looked lovingly at me, the struggle between arithmetic and inclination might become unpleasantly severe" (103). Any relation with Hetty, animal that she is, would be "a lower kind of folly" than even "foolish romance" (172).

In a similar way traditional religion fails Hetty, a character on whom religious doctrines take no hold: "She was one of those numerous people who have had godfathers and godmothers, learned their catechism, been confirmed, and gone to church every Sunday, and yet, for any practical result of strength in life, or trust in death, have never appropriated a single Christian idea or Christian feeling" (385–386). In contrast to this spiritual emptiness, the physical attraction between Arthur and Hetty is palpable. In the woods we sense the "overpowering presence of their first privacy," and something—usually called love—takes possession of these two beautiful young people (129). The force of their attraction blends with the natural energy and pulse informing the limes and beeches, the golden light lingering languidly—"an afternoon in which destiny disguises her cold awful face behind a hazy radiant veil" (129). This "cold awful face" suggests something markedly different from the Romantic view of nature, and Hetty and Arthur are ill-equipped to restrain their passion.

Arthur "was getting in love with Hetty. . . . He was ready to pitch everything . . . for the sake of surrendering himself to this delicious feeling" (132).

Constantly compared to kittens, spaniels, and butterflies, it is easy to lose sight of how efficient Hetty is. When Mrs. Poyser is confined to her room all through January, Hetty manages "everything" downstairs and much of "Molly's place too, while the good damsel waited on her mistress" (362). Thus, Hetty performs the work of three. We know in some detail how demanding this work can be, and we also know what a fine job she does in the dairy. Though reading a novel may be too hard, her skill and organization belie simple-mindedness (135). When the "little minx" flattens her hair and dresses in a black gown and a Methodist high-crowned cap to mimic Dinah, Hetty displays her fine sense of humor. No doubt, she is different, and she is very young, just seventeen, and surely one of the most beautiful of fictional creations.

Peter Allan Dale writes that Eliot thought of her novels as "experiments in life" that repeatedly test the positivist proposition that there is something in our "cerebral structure" that tends to altruism, and that *Adam Bede* is the closest she comes to an "uncritical acceptance of the Comtean paradigm" (83). But how can this be? Through Hetty, Eliot poses a direct challenge to Comte's altruism and especially the prevailing belief in maternal instinct. Early in the novel we are told that Hetty is not fond of children and "would have been glad to hear that she should never see a child again; they were worse than the nasty little lambs . . . for the lambs *were* got rid of sooner or later" (154). In this eerie foreshadowing of the infanticide, Hetty's difference from the simple and faith-abiding members of the Hayslope community intensifies. As a positivist text *Adam Bede* must leave Hetty out, but Eliot cannot and, in fact, forces her in with emphasis until her isolated ego takes full control of the novel's action and emotion.

Taken into the Poyser household with no exchange of deep love or attachment, expected to be grateful and hard working, Hetty does her work tolerably well. In the midst of all the farm animals and the many metaphors comparing her to tempting dogs and downy ducks, however, she is often pushed outside cultural boundaries. She is "no better than a peacock, as 'ud strut about on the wall and spread its tail when the sun shone if all the folks i' the parish was dying: there's nothing seems to give her a turn i' th' inside" (154). Like Mrs. Poyser, Dinah, and Adam, the narrator is drawn to but confused and disturbed by this character who does not fit any pattern, who fails to respond in a way that will confirm their beliefs and restore their sense of well-being and security.

Upon leaving the safety of the Hayslope community, how suddenly Hetty's instinctive nature surfaces. After her wandering, "a hard and even fierce look had come in the eyes." She looked like "a wild woman," "trapesin' about the fields like a mad woman," "clinging to life only as the hunted wounded brute

clings to it" (386, 390–391). Through this swift loss of the veneer of civilization, Eliot captures a widespread Victorian fear concerning the origin and extent of reason, control, and human dignity. In the prison, Dinah wants a
confession of guilt and remorse; the guilt is acknowledged, but Hetty expresses
no Christian remorse. Dinah's intense efforts and Adam's agitation represent
the communal anxiety caused by Hetty's transformed appearance and murderous behavior.

Comte scientifically grounds morality in biology and specifically in animal
instinct. The great problem between the two competing instinctual energies,
the egoistic and altruistic, is subordinating the personal to the social instincts.
The antagonism is addressed through social institutions that educate the affec-
tive instincts so that the "greater energy" of egoism is gradually suppressed by
the "lesser energy" of altruism (Dale, 20). Through the Anglican Church,
Hayslope community, and Poyser family values, it would seem that Hetty has
received the appropriate institutional training, but her altruism remains un-
tapped or absent. She is the exception, an emergent symptom, embodying the
potential to alter traditional beliefs and Comte's positivism. However, rather
than a catalyst for revision within the narrative framework, she is finally cut out
of the story through banishment and death. Still, Adam and Dinah's happy union cannot dispel her haunting presence. In the Methodism of Dinah and Seth,
Irwine's Anglicanism, and the simplistic beauty of the Hall Farm, Eliot represents an old world, but it is a world that Hetty shatters.

HARD TIMES

Charles Dickens wanted to believe that humans had special status and were
born with an instinctive moral sense. When Dickens read about the cannibal-
ism of the 1845 Franklin Expedition, he denied such a possibility, finding it in-
conceivable. In two articles published in *Household Words,* he argued that no
British gentleman was capable of doing what Franklin was accused of doing.
Dickens's novels, filled with phrases from the Bible and the Book of Common
Prayer, resonate with his faith in innate goodness and a transcendental power.

Whereas so many of his contemporaries celebrated advances in science and
technology, Dickens feared that the essential value of feeling would be lost in
the midst of the general enthusiasm for rationalism. Prince Albert referred to
the Great Exhibition of 1851 as "a new starting point from which all nations
would be able to direct their further exertions," but Dickens worried about this
new beginning. In *Hard Times*, published only a few years after the erection of
the Crystal Palace, Dickens argued against an over-reliance on utility and industry, especially targeting Jeremy Bentham's critique of poetry and Thomas
Carlyle's assault on the "lying" fictions of novels.

Organized as a dialogue, the novel presents the utilitarianism of Mr. Grandgrind juxtaposed with the goodness of the laborers and circus people. Through a season of "sowing," "reaping," and "garnering," we witness the effects of competition versus cooperation and reason versus imagination. The dangers of an over-reliance on fact and utility emerge in the education and development of Louisa's depression, Tom's dissipation, and Bitzer's hardness.

Mr. Grandgrind was saddened that the townspeople visiting the Coketown library read Defoe and Goldsmith rather than Euclid and Cocker. With a pair of scales and the multiplication table always in his pocket, Gradgrind "was ready to weigh and measure any parcel of human nature, and tell you exactly what it comes to" (10). Actions in themselves have no moral value. What matters is their effect, and Gradgrind felt confident that he could calculate that effect. It makes sense, then, that his son Tom is always chasing his own pleasure because in the utilitarian system there are no ethical first principles.

If Tom had his way, he would collect all the facts and figures and all the people who found them out and ignite a thousand barrels of gunpowder under them. In a more practical but no less angry way, Tom plans to get his revenge and enjoy himself a little when he goes to live with old Bounderby. His mode of managing and smoothing Bounderby will be to sacrifice his sister Louisa, and he tells her, "I had better go where I can take with me some advantage of your influence, than where I should lose it altogether. Don't you see?" (58). Tom, a pathetic figure who is isolated by anger and neglect, turns to gambling and embezzlement and only escapes prison by fleeing the country.

Bitzer stands as a second logical outcome of the utilitarian approach to education. When asked by Mr. Grandgrind "Have you a heart?" he responds, "The circulation, sir, couldn't be carried on without one. No man, sir, acquainted with the facts established by Harvey relating to the circulation of the blood, can doubt that I have a heart" (286). Brought up in the catechism of self-interest, Bitzer refuses to help Tom escape, having calculated that promotion in the bank is in his best interest. The narrator again notes that in the Gradgrind philosophy, nobody "was ever on any account to give anybody anything, or render anybody help without purchase. Gratitude was to be abolished" (288).

Because Sissy has developed elsewhere in a culture of affection and cooperation, she is resistant to utilitarianism. With no regard for percentages and a stubborn concern for the twenty-five out of a million inhabitants who starve to death, the "greatest happiness of the greatest number" is not the kind of education she can absorb (62–63). As the one character who crosses over from carnival to middle class, Sissy illustrates the redeeming power of feeling. As the antidote to M'Choakumchild's pedagogy, she restores imagination to the Gradgrind family, and, among Tom, Louisa, Bitzer, and Harthouse, it is only Sissy, the real heroine of the novel, who reproduces.

Often locating goodness and decency in members of the lower class, Dickens was not to be outdone in his dissatisfaction with organized religion. Understanding better what his religion was not, there is a conspicuous absence of clergy throughout his novels. Disgusted with the established Church and its "Puseyisms" and described as "aggressively anticlerical, antidogmatic, and antisectarian," his concerns were material and practical. Believing that Jesus was an extraordinary human being rather than the son of God, he joined the Unitarians who, in his words, "*would* do something for human improvement, if they could; and who practice Charity and Toleration" (Kaplan, 175). The crucial issues were the necessity to eliminate poverty and prostitution and provide education and decent living arrangements. In the non-Spencerian world of *Hard Times*, it is not the competition, dogmatism, and arrogance of the industrialists that define survival of the fittest, but the gentleness and cooperation of the circus people.

THE WAY OF ALL FLESH

Although *The Way of All Flesh* satirizes several aspects of Victorian culture such as marriage, public education, and the orthodoxy of Darwin and his followers, the novel's primary target is organized religion. With an Anglican bishop for a grandfather and an Anglican clergyman for a father, Samuel Butler grew and developed from within a system to become one of its fiercest critics. Once the novel's protagonist Ernest Pontifex breaks from the Church, he realizes "that the greater part of the ills which had afflicted him were due, indirectly, in chief measure to the influence of Christian teaching." He had been "humbugged" and hopes for the extinction of Christianity in England within a few months' time (Butler, 307).

Butler's attack focuses on the clergy's arrogance, ignorance, and greed. Theobald Pontifex and, initially, his son Ernest accept without question what they are told about religion. Edward Overton, the narrator, remarks that it "had never so much as crossed Theobald's mind to doubt the literal accuracy of any syllable in the Bible. He had never seen any book in which this was disputed, nor met with anyone who doubted it" (81). And, when Ernest arrives in central London to assume his curacy, "his earlier habit of taking on trust everything that was told him by those in authority . . . returned with redoubled strength" (255). The greater part of his education "had been an attempt, not so much to keep him in blinkers as to gouge his eyes out altogether" (291). Mrs. Jupp, the landlady, confirms the success of this metaphoric gouging by commenting that Ernest at twenty-four "don't know nothing at all, no more than a unborn babe, no he don't; why, there's not a monkey going about London with an Italian organ grinder but knows more than Mr. Pontifex do" (270).

Theobald and Ernest fail to experience any special calling or any desire to be ordained. Theobald's father, George, a well-known publisher of religious books, felt he "should devote at least one of his sons to the Church; this might tend to bring business, or at any rate to keep it in the firm" (60). Instead of deep faith or conviction, getting and spending provide the impetus. When Theobald approaches the time of his ordination, he is frightened and writes his father regarding his doubts, "My conscience tells me I should do wrong if I became a clergyman." Ordination, however, is a necessary step on the road to status and financial security, and George threatens to cut Theobald off completely if he persists in such "folly and wickedness" (66).

For many, like George Pontifex, this secular approach is reasonable and respectable. The poorest Cambridge undergraduates view ordination as "the *entrée* into a social position from which they were at present kept out by barriers they well knew to be impassable; ordination, therefore, opened fields for ambition which made it the central point in their thoughts" (233). In such a practical context, a sincere belief in supernaturalism becomes a vulnerability, often ending in bitterness and disillusion. During his prison stay, it puzzled Ernest "that he should not have known how much he had hated being a clergyman till now" (303).

Frequently, the narrator reminds the reader that Ernest's parents are not exceptional but representative, and Theobald as husband, father, and clergyman is scrutinized in detail. His philosophy as a parent is that the "first signs of self-will must be carefully looked for, and plucked up by the roots at once before they had time to grow" (117). When, as a little boy, Ernest can only say "tum" in place of "come," he is beaten (125). Overton observes that as a child Ernest is "like a puny, sallow little old man," suffering from "*home sickness*," a kind of starving, through being overcrammed with sin, shame, and sorrow (121, 138, 220). Later, Ernest says "as regards his father, he could remember no feeling but fear and shrinking" and "the continual whippings that were found necessary at lesson times" (117). Overton concludes, "The Church of Rome does wisely in not allowing her priests to marry" (136).

"Sadly in want of occupation," Theobold dislikes scholarship and music, and he does not ride, shoot, fish, or play cricket. When he begins instructing his children, "the daily oft-repeated screams that issue from the study during the lesson hours tell their own horrible story over the house" (97). Theobald's boredom, idleness, and cruelty contrast vividly with *Adam Bede*'s Irwine, but in the context of *The Way of All Flesh* Irwine becomes the exception: the "reader, if he has passed middle life and has a clerical connection, will probably remember scores and scores of rectors and rectors' wives who differed in no material respect from Theobald and Christina. . . . I should say I had drawn the better rather than the worse side of the life of an English country parson of some fifty years ago" (102).

Although Butler argues for a kind of human agency rather than mere subjection to natural laws, throughout the novel instinct and habit appear to drive human behavior. Personal choice appears almost beyond the bounds of possibility. A swarm of bees on the Pontifex dining-room wallpaper, which is covered with bunches of red and white roses, illustrates the trouble. Overton describes these bees who

fly up to these bunches and try them, under the impression that they were real flowers; having tried one bunch, they tried the next, and the next, and the next, till they reached the one that was nearest the ceiling, then they went down bunch by bunch as they had ascended, till they were stopped by the back of the sofa; on this they ascended bunch by bunch to the ceiling again; and so on, and so on till I was tired of watching them. As I thought of the family prayers being repeated night and morning, week by week, month by month, and year by year, I could not help thinking how like it was to the way in which the bees went up the wall and down the wall, bunch by bunch, without ever suspecting that so many of the associated ideas could be present, and yet the main idea be wanting hopelessly, and for ever. (127)

Throughout the novel, Christians are compared to these bees, lured and caught by elaborate myth and ritual and doomed to futile repetition without any core reality or spiritual sustenance.

Ernest is able to break away. He had, like his creator, "read Mr Darwin's books as fast as they came out and adopted evolution as an article of faith" (386). In the British Museum Reading Room he sends for *Vestiges of Creation*, and the novel refers to Bacon, Paley, geology, German skepticism, Dickens, Arnold, *Origin of Species, Criticisms on the Pentateuch*, and *Essay and Reviews*. Ernest decides to radically alter the environment of his two illegitimate children, Georgie and Alice, replacing the middle-class values, education and religion of his own upbringing with poor foster parents and the fresh sea air. Similarly, the novel's ideal man, Towneley, is orphaned at the age of two, and in combination with the wealth he inherits, this break with the past is a supreme blessing—the very reason for his perfection. Still, *The Way of All Flesh* is no fairy tale. The good fortune of Georgie, Alice, and Towneley is an anomaly, whereas the damage done to Ernest is commonplace and permanent.

Alongside Butler's brutal honesty stands his refusal to surrender to the naturalism and social Darwinism then so prevalent. He insists that humans can and do participate in shaping their destinies, and, like other skeptical Victorians before him, he reserves a philosophical space for a new kind of faith. Ernest had "lost his faith in Christianity, but his faith in something—he knew not what, but that there was a something as yet but darkly known, which made right right and wrong wrong—his faith in this grew stronger and stronger daily" (321).

JUDE THE OBSCURE

Thomas Hardy noted in his letters that he was "brought up as an orthodox English Churchman" and when young he had "a wish to enter the Church" (Millgate and Purdy, iv, 319; vii, 21). But, like so many, Hardy broke with Christianity and became a self-proclaimed agnostic and critic of organized religion, acknowledging Darwin as a major influence on his philosophy. In an 1885 letter to John Morley, he asked why the religious wants of those who have ceased to believe in supernatural theology are ignored in the public press: "The battle of establishment v. disestabt [*sic*] is there fought out as between the old fashioned nonconformist & the ordinary churchman; whilst of the growing masses of people who for conscientious reasons can enter neither church nor chapel . . . nobody raises up his voice in the schemes for readjustment" (i, 136). In an 1897 letter to Edward Clodd regarding his book *Pioneers of Evolution from Thales to Huxley*, Hardy wrote, "the most striking idea dwelt upon is that of the arrest of light & reason by theology for 16,00 [*sic*] years. The older one gets, the more deplorable seems the effect of that terrible, dogmatic ecclesiasticism—Christianity so called . . . on morals and true religion" (ii, 143). Again, in 1902 he wrote to Clodd regarding the extent to which "Theological lumber" was still allowed to discredit religion:

[I]f the doctrines of the supernatural were quietly abandoned to-morrow by the Church, and "reverence and love for an ethical ideal" alone retained, not one in ten thousand would object to the readjustment, while the enormous bulk of thinkers excluded by the old teaching would be brought into the fold, and our venerable old churches and cathedrals would become the centres of emotional life that they once were. (iii, 5)

Striving for transcendence without God, Hardy wanted to restore church structures to fit the modern spirit. He resented Christianity's enslavement to custom and convention and analyzed many of his concerns through Jude's changing relationship to Christminster.

As a young boy, Jude views Christminster as a "city of light," the "heavenly Jerusalem," and "a castle, manned by scholarship and religion," and he says, "It would just suit me" (26). He even imagines that he might be a bishop some day. The first impediment, however, is the "unvoiced call . . . uttered very distinctly by Arabella's personality." The narrator comments, "She saw that he had singled her out from the three, as a woman is singled out in such cases . . . in commonplace obedience to conjunctive orders from headquarters, unconsciously received" (39). Regarding this scene of sexual selection, Hardy remarked that the "'grimy' features of the story go to show the contrast between the ideal life a man wished to lead, and the squalid real life he was fated to lead. The throwing of the pizzle, at the supreme moment of his young dream, is to sharply initiate this contrast. . . . The idea was meant to run all through the novel. It is, in fact to be discovered in *every* body's life—though it lies less on the surface perhaps than it does in my poor puppet's" (ii, 93).

The morning after Jude arrives in Christminster, in the light of day, the spirits of the great men have disappeared, and his fantastic view shifts quickly to a "more or less defective real." Reading the architecture, Jude comprehends a rottenness in the historical documents; the erections "were wounded, broken, sloughing off their outer shape in the deadly struggle against years, weather, and man" (84). Even more painful to Jude, dressed as a workman in a white blouse, is his complete invisibility to the Christminster students, who in passing "did not even see him, or hear him, rather saw through him as through a pane of glass" (86).

The novel's epigraph, "The letter killeth," emerges explicitly when Jude receives the letter from Biblioll College telling him to stick to stonemasonry (117). Hardy, too, had once received such a letter. Jude adjusts by altering his "vision of the bishopric" to that of a "humble curate." He finds new lodgings and begins work on the Cathedral repairs, "which were very extensive, the whole interior fittings having been swept away, to be replaced by new" (135). Similarly, he replaces his old theological readings with "Newman, Pusey, and many other modern lights" (136).

Newman and Pusey were leaders of the Oxford Movement, which A. Dwight Culler describes as a movement towards celibacy. He notes Newman's belief that it was God's will that he remain single: "Hence the high, severe conception of virginity which he shared with his friend Hurrell Froude and which they tried to institutionalize by gathering their friends into colleges of unmarried priests, and hence the anger which they felt, Newman especially, when these friends fell away from the ideal and married" (ix).

Finally, with no deep-felt inclination to Newman's virginity, Jude acknowledges his physical passion for Sue, "thinking it was glaringly inconsistent for him to pursue the idea of becoming the soldier and servant of a religion in which sexual love was regarded as at its best a frailty, and at its worst damnation" (216–217). As he burns his theological and ethical books, "the sense of being no longer a hypocrite to himself afforded a relief to his mind which gave him calm" (218).

Jude and Sue share a few years of intimacy and contentment, but Father Time's arrival results in communal condemnation of their unconventional relationship. During their subsequent nomadic wandering, Jude develops a strong antipathy to ecclesiastical work due to the incongruity between Christian dogma and his relation with Sue, "hardly a shred of the beliefs with which he had first gone up to Christminster now remaining with him" (310). The immense distance between his youthful idealism and the "grind of stern reality" is captured pathetically in the Christminster cakes he bakes in the shape of college windows, towers, and pinnacles and Sue sells at the Kennetbridge spring fair (312).

Jude knows his Latin, can preach, and is a large-spirited man, and rather than a baker or a stonemason, he is suited for the life of a scholarly divine. Unfortunately, nicknamed the "Tutor of St. Slums," he can only drunkenly display his Latin and preach regrettably on Remembrance Day. Tinker Taylor notes: "One of them jobbing pa'sons . . . wouldn't ha' discoursed such doctrine for less than a guinea. . . . And then he must have had it wrote down for 'n" (327). But, then, the point of this antichurch and antiprovidential novel is that many humans are maladapted, having consciousness and sensitivity in great excess of what is necessary to reproduce the species. Sue imagined that the First Cause had worked like a somnambulist rather than reflectively like a sage, and that there never was contemplated such a "development of emotional perceptiveness . . . as that reached by thinking and educated humanity" (342). In the end, with their overdeveloped nerves and intelligence, Sue breaks and Jude dies, and Arabella, strong in flesh, survives.

Natural law drives *Jude the Obscure* through its repeated inversions of Christianity to its final conclusion, demonstrating how the mix of Christianity with a post-Darwinian view can result in tragedy. Far removed from old-world supernaturalism, Hardy even discerned too much design in Darwin's metaphor of the tree, writing, "History is rather a stream than a tree. There is nothing organic in its shape, nothing systematic in its development. It flows on like a thunderstorm-rill by a road side; now a straw turns it this way, now a tiny barrier of sand that" (225). In considering his transformation of evolutionary theory into literature and in terms of men and women, Hardy understood evolution as well or better than Darwin did.

CONCLUSION

Although numerous representatives of the clergy populate nineteenth-century novels, there is no pervasive feeling that "trailing clouds of glory do we come from God, who is our home." And even though Christian myth and Biblical allusion permeate the narratives, it is myth mined for its familiarity and evocative power rather than for its authority. When Jane Eyre appears unconvinced that Helen Burns has gone to a better place and turns her attention toward that which she can see, Jane announces many of the century's intellectual movements.

Eliot's caution and empathy, Dickens's humor and sentiment, Butler's ferociousness, and Hardy's penetration indicate noteworthy differences. Still, although the impulse to retain the old belief system is present but weak in the early novels, all four express concerns about the inadequacy of orthodox religion to deal with modern issues. In recasting positivism, utilitarianism, and evolutionary theory into novelistic discourse, these writers identify and direct a shift to a new faith. Rather than resignation and constraint, this new faith resides in the potential of science and human agency to create a moral order focused on the release of energies and earthly well-being.

WORKS CITED AND SELECTED WORKS FOR FURTHER READING

Ashton, Rosemary. *George Eliot: A Life*. New York: Penguin, 1996.

Beer, Gillian. *Darwin's Plots: Evolutionary Narrative in Darwin, George Eliot and Nineteenth-Century Fiction*. London: Routledge and Kegan Paul, 1983.

Browne, Janet. *Charles Darwin: Voyaging, Volume 1 of a Biography*. New York: Knopf, 1995.

Butler, Lance St. John. "'Bosh' or: Believing Neither More nor Less—Hardy, George Eliot and God." In *New Perspectives on Thomas Hardy*, pp. 101–116. Ed. Charles P. C. Pettit. New York: St. Martin's Press, 1994.

Butler, Samuel. *The Way of All Flesh*. New York: Penguin, 1986.

Cashdollar, Charles D. *The Transformation of Theology, 1830–1889: Positivism and Protestant Thought in Britain and America*. Princeton: Princeton UP, 1989.

Cockshut, A.O.J., ed. *Religious Controversies of the Nineteenth Century: Selected Documents*. London: Methuen, 1966.

Cole, G.D.H. *Samuel Butler*. London: Longmans, Green, 1961.

Collins, Deborah. *Thomas Hardy and His God: A Liturgy of Unbelief*. London: Macmillan, 1990.

Creighton, T.R.M. "Some Thoughts on Hardy and Religion." In *Thomas Hardy after Fifty Years*, pp. 64–77. Ed. Lance St. John Butler. Totowa: Rowman, 1977.

Culler, A. Dwight. Introduction. *Apologia Pro Vita Sua*. By John Henry Cardinal Newman. Boston: Houghton Mifflin, 1956.

Dale, Peter Allan. *In Pursuit of a Scientific Culture: Science, Art, and Society in the Victorian Age*. Madison: U of Wisconsin P, 1989.

DeLaura, David J. "'The Ache of Modernism.' Hardy's Later Novels." *English Literary History* 34 (1967): 380–399.

Dickens, Charles. *Hard Times*. New York: Penguin, 1995.

Eliot, George. *Adam Bede*. New York: Penguin, 1980.

———. *The Mill on the Floss*. Oxford: Clarendon, 1980.

Guest, David. "Acquired Characters: Cultural vs. Biological Determinism in *The Way of All Flesh*." *English Literature in Transition (1880–1920)* 34.3 (1991): 283–292.

Haight, Gordon S., ed. *The George Eliot Letters*. 9 vols. New Haven: Yale UP, 1954–78.

Hardy, Florence Emily. *The Early Years of Thomas Hardy, 1840–1891*. New York: Macmillan, 1928.

Hardy, Thomas. *Jude the Obscure*. New York: Penguin, 1998.

Harrison, Frederic. "Neo-Christianity." Rev. of *Essays and Reviews*. *Westminster Review*. Oct. 1, 1860. New Series, Vol. 18, pp. 292–332. London: George Manwaring, 1860.

Helmstadter, Richard J., and Bernard Lightman. *Victorian Faith in Crisis: Essays on Continuity and Change in Nineteenth-Century Religious Belief*. Stanford: Stanford UP, 1990.

Hilton, Boyd. *The Age of Atonement: The Influence of Evangelicalism on Social and Economic Thought, 1795–1865*. Oxford: Clarendon, 1988.

Huxley, Leonard. *Life and Letters of T. H. Huxley*. 2 vols. London: Macmillan, 1900.

Johnson, Bruce. "'The Perfection of Species' and Hardy's *Tess*." In *Nature and the Victorian Imagination*. Berkeley: U of California P, 1977.

Kaplan, Fred. *Dickens: A Biography*. New York: William Morrow, 1988.

Levine, George. *Darwin and the Novelists: Patterns of Science in Victorian Fiction*. Cambridge: Harvard UP, 1988.

Logan, Deborah Anna. "Am I My Sister's Keeper?: Sexual Deviance and the Social Community." In *Fallenness in Victorian Women's Writing: Marry, Stitch, Die, or Do Worse*, pp. 92–125. Columbia: U of Missouri P, 1998.

Logan, Peter M. "Conceiving the Body: Realism and Medicine in *Middlemarch*." *History of the Human Sciences* 4.2 (1991): 197–222.

Marx, Karl. "Contribution to the Critique of Hegel's *Philosophy of Right*: Introduction." *The Marx-Engels Reader*. Ed. Robert C. Tucker. New York: W. W. Norton, 1978.

McNees, Eleanor. "Reverse Typology in *Jude the Obscure*." *Christianity and Literature* 39.1 (1989): 35–49.

Meisel, Perry. *Thomas Hardy: The Return of the Repressed*. New Haven: Yale UP, 1972.

Miller, J. Hillis. *The Linguistic Moment: From Wordsworth to Stevens*. Princeton: Princeton UP, 1985.

Millgate, Michael. *Thomas Hardy: A Biography*. New York: Random House, 1982.

Millgate, Michael, and Richard Little Purdy, ed. *The Collected Letters of Thomas Hardy*. 7 vols. Oxford: Clarendon, 1978.

Morton, Peter. *The Vital Science: Biology and the Literary Imagination, 1860–1900*. London: George Allen and Unwin, 1984.

Robb, George. "*The Way of All Flesh*: Degeneration, Eugenics, and the Gospel of Free Love." *Journal of the History of Sexuality* 6.4 (1996): 589–603.

Schacht, Paul. "Dickens and the Uses of Nature." *Victorian Studies* 34.1 (1990): 77–102.

Shuttleworth, Sally. *George Eliot and Nineteenth-Century Science: The Make-Believe of a Beginning*. Cambridge: Cambridge UP, 1984.

Stone, Marjorie. "Dickens, Bentham, and the Fictions of the Law: A Victorian Controversy and Its Consequences." *Victorian Studies* 29.1 (1985): 125–154.

Turner, Frank. "The Victorian Crisis of Faith and the Faith That was Lost." *Victorian Faith in Crisis: Essays on Continuity and Change in Nineteenth-Century Religious Belief*. Ed. Richard J. Helmstadter and Bernard Lightman. Stanford: Stanford UP, 1990.

Turner, Paul. *The Life of Thomas Hardy: A Critical Biography*. Oxford: Blackwell, 1998.

Williams, Raymond. *Culture and Society, 1780–1950*. London: Chatto and Windus, 1958.

Wright, T. R. *The Religion of Humanity: The Impact of Comtean Positivism on Victorian Britain*. Cambridge: Cambridge UP, 1986.

Philosophy and the Victorian Literary Aesthetic

Martin Bidney

The Victorian novel would be a far different and a lesser thing without the stimulation of imaginative and philosophic ideas from Germany, France, Italy, and Russia. Looking, even briefly, at the influences of these countries' respective literary cultures on the works of the Victorian masters will clarify the cultural history of both Britain and the continent, and will enhance informed enjoyment.

GERMANY

Charlotte Brontë admired the verse dramas of Friedrich Schiller. The powerful impact of Schiller's romantic imagination on that of Brontë will have struck readers of *Jane Eyre*. When Jane overhears Mary Rivers reading to Diana, in German, the striking passage from Schiller's *The Robbers* beginning "Then stepped forth one, in appearance like the starry night," followed by Mary's enthusiastic comment, "There you have a dim and mighty archangel set before you!," the reader senses in the "starry night" a prophetic reference to Jane's impending encounter with the Heaven-obsessed St. John Rivers, and in the "dim and mighty archangel" one may feel perhaps an equally foreboding intimation of the later chastened Rochester, his sight more than dimmed, his Vulcan-like figure still mighty though fallen (Brontë, 293). Samuel Taylor Coleridge (who beautifully translated Schiller's *Wallenstein*), Thomas Carlyle (who wrote a *Life of Schiller*), and later George Eliot as well all seem to have begun their study of German with Schiller's heroic plays (Ashton, 147).

But Carlyle valued Johann Wolfgang von Goethe even more highly than he esteemed Schiller. In the semiautobiographical philosophic novel *Sartor Resartus*, Carlyle offered a celebrated argument for the superiority of the ethically mature poet and novelist Goethe to the more hedonistic, sensation-seeking Lord Byron; and by making this argument, Carlyle became chiefly responsible for the increasing preference of Victorians for Goethe over Schiller, Byron, and other literary rivals in the 1820s and afterward (Ashton, 21). George Eliot followed suit: The well-known advice from *Sartor*, "Close thy Byron, open thy *Goethe*," is implicitly echoed in *Middlemarch*, where Eliot tellingly contrasts Lydgate's worries over the miseries resulting from self-indulgent egotism to Dorothea Brooke's more practical realization that loss of a private joy need not deter a person from leading a meaningful, morally active life (Argyle, 42).

Goethe inspired George Eliot in many ways. In *The Mill on the Floss*, she achieves a difficult, subtle moral equipoise whose example is Goethe's novel *Elective Affinities*: Both narratives paradoxically affirm "duty towards established social and familial ties, while exposing the stifling rigidity of that society whose continuing existence depends on strict observance of those ties" (Röder-Bolton, 90). Similarly, Eliot adapts imagery from Goethe's *Faust* to depict the ethical struggle for Gwendolyn's soul in *Daniel Deronda*, while the narrative pattern of moral growth in that novel—beginning with alienation from one's environment and then proceeding, through confusion and near despair, to final "acceptance of self-restriction"—allies both Gwendolyn and Deronda to the hero of Goethe's novel *Wilhelm Meister*, translated by Carlyle and influential upon the entire Victorian tradition of the *Bildungsroman*, the novel of ethical development or character-building (Röder-Bolton, 109, 177). George Henry Lewes, longtime intellectual and emotional partner of George Eliot, not only wrote three novels imitative of *Wilhelm Meister* but, with Eliot's help, authored the first full-length biography of Goethe (McCobb, 23), which he dedicated to Carlyle. It is a lively work still very readable today, and particularly good on the polymathic German poet's optics and biology.

The agnostic moral humanism that informs George Eliot's fiction was partly shaped by German works of Biblical criticism, and of social and moral philosophy, that she translated. By rendering Friedrich Strauss's *Life of Jesus*, Eliot was helped to acquire a skeptical attitude that maintained clear distinctions between ascertainable historic fact and religious dogma. In translating Ludwig Feuerbach's *Essence of Christianity*, Eliot further acquired sympathy with this philosopher's secularizing thesis that "the essence of Christianity is really 'the essence of human feeling' and that the only divinity is 'the divinity of human nature' "; indeed, one Victorian critic found that the protagonist of Eliot's *Romola*, with her surprisingly modern readiness to interpret religious language in humanist or secular ethical terms, was rather more of a philosophical Feuerbachian than we might have expected in fifteenth-century Florence (Ashton, 159, 164). Eliot also translated Spinoza's *Ethics*, and Rosemary Ashton (166) argues that this seventeenth-century philosopher is so very close in spirit to a number of his later German admirers, including poets and thinkers such as Goethe and Schelling, that Spinoza may usefully be included along with Feuerbach and Goethe as, culturally speaking, one more "German" influence on Eliot. Spinoza "had been tolerant of popular religions because they kept men virtuous by means of the imagination where it was not possible by reason; and George Eliot, in *Scenes of Clerical Life* and *Adam Bede*, displayed just such a knowledgeable warmth towards religious doctrines she no longer held and could not approve of intellectually" (Ashton, 159).

George Gissing and Thomas Hardy to some extent reworked, in their fiction, the thought of another German philosopher, Arthur Schopenhauer, who in *The World as Will and Idea* urged his reader to deny or renounce, in Buddhist fashion, the passionate "Will" or Desire, conceived as a blind cosmic life-force whose endless drives meant, for the individual human being, nothing but endless frustration. Gissing partly incorporated the Schopenhauerian program of his essay "The Hope of Pessimism" in depicting Arthur Kingcote, the central character of his novel *Isabel Clarendon*, who, however unsuccessfully, attempts a Schopenhauer-like self-denial through a detached, delicate, but unemotional contemplation of nature (Argyle, 97, 128). (*Workers in the Dawn*, a better novel, shows us another side of Gissing; here he appears as a trenchant social critic stimulated by the thought of German theorists Karl Marx and Ferdinand Lassalle [Argyle, 96].) In Thomas Hardy the thought of Schopenhauer proved aesthetically more fruitful than in Gissing. Hardy was apparently reading the 1883 English translation of the German thinker's *magnum opus* during the time when he was composing *The Woodlanders* (Bailey, 88). "The book which Hardy wrote most immediately after his reading of Schopenhauer, *Tess of the d'Urbervilles*, is the one more widely regarded than any other as his masterpiece, and also the one most replete with Schopenhauerian allusions. Schopenhauer is even mentioned in it by name." In *Tess* we find not only a cosmic pessimism reminiscent of Schopenhauer (the "plight of being alive") but even a likely echo of the latter's conviction that of all types of artistic creator it is the musical composer whose power is the most "strange and godlike" (Magee, 384) because, in Schopenhauer's view, music alone of all the arts (unlike painting, say, or sculpture) does not simply depict individual objects or landscapes but rather evokes the formidable cosmic Will itself in all its surges and swells of

Desire. Further, in *The Dynasts*, Hardy uses the recognizably Schopenhauerian-sounding concept of an "Immanent Will" to form the metaphysical basis for an astonishingly experimental, cinemalike dramatic epic of the Napoleonic wars. As a postscript to these developments, it is worth noting that the narrator Marlow, whom Joseph Conrad in *Heart of Darkness* likens to a "Buddha preaching in European clothes and without a lotus-flower," sums up his horror of primordial nature in a highly Schopenhauerian, neo-Buddhist way when he calls life—the world of desire—a "mysterious arrangement of merciless logic for a futile purpose" (Conrad, 10, 69).

FRANCE

The stereotype-smasher George Sand, who dressed in male garb, maintained unorthodox relationships with a roster of French artistic luminaries, and wrote over a hundred novels, challenged Victorians through her life and works. Charlotte Brontë and George Eliot both preferred Sand's warmer nature to that of the harsh, cynical Balzac—a contrast that Sand herself liked to make (Thomson, 64; Vitaglione, 131). What can be pinpointed as George Sand's "particular legacy" to Charlotte Brontë is "her unswerving belief in the truth of the heart's promptings, and her equally firm disbelief in the chances of attaining perfect happiness in the formal marriage"—an identifiably Sandian blend of "disenchantment about matrimony and dedication to love" (Thomson, 64). After writing *Jane Eyre*, Brontë found herself in the position, familiar to Sand, of being charged with unfeminine coarseness and irreligious radicalism (Thomson, 66). The reader of *Jane Eyre* will also find interesting the plot of Sand's *The Miller of Angibault*, featuring a "maniac sister, La Bricoline, who has been disappointed in love, is kept hidden by her parents but breaks out from time to time and howls like a wolf, tears fowls apart with her nails and ends by setting the *château*, chapel and herself on fire and perishing in the flames" (Thomson, 73). Praising Brontë's "instinct for the tragic use of landscape," Swinburne—himself a Victorian virtuoso of lyric writing—averred, "No other woman that I know of, not George Sand herself, could have written a prose sentence of such exalted and perfect poetry": "The moon reigns glorious, glad of the gale: as glad as if she gave herself to its fierce caress with love" (Thomson, 76). Emily Brontë, described by Mrs. Gaskell as able to read French fluently, also may be reworking George Sand when, in *Wuthering Heights*, she offers a plot (based on two vividly contrasting country houses and temperament-types) reminiscent of the French novelist's *Mauprat* (Thomson, 80–89).

Emily spent nine months in Brussels, and Charlotte's residence there lasted a full two years, so it may not surprise us that both the latter's novels *The Profes-*

sor and *Villette* are set in that Belgian city. (These two works also happen to contain striking echoes of scenes from George Sand's earliest novel, cowritten with her lover Jules Sandeau, called *Rose et Blanche* [Thomson, 74].) The many *devoirs* or homework essays and transcriptions done by Charlotte in her Brussels schooling with M. Heger show what would prove a lasting legacy of French Romantic motifs and stylistic features in her later work. Her transcriptions include passages from Alphonse de Lamartine, Victor Hugo, and (most numerous of all) René de Chateaubriand, whose verbal landscape painting is echoed in the *devoirs* and also "perhaps in the brilliant and sensuous painting of moonlight and storm in Louis Moore's journal in *Shirley*"—including the very same "glad of the gale" passage that Swinburne singled out for praise (Duthie, 231–232, 192–193). Revealingly, the ship on which M. Paul sailed to Guadeloupe at the end of *Villette* was the *Paul et Virginie*, named after a novel by Bernardin de Saint-Pierre, who had schooled both Chateaubriand and Charlotte Brontë in the art of stormy seascape (Duthie, 198, 192).

Returning to George Sand, we note that George Eliot and Thomas Hardy both learned much from her. Before Strauss and Feuerbach, Sand in such novels as *Lélia, Jeanne*, and *Spiridion* had challengingly critiqued the mythological element in religion as manifesting a "less developed phase of humanity"; also attractive to Eliot were Sand's dismissal of ritualism and of ascetic privation, and her praise of imaginative sympathy as the core of religion (Vitaglione, 41, 45). Mordecai, who is Daniel's mentor in Eliot's *Daniel Deronda* as Alexis is Angel's advisor in Sand's *Spiridion*, teaches his protégé a similar lesson about the need to revive the "organic center" of religious fellowship in imaginative empathy (Vitaglione, 54). Eliot's Maggie, Dorothea, and Romola, those "beautiful, ardent, trustful, high-souled" heroines, with their "desire for learning" and "passionate need for affection," mirror not only the protagonists of Sand in such works as *Lélia* but also the French writer's self-portrait as an independent-minded religious quester in her memoir *Histoire de ma Vie* (Thomson, 161). Yet it is to Hardy that we must go if we seek a Sandian love of untamed nature; this is embodied as effectively in the "primitive heath-dwellers" of *Return of the Native* as in those of George Sand's *Jeanne*. "An all-night vigil in the shelter of druid stones, the grotesque effects of flames from a bonfire"—these we find not only in *Tess of the d'Urbervilles* but equally in *Jeanne*; nor should we forget that it was Sand who first thought of creating a man named Angel (Thomson, 198–199). In addition, Sand's wild and rugged Vallée Noire, locus of a sizable group of widely read novels, became an area of fictional topography as well known to French readers as Hardy's Wessex, much later, to British ones (Thomson, 189–191).

The Irish novelist George Moore, an intercultural mediator of great breadth and variety, incorporated a range of French influences in the course of his development. Minute attention to details of background and setting, in the manner of Honoré de Balzac and Émile Zola, lends credibility to the portrayal of the life of actors in *A Mummer's Wife*, but in *Esther Waters* Moore introduced increasingly subtle moral discriminations to avoid what he saw as the monolithic determinism of the Zolaesque novel (Cave, 40, 95). The autobiographical *Confessions of a Young Man* shows Moore at least partly under the spell of Joris-Karl Huysmans, the decadent aesthete author of *A Rebours* (variously rendered *Against the Grain* or *Against Nature*), though there is an ironic undertone to Moore's self-portrayal as apprentice aesthete in the current French style (Cave, 106). By the time of his trilogy of spiritual quest novels, *Evelyn Innes*, *Sister Teresa*, and *The Lake*, Moore had turned to the guidance of his friend Edouard Dujardin for ideas on how to transfer to novel-writing the technique of the *leitmotiv* or symbolic musical phrase pioneered in the operas of Richard Wagner, at that time hugely popular with French novelists and poets. The idea was now to "invest language with the symbolic potency with which Wagner had succeeded in investing music" (Cave, 138). In the three novels mentioned, and most successfully in *The Lake*, Moore—under the vivifying influence of his talks with Dujardin—merged the ideas of *leitmotiv*, symbol, and what James Joyce would later call "epiphany" (Devine, 165). (In fact, Joyce's "epiphanies" are very like Moore's "illuminations" [Cave, 136].) Even in the late Biblical novel *The Brook of Kerith*, with its bold examinations of the mentalities of Jesus, Paul, and Joseph of Arimathea, we find the versatile Moore again stimulated by the shifting interests of the ever-fertile Dujardin, who in the nineties had turned his attention "away from Wagner and Symbolism towards Biblical exegesis," a pursuit Moore followed "with some excitement" (Cave, 199). It is worth pointing out, too, that Walter Pater, who had set a precedent for such writers as Moore in his French-influenced aestheticism or "art for art's sake" philosophy, interestingly gallicizes or "frenchifies," at certain points in his writing, the ambiance of his aestheticist novel set in ancient Rome, *Marius the Epicurean* (an extremely influential book—later a great favorite, for example, with Virginia Woolf). Thus, Pater likens Emperor Antoninus Pius to the French Renaissance essayist Montaigne, while—more important—the Roman novelist Apuleius, whose tale of Cupid and Psyche plays a central symbolic role in the novel, is tellingly compared to a highly influential art-for-art's-sake theorist, the French novelist and poet Théophile Gautier (Conlon, 98).

ITALY

An interest in Italy entered the lives and writings of Charlotte Brontë and George Eliot via the novel *Corinne, or Italy* by the French writer Mme. Germaine de Staël. In this work de Staël exalts Italian nationalism and feminism at once, as, in "a nearly mystic ecstasy," the protagonist "marries herself to her own fate—as poetess of Italy—instead of to that of a man" (Gutwirth, 248). Corinne appears little changed as Zenobia Percy in Brontë's youthful tales about the fantasy-land of Angria (Moers, 178). And *Corinne* also influenced Elizabeth Barrett Browning's novelistic verse epic *Aurora Leigh*, a story of an Italian-born girl, which in turn provides plot features borrowed by George Eliot for the Caterina narrative of "Mr. Gilfil's Love Story" in *Scenes of Clerical Life* (Thompson, 51). Mme. de Staël had helped set in motion powerful Italian-oriented imaginings that would have major literary consequences.

Two additional factors assisted in making Italy, and her national poet, Dante, interesting to Victorian writers such as Eliot. During the *Risorgimento* or resurgence of Italian national feeling, a period lasting roughly from the congress of Vienna (1815) to the unification of Italy in 1860–61, a "*Risorgimento* cult of Dante" was created by the nationalist thinker Giuseppe Mazzini, "drawn by the irresistible temptation to transform Dante from the prophet of medieval Empire to the prophet of the unified nation" of Italy that he wanted so much to help create; and Mazzini's exile, which brought him into contact with figures like Eliot and Lewes in Britain, helped introduce into that country a combined interest in Italy, in Dante, and in Mazzini himself (Thompson, 6, 22, 33). Eliot incorporates the thought of many writers—Lorenzo, Pulci, Machiavelli, Savonarola—in her very thoroughly researched Renaissance Florentine novel *Romola*, but a series of epigraphs Eliot chose (rejected because of problems in serial publication) indicates also a Dantesque plan for the book; indeed, the Romola of the epilogue is a kind of iconic Beatrice (Thompson, 79, 88, 96). In *Felix Holt, The Radical* the Dante-Virgil relationship central to *Inferno* is evoked by that between the "humble disciple Esther and the enlightened mentor Felix," and in *Middlemarch* Will Ladislaw is possibly modeled in part on the poet Dante Gabriel Rossetti, translator of Dante's *La Vita Nuova* (Thompson, 114, 141). In *Daniel Deronda*, finally, Daniel, like Eliot herself, admires, reads, and supports the Italian nationalist leader Mazzini, and there are many parallels in the two men's lives (Thompson, 174–179). There is some force, then, to the argument that "the arc of Italian *Risorgimento* history which is traced over the course of the novel provides a powerful analogue which renders Deronda's Zionist project both more concrete and more credible" (Thompson, 173).

Elizabeth Gaskell, too, shows an interest in Mazzini and in Dante. Over the years, her closeness to "English friends of Mazzini had kept . . . keen" her zeal for Italian nationalism, and "while struggling with the cotton famine and *Sylvia's Lovers*," she took time to write a preface to a work praising the nationalist rebel Garibaldi (Uglow, 535). In *North and South,* Margaret reads Dante, and her sensual fantasies are counterpointed by a quotation from *La Vita Nuova* (translated by Charles Eliot Norton, with whom Gaskell had not quite fallen in love [Uglow, 380, 384, 419]). In *Cousin Phillis*, as a "glamorous engineer" with a good knowledge of Italian offers to aid the title-heroine in reading Dante's *Inferno*, the "stage seems set for a Paolo and Francesca intimacy" (Milbank, 83). Although Holdsworth recommends an alternate text as easier, his suggested substitute reading, Manzoni's *I Promessi Sposi*, ironically proves just as dangerous, as it encourages in Phillis an idealistic belief in his faithfulness of which—too late—she is sadly disabused. As for Charles Dickens, his *Pictures from Italy* has been praised as "quite unlike any other book on Italy" in the "precision and insight," the "pathos" and "hilarity," of its abundant portraits, and his treatment of Italy in *Little Dorrit* gives for the first time a full sense of the stifling sadness of Anglo-Venetian society (Churchill, 137–139).

RUSSIA

Ivan Turgenev was the most popular and influential Russian novelist in Britain throughout the Victorian era: Only in the late 1880s did it first become possible to "discern a Russian, as opposed to a purely Turgenevan, literary impact in England," and his reputation there climbed steadily as the century progressed, rising to a height with the publication of fifteen volumes of his works in translations by Constance Garnett during the years 1894 to 1899 (Turton, 136). Charles Dickens did as much as anyone to initiate this vogue by publishing, in various numbers of his journal *Household Words* in 1855, four imaginatively retitled segments from Turgenev's *Sportsman's Sketches*—"The Children of the Czar," "More Children of the Czar," "Nothing Like Russia-Leather," and "A Russian Singing-Match"—in James Meiklejohn's translation of Ernest Charrière's problematic French rendering, which "shamelessly embroiders Turgenev's style, and in places inserts whole sections of text not present in the original" (Waddington, *Turgenev and England*, 78; Turton, 13). The laudatory introduction to the extracts (whether or not Dickens actually wrote it) effusively compares the Russian writer to Balzac, to Audubon, and to "an eloquent improvvisatore, or Red Indian orator" (Waddington, *Turgenev and England*, 78).

Turgenev's distinctive combination of lyrical warmth, awareness of the embeddedness of individual behavior in class and social setting, and intellectual agility, together with a positively Flaubertian care in choosing the psychologically revealing detail that would imbue a description with the precisely suitable mood, was not easy to emulate, but several British novelists appear to have tried. Godwin Peak in Gissing's *Born in Exile* owes some of his concerns and problems to an equally unhappy intellectual, Eugene Bazarov in Turgenev's *Fathers and Sons*, which Gissing had read six or seven times. Both characters have been called "strong-willed egotists who are also scientific ratio-nalists; within their natures rational negation and irrational self-assertion work in dialectical relationship, the negative mind driving the positive will" (Turton, 130)—though the relationship indicated here might have been better styled "counterproductive" or "conflicted" than "dialectical," in both cases. Elizabeth Gaskell's writing may show more of Turgenev's lyricism than of his preoccupa-tion with the psychological conflicts of the intelligentsia. "Turgenev had vis-ited Manchester in 1859: *Cousin Phillis* has the haunting quality of his 1860 story, 'First Love'; *Fathers and Sons*, translated into French in 1862, may have partly prompted *Wives and Daughters*" (Uglow, 531).

George Moore, John Galsworthy, and Arnold Bennett all tried to incorpo-rate into their work lessons learned from Turgenev. Moore, who likened Turgenev to "a beautifully cultivated islet lying somewhere between the philo-sophic realism of Balzac and the maiden-lady realism of Miss Austen," sought, in what he took to be Turgenev's own manner, for a narrative that would be not a plot but purely a sequence of moods and tones, a "melodic-line narrative." But one critic claims that Moore did not come close to attaining this end until *The Untilled Field*, already a post-Victorian work (Gettmann, 150). Galsworthy, who for over thirty years continued to regard Turgenev as the su-preme master of literary composition, produced in *Villa Rubein* the "prime ex-ample" of Turgenev's "tangible influence upon English novelists of the 1890s"; Constance Garnett saw "the disciple's devotion to the master on every page" (Turton, 172). Arnold Bennett's first novel, the autobiographical *Man from the North*, was read in the light of such essays as his own grateful tribute, "Ivan Turgenev, an Enquiry," and in the overwhelmingly Turgenev-friendly mood of the nineties Bennett's novel was widely compared to Turgenev's work, though it contained little to recall that author except for the "theme of failure" (Turton, 179–180). Tolstoy, of increasing interest in the eighties and nineties, was not yet a major influence on works of British fiction, and the "real vogue for Dostoevsky" was "not to come until the second decade of the twentieth cen-tury" (Turton, 142).

WORKS CITED AND SELECTED WORKS FOR FURTHER READING

Argyle, Gisela. *German Elements in the Fiction of George Eliot, Gissing, and Meredith.* New York: Peter Lang, 1979.

Ashton, Rosemary. *The German Idea: Four English Writers and the Reception of Ger-man Thought, 1800–1860.* London: Libris, 1994.

Bailey, James Osler. *Thomas Hardy and the Cosmic Mind: A New Reading of "The Dy-nasts."* Chapel Hill: U of North Carolina P, 1956.

Brontë, Charlotte. *Jane Eyre*. Ed. Richard J. Dunn. New York: Norton, 1971.

Cave, Richard Allen. *A Study of the Novels of George Moore*. Gerrards Cross: Colin Smythe, 1978.

Churchill, Kenneth. *Italy and English Literature, 1764–1930*. London: Macmillan, 1980.

Collet, Georges-Paul. *George Moore et la France*. Geneva: Droz, 1957.

Conlon, John J. *Walter Pater and the French Tradition*. Lewisburg: Bucknell UP, 1982.

Conrad, Joseph. *Heart of Darkness*. Ed. Robert Kimbrough. 3rd ed. New York: Norton, 1988.

Davie, Donald, ed. *Russian Literature and Modern English Fiction: A Collection of Critical Essays*. Chicago: U of Chicago P, 1965.

Devine, Paul. "Leitmotiv and Epiphany: George Moore's *Evelyn Innes* and *The Lake*." In *Moments of Moment: Aspects of the Literary Epiphany*. Ed. Wim Tigges. Amsterdam: Rodopi, 1999.

Duthie, Enid L. *The Foreign Vision of Charlotte Brontë*. New York: Harper, 1975.

Gettmann, Royal. *Turgenev in England and America*. Urbana: U of Illinois P, 1941.

Gutwirth, Madelyn. *Mme. de Staël Novelist: The Emergence of the Artist as Woman*. Urbana: U of Illinois P, 1978.

Jacquette, Dale. *Schopenhauer, Philosophy, and the Arts*. Cambridge: Cambridge UP, 1996.

Magee, Bryan. *The Philosophy of Schopenhauer*. Oxford: Oxford UP, 1983.

McCobb, Anthony. *George Eliot's Knowledge of German Life and Letters*. Salzburg: Universität Salzburg, 1982.

Milbank, Alison. "Moral Luck in the Second Circle: Dante and the Victorian Fate of Tragedy." In *Dante's Modern Afterlife: Reception and Response from Blake to Heaney*. Ed. Nick Havely. New York: St. Martin's, 1998.

Moers, Ellen. *Literary Women*. Garden City: Doubleday, 1975.

Phelps, Gilbert. "The Early Phases of British Interest in Russian Literature." *Slavonic and East European Review* 36 (June 1958): 418–433.

Röder-Bolton, Gerlinde. *George Eliot and Goethe: An Elective Affinity*. Amsterdam: Rodopi, 1998.

Sadrin, Anny, ed. *Dickens, Europe and the New Worlds*. New York: St. Martin's, 1999.

Smalley, Barbara. *George Eliot and Flaubert: Pioneers of the Modern Novel*. Athens: Ohio UP, 1974.

Thompson, Andrew. *George Eliot and Italy: Literary, Cultural, and Political Influences from Dante to the Risorgimento*. New York: St. Martin's, 1998.

Thomson, Patricia. *George Sand and the Victorians: Her Influence and Reputation in Nineteenth-Century England*. New York: Columbia UP, 1977.

Turton, Glyn. *Turgenev and the Context of English Literature, 1850–1900*. London: Routledge, 1992.

Uglow, Jenny. *Elizabeth Gaskell: A Habit of Stories*. New York: Farrar, Straus, & Giroux, 1993.

Vitaglione, Daniel. *George Eliot and George Sand.* New York: Peter Lang, 1996.
Waddington, Patrick, ed. *Ivan Turgenev and Britain.* Oxford: Berg, 1995.
————. *Turgenev and England.* New York: New York UP, 1981.

Science and the Scientist in Victorian Fiction

Michael H. Whitworth

Summarized in a phrase, "science" in the Victorian period was the theorization of transformation: In "biology," the central concern was the transformation of one species into another; in "physics," the transformation of energy. These generalizations require immediate qualification: One cannot neglect the importance of the impulse to collect and classify, most obviously in the case of Darwin, an "inveterate collector and hoarder," who gathered a vast collection of specimens (Desmond and Moore, 13, 58–59, 208–209). But the case of Darwin is instructive: The impulse of curiosity, which had seemed sufficient justification to the previous generation of gentleman naturalist-collectors, developed into, and was sustained by, an impulse to theorize. The sciences of transformation are interestingly paralleled by Victorian narratives of transformation; if the word "character" had once meant something permanently engraved and unchangeable, as it had been in the picaresque novel, by the Victorian period it had come be "a process and an unfolding" (Eliot, *Middlemarch*, 178). This broad parallel spawns many further questions: Should the similarity be explained as an interchange of discourses between cultures, or of ideas between authors? Is the literary author always the recipient, and, if so, how actively can he or she transform the scientific materials? How far can those materials be transformed before their scientific content becomes irrelevant?

DEFINITIONS

"Science" must remain in quotation marks, because its modern meaning entered the language only in the Victorian period, and the term "scientist" appeared only in 1834. Brief accounts of the semantic development of "science" appear in the *OED* and in Williams (276–280); more detailed inquiries by Ross, Schuster, Sloan, and Morrell appear in Olby, et al. (224–225, 295–313, 799–802, 980–989). Workers in a new science must employ the conceptual tools of their predecessors, and of workers in apparently unrelated, "nonscientific" disciplines. In 1830, the influential geologist Charles Lyell explicitly recommended that followers of his science have a wide range of scientific knowledge, and implicitly constructed that science by analogy with history: The "kingdoms of nature" were like the kingdoms of man, and the record of the rocks like the historian's archive (Lyell, 5–6). We are used to seeing the terms "science" and "religion" presented in opposition, but this obscures the extent to which scientists inherited theological assumptions: Darwin from Unitarianism (Desmond and Moore, 293, 331) and the Scottish physicists from Presbyterianism (Smith, 15–30). Gillian Beer has argued that Darwin also drew on his literary reading. The argument is important, because it suggests that literature is doing more than follow passively in the wake of science, though it has not gone unchallenged (Beer, "Darwin's Reading"; Benton, 74–76).

In transferring concepts across disciplines, scientists are using metaphor. "Metaphor" here is not a matter of superficial decorative language, but, as Lakoff and Johnson have shown, of fundamental concepts. In the world of science, rocks are like an archive, the sun's heat is like God's gifts, and Nature is like a sheep breeder. Although when describing "facts" scientists may attempt to limit the figurative play of language, this play cannot be altogether controlled. When developing theories, they find it positively advantageous, though exactly how far it is advantageous is a matter of some debate (Benton, 71–73). The process of interpreting science and literature is a process of reading texts intensively for their metaphors: not only their vivid, ostentatious metaphors but also those that are "dead" or "dormant" and those embodied in their narrative or poetic form (Beer, *Darwin's Plots*, 79–103; Black, 26). It involves tracing the historical migrations and disciplinary affiliations of key terms and images, terms that may now seem to belong exclusively to one discipline, or to none at all.

This process is best illustrated by particular readings. Though there has been some debate over whether evolution or thermodynamics was the more significant science for literature (Dale, 300, n. 15), evolution is the more readily accessible. It is also debated whether scientific ideas filter through into literature, as part of its conceptual unconscious (Levine), or are more actively appropriated by literary writers (Beer; Shuttleworth). George Eliot and Charles Dickens provide a useful contrast: We know that the former took an active interest in science and *The Origin of Species* (Eliot, *Letters,* iii, 224–228); the evidence for the latter is less clear (Flint, 153).

The publication in November 1859 of Darwin's *The Origin of Species* is often represented as a dramatic event that precipitated a conflict of science and religion and many "crises of faith." Emphasizing the drama of the event has led some readers to underestimate the extent to which evolutionary discourses had been in circulation for several decades. Darwin himself had produced unpublished preliminary sketches of the theory in 1839 and 1844. Thus, the discourse was available through many routes, both before and after 1859. Emphasizing the conflict of Darwinism with creationism oversimplifies the nature of the Christian religion, anachronistically aligning Britain in 1859 with, say, Tennessee in 1925 (Moore, 75–76). In the Victorian period, many Anglicans viewed Biblical fundamentalism as simple-minded faith and subscribed to Paley's view that there had been not one, but a series of "special creations." However, as a God who makes a series of miraculous interventions to correct his mistakes implicitly lacks foresight, the antimiraculous Darwinian theory had much to recommend it. This was noted even in popular accounts ("Species," 176).

GREAT EXPECTATIONS

Although Dickens took a less active interest in contemporary scientific theory than did Eliot, it is well known that he arranged for two articles on Darwin to appear in his weekly periodical *All the Year Round* in 1860: "Species," a sympathetic account of Darwin's key concepts, and "Natural Selection," a more skeptical account, conceding more to religious concerns, and giving Darwin himself more coverage. That *All the Year Round* was relatively slow to tackle evolution might seem to indicate trepidation on Dickens's part, either personally or as a publisher, though these articles have generally been taken to validate discussions of Dickens's Darwinism (Crawford, 637–638; Flint, 152–154). A more complex picture emerges when we consider two neglected earlier articles from *All the Year Round*. Their titles, "English Mutton" and "Pork," seem unpromising, but in fact Dickens's contributors discuss artificial selection, a process of obvious relevance to Darwin. "English Mutton" describes how the breeder Robert Bakewell had "manufacture[d]" the Leicester sheep by "selecting the best specimens" of the Warwickshire breed (58). It explores the apparent paradox of a "fixed type," the Dishley, being not "an aboriginal breed" but an artificial creation. Even when these articles conflict with Darwinian theory, they articulate their disagreements within a vocabulary of "types" and "selection"; in other words, in a discourse that we now term "Darwinian."

That Dickens published these articles is open to a variety of interpretations. The first, predating the publication of *The Origin of Species* by two weeks, cannot be a direct response to it. However, Dickens was possibly anticipating Darwin's publication, treading cautiously but paving the way for later, more scientific expositions. The later article, "Species," made explicit reference to the analogy of natural selection to artificial. It is equally possible that the two articles reflect not a conscious scheme but rather the ubiquitous presence of "Darwinian" discourse in the mid-nineteenth century: That Darwin refers to sheep-breeding (*Origin*, 90) and to Bakewell (*Origin*, 93) need not imply direct influence on *All the Year Round*. Either interpretation validates a reading of *Great Expectations* in terms of Darwin, but the former would suggest that Dickens was more actively interested in contemporary theory than has hitherto been recognized.

"If you want a subject, look at Pork!" (Dickens, 26). Mr. Pumblechook's Christmas dinner sermon is rich with meanings: his intended moral meaning, concerning gluttony; Pip's moral interpretation, concerning a stolen pork pie; and, in the light of the article "Pork," another meaning for the regular reader of *All the Year Round*. "Pip" is but one phonemic mutation away from "Pig," and Pumblechook's rhetorical consideration of what would have happened to the infant had he been born "a four-footed Squeaker" recalls Magwitch licking his lips cannibalistically (4). Taken together, these scenes form part of the novel's larger world picture, one that is compatible both with the "dog-eat-dog" ideology of laissez-faire capitalism, and with one aspect of Darwinian Nature (Flint, 158–162). In the biological as in the economic discourse, every organism is in "severe competition" with every other (*Origin*, 115).

It is true that the reader who could extract all these meanings from Pumblechook's words alone is in some respects an idealized one, for a year had elapsed between the "Pork" article and the Christmas dinner episode. But, however idealized the reader, the possibility of this reading has a very real material existence in the bound volumes of *All the Year Round*, and it should also be asked whether this reader, constructing meanings across discourses, is any less idealized than one who constructs meanings within the narrow confines of a purely "literary" intertextuality. Interpreting science and literature is not a matter of violently yoking together dissimilar discourses but of restoring texts to the fragile webs of their original contexts.

In any case, the original and the modern reader are both given a far more overt clue in the second paragraph of the novel: Pip's five dead brothers are described as having given up trying to get a living "exceedingly early in that universal struggle" (3). The deictic "that" gestures to shared cultural assumptions outside the text: Dickens and his readers would have been aware of the topicality of "struggle," and of the scientific meanings invested in it; Darwin too had referred to the struggle as "universal" (*Origin*, 115).

If the penetration of Darwinian discourse into *Great Expectations* was merely a matter of scattered verbal similarities, one might suspect Dickens of making superficial topical gestures. However, these similarities, inadequate in themselves, authorize further consideration of the relation of Dickens's narrative form to Darwin's ideas. *Great Expectations* is a novel of character development in which the protagonist is subjected to the selective pressure of external forces. "Pip" can be seen not only as a developing seedling but as a mutating species.

We can highlight the Darwinian aspects of *Great Expectations* by reading a Darwinian text, focusing particularly on its narratives and their cultural assumptions. This interpretative strategy is crucial to the practice of reading literature with science. Darwin's concise "Essay of 1844" was unavailable to Dickens, so the interpretative strategy involved here is quite explicitly one of finding analogies rather than searching for "influences." The relevant passage is a deeply anthropomorphic one. Darwin asks his reader to imagine a "Being" watching over all organisms. If its powers of perception and foresight are superhuman, as the capital "B" might imply, they are so by a matter of degree and not of kind ("Essay," 114–116). Darwin supposes that the Being sees "a plant growing on decaying matter in a forest and choked by other plants" (115), and wishes to enable it to live somewhere higher, on the rotten stems of trees. The Being would take advantage of the natural variation in seedlings, and would select those whose berries were more attractive to tree-frequenting birds, and those who had the greatest power of drawing nutriment from rotten wood. He might in time undertake further selections, allowing the future seedlings to grow on sound as well as on rotten wood. He might select specimens with sweeter honey or pollen, to encourage insects to visit their flowers and fertilize their seed. Only at the end of this riddling narrative does Darwin reveal the species under consideration to be mistletoe. The deliberate concealment of this information is interesting, but less immediately relevant than other gaps in the text, the assumptions that Darwin feels it unnecessary to articulate or justify. Why should the Being wish to improve the lot of this struggling plant? Because, Darwin assumes, all beings are motivated by humanitarian concerns. The anthropomorphism here is based on a particularly Victorian variety of anthropoid, the philanthropist. Even though "decaying matter" may provide nutrition for a plant, the narrative makes the anthropomorphic assumption that a plant would wish to escape it and to grow on "sound wood." "Choked" and living in squalor, the plant resembles the urban poor memorably described by Engels in *The Condition of the Working Class in England* (Marx and Engels, iv,

295–596). A similar anthropomorphism informs the assumption that a "higher" position is necessarily better: A lateral move, out of the forest, might have been equally beneficial, but "higher" is a metaphor of social rank. Reading in this way, attending to the unstated assumptions and making connections with other texts, we can recover the metaphorical content of Darwin's scientific text.

The seedling called "Pip" is not literally choking in the manner of the urban poor, but his education is choked—or so Joe alleges—by Mrs. Joe's fears that they "might rise": the term ambiguously suggests both insurrection against her "government," and social advancement (Dickens, 49). The "Being" who raises him from the forest floor is Magwitch, a man who has been, among other things, a sheep-farmer and stockbreeder (317), and who might be expected to possess the Being's powers of perception and foresight. In a novel rich with parallelism, Miss Havisham bears a similar relationship to Estella. Moreover, in the chapter describing Newgate prison, Wemmick seems to bear a similar relationship to his clients. He walks among the prisoners "much as a gardener might walk among his plants" (260). The scene of "Wemmick's greenhouse" is densely packed with Darwinian hints. One of Wemmick's clients, the condemned man called "the Colonel," was a pigeon fancier. His occupation would have been of great interest to Darwin, who considers at great length the "astonishing" diversity of pigeon breeds created through artificial selection (*Origin*, 82).

The Colonel's crime is not columbaphilia but "coining": an act of creation that, like his hobby, requires acute powers of perception and selection, but that, unlike it, aims to minimize variation from the fixed type. By producing perfect imitations, forgery severs the association of the fixed type with "official" creation, divine or governmental. The forgery, like the fixed types created by Bakewell, raises questions concerning the relation of the real and the imitation. Can a forgery which is identical to the original in every material detail be said to be "the same" as the original? Or is there some invisible inner essence which guarantees the identity of the original and differentiates it from the forgery? If so, then the forgery, which lacks this guarantee, will always be in danger of reverting to its real fixed type. Forgery is ubiquitous in *Great Expectations*: When Pip asks why people are sent to the hulks, Mrs. Joe tells him "because they murder, and because they rob, and forge, and do all sorts of bad" (15). Her surprising equation of forgery with murder has a historical legal basis—both were capital crimes—but it also draws attention to the dark symbolic side of Joe's forge, a place that has the power to break and reforge the chain of being.

Dickens's novel is not, however, merely the story of the upwards evolution of a species, nor can its every feature be reconciled with Darwinian theory. Returning from London to Satis House, the newly rich Pip feels that he "slipped hopelessly back into the coarse and common boy again" (235). The seeming inevitability of this process introduces an anti-Darwinian note, a suggestion that nature consists of fixed types to which all variations will eventually revert (*Origin*, 195–197). Biddy had suggested that Pip should be happier remaining where he was (127). Later, the birth of young Pip reminds us that Darwinian evolution occurs only gradually, over many generations: The "miraculous" or "catastrophic" transformation has no place in Darwin's theory. Dickens's text remains ambiguous: Pip's evolutionary change comes from "above," in that it is not self-willed, but the "Being" comes from the bottom of the social pyramid. The novel may be interpreted as rejecting evolution altogether in favor of Biddy's conservative view, or as accepting the idea of change conferred gradu-ally from above, while resisting the politically troubling idea of radical self-transformation (Desmond and Moore, 34).

GEORGE ELIOT

Eliot hints at the Darwinist subtext of *Middlemarch* in the Prologue. Along-side the dominant comparison of Dorothea and St. Teresa is a subordinate one of her and a cygnet reared among ducklings. Furthermore, in the ironic discus-sion of the "indefiniteness" of women's nature, the narrator employs the bio-logical term "variation" (*Middlemarch*, 26). Women are not fixed types, though literature and fashion give that impression. She announces Darwinism less subtly with the pet name that Celia gives to Dorothea: "Dodo" (42). The story then, like *The Mill on the Floss*, is the story of a female organism struggling within an unfavorable ecological niche. In Eliot's earlier novel, the comparison of the heroine to animals was continuing and unavoidable, and the "narrow-ness" of her world (which we would now call her "ecological niche") was re-peatedly emphasized. In *Middlemarch*, comparisons to animals are used more sparingly. When Darwinism emerges explicitly, the narrator uses a more ab-stract and polysemous vocabulary. When Casaubon's will is read, Dorothea feels that her life is taking on a "new form," undergoing a "metamorphosis," in which she develops "new organs"; her world is in "a state of convulsive change" (532). With this combination of terms, some of which could be mythological, geological, or biological, the narrator constructs Dorothea both as a land mass undergoing a volcanic eruption and as a species undergoing change. Eliot's Darwinist discourse not only provides a conceptual scheme for understanding provincial life but a way of realizing abstract emotions with intense physicality.

Dorothea is not the only creature who must endure the narrowness of the Midlands town. Lydgate represents a new variety of medical man among the old varieties of "physician" and "apothecary," and although he is clearly more intellectually advanced than his competitors, "fitness" is not an absolute term but a relative one. Lydgate does not "fit" the town. He also discovers that he and Rosamond are temperamentally dissimilar to the extent that they might as well be "different species" (643). The idea of professional specialization closely resembles Darwinian speciation, as Karl Marx noted in 1862: "Darwin rediscovers, among the beasts and plants, the society of England, with its division of labor, competition, opening up of new markets, 'inventions' and the Malthusian 'struggle for existence'" (Marx and Engels, xli, 381); Eliot's plot is formed around this parallel. However, Eliot's scheme is flexible, and Middlemarch can be represented not only as the environment in which Lydgate's competitors live but also as a voracious competitor itself, one that "counted on swallowing Lydgate and assimilating him very comfortably" (183).

Middlemarch not only employs a scientific vocabulary in its narration but narrates the lives of "scientists." Lydgate's literal scientific quest is to discover the "primitive tissue" that underlies the differentiated tissues of the body, just as "sarsnet, gauze, net, satin and velvet" have all begun "from the raw cocoon" (177–178). This quest runs in parallel to Casaubon's more loosely "scientific" quest to discover the "key to all mythologies." Both men are granted limited approval by the narrator for their patience and their gradual accumulation of data: The idea of gradualism extends from organic variation into scientific process; Eliot herself had praised *The Origin of Species* as being the result of "long years of study" (*Letters*, iii, 227). But accumulation is nothing without selection, and the scientist's selection must be guided by a metaphor or model. Ladislaw makes explicit the misguidedness of Casaubon's approach, and the narrator additionally suggests that his thoughts are entangled in the wrong set of metaphors (111). A parallel passage suggests that Lydgate, in asking for the "primitive tissue," was also asking a question "not quite in the way required by the awaiting answer" (178). Lydgate and Casaubon are not the only characters to leap to conclusions: Dorothea's misreading of her future husband, and Rosamond's of hers, are both analogous to errors of scientific theorization. A good theory must navigate between the opposing perils of non-theorization and reductive theorization. For all four characters, the reductive theorization is also a premature one.

ENTROPY AND DEGENERATION

The narrative of Pip has already provided one fictional adaptation of the idea of reversion to type. In the later Victorian period, the idea of degeneration loomed larger. The optimistic implications of Darwin's theories of evolution were confronted with the pessimistic physical theories of energy and entropy. According to the second law of thermodynamics, all energy in the universe was passing from a highly ordered form to a disordered form. The theory had first been articulated in scientific journals in the 1850s, but its implications took longer to enter into popular consciousness. There were broad similarities between energetics and evolution: Both were sciences of transformation; the branch of energy physics concerned with the age of the sun was, like evolutionary theory, concerned with gradual processes and long time scales. The language employed in thermodynamics was by turns economic and moral: The sun had "reserves" of energy that were being withdrawn but never replenished; the technical name for the process, "dissipation," carried implications of spendthrift and morally dissolute behavior (Whitworth, 47–48). This was not the only possible interpretation that could be made—that the sun radiates its energy could be seen as creating opportunities to turn that energy to useful ends—but this interpretation did not prevail (Smith, 314).

Some manifestations of entropy in Victorian fiction are relatively trivial: for example, the ubiquity of red, decaying suns, particularly as a *fin-de-siècle* emblem of decay, the most spectacular example occurring in H. G. Wells's *The Time Machine* (82–86). Such emblems do not in themselves govern narrative form, though they may give a clue to it: The dying sun in *Bleak House* grants a dubious scientific authority to Dickens's vision of the social mechanism grinding to a halt (Miller, 181).

The more significant manifestations are mediated through biological theories of degeneration (Greenslade, 21–22). The language of "fitness" within evolution had remained ambiguous, implying either a fitness relative to a particular environment, or a fitness according to an absolute scale. Degeneration theories saw the scale as absolute, and progress as perilously insecure. Whereas some theories conceived of degeneration as a process, just as evolution was, others underemphasized the process and dwelt instead on the idea of the "degenerate type," a fixed form. Although today this seems like bad science or pseudoscience, and although there were dissenting voices even in the Victorian period, it was taken seriously at the time.

An interesting test case occurs in Arthur Morrison's *A Child of the Jago*, a text that is open to conflicting interpretations. The Jago, a fictionalized version of the Old Nichol district of East London, is inhabited by characters who are constructed by the narrator within the usual discourse of degeneration: as deindividualized swarms, as rats, and as "savages" (11, 31, 81). At these points the discourse overlaps with that of eugenics, the doctrine of "good breeding" and racial purity; eugenical doctrines are explicitly voiced by the surgeon in the novel (140), as they were by Morrison himself (228). The central character, Dicky Perrot, is also seen in degenerationist terms: He is physically stunted. However, here the ambiguities emerge: Dicky's stature, which in the absolutist terms of eugenics would mark him as "unfit," ironically means that he is well adapted to his career as a pickpocket (84). "Fitness" is a relative term, and as a pickpocket, Dicky thrives.

Scientific discourses were in a state of continuing development throughout the Victorian period. Scientific theories were sites of debate, and the debates were conducted not in purely scientific terms but with metaphors borrowed from contemporary social, religious, and literary discourse. The exploration of scientific discourse sharpens our understanding of the historical nuances of key words but does not necessarily impose a single determinate meaning on the literary text: Rather, it allows us to locate characters and narratives in the center of contemporary debates, and to reveal rich and complex exchanges of ideas.

WORKS CITED AND SELECTED WORKS FOR FURTHER READING

Amigoni, David, and Jeff Wallace, eds. *Charles Darwin's* The Origin of Species: *New Interdisciplinary Essays*. Manchester: Manchester UP, 1995.

Beer, Gillian. *Darwin's Plots: Evolutionary Narrative in Darwin, George Eliot, and Nineteenth-Century Fiction*. London: Routledge and Kegan Paul, 1983.

———. "Darwin's Reading and the Fictions of Development." In *The Darwinian Heritage*, pp. 543–588. Ed. David Kohn. Princeton: Princeton UP, 1985.

Benton, Ted. "Science, Ideology and Culture: Malthus and *The Origin of Species*." In *Charles Darwin's* The Origin of Species: *New Interdisciplinary Essays*, pp. 68–94. Ed. David Amigoni and Jeff Wallace. Manchester: Manchester UP, 1995.

Black, Max. "More about Metaphor." In *Metaphor and Thought*, pp. 19–43. Ed. Andrew Ortony. Cambridge: Cambridge UP, 1979.

Crawford, Iain. "Pip and the Monster." *Studies in English Literature* 28 (1988): 625–648.

Dale, Peter Allan. *In Pursuit of a Scientific Culture: Science, Art, and Society in the Victorian Age*. Madison: U of Wisconsin P, 1989.

Darwin, Charles. "Essay of 1844." *Evolution by Natural Selection*, pp. 91–254. Cambridge: Cambridge UP, 1958.

———. *The Origin of Species by Means of Natural Selection*. Ed. J. W. Burrow. London: Penguin, 1968.

Desmond, Adrian, and James Moore. *Darwin*. 1991. London: Penguin, 1992.

Dickens, Charles. *Great Expectations*. Ed. Charlotte Mitchell. London: Penguin, 1996.

Eliot, George. *The George Eliot Letters*. Ed. Gordon S. Haight. 9 vols. London: Oxford UP, 1954–78.

———. *Middlemarch*. 1870–71. Ed. W. J. Harvey. London: Penguin, 1965.

"English Mutton." *All the Year Round* 2 (12 November 1859): 57–62.

Flint, Kate. "Origins, Species, and *Great Expectations*." In *Charles Darwin's* The Origin of Species: *New Interdisciplinary Essays*, pp. 152–173. Ed. David Amigoni and Jeff Wallace. Manchester: Manchester UP, 1995.

Greenslade, William M. *Degeneration, Culture, and the Novel, 1880–1940.* Cambridge: Cambridge UP, 1994.

Lakoff, George, and Mark Johnson. *Metaphors We Live By.* Chicago: U of Chicago P, 1980.

Levine, George. *Darwin and the Novelists: Patterns of Science in Victorian Fiction.* Cambridge: Harvard UP, 1988.

Lyell, Charles. *Principles of Geology.* 1830–33. Ed. James A. Secord. London: Penguin, 1997.

Marx, Karl, and Frederick Engels. *Collected Works.* 50 vols. London: Lawrence and Wishart, 1975–2000.

Miller, J. Hillis. *Victorian Subjects.* Hemel Hempstead: Harvester Wheatsheaf, 1990.

Moore, James R. *The Post-Darwinian Controversies.* Cambridge: Cambridge UP, 1979.

Morrison, Arthur. *A Child of the Jago.* 1896. Ed. Peter Miles. London: Dent, 1996.

"Natural Selection." *All the Year Round* 3 (7 July 1860): 293–299.

Olby, R. C., G. N. Cantor, J.R.R. Christie, and M.J.S. Hodge, eds. *Companion to the History of Modern Science.* London: Routledge, 1990.

"Pork." *All the Year Round* 2 (10 December 1859): 157–162.

Shuttleworth, Sally. *George Eliot and Nineteenth-Century Science.* Cambridge: Cambridge UP, 1984.

Smith, Crosbie. *The Science of Energy: A Cultural History of Energy Physics in Victorian Britain.* London: Athlone, 1998.

"Species." *All the Year Round* 3 (2 June 1860): 174–178.

Wells, H. G. *The Time Machine.* 1895. Ed. Michael Moorcock. London: Dent, 1993.

Whitworth, Michael. "Inspector Heat Inspected: *The Secret Agent* and the Meanings of Entropy." *Review of English Studies* 49 (1998): 40–59.

Williams, Raymond. *Keywords: A Vocabulary of Culture and Society.* London: Fontana, 1983.

Law and the Victorian Novel

Elizabeth F. Judge

Law and literature scholarship is an interdisciplinary movement that at its origin was characterized as having two branches: law *in* literature and law *as* literature. Although these descriptions are too procrustean to do justice to the variety of projects that come under the law and literature rubric, they serve as a useful starting point. "Law in literature" criticism focuses on representations of law in literature, including its participants, procedures, and substantive statutes, and also embraces literary works that address more general themes of justice and reform. The nineteenth-century novel is a fertile source for such studies. In an age of high-profile legislation, including the three Reform bills, the 1857 Matrimonial Causes Act, the 1870 and 1882 Married Women's Property Acts, and the 1873–1875 Judicature Acts, and legal reformers, including Brougham and Bentham, it is not surprising that the period's novel sharply attends to the law. Legal reform serves as prominent backdrops to *Middlemarch* (1832 Reform Bill) and *Bleak House* (Court of Chancery). The Victorian novel casts memorable lawyers like Dickens's Jaggers and Buzfuz and Trollope's Chaffanbrass. Victorian plots frequently trace law's impact both on public and domestic spheres, as with prisons in *Little Dorrit, Barnaby Rudge,* Charles Reade's *It Is Never Too Late to Mend,* and Edward Bulwer Lytton's *Eugene Aram*; the intricacies of inheritance law in *Wuthering Heights, Felix Holt, The Radical,* and Samuel Warren's *Ten Thousand a Year*; marriage and divorce in *Jane Eyre, Diana of the Crossways, Hard Times,* and *Jude the Obscure*; or the status of women in *The Odd Women.*

"Law as literature" criticism emphasizes the linguistic and narrative qualities of law to argue that law and literature are parallel discourses. Drawing on the hermeneutic philosophy of Martin Heidegger and Hans-Georg Gadamer, law as literature critics assert that with this shared textuality, the disciplines have a joint theoretical interest in representation and interpretation (see generally Levinson and Mailloux; Leyh). If law and literature are parallel texts, then juries and readers are performing similar interpretive roles. From this insight, it follows that law and literature both are concerned with the intercession of a mediating consciousness with the text and thus with the interplay of intention, reader response, and historical and cultural contexts. Law and literature rely on similar devices by which to manage subjectivity and indeterminacy, an assumption that underlies both Fish's discussion of interpretive communities and Dworkin's notion of legal interpretation as a "chain novel." Other theorists, however, caution that the equivalency between law and literature should not be exaggerated. The functions of the texts and objectives of the readers diverge too greatly for a unified theory, according to Posner, or the practices of interpretation in law and literature will differ even where a general theory of interpretation would be valid, according to Kingwell. In its bluntest form, this objection asserts that "adjudication is not interpretation" because legal interpretation as a formal process resolves life, liberty, and property interests and such decisions are enforced by the state through violence and power (see West; Cover). Literature, by contrast, both in practice and in theory can tolerate more ambiguity and multiple interpretations within its interpretive communities.

A third branch, of which this chapter is an example, can be characterized as combining and supplementing the insights of the first two while addressing some of their limitations. As the "law as literature" title suggests, the analogy is more often posed from law's perspective with the objective of testing whether literary criticism can aptly be applied to law. Further, although a central claim of hermeneutic philosophy is that interpretation is always historically and linguistically conditioned, the parallels between legal and literary interpretation tend to be asserted without placing the specific texts in their historical context. The third branch thus agrees that there is a relationship between law and literature but qualifies that it is informed by historical and cultural factors. Alexander Welsh's *Strong Representations: Narrative and Circumstantial Evidence in England,* as an illustration, focuses on the history of evidence law and argues that the nineteenth-century trial and novel shared a narrative model that was constructed from circumstantial evidence.

Nineteenth-century trial procedure, like evidence, is another important but neglected area from which to discuss law and literature's close relationship. By regulating the discourse at trial, procedural rules govern who speaks at a trial, how their stories are told, and how the jury should assess these storytellers. In *The Rise of the Novel*, Ian Watt remarked that jurors' procedures may aptly be applied to the reader as a descriptive model because both are "specialists in epistemology" with similar expectations (31). Watts's observation is a commonplace. Eighteenth- and nineteenth-century critics remarked similarities between the trial and the novel and their respective reading processes, and authors self-consciously invoked the parallel as with Wilkie Collins promising in the preamble to *The Woman in White* that the reader shall hear the story just as a judge would hear it in a court of law. However, the reader and juror parallel can be explored accurately only by studying the legal historical context. Legal procedures do shape expectations for the representation of truth-telling narratives; but, as trial procedures are both local and variable over time, so too are these expectations.

Victorian novelists recognized the parallels between trial procedure and novel conventions such as point of view that, by determining whether characters are heard directly or have their stories mediated through other speakers, influence how information is arranged and then received by the reader. Dickens, Eliot, and Trollope all incorporated representations of trials in novels not simply for reasons of plot or character but to comment about the possibility of truth, the limitations of knowledge, and the subjectivity of narrative interpretation. Several dramatic changes in trial procedures occurred in the nineteenth century and provoked sharp debate not merely in specialist circles of the bar and by Parliamentarians but also by the public who saw procedural changes as representative of, and at times undermining, cultural ideas about "truth" and "facts." Far from dismissing the process for how trials were conducted as a technical and arcane issue best relegated to the bar, the public treated it as having profound cultural implications. In particular, the morality of forensic advocacy was rigorously debated in Victorian periodicals and captured the attention of these novelists as a trenchant vehicle through which to discuss epistemology and hermeneutics.

THE NINETEENTH-CENTURY TRIAL

In 1836, Parliament passed the Prisoners' Counsel Act, which granted felony defendants the right to have a "full" defense at their trials (6 & 7 Wm. 4, c. 114). Before this legislative reform, felony defendants had been restricted in their use of counsel at trial. During the eighteenth century, judges had gradually permitted lawyers to assist defendants by arguing points of law and examining and cross-examining witnesses, but the "storytelling" function of relating the facts directly to the jury had to be done personally by the defendant. The

1836 reform was preceded by lengthy Parliamentary debates beginning in the 1820s, but the rule had been attacked as being unjust from the eighteenth century. Partridge in *Tom Jones* (Fielding, 1749) "thought [it] a little hard, that the prisoner's counsel was not suffered to speak for him" whereas the prosecutor's counsel could speak against him (viii, 411). Only defendants in a specific range of criminal offenses were prohibited from having lawyers tell their stories to the jury: Defendants in trials for civil disputes, and in criminal trials for misdemeanors, less serious than felonies, and treason, the most serious felony, did not have that disadvantage. Moreover, neighboring countries' procedures did not impose this same limitation on their defendants. In the description of Effie's trial in Scott's *Heart of Mid-lothian*, the narrator commends the "humanity of the Scottish law" in this respect because it "not only permits, but enjoins," lawyers "to appear and assist with their advice and skill all persons under trial" (213–214). Those in favor of full representation for felony defendants argued that truth and fairness were undermined by these procedural discrepancies between courts and crimes.

In the Parliamentary debates about lifting the restriction, the members wrestled with the connection between narrators and truth-telling narratives. The proponents for the status quo argued that truth is best elicited by having a person tell a story in his or her own words and that no special skill is required to narrate and arrange the elements of a story. The prosecuting counsel already gave a measured recitation of "the facts," proponents claimed, so defense counsel would have nothing to add. The reformers countered that the trial has its own professional discourse and that, as an amateur storyteller, the defendant is prejudiced by competing against the prosecuting counsel's experience. The reformers dismantled the notion that there was a single definitive narrative to be constructed out of the events or facts and pointed out that even a dispassionate narrative can be a powerful, yet hidden, form of advocacy.

After the legislation passed in 1836, defense counsel took up the defendant's former responsibility of addressing the jury on the facts and the defendant's own speaking role virtually disappeared. The taciturn Fagin standing in the Old Bailey courtroom like a "marble figure," who looks at his counsel in "mute appeal" and breaks his silence only to mutter three times in a whisper that he was an old man when asked if had "anything to say" (Dickens, *Oliver Twist*, 358–360) contrasts sharply with a garrulous Moll Flanders a century before in the Old Bailey who "insisted" and "pleaded" with the court, corrected witnesses, and had "time to say all that [she] would" (Defoe, 361–363). A 1771 treatise described the eighteenth-century juries' experience as like listening to an informal "discussion between the parties" (Eden, 219). With the "lawyerization" of the courts, a nineteenth-century jury heard a more carefully orchestrated trial in which a tighter storyline ordered both witness testimony and counsel speech. This narrative function of selecting and arranging the elements of a trial into a storyline, the "giving order and connection to a mass of facts" (*Second Report*, 10), had been characterized by the reformers as a special skill that lawyers possessed in order to support the reformers' argument that amateur defendants speaking in their own words would be disadvantaged without full professional assistance. The bar endorsed this notion of a professional discourse and promoted it as a key aspect of their own self-definition in the pages of their professional journals by featuring articles on forensic eloquence and hagiographic profiles of barristers who were gifted in oratory and advocacy.

But granting a professional status to storytelling disrupted the presumed links between law and truth and law and morality. The eighteenth-century view of the trial had been that truth would be elicited by defendants speaking in their own words. In the wake of the Prisoners' Counsel Act debates, the reformers and the bar distinguished lawyers' speech as a special discourse and argued that the prosecutor's story had to be countered with an equivalent professional story by the defense. This undermined cultural assumptions about law, narrative, and truth. If lawyers were indispensable because their speech was qualitatively different from that of the defendants, then there was no clear correspondence between defendants' and lawyers' narratives, and the truth value that had been attributed to the former process could not be easily credited to the new process. Further, the prosecutor's recitation of the facts was explicitly recognized as a "version" of what the truth could be whose plausibility must be tested against another "version" that the defense counsel put forth. The change in trial procedure acknowledged that personal skill in arranging and selecting the form of the story could affect the content and reception of a story and that several stories of the "truth" could be constructed and their persuasiveness could vary according to the skill of the storyteller. As a character in *Orley Farm* observed in humorously deconstructing the notion of a single truth-telling narrative, "as if all those lawyers were brought together there—the cleverest and sharpest fellows in the kingdom . . . to listen to a [witness] telling his own story in his own way. You'll have to tell your story in their way; that is in two different ways" (ii, 212–213).

With the increase in the scope of the bar's role as narrator and the increasingly adversarial tenor of the trial came an increase in the public scrutiny of the bar. The focus of the debate shifted subtly from the representation of defendants (in the 1820s and 1830s) to the morality of advocacy (in the 1840s to 1860s), but the second issue pursued the implications of the premises developed in the first. The logic of full representation was tricky, and the defense counsel's two roles, as defendant's representative and legal professional, suggested two different normative standards for the bar. As defendant's proxy "mouthpiece," the lawyer need have no personal conviction in the speeches and owes the full duty to the client. But as speakers of a professional discourse, counsel should be responsible for the content of such personally inflected speech and must balance duties to the client and the court. The first theory received high profile support when Queen Caroline's lead counsel, Henry Brougham, gave an impassioned speech asserting that counsel owed a duty to "that client and none other" and should use "all expedient means" "at all hazards and costs to all others" to fulfill it (*Life and Times*, 405–406). Brougham expanded these views in the unsigned "Rights and Duties of Advocates" in the *Edinburgh Review* (1836), which used the "representative" nature of advocacy to counter criticisms by Swift, Bentham, and Paley that the description of lawyers' services could be reduced to lying for money. The advocate "*is*" the represented party "endowed with legal knowledge [and] . . . the skill of applying it" and "whatever the party could have justly said for himself, the advocate may justly say for him" (159). The counsel impersonates the client, but this "identity" between them counterintuitively absolves the advocate of personal accountability; the advocate serves neither as an arbiter nor a conscience for the client.

Thomas Talfourd in "On the Principle of Advocacy as Developed in the Practice of the Bar" in *Law Magazine* (1846) supported advocacy in the more moderate terms of the second theory, which balanced duty to the client with the counsel's responsibilities to the court, both in the sense of decorum in the courtroom and to justice. His definition of advocacy resembles Brougham's in saying that advocates do on their clients' behalf all that they might do for themselves "if gifted with sufficient knowledge and ability," but with the important qualification that the duty must be exercised "with fairness to their opponents" (2). Talfourd defended advocacy as consistent with personal integrity on the epistemological grounds that knowledge is limited and all perception is biased. "Human nature is essentially partisan" (7), and thus lawyers, historians, and authors alike cannot escape the imputation of being advocates. Those who castigate lawyers for accepting particular cases erroneously assume that the truth about the merits is accessible to the lawyer before the trial and that in criminal cases "guilt" or "innocence" was transparent. However, bias affects all perceptions, from the defendant to the disinterested witness, and this bias is compounded by the lawyers' natural sympathy for clients that the practice of law fosters. Both theories supported advocacy's broad principle that litigants should have professional representation as being essential to the adversarial system.

Two instances of defense counsel behavior particularly exercised the press and exacerbated the controversy about advocacy. At François Courvoisier's 1840 trial, Charles Phillips tested the limits of Brougham's "that client and none other" advocacy duty, when he mounted a vigorous defense that included character aspersions on the prosecutor's witnesses despite having heard his client confess to him at the trial; the confession became well known after the conviction, and Phillips was accused of overstepping whatever the ill-defined boundaries of advocacy were by insinuating during the trial that his client was innocent. Another much cited example of unseemly advocacy was the 1845 trial of John Tawell for murdering his wife in which counsel Fitzroy Kelly dissolved into tears on behalf of his client; he was derided for simulating the display on cue. The press, including the *Times, Punch*, and the *Examiner*, seized on such examples to season their campaign about the immorality of advocacy, and particularly focused on the Old Bailey criminal bar as the most egregious offenders for their repertoire of browbeating witnesses in virulent cross-examinations and misleading the jury. The bar was ill-equipped to defend itself because their own theory of advocacy was still inchoate and some writers disassociated themselves from the Old Bailey criminal bar and conceded it to be a "disreputable" class of the profession ("Old Bailey and Its Practices"; Parker).

ADVOCACY AND REPRESENTATION IN THE VICTORIAN NOVEL

Trial scenes in Victorian novels must be situated within this public debate about advocacy and representation. At the same time that advocacy captivated writers for general and legal periodicals, forensic procedures were prominently featured by Eliot in *Felix Holt* and *Adam Bede*, Trollope in *Orley Farm* and *Phineas Redux*, Gaskell in *Mary Barton*, and Dickens in *A Tale of Two Cities, Oliver Twist*, and *Great Expectations*, among others. Such sustained discussions caught the attention of legal contemporaries, like Fitzjames Stephen, who credited novelists whose works included fictional representations of the law with being influential, albeit sometimes irresponsible, participants in the conversation about advocacy. Stephen objected that the novelists' portrayal of law was inaccurate—"it is only in novels that people engage in lawsuits with the conviction that they are in the wrong"—and dangerously misleading because the fictional misrepresentations, like the press's skewed selection of "Fool v. Knave" cases, "beget hasty generalizations and false conclusions" ("The Morality of Advocacy," 456–458; "License of Modern Novelists," 125). Stephen singles out the trial in *Mary Barton* for special condemnation for depicting immoral advocates as the norm and suggesting that such techniques have the bar's imprimatur ("The Morality of Advocacy," 453–54). His worry was that the novelists' license to "suppress all that is dull" would be misread by the public as an accurate picture of the workings of the courts ("License of Modern Novelists," 125).

Modern interpretations of these trial scenes likewise understand the novelists to be censuring the law. To be sure, a catalogue of reproofs can be compiled,
especially against the criminal defense bar's "art" of browbeating witnesses; but
many of these are captious snipes rather than considered criticisms, as when
Trollope equates Chaffanbrass with a hired assassin (*Orley Farm*, 359). To position the argument as the bar versus novelists overstates the opposition. One
common interpretation of Trollope, for example, has been that he misunder-
stood or willfully ignored the idea of advocacy (see McMaster, 8; Lansbury,
158). However, the Victorian bar itself had not internalized a theory of advocacy. Without a description of advocacy in place, the debates did not reflect a
divide between proponents and opponents of advocacy but rather concerned
different normative ideas about how advocacy should be practiced. The Victorian bar had not yet articulated the appropriate duties and behavioral parame-
ters for its members nor, by implication, what conduct constituted an abuse or
excess of advocacy. The bar's disciplinary and educational functions were dormant and thus did not give guidance to its members. The bar members for
whom the appropriate scope of the advocacy posed the most pressing ethical
questions were the criminal defense barristers, such as Trollope's Chaffanbrass
and Dickens's Jaggers; but this group was frequently dismissed as an embarrassment by the senior members of the bar and excluded from leadership positions.
As there was no consensus within the bar on "advocacy," nor on "representation" in the Prisoners' Counsel debates of the preceding decades, novelists were
entering an ongoing discussion rather than dissenting from the bar's policy.

THE PRISONERS' COUNSEL ACT, REPRESENTATION, AND REFORM

Eliot's *Felix Holt* (1866) interestingly highlights the change in
epistemological theories that informed the shift from "representation" during
the Prisoners' Counsel debates to "advocacy" at mid-century. The book is set
before felony defendants were granted full defense representation but written
during the later advocacy debates. By the 1850s and 1860s, the Prisoners'
Counsel reform had slipped from the public consciousness. A writer for Dickens's *Household Words* guessed in 1851 that many readers did not know that in
the very recent past felony defendants had to address the jury personally
("Bringing out the Truth," 38). Eliot includes a contextual interpolation in
Adam Bede (1859) that in the "stern times" of the late eighteenth century, defendants were not granted the "favor" of having counsel speak for them (437);
however, she only learned that the restriction was still in effect into the nineteenth century when she was researching *Felix Holt* (Haight, 259–260).

During the manuscript phase of *Felix Holt*, Eliot's own presence in the swirl of 1860s anti-advocacy talk colors her depiction of her novel's early 1830s setting. Felix speaks on his own behalf, as of course he must before the passage of the Prisoners' Counsel Act, but the narrator comments that "even if" counsel had been permitted, Felix "would have declined it: he would in any case have spoken in his own defense." He had a "simple account" and no need for "legal adroitness" (355). In the author's present, allegations about advocacy excesses led to suspicion that professional narrators undermined the ability to discern the truth. Thus, to illustrate that a character had integrity, an author might have him choose self-representation as the "pure" defense and his courage would be emphasized by other characters mocking the decision as "fanatical." Other characters in novels written during the advocacy debates similarly voice their desire to speak on their own behalf: *Bleak House*'s George Rouncewell, for one, initially adamantly refuses counsel after being arrested for Tulkinghorn's murder because counsel would silence him and prevent the truth from coming out (Chapter 52).

But in the early 1830s, defendants spoke by necessity, not by choice, and thus the procedural restriction from the contemporary reformers' point of view was more properly characterized as unjust rather than strategically "injudicious," as Eliot's original manuscript stated (538, n. 3). In 1826 Sydney Smith, for example, extolled the mercies of the Prisoners' Counsel bill that would obviate the "blush" of the sympathetic on hearing defendants told "your counsel cannot speak for you, you must speak for yourself" (85). There was a significant overlap between Parliamentarian supporters of the Prisoner's Counsel bills that were introduced in the 1820s and 1830s and those who were abolitionists, opponents of capital punishment, and advocates of other law reform efforts (Beattie, 250–251). Thus, although the novel's time period of the early 1830s would otherwise aptly connect the Prisoners' Reform Bill with similar humanitarian law reform efforts, including the first Reform Bill, Eliot disassociates them. With the passage of time, the reformers' arguments that full defense representation ensures truth and equality by granting amateur defendants access to professional skills of narration had been lost. When Eliot reconstructs the time immediately preceding the Prisoner Reform, she reads back her own period's anxiety that professional advocacy undermines truth and in effect endorses the eighteenth-century epistemology that truth is best elicited when people speak in their own words.

ADVOCACY, KNOWLEDGE, AND INTERPRETATION

Novelists' critiques generally are not against advocacy per se but rather are consistent with Stephen's view that "the shocks given by the practice of advocacy to the sentiment of justice, and the hardships inflicted by it on individuals, which are inseparable from advocacy, are drawbacks from its advantages, and not objections to its existence" ("The Morality of Advocacy," 452). It is Brougham's then extreme view of advocacy as an absolute duty owed to "that client and none other" that is targeted by the novelists. Dickens, for example, in letters to the *Morning Chronicle* critical of Phillips's defense in the *Courvoisier* case, conceded an advocate's right "to do his best to save" his client while "keeping within due bounds" (91). By recognizing nonclient interests as part of the advocacy calculus, Dickens's view is consonant with the moderate definition of advocacy proposed by Talfourd.

Talfourd's emphasis on epistemology and hermeneutics also resonates with the Victorian novelists' interests. The fictional trial scenes pick up on topical issues about the application of advocacy in the courts. For example, Chaffanbrass and Jaggers assiduously avoid having any certain knowledge of their client's guilt imputed to them so as to elude the specter of the ethical dilemma that haunted Phillips in *Courvoisier;* another concern to which these scenes typically allude is the Old Bailey lawyers' aggressive cross-examinations of witnesses. More importantly, however, the trial scenes are ways to explore ideas about knowledge and interpretation and the cultural implications of courtroom hermeneutics. Talfourd rehabilitated the advocate by correcting assumptions that their intellectual position involves a direct choice between truth and falsehood. As human nature is essentially partisan, self-deceptive, and sympathetic, no perceptions are free from bias. Eliot includes a strikingly similar observation in *Felix Holt* in defense of the judge's summary to the jury: "Even the bare discernment of facts, much more their arrangement with a view to inferences, must carry a bias: human impartiality, whether judicial or not, can hardly escape being more or less loaded" (449). Frustration with epistemological limitations, these comments suggest, rather than defects in the procedures themselves, may inspire the criticisms about advocacy.

Fictional trial scenes then become pedagogical devices to teach readers about human fallibility. Trollope and Eliot remind readers that they enjoy a privileged hermeneutic position of access to characters' thoughts, narrators to guide their impressions, and the comfort of certain knowledge, as contrasted with the characters within the fictional frame who labor under the hermeneutic restrictions of limited knowledge, inability to attain certain truth, and fallible impressions. Trial scenes make this juxtaposition concrete, particularly when verdicts do not comport with the readers' knowledge of the truth, as with the legal resolutions in *Pickwick Papers* and *Orley Farm*. The law internalizes the truth that the best that the trial can achieve is something short of certainty: "The man is to be hung not because he committed the murder,—as to which no positive knowledge is attainable; but because he has been proved to have committed the murder,—as to which proof, though it be enough for hanging, there must always be attached some shadow of doubt" (*Phineas Redux,* ii, 178). But *Orley Farm*, *Phineas Redux*, and *Felix Holt* prompt readers to accept that same imperfectability, that "shadow of doubt," as an inevitable aspect of their own social practices when they are outside the discursive conventions of the novel. The adversarial system and legal rules of procedure and evidence merely formally accommodate the fact that partisanship and fallible impressions describe human nature generally.

As Trollope clarifies, the "shadow of unbelief" does not just darken the courtroom but hangs over all interpretive practices. Characters, dissatisfied that the law distinguishes between verdicts and certain truth and that their counsel separate duty from personal belief, turn to the alternate forum of public opinion but find the same constrictions there. Phineas Finn, like Pickwick, breaks convention to meet with his counsel before trial to iterate his innocence but finds Chaffanbrass disregarding his protestations to insist on the verdict as the relevant measure (*Phineas Redux*, ii, 60; *Pickwick Papers*, Chapter 31). Yet Phineas meets with a similar reception from an acquaintance who "rationally" remarks that "I as your friend was bound to await the result,—with much confidence, because I knew you; but with no conviction, because both you and I are human and fallible" (ii, 250). Trollope adeptly moves the characters in and out of the courtroom during the several day trial scene in *Orley Farm* to draw parallels between judicial and social interpretive practices. Though the trial does conclude with an "inaccurate" verdict, the process correctly effects changes in the characters' beliefs about Lady Mason's guilt. Meanwhile, the characters practice interpretation in nonlegal social settings and only haltingly arrive at the knowledge the reader possesses. The narrator in *Orley Farm* chides readers who judge these characters' learning process unfairly and forget that readers get to cheat; indeed, the narrator gently reminds the reader not to mock the characters because their interpretive stumbles and inferences from misimpressions reflect the reader's reality when he or she moves outside the interpretive boundaries of the novel.

Law and literature's "storytelling" parallels therefore should themselves be interpreted carefully. The reader/juror analogy can be instructive but only when informed by legal history and only when it is not taken to mean that the hermeneutics of the courtroom and the novel are precisely comparable. Instead, Victorian novelists embed the trial model within the novel in order to show readers that law must approach truth only through probabilities and that likewise the reader's position, once outside the hermeneutic conventions of the novel, operates under the "shadow of doubt." For "we interpret signs of emotion as we interpret other signs—often quite erroneously, unless we have the right key to what they signify" (*Felix Holt*, 463).

WORKS CITED AND SELECTED WORKS FOR FURTHER READING

Abel-Smith, Brian, and Robert Stevens. *Lawyers and the Courts: A Sociological Study of the English Legal System, 1750–1965.* Cambridge: Harvard UP, 1967.

Beattie, J. M. "Scales of Justice: Defense Counsel and the English Criminal Trial in the Eighteenth and Nineteenth Centuries." *Law and History Review* 9 (1991): 221–267.

"Bringing out the Truth." *Household Words* 4 (1851–52): 38–40.

[Brougham, Henry.] *The Life and Times of Henry Lord Brougham Written by Himself.* Vol. 2. London: Blackwood, 1871.

———. "Rights and Duties of Advocates." *Edinburgh Review* 64 (1836–37): 155–168.

Cairns, David J. A. *Advocacy and the Making of the Adversarial Criminal Trial, 1800–1865.* Oxford: Clarendon, 1998.

Cocks, Raymond. *Foundations of the Modern Bar.* London: Sweet and Maxwell, 1983.

Colaiaco, James A. "The Politics of Literature." In *James Fitzjames Stephen and the Crisis of Victorian Thought,* pp. 49–60. New York: St. Martin's, 1983.

Cornish, W. R., and G. de N. Clark. *Law and Society in England, 1750–1950.* London: Sweet and Maxwell, 1989.

Cover, Robert. "Nomos and Narrative." In *Narrative, Violence and the Law: The Essays of Robert Cover,* pp. 95–172. Ed. Martha Minow, Michael Ryan, and Austin Sarat. Ann Arbor: U of Michigan P, 1992.

Defoe, Daniel. *Moll Flanders.* 1722. Ed. David Blewett. London: Penguin, 1989.

Dickens, Charles. Letter. *Morning Chronicle* 29 June 1840. In *The Letters of Charles Dickens.* Ed. Madeline House and Graham Storey. Vol. 2, 90–91. Oxford: Clarendon, 1969.

———. *Oliver Twist.* 1838. Ed. Kathleen Tillotson. Oxford: Clarendon, 1966.

Dolin, Kieran. *Fiction and the Law: Legal Discourse in Victorian and Modernist Literature.* Cambridge: Cambridge UP, 1999.

Duman, Daniel. *The English and Colonial Bars in the Nineteenth Century.* London: Croom Helm, 1983.

———. "Pathway to Professionalism: The English Bar in the Eighteenth and Nineteenth Centuries." *Journal of Social History* 13 (1980): 615–628.

Dworkin, Ronald. "How Law Is Like Literature." In *A Matter of Principle,* pp. 146–166. Cambridge: Harvard UP, 1985.

Eden, William. *Principles of Penal Law.* London, 1771.

Eliot, George. *Adam Bede.* 1859. Ed. Stephen Gill. New York: Penguin, 1985.

———. *Felix Holt, The Radical.* 1866. Ed. Lynda Mugglestone. New York: Penguin, 1995.

Fielding, Henry. *The History of Tom Jones.* 1749. Ed. R.P.C. Mutter. New York: Penguin, 1985.

Fish, Stanley. *Doing What Comes Naturally: Change, Rhetoric, and the Practice of Theory in Literary and Legal Studies.* Durham: Duke UP, 1989.

Haight, Gordon S., ed. *The George Eliot Letters.* New Haven: Yale UP, 1954–78.

Kingwell, Mark. "Let's Ask Again: Is Law Like Literature?" *Yale Journal of Law and the Humanities* 6 (1994): 317–352.

Lansbury, Coral. *The Reasonable Man: Trollope's Legal Fiction.* Princeton: Princeton UP, 1981.

Levinson, Sanford, and Steven Mailloux, ed. *Interpreting Law and Literature: A Hermeneutic Reader.* Evanston: Northwestern UP, 1988.

Lewis, J. R. *The Victorian Bar.* London: Robert Hale, 1982.

Leyh, Gregory, ed. *Legal Hermeneutics: History, Theory, and Practice.* Berkeley: U of California P, 1992.

McMaster, R. D. *Trollope and the Law.* New York: St. Martin's, 1986.

"Old Bailey, and Its Practices." *Law Magazine and Review* 1 (1872): 326–334.

[Parker, Francis.] "The Profession of Advocacy." *Cornhill Magazine* 12 (1865): 105–115.

Petch, Simon. "Legal." In *A Companion to Victorian Literature and Culture,* pp. 155–169. Ed. Herbert F. Tucker. Oxford: Blackwell, 1999.

Posner, Richard A. *Law and Literature.* Rev. ed. Cambridge: Harvard UP, 1998.

Scott, Sir Walter. *The Heart of Midlothian.* 1818. Ed. Claire Lamont. Oxford: Oxford UP, 1982.

Second Report from His Majesty's Commissioners on Criminal Law. Parliamentary Papers 36.183. 1836.

[Smith, Sydney.] "Counsel for Prisoners." *Edinburgh Review* 45 (1826–27): 74–95.

[Stephen, James Fitzjames.] "The License of Modern Novelists." *Edinburgh Review* 106 (1857): 124–156.

———. "The Morality of Advocacy." *Cornhill Magazine* 3 (1861): 447–459.

[Talfourd, Thomas Noon.] "On the Principle of Advocacy as Developed in the Practice of the Bar." *Law Magazine* 35 (1846): 1–34.

Trollope, Anthony. *Orley Farm.* 1862. London: Oxford UP, 1951.

———. *Phineas Redux.* 1874. London: Oxford UP, 1973.

Watt, Ian. *The Rise of the Novel: Studies in Defoe, Richardson, and Fielding.* 1957. London: Hogarth, 1987.

Welsh, Alexander. *Strong Representations: Narrative and Circumstantial Evidence in England.* Baltimore: Johns Hopkins UP, 1992.

West, Robin L. "Adjudication Is Not Interpretation: Some Reservations about the Law-as-Literature Movement." *Tennessee Law Review* 54 (1987): 203–278; reprinted in *Narrative, Authority, and Law,* pp. 89–176. Ann Arbor: U of Michigan P, 1993.

Intoxication and the Victorian Novel

Kathleen McCormack

Two years before the coronation of Queen Victoria, Charles Dickens began writing *The Posthumous Papers of the Pickwick Club*, a long, serialized work now regarded as a novel, which triumphantly established the young Londoner's reputation. Among the most important of early Victorian novels, Dickens's episodic romp largely celebrates rather than condemns intoxication. It contains enormous amounts of convivial drinking, a number of repeatedly intoxicated but admirable characters, and dozens of peaceful and benevolent drinking-place settings. In *Pickwick*, alcohol causes accidents, poor performances at sport, and aggressive confrontations, but it also relaxes the drinkers, creates hilarity, and solidifies friendships.

Opium, on the other hand, in *Pickwick* as in most Victorian novels, results in a different kind of intoxication regarded with less tolerance by the narrator. The second most popular intoxicant of the period, opium, rather than contribute to the pleasures of a picnic or the coziness of an inn, produces only a too-tranquil sleep. The worldly wise servant Sam Weller invokes its tranquilizing effects in one of his characteristic comparisons: "There's nothin' so refreshin' as sleep, sir, as the servant-girl said afore she drank the egg-cupful of laudanum" (212). Weller also shocks the gentle Mr. Pickwick with his information that electioneering tactics during the Eastonswill election have included adding laudanum to the brandy of independent voters. Their drugged sleep causes them to miss the polling entirely.

The contrast between the two drugs manifested in the Pickwickians' joyful tipsiness and Sam Weller's description of the narcotizing opium becomes rarer in later Victorian novels. As industrialism not only continued to increase the crowding, tedium, and despair that turned many people to chemical escape, it also helped ensure the perniciousness of inebriation in fiction. The Condition of England novels that became popular in the 1840s usually treated working-class drunkenness as a hazard of industrialism. Meanwhile, especially in the novels of the Brontë sisters, the characters most likely to drink too much (Byronic young profligates with Romantic literary predecessors) were losing any glamor that lingered after the end of the Regency. Victorian novels usually punish them severely with sickness, death, or poverty. Consequently, as the century advances, drinking loses its innocuousness in fiction and becomes linked with opium as the two drugs that demoralize poor people and debauch more privileged characters into mindless irresponsibility.

The most respected Victorian novels embody a realism that carries aesthetic as well as moral implications about intoxication. The realist aesthetic requires rendering the physical world in great detail and examining the causes and consequences of events with scientific accuracy. Successful protagonists must abandon befuddled perceptions and romantic escape in favor of clear moral vision and earnest commitment to solving the problems of day-to-day reality. This kind of realism prompted authors to associate intoxication with the youthful periods of ignorance or delusion from which characters begin their progress toward insightful maturity. Because intoxication clouds perceptions and results from self-indulgence, it takes its place with other impediments (romantic love, faulty education) to a character's development of maturity. At the same time, realism demands narrators who refuse to dress up the behavior of their characters. Hence many Victorian novelists include scenes of drunkenness out of a sense of moral responsibility as well as out of fidelity to the Victorian realist aesthetic.

Dickens himself, while continuing to present scenes of conviviality in many of his works, also wrote novels that engaged the severe social problems of his times, including intoxication-related problems. Even in *Pickwick*, as the novel advances, intoxication produced by alcohol takes on a more dangerous aspect. Sam Weller's hangover reduces his competence so that Mr. Jingles can execute the plan to embarrass Mr. Pickwick on the premises of the girls' school at Bury St. Edmunds. Later, in the Fleet, Pickwick isolates himself from the other prisoners when the sale of alcohol there disgusts him. Finally, the drunkenness of Bob Sawyer and Ben Allan jeopardizes Winkle's post-elopement reconciliation with his father. While Pickwick attempts to win over the laconic Mr. Winkle, the two medical students flirt with the maid, make funny faces, and fall asleep, and, as the bride's brother Ben especially appalls the disappointed father. Such events anticipate the nonconvivial intoxication in later novels by Dickens.

THE DRUGS OF THE PERIOD

Overwhelmingly, the two favorite drugs of the Victorians were alcohol and opium. At the time of the Reform Bill of 1832, both were freely available, sold over the counter in chemists' shops, public houses, and elsewhere. Both came in a variety of forms that made them available to members of all social groups. Brandy, spirits, and wine, imbibed on their own or mixed in punches, satisfied the upper classes, whereas their social inferiors turned to gin and beer. Opium could be smoked, consumed as a liquid, mixed with alcohol, swallowed in capsules, or applied as an ointment. Physicians recommended both alcohol and opium for a number of legitimate medicinal purposes. The intoxication proceeding from either or both suited them as preparations for a variety of activities: to face the ordeals of surgery, dentistry, or childbirth; to ease the anxieties connected with courting or public speaking; and to create disturbances of the public order, especially during post-reform elections or labor-related protests. Opium remained entirely legal until 1868. Meanwhile, distilleries and breweries increased in size and number—and created huge fortunes.

Regarding alcohol and opium as medicines enabled drug-taking Victorians to mask their uses for purposes other than disease or pain, further suiting them for consumption by everyone. If women rarely joined the company at the ale houses, they could still, with legitimacy, avail themselves of patent medicines composed almost entirely of alcohol and opium. Parents dosed their children with tonics such as Daffy's or Godfrey's, also made up largely of opium, and although Virginia Berridge and Griffith Edwards's classic study *Opium and the People* questions their objectivity, stories persist of workers who overdosed their babies to quiet them during their absences at the mills (97). Drug companies advertised their products extensively on the front pages of newspapers, on the side panels of coaches, and in the back pages of the novels themselves.

As the century advanced, efforts to solve England's social and political problems included strategies for reducing consumption of intoxicants, especially among poor people. During the 1830s, both teetotal and anti-opium groups formed to advocate abstinence and ways of reducing legal trade in alcohol and opium. The 1868 Pharmacy Act restricted the sale of opium; licensing acts passed in the 1870s limited the availability of alcohol. Medical theory, meanwhile, began moving toward regarding constant intoxication as a disease rather than a moral weakness and expanding the concept of addiction to apply to other compulsive behaviors. By the end of the century, the Defense of the

Realm legislation aimed at sobering up the kingdom in preparation for war lay in the near future. Meanwhile, novelists had two widely available substances with which to dramatize the weakness or criminality of their characters.

CHANGING SETTINGS FOR CHANGE

Probably Victorian characters become intoxicated more often at home than in any location specifically designed for the distribution of alcohol or opium. Nevertheless, coaching inns and public houses make useful settings in early Victorian fiction; opium dens appear later in the century. Volatile political groups met at taverns, and, as campaign headquarters where candidates treated voters and nonvoters alike, public houses offered an ideal setting for public demonstrations that turned into riots. Drinking places, from the Bugle Inn in William Makepeace Thackeray's *Catherine* (1839–40) through Rolliver's in Thomas Hardy's *Tess of the d'Urbervilles* (1891), often accommodate dangers, especially dangers connected with rapid social and/or political change. Thackeray's Catherine aspires to social advancement from behind the bar of the Bugle. At Rolliver's, Tess's parents plan to change her class status by insisting she "claim kin" (27) with the family of new-made d'Urbervilles.

Many novelists of the 1830s and '40s repeat fictional techniques and settings favored by their predecessors. In Newgate novels, Harrison Ainsworth and Edward Bulwer-Lytton create traveling rogue characters in the picaresque tradition, and Fieldingesque protagonists like Thackeray's Barry Lyndon travel along fictional coach roads at a time when their creators were already journeying by railway. Novelists such as Dickens, Thackeray, and George Eliot all liked settings in the near or distant past, during times when travel required that all passengers, regardless of age, gender, or social status, stop at inns along the road. The multiple functions of public houses within villages or towns early in the century also legitimized the visits of various members of the community who had business there other than drinking. As banks, libraries, cookhouses, museums, transport terminals, surgeries, morgues, employment bureaus, gambling halls, auction rooms, theaters, ballrooms, campaign headquarters, and meeting rooms, they offered services to people from all but the highest and lowest status levels and provided an area where changes occurred rapidly enough to propel plot action quickly. But, like the coaching inn, the multifunction public house also yields to other settings as the century goes on. Later in the period, public houses became more exclusively associated with drinking because town halls, libraries, hospitals, and museums began to accommodate the nondrinking activities previously pursued there. Meanwhile, Dickens's Mr. Dombey in *Dombey and Son* (1847), Anthony Trollope's

Septimus Harding in *The Warden* (1855), and Mary Elizabeth Braddon's Robert Audley in *Lady Audley's Secret* (1862) all travel by the railway.

If the volatility of events at public houses suits them for advancing plots quickly, their signs offer a creative opportunity to construct character. Few novelists resist exploiting the names of the public houses where their characters drink. Both pictorial and linguistic, public house signs can also carry historical meanings, bits of narratives of past events that might parallel what happens in a novel or render it ironic. Typically, the sign of the Quiet Woman in Hardy's *The Return of the Native* makes an implied reference to Anne Boleyn and anticipates the destruction of Eustacia Vye. It draws additional meaning from its caption, which links the decapitation with gender and political conflicts, "Since the woman's quiet/Let no man breed a riot" (61). The peculiar history of pub signs also increases the possibilities for linguistic play and for implications about religion and parenthood. Signs such as the Angel and the Cross Keys survived the iconophobia of newly Protestant Tudor England through the removal of ecclesiastical figures, in these cases the Virgin recipient of the Angel Gabriel's annunciatory message in the one and St. Peter who leaves his keys behind him on the other. Many signs bore the arms of the neighboring nobility who had assumed the duties of hospitality abandoned by monks when Henry VIII dissolved the monasteries. The absence of arms therefore indicates irresponsibility in the local nobility and, by implication, in all authority. Consequently, the most popular of the signs harbor potential for allusions to class-related, political, and religious matters because of the absence of something previously or otherwise there.

The remainder include enough oddities to draw attention to the faults of the characters who frequent them. The Three Cripples in *Oliver Twist* displays a sign that adequately describes the moral atrophy of Bill Sikes and his associates. In *The Moonstone*, the climactic wild night of disguise, murder, theft, and, ultimately, revelation of guilt occurs at the Wheel of Fortune, whose sign also represents drastic change. Although the gentry and aristocracy—for example Jos Sedley in Thackeray's *Vanity Fair* and Lord Felix in Trollope's *The Way We Live Now*—drink more in clubs than in public houses, the sudden changes that occur in these settings parallel those at public houses, and the name of Trollope's Beargarden blatantly describes the young drinkers who gamble themselves to destruction there.

Fictional opium dens have little in common with inns and public houses. They begin appearing in late-Victorian fiction, not to replace the diminishing numbers of drinking places but to add an unambiguously evil setting and one that carries strong implications about British Imperialism. Berridge and Edwards believe that Dickens begins the transfer of this setting from Victorian journalism to fiction in the dramatic opening chapter of his last (unfinished)

novel, *The Mystery of Edwin Drood* (1870), which they describe as "the beginning of a more melodramatic presentation of the subject" (196), followed by
later sensational opium-den settings in A. Conan Doyle's fiction and in Oscar
Wilde's *The Picture of Dorian Gray*.

Most authors who write about nineteenth-century opium (Berridge and
Edwards, Barry Milligan, Julian North) agree that Thomas DeQuincey initiated during the 1820s a pattern of Orientalizing opium that expresses anxieties
over British imperialism. *Confessions of an English Opium-Eater* established
patterns Victorians sustained in their fiction, primarily patterns that associate
opium with exotic and sinister foreigners who smoke, eat, drink, convey, and
dispense opium to decent Englishmen.

INTOXICATED PEOPLE: NARRATORS

The most common heavy-drinking or drug-taking characters in Victorian
fiction include profligate young men, irresponsible landowners, lower-class
males often assembled in mobs, and completely abandoned women. Indeed of
all the people in Victorian novels, the least likely drinkers or opium consumers
are the responsible, didactic narrators. Nevertheless, intoxicated narrators
sometimes occur in alternate voices and even in first-person narratives. When
this happens, the condition of the intoxicated narrator undermines the reliability of the primary/sober narrator. Subtextually, the narrative situation calls
into question the benefits of abstinence or moderation.

Although primary narrators in Victorian novels generally maintain the utmost sobriety in order to sustain their authority, occasionally an intoxicated alternate narrator becomes the voice. In *The Pickwick Papers*, the traveling
salesman Dickens calls the "one-eyed bagman" (662) has another drink of
negus before delivering his interpolated tale. In Wilkie Collins's *The Moonstone*, the many narrators all praise the first, the reliable senior servant Gabriel
Betteredge who introduces his successor by noting her "pretty taste in cham-
pagne" (176). When Miss Clack undertakes the narration a few pages later, her
hysterical tone remains consistent with her introduction as a drinker by
Betteredge. At the end, Betteredge further complicates the issue by revealing
his own enthusiasm for taking "a drop" (426). Despite the dramatic irony,
Betteredge, Miss Clack, and the bagman, like other intoxicated narrators, deliver well-shaped coherent stories that boost their reliability regardless of their
condition at the time.

Similarly, when first-person primary narrators become intoxicated, they too
maintain reliability. David Copperfield reports his drunken night with
Steerforth as an older, wiser man, but as he does, he remembers a long sequence
of events, bits of conversation, and embarrassing mishaps with perfect clarity.

He also re-creates with accuracy the disjointed perceptions of a drunkard through sophisticated techniques such as tense shifts and repetitions. Charlotte Brontë's drugged Lucy Snow describes in detail her night out in *Villette*: the people she sees at the fête, the Egyptian decorations of the gardens, and her careful strategies to avoid detection. Despite the effects of the opiate, she makes only one error during her night out: She concludes that Mme. Beck and her associates design M. Paul for Justine-Marie who turns out to be already engaged.

In these examples, the voices that deliver their stories while intoxicated do not, as consistency would dictate, lose their reliability. Despite direct or indirect admissions of intoxication, they devise detailed, coherent, often perceptive narratives. In this way the first-person and alternate narrators can undercut the reliability of the narrations as a whole. If a story comes across fully and accurately when delivered by an intoxicated voice, the virtues of sobriety become less clear, and an acknowledgment of the possible benefits of the intoxicated state creeps into the otherwise temperance-advocating narratives.

INTOXICATED PEOPLE: CHARACTERS

The characters in Victorian novels rarely succumb to the ambiguity that affects the narrators, for few sympathetic portrayals of intoxication or dependence survive the disapproval of narrators who warn against dangers to sobriety, responsibility, self-reliance, chastity, moderation, perception, and domesticity. Characters associated with the early-period roadside settings include susceptible barmaids, scurrilous publicans, and nostalgic coachmen who lament the arrival of the railways. Young men who take over the reins provide another DeQuincey association since the persona of "The English Mail Coach" courts disaster by driving after taking a dose of opium. Characters who aspire to own public houses earn consistent scorn, especially if they hope to marry into an already established business. Because the first generation of Victorians believed that their parents drank far more than they, a group of intoxicated parents also appears. Dickens's Mr. Wickfield, George Eliot's Thias Bede, Braddon's drinking grandfather, and Elizabeth Gaskell's John Barton all trouble their children because of their habitual intoxication. Young profligates, people in mobs, and intoxicated women also earn their narrators' severity on the topic.

By 1832, the Byronic rakehell character popular during the first decades of the century and associated in Romantic culture with both drinking and opium was already losing his glamor. Byron himself had died in 1824. The Prince Regent, whose indulgences popularized excess, had succeeded to the monarchy and himself died. Political reform, removing some of the power of the aristocratic classes, was underway. Although male novelists such as Trollope and Thackeray also created young blades in need of reform, the novels of the

Brontë sisters contribute most directly to the deglamorization of the Romantic hero in Victorian fiction.

The novels written by the Brontë sisters can differ as drastically from each other as does Emily Brontë's Gothic *Wuthering Heights* from her youngest sister's Georgian *Agnes Grey*, yet all three sisters create addicted characters reminiscent of their brother Branwell. Despite Charlotte Brontë's construction of the Byronic romantic hero Mr. Rochester in *Jane Eyre*, she does not omit chastising the profligate drunkard in the character of John Reed. E. Brontë creates a specifically fraternal alcoholic in Hindley Earnshaw of *Wuthering Heights*. But of all the Brontë characters whose behavior repeats Branwell's, Anne Brontë's Arthur Huntingdon in *The Tenant of Wildfell Hall* presents life with an unreformable rakehell in the most detail. Each step in his degeneration betrays its author's intimate knowledge of daily life with an alcoholic and warns young women attracted to wild suitors that possibilities for reforming the rake lie out of her power. Whether addicted to alcohol or opium or both, the profligate characters of the Brontë sisters help rewrite the popular figure of the Regency rakehell in terms that express the Victorian lack of tolerance for excess.

Like unreformable rakehells, working-class rioters drink to excess in scenes of volatility, disorder, and destruction. In *Shirley*, C. Brontë varies the drunken rakehell characters she and her sisters favor elsewhere, characters likely to belong to the upper classes, with a mob led by drunken working-class Methodists. In *Felix Holt*, George Eliot's election-day mob not only get drunk on beer provided by the election agents, they attack public houses and target the town brewery before Felix diverts them away from Slaughter Lane. Incited by the title character's uncontrollably emotional response to his audience, the mob in Charles Kingsley's *Alton Locke* includes "drunkards, a woman or two among them, reeling knee-deep in the loose straw among the pigs" (212). Kingsley's insistence on mentioning the few women together with the pigs in his mob conforms to practices of intensifying an evil by adding gender implications.

Indeed when Victorian novelists want to signal complete baseness, they, often gratuitously, attribute alcohol and opium use specifically to women characters—for example, Thackeray's Becky Sharp or the hopeless wife of Stephen Blackpool in Dickens's *Hard Times*. When Farmer Porter drives Alton Locke toward Cambridge, he specifies women as purchasers of the opium for which the fen area maintained a kind of fame "yow goo into druggist's shop o' market-day into Cambridge, and you'll see the little boxes, doozens and doozens, a' ready on the counter; and never a ven-man's wife goo by, but what calls in for her pennord o' elevation to last her out the week" (97). George Eliot attempts a sympathetic treatment of a drinking woman in her 1857 short-fiction "Janet's Repentance," but the story so disturbed her publisher that she never directly touched the issue again. Not until George Gissing's *The Odd Women* (1893), does a sympathetic representation of a woman alcoholic enter Victorian fiction.

HUMOR, SUBTEXT, METAPHOR

Because Victorian didacticism refuses to acknowledge any pleasures or nonmedical benefits of the two most popular drugs of the period, harmless examples of drinking or drugs seldom occur at the level of plot or character in the novels of the time. Nevertheless, novelists draw on them as resources for the creation of humor, subtext, and metaphor. The circumlocutions of narrators encourage mock-heroic descriptions of intoxication whose humor proceeds from the attempts of the drunkard to appear sober. In *Martin Chuzzlewit* (1844), Sairy Gamp makes herself foolish by the pomposity of her language. George Eliot's *Middlemarch* narrator comments with elaborate mock courtesy on the condition of Raffles: "To say that Mr. Raffles' manner was rather excited would be only one mode of saying that it was evening" (501). David Copperfield reports of himself and the visiting trio from Oxford: "We went downstairs, one behind another. Near the bottom, somebody fell, and rolled down. Somebody else said it was Copperfield. I was angry at that false report, until, finding myself on my back in the passage, I began to think there might be some foundation for it" (301). The humor of his conclusion proceeds from the contrast between the rationality he exercises in evaluating the evidence and his position flat on his back.

Subtextually, drug references can signal guilt, create foreshadowings, or suggest intoxication in characters not obviously impaired. In characters named Godfrey, as in George Eliot's *Silas Marner* and Wilkie Collins's *The Moonstone*, the association with the most popular children's opiate prefigures the flaws of the two men, one a selfish and irresponsible parent, the other a hypocritical villain. Dickens mounts his attack on Victorian breweries in *Great Expectations* where Miss Havisham's name rhymes with Faversham, a brewing town near the novel's Kentish setting. George Eliot's narrator in *The Mill* never describes Maggie's Aunt Pullet as inebriated, but the quantities of drugs she consumes indicate that she must remain constantly impaired during the scenes of Maggie's childhood.

Indeed, whereas Dickens relies heavily on intoxicated characters, plots, and settings throughout his *oeuvre*, the novels of George Eliot, because of the comprehensiveness of her representations of drugs at every semiotic level, offer numerous typically Victorian examples of the metaphorical potential of intoxicants and intoxication. Most typically, she applies intoxication metaphors to the condition of being in love. In *Adam Bede*, Adam fails to produce in Hetty "the sweet intoxication of young love" (86), but her earliest awareness of Arthur creates "a pleasant narcotic effect" (86). In *The Mill on the Floss*, she rep-

146

resents Maggie's romantic literature and waking dreams as opiate. Like Hetty, Maggie also succumbs to intoxication in her passion for Stephen. George Eliot's metaphors also conform to the Victorian tendency to figure politics, especially reform, as a drug. In *Middlemarch*, Farmer Dagley has not only drunk too much on market day, "he had also taken too much in the shape of muddy political talk" (379).

DRUGLESS INTOXICATION

Not all fictional Victorian intoxication results from alcohol and opium. More mysterious intoxicants occur in late Victorian novels set in other worlds, whether magic realms, future utopia/dystopias, or outer space. The respect for scientific rationalism that accompanied ever more sophisticated nineteenth-century geology, physiology, zoology, and botany coexisted with an impulse to reclaim the charm and power of magic, fantasy, spiritualism, and other anti-Positivistic impulses to seek nonrational ways of knowing. Seances and mesmerism were popular, and people believed in the presence of departed spirits moving within the rooms of nineteenth-century buildings side-by-side with the contemporary inhabitants. Such beliefs can sometimes detoxify drugs by accepting them as a means to achieve a more intense susceptibility to spiritual influences.

In 1865, Charles L. Dodgson (Lewis Carroll) made one of the most long-lasting literary evocations of the ambiguous allure of magic potions and fantastic landscapes. Down the rabbithole, in *Alice's Adventures in Wonderland*, Alice radically distorts and alters her size and thus her perspective by consuming food and drink, and the caterpillar with his hookah conforms to the pattern of Orientalized drug-taking. Indeed the cultural potency of Dodgson's text arises a good deal from the nonspecificity and therefore the adaptability of what Alice consumes. As the twentieth-century pharmacy has expanded to include a greater variety of recreational drugs, the substances that change Alice can be adapted to represent the variety.

Late-Victorian science fiction also contains intoxicants beyond what was available in nineteenth-century Britain. When protagonists of novels such as Bulwer-Lytton's *The Coming Race* or Percy Greg's *Across the Zodiac* travel to other universes, they usually encounter substances or forces foreign to earthlings. In *Across the Zodiac*, the narrator of life on Mars reports that "no fermented liquors form part of the Martial diet; but some narcotics resembling haschisch and opium are much relished" (212). In the subterranean world, Bulwer-Lytton's American finds that vril, a force rather than a fluid, can change temperatures, send people to sleep, destroy or heal them, and impart new knowledge. He describes his first taste: "In place of my former terror there passed into me a sense of contentment, of joy, of confidence in myself" (17).

Removed from their Victorian contexts, these intoxicants retain dangerous but also potentially narcotic, anaesthetic, or euphoric sides. The futurism of *fin-de-siècle* science fiction includes hopes for miracle cures and limitless sources of energy and acknowledges the power and usefulness of present or future drugs partly by removing from them the disapproval signaled by specific references to alcohol and opium.

INTOXICATION AND INSPIRATION

The requirements of Victorian publishing, especially of circulating libraries and periodical serialization, contributed to the marketability of Victorian novels that express a moral severity that did not necessarily correspond to the actions and beliefs of their authors. Many novelists violated in life the Victorian sexual codes they advance thematically in their novels. Similarly, most of the novelists mentioned here drank alcohol at least moderately, and some of them, notably Wilkie Collins, maintained opium habits. Occasionally they insert in their novels suggestions that they may not share the horror of their narrators toward drugs. Collins himself creates the enslaved but heroic Ezra Jennings in *The Moonstone*. In *Middlemarch*, George Eliot applies a wine metaphor to the irreproachable Dorothea in the motto to Chapter 55: "Hath she her faults? I would you had them too. / They are the fruity must of soundest wine" (521). In mid-Victorian novels (aside from Dickens's), despite the activities of the authors, these acknowledgments of the pleasures of intoxication occur at the subtextual or metaphorical level of the novels.

Most importantly, Victorian literature, at least temporarily, severs the Romantic connection between intoxication and artistic creativity. Unlike both their Romantic predecessors and their Modernist successors (who could and did draw stimulation from a much expanded pharmacy of medical and recreational agents), the Victorian novelists rarely make a point of seeking inspiration through intoxication. Authors of the Victorian period recoiled from the irresponsibility and self-preoccupation of Romantic excess and escapism, but the Modernists reacted even more violently against Victorian prudery, including the prudery of moderation or abstinence. With Coleridgean Romanticism behind them, and the revival of the archetype of the half-mad artist drunk on honeydew ahead, the Victorians create an interlude of sobriety in novels if not in life.

WORKS CITED AND SELECTED WORKS FOR FURTHER READING

Berridge, Virginia, and Griffith Edwards. *Opium and the People.* New Haven: Yale UP, 1987.

Bulwer-Lytton, Edward. *The Coming Race*. London: Alan Sutton, 1995.

Collins, Wilkie. *The Moonstone*. London: Wordsworth, 1999.

Dickens, Charles. *David Copperfield*. London: Penguin, 1994.

———. *The Pickwick Papers*. London: J. M. Dent, 1998.

Eliot, George. *Adam Bede*. Boston: Riverside, 1980.

———. *Middlemarch*. London: Penguin, 1994.

———. *The Mill on the Floss*. Boston: Riverside, 1961.

Greg, Percy. *Across the Zodiac: The Story of a Wrecked Record*. London: Trübner, 1880.

Hardy, Barbara. "*The Mill on the Floss*." In *Critical Essays on George Eliot*. New York: Barnes and Noble, 1970.

Hardy, Thomas. *The Return of the Native*. London: Macmillan 1995.

Harrison, Brian. *Drink and the Victorians: The Temperance Question in England, 1815–1872*. Pittsburgh: U of Pittsburgh P, 1971.

Hewett, Edward, and W. F. Axton. *Convivial Dickens: The Drinks of Dickens and His Times*. Athens: Ohio UP, 1983.

Kingsley, Charles. *Alton Locke, Tailor and Poet: An Autobiography*. London: Macmillan, 1889.

McCormack, Kathleen. *George Eliot and Intoxication: Dangerous Drugs for the Condition of England*. New York: St. Martin's, 2000.

Milligan, Barry. *Pleasures and Pains: Opium and the Orient in Nineteenth-Century British Culture*. Charlottesville: UP of Virginia, 1995.

North, Julian. "The Opium-Eater as Criminal in Victorian Writing." In *Writing and Victorianism*. Ed. J. B. Bullen. London: Longman, 1997.

Ricks, Christopher. "Pink Toads in *Lord Jim*." *Essays in Criticism* 31 (April 1981): 142–144.

III

Victorian Genres

Ghosts and Hauntings in the Victorian Novel

Lucie J. Armitt

The Victorian period is almost synonymous with the literature of ghosts. During a period in which occultism is competing with science and technology for the large answers to cultural questions, even early photography meets its true popularity in relation to the spirit world, as charlatan photographers set up studios on the proceeds of providing grieving parents with "photographs" of their dead children's ghosts. Yet this connection is continually masked by a literary truism that the nineteenth century is the great era of the realist novel. Though one might choose, as a rough rule of thumb, to assign ghost stories to the popular or shadow-side of nineteenth-century writing and realism to its serious or "legitimate" side, ghosts and hauntings also feature repeatedly in the latter. In this chapter I take two such "serious," predominantly realist works—Charles Dickens's *Great Expectations* (1860–61) and Anne Brontë's *The Tenant of Wildfell Hall* (1848), and show how that realism is underwritten by a pattern of haunting borrowed directly from the popular ghost story, which proves intrinsic both to their narrative structures and their social significance.

GHOSTS IN RELATION TO NARRATIVE STRUCTURE

For R. A. Gilbert, the popularity of ghost stories (much like that of spirit photography) derives from society's desire to "evad[e] the larger, and infinitely more unpleasant, issue of death and what may lie beyond it" (Gilbert, 69). Though this may well be true, it does not fully explain the role of the fictive ghost, nor its relationship with literature as a whole. In *Over Her Dead Body: Death, Femininity, and the Aesthetic*, Elisabeth Bronfen devises an intriguing and complex argument in which she claims the act of storytelling itself to be always and inseparably linked with death in the reanimation of characters and the resulting temporary suspension of social life enacted upon the reader. Readers, we might suggest, exist in a zombielike state while engaged with the text. Similarly, Bronfen claims, the narrator of a story is "absent from the world and therefore 'dead' as a social person . . . producing fictions that in turn are alive in the realm of the imaginary but immaterial in respect to social reality" (Bronfen, 349). In these terms all narratives and their characters become "ghost-like," while "storytellers are like revenants in that the liminal realm between life and death inspires and produces fictions" (Bronfen, 349). David Punter's recent work on *Gothic Pathologies* takes a similar line, viewing haunting as, to some extent, a phenomenon characteristic of all narrative fictions. If, he argues, the Gothic is determined by the presence of Otherness, "all writing is 'haunted' by the shapes of all that it is not" (Punter, 2). This being true, it stands to reason that the status of ghosts in literature is not the same as their status in real life. In reality the sighting of a ghost brings us into direct contact with "the other side" and, as a result, a prefiguring of our own death. In literature, however, if all characters hover in a realm somewhere between life and death, being neither animate nor inanimate, how does one convey the uncanniness of the fictive ghost as opposed to any other character in the text?

In a popular ghost narrative this conveyance of the thrill/chill factor becomes the author's paramount concern. In the serious novel there must be more to the presence of the ghost than this, and, if so, the larger and more salient question lies in asking what purpose the literary ghost serves. The answer may lie less with the ghost itself and more in the nature of its hauntings. In Dickens's *A Christmas Carol* (1843), for example, the ghost is a mere projection of Scrooge's otherwise buried conscience. Though still uncanny to a degree, the generic orderliness of this festive piece of consolation always outweighs the supernatural disturbance. In *Great Expectations*, on the other hand, the status and function of the haunting is different, more disturbing and—because of its lack of generic conformity—always more genuinely disruptive.

GREAT EXPECTATIONS: THE GHOST AS DOUBLE

Bronfen's reading of the storyteller as ghost is surely best made in the context of the third-person omniscient narrator. Such a figure does, indeed, stand in as a shadowy presence, both there and not there: invisible but evident in the skinless membrane it inhabits. Neither proper to the time of the novel nor the time of the reader, this narrator is stranded, specterlike, in no-time and no-place. Bronfen, however, shuns the role played by omniscience and, in her own choice of illustrative text (again, *Great Expectations*), does not dwell on narrative structure as such, slipping instead among author, reader, and characters, centering her focus on Miss Haversham. Setting her up as a kind of self-fashioning creator, she claims that this antagonistic villainess "link[s] femininity, death and the emergence of fiction over the body of a revenant bride. . . . Miss Haversham [is] a woman who remains beyond her social death to provoke a mystery and inspire a tale" (Bronfen, 349).

Bronfen is, of course, right insofar as Miss Haversham is a fictive author: author of the "great expectations" that name the novel in which she is buried alive. Nevertheless, it is the central protagonist, Pip, not Miss Haversham, who (re)writes that particular story, persuading himself of its facticity, irrespective of to what extent she tacitly encourages his delusions. Bronfen is also right, insofar as *Great Expectations*, though set up as the story of Pip, is hijacked by Miss Haversham, for, paradoxically, it is she who lives on most vividly in our minds. And yet, however seductive Bronfen's argument, Miss Haversham's tale is not her own: It remains filtered through the voice of another Pip, not the central protagonist this time, but the more mature frame narrator, who tells his own story (within which hers lies), taking a first-person retrospective stance throughout. Pip is, himself, therefore, "ghosted" in the sense that a screen image is ghosted: doubled or echoed by another shadow-self. As I have already implied, his doubling is further doubled as Pip and Miss Haversham become parasitically inseparable—just who is feeding off whose story? Bronfen continues: "Disempowered in life, [Miss Haversham] gains demonic power by speaking from the position of an empty grave" (349). Her reading, nevertheless, once again implicates Pip, for his narrative opens, not with an empty grave but a full one:

As I never saw my father or my mother, and never saw any likeness of either of them . . . my first fancies regarding what they were like, were unreasonably derived from their tombstones. The shape of the letters on my father's, gave me an odd idea that he was a square, stout, dark man, with curly black hair. From the character and turn of the inscription, "*Also Georgiana Wife of the Above*," I drew a childish conclusion that my mother was freckled and sickly. (Dickens, 35)

Great Expectations is simultaneously a journey into the past and into the future. Though the reader experiences the narrative trajectory as a projection into Pip the protagonist's future, it is, for Pip the frame narrator, one that projects backwards into his past and, at this initial point, poses questions about origins that project us still further back in time and, necessarily, remain unanswered. I began by suggesting that the ghost often functions to evoke larger cultural questions: Its role in *Great Expectations* follows this paradigm. Hence, in the larger context of origins inspired by the narrative opening, Pip's journey takes him into and repeatedly returns him to a space ironically echoing postlapsarian Eden. Banished from Satis House, he finds himself in "a rank garden . . . overgrown with tangled weeds" (Dickens, 93) adjoining the yard of a disused brewery. Here, Pip searches out his own fallen Eve:

There was a track upon the green and yellow paths . . . [and] Estella was walking away from me even then. But she seemed to be everywhere. For, when I yielded to the temptation presented by the casks, and began walking on them, I saw *her* walking on them at the end of the yard of casks . . . pass[ing] out of my view directly. So, in the brewery itself . . . when I first went into it, and, rather oppressed by its gloom, stood near the door looking about me, I saw her pass among the extinguished fires, and ascend some light iron stairs, and go out by a gallery high overhead, as if she were going out into the sky.

It was in this place, and at this moment, that a strange thing happened to my fancy. I thought it a strange thing then, and I thought it a stranger thing long afterwards. I turned my eyes—a little dimmed by looking up at the frosty light—towards a great wooden beam in a low nook of the building near me on my right hand, and I saw a figure hanging there by the neck. . . . [T]he face was Miss Haversham's, with a movement going over the whole countenance as if she were trying to call to me. In the terror of seeing the figure, and in the terror of being certain that it had not been there a moment before, I at first ran from it, and then ran towards it. And my terror was greatest of all, when I found no figure there. (Dickens, 93–94)

The passage is worth quoting at length because of the progression that is developed therein. Whatever the erroneous nature of Pip's expectations, neither he nor we are led to expect this. In that sense, it embodies the false (apparitional) hopes Pip has placed upon Miss Haversham, which take the shape of Estella, even if here Estella merges into and out of the shape of Miss Haversham. Or, to put it in Punter's terms, this vision confronts Pip with his own arrogance: "Gothic heroes [(of which, surely, Pip is one)] share a tendency to think that, if there is distortion in the world, it is they themselves who are producing and controlling it" (Punter, 7). Here the distortions are put down to another understanding of the word "spectral," namely deriving from the spectrum, as the play of light causes optical illusions and the occult to merge. Pip's eyes are "a little dimmed by looking up at the frosty light," sufficiently so to cast doubt upon whether he is seeing a ghost or experiencing a hallucination.

In one sense Miss Haversham is corporeality in excess, living in a state of ongoing rot, decay, and infestation. In this scene, however, rather than the removal of her body in death, the projected death of the living corpse that is Miss

Haversham simply replicates her image many times over, as she, like Pip, ghosts her own story here, as if projected onto the spirit photographer's lens. The passage begins in the realms of realism as the real, flesh-and-blood Estella recedes from Pip's gaze. As she does so, not only do her outlines blur, it seems as if another moves into the frame to supplant her. The "she" of the following sentence appears ambiguous—does it point to Estella or someone else? We know where Estella is at this point, so who is this "she" who appears to be everywhere? Once the ensuing sentence employs the italicized pronoun "*her*" in such an emphatic manner, we strongly start to suggest that, blurring into and out of, part of yet distinct from, Estella is Miss Haversham herself. It is not that Estella leads Pip to the specter of Miss Haversham here, but that the specter of Miss Haversham merges into and out of the image of Estella throughout the novel. Indeed, Miss Haversham is the creator of Estella, painting her onto the canvas of her own past.

This theme of fictive doubling—the overlaying of characters and storytellers, one upon another—also defines an additional story analyzed by Bronfen, Edgar Allan Poe's "The Oval Portrait" (1842). Poe's story, again a first-person narrative, is told by a visitor to a chateau in the Apennines, who finds himself in a bedchamber lined with paintings, accompanied by a written guidebook laid conveniently on his pillow. As he drifts off to sleep, the candlelight suddenly illumines a portrait of a young woman that seems, to the dimming gaze of the dozing voyeur, alive. Bolt upright in fear, he stares fully at the painting until he has reassured himself that the trick played upon him is merely that of the mastery of the painter's art. Then he turns to the guidebook for further illumination. In it he reads of a young bride whose marriage to a painter was haunted by her jealousy of the ardor with which he pursued his art. Sitting for her own portrait, she resents the canvas that obscures his face from her and yet, being "humble and obedient," she "smiled on and still on, uncomplainingly" (Poe, 252). As completion nears, the guidebook's own (ghostly?) omniscient narrator obliquely criticizes the artist:

He *would* not see that the tints which he spread upon the canvas were drawn from the cheeks of her who sat beside him. . . . And [w]hen the [final] brush was given, and . . . the [final] tint was placed . . . the painter stood entranced before the work which he had wrought; but in the next, while he yet gazed, he grew tremulous and very pallid, and aghast, and crying with a loud voice, "This is indeed *Life* itself!" turned suddenly to regard his beloved—*She was dead!* (Poe, 252–253)

Although the gender balance of the two relationships is different, Miss Haversham's control over Estella is as vampiric as Poe's artist's predatory talent. Both tales act out the possible dangers facing nineteenth-century brides, but

Dickens, unlike Poe, doubles the jeopardy in setting up Estella as the second victim of this perverse nuptial feast. On one of Pip's visits he observes, "As Estella looked back over her shoulder . . . Miss Haversham kissed [her] hand to her, with a *ravenous* intensity that was of its kind quite dreadful" (Dickens, 261; emphasis added). On another, he notices, "She *hung* upon Estella's beauty, *hung* upon her words, *hung* upon her gestures . . . while she looked at her, as though she were *devouring* the beautiful creature she had reared" (Dickens, 320; emphasis added). In creating an *objet d'art* of impossible beauty, Miss Haversham, like Poe's artist, refuses Estella life. In addition to the presiding vocabulary of eating and feasting, we can hardly overlook the repeated use of the word "hung" in the second quotation, a verb linking art with domestic incarceration as the portrait is fastened to the wall of the mansion. Recalling the earlier haunting scene, it also of course reinvokes the apparition of the "hanged" Miss Haversham, a vision in this case that projects Estella into the role of artist and Miss Haversham as image. According to Bronfen, the power relations of "The Oval Portrait" are relatively straightforward: "The masculine artist, incorporating the feminine power of creation engenders and requires the decorporalization of the woman who had inspired the artist as model and whose capacities to give birth are what the painting sessions imitate" (Bronfen, 112). In *Great Expectations*, the dynamics of power in relation to gender are far more complexly interlaced.

At the end of the novel Estella, sitting with Pip on a bench in the garden, refuses to play the romantic game: "I little thought . . . that I should take leave of you in taking leave of this spot. I am very glad to do so" (Dickens, 493). The ambiguity of Estella's words seems both deliberate and deliberately hurtful: Pip, we presume, is once again being rejected. Pip, however, baulking at her intentions, determines to hear nothing but his own desired ending: "I took her hand in mine, and we went out of the ruined place; and, as the morning mists had risen long ago when I first left the forge, so the evening mists were rising now, and in all the broad expanse of tranquil light they showed to me, *I saw no shadow of another parting from her*" (Dickens, 493; emphasis added). This ending is, we know, not the original one Dickens wrote. In the first and preferable version, Pip remains unmarried and separate from Estella, channeling his energies into working for Herbert and Clara. Only at the last moment prior to first publication did Edward Bulwer-Lytton persuade him to provide a conventional happy ending for the consolation of readers. So Dickens exchanged it, as he told his biographer, John Forster, for "as pretty a little piece of writing as I could" (Calder, 494). The kitsch language Dickens employs here is surely no more lost on us than the inferior quality of its replacement. However, according to Angus Calder, Dickens's affirmation ghosts a "buried meaning" dependent upon the reader hearing what Pip does not say in the second version: "At this happy moment, I did not see the shadow of our subsequent parting looming over us" (Calder, 496). Calder's view is certainly persuasive, not least because no character portrayal is offered of Dickens's frame narrator, hence leaving a deliberate lack of any corroborating evidence as to whether Pip the frame narrator is or was married and, if married, to whom. But, in addition to this ambiguity, there is a further one, in that the phrase "another parting" also reinvokes the predatory doubling/haunting of Estella by Miss Haversham. In this case what Pip does not (wish to) entertain is his own impotence to prevent Estella from continuing to be haunted. Hence his failure, here, to perceive "another [person—Miss Haversham—(de)]parting from her." This second meaning is reinforced by the fact that the ending leaves us in the same misty world of shadows that provided the backdrop to the earlier hanging scene. Even in the terms of the second, so-called "happy" ending, Estella, haunted by Miss Haversham, will always be a ghost(ed) bride. Compare this structure with that imposed by the frame narrator of *The Tenant of Wildfell Hall*.

THE TENANT OF WILDFELL HALL: THE GHOST-WRITTEN TEXT

I began this chapter by arguing that it is the omniscient narrator who best inhabits Bronfen's realm of the ghostly storyteller. What happens when, as in Brontë's novel, that narrative structure is more complexly overlaid with competing narrative voices? Like *Great Expectations*, *The Tenant of Wildfell Hall* is retrospectively told in the first person by a frame narrator, Gilbert Markham, who ghosts his own role as protagonist, but unlike in *Great Expectations*, this voice is, itself, ghosted by another: Helen Graham's as reproduced in her journal in Chapters 16–44 and her letters to her brother Frederick in Chapters 47–49 (disclosed to Gilbert without her permission). Unlike Dickens's seclusion of the frame narrator Pip, however, Brontë gives us a relatively clear image of the older Gilbert Markham. He is, it seems, a sedate, reliable, contemplative figure who,

having withdrawn my well-roasted feet from the hobs, wheeled round to the table, and indicted the above lines to my crusty old friend, [is] about to give him a sketch—no, not a sketch,—a full and faithful account of certain circumstances connected with the most important event of my life. (Brontë, 34)

This passage establishes Gilbert as a steady, reassuring, fatherly figure. However, fathers are given a rather bad press in this novel, and almost as soon as the narrator's reliability is communicated, it is undermined. This Gilbert is no more than a pale shadow of his character double, the sulky but endearingly

boyish, hotheaded, impetuous (perhaps overly so), all-action Gilbert
Markham who, though at one moment "vault[ing]" a "barrier" (Brontë, 124),
at the next is "leap[ing] or tumbl[ing] over [a] wall" (Brontë, 125), and again
"cutting away across the country, just as a bird might fly—over pasture-land
and fallow, and stubble, and lane—clearing hedges and ditches, and hurdles"
(Brontë, 464).

Secrets and half-truths are the narrative tone from the start. Gilbert's excuse
for telling the tale is that it is payment in kind, gossip imparted in exchange for
a whispered confidence, formerly imparted to him by Jack Halford but, importantly, never divulged to us. Like Pip, Gilbert claims to be telling his own story
in revealing the contents of "musty old letters and papers" and "a certain faded
old journal *of mine*" (Brontë, 34; emphasis added). Instead, what he goes on to
reveal are the contents of private letters and diaries belonging to his wife. That
Helen is absent from the house at the point of telling (Gilbert informing
Halford that "the family are absent on a visit" [Brontë, 34]) shows Gilbert having as little regard for his wife's privacy in middle-age as he had for it in reading
her letters to Frederick while a young man. None of this detracts from the
reader's own voyeuristic pleasure, of course—far from it. Its purpose is to act, at
least in part, as a rider to another forced happy ending: "As for myself, I need
not tell you how happily my Helen and I have lived and loved together, and
how blessed we still are in each other's society, and in the promising young sci-
ons that are growing up about us" (Brontë, 490). Again, then, it is nineteenth-century marriage that facilitates the larger cultural hauntings.

According to Nickianne Moody, nineteenth-century ghost stories provide
their authors with a way of exploring the underside of culture we may wish to
deny. For the Victorian woman writer in particular it was marriage that epito-
mized this underside, often leading to abuse, self-denial, a living death. Helen
Graham, married to the boorish, womanizing drunk Arthur Huntingdon,
epitomizes that plight while confronting Victorian patriarchy with its own un-
acceptable face. Arguably, in fact, Wildfell Hall represents in architectural
form the double standards of Victorian marriage, being "venerable and picturesque to look at, but doubtless, cold and gloomy enough to inhabit, with its
thick stone mullions and little latticed panes, its time-eaten air-holes, and its
too lonely, too unsheltered situation" (Brontë, 45). And yet, though the mansion attracts "ghostly legends and dark traditions" (Brontë, 46), and despite
Gilbert's old childhood nurse referring to it as "the haunted hall" (Brontë, 46),
Stevie Davies insists that "neither uncanny presences, violent usurpation nor
extremes of possessive hatred and need haunt [it]" (Davies, x). I disagree:
though no creeping figure clanking chains paces its corridors, Helen herself
continually associates Wildfell Hall with "the *haunting* dread of discovery"
(Brontë, 397; emphasis added), her place of refuge being continually threat-

ened by exposures of a variety of kinds that, though taking no very clear shape, always cohere around what Moody sees as the most affecting phantom of all: "a return of . . . the past" (Moody, 77). Nor is it only following their separation that Helen makes such connections. In the opening to the middle section of the novel, when her liaison with Arthur still takes the shape of a clandestine or furtive secret, Arthur surprises Helen as she takes a solitary walk, her immediate response being to compare him with an "unexpected . . . apparition" that, she muses, she might have attributed to "the creation of an over-excited imagination, had the sense of sight alone borne witness to his presence" (Brontë, 187).

The Tenant of Wildfell Hall is, therefore, a story about specters, but, in addition, its very structure is "ghosted" in a similar manner to *Great Expectations*. In both novels, we read the story of a woman (Miss Haversham/Helen Graham), closeted away from society until her story is not only told by a fictitious male (Pip/Gilbert Markham) but told in the guise of being a story about him. In Brontë's case, of course, there is a further layer of irony in that Acton Bell, the false signatory, ghosts the shadow-self of Anne Brontë, telling her story as if it were also "his" own. Like Brontë herself, Helen signs her work (here painting) with a false signature but has an even more slippery relationship with names than her author. Beginning the novel as Mrs. Graham, entry into her journal severs her from any reference to the patronymic altogether, her name being concealed behind the pseudonymous "I." Though we later, through our own inference, realize that her maiden name must have been Helen Lawrence (for we discover eventually that she is sister to Frederick Lawrence), the schism with her father—repeatedly hinted at but never fully explained—casts doubt even upon this, she being separated from the family home and brought up by her aunt and uncle. Her first marriage names her as Helen Huntingdon, but, on leaving Arthur, she adopts her mother's maiden name returning, again, to the name Mrs. Graham. Finally, of course, Helen the wife of our frame narrator must also be Helen Markham, though we never encounter this name in print.

In fact, Brontë continually stresses the enforced relationship between closeted duplicity and female creativity, the most significant illustration of the theme occurring early on and, once again, in the context of Helen's courtship with Arthur Huntingdon. Nervously watching Arthur scrutinize her work, Helen muses:

So far, so good;—but, hearing him pronounce, *sotto voce*, but with peculiar emphasis concerning one of the pieces, "THIS is better than all!'—I looked up, curious to see which it was, and, to my horror, beheld him complacently gazing at the back of the picture—It was his own face that I had sketched there and forgotten to rub out! . . .

Then, drawing a candle close to his elbow, he gathered all the drawings to himself . . . and muttering, "I must look at *both* sides now," he eagerly commenced an examination. . . . I was sure that, with that one unfortunate exception, I had carefully obliterated all such witnesses of my infatuation. But the pencil frequently leaves an impression upon cardboard that no amount of rubbing can efface. Such, it seems, was the case with most of these; and I confess I trembled when I saw him holding them so close to the candle, and poring so intently over the seeming blanks. (Brontë, 171–172)

Significantly, Chapter 18, in which this scene takes place, is titled "The Miniature," for here we have, in microcosm, the true significance of the specter to women's writing of the period. Ghosting the surface lies a coded subtext, or palimpsest, signaling risk, danger, but also the necessity of taking a chance if women were to fill the "seeming blanks" of women's intervention into the nineteenth-century literary marketplace.

If these novels are not, then, exactly ghost stories, they are stories about the ghosts of Victorian culture. S. L. Varnado observes that "in the most common ghost stories, the human protagonist is often an innocent victim . . . [or] a harmless, conventional individual . . . sitting quietly in an easy chair" (3). Though the first part of this quotation applies equally well to Pip and Helen Graham, the second most clearly sums up Brontë's frame narrator, Gilbert Markham. These characters are not particularly extraordinary in themselves, and although all three become embroiled in extraordinary stories, the central theme—the destructiveness of Victorian marriage—is ordinary enough. Gary Day claims it to be less specters themselves that unsettle readers of ghost stories and more "the absence, or nothingness, from which they emerge" (28). Few "voids" carry more resonance than the echoing structures of Dickens's ironically named Satis House, promising fulfilment while offering an apparently never-ending emptiness. Few "career choices" promised nineteenth-century middle-class heroines like Helen Graham more, while giving them less, than the double-standards of Victorian marriage.

WORKS CITED AND SELECTED WORKS FOR FURTHER READING

Botting, Fred. *Gothic*. London: Routledge, 1996.

Bronfen, Elisabeth. *Over Her Dead Body: Death, Femininity, and the Aesthetic*. Manchester: Manchester UP, 1992.

Brontë, Anne. *The Tenant of Wildfell Hall*. Ed. G. D. Hargreaves. London: Penguin, 1979.

Buse, Peter, and Andrew Stott, eds. *Ghosts: Deconstruction, Psychoanalysis, History*. London: Macmillan, 1999.

Byron, Glennis, and David Punter, eds. *Spectral Readings: Towards a Gothic Geography*. London: Macmillan, 1999.

Calder, Angus. "Appendix A: The End of the Novel." In *Great Expectations*, by Charles Dickens, pp. 494–96. Ed. Angus Calder. London: Penguin, 1965.

Davies, Stevie. Introduction. In *The Tenant of Wildfell Hall*, by Anne Brontë, pp. vii–xxxii. London: Penguin, 1996.

Day, Gary. "Figuring Out the Signalman: Dickens and the Ghost Story." In *Nineteenth-Century Suspense: From Poe to Conan Doyle*, pp. 26–45. Ed. Clive Bloom, et al. London: Macmillan, 1988.

Dickens, Charles. *Great Expectations*. Ed. Angus Calder. London: Penguin, 1965.

Gilbert, R. A. "Ghost Stories." in *The Handbook to Gothic Literature*, pp. 68–69. Ed. Marie Mulvey-Roberts. London: Macmillan, 1998.

Goodwin, Sarah Webster, and Elisabeth Bronfen, eds. *Death and Representation*. Baltimore: Johns Hopkins UP, 1993.

Graham, Kenneth W., ed. *Gothic Fictions: Prohibition/Transgression*. New York: AMS, 1989.

Moody, Nickianne. "Visible Margins: Women Writers and the English Ghost Story." In *Image and Power: Women in Fiction in the Twentieth Century*, pp. 77–90. Ed. Sarah Sceats and Gail Cunningham. London: Longman, 1996.

Poe, Edgar Allan. "The Oval Portrait." In *The Fall of the House of Usher and Other Writings: Poems, Tales, Essays and Reviews*, pp. 250–253. Ed. David Galloway. London: Penguin, 1986.

Punter, David, ed. *A Companion to the Gothic*. Oxford: Blackwell, 2000.

———. *Gothic Pathologies: The Text, the Body, and the Law*. London: Macmillan, 1998.

———. *The Literature of Terror: A History of Gothic Fictions from 1765 to the Present Day—Vol. 1: The Gothic Tradition*. 2nd ed. London: Longman, 1996.

Varnado, S. L. *Haunted Presence: The Numinous in Gothic Fiction*. Tuscaloosa: U of Alabama P, 1987.

The Victorian Gothic

Peter J. Kitson

DEFINING GOTHIC

In terms of its mass appeal as a cultural phenomenon, the Gothic novel has probably three high points: Mary Shelley's *Frankenstein* (1818), Robert Louis Stevenson's *The Strange Case of Dr. Jekyll and Mr. Hyde* (1886), and probably the most weirdly epiphanic of all, Bram Stoker's *Dracula* (1897). This eerie triumvirate, however, conceals a long-running and reflexive tradition of imaginative writing. *Dracula* and *Jekyll and Hyde*, written just over a hundred years ago, are both belated texts in that they are responses to a resurgence of cultural unease in the latter half of Victoria's reign. They, along with many other similar fictions, function as a revivification of a form of novel unfashionable and largely moribund since the mid-1820s when the last great Gothic novel of the old stamp, Charles Maturin's *Melmoth the Wanderer* (1826), made its appearance. Both the styles and subject matter of *Dracula* and *Jekyll and Hyde* hark back to an older kind of writing.

The Gothic novel used to be regarded as a popular form of fiction that did not require a great deal of critical exegesis. In recent years, however, there has been a huge increase in critical interest in this form of writing that has been rediscovered, redefined, and subjected to just about every possible critical approach possible—Marxist, cultural, poststructural, and psychoanalytical. The redefinition carried out by a series of critics of the genre has widened our understanding of the term, extending its range beyond the narrowly novelistic to encompass the range of genres from, and including, poetry and melodrama (see Botting; Mighall; Miles). Gothic is no longer constrained to a form; it can also be regarded as a mode or kind of treatment of a subject that is apparent in the works of writers such as Sir Walter Scott, Charles Dickens, Charlotte and Emily Brontë, and the sensation novel and detective fiction of Wilkie Collins, Mrs. Henry Wood, and Mary Elizabeth Braddon. However, the origins of the term "Gothic" as applied to the novel lie back in the late eighteenth century, and it is important to realize that Victorian Gothic is not an original form but a rediscovery of modes of fiction that had become less popular by the mid-1820s.

There are many definitions of "Gothic." Originally, it denoted the archaic and medieval, deriving from the late-eighteenth-century interest in pre-Reformation subjects and aesthetic styles as demonstrated in Richard Hurd's *Letters on Chivalry and Romance* (1762). This fashionable interest in medieval romance found its most influential voice in Horace Walpole's *The Castle of Otranto* (1764), allegedly a sixteenth-century manuscript of an eleventh-century tale of murder, usurpation, incestuous desire, persecuted maidens, ghosts, and supernatural events set in a labyrinthine Spanish castle. These gothic elements that Walpole crafted into a thrilling romance were to resurface throughout the history of Gothic writing, and they still appear, in different manifestations, in gothic fictions of today. Even in the years after *Otranto*, however, the Gothic was adapted by male and female writers to suit their own interests and audiences. Clara Reeve more or less abandoned the supernatural aspects of the form, concentrating on the historical dimensions in works such as *The Champion of Virtue* (1777). William Beckford grafted Gothic on to the fashionable interest in the East as a site of magic and desire, pioneering a kind of "Oriental Gothic" in his Arabian Night tale, *Vathek* (1786). Ann Radcliffe added substantial picturesque and sublime scenery to her tales of heroines persecuted by patriarchal oppressors in her more polite and highly literary novels *The Mysteries of Udolpho* (1794) and *The Italian* (1797), the latter bringing the novel close to the contemporary with its setting in the year 1756. Radcliffe eschewed the supernatural, preferring to explain apparent apparitions by natural explanations; not so the full-bloodied Gothic of Matthew Lewis's *The Monk* (1796) (and his poems and dramas), which dealt with the tormented Abbot Ambrosio, tempted by Satan to follow a downward slope of insatiate desire, until trapped into murdering, unknowingly, his own mother and raping his sister. Lewis's unabashed acceptance of the supernatural and his Romantic concern with the divided self in the character of the Ambrosio, outwardly the holiest man in Madrid, but inwardly a seething mass of perverse desire, would find echoes in Stoker's *Dracula* and Stevenson's *Dr. Jekyll and Mr. Hyde*. Mary Shelley's *Frankenstein* (1818), which like Radcliffe's fiction uses a nearly contemporary setting and deals with the unnatural, not the supernatural, comes toward the end of the first eruption of the Gothic upon the British literary scene. Shelley's concern is with anxieties concerning contemporary scientific debates rather than the medieval.

Another way to define Gothic is not to look in terms of the forms and content of the fictions, but rather to elucidate the effects these fictions have in raising the anxieties of its audience (see Moretti; Punter). Freud pioneered this approach in his critically influential essay on the "uncanny" *das Unheimliche* (1919). Freud argued that the unease, the feeling of the uncanny that certain kinds of occurrence or of literature occasions relates to our own repressed desires and fears, originating from the primal scene of the Oedipal family romance. Certainly, there are recurrent themes and subjects that unify Gothic from its earliest to its present-day manifestations. Themes such as disease, infection, transgressive or taboo desires (incest, homosexuality), madness, monstrosity, xenophobia, and so on are common in Gothic, appealing to different forms of transhistorical anxieties. Subjects including hauntings, doubles, vampires, demonic females, patriarchal tyrants, old labyrinthine houses, castles, cities, and so on are common in Gothic writing. Also recurrent is the fragmented or confusing narrative structure of these tales, often readily creating anxiety and uncertaintly, the true test of what Tzvetan Todorov refers to as the fantastic (Todorov). Gothic narratives often take their form from the style of Gothic architecture and landscape gardening with an overall unity masked by digressions, detours, and prolixity. They are frequently told through multiple narrators with no comforting third-person authorial presence, and they are usually distanced from the reader by a series of narrative frames.

THE GOTHIC REVIVAL

If the Gothic novel was less apparent after the 1820s, it did not disappear. It survived as a form of popular melodrama and also in the working-class fictions of the penny dreadfuls, such as *Varney the Vampyre: or, the Feast of Blood* (1846) (Frayling, *Vampires*; James). It was to find a home in the writing of Edgar Allan Poe, Nathaniel Hawthorne, and others in America. It survived as a mode in the writings of the Brontë sisters, whose heroes Edmund Rochester and Heathcliff owe much to the traditions of the Gothic hero-villain. It abounds in the works of Charles Dickens who replaces the Gothic abbeys and castles with the labyrinth of the fog-bound and decaying city of London in numerous novels, such as *Bleak House* (1852–53), *Little Dorrit* (1855–57), and, darkest and most Gothic of all, *Our Mutual Friend* (1864–65). So too are the excesses of gothic melodrama present in his fictions of concealed crimes and mistaken or disguised identities. The spur to the revival of Gothic writing, however, was applied most obviously by sensation novelist and friend of Dickens, Wilkie Collins, whose *The Woman in White* (1859) began a literary fashion that led to the return of the full-bloodied Gothic in the later nineteenth century. Collins revived the narrative style of the epistolary novel, much used by the early Gothic writers to tell his tale of a corrupt baronet, Sir Percival Glyde who, born a bastard, is not the true heir to his estate and who has falsely imprisoned his wife, "Anne Catherick," in a lunatic asylum. The text is pieced together by the narrator and editor-investigator Walter Hartright, who attempts to solve the mystery with which he is confronted. It is composed like a legal case, including a number of genuine legal documents, such as medical records and birth, marriage, and death certificates, a style of novel writing Stoker's *Dracula* was to imitate. Collins's novel contains several other stalwarts of the gothic genre—the doubles of the two women, Anne and Laura, and the cultured, charismatic, and dangerous villain, the elephantine, anarchistic Count Fosco whose inordinate fondness for his pet mice conceals a vicious, ruthless, and cruel nature. Fosco, representing the foreign and dangerous, appealed to that odd mixture of xenophobic repulsion and exotic admiration that was also to be enkindled in Stoker's East European vampire count. So too is the setting of the novel largely Gothic, in the lowering gloom of Sir Percival's estate, Blackwater Park. *The Woman in White* is widely and justifiably regarded as the first novel of its kind. Among Collins's many other novels, *The Moonstone* (1860), an investigation of the plundering criminal policies of British India, with its themes of oriental vengeance, also prefigures the Imperial Gothic, which reaches its climax in the work of Sir Henry Rider Haggard. *The Moonstone* also applies ideas from the new science of criminal anthropology, which would inform Abraham Van Helsing's racial-criminal categorization of *Dracula* and the detective fiction of Sherlock Holmes.

Dickens and Collins to some extent domesticated the Gothic novel and brought it into the sphere of Victorian family relations, exploiting Victorian middle-class fears of the social and political forces that constrained and threatened their lives. Collins's massive sales encouraged others to write sensation and neo-Gothic fiction. Perhaps the first, true Victorian neo-Gothic novel was that by the Anglo-Irish writer Joseph Sheridan LeFanu. LeFanu, a product of the same Anglo-Irish Protestant ascendancy that had produced Maturin, was to write a novel with an unmistakably Gothic theme, *Uncle Silas* (1864–65), and to contribute one of the most haunting examples of the nineteenth-century demonic female, the beautiful but languid vampiress, the Countess Mircalla Karnstein. *Uncle Silas* tells the story of Maud Ruthyn, who, on the death of her father is obliged to go and live with Silas, her uncle. Silas is an ill and gloomy religious fanatic who had been ostracized by his family because of some past misdeed, possibly relating to an unexplained murder. His gloomy and forbidding house, Bartram-Haugh, contains his rough and unpleasant son, and a monstrous governess, Madame de Rougierre.

LeFanu's most famous Gothic creation, however, belongs to a series of supernatural tales, many collected in 1872 under the title *In a Glass Darkly* (Auerbach; Briggs; Gelder). This collection preempts the kind of psychoanalytic practice that Freud was later to pioneer, in that the tales are allegedly the case histories of one German physician of the mind, Dr. Martin Hesselius, the editor of the text being his young, unnamed medical secretary. The ghost stories are genuinely disturbing and weird; the best of them—"Green Tea," "The Familiar," "Mr. Justice Harbottle," and "The Room in the Dragon Volant"— concern eruptions into everyday life of unpleasant supernatural creatures, such as the malevolent monkey that possesses the narrator of "Green Tea." However, it is the novella "Carmilla" that is most striking for its quasi-sympathetic treatment of a vampire. The tale is told by Laura, a young woman, the daughter of an English father and an East European mother, now deceased. Laura recounts events that took place ten years ago at her home in a Styrian schloss, and recalls how she was bewitched and mesmerized by a beautiful young woman, Carmilla, who is deposited at her home as the result of an arranged traveling accident. Laura both loves and fears Carmilla, an aristocratic vampire who devotes herself to her new victim. LeFanu's sensitive and highly eroticized depiction of the vampire's embraces, told from Laura's point of view, are new to vampire fiction. Ultimately, Carmilla's true identity is revealed as the Countess Mircalla Karnstein, and she is dispatched by a posse of male professionals in a brutally clinical climax, but her influence on the adult Laura still persists as the memories of her strange lover haunt her in the present. The tale is also notable for the character of Baron Vordenberg, an ugly and unprepossessing figure, the first vampirologist in Gothic fiction and the ancestor of Stoker's Van Helsing.

LeFanu's tale of transgressive desires and fears may have appealed to the repressed areas of Victorian life. Another text that depicted the repression of middle-class Victorian professional men was Robert Louis Stevenson's *The Strange Case of Dr. Jekyll and Mr. Hyde* (1886). Stevenson, who grew up in a Scottish Calvinist household, knew himself the tensions existing between outward conformity and inner desires. His fable of a divided self updated the career of Matthew Lewis's damned monk Ambrosio in the context of Victorian society, replacing medieval labyrinthine buildings and the temptations of the Devil with the urban Gothic of London and the possibilities of science. Henry Jekyll is a complacent and likeable middle-aged medical man who discovers a potion that allows him to free his other self (though Jekyll muses that the number of selves may be multiple rather than twofold). In the character of the indescribable but unforgettable young man, Edward Hyde, Jekyll commits a series of, largely unnamed, misdemeanors, the most horrific of which are the brutal assault and stamping of a child and the vicious murder of an apparently harmless old gentleman, the MP Danvers Carew.

The story is told with an extraordinary degree of narrative panache as Stevenson adopts a fragmented and multiple narrative style to develop his plot. Half the tale belongs to a dramatized but unnamed narrator (not Stevenson) who filters the events through the mind of the lawyer Utterson, a man similarly tormented by his own unrealized desires; a man who enjoys the theater but has not seen a play for twenty years and who has a taste for fine wine, which he mortifies by imbibing gin. The latter half of the novella belongs to the poignantly fragmenting self of Henry Jekyll as he details his initial excitement and pleasure in Hyde's disguise, followed by his horror and despair as he loses control of the fortress of his identity to the younger and powerful resurgent alter ego. Stevenson's story disturbs by problematizing our notions of a stable identity that in Jekyll's case is fluid and multiple. The novella has been interpreted in a variety of ways. The Victorians themselves saw the tale as one of good and evil, demonstrating the traditional Christian conflict between the body and the soul. Freudian critics see *Jekyll and Hyde* as preempting Freud's division of the human psyche into a conscious and social scheme of morality, the Super-Ego, and a collection of primal and atavistic desires, the Id. Other critics have seen the Hyde as a representative of more specific Victorian anxieties. The ugly, deformed, apelike, but sprightly young man has been seen as reflecting Victorian fears about Darwinian evolutionary theories of humanity's descent from the ape, or about fears of the newly enfranchised working classes. Most recently, the hysterical Hyde, with his light and tripping step, has been interpreted as homosexual rough trade, representing the unmarried and middle-aged Jekyll's own repressed homosexuality (see Frayling, *Nightmare*; Herdman; Showalter, *Sexual Anarchy*; Veeder and Hirsch). However one interprets Stevenson's story of the duality of humanity, the shimmering ambiguities of the text defies any authoritative or final reading.

THE 1890S

In the 1890s, the form of the Victorian neo-Gothic novel appeared in its most characteristic forms. The reasons for this are complex and speculative, but it is clear that, in *fin de siècle*, certain anxieties and uncertainties were fueling its success (Arata; Dijkstra; Ledger; Stott). The end of the century brought with it the kinds of uneasiness that is common at such times with the feeling that things were becoming worn out and breaking down. Concerns about the sorts of decadence that corrupted the Roman Empire were apparent in a number of contemporary scandals. The British Empire, which dominated roughly one quarter of the world's surface, also brought with it anxieties about contamination, especially in the context of growing resistance by subject peoples. Fears of economic depression and the imperial rivalry of German and the United States also fed this uncertainty. This was to lead to the growth of the subgenre of the Gothic novel, Imperial Gothic, and its most celebrated manifestations in Rider Haggard's *She* (1886) and Bram Stoker's haunting *Jewel of Seven Stars* (1903).

In the domestic sphere, there were anxieties treating to the emergence of new political and social trends, the growth of unionism, and the phenomenon of the "New Woman." The figure of the demonic female, a supernatural and powerful creature feeding off the life force of the male, figures prominently in literature of this period in a number of works, plays, and poems. Most argue that the literary representations of this creature are a kind of demonization by worried males of those independent women who appeared at the turn of the century, refusing to play the role of Victorian wife and mother. This newly articulated feminine consciousness is apparent in Sarah Grand's *The Heavenly Twins* (1893), which coined the term "New Woman." This woman espoused the cause of female autonomy and eschewed Victorian beliefs in domestic and maternal values, challenging the marriage and divorce laws and arguing for sexual and social autonomy for women, for their access to higher education and to the professions. The deadly, poisonous, and sexually aggressive females of 1890s Gothic may well represent fears of challenges made by this "New Woman" to Victorian patriarchal culture.

A newly emergent form of female sexuality was not the only challenge to Victorian patriarchal values in the period. If women were behaving as men, men were also becoming tainted with female traits. We have already noted Edward Hyde's proneness to hysteric outbursts, and certainly fears about the emasculation and feminization of men were rife in the 1890s, occasioned, in part, by the Aesthetic and Decadent artistic movements that argued for a submission to feeling and pleasure rather than the stoic brand of Christian manliness that predominated in the Victorian masculine ideal. Homosexuality, a taboo desire exploited by Gothic writing, was under investigation. The term "sexual inversion" enters discourse in the period in such texts as John Addington Symonds's *A Problem in Greek Ethics* (1883), Edward Carpenter's *Homogenic Love* (1894), and Havelock Ellis's *Sexual Inversion* (published, then suppressed in 1893). The phenomenon of "male hysteria" is discussed by the new breed of professional doctors of the mind, like Freud. The 1890s Gothic clearly responds to these fears about the feminization of males and the blurring of socially constructed gender boundaries.

The widespread sense of cultural malaise in the 1890s found confirmation in contemporary scientific theories of degeneration. Evolutionary theories, popularized by the Darwinian materialist, Thomas Henry Huxley, had postulated that humanity was descended from the ape-kind with no special, providential design or morality attaching to the species. The boundary between human and animal was confused. Karl Marx's economic theories postulated the catastrophic collapse of the capitalist system which underpinned Victorian prosperity, as well as argued for a kind of economic determinism subversive of Victorian moral and spiritual values. Freud's theories of the "unconscious" motivations that determine human actions—chiefly, though not exclusively, sexual—added to this unease. Of course, if individuals and societies could evolve, they could also degenerate, and this notion of the "degeneration" of individuals, races, and societies was to haunt the late Victorian period. The discourses of degeneration spanned many fields, including economics, anthropology, psychiatry, eugenics, and criminology. In particular, the criminal anthropology of Cesare Lombroso used the "science" of phrenology to argue that there were in existence determinable physical types, habitual criminals, throwbacks to primitive racial groupings (see Arata; Mighall). Lombroso's theories were utilized by Max Nordau, who in *Degeneration* (1895), argued that a general racial and artistic regression was occurring, attacking contemporary artists for their excessive fostering of emotion and feeling. Both the theories of Nordau and Lombroso inform Stoker's characterization of Dracula and figure in Van Helsing's attempt to make sense of the polymorphously perverse vampire.

Practically all the fears and anxieties of the 1890s are contained in Bram Stoker's extraordinary novel *Dracula*, published in the sixtieth year of Victoria's reign. Stoker, like Maturin and LeFanu, was an Anglo-Irish writer (Frayling, *Nightmare*; Glover). He was born in Dublin and educated at Trinity College. Though his early profession was as a civil servant at Dublin Castle, Stoker had an artistic and imaginative side to his life, demonstrated by his adoration for the great Victorian actor manager, Sir Henry Irving. Stoker met Irving in 1876 and shortly afterwards became his manager at the Lyceum Theatre, London, functioning as his general factotum. *Dracula* famously originated in a dream Stoker had in 1890 in which he was menaced by three women, who were interrupted by the intrusion of a commanding male figure claiming "This man belongs to me!" The sexual anxieties of this dream were to resurface in the famous scene of Jonathan Harker's menacing by Dracula's brides and the hint of male homosexual desire in Dracula's proprietary claim on the recumbent male.

Dracula is the quintessential Victorian neo-Gothic novel. It has all the hallmarks of the tradition from whence it sprang, updated for a late-nineteenth-century world of science and technology. The narrative style of the novel betrays its origins by its use of multiple narrators. The novel purports to be a collection of letters, journals, newspaper cuttings, telegrams, and legal and other documents, in the manner of Collins's *Woman in White*. These documents have been collected and, in some cases retyped and reconstructed, by the industrious Mina Harker as a record of the Count's invasion. The only main character who does not have a voice is, of course, Dracula himself, a figure of excess and multiple forms. The novel is very contemporary, beginning with Jonathan Harker's journey to Castle Dracula on 3 May 1893. Harker's journal is wonderfully ambiguous as we leave the certainties of the Western world with its science and progress to embark on a long journey into the heart of East Europe where "every known superstition in the world is gathered into the horseshoe of the Carpathian mountains" (Stoker, 32). It is here that all the values of Victorian reason break down, weird things happen, phantasmic blue lights appear, people seem to be transparent, mirrors cast no reflection, and Harker enters a world of the irrational where dreaming and reality merge into each other and where the normal routines of everyday are reversed. It is here that Harker meets Dracula, that embodiment of all the fears, anxieties, and repressed desires of the Victorian age. Dracula is apparently near immortal, 476 years old. At the beginning of the novel he is an ancient racial other, defined in terms of his physical and animal characteristics. His nose is "aquiline," his ears are "extremely" pointed, his hands are hairy on the palm, his mouth conceals rodentlike "sharp white teeth" (48). Dracula is an aristocrat, the once "Voivode" of Wallachia, a brutal and ruthless, but Christian, soldier who fought for the country he led against the Turks, before somehow becoming a vampire (the text is not explicit on this point). Dracula, who fought to maintain the borders of Christianity against the Islamic empire, now becomes engaged in a process of reverse colonization as, exhausting the blood of his own lands, he seeks to move from the margins back to the nineteenth-century imperial center London and to found his own dark empire (Arata; Brantlinger). If Dracula crystallizes fears of reverse colonization and racial threat, his body provides proof of racial degeneration. He is a throwback to a primitive and criminal race, antagonistic to the contemporary science and progress that must unite in all its manifestations to defeat him. Toward the end of the novel this apparently supernatural and powerful demon is reduced to the categories of the current theories of criminal anthropology. Mina, parroting what she has learned from Van Helsing, scientifically reduces Dracula to the types of the criminal anthropology: "The Count is a criminal and of a criminal type. Nordau and Lombroso would so classify him" (Stoker, 383).

Dracula functions as a dark mirror within which are reflected the other sides of the Victorian imperial project. But the novel is not simply Imperial Gothic. In his depiction of female characters, Stoker also taps into the concerns of the day. The two main women in the novel differ. Lucy Westernra (a significant name, given the novel's imperial theme) is the white woman every foreigner allegedly would like to possess. But she is also culpable in the novel's scheme. She is a little flighty and a debutante. She attracts the attention of several men and muses that she would like to marry all, if the law would allow. She becomes Dracula's first Western victim on his arrival in Whitby. Soon transformed into a vampire, she becomes a sexually voracious and predatory creature. She rejects the Victorian ideal of womanhood as the "angel in the house" and preys on children. Ultimately, she must be exorcised and staked in a disturbingly violent scene in which her intended husband, Arthur Godalming, the perfect Victorian bourgeoisie aristocrat, transfixes her in a grim parody of the marital scene, restoring her purity and virtue. Mina Harker, of course, is the perfect Victorian woman—almost. She becomes Jonathan's wife after his return and nurses him back to health. At the end of the novel she produces a child, Quincey Harker. She is an assistant schoolmistress then helpmate to Jonathan and the vampire hunters, making clear that she is not one of those "New Women" writers who "some day will start an idea that men and women should be allowed to see each other asleep before proposing or accepting" and who will "do the proposing herself" (Stoker, 89). Aware of her own fallen nature, she accepts the rationale of her pollution by Dracula, a victim who participates in the blame of an attack she does not consciously wish. Mina is herself somewhat masculine and, indeed, Van Helsing acknowledges that she is at times, more than woman, possessed of "a man's brain."

The attractions and repulsion of the demonic female are also dramatized in Harker's encounter with Dracula's vampire brides. Disobeying the Count's injunction not to wander freely in the castle by night, Harker comes across three female vampires, two dark and one fair. Though disturbed by the women, Harker is also clearly aroused, feeling a "wicked, burning desire that they would kiss me with those red lips." The fair girl, whose face Harker seems to know "in connection with some dreamy fear," advances first (Stoker, 69). The girl's Saxon features, out of context with the racial distinctness of the other vampires, and Harker's vague preknowledge of them, has led many to suggest an Oedipal reading for the passage. These demons with their human forms and animal desires are interrupted by the Count who compensates them for their disappointment with a half-smothered child he has stolen. Rather than succor the child with mother's milk and care, the women feed off it, draining it of blood, heedless later of the mother's agony. Harker cannot pity the woman as "she was better dead" now that she is no longer a mother. Stoker was to return to the theme of the powerful, supernatural woman in his later adventure tale *The Lady of the Shroud* (1902), the Egyptian romance *Jewel of Seven Stars* (1903), and in his final novel *The Lair of the White Worm* (1911), a deeply misogynist and racist work, telling of the career of Lady Arabella March, female temptress and serpent creature.

Dracula is also a novel about masculinity, a key theme of 1890s Gothic. To counter the incursions of the Eastern, irrational forces into the contemporary Victorian world, the West has to reply with a coalition of attributes. The posse that tracks down Dracula is white, Anglo-Saxon, scientific, professional, and modern: Harker is a lawyer, Seward a psychiatrist, Holmwood a bourgeois Lord, and Quincey P. Morris an American. The bizarre Abraham Van Helsing who shares much in common with Dracula (his arcane knowledge and his idiomatic English) heads the group. As well as awakening the dormant sexuality of the women, *Dracula* also renders the men feminine. His possession of the lunatic R. M. Renfield turns him into a coquettish and jealous masochist, only redeemed by the return of his heterosexual passion for Mina, which leads him to face down Dracula for the first and last time. Dracula paralyzes Harker when he steals into the couple's marital bed and assaults her. In the castle itself, Dracula claims Harker as his property, "This man belongs to me!" and he earlier makes a grab at Harker's throat when the latter cuts himself shaving. Dracula prefers females, but he desires all blood and like all vampires is "bisexual." Stoker, who adored Irving despite the abuse and humiliations visited on him, must himself have wondered about his own possible homosexual feelings, demonstrated in the shock he felt after awakening from the dream of Dracula (Craft; Frayling, *Nightmare*).

Such fears and uncertainties about the male self and its coherence in the 1890s are also reflected in Oscar Wilde's treatment of the double theme in *The Picture of Dorian Gray* (1890), though from a markedly different perspective. Wilde uses the tale of a beautiful young man who is granted his wish to remain young while his alter ego, a portrait, ages, to explore ideas about art and life. The novella derives from Wilde's interest and commitment to the Aestheticism of Walter Pater and Decadence of Baudelaire and Huysman. The innocence of Gray is framed alongside the morality of the tormented artist, Basil Hallward, who paints the portrait and is clearly in love with its subject, and the irresistibly cynical dandy, Lord Henry Wooton, who teaches Gray that the only proper object in life is the pursuit of beauty. As Gray succumbs to the temptations supplied by Wooton, he is led into a life of decadence, an immorality the signs of which mark his portrait but not his person. On this downward slope of decadence, Dorian commits several unnamed acts of depravity leading to the murder of Hallward in a fit of rage. Shocked by his own cruelty and enraged by the power of the portrait, Gray finally dies in an attempt to destroy it. Much of the novella's power resides in Wilde's depiction of the hypocrisies of Victorian society as wealth and status cloak vice and immorality, as well as the fatalistic logic of human sin.

IMPERIAL GOTHIC

We have seen how Stoker's *Dracula* deals with fears of racial degeneration and reverse colonization and how it exploits the *fin-de-siècle* concern with the demonic female. Such fears found memorable expression in an earlier text, the extraordinary *She* (1887) by Sir Henry H. Rider Haggard (Brantlinger). Haggard, who spent much of his life in South Africa at the time of the Zulu Wars and the first Boer War, constructed a narrative about an immortal, powerful, and beautiful woman, the ruler of a forgotten civilization in the heart of Africa. The story is told by Ludwig Horace Holly, a highly intelligent but abnormally ugly character who befriends a handsome young man, Leo Vincey. Leo's ancestry is traced back to ancient times, his lineage descending from a priest of Isis, Kallikrates. The two men, along with Leo's faithful servant, Job, go on a quest relating to the Vincey family legend detailing the existence of the beautiful white queen in central Africa. After a series of adventures and an encounter with the cannibal Amahagger people, in which the trio are nearly eaten, they arrive at the ancient kingdom of Kôr ruled over by Ayesha, "*She-who-must-be-obeyed.*" It transpires that Leo embodies her ancient lover Kallikrates and that She, by the power of her will, has called Leo back to reincarnate this lover. Once this occurs, She will confer immortality on him by bathing in sacred flames and found an empire between them, invading the West. Like Dracula, Ayesha represents a demonic parody of the British Empire, replacing an allegedly liberal and progressive order with an absolutist and tyrannical regime. Ultimately the flame robs Ayesha of her immortality, reducing her to the ghastly shape of a bestial and withered monkey.

The figure of the powerful, beautiful female who erupts from the past into the progressive present is also the subject of Bram Stoker's evocative and poignant *Jewel of Seven Stars* (1903), which exploits the romance and mystique of Egypt and the new science of Egyptology (Glover, 58–92). It concerns the attempts of an ancient Egyptian queen, Tera, to return to life in the present day through the body of a young woman, Margaret Trelawny, the daughter of the archaeologist who discovered her tomb. Like *Dracula*, the novel dramatizes the attempts of a group of professional men to unravel the mystery of the dead queen and to prevent her from accomplishing her purpose, which is to re-establish her kingdom. The narrator of the tale, Malcolm Ross, is a barrister infatuated with Margaret, who recounts the events of the novel in a dreamy and nostalgic manner. Tera, however, is an ambiguous figure, shadowy and herself a victim of the jealousy of male priests. The Egyptologist Trelawny, along with his sinister, estranged friend Corbeck, is conducting an experiment to resurrect Tera. Stoker's original ending for the tale was tragic and apocalyptic, with no sure sense of whether Tera had returned to life, or what the fate was of the experimenters. He was, however, obliged to replace it with a happier ending in which the restored Margaret and Ross wed.

Imperial Gothic was a pervasive mode in the late nineteenth and early twentieth centuries. It features in a number of works from Richard Marsh's *The Beetle* (1897), the tale of an eastern mystery cult with its strange leading member, a creature of androgynous appearance who metamorphosizes into a giant beetle and back, to the colonial and imperial fictions of Joseph Conrad and Rudyard Kipling. In tales such as "The Phantom Rickshaw" and "The Mark of the Beast," Kipling figured India as the site of the uncanny. Conrad's Kurtz from *Heart of Darkness* (1900) is himself a kind of Dracula figure, a Christian warrior sent to the frontiers of the empire who is corrupted, sending back a message of primal savagery and moral confusion.

Victorian Gothic, therefore, was a many-splintered thing, fashioned from all kinds of cultural fears and anxieties. It was a synthetic form, combining the established traditions of earlier Gothic with the recent innovations of sensation fiction, marketing these attributes for a Victorian-reading public both awed and exhilarated by the process of change and improvement but terrified by fears of degeneration and decay. Victorian Gothic deals with the darker sides of the Victorian mind, those anxieties and desires that could not find open expression in the contemporary climate.

WORKS CITED AND SELECTED WORKS FOR FURTHER READING

Arata, Stephen. *Fictions of Loss in the Victorian Fin de Siècle.* Cambridge: Cambridge UP, 1996.

Auerbach, Nina. *Our Vampires, Ourselves.* Chicago: U of Chicago P, 1995.

Barreca, Regina, ed. *Sex and Death in Victorian Literature.* London: Macmillan, 1990.

Bloom, Clive, ed. *Nineteenth-Century Suspense from Poe to Conan Doyle.* London: Macmillan, 1988.

Botting, Fred. *Gothic.* London: Routledge, 1996.

Brantlinger, Patrick. *Rule of Darkness: British Literature and Imperialism, 1830–1914.* Ithaca: Cornell UP, 1988.

Briggs, Julia. *Night Visitors: The Rise and Fall of the English Ghost Story.* London: Faber and Faber, 1977.

Byron, Glennis, ed. *Dracula: Contemporary Critical Essays.* London: Macmillan, 1999.

Carter, Margaret L. *Dracula: The Vampire and the Critics.* Ann Arbor: UMI Research, 1988.

Craft, Christopher. *Another Kind of Love: Male Homosexual Desire in English Discourse, 1850–1920.* Berkeley: U of California P, 1994.

Dijkstra, Bram. *Idols of Perversity: Fantasies of Feminine Evil in Fin-de-Siècle Culture.* Oxford: Oxford UP, 1986.

Frayling, Christopher. *Nightmare: The Birth of Horror.* London: BBC Books, 1996.

————. *Vampires: Lord Byron to Count Dracula.* London: Faber and Faber, 1991.

Gelder, Ken. *Reading the Vampire.* London: Routledge, 1994.

Glover, David. *Vampires, Mummies and Liberals: Bram Stoker and the Politics of Popular Fiction.* Durham: Duke UP, 1996.

Heath, Stephen. "Psychopathia Sexualis: Stevenson's Strange Case." *Critical Quarterly* 28.1–2 (1986): 93–108.

Herdman, John. *The Double in Nineteenth-Century Fiction.* London: Macmillan, 1990.

James, Louis. *Fiction for the Working Man, 1830–1850.* Oxford: Oxford UP, 1958.

Ledger, Sally. *The New Woman: Fiction and Feminism at the Fin de Siècle.* Manchester: Manchester UP, 1997.

Malchow, H. L. *Gothic Images of Race in Nineteenth-Century Britain.* Stanford: Stanford UP, 1996.

Marsh, Richard. *The Beetle.* Ed. William Baker. Dover: Alan Sutton, 1998.

Mighall, Robert. *A Geography of Victorian Gothic Fiction: Mapping History's Nightmares.* Oxford: Oxford UP, 1999.

Miles, Robert. *Gothic Writing, 1750–1820: A Genealogy.* Manchester: Manchester UP, 1993.

Moretti, Franco. *Signs Taken for Wonders: Essays in the Sociology of Literary Forms.* London: Verso, 1988.

Punter, David. *The Literature of Terror.* 2 vols. 2nd ed. Harlow: Longman, 1996.

Showalter, Elaine. *Sexual Anarchy: Gender and Culture at the Fin de Siècle.* London: Bloomsbury, 1990.

————, ed. *Daughters of Decadence: Women Writers of the Fin de Siècle.* London: Virago, 1993.

Spencer, Kathleen L. "Purity and Danger: *Dracula*, the Urban Gothic, and the Late Victorian Degeneracy Crisis." *ELH* 59.1 (1992): 197–225.

Stoker, Bram. *Dracula.* Ed. Glennis Byron. Peterborough: Broadview, 1998.

Stott, Rebecca. *The Fabrication of the Late-Victorian Femme Fatale: The Kiss of Death.* London: Macmillan, 1992.

Todorov, Tzvetan. *The Fantastic: A Structural Approach to a Literary Genre.* Ithaca: Cornell UP, 1975.

Veeder, William, and Gordon Hirsch, eds. *Dr. Jekyll and Mr. Hyde after One Hundred Years.* Chicago: U of Chicago P, 1988.

Victorian Detective Fiction

Lillian Nayder

Between September 1829 and May 1830, seven years before Queen Victoria ascended the throne, 2,906 uniformed constables of the newly established Metropolitan Police force took to the London streets, and their two commissioners established their offices in Scotland Yard; twelve years later, the Detective Department of the Metropolitan Police was formed (Emsley, 216; Tobias, 82–84). As these developments suggest, Victorians were preoccupied with the problem of crime, its prevention, and its detection, and their preoccupation helps to explain the creation and popularity of a new narrative subgenre: detective fiction. Living in what historians and critics have termed an "age of sensation" (Altick, 3), Victorians eagerly followed accounts of thefts, assaults, and murders in the daily press, crimes often reported in lurid detail (Boyle, 3–4). They read highly fictionalized reminiscences of police officers and became armchair detectives themselves as they puzzled through the tales of crime and exposure written by such novelists as Charles Dickens, Wilkie Collins, and Mary Elizabeth Braddon, among the dozens of authors who helped shape the new subgenre.

A hybrid form, Victorian detective fiction typically includes the figure of a sleuth, whether amateur or professional, but it cannot be neatly distinguished from sensation fiction, another product of the Victorian period. Rather, the two subgenres often merge in novels that sensationally expose crimes committed within respectable, middle-class homes and that reinvent the Gothic tradition by Anglicizing the villainous characters and schemes found in the works of Ann Radcliffe and Matthew Lewis, giving them a new and disturbing "proximity" to English readers (Hughes, 18).

As one Victorian reviewer advised the aspiring novelist of his day, "Let him only keep an eye on the criminal reports of the daily newspapers, marking the cases which are honored with the special notice of a leading article, and . . . he has the outline of his story not only ready-made, but approved beforehand as of the true sensation cast" (quoted in Altick, 157). Indeed, Victorian writers consistently drew on sensationalized criminal cases in producing their detective fiction, making use of the poisoners Pritchard and Palmer, among other notorious murderers, as Ian Ousby notes: "The Manning case is echoed in *Bleak House*, while the Constance Kent case gave Wilkie Collins several hints for the plot of *The Moonstone*" (81). Victorian detective fiction is indebted to the divorce court (established in 1858) as well as the criminal court, and a number of well-publicized cases of adultery and bigamy inform both Braddon's *Lady Audley's Secret* (1861–62) and Arthur Conan Doyle's tales of Sherlock Holmes. Drawing on famous detective figures in addition to notorious criminals and trials, Collins models Sergeant Cuff of *The Moonstone* (1868) on Inspector Jonathan Whicher of the Metropolitan Police, and Dickens models Mr. Bucket of *Bleak House* (1852–53) on Whicher's colleague, Inspector Charles Frederick Field.

Yet in searching for source materials and prototypes, we should not lose sight of the larger aims of Victorian detective fiction, which takes crime and policing as its theme but uses this theme to investigate a number of broader social issues: the origins and construction of social identity, for example, the integrity and violation of social boundaries, and the status of women. Thus in *The Law and the Lady* (1874), Collins draws on newspaper accounts of the alleged female poisoner, Madeleine Smith, whose 1857 trial for murdering her lover with arsenic ended with a Scottish verdict of "not proven," yet complicates Smith's case, using a lady poisoner to examine not only female criminality but also the oppression of women. His plotline hinges on the fact that arsenic was recommended as a beauty treatment for women with flawed complexions, connecting feminine ideals with self-destruction, and revealing the harm that Victorian women were apt to inflict on themselves when they felt unattractive, slighted, or wronged.

As this example suggests, Victorian detective fiction sometimes clouds rather than clarifies the distinction between victim and victimizer. Even more significantly, it blurs the boundary between detection and crime. The most suspicious figures in Victorian detective fiction often prove to be the detectives themselves: Men of working-class origins who intrude into the genteel world of their social superiors in the course of their investigations, and women from various social classes who cross gender boundaries and assume male prerogatives in their search for truth. Although its ostensive subject is the commission and discovery of specific crimes, Victorian detective fiction is engaged in a much more general and wide-ranging investigation into class and gender relations, and the potential criminality or injustice of the social status quo. Thus, when detective stories employ such forensic techniques as fingerprint technology and crime photography, Ronald R. Thomas observes, their aim is twofold: to examine not only the "individual anatomy" of particular characters but also the "general condition of the body politic itself" (4).

As the Victorian literary detective frequently discovers, the body politic appears to be in a failing state, a condition that some writers attribute to class inequities. "The clergyman said in his sermon, last Sunday evening, that all things were ordered for the best, and we are all put into the stations in life that are properest for us," Collins's working-class sleuth observes at the beginning of "The Diary of Anne Rodway," a story first published in Dickens's *Household Words* in 1856: "I suppose he was right, being a very clever gentleman who fills the church to crowding; but I think I should have understood him better if I had not been very hungry at the time, in consequence of my own station in life being nothing but Plain Needlewoman" (Collins, "Diary," 129). A murder mystery investigated—and narrated—by a detective who does not have enough to eat, "The Diary of Anne Rodway" examines the issue of class relations and suggests, initially at least, that feelings of discontent and resentment among impoverished workers are well founded, whatever well-fed clergymen may say to the contrary. By the end of the narrative, however, Collins has largely undermined his political critique, in a conservative turn that characterizes many Victorian detective stories.

Collins's story centers on the friendship between Anne Rodway and Mary Mallinson, both poor needlewomen, the latter of whom is killed by a blow to the head. At the inquest into Mary's death, the authorities conclude that she was fatally injured when she fell, exhausted, in a London street, while returning to her lodgings from work. Although the jurors reach a verdict of "Accidental Death," they hold Mary's unfeeling and exploitative employers indirectly responsible for it: "They reproved the people where Mary worked for letting her go home alone, without so much as a drop of brandy to support her, after she had fallen into a swoon from exhaustion before their eyes. The coroner added, on his own account, that he thought the reproof was thoroughly deserved" (143). As the physician who first examined Mary tells Anne, "The only ill-usage to which the poor girl was exposed was the neglect she met with in the work-room" (141).

Despite the conclusions reached by these authorities, and her own experience of economic hardship and exploitation, Anne Rodway suspects that her friend was actually murdered, having found "an end of a man's cravat" clutched in the dying woman's hand (137). When the police tell her that "they could make no investigations with such a slight clue to guide them" (143), Anne investigates the case herself, tracking down the cravat in a rag and bottle shop, and then identifying the man who wore it on the night that Mary was fatally injured. What she discovers deflects blame for Mary's death away from her middle-class employers, instead fixing it on brutal men of her own class. Having been beaten by her alcoholic father as a child, Mary is finally killed by one of her father's former associates, a drunkard who purposely trips her when she gets in his way on the street, and then strikes her down with his fist when she calls him a "brute" (154).

Thanks to the detective work of Anne Rodway, the murderer is identified, convicted, and transported for life, and Mary's employers are effectually acquitted, a solution that undermines the radical implications of Collins's investigation into class relations. The fate of the female sleuth serves an equally conservative end. Despite her success as a detective—a role that requires her to cross gender boundaries at times—Anne is forced to hand over the investigation to her fiancé Robert upon his return from America. Told that her "strength and resolution had been too hardly taxed already" (156), Anne is rewarded for her detective efforts with a marriage that elevates her to the middle class but that leaves her an unwaged woman in the private sphere, wholly dependent on her male provider. As Collins constructs his plotline, his heroine simultaneously discovers the identity of Mary's murderer and finds her own "proper place" as a wife, suppressing her manly capabilities as a detective. Not until the appearance of Catherine L. Pirkis's *The Experiences of Loveday Brooke* (1894), George R. Sims's *Dorcas Dene* (1897), and M. McDonnell Bodkin's *Dora Myrl* (1900) did the female detective receive a more explicit endorsement in Victorian fiction, and even here the lady sleuths often prove subordinate to their husbands or their male colleagues.

In his portrait of Anne Rodway, a working-class sleuth who exposes the brutality of those in her own walk of life, Collins presents a variation on what was becoming a standard motif in Victorian detective fiction—the confrontation between the lowly policeman and his transgressive social superiors, particularly genteel women, the so-called "angels of the house," who sometimes prove to be female fiends. As Anthea Trodd observes, depictions of domestic crime in Victorian fiction invest the "semi-servile" policeman with "unusual authority" over the ladies and gentlemen whose homes he enters and whose actions he scrutinizes (6), enabling writers to examine class differences and the interrelation of class and gender identities, to dramatize the threat posed to social order by class mobility, to scrutinize ideals of feminine behavior, and to test the boundary separating the private from the public sphere.

Dickens's representation of Mr. Bucket in *Bleak House* clearly illustrates this range of interests and concerns. First appearing as a "sharp-eyed" detective officer (363), later as "a very respectable old gentleman"—a physician "with grey hair" (403)—and even later as an amateur singer and musician (731–732), Bucket adopts a host of disguises in the novel, masquerading as a family man and a private friend when he is, in fact, engaged in an official and public cause. Slipping in and out of roles, Bucket actively constructs and reconstructs his social identity. Establishing an "intimacy" with those he hopes will prove useful to his investigations (363), employing his wife as a spy, and making his home into a "prison" for his criminal lodger (796), Bucket collapses the cherished distinction between private and public life, challenging the Victorian ideal of the morally pure domestic haven.

A man of humble social origins, Bucket makes himself at home among the English gentry as well as the impoverished residuum of London, moving from the slums of Tom-all-Alone's to Chesney Wold, Sir Leicester's landed estate. Eroding class barriers, he claims that "every person should have their rights according to justice" (363). More often than not, Bucket works for affluent solicitors and baronets, and he persecutes the homeless crossing sweeper Jo, forcing him to leave the shelter that Mr. Jarndyce provides for him at Bleak House. Yet the detective officer retains his class allegiances and seems animated by class resentment on occasion. Although a murder is committed in the novel, Bucket appears less concerned with apprehending the working-class Frenchwoman who commits the crime than he is with investigating the gentlewoman whom she once served. Rather than concentrating his powers of surveillance on the lady's maid, Mademoiselle Hortense, Mr. Bucket focuses on Lady Dedlock, investigating her sexual past, and helping to discover the love affair that preceded her marriage to Sir Leicester and that produced an illegitimate daughter.

Hired by the baronet to find and save the suicidal Lady Dedlock after her sexual fall is brought to light, Bucket loses track of the wayward woman long enough to ensure her death. To Anthea Trodd, this surprising failure on the part of a seemingly omniscient detective points to the limits imposed on such figures by their class origins: Bucket proves unable to fully understand and outwit a member of the gentry. "He can see and oversee society's derelicts," Trodd argues, "but Lady Dedlock remains invisible to him" (33). More subtly, however, Bucket's failure to save Lady Dedlock suggests his antipathy toward his social superiors while also signifying his patriarchal function in the novel: what Laurie Langbauer sees as Bucket's "control of women's supposed errancy," and his desire to keep wayward women "'in train'" (153). In this regard, Bucket resembles the generality of Victorian literary detectives, who assume "that women [are] inherently the more criminal sex" when they investigate a case (Trodd, 96). As Sherlock Holmes warns Dr. Watson in *The Sign of the Four* (1890), "Women are never to be entirely trusted—not the best of them" (70): "The most winning woman I ever knew was hanged for poisoning three little children for their insurance-money" (15–16).

Indeed, the detectives of Victorian fiction are sometimes misogynistic figures set on exposing the criminal failings of female nature, pursuing investigations that serve to rehabilitate their own imperiled manhood and shore up conventional gender boundaries. Braddon's *Lady Audley's Secret* provides a case in point. At the outset of Braddon's story, her hero, Robert Audley, is an effeminate gentleman too indolent to practice law; he prefers reading French novels to hunting, and eats toast and marmalade rather than beef. But once he assumes the role of amateur sleuth and begins to investigate the young, second wife of his uncle, Sir Michael Audley, Robert learns to become a "real" man at the same time that he uncovers the "hellish power" (274) of a seemingly angelic woman. Exposing the crimes of Lady Audley—a bigamist, an arsonist, and a would-be murderess—Robert generalizes from her case. With "a shiver of horror, . . . he remembered the horrible things that have been done by women, since that day upon which Eve was created to be Adam's companion and help-meet in the garden of Eden" (273–274).

Assumptions about the inherent criminality and fallenness of women underlie the inquiry launched by Collins's Sergeant Cuff just as they guide those of Inspector Bucket and Robert Audley, although Collins questions stereotypes of female errancy much more vigorously than either Dickens or Braddon do. In *The Moonstone*, Collins tells the story of a sacred Hindu diamond that is looted from the treasury of the sultan Tippoo during the British Siege of Seringapatam in 1799. John Herncastle brings the gem back home to England, bequeathing it to his niece, Rachel Verinder, who receives it on her eighteenth birthday, 21 June 1848. That night, it disappears from her rooms at the family's Yorkshire estate, and Sergeant Cuff is called in from Scotland Yard to investigate. His suspicion soon falls on Rachel herself, whom he believes has stolen her own diamond to pay off debts, acting in collusion with Rosanna Spearman, a housemaid with a criminal past. "Miss Verinder has been in secret possession of the Moonstone from first to last," Cuff informs Rachel's mother, Lady Verinder, "and she has taken Rosanna Spearman into her confidence, because she has calculated on our suspecting Rosanna Spearman of the theft. There is the whole case in a nutshell" (173).

As events prove, however, the celebrated Cuff is entirely mistaken in his judgment. Undermining Cuff's suspicions, Collins identifies the housemaid Rosanna as the better sleuth of the two. In gathering together the family's dirty linen for wash day—a job that suggests why domestic servants make particularly good detectives in Victorian fiction—Rosanna discovers an incriminating stain on the nightclothes of the gentleman whom Rachel loves: her cousin Franklin Blake. Blake rather than Rachel has taken the diamond from her rooms, we learn. But he has done so under the influence of laudanum, an opiate secretly administered to him by a medical man to prove a point; thus he is unaware of his theft. Furthermore, Blake took the Moonstone to protect Rachel and her property—because he was fearful of the three Hindu priests who had followed the diamond from India to England in order to reclaim it, and who appear at the Verinder estate on Rachel's birthday. With Blake "guiltless, morally speaking, of the theft" (441), the most culpable figure in the novel proves to be a third cousin, Godfrey Ablewhite, to whom Blake handed the Moonstone for safekeeping while in his opium trance. A philanthropist who lives a double life, embezzling trust funds and keeping a mistress in an expensive suburban villa, Ablewhite chooses not to deposit the diamond in his father's bank, as Blake requested, instead arranging to have it cut into separate stones and sold to pay off his debts. Before Ablewhite can do so, he is caught and murdered by the three Hindus, who regain their gem intact and restore it to an Indian shrine in the province of Kattiawar.

Understood as an investigation into Victorian social relations, *The Moonstone* dispels sexual stereotypes by acquitting Rosanna and Rachel of the charges leveled against them while also revealing the class inequities that divide the housemaid from the young lady of the house. As Rosanna puts it, "Young ladies may behave in a manner which would cost a servant her place" (363). Although Rosanna, like Rachel, loves Franklin Blake, her affection for the gentleman is perceived as "monstrous" by the Verinders' steward, Gabriel Betteredge, and by his daughter Penelope, a lady's maid (185), and it goes completely unrecognized by Blake himself. Misconstruing Rosanna's behavior, he only learns of her love from her suicide note, which expresses her affection for Blake as well as her class resentment, a feeling more fully articulated by her friend Lucy Yolland, who considers the gentleman a "murderer" and looks ahead to "the day . . . when the poor will rise against the rich" (226–227).

Collins does not endorse Lucy's call for revolution or hold Blake directly responsible for Rosanna's suicide, but he traces the crimes perpetrated in his novel to the English upper classes and to the privileges enjoyed by men. Incriminating Godfrey Ablewhite, Collins exonerates Franklin Blake of the theft of the Moonstone, yet he leaves us with the uncomfortable suspicion that Blake has injured Rosanna and Rachel alike: that Blake has driven the housemaid to suicide through his indifference toward his social inferiors, and has violated the gentlewoman he loves and eventually marries in the very process of protecting her—by appropriating the precious jewel that symbolizes Rachel's virginity in the view of many Collins critics. Comparing Blake's efforts to protect Rachel from a seduction or a rape, Collins points to the criminality of the sexual status quo and the laws governing Victorian marriage, which rob women of their legal identity and property, and encourage men to "marry . . . for [their] own selfish and mercenary ends" (318). Stipulating that wives were guarded or "covered" by their husbands, the common law doctrine of coverture denied married women legal autonomy and property rights, and it enables the male characters in *The Moonstone* to treat Rachel's desire for independence as an unfortunate "defect" in her character (87) rather than as a valid response to gender inequities.

In *The Moonstone*, Collins draws a parallel between Rachel's angry resistance to male protection and control and that of the Indians to imperial rule and exploitation. Writing a decade after the Indian Mutiny (1857–58) revealed that Hindus and Muslims were profoundly dissatisfied with the British Raj and capable of violent insurrection against it, Collins begins his detective novel by constructing a colonial crime scene in which the Indians are victims of British rapacity and violence. Set fifty years before the main narrative, Collins's Prologue depicts British troops looting a Muslim treasury after they storm Seringapatam, and identifies John Herncastle as a thief and murderer. To gain possession of the Moonstone, set in the handle of a dagger, Herncastle kills the three Hindu priests guarding it. As a second English officer recalls, "The dying Indian sank to his knees, pointed to the dagger in Herncastle's hand, and said, in his native language:—'The Moonstone will have its vengeance yet on you and yours!'" (37).

Opening his novel with a call for Indian retribution against the British, Collins identifies Herncastle's imperial crime as the origin of all those that follow. Referring to Herncastle as "the Honorable John" (66), the nickname of the East India Company, Collins broadens his indictment, offering a critique of imperialism that extends beyond the actions of one particular officer to incriminate the policies and practices of the British empire as a whole in the years leading up to the Indian Mutiny. Although the English characters in the novel are apt to forget that "the Indians . . . originally owned the jewel" (72), Collins reminds us of this fact in his Epilogue, by restoring the Moonstone to what he suggests is its rightful place in an Indian shrine. The English may view the Moonstone as a "fortune of war" (68) or as "a marketable commodity" (512), but it is finally seen "in the forehead of the deity" (526), a gleaming and sacred Hindu gem.

As *The Moonstone* makes clear, Victorian detective fiction investigates imperial relations as well as class and gender relations, although its sleuths often uncover the innate criminality of the so-called "subject races" rather than the guilt of British imperialists. Like *The Moonstone*, Conan Doyle's *The Sign of the Four* centers on a stolen treasure of Eastern jewels and connects a murder committed in England to crimes perpetrated in India years before. More anxious than Collins to defend the empire, however, Conan Doyle highlights the savagery of the Indians rather than the British, and represents forms of violence that are pointedly un-English. As Holmes observes, "The case . . . breaks fresh ground in the annals of crime in this country—though parallel cases suggest themselves from India and, if my memory serves me, from Senegambia" (41).

Recalling Collins's detective novel, Conan Doyle's story hinges on the greed of an English officer, Major Sholto, who retrieves a hidden treasure stolen by another Englishman, Jonathan Small, and three Indian confederates during the Indian Mutiny. Incarcerated in the Adaman Island prison where Sholto commands the guard, Small confides in him and his friend Captain Morstan on the understanding that the two officers are to share the treasure with the English convict and his Indian confederates. After Sholto betrays them and returns to England, Small escapes there. Before he can exact his revenge, Sholto dies, but Small recovers the treasure with the help of Tonga, a faithful yet fierce aboriginal. During the police pursuit that leads to his capture, however, Small dumps the treasure into the Thames rather than "give it up to those who have never earned it" (96).

Instead of focusing on the criminality of Jonathan Small, Conan Doyle distinguishes the Englishman's relatively civilized behavior from what he represents as the much deeper depravity of the natives, foregrounding the "savage instincts" of Tonga, the Adaman Islander, who unnecessarily kills Major Sholto's son with his blowpipe and poisoned darts, much to Small's disgust: "I give you my word on the book that I never raised hand against Mr. Sholto," he assures Holmes. "It was that little hell-hound, Tonga, who shot one of his cursed darts into him. I had no part in it, sir. I was as grieved as if it had been my blood-relation" (89). As Holmes tells Watson, the members of Tonga's aboriginal race are "naturally hideous," "so intractable and fierce . . . that all the efforts of the British officials have failed to win them over in any degree. They have always been a terror to shipwrecked crews, braining the survivors with their stone-headed clubs, or shooting them with their poisoned arrows. These massacres are invariably concluded by a cannibal feast" (68–69). When Holmes and Watson finally see the cannibal, shortly before they kill him in self-defense, they are struck by the "bestiality and cruelty" that "deeply mark" his features (86–87). Set apart from his Muslim confederates as well as from the primitive Tonga, Small explains to Holmes that the Sikhs forced him into league with them at knifepoint during the mutiny; although he helped them trap the merchant Achmet, he did not himself strike a single blow.

Acknowledging his debt to *The Moonstone* at the same time that he reworks its representation of empire and crime, Conan Doyle includes a character named Abel White in *The Sign of the Four*, a kindly indigo planter who is slaughtered by the Indian mutineers. These "black devils" make the colony "a perfect hell," murdering civilian Englishmen and cutting Englishwomen "into ribbons" (97–98). Transforming Collins's English villain into a martyr of sorts, and identifying natives rather than Englishmen as the enemies of the women, Conan Doyle reinforces racist stereotypes of Indian lawlessness and treachery, defending the empire against its critics and implicitly justifying British rule.

At a time in which European and American rivals were challenging Britain's imperial supremacy, Victorians found Conan Doyle's detective hero particularly reassuring. Not only could Holmes track down and exterminate savage invaders; he could protect defenseless women from persecution and expose class transgressions. The remarkable popularity of Sherlock Holmes is largely due to the conservatism that informs his fictional adventures—stories that defend the status quo at home as well as in the colonies. In a subgenre in which working-class detectives often threaten to subvert traditional class relations, Holmes is a gentleman who defines himself against vulgar and incompetent upstarts from Scotland Yard. A hero of the 1890s, the decade in which the "New Woman" first appeared in English fiction, advocating women's rights and refusing to marry, Holmes helps to revive an ailing patriarchy and keep women in their place. Impervious to female wiles, he acts as a responsible and reassuring father figure to the helpless young women who appear at his door, seeking his aid and protection.

Long considered a suspect literary subgenre by scholars and critics—a lowbrow form associated with the even more disreputable subgenre of sensation fiction—Victorian detective fiction has found its advocates in recent years, thanks largely to changes in the field of literary studies and in our understanding of literary value. Immensely popular among Victorians, the detective stories of Arthur Conan Doyle, Grant Allen, and Arthur Morrison reached a circulation of 500,000 readers in the *Strand Magazine*, first published in 1891. Yet the very popularity of these stories was used against them when critics evaluated their artistic worth. Since the 1980s, however, critical interest in popular culture, modes of literary production, and the process of literary canonization has led to a reappraisal of Victorian detective fiction. The detective novels of Dickens, Collins, and other Victorian writers are now used by critics to illustrate the theories of deconstruction, semiotics, and psychoanalysis, the process of gender construction, and the principles of modern surveillance first described by French historian Michel Foucault. Perhaps most importantly, critics now see that Victorian detective fiction can help them to uncover the often hidden workings of the culture that produced it, illuminating the social anxieties, ideologies, and political aims that characterize the period.

WORKS CITED AND SELECTED WORKS FOR FURTHER READING

Altick, Richard D. *Deadly Encounters: Two Victorian Sensations.* Philadelphia: U of Pennsylvania P, 1986.

Belsey, Catherine. "Deconstructing the Text: Sherlock Holmes." In *Popular Fiction: Technology, Ideology, Production, Reading,* pp. 277–288. Ed. Tony Bennett. London: Routledge, 1990.

Boyle, Thomas. *Black Swine in the Sewers of Hampstead: Beneath the Surface of Victorian Sensationalism.* New York: Viking, 1989.

Braddon, Mary Elizabeth. *Lady Audley's Secret.* Ed. David Skilton. Oxford: Oxford UP, 1992.

Collins, Wilkie. "The Diary of Anne Rodway." In *Mad Monkton and Other Stories,* pp. 129–64. Ed. Norman Page. Oxford: Oxford UP, 1994.

———. *The Moonstone.* Ed. J.I.M. Stewart. London: Penguin, 1986.

Craig, Patricia, and Mary Cadogan. *The Lady Investigates: Women Detectives and Spies in Fiction.* New York: St. Martin's, 1981.

Dickens, Charles. *Bleak House.* Ed. Norman Page. London: Penguin, 1985.

Doyle, Arthur Conan. *The Sign of the Four.* Ed. Christopher Roden. Oxford: Oxford UP, 1993.

Emsley, Clive. *Crime and Society in England, 1750–1900.* 2nd ed. London: Longman, 1996.

Hughes, Winifred. *The Maniac in the Cellar: Sensation Novels of the 1860s.* Princeton: Princeton UP, 1980.

Jaffe, Audrey. "Detecting the Beggar: Arthur Conan Doyle, Henry Mayhew, and 'The Man with the Twisted Lip.'" *Representations* 31 (Summer 1991): 96–117.

Kestner, Joseph A. *Sherlock's Men: Masculinity, Conan Doyle, and Cultural History.* Aldershot: Ashgate, 1997.

Klein, Kathleen Gregory. *The Woman Detective: Gender and Genre.* 2nd ed. Urbana: U of Illinois P, 1995.

Langbauer, Laurie. *Women and Romance: The Consolations of Gender in the English Novel.* Ithaca: Cornell UP, 1990.

Miller, D. A. *The Novel and the Police.* Berkeley: U of California P, 1988.

Most, Glenn W., and William W. Stowe, eds. *The Poetics of Murder: Detective Fiction and Literary Theory.* New York: Harcourt, Brace, Jovanovich, 1983.

Ousby, Ian. *Bloodhounds of Heaven: The Detective in English Fiction from Godwin to Doyle.* Cambridge: Harvard UP, 1976.

Porter, Dennis. *The Pursuit of Crime: Art and Ideology in Detective Fiction.* New Haven: Yale UP, 1981.

Thomas, Ronald R. *Detective Fiction and the Rise of Forensic Science.* Cambridge: Cambridge UP, 1999.

Tobias, J. J. *Crime and Police in England, 1700–1900.* New York: St. Martin's, 1979.

Trodd, Anthea. *Domestic Crime in the Victorian Novel.* New York: St. Martin's, 1989.

The Victorian Social Problem Novel

James G. Nelson

That awesome phenomenon known as the Industrial Revolution appeared first in the United Kingdom in the later eighteenth century. Technological developments such as James Watt's steam engine and inventions like the power loom and the spinning jenny, coinciding with the rapid rise in population, created the conditions for an industrial transformation of Britain that was surprisingly well advanced by the 1830s. Such a revolution had far-reaching effects, none more so than the rapid rise of cities, especially in the English midlands. Having been small market towns before the nineteenth century, Birmingham, Manchester, and Leeds, among others, burgeoned into large industrial centers in the early decades of the century as agricultural laborers from the impoverished countryside flooded into the new industrial towns in search of work in the textile mills.

So massive and rapid was the onset of the revolution that it created unprecedented and unfamiliar social and economic problems to be solved by the kingdom's governing bodies. As the nation was plunged into the first great industrial depression in the mid 1830s (which lasted well into the 1840s), the increasing economic and social distance between the rich and the poor, as well as other ill effects of industrialization, gave rise to the so-called "Condition of England Question." This debate, which dominated the minds of the British people for many years, was central to a new form of the novel that rose to prominence in the 1840s, a form of fiction that was unique in its focus on the social, economic, political, and even religious upheavals occurring throughout the kingdom. Quite different from the historical novel inaugurated by Sir Walter Scott and the novel of manners one associates with Jane Austen—both forms well-established in the early decades of the nineteenth century—the "social-problem" novel—as later critics came to name it—was practiced by such novelists of note as Benjamin Disraeli, Elizabeth Gaskell, Charles Kingsley, and Charles Dickens.

Popular in the mid-Victorian period, the social-problem novel was first identified as such by Louis Cazamian in his pioneering study, *The Social Novel in England, 1830–1850* (1903). However, the novel received little further study until the second half of the twentieth century, led by Kathleen Tillotson's essay on Mrs. Gaskell's *Mary Barton* in her celebrated *Novels of the Eighteen-Forties* (1956). The social-problem novel has continued to receive considerable attention from students and critics in recent years as a result of its appeal to various critical circles, in particular, Marxist and feminist theorists. Marxist readings of note are found in Arnold Kettle's "The Early Victorian Social-Problem Novel" in *From Dickens to Hardy*, which appeared in 1958, and Raymond Williams's chapter on what he termed the "industrial" novel, published in the same year. Among the notable feminist approaches to the social-problem novel are Rose-Marie Bodenheimer's *The Politics of Story in Victorian Social Fiction* (1988) and Susan Morgan's *Sisters in Time: Imagining Gender in Nineteenth-Century British Fiction* (1989).

The social-problem novel as it developed during the mid-Victorian period is a complex story, its variety and essential characteristics being manifold. Nevertheless, its central thrust, perhaps, can best be understood in short compass by discussing in some detail three novels that, though clearly within the canon, differ in their emphasis: Disraeli's *Sybil* (1845), Dickens's *Hard Times* (1854), and Gaskell's *North and South* (1855). Disraeli's *Sybil* is an excellent example of how the social-problem novel was used to promote a novelist's political agenda. A leader of the Young England movement, a conservative body of young men arguing for a nation led by a renewed and energized aristocracy, Disraeli (the future Tory prime minister who would make Queen Victoria Empress of India) employed the poverty-stricken state of the laboring poor and the uncaring posture of the idle nobility during the "Hungry Forties" to energize a debate about the Condition of England Question, a debate conjoined in the romantic setting of Marney Abbey where the novel's hero, the young nobleman Charles Egremont, encounters some strangers viewing the gothic ruins: Stephen Morley, a proponent of the Chartist Movement; his friend, Walter Gerard, a factory inspector; and his daughter Sybil.

Egremont, young, idealistic, and of the opinion that Britain under the young Victoria is the most prosperous, progressive, and free nation in the world, echoes the Whig view of history as expounded by the popular, influential liberal statesman of the day, Thomas Macaulay, in such essays as "Francis Bacon" and "Robert Southey." Stimulated by their medieval surroundings, Morley and Gerard recall an idealized, Tory view of the Middle Ages, a past time when the people and their leaders existed in harmony with one another and a sense of community and good will prevailed. How different, Morley and Gerard lament, the present state of the nation. Skeptical of so romantic a view that flies in the face of his Whig sympathies, Egremont confidently asserts: "'Say what you like, our Queen reigns over the greatest nation that ever existed,'" an assertion that is countered by Morley's arresting question: "'Which nation? . . . for she reigns over two.'" Perplexed, Egremont hesitatingly asks: "'You speak of—'" and Morley replies: "'The *Rich and the Poor*'" (Book 2, Chapter 5). This famous exchange, the best-remembered statement in the novel, introduces Disraeli's theme of social polarization.

As the plot of the novel unfolds, the novelist amply illustrates this theme through skillfully alternating chapters focused on the rich and the poor, thus vividly contrasting the palatial domiciles and idle, frivolous lifestyles of the nobility with that of the miserable dwellings and hard-working, deprived existences of both the industrial laborers crowded together in the slums of the factory town of Mowbray and the agricultural workers returning to their squalid hovels in the farming village of Marney. Few novels of the period depict so graphically the conditions in which England's laboring classes lived during the "Hungry Forties."

In exposing the rather sordid, disreputable backgrounds of the two aristocratic families—that headed by the Earl of Marney (Egremont's elder brother) and that led by Lord Mowbray (Book 1, Chapter 3)—Disraeli illustrates the Tory view that the present English nobility is composed of a new species of middle-class interlopers posing as aristocrats, having obtained their lands and fortunes as well as titles through the rise of the Whig oligarchy, which diminished the monarchy, degraded the people, and displaced the old Norman aristocracy during the later seventeenth and early eighteenth centuries. Lacking any sense of *noblesse oblige*, the feeling of obligation to the people and a commitment to seeing after their welfare, which the old nobility responsibly maintained, the new Whig aristocracy has left the people to their own devices, abdicating its responsibility—thus the perilous gulf that has yawned between their leaders and the people.

Disraeli's hope—shared by many Victorians—that there still existed in Britain a saving remnant of the old aristocracy that could rescue society from the clutches of the idle rich is embodied in Egremont, whose rambles through the countryside and factory towns of England, disguised as a reporter, lead him to shed his Macaulayesque, Whiggish optimism and open his eyes to the shameful plight of the nation's poor as well as to its cause and cure. Gradually enlightened about past history and the causes of the present unrest by Morley and Gerard and, more significantly, by his growing admiration and love for Sybil, Egremont, at the conclusion of the novel, stands as Disraeli's beacon of hope for the future.

Although the brother of the loathsome Lord Marney and therefore sharing his bogus credentials as a true aristocrat, Egremont is legitimized, so to speak, by his marriage to Sybil, who turns out in the end to be the scion of a great Norman family whose lands and titles were usurped by the upstart Mowbrays. During a climactic scene in which Mowbray castle is besieged and burned by a desperate mob of laborers led by Gerard and Morley, Gerard succeeds in breaking into the castle's keep where he finds papers that—as he had long suspected—prove that he and his daughter are indeed the true aristocratic owners of the Mowbray estates and, therefore, the rightful leaders of the people.

Disraeli believed deeply when he wrote *Sybil* that the people could not lead themselves. In one of the most appalling chapters of his novel (Book 3, Chapter 4), he drives this message home, describing in grim detail the filthy, lawless, churchless town of Wodgate, a hellhole in which the people, left unguided, have degenerated into anarchy, drowning in their own ignorance and bestiality. The people, he felt, needed a noble aristocracy of men who would put the people's welfare before personal wealth and comfort and would lead them out of the mire of incivility and protect them from their brutish instincts. This paternalistic or patriarchal view, which was widespread, is memorably expressed by Disraeli's contemporary, the poet, Alfred Tennyson, whose old Ulysses speaks of the labor he leaves to his son Telemachus: "by slow prudence to make mild / A rugged people, and through soft degrees / Subdue them to the useful and the good" ("Ulysses," ll, 36–38).

Both Disraeli and Dickens were influenced in their assessment of society and its problems during the mid-Victorian years by Thomas Carlyle, the Scots sage whose writings such as *Past and Present* (1843) exuded a sharp sense of crisis. Both men shared Carlyle's uneasiness about the coming of democracy, and both seemed persuaded by his argument that his idealized paternalistic society of the Middle Ages was the proper model for the country, which, falling deeper and deeper into a state of anarchy, was ruled by a heartless philosophy known as Utilitarianism, a godless system of thought and action that denigrated emotion while it exalted reason and intellect. Needless to say, to Carlyle, Utilitarianism was anathema. Dedicated to Carlyle, Dickens's *Hard Times* is a powerful and penetrating critique of both the stultifying effects of Utilitarianism on mid-Victorian society and the baleful effect of industrialization on the laboring poor.

As we have seen, Great Britain not only had the manpower and the tools to launch an industrial revolution, it also possessed a rising middle class ready and willing to take advantage of it and manage it. The British middle class, which had risen out of the skilled artisans and shopkeepers of the nation's past, was characterized by its practical intelligence; down-to-earth, no-nonsense attitude of mind; and a Protestant religion that taught its adherents that through hard work and sober living, success in this world could be attained. Material prosperity was a sign of godliness. Unlike the idle, dandified aristocracy that Carlyle railed against in his writings, the middle class seized the opportunity the Industrial Revolution provided and energetically set about organizing and managing it.

Given their empirical approach to life, the middle class largely embraced some form of the new philosophy of Utilitarianism that, ready to hand, sanctioned its hardheaded approach to organizing and dealing with the labor force as well as its mode of raising its families and educating its children. It is this latter element in the new dispensation for which Dickens shows much concern in *Hard Times*. By the 1850s, when he wrote his novel, Dickens was well aware that the new system of education developing in Britain in a desperate effort on the part of the nation's leaders to "educate our masters" before the coming of democracy was not only a system increasingly secular but one increasingly Utilitarian in its content and orientation. Consequently, in *Hard Times*, Dickens is as concerned about the effects of Utilitarianism on the education of the nation's children as he is about the effects of industrialization on the workers.

As a consequence of this dual concern, the novel has two major plots: one having to do with education, centered in the family of the prosperous middle-class Thomas Gradgrind, a recently retired hardware dealer; the other, having to do with industrialization, centered on Josiah Bounderby, a wealthy mill-owner. The two plots, of course, are neither wholly divorced from one another in the novel, nor are the characters, since, for instance, both Gradgrind and Bounderby are ardent Utilitarians—Gradgrind conducting his home, Stone Lodge, and his family according to strict Utilitarian principles as does Bounderby his mill.

Set in Coketown, a fictional name for one of the numerous new industrial cities in England's Midlands, *Hard Times* moves forward along these two plot lines. The centrality of what I shall term the education plot is indicated by the structure of the novel, arranged by Dickens in three parts titled Sowing, Reaping, Garnering—metaphorical language drawn from agriculture that represents the children as plants whose growth depends upon the kind of soil they are placed in and the kind of nurturing they receive as they grow toward maturity. The children about whom the reader is concerned in *Hard Times* are students in a model school set up through the generosity of Gradgrind, two of whose own children, Louisa and Tom, attend.

Another indication of the importance of the education plot is the opening scene in Book 1, Chapter 1, set in "a plain, bare, monotonous vault of a schoolroom," filled with children seated on an inclined plane. Before them is Gradgrind himself; M'Choakumchild, the new teacher; and another gentleman, a government inspector whose intent is to see that education follows the new Utilitarian line. In giving the charge to the teacher, Gradgrind reveals his Utilitarian colors, admonishing M'Choakumchild to teach facts: "Stick to Facts, Sir! . . . In this life, we want nothing but Facts, Sir; nothing but facts!" Drawing for the reader his portrait of a Utilitarian, Dickens provides Gradgrind with a "square wall of a forehead, which had his eyebrows for its base, while his eyes found commodious cellarage in two dark caves, overshadowed by the wall." As one observes, Gradgrind here and throughout *Hard Times* is symbolized by sharp-angled geometric forms—as is the schoolroom itself. A near-tragic figure, Gradgrind, as indicated by this description of his eyes, has a tragic flaw: blindness, an inability to see the dangerous limitations of the philosophy he lives by.

This opening scene—the most memorable in the novel—acquaints the reader with the education. That Dickens is not so much concerned with what is taught in this schoolroom—specific subjects are not listed—but how it is taught is concretely demonstrated, that is, "shown," in the famous "put-down" of Sissy Jupe, a poor girl from Sleary's Circus Troupe camped on the outskirts of Coketown, by Gradgrind as he drives home his point that knowledge must be packaged in terms of facts and abstract definitions. "Squarely pointing" to the child "with his square forefinger," Gradgrind calls on "girl number twenty" (Sissy) to define a horse. Astonished and rendered speechless by a question so alien to her nature and experience, Sissy is held up to the class by her censorious interrogator as one "'possessed of no facts, in reference to one of the commonest of animals! Some boy's definition of a horse,'" he commands. "'Bitzer, yours.'"

In a fashion reminiscent of the future D. H. Lawrence, Dickens, skillfully employing the symbolism of light and dark, turns the spotlight on a pale, cold-eyed boy whose "skin was so unwholesomely deficient in the natural tinge, that he looked as though if he were cut, he would bleed white." In contrast, Sissy, "irradiated" by a ray of sunshine, is "dark-eyed and dark-haired" and seems "to receive a deeper and more lustrous color from the sun" (Book 1, Chapter 2). The conclusion is obvious, of course: Bitzer has been taught to package knowledge in terms of definitions and abstractions, to deal with objects in general/universal terms rather than concrete, particular/individual terms. Sissy, who has known horses firsthand all her life—her father belonging to what she calls "the horse-riding" in Sleary's circus—fortunately can only know a horse or any other object in terms of a close, intimate, sympathetic, and emotional involvement with it as an individual not as a generalization.

Bitzer, of course, rattles off the definition Gradgrind requires: "'Quadruped. Graminivorous. Forty teeth, namely twenty-four grinders, four eye-teeth, and twelve incisive. Sheds coat in the spring; in marshy countries, sheds hoofs, too. Hoofs hard but requiring to be shod with iron. Age known by marks in mouth.'" Triumphant in his obtuse and blind perspective, Gradgrind proclaims: "'Now girl number twenty . . . You know what a horse is.'" Dickens's irony is powerfully effective here as it is throughout the novel.

The chapters that follow in Book 1 show graphically that in Dickens's view Utilitarianism destroys children's emotional apparatus, leaving them frustrated, drained of imagination, and emptied of spirit. For example, much to Gradgrind's shock and mortification, after school, walking full of self-satisfaction toward Stone Lodge, he comes upon the circus encampment, a performance in full swing. Although his intention is to pass by without noticing so frivolous and useless an event, Gradgrind catches sight of a group of children who "were congregated in a number of stealthy attitudes, striving to peep in at the hidden glories" of the circus. Approaching to shoo them off, with horror, he sees "his own metallurgical Louisa, peeping with all her might through a hole in a deal board, and his own mathematical Thomas abasing himself on the ground to catch but a heel of the graceful equestrian Tyrolean flower-act!" Needless to say, both children rise "red and disconcerted. But, Louisa looked at her father with more boldness than Thomas did" (Book 1, Chapter 3), Dickens's implication being that Louisa will not accompany her father home, as Tom does, like a machine, but like a human being still alive with passion and emotion.

Book 1 rises to its climax in the penultimate Chapter 15, a scene between Gradgrind and his now grown Louisa in which the father's blindness leads to near-tragic consequences for himself and his daughter. Bounderby, although old enough to be her father, has asked Gradgrind for Louisa's hand in marriage. Having summoned Louisa to his study (which Dickens ironically likens to an astronomical observatory without any windows), Gradgrind prefaces his announcement of Bounderby's proposal with the presumption that Louisa is, indeed, the machine he has made her: "'You are not impulsive, you are not romantic, you are accustomed to view everything from the strong dispassionate ground of reason and calculation.'" But when Louisa asks the inappropriate and embarrassing question—" 'Do you think I love Mr. Bounderby?' "—Gradgrind, disconcerted, waves the question aside and, blind to his daughter's obvious feelings of distaste for Bounderby, reduces the whole matter to a question of plain fact: "'The question of Fact you state to yourself is,'" he advises his daughter, "'does Mr. Bounderby ask me to marry him? Yes, he does. The sole remaining question then is: Shall I marry him?'"

As if her whole education has come down to one final examination question—"'shall I marry him?'"—Gradgrind is certain Louisa's answer will be the correct one, confirming beyond doubt the efficacy of the education and upbringing he has provided her, that she will make her decision on the basis of fact and reason alone. Having received from her own lips the correct response, that she will indeed marry Bounderby, Gradgrind, with an unwonted show of emotion, embraces his daughter, exclaiming, "'My dear Louisa . . . you abundantly repay my care. Kiss me, my dear girl.'" And so she gives her father what, in effect, is a Judas kiss—a kiss of betrayal. Blind to the fact, Gradgrind concludes the interview in triumph unaware that his daughter has made her decision not on the basis of fact and reason but on the basis of emotion—her aberrant love for her ne'er-do-well brother Tom and her altruistic hope of being of service to him as Mrs. Bounderby.

Book 1, Chapter 10, opens with a celebrated passage of description, a dramatically vivid, graphic portrait of Coketown and its inhabitants. In form, a lengthy periodic sentence, it concludes with the introduction of one of the novel's major characters:

In the hardest working part of Coketown; in the innermost fortifications of that ugly citadel, where Nature was as strongly bricked out as killing airs and gases were bricked in; at the heart of the labyrinth of narrow courts upon courts, and close streets upon streets, which had come into existence piecemeal, every piece in a violent hurry for some one man's purpose, and the whole an unnatural family, shouldering, and trampling, and pressing one another to death; in the last close nook of this great exhausted receiver, where the chimneys, for want of air to make a draught, were built in an immense variety of stunted and crooked shapes, as though every house put out a sign of the kind of people who might be expected to be born in it; among the multitude of Coketown, generically called "the Hands,"—a race who would have found more favor with some people, if Providence had seen fit to make them only hands, or, like the lower creatures of the seashore, only hands and stomachs—lived a certain Stephen Blackpool, forty years of age.

Stephen, along with his devoted friend Rachel, represents the laboring poor of Coketown. Stephen is (as he continuously complains) always in a "muddle." As he informs Rachel: "'That's where I stick. I come to the muddle many times and agen, and I never get beyond it.'" Caught as he and his fellow Coketown laborers are between the indifference, greed, and harsh treatment of the mill owner Bounderby and the machinations of the unscrupulous labor organizer

Slackbridge—both of whom are bent on using the workers for their own ulterior purposes—Stephen is characterized by his gentle, childlike nature. Like most of his fellow mill hands, he has come into Coketown from the country where he has been brought up in a paternalistic society in which the simple folk look to the local nobility for protection and guidance, seeing their relationship to the lord of the manor as that of a child to his father. In this respect, he is allied in the novel with the members of Sleary's circus, which is a microcosm of the patriarchal macrocosm, Sleary being the father of a family—that is, Sissy and the circus performers. Stephen and Sissy are aliens in the Bounderby/Gradgrind world of Coketown. Consequently, Stephen finds no such relationship in the Utilitarian society of Coketown, where no sense of community exists. Dickens, as the reader is soon aware, symbolizes these two different societies by the geometrical forms of the circle (Sleary's horse-riding) and the square/rectangle (Coketown). Bounderby and his ilk recognize only what was known as the cash nexus and spurn all other links and relationships with their hands.

In fact, the world of Coketown is divided by an unbridgeable gulf between two classes: the laboring poor and the well-to-do ruling middle-class (i.e., Disraeli's rich and poor), the aristocracy significantly having all but vanished. Only a remnant remains in the form of a bedridden old woman, Lady Scadgers, whose "mysterious leg" has refused to get out of bed for the last fourteen years (a fitting icon for Dickens's middle-class view of the aristocracy). Nevertheless, Stephen, steeped in a patriarchal tradition, instinctively turns to the mill owner Bounderby for help when he finds himself in a deeper muddle than usual. His wife, having refused to assume the role of the Victorian "angel in the house," and having tired of the monotonous drudgery of a mill hand, has deserted her husband some years before, traveling to another town and, inevitably, falling into a life of drink and prostitution. Nevertheless, she exercises a modicum of power by defying her husband and returning to him from time to time. Her latest return (in a state of grim intoxication) to Stephen's dark and ill-appointed rooms has made him desperate to be rid of his wife. Seeing in Bounderby the Coketown equivalent of the lord of the manor, Stephen approaches him for guidance and advice about obtaining a divorce from a woman who stands in the way of his marrying Rachel who, given her meek and self-effacing demeanor, will accept the role of angel.

Bounderby, rather than being one of the Carlylean "Master-Workers" who do, indeed, seek to assume the role of the feudal baron in the lives of their retainers, is more like what Carlyle termed a "Bucanier" or a "Chactaw Indian," who is out for booty, plunder, scalps, money (*Past and Present*, Book 4, Chapter 4). Lacking any semblance of chivalry, Bounderby treats Stephen's request for advice with contempt, finding his mill hand's desire to obtain a divorce preposterous and, along with his pretentious and sycophantic old housekeeper, Mrs. Sparsit, altogether shocking. Having been dismissed with the warning that he sees in his employee's behavior, "traces of turtle soup, and venison, and gold spoon," as well as a desire to ride in a "coach and four," Stephen leaves Bounderby's house cast down and more in a muddle than ever.

Stephen's allegiance to the idea of paternalism has failed him in his search for a way out of his muddle, and its firm hold over his mind and heart is further indicated by another highly significant episode in *Hard Times*. By the 1850s, early forms of the present-day labor unions were attempting to organize and attend to the needs of the poor mill workers. In Coketown the United Aggregate Tribunal has been formed to which all the men working in Bounderby's mill have been pressed to join (women were excluded). Stephen, however, is the lone holdout. In the opening scene of Book 2, Chapter 4, the entire union membership is gathered to consider what to do about Stephen. Haranguing the workers is the labor organizer, Slackbridge, newly arrived in Coketown to rouse the workers of Bounderby's mill to strike. The rhetoric Dickens puts in his mouth is clearly that of a rabble-rouser. Dickens not only speaks slightingly of Slackbridge directly to the reader but also adroitly interlaces his speech with responses from the Tribunal's membership, which contrast markedly in terms of rhetoric and moderation of tone and content with that of the labor organizer. Clearly bent on having Stephen openly chastised and "sent to Coventry" (i.e., shunned by the entire membership), Slackbridge refuses to allow Stephen to speak in his own defense. He is overruled by the chair of the meeting. Stephen speaks to the gathering. However, he concludes by saying simply that he has his reasons—"'mine, yo see—for being hindered [from joining the union]; not on'y now, but awlus—awlus—life long!'" (Book 2, Chapter 4)—Stephen gives his fellow workers no choice but to go along with Slackbridge and send him into the cold, murky streets of Coketown a pariah.

Although Stephen refuses to reveal his reasons to the Tribunal, he later tells Bounderby that he had made a promise not to "come in." And although to whom he made that promise is not revealed in the published novel, Dickens's manuscript contains a passage that reveals that his promise was made to Rachel who had counseled him to "'let things be. . . . They only lead to hurt. Let them be.'" Stephen's brief speech in his own defense echoes Rachel's words when he doubts that the Tribunal's regulations and intended course of action against Bounderby will do the membership "onny good. Liker they'll do you hurt."

In truth, Stephen instinctively mistrusts the union as he mistrusts any organization that threatens the social fabric of paternalism. Continuing, as he does, to see Bounderby in terms of the feudal baron, the union—led by so unsavory a character as Slackbridge—cannot serve as a viable alternative. That Stephen assigns the cause of his muddled state of mind to the lack of fit leadership in either Bounderby or Slackbridge is seen in his final interview with Bounderby, who, having failed to force Stephen to provide him with information about the Tribunal, sacks him.

Agreeing with Bounderby that union leaders like Slackbridge are bad, Stephen pointedly observes to him that the workers "take such as offers. Haply 'tis no' the sma'est o' their misfortune when they can get no better." The interview concludes with the overbearing and intimidating Bounderby's posing the question to Stephen: How would you "'set this muddle (as you're so fond of calling it) to rights?'" Stephen's ready reply is significant: "I donno, Sir. I canna be expecten to 't. 'Tis not me as should be looken to for that, Sir. 'Tis them as is put ower me, and ower aw the rest of us. *What do they tak upon themseln, Sir, if not to do 't?*"(Book 2, Chapter 5; emphasis added). The implications are clear: It is not the workers' duty to set things right. It is the duty of those men God set above them. Stephen is in a muddle, as are his misguided fellows, because they are not provided the kind of leadership they *deserve*.

Having been literally run out of Coketown by the mill hands, their leaders, and Bounderby, and having wandered about the countryside for sometime, Stephen, returning to Coketown to refute the charge that he had robbed the bank, wanders blindly through the night across the pock-marked coal fields of the Midlands when he falls into the uncovered entrance to a mine, known locally as the Old Hell Shaft, the sad import being—yet again—that without paternal guidance, the laboring poor will inevitably find themselves at the bottom of a symbolic Old Hell Shaft.

Lying mortally wounded at the bottom of the pit, Stephen fixes his eyes upon a star shining high above the shaft, Dickens's use of light and dark imagery throughout *Hard Times* culminating in this bright orb beaming clear in the dark sky. The dying man associates it with heaven. As he says to Rachel, who, with others, has rescued him from the pit: "'Often as I coom to myseln, and found it shinin' on me down there in my trouble, I thowt it were the star as guided to Our Saviour's home. I awmust think it be the very star!'" As his body is carried away, Dickens observes: "The star had shown him where to find the God of the poor; and through humility, and sorrow, and forgiveness, he had gone to his Redeemer's rest" (Book 2, Chapter 6). How apropos to the close of Stephen's life that both he and Dickens associate the star with a religion that sanctions and provides the model for the entire fabric of paternalism.

Just as Stephen, the son of the laboring poor, comes to a disastrous end, so, too, Louisa, a daughter of the prosperous, self-assured middle class. As Mrs. Bounderby, Louisa finds herself living in an even less heart-warming house than Stone Lodge. Her husband—self-centered, self-serving, and totally without feelings, a man who espouses Utilitarian principles as an excuse to starve his workers and hoodwink the public—is incapable of love, in fact, incapable of any genuine human emotions. The arid, uncongenial atmosphere of Bounderby's house intensifies Louisa's sense of imaginative and emotional frustration, further undermining her desperate inner struggle to redeem herself from the ravages of her utilitarian education and upbringing. Louisa's life in Bounderby's house is made even more unpleasant by the housekeeper, a bitter old hanger-on, Mrs. Sparsit, who had for years nourished the preposterous notion of one day becoming Mrs. Bounderby herself. With the advent of Louisa, her jealousy and envy know no bounds. Not a poetical woman (as Dickens with some irony informs us), she, nevertheless, has it in her to construct in her mind a fanciful staircase that day by day she, with considerable relish (and no little malice), sees Louisa, the bride of Bounderby, descending. At the bottom of this staircase, Sparsit imagines "a dark pit of shame" (Book 2, Chapter 10).

Louisa's descent is hastened when the handsome, cultivated, urbane James Hearthouse enters her life. Offering her the fulfillment of her heart's desire, Hearthouse poses the emotionally starved Louisa with the most insidious temptation possible. Yielding to his offers of love, Louisa agrees to run away with him. However, poised to step off Sparsit's stairs into the dark pit of shame, Louisa (in a scene comparable to one in the best sensational novels) flees to Stone Lodge in the midst of rain, thunder, and lightning, breaks into the sanctity of her father's study, and throws herself at his feet, demanding that he come to her rescue: "'All I know is,'" she exclaims to Gradgrind, "'your philosophy and your teaching will not save me. Now, father, you have brought me to this. Save me by some other means!'"

In the dramatic interview leading up to this demand, Louisa's heroic nature expresses itself as she relates to her astounded father her life-long inner struggle to save what she terms her "better angel" from being crushed "into a demon." With much passion she explains: "'With a hunger and thirst upon me, father, which have never been for a moment appeased; with an ardent impulse towards some region where rules, and figures, and definitions were not quite absolute; I have grown up, battling every inch of my way.'" His eyes at last opened to his daughter's heroic struggle and her miserable plight, Gradgrind, his old certainty gone, stands helpless as he sees "the pride of his heart and the triumph of his system, lying, an insensible heap, at his feet" (Book 2, Chapter 12).

Although the social-problem novel presented a diversity of views on the many problems—as its name suggests—to which the industrialization of Britain gave rise, most novelists agreed that division must yield to communication and understanding between adversaries. Elizabeth Gaskell is no exception, her novel *North and South* showing that by mediating their differences through dialogue, masters and men, utilitarians and paternalists, north and south, can reach a satisfactory solution to their problems. *North and South* focuses on the developing relationship between John Thornton, the northerner and Margaret Hale, the southerner. Thornton is a wealthy, highly regarded mill owner in Milton-Northern (Manchester), a factory town to which Margaret recently has moved with her parents from the village of Helstone in the south of England where her father was the parish priest. Having formed doubts about certain church doctrines, the Rev. Mr. Hale has resigned his benefice. The relationship between Thornton and Margaret is paralleled by Thornton's developing relations with his mill hands, both relationships centering in the ability of Thornton and Margaret, on the one hand, and master and men, on the other, communicating and, through communicating, coming to understand one another.

Like Elizabeth Bennett and Darcy in Jane Austen's *Pride and Prejudice*, the first contacts Thornton and Margaret have with one another are decidedly negative. Their first meeting in a hotel in Milton-Northern, where Margaret and her father are staying while house hunting, is anything but comfortable and, moreover, complicated by false first impressions on both sides. Her father briefly away on business, Margaret reluctantly meets Thornton when he calls at their rooms, Thornton having been solicited by a mutual friend of both parties to help facilitate the Hales' move north. Being met not by a middle-aged clergyman but by a handsome, dignified, socially adept young woman, John is disconcerted as he is invited to take a seat while he awaits the return of Mr. Hale. As the narrator observes, Thornton, who was in the habit of dominating most situations in which he found himself, is aware that Margaret had "assumed some kind of rule over him at once. . . . Her movements, full of soft feminine defiance gave" her visitor "the impression of haughtiness." He, himself, felt that he must appear to this refined young lady like "a great rough fellow, with not a grace or a refinement about him." Later, to her mother, Margaret describes Thornton as "'not quite a gentleman. . . . Altogether a man who seems made for his niche . . . sagacious, and strong, as becomes a great tradesman'" (Chapter 7).

Later, when Thornton comes to tea at the Hale's, Margaret attends but little to the conversation between her father and the mill owner. But when he rhapsodizes about the glories of Milton-Northern, extolling the energy and inventiveness of its people, the wonders of its machines and productivity, viewing the town as a showplace of science and industry, Margaret listens attentively. Homesick for her native south and offended by the dirt and smoke of Milton-Northern and its boisterous, unruly, ignorant, and sexually risqué working-class population who crowd her in its streets, she hears Thornton with distaste. And when he tells her father that he "would rather be a man toiling, suffering—nay, failing and successless—here, than lead a dull prosperous life in the old worn grooves of what you call more aristocratic society down in the South, with their slow days of careless ease," observing: "One may be clogged with honey and unable to rise and fly," Margaret feels constrained to contradict the guest.

"You are mistaken," said Margaret, roused by the aspersion on her beloved South to a fond vehemence of defense, that brought the color into her cheeks and the angry tears into her eyes. "You do not know anything about the South. If there is less adventure or less progress—I suppose I must not say less excitement—from the gambling spirit of trade, which seems requisite to force out these wonderful inventions, there is less suffering also. I see men here going about in the streets who look ground down by some pinching sorrow or care—who are not only sufferers but haters. Now, in the South we have our poor, but there is not that terrible expression in their countenances of a sullen sense of injustice which I see here. You do not know the South, Mr. Thornton." (Chapter 10)

Although Margaret lapses into a determined silence, angry with herself for having said so much, she once again is roused to take issue with Thornton, who goes on to express his laissez-faire economic views to Mr. Hale. Unlike Bounderby, Thornton, a true believer and an honest proponent of the principles of the current political economy, one who sees the relations between master and men as a battle, argues that it is good for the masters and men to vie with one another, an activity that he considers salutary and productive of prosperity and wealth for all. "'Now,'" he points out to his listeners, this battle "'is pretty fairly waged between us. We will hardly submit to the decision of an umpire, much less to the interference of a meddler with only a smattering of knowledge of the real facts of the case, even though that meddler be called the High Court of Parliament.'" Both Margaret and her father, however, take exception to Thornton's viewing the relations between masters and men in terms of the battle metaphor. "'Is there any necessity for calling it a battle between the two classes?'" Mr. Hale inquires, Margaret, again entering the conversation "in a clear, cold voice": "'You consider all who are unsuccessful in raising themselves in the world, from whatever cause, as your enemies, then, if I understand you rightly.'"

Misconstruing Thornton's gesture of extending his hand to her in parting, Margaret "simply bowed farewell; although the instant she saw the hand, half put out, quickly drawn back, she was sorry she had not been aware of the intention." On his part, Thornton, interpreting her behavior as a mark of haughtiness, draws himself up to his full height, walks off, muttering to himself—" 'A more proud, disagreeable girl I never saw. Even her great beauty is blotted out of one's memory by her scornful ways' " (Chapter 10).

Margaret's distaste for Thornton's battle metaphor and her sense that it is wrongheaded to so view the relations between master and men, is reinforced over the next few weeks through her acquaintance with one of the local mill hands, Nicholas Higgins, and his dying daughter, Bessy. Having met casually and by chance, Margaret, Higgins, and Bessy become good friends, Margaret having readily made the effort to overcome the problems language and gesture inevitably present to a young lady from the south, new not only to the north but to another class of people. As his distrust of her fades, Higgins speaks more openly with her about the plight of the mill hands and their feeling that they are being unfairly treated by the masters. Sympathetic to and understanding of the workers' views and demands, Margaret finds herself playing the role of mediator as the threat of a strike looms over Milton-Northern. In contact with Thornton from time to time, not from choice but from circumstance, she comes to understand thoroughly the masters' position as well as that of the workers.

Having from an early age been accustomed to visiting the poor as the daughter of the parish priest, listening to their concerns and ministering to their needs, Margaret is used to entering the so-called social sphere, a space between the public and the private spheres, and sharing to some extent in both. An energetic, intelligent young woman of some independence of thought and action, she comes to Milton-Northern unwilling to remain—as so many Victorian women were constrained to do—immured within the confines of the home. Her father, disoriented and distracted by his theological problems, her brother afar in foreign lands, and her mother enfeebled and increasingly ill, Margaret is relatively free of paternalistic restraints. Her freedom to visit the Higginses and her contacts with Thornton place Margaret in a position to mediate between the masters and men of Milton-Northern at a critical point in their "battle."

Margaret sees the battle lines drawn between Thornton and other mill owners on one side and the textile laborers and their union on the other. The masters all stand together in allegiance to the orthodox laissez-faire doctrines of the day, central among them the cash-nexus—cash pay for labor done. No other contact between masters and men need exist; workers' pay and hours of labor required, dependent entirely on the laws of supply and demand. The mill hands stand together in their hatred of the masters who, they feel, treat them unjustly and refuse to have any meaningful contact with them other than the cash-nexus. Although both sides talk to her, neither side is willing to talk to one another. Hence the inevitability of serious labor trouble in Milton-Northern.

These troubles come to a head when the union representing the mill hands initiates a strike. And despite the fact that Higgins and his fellow members of the strike committee intend the labor action to be free of any violence lest the public turn against their cause, a huge mob of strikers, having found that

Thornton has imported into his mill Irish laborers, take to the streets of Milton-Northern, their goal the home of the mill owner, which sits on the premises of the mill itself. Unaware of the impending event, Margaret, on an errand of mercy to the Thornton mansion to secure the loan of a water bed for her dying mother, finds herself trapped in the house with Thornton by the rapidly gathering mob, along with his mother and sister. During this, the most dramatic and in many ways the most significant scene in the novel, Thornton, having summoned the militia, intends simply to "sit it out," hoping that the mob's threats to his home and its occupants will not materialize. However, Margaret, watching with Thornton from an upstairs window the raging multitude of workers below, is concerned not only for the Thornton family but for the rioters themselves. Aware that a clash between the mob and the militia would bring serious injuries, even death, Margaret urges Thornton to go down and face his enraged mill hands in an effort to avoid the impending violence: "'Speak to your workmen as if they were human beings,'" she exhorts him. "'Speak to them kindly,'" she advises. "'Don't let the soldiers come in and cut down poor creatures who are driven mad. . . . If you have any courage or noble quality in you, go out and speak to them, man to man!'" (Chapter 22).

Thus urged by Margaret, Thornton fearlessly rushes below and confronts the mob, leaving Margaret to bar the door behind him. Despite their master's appearance before them, the maddened rioters rage worse than ever. Watching anxiously from above, Margaret, seeing lads removing their heavy clogs, "the readiest missile they could find," intuitively is aware that it is figuratively "the spark to the gunpowder, and, with a cry . . . she rushed out of the room, down stairs . . . had thrown the door open wide—and was there, in face of that angry sea of men, her eyes smiting them with flaming arrows of reproach." Quelled but for a moment, the mob rages into action, slinging clogs in Thornton's direction. In an effort to save him, Margaret throws her arms around him. In a scene replete with sexual meaning, Thornton shakes her off, bidding her to go away. Determined to remain, while missiles fly, Margaret clings to Thornton's arm. Thus exposed, she is struck by a pebble that grazes her forehead and cheek causing the blood to flow "and drawing a blinding sheet of light before her eyes. She lay like one dead on Mr. Thornton's shoulder." The sight of the injured Margaret, red blood running down her face, has the effect on the rioters that no words from her or Thornton has had. Reluctant to resort to any further physical violence, the mob slowly begins to disperse.

Margaret's actions are interpreted not only by Thornton, himself, but his stern mother, as well as the public, as a sign of the young woman's affection for the mill owner. Stung by such an apparent misreading of her intentions, Margaret insists that she was acting dispassionately to save bloodshed on both sides, describing her behavior as "woman's work" (Chapter 23). Nevertheless, berating herself for acting "'like a romantic fool,'" Margaret is in no mood to entertain a proposal of marriage that Thornton tenders the following day. She rejects his suit after a heated, angry exchange of words, but, significantly, "when he was gone," the reader is told, Margaret "thought she had seen the gleam of unshed tears in his eyes; and that turned her proud dislike into something different and kinder, if nearly as painful—self-reproach for having caused such mortification to anyone" (Chapter 24). Although in this proposal scene Margaret has told Thornton that she does not wish to understand him, he then, accusing her of being unfair and unjust, Margaret, as the complex plot unwinds, does come to understand her lover, and, in the end, to treat him fairly and justly. Similarly, Thornton comes to better understand his mill hands, as they him, through the continued efforts of Margaret as mediator.

For example, when, after the strike, Higgins, having been one of the union leaders, loses his job in the mill, Margaret suggests that he seek employment with Thornton. Although Higgins abhors the thought of asking Thornton for work, he decides to do so because he has undertaken the care of the wife and children of his friend, Boucher (the renegade union member, who, having led the mob in the scene before Thornton's house, committed suicide). Meanwhile, in a conversation with her father, Margaret indicates the grounds on which the two men—as well as all masters and men—can come together: If Higgins and Thornton, she observes, "'would speak out together as man to man—if Higgins would forget that Mr. Thornton was a master, and speak to him as he does to us—and if Mr. Thornton would be patient enough to listen to him with his human heart, not with his master's ears,'" the interview could be a success (Chapter 37).

After Higgins has patiently waited five hours to see Thornton, this first interview between the two men is tense, angry, and contentious. Yet in the course of the frank discussion, Higgins reveals information about his motives and actions during the strike and his commitment to undertake the care of the destitute Boucher family. Having refused Higgins's request for a job and dismissed him, Thornton has second thoughts. Soon after, as Higgins tells Margaret of the conversation with Thornton, the man himself appears at the door of the Boucher hovel. Margaret hastens from the room leaving Thornton and Higgins to their second interview. Thornton had taken the time to confirm that all Higgins had told him was true. "And then," the reader is told, "the conviction went in, as if by some spell, and touched the latent tenderness of his heart; the patience of the man, the simple generosity of the motive [for caring for the Boucher family] . . . made him forget entirely the mere reasonings of justice, and overleap them by a diviner instinct" (Chapter 39). The second interview having promoted further understanding between the master and the man, Higgins has his job.

That Thornton has a heart as well as a sense of justice is confirmed by his putting several of the Boucher children to school, and his growing interest in his mill hands' welfare. Moreover, he pursues several schemes—always with the input and approval of the workers—one of which grows out of his awareness of how ill-nourished his hands are, especially at a time when the price of food has risen so high. With Higgins, he draws up a scheme for a kind of dining club that requires him to build a dining room at the mill, to provide a cook, and to purchase the food wholesale. The success of this venture leads him to envision launching what he describes as "experiments" that might further facilitate a master's relations with his men.

Ironically, it is at this crucial time when he, at last, welcomes an "opportunity of cultivating some intercourse with the hands beyond the 'cash nexus'" (Chapter 51) that Thornton, a year and a half after the strike against the mill owners has ended, suddenly realizes the unthinkable: that his business is in serious financial difficulty due to the after effects of the union action and a down-turn in the nation's economy.

Unable to find financial support in Milton-Northern, Thornton in desperation travels to London in search of a backer. There by chance at an evening party he meets Margaret, who is staying with the wealthy aunt with whom she had lived for some years before her move to Milton-Northern. Having recently inherited a great fortune left her on the death of her godfather, Mr. Bell, Margaret wants to put her wealth to good use. Restless and disoriented by the deaths of her father and mother and her subsequent removal from Milton-Northern, she anxiously looks for some worthy enterprise in which to immerse herself. Asked by another gentleman if he thinks his experiments in communicating with the mill hands will prevent the recurrences of strikes, Thornton replies: "'Not at all. My utmost expectation only goes so far as this—that they may render strikes not the bitter, venomous sources of hatred they have hitherto been. A more hopeful man might imagine that a closer and more genial intercourse between classes might do away with strikes. But I am not a hopeful man.'"

Suddenly on impulse Thornton crosses over to where Margaret is sitting, aware that she has been listening to his conversation about his experiments as well as about his financial losses. Informing her that he has had a letter from Higgins and other mill hands stating their wish to work for him if he is able to start anew, Thornton asks: "'That was good, wasn't it?'" "'Yes. Just right. I am glad of it.'" The following day, Margaret pledges her wealth to re-establish Thornton in business. All misunderstandings and prejudices gone, Margaret and Thornton are married, the two settling down as husband and wife in the great house before which several years earlier the couple had stood defenseless, facing the maddened mob of rioters.

In providing *North and South* with a conventional close, Gaskell not only wished to gratify her Victorian readers with a happy marriage, but she also wanted to leave them with an *unconventional* marriage, a marriage in which there is less inequality, a marriage in which the partners communicate with one another as mature adults, working together in an enterprise of social betterment to which each has something important to contribute. In so doing, Gaskell displaces the father/child relationship of paternalism as the model for master and men with the adult/adult relationship of marriage, an arrangement that implies a more equal as well as a more interactive relationship between capital and labor.

Although *Sybil, Hard Times,* and *North and South* offer their Victorian readership different solutions to the problems the Industrial Revolution brought to the United Kingdom, these social-problem novels are in agreement about one thing: that the most alarming and dangerous problem facing the nation, the growing division between the rich and the poor, between master and men, must end. Though none of these novels advocates either the eradication of class distinctions or placing of the classes on an equal footing (or of the sexes, for that matter), they argue for closer ties between capital and labor that hopefully will promote mutual respect and good-will, a sameness of purpose, a sense of unity. Only through community will prosperity and peace reign again in the nation.

WORKS CITED AND SELECTED WORKS FOR FURTHER READING

Bodenheimer, Rose-Marie. *The Politics of Story in Victorian Social Fiction.* Ithaca: Cornell UP, 1988.

Cazamian, Louis. *The Social Novel in England, 1830–1850.* 1903. London: Routledge and Kegan Paul, 1973.

Dickens, Charles. *Hard Times.* New York: Penguin, 1995.

Disraeli, Benjamin. *Sybil.* Ed. Sheila M. Smith. Oxford: Oxford UP, 1980.

Ford, Boris, ed. *From Dickens to Hardy.* London: Penguin, 1958.

Gaskell, Elizabeth. *North and South.* London: Penguin, 1970.

Hill, Robert. W., Jr., ed. *Tennyson's Poetry.* New York: W. W. Norton, 1971.

Morgan, Susan. *Sisters in Time: Imagining Gender in Nineteenth-Century British Fiction.* Oxford: Oxford UP, 1989.

Past and Present. Oxford: Oxford UP, 1960.

Tillotson, Kathleen. *Novels of the 1840s.* Oxford: Clarendon, 1956.

Williams, Raymond. *Culture and Society, 1780–1950.* London: Chatto and Windus, 1958.

The Victorian Sensation Novel

Helen Debenham

SENSATION FICTION

"Sensation fiction"—or "sensational fiction," the terms were often used interchangeably—was the generic name given to the hugely popular novels of crime and passion that scandalized and enthralled reviewers and the British reading public in the 1860s. Both a reaction against the domestic fiction, which dominated the previous decade ("domestic," as Charles Reade pointed out in 1859, "is Latin for tame") and a response to the tensions and anxieties of a society in a state of rapid change, sensation novels were also very much a product of the growing commercialization of the literary marketplace, and one that marked the emergence of a real distinction between "serious" and "popular" fiction. In their own time they generated a moral panic among reviewers and social commentators, and it is this as well as the novels themselves (some still eminently readable, others rightly described as feeble and ephemeral) that attracts attention today. The resurgence of the genre as an area of scholarly investigation, after a century of being largely ignored in canonical literary histories, has been concurrent with the rise of feminist and cultural studies and forms part of a wider revaluation of popular literature and its role in the formation and negotiation of cultural ideologies.

Wilkie Collins is generally credited with beginning the sensation vogue when *The Woman in White,* with its racy plot exposing the dark underside of a supposedly respectable society, "exploded on its British readership like a bombshell" in 1859–60 (Sutherland, vii). His example was quickly followed and expanded by Ellen (Mrs. Henry) Wood with *East Lynne* in 1861 and Mary Elizabeth Braddon with *Lady Audley's Secret* in 1862 and *Aurora Floyd* in 1863. The immediate and enormous success of these novels (all eventually ranked among the best-selling works of the century) prompted a spate of imitators and provided reviewers with a focus for their many concerns about the "flood of novels" that was "pouring over" the land at this time (Oliphant, "Novels," 168). Whereas the "silly novels by lady novelists" that George Eliot had attacked in 1856 could be regarded as relatively harmless, this new phenomenon of "sensational" fiction, though not without defenders, was widely seen as a symptom of national decline. Works aimed at producing "[e]xcitement, and excitement alone" and appealing to "the nerves instead of the judgment" could only be "indications of a widespread corruption," evidence of and a stimulus for "the cravings of a diseased appetite," declared H. L. Mansel in 1863 (482, 483). His lengthy article in the influential *Quarterly Review,* the first extended analysis of sensation fiction as a cultural phenomenon, was typical in its near-hysterical metaphors of drugs and disease. Throughout the 1860s and into the 1870s, sensation novels and outraged alarm at their possible threat to the nation's well-being flourished side-by-side, both gradually fading from prominence thereafter (though never entirely disappearing) as other forms of popular fiction evolved to provoke other causes for concern.

CHARACTERISTICS

To its contemporary critics, the sensation genre was simultaneously homogeneous—"each game is played with the same pieces, differing only in the moves"—and hydra-headed in its compulsive quest for "new methods of awakening the interest of their readers" (Mansel, 486, 485). Once they moved beyond the obviously formulaic, reviewers disagreed about which authors or works should be described as sensational. Charles Dickens's *Great Expectations* (1861) was damned as sensational by some and excluded from the taint by others, while Rhoda Broughton's *Cometh Up as a Flower* was, in the same magazine, pronounced "entirely devoid of affectation or 'sensation'" in 1867 ("Literature," 478) and denounced for "outraging morality, sense and decency" in 1868 ("Reviews," 187). Recent scholars, who are themselves divided about the boundaries of the genre, recognize that generic labels often tell less about "the intrinsic properties of particular texts than the needs and concerns of the readers reading those texts" (Gilbert, 3–4), and that the most constant factor in nineteenth-century usage of the term "sensation novel" is the users' fear and dislike of mass culture. Nonetheless, they generally agree that sensation fiction's most crucial effects derived from the "mystery, entanglement, surprise, and moral obliquity" (Hardy, v) with which it assaulted the readers' nerves. For the most part these entailed complex plots depicting crime, deception, secrets, and their almost inevitable concomitant, detection, with its overtones of spying and betrayal. Murder and attempted murder, arson, fraud and forgery, real and imagined bigamy, impersonations and disguises, illegal incarcerations, inherited and imputed insanity, seduction and betrayal, all abound in sensation novels, along with often exhaustive explorations of the implications for victims and perpetrators alike. The "sensation," the special *frisson* of horror that thrilled the reader, lay not so much in the existence and unraveling of the crime as in its proximity and its contemporaneity. These crimes were not distanced by time or geography like those of Gothic fiction; they occurred within "ordinary" modern society, hinting that the man or woman next door might be harboring some guilty secret or plotting some dastardly deed.

An extra "turn of the screw" (Henry James's 1898 novella of this name is one of many later works indebted to the sensation genre) came from the frequency with which the crimes and secrets were attributed to women, challenging conventional assumptions about women's roles and women's nature. The prevailing ideology of separate spheres, according to John Ruskin's supposedly reassuring summary, decreed that "within [the man's] house, as ruled by [woman], *unless she herself has sought it,* need enter no danger, no temptation, no cause of error or offence. This is the true nature of home—it is the place of Peace; the shelter, not only from all injury, but from all terror, doubt and division" (122; emphasis added). Sensation fiction not only featured women courting danger, temptation, and offense; it also was very often written by women and was believed to be most eagerly devoured by female readers, who were considered psychologically and even physiologically more at risk from their reading than men. Increasingly throughout the 1860s the threat to home and society was seen as coming from women's emotional susceptibility, from transgressive passion rather than criminal activity, and hence from a quality more easily transferred from text to reader. Braddon's Lady Audley is a bigamist, would-be murderer, and arsonist, but sexual desire forms no part of her motives; by 1867 to the deep dismay of Margaret Oliphant, one of the genre's most trenchant critics, the typical sensational heroine "waits now for flesh and muscles, for strong arms that seize her, and warm breath that thrills her through." Even worse, books representing these "sensuous raptures" as "the natural sentiment of English girls" were "read everywhere, and . . . not contradicted" ("Novels," 259). Such concern needs to be seen in the context of intensified public agitation about the "condition of women" at this time—the 1860s saw the first major campaigns for married women's property rights, for the female franchise, and for higher education and wider employment opportunities for women—which also threw into question stereotypes of femininity and issues of gender identity.

SOURCES AND SIGNIFICANCE

As the anxiety implies, behind the desire to reject the sensational depiction of life lay a fear that it might be true. Despite their implausible plots, the novels did contain "close representations of events passing around us" ("Sensational Novels," 458). When Oliphant used the term "sensation" in relation to fiction in 1855 (566), she was drawing on its association with the contemporary "sensational" theater, where melodrama with its emphasis on extreme emotions, extraordinary incidents, and spectacular special effects reigned supreme. Although this remained its primary referent, it gained quasi-scientific force from contemporary medical suppositions concerning connections between the nerves, heart, and brain. Newspapers also adopted the term, however, to indicate the effect in the courtroom of particularly shocking evidence in the criminal and (after 1857) divorce cases that they reported in graphic detail, and, unlike melodrama, these real-life dramas could not be simply dismissed as unreal or irrelevant to middle-class experience. Sensation fiction flaunted its "realism" in its use not only of real court cases and newspaper reports to inspire its plots ("newspaper novels" was another name for the genre) but also of "real" material in the form of railway timetables and telegraphed messages, references to current events, support for current "causes," and other self-consciously topical detail. "Realist" and "sensational" were for some critics equivalent terms of abuse as they struggled to demonstrate that "truth" was something different from "fact." This issue, too, was gendered because women writers were thought innately more inclined than men to "dwell on the little points which convey the sense of reality and minister to the craving for it" without discerning any "living and intelligible connection between them" (Maurice, 5). Yet the critics themselves saw their age as one of "sensation," using the word to "encapsulat[e] the experience of modernity itself—the sense of continuous and rapid change, of shocks, thrills, intensity, excitement" in what was deemed an age of "events" (Taylor, 3). Sensation, Peter Edwards observes, was seen to be "taint[ing] drama, poetry, art, auction sales, sport, popular science, diplomacy, and preaching," with the result that "[t]he nervous system of the nation seemed to be under attack in every direction" (4). The nation, in other words, was being feminized.

Literary sources for sensation are numerous. What was new about it was not so much particular aspects of content and technique as their combination in new and different forms. As Lyn Pykett explains, "the sensation novel's power to disturb derived substantially from its adventurous and opportunistic mixing of formulas, and its blurring and crossing of generic, stylistic and other boundaries" (*Sensation*, 9). Melodrama and Gothic fiction have already been mentioned as points of comparison and contrast; both genres through their affinities with romance enabled the articulation of fears and anxieties not otherwise easily expressible in a rational age. A more immediate ancestor could be found in the Newgate novels, which flourished between about 1830 and 1847 and stirred great controversy about the propriety of representing criminal behavior, otherwise relegated to the lower-class penny dreadful, in fiction intended for the middle-class reader. Critics also looked abroad for corrupting influences, to America where "fierce expedients of crime and violence" and "the wild devices of a romance" dominated "the higher class of fiction" (Oliphant, "Sensation Novels," 565), and of course to France, the home, to xenophobic English minds, of all manner of social and literary dangers. (Some comfort was derived from seeing the English preference for bigamy in fiction, whereas the French favored adultery as an indication of moral superiority.) Those defending sensation fiction looked for parallels in Elizabethan drama, in Shakespeare especially, and in the novels of Walter Scott and other "respectable" authors; Charlotte Brontë's *Jane Eyre* was cited both positively and negatively for introducing passion to the English novel, as well as for popularizing bigamy and concealed first wives.

The boundaries crossed by sensation fiction were those of class as well as genre, and in this lay its greatest perceived threat. Because the novels were so popular—equally attractive to the cook and her mistress, to say nothing of valet and master—they broke class barriers, eroding distinctions of education and taste. Available everywhere in weekly magazines (many appeared first in serial form, and new periodicals proliferated to meet expanding demand), in lending libraries (also expanding), and in railway bookstores (that very literal Victorian symbol of the spread of literacy), their apparently infinitely repeatable variations on a theme reduced literature from an art form to a mass-produced commodity. Without culture what protection was there against anarchy? If literature "capitulate[d] to the desires of the mass reading public" (Brantlinger, *Lesson*, 143), a middle class nervously confronting the idea of an extended franchise in the lead up to and immediate aftermath of the Second Reform Act of 1867 could no longer be certain of its own values, let alone of how to prepare the lower classes for political power.

On a more personal level, sensation novels queried the degree to which individuals could be held responsible for their actions. Some, with overtly didactic or propagandist intent, blamed a specific social, legal, or political wrong for their protagonists' plight (Mansel found Dickens a "grievous offender in this line" [488]), but even the most conservative in their proclaimed moral stance—and many sensation novels were highly moralistic—tended to show characters as the victims of circumstance, their lives determined by fate or the intrigues of others rather than their own actions. At the same time, by naturalizing extreme situations and emotions and by inviting sympathy for transgressors, such fictions blurred the distinctions between heroes and villains and cast doubt on normal definitions of guilt and innocence. In these respects, the novels, whether lightweight or more serious, raised issues that impinged on major debates in the realms of ethics and politics, about absolute or relative standards of right and wrong, and about the respective responsibilities of the individual and the governing authorities for rectifying wrongs and abuses.

NOVELS AND NOVELISTS

Collins, Braddon, and Wood, the three novelists whose huge successes in the early 1860s helped to shape the sensation genre and the associated panic, are still today the most read by the general public and critics alike. In modern studies, changing definitions and the changing value attached to the genre, as well as the differing theoretical approaches of critics, have largely determined which other writers, and especially whether male or female writers, are given most attention. So Charles Reade features prominently in accounts where melodramatic effects and swinging attacks on abuses are key criteria, or where Dickens is seen as the prototype sensationalist, whereas Broughton, whose sensationalism lies in thrilling emotion, tends to be excluded if the focus is on crime and detection. Sheridan LeFanu and Ouida, veering respectively towards the Gothic and the high-society romance, often help to demarcate borderlines. Some feminist criticism, echoing Elaine Showalter's dismissal of "male sensationalism" as "relatively conventional" (*Literature*, 162), examines the genre almost exclusively in terms of a subversive female tradition. Given the genre's fluid boundaries, the following sketches can suggest only something of the variety of sensation novels, and of the issues they raise.

William Wilkie Collins (1824–89), whose reputation rests principally on the four novels he wrote in the 1860s, has always been the most highly regarded of the sensation writers. He was known for ingenious plots, "modern" subject matter, and dramatic presentation before 1860; what gave *The Woman in White* its immediate sensational success was the exceptional control of suspense and surprise, an innovative narrative method and a wholly new type of villain, all of which helped to make it both much imitated and essentially inimitable. The basic ingredients of its plot reappear in many other sensation novels: mercenary marriage, greed, inherited property, family secrets involving issues of legitimacy and sanity. In any hands these topics, and the counternarratives of detection and true love, may raise questions concerning marriage and the family as social institutions and the laws and conventions that uphold them; and any novels that achieve their "sensational" effects by showing authority, convention, and morality being questioned can appear subversive even where the challenges are overcome and conventional order finally restored. Collins's novels self-consciously reveal the hypocrisy, equivocations, and contradictions in Victorian morality, but it is their conscious and unconscious revelation and interrogation of the processes by which bourgeois society itself, and within it individual identity, are shaped and maintained that have attracted most recent critical attention.

Thus, in *The Woman in White*, underlying the immediate mysteries—who the "woman in white" is and what she might know about the wicked Sir Percival Glyde—is a deeper question of identity centering on the interchangeability of the deranged, illegitimate "woman in white," Anne Catherick, and the heiress and putative heroine, Laura Fairlie. Laura's quintessential feminine virtues—purity, innocence, and passivity—offer no protection from evil; rather they are precisely what make her vulnerable to it and her home a potential place of "terror, doubt and division." Stripped of the trappings of her class, Laura can be substituted for Anne in an asylum that, as is made clear, merely echoes the various imprisonments that constitute the domestic life of the dutiful daughter and wife. At the same time, feminine vulnerability is shown to be essential to the construction of masculine identity. Walter Hartright, the principal narrator, who begins the novel in the somewhat feminine role of impoverished art tutor, earns his eventual promotion to landed patriarch by rescuing Laura, uncovering evils and restoring order, and arguably by containing the potential threat to his own masculinity of Laura's enterprising and independent stepsister Marian. The text is deeply ambivalent about Marian, allowing her to give voice to the constraints of a life in petticoats and the repressive effects for women of marriage, yet associating her intelligence and capacity for action with ugly "masculine" features (32), and reducing her finally to the status of unmarried aunt, family help, and perhaps erotic side-interest for Hartright. Readers who think they judge her better than Hartright find themselves paired in their appreciation of her with the self-styled "Napoleon of crime," Count Fosco.

Fosco typifies Collins's most open exploitation of the dialogic nature of the novel. As the fascinating foreign villain behind the stereotypical wicked baronet, he is uncomfortably persuasive in demonstrating the complicity between English society and the crime it professes to deplore, a claim repeated in *No Name* (1862) by the swindler Captain Wragge, and in *Armadale* (1866) by the villainess Lydia Gwilt and her accomplices. More pervasively, Collins's disruption of narrative authority (often through multiple narration), his emphasis on "play, doubling and duplicity" (Taylor, 1), and his intermingling of the real and the fantastic undercut the eventual victories of rationality and right. The rejection of omniscience in fiction of this period has been linked to a wider crisis of authority in Victorian literature and society, related to both the general decline of religious faith and the loss of what Raymond Williams has called the "knowable community" (16). In this modern, changing, expanding world, Collins's characters typically lose, change, and share their identities with remarkable facility: Magdalen Vanstone in *No Name*, deprived by illegitimacy of legal identity, becomes a virtuoso impersonator; Lydia Gwilt, steeped in evil from her servant childhood, passes for a perfect lady and is (almost) transformed by love; Alan Armadales proliferate; in *The Moonstone*, Franklin Blake is significantly ignorant about himself. The problems of knowing others and being known (rightly or wrongly) by them, even of accurately knowing oneself in a world where appearances persistently belie reality, are almost everywhere in sensation fiction inseparable from the key activities of uncovering secrets and detecting crime. In Collins's work the possibility of self-determination—the cornerstone of both the Victorian ethic of self-help and the conventional realist plot—is further undermined by eerie settings, uncanny events, prophetic dreams, and repeated references to fate and destiny.

The writer closest to Collins in terms of social critique is Mary Elizabeth Braddon (1835–1915) who was, following the appearance in rapid succession of *Lady Audley's Secret* and *Aurora Floyd* at the start of her career, irrevocably associated with the sensational transgressive heroine. In both these works the heroine's appearance and ostensible character contradict conventional stereotypes and question normative ideas of femininity: The angelic golden-haired Lady Audley is a scheming, bigamous, murderous "fiend"; the passionate, inadvertently bigamous, whip-wielding, dark-haired Aurora is ultimately a more satisfactory "proper woman" than her meekly virtuous cousin Lucy. Like Collins, Braddon eventually endorses conventional domesticity, but not before the dramatic display of feeling, or "melodramatic excess," and the shifting narrative perspectives and tones disrupt and destabilize the orthodox moral. Whether or not they are criminals like Lady Audley, all Braddon's sensation heroines are women with secrets, which, by their very existence, reveal the inconsistencies of the domestic ideology.

Lady Audley, who, in Ann Cvetkovich's words, "represents the [sensation] genre in microcosm" (46), is notable for the range of Victorian anxieties—about gender, class, madness, and the family generally—that her secrets embody. As a lower-class woman, her skill in acting the perfect lady threatens class boundaries; as a trophy wife, she makes explicit the commercial basis of a marriage that convention would sentimentalize; and, most famously, she exposes the Victorian conflation of feminine assertion with madness. Collins's

Laura was an angel in the asylum; Lady Audley is the madwoman in the drawing room, except, of course, that, according to the doctor brought in to diagnose her condition, she is not mad but dangerous. Her actions, far from showing the inherited insanity she claims in extenuation, are chillingly logical in a world where women are wholly dependent on men and on whatever advantages their looks can bring them, and where "'insanity' is simply the label society attaches to female assertion, ambition, self-interest, and outrage" (Showalter, *Malady,* 72). True madness, the novel suggests, is everywhere, part of the modern Zeitgeist in which all certainties are dissolved and anyone can be "mad today and sane tomorrow" (403). Robert Audley, who, even more overtly than Walter Hartright, discovers his manhood by restoring patriarchal order, ascertains his own sanity by expelling Lady Audley to a continental asylum that tellingly combines prison, nunnery, and bourgeois home. Unlike Collins, Braddon mocks the domesticity that is Robert's reward in a satirically ingenuous ending that leaves "the good people all happy and at peace" (447).

Lady Audley's artful impersonation of the ideal woman, for feminist critics, reflects the duplicity forced on middle-class women by an ideology that required them to suppress their selves in order to serve others, a necessity that could, in life and in fiction, lead to insanity. Olivia Arundel, in Braddon's *John Marchmont's Legacy* (1863), is driven mad by endless rounds of doing her duty and the frustration of unrequited love, and so attempts to destroy the lives of all around her. On the other hand, Ellen Wood associates the inherited insanity of Charlotte St. John, in *St. Martin's Eve* (1866), with lack of discipline as a child and undisciplined maternal feeling as an adult. Although some sympathy is generated for Charlotte as a second wife whose child will not inherit, her action in locking her five-year-old stepson in a burning room is too gruesome to be seen, like the "carefully controlled female fantasy" of *Lady Audley's Secret* (Showalter, *Literature,* 163), as a justifiable retaliation on the patriarchal society that has wronged her.

Wood (1814–87), whose first novel was a tub-thumping temperance tract, made her name with another horrid warning for transgressive women, Lady Isabel in *East Lynne,* who elopes from home and family only to return unrecognized as governess to her children, suffer at length, and die. Wood seized with some genius upon the possibility of exploiting sensation in the name of morality. *East Lynne* has the usual sensation elements of murder, false accusations, disguises, and detection but reserves its most powerful effects for its elaborate dramatization of the consequences of transgression as Isabel is forced to watch her former husband and his second wife repeatedly reenact the scenes of marital bliss she once enjoyed and to nurse her dying son without disclosing their relationship. The melodramatically emphasized moral is that women must suffer any trial in marriage or be "plunged into an abyss of horror, from which there [is] never more to be any escape; never more, never more" (289). Isabel's fate is so overdetermined, however, and the novel's investment in the spectacle of female suffering so extreme that Wood appears oblivious to other possibilities within her text, including its devastating depiction of patriarchal tyranny and fantasized female revenge. More transparently than the novels of Collins and Braddon, *East Lynne* simultaneously expresses and contains potentially subversive social criticism, particularly, as Cvetkovich has shown, by deflecting attention from the underlying social causes of Isabel's problems onto her personal vulnerability, allowing the reader the relief of tears without offering any grounds for real change.

Rhoda Broughton (1840–1920) made a doubly sensational debut, with two novels appearing almost simultaneously in 1867 after book publication of her first novel, *Not Wisely but Too Well*, was delayed by demands that she tone down its "hot-blooded passion" (Jewsbury). The much-criticized sensuality of Braddon's heroines in fact often lies in the voyeuristic eye of beholders, including those of the narrator who dwells with relish on female appearance. In general, as Brantlinger notes, "the mysteries of sensation fiction . . . *hint* at a hidden, steamy or perverse sexuality that may itself never be described or explained" (*Lesson*, 159, emphasis added). Broughton makes sexuality explicit and central. Her plots are love stories, not always happy (though surprisingly funny), with few secrets. Her first two heroines yearn through three volumes for unavailable men, whose own physical charms are vividly delineated. Kate Chester, "soft" and "round" of figure, with the characteristic sensational mass of hair, refuses her married lover's burning entreaties, espouses philanthropy, retreats to a convent and dies. Nell Lestrange marries to save her father from ruin, graphically describes the physical repulsiveness of her old husband, unsuccessfully entreats her lover to take her away, and looks forward to early death. These heroines were perhaps more shocking to contemporaries because they are otherwise cheerful, "modern," outstandingly ordinary girls. Broughton's aim was clearly to reclaim the intensity of feeling associated with female sexuality from the world of crime and melodrama and to relocate it in the world of ordinary middle-class life, while demonstrating by extensive reference to poetry and paintings that it was already a proper subject for "high" art.

SENSATION AFTER 1870

The decline of the sensation phenomenon has been linked to the shifting interests of major practitioners and to changes in the economic and political climate and in the circumstances of literary production. As Jenny Bourne Taylor suggests with reference to Collins, the 1860s was a period "when a particularly productive range of constraints and possibilities converged" (209); as these dispersed inevitably, so too did the genre's power to shock. Sensation's continuing influence can be seen in works by Anthony Trollope and Thomas Hardy among others, and Gwendolen Harleth in Eliot's *Daniel Deronda* may be a response to it. Of the newer cultural "commodities" that emerged in the increasingly specialized popular fiction market, the detective novel is usually considered sensation's most direct offspring, with the thriller a more distant descendant.

Over the last twenty years, attention to sensation fiction has focused largely on the relation between text and context, reading the novels and reactions as interventions in mid-Victorian literary and social debates, and in the light of a variety of critical theories and approaches. Peter Brooks's work on the "melodramatic imagination," for example, has been used to illuminate specific sensation techniques and motifs and the differing kinds of ideological work the genre can perform. Marxist criticism emphasizes the significance of modes of production and explores the novels for evidence of how "crises are managed and resolved in the popular imagination" (Rance, 105). Secrets, detection, and surveillance have attracted Foucauldian and psychoanalytic analysis, and explorations of the gaze informed by film theory have further helped to explain power relations within the novels and have highlighted the narrow line, in some instances, between sensation and pornography. The roles of real and implied readers are also attracting attention, especially, given the construction of the genre as feminine, from feminist critics. Most recent critical work in fact adapts and combines approaches, and no summary does justice to the scope and sophistication of discussions. If, as has been argued, the sensation genre was constructed by its critical reception in the 1860s, its reconstruction in modern criticism suggests how much these highly entertaining novels contributed to the formation of mid-Victorian culture.

WORKS CITED AND SELECTED WORKS FOR FURTHER READING

Boyle, Thomas. *Black Swine in the Sewers of Hampstead: Beneath the Surface of Victorian Sensationalism.* New York: Viking, 1989.

Braddon, Mary Elizabeth. *Lady Audley's Secret.* Oxford: Oxford UP, 1992.

Brantlinger, Patrick. "What Is Sensational about the 'Sensation Novel?'" *Nineteenth-Century Fiction* 37 (June 1982): 1–28.

———. *The Reading Lesson: The Threat of Mass Literacy in the Nineteenth-Century British Fiction.* Bloomington: Indiana UP, 1998.

Brooks, Peter. *The Melodramatic Imagination: Balzac, Henry James, Melodrama, and the Mode of Excess.* New York: Columbia UP, 1985.

Collins, Wilkie. *The Woman in White.* 1860. In *The Works of Wilkie Collins.* Vol. 1. New York: AMS, 1970.

Cvetkovich, Ann. *Mixed Feelings: Feminism, Mass Culture, and Victorian Sensationalism.* New Brunswick: Rutgers UP, 1992.

Edwards, Peter. *Some Mid-Victorian Thrillers: The Sensation Novel, Its Friends and Foes.* Queensland: U of Queensland P, 1971.

Flint, Kate. *The Woman Reader, 1837–1914.* Oxford: Oxford UP, 1993.

Gilbert, Pamela K. *Disease, Desire, and the Body in Victorian Women's Popular Novels.* Cambridge: Cambridge UP, 1997.

Hardy, Thomas. Prefatory Note. In *Desperate Remedies: A Novel,* pp. v–vi. By Hardy. London: Macmillan, 1951.

Hughes, Winifred. *The Maniac in the Cellar: Sensation Novels in the 1860s.* Princeton: Princeton UP, 1980.

Jewsbury, Geraldine. Letter, 2 July 1866. Readers' Reports. Bentley Archive. British Library.

"Literature." *The Victoria Magazine* 9 (September 1867): 475–480.

Loesberg, Jonathan. "The Ideology of Narrative Form in Sensation Fiction." *Representations* 13 (1986): 115–138.

[Mansel, H. L.] "Sensation Novels." *Quarterly Review* 113 (1863): 481–514.

Maurice, F. D. "The Education of Girls." Paper read to the Ninth Annual Meeting of the Association for the Promotion of Social Science. Reported in "The Social Science Congress," *The Victoria Magazine* 6 (November 1865): 1–22.

Miller, D. A. *The Novel and the Police.* Berkeley: U of California P, 1988.

[Oliphant, Margaret.] "Modern Novelists—Great and Small." *Blackwood's Edinburgh Magazine* 77 (May 1855): 554–563.

———. "Novels." *Blackwood's Edinburgh Magazine* 94 (1863): 168–183.

———. "Novels." *Blackwood's Edinburgh Magazine* 102 (1867): 257–280.

———. "Sensation Novels." *Blackwood's Edinburgh Magazine* 91 (1862): 564–584.

Pykett, Lyn. *The "Improper" Feminine: The Woman's Sensation Novel and the New Woman's Writing.* London: Routledge, 1992.

———. *The Sensation Novel from* The Woman in White *to* The Moonstone. Plymouth: Northcote, 1994.

Rance, Nicholas. *Wilkie Collins and Other Sensation Novelists: Walking the Moral Hospital.* Rutherford: Fairleigh Dickinson UP, 1991.

"Reviews of Books." *The Victoria Magazine* 12 (December 1868): 172–192.

Ruskin, John. *Sesame and Lilies.* 1865. *The Works of John Ruskin.* Ed. E. T. Cooke and Alexander Wedderburn. Vol. 18. London: George Allen, 1905.

"Sensational Novels." *The Victoria Magazine* 10 (March 1868): 455–465.

Showalter, Elaine. *The Female Malady: Women, Madness and English Culture, 1830–1980.* London: Virago, 1987.

———. *A Literature of Their Own: British Women Novelists from Brontë to Lessing.* Princeton: Princeton UP, 1977.

Sutherland, John. Introduction. *The Woman in White,* pp. vii–xxiii. By Wilkie Collins. Oxford: Oxford UP, 1996.

Taylor, Jenny Bourne. *In the Secret Theatre of the Home: Wilkie Collins, Sensation Narrative, and Nineteenth-Century Psychology.* London: Routledge, 1988.

Williams, Raymond. *The English Novel from Dickens to Lawrence.* London: Hogarth, 1984.

Wood, Ellen [Mrs. Henry]. *East Lynne.* London: Dent, 1984.

Victorian Juvenilia

Christine Alexander

Victorian juvenilia offer a new perspective on the culture of the period. Because children learn largely by imitation, their early writings represent a microcosm of the larger adult world, disclosing the concerns, ideologies, and values of the age. Yet the child was to be seen and not heard. Displayed in paintings, greeting cards, advertisements, and novels, the child was both a prominent symbol of innocence and a neglected figure in Victorian society. Despite a popular concern with education and child development, interest centered on the adult response to childhood. Novelists like Dickens, in *Hard Times* (1854), and Lewis Carroll, in the *Alice* books (1865 and 1871), understood the importance of fantasy for children, but there is little evidence of any general understanding of the needs of children or a readiness to listen to their point of view.

It is time the voice of the child was heard. The recovery, publication, and critical exploration of youthful writings (generally those produced before the age of twenty) is now under way, providing a large enough sample of individual studies to allow us to speak of juvenilia as a subgenre of literary culture. Scholarship to date has centered on the early works of a given writer with a view to examining their relationship to later work, and therefore revealing the writer's route to maturity. Numerous nineteenth-century children who wrote papers and diaries, however, never became adult authors; and some, like nine-year-old Daisy Ashford (*The Young Visiters* [1890]) achieved lasting fame by their youthful works alone. Such works are of interest in themselves, both for their own literary merit and for their biographical and historical value.

The Victorian era is particularly rich in juvenile writings that portray a passion and impetuosity that is lacking in the adult-directed longer works. The exotic African sagas of the Brontës, the teenage historical fictions of George Eliot, the whimsical contributions by the young Lewis Carroll to his own family magazines, and the experimental early journalism of the Stephen children survive as witness to the imaginative life of the child writer. They demonstrate the young author's appropriation of the adult world and the assumption of a power they would not otherwise have in a world where children were denied quite basic human rights, let alone a voice. They offer a window onto the development of self, uniquely documenting the apprenticeship of the youthful writer.

SOCIAL POSITION AND EDUCATION OF THE CHILD AUTHOR

Because literacy is a prerequisite for writing, Victorian literary juvenilia are middle- and upper-class phenomena. No records of stories by Victorian working-class children have yet come to light, suggesting that their imaginative life belonged chiefly to an oral tradition. Increasing concern throughout the century for child labor in mines, factories, and other industrial sites improved working conditions, and concern for "street children" led to reformatories for young delinquents, "ragged schools" for the homeless, and "barrack schools" where children were taught life skills and the values of middle-class reformers. Gradually a series of Education Acts, in particular that of 1870, extended the number of hours and categories of children attending school. Literacy improved, but the working class could not afford the luxury of the extended childhood of the more privileged. Although child labor in mines decreased by half from 1841 to 1881 as a result of legislation, children working as servants nearly doubled during the same period (Jordan, 126). The means and leisure to read and write were the preserve of the middle- and upper-class child.

The classic images of Jane Eyre and David Copperfield mistreated by their guardians, however, suggest that the life of even the more privileged child was not without its difficulties. They were not immune from abuse or neglect. There was minimal contact with parents, and children were left in the care of nursemaids, governesses, and tutors, or, if they were lucky, to their own devices. In 1851, some 50,000 children, mainly girls, were in the charge of governesses (Jordan, 155). From the age of seven, boys were increasingly likely to be boarders at preparatory or public schools, especially after the reforms of Thomas Arnold, headmaster of Rugby from 1828 to 1841, took root. The letter home was often the first literary effort of these young schoolboys. Many of these early writings are painfully self-conscious, reflecting the adults to whom they are addressed as much as the children who wish to please. Yet amongst the artifice there are revelations of self impossible to conceal. Twelve-year-old Charles Kingsley writes sententiously of his Bible reading at school, concealing his longing to return home:

I am now quite settled and very happy. I read my Bible every night, and try to profit by what I read, and I am sure I do. I am more happy now than I have been for a long time; but I do not like to talk about it, but to prove it by my conduct. (Kingsley, 8)

Robert Louis Stevenson, at the same age, is blunter about his dislike of Spring Grove School: "My dear Papa you told me to tell you whenever I was miserable. I do not feel well and I wish to get home. Do take me with you" (Booth and Mehew, 98). The letters of Lewis Carroll (or Charles Lutwidge Dodgson as he was then at twelve), from his first boarding school, describe his resilience when the boys played tricks on him and record his need of a toothbrush, blotting paper, and a shoehorn. "The chief games," he reported, "are football, wrestling, leap frog, and fighting" (Collingwood, 22). The details recording the social life of the child are as revealing as anything in *Tom Brown's Schooldays*. One wonders what lies behind the twelve-year-old Macaulay's "tolerably cheerful," "takes my part," and "quite a friend" in his letter home: "With respect to my health, I am very well, and tolerably cheerful, as Blundell, the best and most clever of all the scholars, is very kind, and talks to me and takes my part. He is quite a friend of Mr. Preston's" (Trevelyan, 40). Thackeray's childhood letters, too, written to his mother in India, after he was sent at the age of five to board with relatives in England, are revealing documents of the child's reaction to adult behavior: "Your old acquaintances are very kind to me and give me a great many Cakes, and great many Kisses but I do not let Charles Becher kiss me I only take those from the Ladies" (Ray, i, 8).

Agitation for better secondary schools for girls led by 1894 (as recorded by the Bryce Commission on Secondary Education) to at least 218 endowed and proprietary schools for girls, most founded since 1870 (Pedersen, 36). More numerous still were the private schools that had existed since the previous century, owned by an individual or family, like the one the Brontë sisters attended at Roe Head in Mirfield, Yorkshire, and to which Charlotte Brontë later returned as a governess-teacher. Benign as the system was at Roe Head and beneficial to a young pupil eager for self-improvement, Brontë still records in her Roe Head journal her frustration at the lack of time for imaginative play, or "making-out" as she calls the creative process in her early writing. Only in her home at Haworth Parsonage could she find the space, mentally and physically, to indulge in the writing of fiction.

For Emily Shore there was no threat of school competing with her imaginative life, no necessity to prepare for financial independence. Taught and nurtured at home by an exceptional Victorian father and supportive family, writing for Emily Shore was play or leisure-work through which she explored her experiences of the world and her very self. Her learning is recorded in her remarkable *Journal*, begun in 1831 when she was eleven and continued to within a few weeks of her death from consumption when she was nearly twenty. It is "a memoir of my character, and the changes and progress of my mind—its views, tastes, and feelings," which moves from a record of the young intellectual with a voracious appetite for knowledge, to the exploration of a spiritual voyage where the young self struggles with imminent death (Gates, xx–xxv). As a journal-keeper she is self-conscious and self-critical. In February 1835, for example, she alters her methods for studying botany: "I have hitherto been a very superficial botanist, attending to little besides the classification, and not studying the habits, properties, and uses of plants, as I do the habits of birds" (Gates, 89). Her minute observation of and fascination for the natural world rivals that of the young Edmund Gosse, and her output of histories, novelettes, verse, and journal documents a literary world as absorbing as that of the Brontës.

IMAGINARY WORLDS AND COLLABORATIVE PLAY

Pretence or make-believe extended for some Victorian children into a private world that they elaborated, systematized, and documented. Such highly organized imaginative activity was part of the childhood of brilliantly creative minds like Thomas de Quincey, Hartley Coleridge, the Brontës, Anthony Trollope, and Robert Louis Stevenson. Fragmentary evidence is all we have of Trollope's "castle in the air firmly built within my mind" (Trollope, 36) or of the tantalizing kingdom of Hartley Coleridge's Exjuria (*Essays and Marginalia*, ii, 265); but records of the most famous and most extensive imaginary world of the period still survive: the Brontë's "web in childhood" (Alexander, *An Edition*, ii, 379), as Charlotte Brontë referred to her family's creative enterprise.

Like all normal children, the Brontës' earliest games were physical: They encountered the adult world by re-enacting historical stories, chiefly derived from Scott's *Tales of a Grandfather,* which they read at an early age. There are reports of Emily Brontë breaking the branch of her father's favorite cherry tree while pretending to be Prince Charles escaping from the Roundheads. Their games centered on Branwell Brontë's toy soldiers, and one set in particular, brought from Leeds in April 1826, provided the catalyst for the "Young Men's Play," which (together with other plays) developed into the legendary Glass Town and Angrian sagas, set in the exotic new world of West Africa. Within this imaginary frame, they chronicled the rise and fall of political parties, of literary and artistic coteries, of heroes and heroines. Their choice of Africa as a site of play and their childhood construction of a new "British" society in that so-called dark continent is vivid testimony to how far the colonial experience had penetrated the psyche of the British public at that time (see Alexander, "Imagining Africa," 201–219).

After 1831 Emily and Anne Brontë formed their own mythical world of Gondal, few manuscripts of which still exist; but Charlotte and Branwell continued to write their Angrian saga for another eight years, until Charlotte was twenty-three. Their writings, all of which have now been published, develop an elaborate world of aristocratic intrigue based on the rival factions of their favorite characters: the Duke of Zamorna (son of the Duke of Wellington) and Alexander Percy, Lord Northangerland (based on the Northumberland Percys). As the children grew older, their saga became more sophisticated, mirroring an increasingly complex world. Material from real life—politics, newspapers, religious debates—was increasingly absorbed into their play, and they assumed a power and authority over their creation that no one could achieve in real life. The imaginary sagas absorbed their authors over such a length of time and to such an intensity of commitment that all happiness for two at least of the young writers was inextricably bound up with playing the game. Branwell never escaped his fictitious Angrian world, and Emily continued to play the Gondal game until the year of her death: It informs at least half her poetry and provided the inspiration for much of *Wuthering Heights*.

Many Victorian novelists owe their sense of literary assurance to such early collaborative play. Amy Levy, for example, gained her apprenticeship as a writer in the 1870s through her collaboration with a group of middle-class Jewish children. She organized a series of journals during her school days until her matriculation in 1879 as the first Jewish woman at Newnham College, Cambridge. Her later advocacy of female social and sexual emancipation is clearly illustrated in her teenage sketches for one of the stories in "Harum Scarum": The left sketch shows an attractive young bride, kneeling in tears at the altar of a church opposite a grotesque old man with bulging money bags behind him; the right hand cameo, titled "office," portrays the "new woman" sitting at her desk, plainly dressed, her hair tied back, and looking absorbed but contented (Naomi Hetherington, work in progress on the Levy archives). Levy's short story "Euphemia: A Sketch," published in an 1880 issue of the *Victoria Magazine*, was originally written for her juvenile magazine *Kettle Drum* and appears in rough draft in her Cambridge notebooks, illustrating the key role her collaborative juvenilia played in her career as "new woman" journalist and novelist.

The earliest literary efforts of Virginia Woolf (née Stephen) and her siblings also developed from collaborative play and storytelling sessions in the nursery. There is one story that was constantly retold in ever more elaborate versions about the Dilke family next door, who could not pronounce their "Rs" and who were conspicuously richer than the Stephens. The fashionable Mrs. Ashton Dilke was also "tainted'—we are told by the nine-year-old Virginia in her diary—by her "connection with women's rights," an opinion the young author had obviously acquired from her mother (quoted in Lee, 37). Unlike the Brontës, however, there was no construction of a secret self-reflexive imaginary world. The Stephen children's literary play depended on family news and gossip, visits to concerts and plays, collaborative reading and discussion of books, riddles and games. In "A Sketch of the Past," Virginia recorded her method of obtaining copy from "the grown-up world into which I would dash for a moment and pick off some joke or little scene and dash back again upstairs to the nursery" (105). Above all, their creative efforts required parental approval. The Stephen children would watch in suspense from the next room for their parents' reactions to their latest issue of the "Hyde Park Gate News," their family journal, which they would place with trepidation on the breakfast table. Such a material adult audience had a marked effect on the editorial policy of the youngsters. Correct language and etiquette had to be observed, and adult taste pampered to, with the requisite "Article on Chekiness" [*sic*] which "should be nipped in the bud" if it is not be become "a great hindrance to mankind" ("Hyde Park Gate News," British Library). There is a self-conscious cleverness in the children's verbal play that again reflects their audience and their own sense of performance.

Written weekly, on and off, from 1891 until 1895, "The Hyde Park Gate News" is a valuable source of Stephen family culture, already mined by biographers. Toby and increasingly Virginia (as Toby was away at boarding school) were the main authors, with Vanessa and Adrian contributing. The stories by various family members share a tone and sense of humor. There is a mock seriousness and satire that rivals the best of Jane Austen's juvenilia. Virginia's fascination with the "marriage market," in particular, equals that of the young Austen: "Oh Georgina darling darling" is the opening to a proposal of marriage made at the monkey house at the zoo. "I love you with that fervent passion with which my father regards roast beef but I do not look upon you with the same eyes as my father for he likes Roast Beef for its taste but I like you for your personal merits" ("Hyde Park Gate News," British Library). This series of love letters from imaginary people to each other licensed the children to play at adult lovemaking, gleefully reflecting their embarrassment and scorn at such silly behavior. "You have jilted me most shamefully," writes Mr. John Harley to Miss Clara Dimsdale, who replies: "As I never kept your love-letters you can't have them back. I therefore return the stamps which you sent." As with the young Brontës, literary play provided the Stephen children with the license both to act out adult roles and to satirize them.

APPROPRIATION OF THE ADULT WORLD

Imitation, involving the reworking and experimentation with an original (rather than simply copying), is a major feature of literary juvenilia. It is one of the chief ways in which a child learns. The first imitative exercise in fiction of Mary Ann Evans (the young George Eliot) was a rewriting of Scott's *Waverley* at eight years old. The manuscript has not survived, but she records the event in the epigraph to Chapter 57 of *Middlemarch*, describing her juvenile writing "in lines that thwart like portly spiders ran" (465). In *The Mill on the Floss*, Chapter 33, Maggie Tulliver tells of a similar experience when reading Scott's *The Pirate*: "O, I began that once; I read to where Minna is walking with Cleveland, and I could never get to read the rest. I went on with it in my own head, and made several endings; but they were all unhappy" (306). A later literary effort, written at fourteen in a school notebook, has survived: Entitled "Edward Neville" and dated "March 16th 1834," it is a fragmentary novelette set during the English Civil War of 1650, featuring the historical regicide Henry Marten as the uncle of her fictional hero. Again, Scott is the model with the hero of *The Pirate*, Cleveland being rewritten as "the determined and haughty character" Edward Neville. There are strong parallels, too, with several novels by the "Historiographer Royal" to William IV, G.P.R. James, which the young George Eliot had read, confirming her early penchant for historical narrative (McMaster, *Neville*, vii).

In children's writing there is no contradiction between the literal and the fantastic. The Glass Town battles between the Brontës' "young men" and the native Ashantee tribes often read like dispatches from the Peninsula Wars, reported in local Yorkshire newspapers, until the heroes are miraculously "made alive" again by the Chief Genii (the controlling authors themselves). Likewise, fabulous accounts of the federal capital of Glass Town—a city of marble pillars, solemn domes, splendid palaces, and mighty towers, raised not by mere mortals but by "supernatural power"—and suggested by the grandiose perspectives of the Victorian historical painter John Martin, alternate with Dickensian descriptions of factories and slums and accounts of colonial expansion reworked from *Blackwood's* of the 1820s and 1830s. Charlotte Brontë makes no apology for interrupting her "Tales of the Islanders" with a breathless account of the passing of the Catholic Emancipation Act in the British Parliament in April 1829. Her father's support for the Bill is reflected here, although the general

Yorkshire anti-Catholic stance (that surfaces later in *Villette*) is appropriated elsewhere in her juvenilia.

The literary allusions of early childhood writings are surprisingly rich and varied. They are an important source of evidence for an author's formative reading. Mary Arnold's adolescent stories written between 1864 and 1869, for example, show a stylistic dependence on the novels of Bulwer-Lytton, Charlotte Yonge, Elizabeth Gaskell, and George Eliot that laid the foundations for the twenty-five novels she later produced as Mrs. Humphry Ward. Lewis Carroll's early parodies extend not only toward the great writers he studied at school (Shakespeare, Milton, Scott) but also toward visual icons of the establishment. In "The Rectory Umbrella" his pictures and text satirize paintings in the Vernon Gallery in London, images reproduced in *The Vernon Gallery of British Art* (1849–50). "The Scanty Meal," the seventeen-year old Carroll tells us, is intended "to illustrate the evils of homeopathy," currently popular amongst the intellectual elite in London. The old woman in Carroll's sketch is so thin because her husband "helped her to *nothing* instead of a nonillionth," a coinage Carroll footnotes as a mathematical fraction: one over a row of zeros, to throw fun at homeopathy's infinitely small medicinal doses (14). Such Victorian juvenilia exhibit a rich intertext of literary and social practice, which extends to the very shape and titles of the works, as the title-page of Emily Shore's first booklet attests. In a clear childish hand she prints in capitals: "Natural History, by Emily Shore, being an Account of Reptiles, Birds, and Quadrupeds, Potton, Biggleswade, Brook House, 1828, June 15th. Price 1 shilling" (Gates, viii).

PERIODICALS AND THE CREATION OF AUTHORSHIP

The periodical press was especially effective in initiating young readers into authorship. Family reading encouraged discussion of texts, and children imitated the self-conscious authors in such periodicals as *Blackwood's Edinburgh Magazine* and *Fraser's*. Contemporary juvenile magazines, published by the Religious Tract Society and Sunday School Unions for edification rather than entertainment, were less appealing. *The Boys' Own Magazine* (1855) and *Aunt Judy's Magazine* (1866) brought a lighter tone to children's periodicals, and by the end of the century *Our Young Folks* and *St. Nicholas Magazine* were soliciting contributions from children and encouraging aspiring child-authors.

Very little, if any, of this journalism for children actually inspired imitation by young authors. It was the adult papers, *Punch* and *The Times*, that provided the journalistic models for the family magazines of the young Lewis Carroll. *Punch* also had a strong influence on the Stephen children, but the favorite journal of Vanessa and Virginia as young girls was *Tit-Bits*, a mixture of announcements, stories, and correspondence. For the Brontës, *Blackwood's* and later *Fraser's* was crucial. Their first experience of journalism was *The Children's Friend*, edited by the Rev. Carus Wilson (the infamous model for the Reverend Brocklehurst in *Jane Eyre*). Its repetitive tales of the sanctimonious deaths of little children were no competition for the racy dialogue, reviews, and stories of *Blackwood's*. The colorful accounts of African and Arctic exploration; gothic tales; political, artistic, and philosophical debates; and the witty dialogue of *Blackwood's* fictitious and opinionated narrators—"Christopher North" and his gang—all found their way into the early writings of the Brontës (see Alexander, "Readers and Writers," 54–69).

Blackwood's provided more than simply content for the young Brontës' play. It converted their imaginative world into a literary enterprise, providing the necessary model for editorial notes, contents pages, letters to the editor, advertisements, serialized stories, poems, reviews of paintings and books. "Blackwood's Young Men's Magazine," edited first by Branwell and then by Charlotte, was a miniature replica of its namesake: hand-printed in minuscule script to imitate newsprint, with contributions signed by fictitious Glass Town authors, and measuring only 54 × 35 mm, a size proportionate to the original toy soldiers who were fast becoming a purely literary fiction.

Magazine culture also provided models for the early literary experience of Lewis Carroll. At twelve, he had already published a story entitled "The Unknown One" in the *Richmond School Magazine* (1845), and he insisted that the series of family magazines he edited between 1845 (when he was thirteen) and 1862 (when he was a talented Oxford undergraduate in his early twenties) should be of an equally professional standard. Four of the eight magazines survive: "Useful and Instructive Poetry," "The Rectory Magazine," "The Rectory Umbrella," and "Mischmasch"; and although they were addressed especially to the young members of the Croft Rectory, they also included an adult audience who occasionally contributed. Like the Brontës, Carroll assumed multiple personalities, wrote under different pseudonyms, and was an exacting editor. In "The Rectory Magazine" he castigates his siblings in an editorial entitled "Rust": "We opened our Editor's box this morning, expecting of course to find it overflowing with contributions and found it—our pen shudders and our ink blushes as we write—empty!" (38). He concludes with a drawing of a bovine-eyed figure with the caption "Ox-Eyed," a homonym for the "oxide" (his caustic wit) used against his rusty contributors in the article itself. The same stylistic idiosyncrasies—the flights of fancy, parody, punning, nonsense, and logic—that we associate with *Alice in Wonderland* can all be found in these early magazines.

The power of the editor could be exhilarating for the nascent writer, especially for the adolescent girl who might otherwise be relegated second place to that of her brother. Despite her legendary diffidence, Virginia Stephen seems to have relished the game of "publication" and her role as editor. Initially following the lead of her brother Toby in playing with words and phrases, and in adopting an authoritative adult voice in the many numbers of the "Hyde Park Gate News," she gained the confidence to survey her world with ease. The recognition of a successful literary performance, Virginia tells us, was "like being a violin and being played upon" ("A Sketch of the Past," 106). She was neither a decorative nor a useless object. In her role as author she was recognized as the equal of her elder brother.

EARLY WRITINGS AND NEGOTIATION OF GENDER BOUNDARIES

The early partnership of Charlotte and Branwell Brontë played a crucial role in the sister's development as a novelist. Although younger, Branwell, with the assurance of an idolized only son, initiated much of the structure and documentation of their imaginary world. He was the first editor of their magazines, handing over to Charlotte when he lost interest and preferred to "edit" newspapers for Glass Town. But this did not prevent him from complaining about his sister's inferior performance: She includes fewer drinking songs, more tales about magic, and dramatically decreases reports of bloodthirsty murders. With the assumption of several male pseudonyms, however, Charlotte quickly asserted her own authoritative voice, and a productive rivalry developed in which fictitious poets, historians, and politicians (the pseudonyms of both siblings) jockeyed for the Glass Town public's attention by writing scurrilous tales and reviews on each other's work, not unlike the *Blackwood's* review that so savaged the youthful Keats. For Charlotte, the adoption of a male pseudonym and in particular of a male narrator for her first novel, *The Professor*, was not only to mask the woman writer but was also a part of that assumption of literary authority practiced since childhood.

David Cohen and Stephen A. MacKeith suggest that girls' fantasy worlds tend to be more personal, more centered in romance and drama between various characters (104). In Charlotte Brontë's manuscripts the focus is on her hero Zamorna. His Byronic character, political machinations, and sensual encounters, legitimate and otherwise, are the focus of her attention. While her brother chronicled the development of Angria as a nation, its population statistics, the parliamentary debates, and business deals, the civil wars precipitated by the Satanic Percy and the external conflicts with the neighboring Ashantee tribes, Charlotte Brontë reveled in "soap-opera" romance. Increasingly influenced by Byron and by newspaper gossip of his affairs, she became intimately involved in the predicament of her heroines and their fascination for her aristocratic hero and his new kingdom of Angria. Her early literary interests were often as action-packed and brutal as those of Branwell, but her later concerns reflect a maturing adolescence. She became increasingly conscious of the "sinful" nature of her "world below" yet, until the age of twenty-three, she was content to revel with her brother in their amoral world, rivaled only by the violence and anarchy of their sister Emily's Gondal saga.

The Brontë juvenilia also reflect the different stereotypical educations accorded to different sexes. Although Emily Brontë took some lessons in the classics, as her fragmentary translation of Virgil attests (manuscript in the Kings School, Canterbury), there is a marked preponderance of classical allusion in Branwell's juvenilia compared to those of his sisters. The imitation of classical models was one of the first educational exercises for Victorian males, whereas the classics (like mathematics) were generally considered too strenuous for the female mind and at odds with future marriage prospects. Elizabeth Barrett Browning's experience was exceptional; her father employed a classics tutor for her and her brother, at ten she read Homer and Virgil with "delight inexpressible" (Kelley and Hudson, 350) and four years later she wrote her own epic, *The Battle of Marathon*. Her proud father had fifty copies privately printed and referred to his daughter as the Poet Laureate of Hope End, the name of their house.

Elizabeth Barrett wrote no fantasy fiction. Parental approval was important, and she masked her inner self in her strangely cynical early lyrics. The Brontës deliberately hid their secret world from prying adult eyes in the minuscule script and tiny size of their manuscripts, although their father could not help but be aware of their industry. Children like Elizabeth Barrett and John Ruskin, whose parents supervised their every move, produced chiefly imitation of the classics or nonfictional prose. It is no surprise that Ruskin's first published prose, at the age of fifteen, was an essay in Lou's *Magazine of Natural History* (1834), "On the causes of the colour of the Rhine." Yet it is remarkable that despite his mother's efforts to curtail his juvenile writing, Ruskin managed to publish some twenty-seven pieces of poetry and prose in the annual *Friendship's Offering* between 1835 and 1844, together with similar works in the *Amaranth*, the *Keepsake*, and the *Book of Beauty*. Sheila Emerson has analyzed Ruskin's textual strategies in the juvenilia for generating energy through resistance to boundaries, and David C. Hanson is exploring the perversely productive response of Ruskin in the juvenilia to psychological conflict and his mother's interference.

In "Recollections of My Childhood," Louisa May Alcott reflected on the very different parental influence of her philosopher father: "My father taught in the wise way which unfolds what lies in the child's nature, as a flower blooms, rather than crammed it, like a Strasburg goose, with more than it could digest" (quoted in Cheney, 29). In the evenings the house in Concord, Massachusetts, would be transformed into a theater and storytelling, games, or impromptu dramatics would be performed to admiring friends like Ralph Waldo Emerson. Louisa and her sister Anna were not only actors but usually the authors of such melodramas as "The Captive of Castile" or "Norna; or the Witch's Curse," recently published by the Juvenilia Press (McMaster). The editors of this volume draw attention to the frequency with which Alcott's heroines adopt masks in order to ensure social survival, a practice the future author of the very proper *Little Women* and the "Children's Friend" would employ despite her inclination for the sensational tales of her juvenilia. A nurturing family clearly challenges the negative effects of gender stereotypes, but with the onset of adolescence and the ambition to publish, the youthful female author encounters the "separate spheres" of the Victorian era.

Nevertheless, writing held out the prospect of a respectable career for young girls whose only alternative was working as a governess. For Rosa Praed, living on a remote sheep-station in Queensland, Australia, reading and writing became "living realities in the solitude and monotony of existence among the gum-trees" (i, 176). She was determined to be a novelist and devoured the English periodicals that arrived each month, especially *Blackwood's* and the *Illustrated London News*. At fifteen, encouraged by her mother, she edited a family journal, *The Marroon Magazine* (1866–68), inspired by the young Brontës' magazines that she had read about in Elizabeth Gaskell's biography of Charlotte Brontë. Here the future Rosa Praed, novelist and spiritualist in late Victorian London, began her literary career. Her serial, "Constance Vere," has all the hallmarks of her later writing, romantic in theme but often ironic in her portrayal of the social milieu of London's "Upper Bohemia." The early practice of writing provided intellectual, emotional and spiritual continuity for this young woman from colonial Queensland as she entered an adult life fraught with hardship and dislocation.

Financial independence was the prime motive for the early writings of Praed's compatriot, Ethel Turner. Her stepfather considered it inappropriate for her to work in a shop or as a governess, so within three months of leaving the Sydney Girls' High School at the age of eighteen, she and her sister Lilian became founders and joint editors of a magazine, *Parthenon*. It ran for three years (1888–1890), funded by advertisements and subscriptions, was reviewed favorably in the *Sydney Morning Herald*, and included contributions by several eminent Australian writers. It was hard work for the two girls to run a monthly with few business or literary connections and often having to supply all the copy themselves. Yet it gave Ethel Turner the security she needed and valuable experience of the realities of journalism, which was to provide her basic income for forty years, even after she became a famous children's novelist.

EXPLORATION OF THE SELF

In the intense religious climate of the nineteenth century, especially after Darwin's theories on evolution rocked previously held beliefs, many fiction writers turned to the portrayal of the child and the child's experience of growing up as a means of interpreting themselves, of understanding their own origins and relationship to the world. Edmund Gosse's *Father and Son* is perhaps the best example of this genre of semiautobiographical fiction, yet many children themselves had already begun the "self-analysis" that Harriet Martineau remarked was "the spirit of the times" (*Autobiography*, iii, 3). At fourteen, Elizabeth Barrett wrote "Glimpses into My Own Life and Literary Character," a manuscript in which she claimed that "at four I first mounted Pegasus" and "at six I thought myself privileged to show off feats of horsemanship" (Kelley and Hudson, 348). Her adolescent awareness of her scholarly shortcomings was acute: She records her tears of "contempt and anguish" when she compared her epic, *The Battle of Marathon*, with that of Homer. Her self-analysis is both precocious and amusing:

I was always of a determined and if thwarted violent disposition—My actions and temper were infinitely more inflexible at three years old than now at fourteen—At that early age I can perfectly remember reigning in the Nursery and being renowned amongst the servants for self love and excessive passion—When reproved I always considered myself as an injured martyr and bitter have been the tears I have shed over my supposed wrongs. At four and a half my great delight was poring over fairy phenomenons and the actions of necromancers—and the seven champions of Christendom in "Popular tales" has beguiled many a weary hour. At five I supposed myself a heroine and in my day dreams of bliss I constantly imaged to myself a forlorn damsel in distress rescued by some noble knight and often have I laid awake hours in darkness, "THINKING," as I expressed myself, but which was nothing more than musing on these fairy castles in the air!

I perfectly remember the delight I felt when I attained my sixth birthday I enjoyed my triumph to a great degree over the inhabitants of the nursery, there being no UP-START to dispute my authority. (349)

Exaggerated as this may be, such infant termagants are, by their own admission and example, very different from the ideal children—the quietly religious, diligent, submissive girls and their more lively, superior, and honorable brothers—in the contemporary writing for children by Juliana Ewing, Louisa Molesworth, Elizabeth Sewell, Charlotte Yonge, and others. Nor are the girls the embodiments of disinterested goodness that we often encounter in the novels of male authors like Dickens. Victorian literary juvenilia provide a valuable corrective to these myths of childhood. There is no evidence in these writings of the fictional convention of the sentimentalized, innocent child who affects a change in adults. Lewis Carroll's heroes bear no relation to Little Lord Fauntleroy. Instead the child narrator turns her gaze onto the adult world, experiencing vicariously an authority and lifestyle beyond her reach and testing the boundaries of the self in a variety of fictional relationships.

The Victorian period is notorious for its surveillance of the child. In his 1878 essay on "Child's Play," Robert Louis Stevenson attacked the tyranny with which adults tried to control even the child's perceptions of reality. He argued that children are not truth-tellers; they are fantasists. Whereas adults are constrained by their own inability to pretend, the play of children will by its nature be distinct. The same can be said of writing by children, unconstrained as this writing (which embodies play) often is by self-consciousness, by a judgmental audience, or by deference to social mores. We find in the manuscripts of child authors an audacity and humor that is often lacking in their adult productions. Virginia Woolf noted this in her essay on Jane Austen, and Katherine Mansfield recognized the freedom of the child author in her review of that remarkable work by the nine-year-old Daisy Ashford at the close of the Victorian period, *The Young Visiters*. She notes, "It is one of the most breathless novels we have ever read, for the entirely unmerciful and triumphant author seems to realize from the very first moment that she can do what she likes with us, and so we are flung into the dazzling air with Bernard and Ethel, and dashed to the earth with poor Mr. Salteena, without the relief of one dull moment" (400). Like the young Brontës, Lewis Carroll, and the Stephen children before her, Daisy Ashford unabashedly negotiates the adult world with its class anxiety and its erotic excitement. In an age characterized by a studied hypocrisy and concealment of the inner life, Victorian juvenilia provide revealing documentary evidence of the development of self and society.

WORKS CITED AND SELECTED WORKS FOR FURTHER READING

Alexander, Christine. *The Early Writings of Charlotte Brontë*. Oxford: Blackwell, 1983.

———. "Imagining Africa: The Brontës' Creations of Glass Town and Angria." In *Africa Today: A Multi-Disciplinary Snapshot of the Continent*, pp. 201–219. Ed. P. Alexander, R. Hutchinson and D. Schreuder. Canberra: Humanities Research Centre, 1996.

———. "Readers and Writers: *Blackwood's* and the Brontës." *The Gaskell Society Journal* 8 (1994): 54–69.

———, ed. *An Edition of the Early Writings of Charlotte Brontë*. 2 vols. Oxford: Blackwell, 1987–91.

Ashford, Daisy, *The Young Visiters, or, Mr. Salteena's*. London: Chatto and Windus, 1951.

Booth, Bradford A., and Ernest Mehew, eds. *The Letters of Robert Louis Stevenson.* Vol. 1. New Haven: Yale UP, 1994.

Carroll, Lewis. *The Rectory Magazine.* Austin: U of Texas P, 1975.

———. *The Rectory Umbrella and Mischmash.* Ed. Florence Milner. London: Cassell, 1932.

Cheney, Edhah D. *Louisa May Alcott: Her Life, Letters, and Journals.* 2nd ed. London: Sampson Low, 1890.

Cohen, David, and Stephen A. MacKeith, *The Development of Imagination: The Private Worlds of Children.* London: Routledge, 1991.

Coleridge, Hartley. *Essays and Marginalia.* 2 vols. 1851. Ed. Rev. Derwent Coleridge. Plainview: Books for Libraries P, 1973.

Collingwood, Stuart Dodgson, ed. *The Life and Letters of Lewis Carroll.* Detroit: Gale Research, 1967.

Eliot, George. *Middlemarch.* Ed. David Carroll. Oxford: Oxford UP, 1988.

———. *The Mill on the Floss.* Ed. Gordon S. Haight. Oxford: Oxford UP, 1980.

Emerson, Sheila. *Ruskin: The Genesis of Invention.* Cambridge: Cambridge UP, 1993.

Gates, Barbara Timm, ed. *Journal of Emily Shore.* Charlottesville: UP of Virginia, 1991.

Hanson, David C. "The Psychology of Fragmentation: A Bibliographic and Psychoanalytic Reconsideration of the Ruskin Juvenilia." *Text* 10 (1997): 237–258.

Jordan, Thomas E. *Victorian Childhood: Themes and Variations.* Albany: State U of New York P, 1987.

Kelley, Philip, and Ronald Hudson, eds. "Glimpses into My Own Life and Literary Character." *The Brownings' Correspondence.* Vol. 1. Winfield: Wedgestone, 1984.

Kingsley, Charles. *Charles Kingsley: His Letters and Memories of His Life.* 12th ed. London: Kegan Paul, 1882.

Lee, Hermione. *Virginia Woolf.* London: Chatto, 1996.

Mansfield, Katherine. "A Child and Her Note-Book." *The Athenaeum* (30 May 1919): 400.

Martineau, Harriet. *Autobiography.* 3 vols. London: Smith, Elder, 1877.

McMaster, Juliet, ed. *Edward Neville.* Alberta: Juvenilia, 1995.

———. *Norna; or The Witch's Curse.* Alberta: Juvenilia, 1994.

Neufeldt, Victor, ed. *The Works of Patrick Branwell Brontë: An Edition.* 3 vols. New York: Garland, 1997–99.

Pedersen, J. S. *The Reform of Girls' Secondary and Higher Education in Victorian England: A Study of Elites and Social Change.* New York: Garland, 1987.

Praed, Rosa. *The Head Station: A Novel of Australian Life.* 3 vols. London: Chapman and Hall, 1885.

Ray, Gordon N., ed. *The Letters and Private Papers of William Makepeace Thackeray.* 4 vols. Cambridge: Harvard UP, 1945–46.

Shealy, Daniel. *Louisa May Alcott's Fairy Tales and Fantasy Stories.* Knoxville: U of Tennessee P, 1990.

Stevenson, Robert Louis. "Child's Play." *Virgin Puerisque: Familiar Studies of Men and Books*. London: Dent, 1925.

Trevelyan, George Otto, ed. *The Life and Letters of Lord Macaulay*. London: Longmans, Green, 1876.

Trollope, Anthony. *An Autobiography*. Ed. Michael Sadleir. Oxford: Oxford UP, 1953.

Woolf, Virginia. "Hyde Park Gate News." Manuscript 70725, British Library.

———. "Jane Austen." *Jane Austen: A Collection of Critical Essays*. Ed. Ian Watt. Englewood Cliffs: Prentice-Hall, 1963.

———. "A Sketch of the Past." In *Moments of Being*. Ed. Jeanne Schulkind. Sussex: Sussex UP, 1976.

Moving Pictures: Film and the Representation of Victorian Fictions

Todd F. Davis

My task which I am trying to achieve is, by the powers of the written word, to make you hear, to make you feel—it is, before all, to make you *see*. (708)

—Joseph Conrad, "The Condition of Art"

It would take much more courage than I possess to intimate that the form of the novel as Dickens and Thackeray (for instance) saw it had any taint of incompleteness. (391–392)

—Henry James, "The Art of Fiction"

I hold myself supremely blest—blest beyond what language can express. (396)

—Charlotte Brontë, *Jane Eyre*

Certainly, many novelists have as a goal the idea that they might in some way, as Joseph Conrad suggests, make the reader *see* the world created by the alchemy of their words. For these writers, the success a given work achieves is based largely upon the novelist's ability to represent some part of the world and the characters who act upon its stage in a manner that draws a reader into the fabricated reality of its fiction, implicating the reader in the very action of the narrative itself. To this same end, then, the filmmaker attempts to translate the text of a screenplay—at times adapted from a novel—into a representation that visually re-creates a world and its people in such a fashion that the viewer truly sees what transpires in the film's events and, as Conrad also suggests, feels what the characters feel. With film, the viewer is at once removed yet intimate with the characters and their trials; as both a voyeur and participant, one watches a film to enter into a kind of relationship where identification with a given character's joys or sufferings takes on such power that, as Wayne Booth suggests in *The Company We Keep: An Ethics of Fiction* (1988), a friendship of sorts develops. Of course, Conrad's selective and directed use of the word *see* reveals his intention as a novelist: Conrad's notion of an artist focuses on a desire to bring the reader into an empathetic relationship with the lives of those created by his text, both as observer and vicarious participant. Perhaps the conventions of the Victorian novel—what Harold Bloom calls "the canonical novel at its strongest" (310)—with its penchant for depth of feeling, its efforts at identification, and its voluminous and encyclopedic attention to cultural customs and ephemeral detail, seems well suited to Conrad's desire for sight and, consequently, insight. The breadth and depth of much Victorian fiction, as Henry James argues, does not have the "taint of incompleteness."

Not surprisingly, then, over the course of the twentieth century, the shape of film narratives has been informed most radically and profoundly by Victorian ideas about the nature of story. As the Victorian age drew to a close, the development of the very technology that would allow for a new narrative medium flourished and later was co-opted by the Hollywood studio system. It is within this system that many directors and writers looked to the conventions of the nineteenth-century novel—both for artistic and financial reasons—as they began to construct cinematic narratives. In *Novel to Film: An Introduction to the Theory of Adaptation* (1996), Brian McFarlane explains that "as soon as cinema began to see itself as a narrative entertainment, the idea of ransacking the novel—that already established repository of narrative fiction—for source material got underway, and the process has continued more or less unabated for ninety years" (6–7). Even though the filmic possibilities of form and structure have expanded dramatically over the last century, many feature filmmakers continue to subscribe to these earlier conventions, and, not surprisingly, film adaptations of Victorian texts continue to appear regularly in Hollywood.

According to Teresa De Lauretis, the success of such adaptations appears to hinge upon a film's ability to please. In *Alice Doesn't: Feminism, Semiotics, Cinema* (1984), De Lauretis contends that a film may "please" its spectators in a variety of ways—by its technical, artistic, or critical interest—but that the most effective films satisfy the spectator's desire "to know" and "to see" (136). Like Conrad and other Victorians, it appears that De Lauretis uses the terms "to know" and "to see" to suggest that our desire for human connection remains at the root of our involvement with narrative, and that narrative alone has the ability to satisfy or thwart such desire. Speaking specifically about film narratives, Vivian Sobchack contends that film "more than any other medium of human communication . . . makes itself sensuously and sensibly manifest as the expression of experience by experience" (37). Thus, our desire for connection with other humans, our longing to be moved as we experience vicariously what a film or novel's protagonist experiences, may be the primary impetus for the marked success of Victorian novel adaptations to the screen. In contrast, postmodern novels and films often use highly stylized conventions to create distance between the viewer and the narrative. The use of metafictional techniques highlights the constructed nature of the medium and, in turn, thwarts the spectator's desire to know and to see in any conventionally Victorian sense. Although postmodern theorists and artists might argue that the conventions of metafiction have more philosophical integrity, such conventions do not address the distress or anxiety that the postmodern paradigm shift creates for many in the reading and viewing audience. Interestingly, some contemporary filmmakers and novelists attempt to wed such Victorian and postmodern concerns, creating unusual, provocative, and heartfelt works like John Irving's *The World According to Garp* (1976) and *The Cider House Rules* (1985), Sam Mendes's *American Beauty* (1999), or Paul Thomas Anderson's *Magnolia* (1999).

Of course, we also must acknowledge that the artists who help translate Victorian novels to the screen do not live outside the strictures of the present moment either. The decision to make a film based upon a Victorian text in the contemporary landscape, as Franco Zeffirelli did with *Jane Eyre* (1996), cannot be judged as either naïve or nostalgic, nor can it be seen as a deliberate attempt to ignore the boundaries or strictures of our own place in time. Certainly, Zeffirelli's ideas about art have been informed by the more than 150 years that have passed between the publication of Brontë's novel and his resolve to adapt it to the screen. In the transformation of the novel from a print text to a visual text—a metamorphosis that rivals the caterpillar's own dramatic and decisive evolution into a butterfly—Zeffirelli clearly imparts his own twentieth-century imprint. Making good use of Brontë's first person narration, Zeffirelli offers Jane's point of view as the driving narrative force, highlighting her strength in a way undoubtedly affected by the significant and abundant feminist criticism devoted to Brontë's text over the past forty years. Though no filmmaker could translate the sheer weight of Jane's suffering, her endurance, and faithfulness—as Henry James intimates in his comment about Dickens and Thackeray, the Victorian novel's length allows it a completeness, a breadth, that contemporary forms of narrative cannot approach—nonetheless, Zeffirelli captures the attention and empathy of his audience by allowing us to see what Jane sees, to feel what Jane feels. He does not attempt to explain away the enigmatic quality of the morose and, at times, foreboding Rochester; nor does he strive to transform Jane's beauty in some cliché manner as the film concludes, a theatrical move included in Robert Stevenson's 1944 interpretation of *Jane Eyre* that offered a classic Hollywood glamor shot of Joan Fontaine. As one would expect from a contemporary reworking of *Jane Eyre*, ideas of beauty have been altered radically by the feminist revolution, and now the viewer comes to see that Jane has been beautiful all along, that her beauty comes from a spiritual strength too often overlooked, and that our inability to see her beauty demonstrates how in some ways we are more like Rochester than Jane. The conclusion of Zeffirelli's *Jane Eyre*, like the novel's, moves the viewer toward a form of catharsis, an expiation of angst over her long suffering. But perhaps more than the novel, Zeffirelli's film emphasizes the dramatic shift in power that has occurred in the relationship between Jane and Rochester; Zeffirelli stresses that Jane's ability to stay true to herself, to her ideas of womanhood, has made all the difference in the world. Hence, when one compares the redemptive narrative structure of the book and the film, the resonance depends more on intertextual dialogue than upon a crass transliteration of its images and ideas.

A director's fidelity to the original print text, however, continues to be at the root of much critical disenchantment with Victorian film adaptations. As McFarlane explains, since the very first film adaptation, the "discussion . . . has been bedeviled by the fidelity issue, no doubt ascribable in part to the novel's coming first [and] in part to the ingrained sense of literature's greater respectability in traditional critical circles" (8). How true is a given film to the text upon which it is based? Does Zeffirelli capture the original intention or meaning of Brontë's novel? Is Jane Campion's *Portrait of a Lady* (1996) Jamesian in its ethos and ambience, or has she shifted the work to fit her own ideological concerns? Can the strength and darkness of Thomas Hardy's prose be translated into film by Roman Polanski? And has Michael Winterbottom changed more than just the name of Hardy's novel in his film *Jude* (1996)? Such questions in and of themselves seem odd in contemporary critical circles when we stop and consider that any idea of a single, correct meaning or interpretation of a text was dismissed within the profession long ago. Even more, the idea of fidelity so narrowly defined seems frighteningly similar to a fundamentalist reading of a sacred text: literalist and dogmatic, bound to cause injury. Certainly such critics should attempt to gain a bit of distance by first admitting that no feature film can encompass the breadth of any Victorian text. Even those novels adapted by the BBC in series form cannot adequately translate the text of a novel. There is not enough time, enough space, or enough funding to make it happen. Moreover, the shift from one medium to another—even if there were sufficient money and time to film the novel's every detail, every action—simply and conclusively demands that the narrative undergo a sea change. One might as well ask if a painting—another form of visual art—can capture effectively the "contents" of a novel. Although we might judge whether the translation of a novel into a visual art form is more or less effective in its re-creation of the mood or ethos of a given work, it can never be said that one art form may take the place of another. Rather, the translation should be seen as something new, similar to the translation of a print text from French to English or from English to Spanish, for example. There is a relationship between the two texts, but the translation should be judged independently by those who understand best the new art object's language—in our case, the language of film.

In his thoughtful essay, "Adapting and Being Adaptable," the novelist Malcolm Bradbury explains that for some purists "a good novel is quite simply irreducible; it exists already, as the right words in the right order, its aesthetic existence complete, and it can only be corrupted by being transliterated or translated into another medium" (300–301). But Bradbury, who has worked at film adaptation himself, does not subscribe to such ideas. Rather, he suggests that even though "fictions may possess a powerful distinctiveness and originality . . . they are also part of a shared community of story. . . . The habit of transfer and translation of story from one medium to another and one language to another is part of the essential history of forms" (301). What, then, might be the single characteristic that virtually all film adaptations of Victorian novels share in their shift from one form to another? Not surprisingly, given many Victorian novelists' penchant for and use of emotion, I would argue that it is the desire and ability of Victorian narratives to move an audience, to make that audience empathize and to be transformed emotionally in some way by the joys and sorrows of human life that makes the crucial difference. Discussing Charles Dickens's *Bleak House*, Harold Bloom confesses that "each time I re-read the novel, I tend to cry whenever Esther Summerson cries, and I don't think I am being sentimental." Bloom insists that the "reader must identify with her or simply not read the book in the old-fashioned sense of reading, which," according to Bloom, "is the only sense that matters. . . . Esther weeps at every mark of kindness and love that she encounters," explains Bloom, and "at our best, when we are not caught in death in life, we are tempted to weep also," he concludes (311).

Therefore, when Polanski brings Hardy's *Tess of the d'Urbervilles* (1979) to the screen, a film he directs not long after the success of *Chinatown* (1974), he must find a new language to translate Hardy's text. The existential angst that swells beneath *Chinatown*'s film-noir façade, the swirling bewilderment that is at the center of that film's penultimate moment, has little place in Hardy's landscape. Although in *Chinatown* Polanski makes us feel something for Evelyn Cross Mulwray (Faye Dunaway), it has little to do with empathy. We do not weep for her. We may be pained by the perverse situation that has wronged her; we may be outraged by her father's actions; but Polanski does not tell the story in such a way that we are moved to tears, as Bloom suggests. We are not encouraged to feel with her, to believe that we too might have been subjected to such pain, except for the blind blessing of chance. In *Tess*, however, Polanski's technique shifts radically. In this film, the director's goal rests squarely upon the idea that empathy may transform a viewing audience. Instead of the stylized trappings of film noir—with its aesthetics of objectification and voyeurism—*Tess* explores the tragedy and victimization of one we are made to identify with. Polanski hopes to construct a relationship between the viewer and Tess, as Hardy does over the course of his novel, so that in the end the narrative enters through our heart first, not our intellect. In "Polanski in Wessex," William Costanzo affirms the director's decision, explaining that Polanski wished to film a story that belonged to "the universe of those authors who tell about certain things, the deepest human sentiments" (74), and judging from the response of both the critical and popular audience, Polanski achieved just that.

Clearly, the work of Charles Dickens attempts to describe human sentiment in much the same way, and his continued popularity—demonstrated in part by over 100 film adaptations of his work—offers a convincing example of the role of emotion in the "success" of a given text with a general reading or viewing audience. In "The King of the Novel," John Irving contends that "the intention of a novel by Charles Dickens is to move you emotionally, not intellectually" (349). In his efforts to make his characters incredibly alive and indispensable, Dickens sees the tools of sentiment and emotion as the most powerful and engaging, and many of the finest film adaptations of his work depend primarily upon these very qualities. Is it any wonder that *A Christmas Carol* (1843) has been adapted to film no less than twenty-eight times over the course of the past century? When one stops to consider the treacherous sorrow that Scrooge casts upon those who live and work with him and, subsequently, the tremendous joy shared by all at the advent of his unlikely redemption, it is no surprise that the power of emotional transformation manifests itself not only in the lives of Dickens's characters but also in those of the film's viewers. Similarly, *Great Expectations* (1861)—a novel adapted to the screen on at least eight occasions—relies less upon a specific historical or cultural setting and far more upon the idea of how we may react to the sorrow and duress of Pip, regardless of time and place. Such translations imply—by their very decision to change locales and time frames—that Victorian cultures, as is the case with any other cultural period, find strength not in their idiosyncrasies but in their common human desires. For this reason, Alfonso Cuarón's 1998 translation of

Great Expectations—which shifts the time and setting of the novel from Victorian England to a decaying Neo-Gothic Mansion in 1960s Florida and later to the present-day art world of New York City—seems less a violation of Dickens's vision than some of the more radical film translations of Shakespearean texts, for instance. The film is a successful translation, not because it remains true to the letter of the text but because it is faithful to the spirit of the text—to the sorrows and joys of Pip and the ultimate sadness of Estella when she finally realizes that the obsessions of Miss Havisham have become her own.

During the 1990s, Henry James received more attention from Hollywood than perhaps any other Victorian author. No less than ten films find their origins in the urbane, suave, and psychologically sophisticated texts of James, an author concerned with the tensions between the customs of class and money often associated with Europe and the new social liberties emerging on the horizon of the American landscape. "What to do with James," bemoans critic Daphne Merkin, "who, by his own admission, had trouble with what he called the 'solidity of specification,' and whose unique skill was his self-professed 'appeal to incalculability'—for intimating, in other words, that which is psychologically most oblique" (121). What to do, indeed? Despite the many obstacles that might stand in the way of translating James to the screen, directors as diverse as Jane Campion and Agnieszka Holland have delved into the prodigious textual worlds James created, often in an attempt to wed their own vision to his. Campion's *Portrait of a Lady*, for example, has been characterized as a film that "translates the intellectual vigor of James's prose into an imaginative visual style" (Sterritt, 13), excavating "a gothic element . . . that is often overlooked" (Pawelczak, 78).

Whether in praise or in criticism, however, virtually all reviews of Campion's adaptation note that the film carries with it a feminist reinvention of James's ideas, that the text does not speak with one voice but takes on a multivocality that accounts for the dramatic shifts in thought concerning liberation and gender that have occurred over the course of the past century. Such alterations should not be seen as a distortion or violation of James's text, however, but, rather, as the inevitable outcome of the act of interpretation. As a director interprets the work of an author, her own cultural and ideological position must play a role, and the narratives created from the interplay of the director and the author proffer a hybrid whose fruit only grows in richness. This coalescing of vision is demonstrated quite powerfully in Holland's *Washington Square* (1997). In this film, the Polish-born director brings the same passion and intensity she demonstrated in *Europa, Europa* (1990) to a tale of an heiress's romantic misfortunes. David Denby contends that in *Washington Square* Holland "gives every emotion its full stop. . . . People run up and down stairs, tremble, and shout," Denby writes. "The filmmakers seem determined to expose the elements of melodrama and erotic anguish beneath James's powerfully urbane manner" (92). Deliberately changing tone and style, Holland searches out the undercurrent of James's voice, and, in the process, creates a new text, one cognizant of the role emotion may play in examining the psychology of cultural transition.

Whether it be the work of James, Brontë, Hardy, or some other Victorian novelist, film passes before light in the darkened space of the cinema, casting its images upon the screen of our imaginations. Pictures literally move before us and, in those special moments, metaphorically move within us, helping us to feel, to experience what is beyond our own limited world. Victorian novelists often sought to engage their audiences by means of emotion and empathy—as a heroine suffered, so too did the reader; as she sought and found redemption, the reader also was renewed. Perhaps the merging of Victorian narratives with film marks the natural progression of this very human aspiration. Describing Michael Winterbottom's *Jude*, Rocco Simonetti might have been speaking of our encounter with any number of films adapted from Victorian texts. "Watching it is an *experience*, by which I mean one gets caught up in its stream of life depiction of the characters, their time and place," Simonetti explains. "We never feel . . . as if the story has been designed merely to push our buttons, to go for only the most predictable emotional responses" (73). Herein lies the secret to the success of many films based upon Victorian fictions: Their stories remain the most human—always unpredictable, yet always connected to the heart.

WORKS CITED AND SELECTED WORKS FOR FURTHER READING

Ashton, Jean. "Reflecting Consciousness: Three Approaches to Henry James." *Literature/Film Quarterly* 4 (1976): 230–239.

Atkins, Elizabeth. "*Jane Eyre* Transformed." *Literature/Film Quarterly* 21.1 (1993): 54–60.

Aycock, Wendell, and Michael Schoenecke. *Film and Literature: A Comparative Approach to Adaptation*. Lubbock: Texas Tech UP, 1998.

Bloom, Harold. *The Western Canon: The Books and School of the Ages*. New York: Harcourt Brace, 1994.

Booth, Wayne C. *The Company We Keep: An Ethics of Fiction*. Berkeley: U of California P, 1988.

Bradbury, Malcolm. *No, Not Bloomsbury*. New York: Columbia UP, 1988.

Bradley, John R. *Henry James on Stage and Screen*. New York: Palgrave, 2000.

Brontë, Charlotte. *Jane Eyre*. New York: Norton, 1987.

Campion, Jane. *The Portrait of a Lady*. With Nicole Kidman, John Malkovich, and Barbara Hershey. Gramercy, 1996.

Cartmell, Deborah. *Adaptations: From Text to Screen, Screen to Text*. London: Routledge, 1999.

Conrad, Joseph. "The Condition of Art." In *The Portable Conrad*, pp. 705–716. Ed. Morton Dauwen Zabel. New York: Penguin, 1976.

Costanzo, William. "Polanski in Wessex." *Literature/Film Quarterly* 9.2 (1981): 72–77.

Cuarón, Alfonso. *Great Expectations*. With Ethan Hawke, Gwyneth Paltrow, and Anne Bancroft. Twentieth-Century Fox, 1998.

De Lauretis, Teresa. *Alice Doesn't: Feminism, Semiotics, Cinema*. Bloomington: Indiana UP, 1984.

Denby, David. Review of *Washington Square*, directed by Agnieszka Holland. *New York*, 13 October 1997, 92.

Giddings, Robert. *Screening the Novel: The Theory and Practice of Literary Dramatization*. New York: St. Martin's, 1990.

Giddings, Robert, and Erica Sheen. *The Classic Novel: From Page to Screen*. New York: St. Martin's, 2000.

Gott, Richard. "We Must Stay True to the Real Henry James." *New Statesman* (30 January 1998): 46.

Holland, Agnieszka. *Washington Square*. With Jennifer Jason Leigh, Albert Finney, and Maggie Smith. Buena Vista, 1997.

Irving, John. "The King of the Novel." In *Trying to Save Piggy Sneed*, pp. 347–81. New York: Arcade, 1996.

James, Henry. "The Art of Fiction." *The Portable Henry James*, pp. 391–418. Ed. Morton Dauwen Zabel. New York: Viking, 1960.

Klein, Michael, and Gillian Parker. *The English Novel and the Movies*. New York: Ungar, 1981.

Lupack, Barbara Tepa. *Nineteenth-Century Women at the Movies: Adapting Classic Women's Fiction to Film*. Bowling Green: Bowling Green State UP, 1999.

McFarlane, Brian. *Novel to Film: An Introduction to the Theory of Adaptation*. Oxford: Clarendon, 1996.

Merkin, Daphne. "The Escape Artist." *The New Yorker* (10 November 1997): 121–122.

Moore, Gene M. *Conrad on Film*. Cambridge: Cambridge UP, 1998.

Naremore, James. *Film Adaptation*. New Brunswick: Rutgers UP, 2000.

Pawelczak, Andy. Review of *The Portrait of a Lady*, directed by Jane Campion. *Films in Review* (2 January 1997): 78.

Peary, Gerald, and Robert Shatzkin. *The Classic American Novel and the Movies*. New York: Unger, 1977.

Polanski, Roman. *Tess*. With John Collin, Tony Church, and Nastassja Kinski. Columbia, 1979.

Sadoff, Dianne F. "'Intimate Disarray': The Henry James Movies." *Henry James Review* 19.3 (1998): 286–295.

———. "Looking at Tess: The Female Figure in Two Narrative Media." *The Sense of Sex: Feminist Perspectives on Hardy*, pp. 149–171. Ed. Margaret R. Higonnet. Urbana: U of Illinois P, 1993.

Simonetti, Rocco. Review of *Jude*, directed by Michael Winterbottom. *Films in Review* (2 January 1997): 73.

Sobchack, Vivian. "Phenomenology and the Film Experience." In *Viewing Positions: Ways of Seeing Film*. Ed. Linda Williams. New Brunswick: Rutgers UP, 1994.

Sterritt, David. Review of *The Portrait of a Lady*, directed by Jane Campion. *Christian Science Monitor*, 24 December 1996, 13.

Stevenson, Robert. *Jane Eyre*. With Orson Welles, Joan Fontaine, and Margaret O'Brien. Twentieth-Century Fox, 1944.

Winterbottom, Michael. *Jude*. With Christopher Eccleston, Kate Winslet, and Liam Cunningham. Gramercy, 1996.

Zeffirelli, Franco. *Jane Eyre*. With William Hurt, Charlotte Gainsbourg, Joan Plowright, and Anna Paquin. Miramax, 1996.

IV
Major Authors of the Victorian Era

Religion in the Novels of Charlotte and Anne Brontë

Marianne Thormählen

Reading the Brontë novels without any awareness of the religious context in which they were created is not only perfectly possible, it is what the vast majority of academic critics, not to mention "common readers," have done for decades. In other words, it has the legitimacy of practice, and the practice has often been both fruitful and exciting. When the religious dimension is brought into the picture, however, the canvas expands and perspectives change. Relationships between men and women remain crucial, but power structures are no longer the main issue. Psychological processes still engage the reader's interest, but their origins and directions appear in a different light, and so do the moral dilemmas confronted and resolved by the fictional characters. The ensuing discussion revisits some familiar scenes and events in the novels of Charlotte and Anne Brontë, suggesting how a degree of acquaintance with the religious climate and the theological debate of the mid-nineteenth century might modify the twenty-first-century reader's response to them.

OBEYING THE LAWS OF GOD

If present-day commentators on *Jane Eyre* take an unfavorable view of Mr. Rochester, it is usually because they regard him as a kind of Bluebeard who would, if he had managed to make Jane his mistress (whether or not he was bigamously married to her), have turned her into a second Bertha Mason, or at least another Céline or Clara. For anyone who sees him in that light, he is an oppressor of women whose dangerousness is only broken by blindness and mutilation. Student readers of the novel, however, often find Jane's desertion of him hard to understand: To generations used to the idea that people who love each other are entitled to living together, her renunciation makes little sense.

The agonized deliberations that precede Jane's departure contain insights that are immediately comprehensible from a purely worldly point of view, above all the conviction that if she were to yield to Rochester's pleas, he would one day come to think of her with the same contempt that he expressed towards his cast-off mistresses (III, i, 316). However, it is significant that Jane commits that realization to her "heart, that it might remain there to serve . . . as aid in the time of trial."

In the most decisive moments of Jane Eyre's life, neither conscience, nor reason, nor feeling is powerful enough to direct her on its own. Her guide, to which these qualities in combination help her respond, is a "voice within" (III, i, 301). That voice is activated by thought: Tired of her "servitude" at Lowood, she "proceeded *to think*" (I, x, 87); alone in her room after the abortive wedding, she is able to disengage herself from the events that had dragged her along, "and now I thought . . . but *now, I thought*" (II, xi, 298); and after St. John's proposal, she demands "a quarter of an hour to think" (III, viii, 409).

Necessary as a preliminary, reflection stops short of setting Jane on the right course. When the inner voice dictates her actions, it speaks through her heart, not her reason, and its utterance is a response to a religious impulse. Thinking could not save her from the flood of despair in her chamber at Thornfield, nor from the confusion and uncertainty that beset her on the brink of yielding to St. John. In the first instance, "a remembrance of God . . . begot an unuttered prayer" (II, xi, 299); the second crisis is resolved as a result of her "[entreaty] of Heaven," "Shew me—shew me the path!" Without those impulses, Jane would not have possessed the strength to "do what was right; and only that" (III, ix, 424). Thus summoned and prepared for by principled reflection, God's guidance never fails to materialize and to sustain the petitioner through the crisis.

Blind and maimed, Rochester at Ferndean goes through the same process. Seeing and acknowledging that his "doom" was just, he begins to repent and conceives a "wish for reconcilement" with God (III, xi, 452). The next step is "sincere" prayer, followed by the "mysterious summons" that rescues Jane from St. John and returns her to him. To a reader for whom religion is irrelevant, Rochester's chastisement may seem overly harsh. His catalogue of past sins is a very substantial one, though. Above all, previous setbacks failed to make him realize that "[t]he human and fallible should not arrogate a power with which the divine and perfect alone can be safely entrusted," and that every occasion on which he has said of any strange, unsanctioned line of action, "Let it be right" (I, xiv, 139), has had hellish consequences.

It was this man, her idol, who almost became Jane's "hope of heaven" and "stood between [her] and every thought of religion, as an eclipse intervenes between man and the broad sun" (II, ix, 277). Her transgression against God, though less spectacular and deliberate than his, was hence not inconsiderable, especially when viewed in the context of Protestant Christianity in which spiritual progress rests on direct communication between God and man/woman.

The Brontës were raised in a household where religious inquiry was constantly pursued. A combination of Evangelical Anglicanism and Wesleyan piety formed Patrick Brontë's spiritual base and laid the foundations for the theological explorations of his children. They sometimes moved far away from that base; the Brontës' novels, poems, and letters testify to their acquaintance with different denominations and a variety of more or less unorthodox theological views. In one respect, though, the Evangelical heritage is discernible throughout the Brontë fiction, especially Charlotte's and Anne's: Evangelicalism, "the religion of the heart," was peculiarly concerned with engaging the passions, and the link between faith and love is manifest throughout the work of these authors.

It is when Jane Eyre realizes that St. John, who has taken away her "liberty of mind" (III, viii, 402) with his persistent demands, is not interested in her heart that her fear of him evaporates: "He had held me in awe, because he had held me in doubt" (III, viii, 411). The first time she heard him preach, she knew that he was as far from spiritual harmony as she (III, iv, 357); now, encouraged by his "fallibilities," she sees him as a human being with whom she can feel free to disagree. A marriage where the husband wants no more from his wife than the labor of a comrade and "a neophyte's respect and submission to his hierophant" (III, viii, 413) must be rejected by a woman whose whole being is centered in her heart. When Jane returns to Rochester, she makes it clear that she does so without any restrictions or reservations: "She is all here: her heart, too" (III, xi, 439); "All my heart is yours, sir" (III, xi, 449).

The word "hierophant," used twice of St. John in relation to Jane (see also III, ix, 423), also strikes an ominous note to a reader familiar with the theological context of the Brontë fiction: A hierophant is an interpreter of sacred mysteries, and Charlotte Brontë followed Thomas Arnold in rejecting the idea that the Christian needs such an intercessor between himself/herself and God. "Priesthood is essentially mediation," said Arnold, and to the Protestant Christian worship does not require such sacerdotal services. The main reason for Charlotte Brontë's hostility towards the Church of Rome is found in her aversion to the idea that the individual's spiritual progress should be directed and supervised, and hence obstructed, by priests (see later discussion). For Jane Eyre, surrendering her "unblighted self" to St. John would entail submission to his control not only of her daily life and labors but of that "heart and mind" that are the Christian's vehicles for communication with God. In view of her cousin's "imperfection" (III, viii, 411) both as a clergyman and as a human being, such a step would be "an error of judgment" (III, ix, 423) that might have cost her more than life and happiness.

Much has been written about the oppressive tactics to which both Rochester and St. John submit Jane Eyre; but it is rarely observed that she regards herself as their "equal" as a spiritual being (II, viii, 256; III, viii, 411), and that neither man is able to assert his domination over her once she has barricaded herself in this realization. Indeed, Rochester is forced to acknowledge that although he could easily conquer Jane physically, it is her spirit he really wants, and he is powerless to command it: It "would escape to heaven before [he] could call [himself] possessor of its clay dwelling-place" (III, i, 322).

The differences between the two leading male characters in *Jane Eyre* and the young heroine of *The Tenant of Wildfell Hall* would appear to be large enough to blot out any similarity. From a theological point of view, though, the disillusioned landowner, the ambitious clergyman, and the infatuated teenage girl commit the same kind of sin: They believe themselves authorized not only to interpret God's wishes for other human beings but to implement those wishes regardless of protests and warnings and without any consideration for the duty of the desired object to assume responsibility for her/his own spiritual welfare. Rochester announces, "It will atone—it will atone. . . . It will expiate at God's tribunal. I know my Maker sanctions what I do" (II, viii, 258) and withholds knowledge of his bigamous project from Jane. St. John fails to acknowledge the force of Jane's objection to his scheme when, distressed at the silence of her inner voice, she repeats "My heart is mute": Like Rochester on a previous occasion, he "arrogate[s] a power with which the divine and perfect alone can be safely entrusted" and has the temerity to reply, "Then I must speak for it" (III, viii, 407). Young Helen in Anne Brontë's second novel, in the full flush of first love and confident of her superior powers, ignores her appalled aunt's incontestable statement, "Mr. Huntingdon . . . is not without the common faculties of men: he is not so light-headed as to be irresponsible: his Maker has endowed him with reason and conscience as well as the rest of us; the scriptures are open to him as well as to others" (XX, 166). Helen is bent on saving him, forgetting that no human being can intercede between another person and God.

The punishments that follow come close to destroying Helen Huntingdon, and any reader may be excused for finding them exaggerated; but she herself never wallows in self-pity. She knows of her transgression and makes no attempt to exculpate herself. The lowest point in her life is reached when she realizes that far from being able to save her "scapegrace" husband, she and their little son are actually in danger of being dragged down with him. So powerless has the radiant would-be savior of another become that she comes close to doubting her ability to save herself.

However, Helen manages to steer clear of the sin of despair in throwing herself on God's mercy (see, for instance, XXXIII, 292; XXXVI, 312; and XXXVII, 321). As her marriage to Arthur Huntingdon ceases to be anything but wretched cohabitation, Walter Hargrave mounts a campaign to seduce her, and she is not wholly invulnerable to it: Hargrave's tastes are akin to her own, he aids her attempts to protect her son from his vicious father's influence, and he showers the harassed and humiliated woman with expressions of adoration. Besides, she cannot but register that he does love her, and there are indications that she is not indifferent to him—not least the danger she herself perceives in his endeavor. However, Helen's disastrous marriage has taught her enough about the dangers of believing herself in possession of special religious insights that would authorize her to act against the rules of her Church. Neither Hargrave nor Gilbert Markham, who also attempts to persuade her that "that man is *not* your husband" (XLV, 384), can bring her to the point where she would disobey what Jane Eyre in a similar situation called "the law given by God; sanctioned by man" (III, i, 321).

UNIVERSAL SALVATION

Helen's reluctance to console her dying husband by dwelling on her secret persuasion that salvation eventually comes to every man, even the vilest sinner, should be seen in connection with the brutal and protracted process in the course of which she is stripped of every shred of spiritual vanity. Even as a girl, she was aware that there was "danger" in the belief that the fire for which sinners were bound after death was not eternal but long-lasting, and that it purified rather than punished; she told her aunt that she "would not publish it abroad, if [she] thought that any poor wretch would be likely to presume upon it to his own destruction." As a woman, she retains the "glorious thought" (XX, 167) but is so far from any idea of "publishing it abroad" that she refrains from trying to comfort Arthur along such lines, even when he is frantic with fear of what awaits him after death. Whatever private hopes she may have, she is no intercessor between God and man—like Thomas Arnold, she holds that only Jesus Christ can serve in that capacity (XLIX, 430)—but a demonstrably fallible human being. As such, she cannot take it upon herself to divert any impulse to repent on her husband's part by suggesting that it might not after all be necessary. It is true that she once—provoked by his bitter accusations—states that if she were indeed able to "look complacently on" while he was "howling in hell-fire," it would only be "from the assurance that [he was] being purified from [his] sins, and fitted to enjoy the happiness [she] felt" (XLIX, 425). The sufferer fails to seize on the conditional consolation, though, which is perhaps not to be wondered at. After all, the likelihood that he will burn after death is not questioned, and to anyone who confronts that prospect, the difference between eternal hellfire and long-lasting purgatorial flames is hardly radical enough to induce instant optimism. At this stage, Arthur Huntingdon still prefers to take refuge in the contention that "it's all a fable."

   To mid-nineteenth-century readers, however, this exchange will have seemed remarkable for several reasons. To begin with, Arthur Huntingdon quotes Luke 16: 19–31 in the course of it, and Helen picks up the allusion in her reply. The story of Lazarus and Dives is one of the best-known Biblical passages on salvation versus damnation, and Anne Brontë's way of using it indicates that she was aware of its significance in the eschatological debate of centuries. The notion that the blessed contemplate the sufferings of the damned with approbation—referred to as "the abominable fancy" by a Victorian theologian—was obsolete as doctrine at the time when *The Tenant of Wildfell Hall* was written; but it was "around" as an idea, and theologically competent readers will immediately have reacted to its manifestation in a novel that explicitly and repeatedly argues that there is no such thing as eternal punishment.

   This conviction, commonly referred to as "universalism," was the subject of intense debate in the mid-nineteenth century. If the "abominable fancy" was widely rejected, the contention that the wicked will undergo endless torment after death still prevailed. Clergymen who maintained that the Atonement of Christ opens the door to Heaven for everybody, though they may have disagreed on the exact nature of the commitment and awareness required in those to whom salvation was to be extended, faced expulsion from their posts. Anne and Charlotte Brontë hence took a courageous stand when they permitted Helen Huntingdon and Helen Burns (see *Jane Eyre* I, vi, 59; II, vi, 239–240) to express the idea that God would not allow the human soul "to degenerate from man to fiend" (*Jane Eyre*, I, vi, 59). It was also brave of Anne to place the received theological wisdom on the subject of perdition in the mouth of her archsinner, who echoes a number of clerical writers on the last things in inquiring:

"Are we not to be judged according to the deeds done in the body? Where's the use of a probationary existence, if a man may spend it as he pleases, just contrary to God's decrees, and then go to Heaven with the best[?]" (*The Tenant of Wildfell Hall,* XLIX, 429)

The fact that the belief that Helen Huntingdon "cherishes in [her] own heart" (XX, 167) amounts to subscribing to the idea of Purgatory lends special emphasis to the theological boldness of the Brontës. Never part of orthodox Protestant theology, Purgatory was constantly decried by early-Victorian anti-Catholic writers, along with such offensive (to them) doctrines and practices as the worship of saints, transubstantiation, and Papal supremacy. It was extremely radical for a daughter of an Anglican clergyman rooted in Evangelicalism to give currency, albeit through a fictional character, to the idea of a stage of purgation leading to heavenly bliss for all human beings. Nor was this view sure to offend Evangelicals and middle-of-the-road Anglicans only; the implicit negation of the doctrine of predestination was an affront to Anglicans with Calvinist leanings, of whom there were many in the Church of England in the Brontës' lifetime, not least in their part of the country and among clergymen they knew personally.

CHARLOTTE BRONTË'S ANTI-CATHOLICISM

It is noteworthy that Charlotte Brontë, whose *Villette* expresses disapproval of the notion of Purgatory, does not permit Jane Eyre to solve the problem of how to envisage the same destination for two such dissimilar souls as Helen Burns's and Mrs. Reed's. Charlotte's anti-Catholicism has often been remarked on and sometimes studied. Several commentators have called her opposition to the Roman Catholic faith and its manifestations bigoted. To some extent, the question of whether it deserves that characterization is a matter of taste. However, it should be pointed out that when contemplated in its historical context, Charlotte's aversion against Roman Catholicism comes across as a phenomenon that is broadly typical of its time (transferring the bigotry issue to mid-nineteenth-century Anglicans in general), and that it is more mildly articulated than the sentiments expressed by large numbers of anti-Catholic authors, clerical writers and novelists alike.

The growth of Roman Catholicism in the British Isles during the second quarter of the nineteenth century alarmed many people associated with the Church of England, including comparatively tolerant ones who had supported the emancipation of the Irish Catholics (Patrick Brontë, for one). The influx of Irish immigrants was one factor; another, and one that caused greater concern among the educated classes, was the burgeoning Oxford Movement and the conversions to Rome of some its most prominent members. Converts were also frequently attracted by the medieval charm of Roman Catholicism and/or repelled by the fundamental link between Church and state that the Church of England stood for. Around the middle of the nineteenth century, Rome intensified its operations in England (the so-called Papal Aggression). Anglican clergymen responded with spates of vehemently anti-Catholic treatises and pamphlets, and Anglican writers of fiction turned out novel after novel warning their readers against the fatal wiles of Rome's agents, from beautiful ladies of rank and foreign governesses to insidious priests.

Like all these works, Charlotte Brontë's *The Professor* and *Villette* contain expressions of disapproval directed against Roman Catholic services and the lavish ornamentation associated with them ("mummeries" being the standard term of abuse), as well as against aspects of Roman Catholic doctrine. The tone of these censorious passages is usually fairly light, though, and Charlotte's main problem with Roman Catholicism is found on another plane.

In Madame Beck's school, the girls are brought up in physical comfort and even indulgence, but the price they have to pay for their pleasant existence consists in surrendering their minds to the guidance of the Roman Catholic Church: "There, as elsewhere, the CHURCH strove to bring up her children robust in body, feeble in soul, fat, ruddy, hale, joyous, ignorant, unthinking, unquestioning. 'Eat, drink, and live!' she says. 'Look after your bodies; leave your souls to me. . . . I guarantee their final fate' (*Villette*, XIV, 157). People whose minds are reared in slavery never plumb the depths of remorse at their own failings and never experience the glory of divine grace dispensed directly by God to the human soul that turns to him, humbly begging a loving father's forgiveness. Only a person to whom spiritual liberty was more important than material comfort could have attacked this miserable bargain as bitterly as Charlotte Brontë did. It was not, at least not primarily, a faith or an institution that she reviled, but an oppressive mechanism that seemed to her to excuse human beings from the duty to assume responsibility for their own lives, both in this world and in the next.

THE INDIVIDUAL'S OBLIGATIONS TO HERSELF

Obligation to self is a duty that no Brontë heroine is allowed to shirk. Struggling with it, Lucy Snowe tries to derive strength from the thought that under God's great plan, some people must suffer more than others, and that "of that number, [she is] one" (*Villette*, XV, 194; see also XXXI, 453 and XXXVIII, 548). In *Shirley*, neither of the two main characters escapes it: The energetic and independent Shirley Keeldar places herself under the guidance of her conscience, taking care to foster her generous impulses; and Caroline Helstone, whose thwarted love erodes her physical strength, does not permit her troubles or her uncle's power over her to obscure her obligation to make the best of her situation, and to be wise if she cannot be good. Similarly, Agnes Grey forbids herself to surrender to the depression that comes over her as she believes that she has lost the love of her life. After a period of self-neglect, she takes up the burden of existence again:

"Should I shrink from the work that God had set before me, because it was not fitted to my taste? Did not He know best what I should do, and where I ought to labour? and should I long to quit His service before I had finished my task, and expect to enter into His rest without having labored to earn it? 'No; by His help I will arise and address myself diligently to my appointed duty.'" (XXI, 172)

TRUST IN AND LOVE OF GOD

The preceding review of religious dimensions in the fiction of Charlotte and Anne Brontë may seem weighted towards somewhat melancholy perspectives, but the forbidding aspects are offset by a trust in God that invariably proves justified. Helen Huntingdon's finding strength and solace in her religion has already been referred to, but she is not the only Brontë character whose faith is thus rewarded. For instance, Jane Eyre, looking up to the night sky and becoming aware of God's omnipotence and omnipresence, is relieved of her greatest fear in leaving Thornfield: that Rochester will be destroyed without her. "Sure was I of His efficiency to save what He had made.... I turned my prayer to thanksgiving.... Mr. Rochester was safe: he was God's, and by God would he be guarded" (III, ii, 329). Later, realizing that she will not survive the bitter night outside Moor House, Jane commits herself to God: "I can but die ... and I believe in God. Let me try to wait His will in silence" (III, ii, 340). St. John answers her out of the dark and admits her to the house that turns out to harbor the family affection that the orphan had longed for all her life. Lucy Snowe, also close to destitution, believes that it is God who guides her to Villette and Madame Beck's *pensionnat*, and her nocturnal prayers are "all thanksgiving" (VIII, 84). It is impossible to experience that kind of trust in a God who cannot be relied on to love all his created beings, and confidence in this all-encompassing love accounts both for the Brontës' rejection of predestination and for their universalism. God's love and the love of God are at the core of Evangelical Anglicanism, and the ten pages on the subject that form a kind of centerpiece in *Agnes Grey* neatly summarize the view of it that was expounded by leading theologians associated with "the religion of the heart." If the Brontë novels had not been love stories, they would not have won millions of new readers all over the world with every new generation. Most of those readers are unaware of the fact that a human love that does not harmonize with God's law, and thus offends against the highest love, is never allowed to fructify in the fiction of the Brontës, and having it pointed out may not make much difference to them. After all, as I suggested by way of introduction, the tribulations of Brontë lovers may be perceived from a number of intriguing perspectives, including, of course, the pressure of external forces of various kinds. However, I hope to have shown that a further dimension is brought into play when the novels are read in the context of nineteenth-century religion in England, and I like to think that that dimension will become more richly orchestrated as a result of future scholarship.

WORKS CITED AND SELECTED WORKS FOR FURTHER READING

Barker, Juliet. *The Brontës*. London: Weidenfeld and Nicolson, 1994.

Brontë, Anne. *Agnes Grey*. Ed. Robert Inglesfield and Hilda Marsden. Oxford: Oxford UP, 1992.

———. *The Tenant of Wildfell Hall*. Ed. Herbert Rosengarten. Oxford: Oxford UP, 1998.

Brontë, Charlotte. *Jane Eyre*. Ed. Margaret Smith. Oxford: Oxford UP, 2001.

———. *The Professor*. Ed. Herbert Rosengarten. Oxford: Oxford UP, 2000.

———. *Shirley*. Ed. Herbert Rosengarten. Oxford: Oxford UP, 1998.

———. *Villette*. Ed. Margaret Smith. Oxford: Oxford UP, 1998.

Chadwick, Owen. *The Victorian Church, Part One, 1829–1859*. London: A. & C. Black, 1966.

Clark-Beattie, Rosemary. "Fables of Rebellion: Anti-Catholicism and the Structure of *Villette*." *ELH* 53 (1986): 821–847.

Cunningham, Valentine. *Everywhere Spoken Against: Dissent in the Victorian Novel*. Oxford: Clarendon, 1975.

Duthie, Enid. *The Foreign Vision of Charlotte Brontë*. London: Macmillan, 1975.

Jay, Elisabeth. *The Religion of the Heart: Anglican Evangelicalism and the Nineteenth-Century Novel*. Oxford: Clarendon, 1979.

Jedrzejewski, Jan. "Charlotte Brontë and Roman Catholicism." *Brontë Society Transactions* 25.2 (2000): 121–135.

Lonoff, Sue, ed. *The Belgian Essays, Charlotte and Emily Brontë: A Critical Edition*. New Haven: Yale UP, 1996.

Maison, Margaret M. *Search Your Soul, Eustace: A Survey of the Religious Novel in the Victorian Age*. London: Sheed and Ward, 1961.

Martin, Robert Bernard. *The Accents of Persuasion: Charlotte Brontë's Novels*. London: Faber and Faber, 1966.

McGlamery, Gayla. "'This Unlicked Wolf-Cub': Anti-Catholicism in Charlotte Brontë's *Villette*." *Cahiers Victoriens et Édouardiens* 37 (1993): 55–71.

Myer, Valerie Grosvenor. *Charlotte Brontë: Truculent Spirit*. London: Barnes and Noble, 1975.

Norman, Edward. *Roman Catholicism in England from the Elizabethan Settlement to the Second Vatican Council*. Oxford: Oxford UP, 1985.

Phillips, Marion J. "Charlotte Brontë and the Priesthood of All Believers." *Brontë Society Transactions* 20.3 (1991): 145–146.

———. "Charlotte Brontë's Concepts of Transcendence and of Authority in Religion as Manifested in Her Correspondence." Diss. King's College, University of London, 1991.

Reardon, Bernard M. G. *From Coleridge to Gore: A Century of Religious Thought in Britain*. London: Longman, 1971.

Storr, Vernon. *The Development of English Theology in the Nineteenth Century, 1800–1860*. London: Longman, 1913.

Thormählen, Marianne. *The Brontës and Religion*. Cambridge: Cambridge UP, 1999.

Winnifrith, Tom. *The Brontës and Their Background: Romance and Reality*. London: Macmillan, 1973.

Wolff, Robert Lee. *Gains and Losses: Novels of Faith and Doubt in Victorian England*. London: John Murray, 1977.

Victorian Professionalism and Charlotte Brontë's Villette

Russell Poole

In seeking to comprehend this most involuted of novels, one of the crucial issues has been how to synthesize the livelihood and the inner life of its protagonist, Lucy Snowe, into a single dynamic. How do the "enterprising individualist" and the "helpless victim" (Eagleton, *Myths of Power*, 64–65) engage within the individual subject? To what extent is Lucy's status as an emerging professional significant across the gender divide? In looking at *Villette*, Charlotte Brontë's last completed novel (1853), I begin with its story of female achievement and later consider how far it relates to Victorian professionalism more generally. Though naturally neither an exhaustive analysis of the novel nor a full account of the criticism and scholarship is feasible, I refer along the way to some of the distinctive features of this work and some of the leading critics and scholars who have written about it.

A CAREER WOMAN

As a woman with a mind "a good deal bent upon success" (146), Lucy clearly expresses aspirations to a career. "I am a rising character: once an old lady's companion, then a nursery-governess, now a school-teacher," she tells Ginevra Fanshawe, an elegant young lady with no career aspirations whatever (394). By the end of the book, Lucy has risen to become what we might term a

capitalist owner-operator. By undertaking senior teaching among her responsibilities, from a comparatively early stage, with little experience and no training by way of foundation, she lays claims to proficiency in her vocation and
therefore to a place on the border of fully professional status. In accordance
with the separation of public and private spheres (Heyck, 195), women could
work as nurses, teachers, and governesses, while maintaining a safely respectable quasi-domestic or pastoral role, whereas the professions of journalism,
theater, and office work were too uncompromisingly public. Within that spectrum, Lucy's job description is comparatively conformist, because boarding
schools for girls, run by ladies, were a common form of education in England at
the time of writing, and her role scarcely anticipates the more controversial establishment, after the mid-century, of girls' public schools. Nevertheless the
novel views Lucy's transgression, however mild, with a characteristic ambivalence, where opportunity and anxiety are represented with equal vividness.

On the side of opportunity, the text engages in what we might call a campaign of justification, some parts of it more overt than others, for women entering the public sphere. Implicit is the point already noted, that the transition
can be made to seem beguilingly gradualistic. Lucy glides into the role of
teacher from the contiguous roles of lady's companion and mother-substitute
(cf. Jacobus, 45). This liminality of status is symbolized in the architecture of
the *pensionnat* where Lucy teaches, with its uncertain boundaries between private and public space. Although the core premises are conventual in design and
ethos, protective of female privacy and chastity (cf. Gates), day pupils and outside teachers readily pass through its entrance. Equally, the premises chosen by
M. Paul for Lucy at the conclusion compromise between the privacy of the
home and the openness of the school (Kavaler-Adler, 42).

Some of the challenge inherent in the novel's discussion of unmarried and
independent womanhood is toned down by one or other literary means. For
instance, such womanhood is persistently associated with nunhood, and, at
that, the silent nunhood practiced by the sequestered Carmelites rather than
the public campaigning of a Saint Theresa. The powers of the actor Vashti,
though transcendent, are ultimately ironized in the narrative by the small fire
that frightens off her audience. Lucy's own foray into theatricals is enforced by
her senior male colleague, M. Paul, and never amounts to more than an amateur endeavor. Amid the anxieties of preparation for the play, great emphasis is
laid upon her refusal to assume totally masculine clothing (Surridge, 6). Lucy's
winning and retaining the cigar case, a decidedly "mannish" accessory in the
context of this book, is likewise reduced in its symbolic charge by an emphasis
on incongruity and personal whim. And Lucy correspondingly avoids appropriation of the moral essayist's stereotypically male voice in her examination essay, instead adopting an extravagantly novelistic mode more consonant with

female authorship (Edgecombe, 820). In sum, we can fairly say that Lucy's position vis-à-vis gender demarcations is equivocal. At the same time, however, we should recognize that this equivocation, beneath its dissimulation of modesty and decorum, has enabling effects.

The traditional Christian imagery of the soul as exile, "tired wayfarer" (534), and pilgrim through life that we find in this novel (Stoneman, 92) also lends itself to advocacy of specifically female excursions. Arriving in London, as the first step toward a renewal of her life (cf. Stewart, 58), Lucy confronts a "Babylon and a wilderness" clamorous with the "strange speech of the cabmen" (106). She then extends her incursion into the male world to the coffee house, her uncles' favorite accommodation. Lucy feels "real pleasure" (109) in the legitimately workful City, rather than the comparatively indolent West End. She buys a book from a "Mr. Jones, a dried-in man of business" who seems to her "one of the greatest . . . of beings" (109). Her sentiments, however ironically handled, are in tune with an ethic of work that by mid-century was making its mark on even the upper reaches of English society (Collini, 32). Altogether, these motifs function as persuasion that she acts justifiably upon the "Evangelical impulse to avoid the 'cowardly indolence' of shrinking from life" (Eagleton, "Class," 235), and that other women might learn from her example. This would be especially so if men have defaulted as their protectors or if, as in Lucy's case, her "primary group" has collapsed around her.

Despite these legitimations, the fear of intruding into the male professional world figures strongly in Brontë's writings. In a letter to W. S. Williams (12 May 1848) she inquires, "Is there any room for female lawyers, female doctors, female engravers, for more female artists, more authoresses?" (Wise and Symington, ii, 215–216). Correspondingly, Lucy is profoundly ambivalent about the "*Bildung*/ambition plot" (Watkins, 222). The invocation of the Styx, Charon, and the "Land of Shades" (111) suggests entry "into a dark new world or afterlife" (Shuttleworth, "Dynamics" 347), not into the bright new world of self-advancement. In similarly eschatological terms, M. Paul makes Lucy feel "vaguely threatened with, I know not what doom, if I ever trespassed the limits proper to my sex, and conceived a contraband appetite for unfeminine knowledge" (440).

Not merely Brontë but the later, more socially attuned George Eliot exhibited a fear of stigmatization as the "public woman," with the automatic associations of self-display, working for money, and prostitution (Bodenheimer, 8). The symbolism of Lucy's arrival in the foreign city expresses this anxiety. Obliged by the misadventure with her luggage to make her way alone at night, she becomes a kind of "street-walker." The prowlers who pursue her are depicted as hypermasculine, mustachioed and smoking cigars, and they obviously construe Lucy as fair game: They are "hunters" (125) pursuing what we would call a "job-hunter," in a symbolic punishment of Lucy for her adventurism. Simultaneously, though, their interference means that Lucy's finding the place of her subsequent employment comes about by sheer accident. If we feel that Providence guides Lucy in this and other excursions (cf. Boumelha, 105), what better defense against the routine accusation that women dissatisfied with the private sphere were rebels against Providence?

SURVEILLANCE

Lucy, then, is committed to a performance as a would-be teacher, where her personal, private life will become indissolubly entangled with her professional, public life. Partly through the coercion of M. Paul (itself another legitimating ploy in the narration), partly through her own volition, she stands upon a stage of sorts. The classrooms are large open spaces, where teachers fixate pupils and pupils fixate teachers. But in this ambiance of exposure, Lucy's characterization is as someone preternaturally sensitive to spectators. I would submit that the effect is to signal, through the construction of an extreme case, what it will cost the individual subject, most immediately the female subject, to engage in a fully modern livelihood under a fully modern regime of surveillance.

In its most graphic form, Lucy's sensitivity would be termed "dysmorphophobia" by some present-day psychiatrists, meaning a morbid anxiety concerning one's face, hair, and other aspects of physical appearance. She represents her complexion as having "no natural rose" (200), her hair as brown but apparently not copious and consisting of "indifferent materials" (199), and her total appearance as a "blank" (200). Any such preoccupation gained a spurious scientific legitimacy from the Victorian fad for physiognomy and phrenology (Dames). For Lucy, to intercept her own gaze in a mirror or to confront M. Paul's or the nun's gaze, gazing at her gaze, is to incur trauma. That trauma proliferates out into numerous "hauntings" (Cheng, 77; Shuttleworth, *Victorian Psychology*, 236) as Lucy bends her gaze towards young Polly (Gilbert and Gubar, 404) and even the king of this pocket-handkerchief state, each of whom have their own ghostly or spectral aspects.

The trauma impresses itself upon the narration when we as readers register how Lucy compulsively blinds and hoodwinks us, in addition to inadvertently but symptomatically breaking M. Paul's spectacles (Hoeveler, 27). She cultivates a systematic reserve (for examples see Auerbach, 340; Lawson, 57; Nestor, 87; Thomas, 569) and, although so virulently opposed to Jesuits, narrates with "mental reservations." Readers must engage in questioning, while incurring antagonism (O'Dea, 41; Silver, 93; Stewart, 52). Blankness regarding her appearance extends into comparable evasions about her childhood, her confession to Père Silas (Boumelha, 107), and her fiancé's fate (Carlisle, 152).

Instrumental here apparently is "the panic of being *known*, so very close to the simple panic of being *knowable*" (Dames, 383). Ginevra's baffled questions, "Who *are* you, Miss Snowe? . . . But *are* you anybody?" (392 and 394), demonstrate that the unknowability of Lucy extends to her exact social status.

When surveillance is under critique, acknowledgment is duly made to its claims to be caring. It is systematically aligned with the novel's three main professions of education, church, and medicine, each of which is shown as beneficent according to its own lights. Through Mme. Beck's inspection, Lucy advances from the nursery to the classroom (Gezari, 151). Through M. Paul's attentions, she is kept in sustenance and improving reading matter. Through Père Silas's elicitation of a confession, she gains solace and pastoral care. Through Dr. John's observation, she is helped with her nervous disorder (Shuttleworth, *Victorian Psychology*, 9).

Nevertheless, it is the intrusive, not to say abusive and voyeuristic aspects of surveillance that dominate the narrative. When Mme. Beck admits the young men to the school ball, the occasion serves to "draw out madame precisely in her strongest character—that of a first-rate *surveillante*" (213)—a "madame" who insinuates "rattlesnake"-like young men into the company of precociously nubile young women. Her snooping into Lucy's private letters for reassurance that Lucy is not her rival for Dr. John suggests dubious sexual curiosity. When M. Paul places his hand, as Lucy remarks, "on intimate terms with my desk" (430)—indeed smokes his cigars into her desk while perusing her books—the language suggests sexual harassment. The male gaze is invested with further phallic connotations in the scene where M. Paul throws his spent cigar into the shrubbery. "Look at it," he says, "is not that spark like an eye watching you and me?" (456).

Repudiating surveillance, Lucy locates it in a Catholic ethos that schemes to defeat Protestant reserve. In one tendentious image, Père Silas so contrives events that what seems a mere "handful of loose beads" is "threaded by that quick-shot and crafty glance of a Jesuit-eye" (486) so as to form a rosary. Lattices are the medium for both the elicitation of confessions and M. Paul's spying upon his colleagues and neighbors (Shuttleworth, *Victorian Psychology*, 225). "Monsieur," Lucy remonstrates, invoking the doctrine of Original Sin against him, "I tell you every glance you cast from that lattice is a wrong done to the best part of your own nature. To study the human heart thus, is to banquet secretly and sacrilegiously on Eve's apples. I wish you were a Protestant" (455–456). M. Paul, along with the entire purportedly alien culture of surveillance, stands convicted theologically as a heretical trespasser upon the Tree of Knowledge.

But complementarily the text constructs surveillance as located not merely within the foreign Other but also within Lucy herself. She institutes surveillance even as she resists it. It contains within itself fear and empowerment in equal measure, as we learn when Lucy avers that she "liked to penetrate to the real truth; I like seeking the goddess in her temple, and handling the veil, and daring the dread glance. . . . [O]ur heart shakes, and its currents sway like rivers lifted by earthquake, but we have swallowed strength. To see and know the worst is to take from Fear her main advantage" (564). Just as Dr. John monitors her symptoms, so she diagnoses the king's hypochondria. It is easy to see the element of projection here, but we should not neglect the point that simultaneously Lucy is emulating professional practices of observation.

As a practitioner in surveillance, Lucy competes more than adequately with her colleagues. Mme. Beck, who qualifies as an irregular "superintendent of police," is scarcely more on the watch than Lucy (Jacobus, 45), who spies on her even while being spied upon (Litvak, 474). The priest may observe her, but simultaneously she observes and sums him up through the lattice: "I saw by his profile and brow he was a Frenchman" (233), says Lucy, expressly applying her knowledge of physiognomy.

THE STATUS OF VICTORIAN PROFESSIONALS

This is an appropriate point at which to remind ourselves that throughout Brontë's work the realm of the foreign functions as a medium through which she can explore disturbing elements within indigenous Victorian culture (Shuttleworth, "Dynamics," 350–351), perhaps especially as these "bear upon the feminine soul" (Larson, 336–337) but not exclusively so. *Villette* testifies to unease about the intensified process of monitoring and inspection that occurred in the Victorian era, consistent with the development of modern government and administration. As the site of a contestation concerning surveillance, Lucy might therefore be seen as representative of anxieties about this aspect of the professional ethos that are voiced in such other well-known novels as Dickens's *Hard Times* and Gaskell's *North and South*.

It is common in Victorian fiction for professionals to be shown constructing themselves as "unobserved observers," like Lucy herself (Kazan, 552) or Physician in *Little Dorrit*. Lucy strives for "the power to objectify and scrutinize others while exempting oneself from similar treatment" (Litvak, 476). Secrecy and reserve are "potentially empowering" (Preston, 394). By preserving them, she can make herself radically inaccessible to the alien culture that would otherwise determine her (cf. Miller, 195). An instance is her practice of excusing herself from the nightly recital of saints' lives at the school—so instrumental a mythology in acculturating the individual subject. Correspondingly, she elevates herself to the status of protagonist in a modern Protestant saint's life, where inducements and temptations cannot divert her from the values of individualism, decorum, and privacy. She implicitly likens herself to Joan of Arc, whose "jailers tempted her with the warrior's accoutrements and lay in wait for the issue" (442). She is enabled to stand outside society (Kucich, 935), the culmination of this tendency being her alienated "attendance" at the national festival, where everyone except herself forms part of an animated community commemorating the "patriots and martyrs" (551) that have secured the future of this society. Although Lucy here appears to be a neglected Cinderella, a "helpless victim," in fact the mechanisms of plot and characterization that contribute to her victimhood, in this case the bungled administration of the opiate and the resistant traits thanks to which Lucy evades its full effects, are simultaneously enabling. In common with her voluntary actions, they maneuver her into the attainment of a selfhood built upon observation, opportunity, stealth, and reserve.

Nonetheless, like her counterparts in the Victorian teaching profession, Lucy cannot enjoy the full luxury of so resolutely reserved a subject position. Inspection and examination were becoming key elements in the code of practice. Though it is true that Sir James Kay-Shuttleworth set up Her Majesty's Inspectorate with the role of providing advice and encouragement rather than engaging in inquisitions and dictatorship (Dent, 7; Evans, 20), nevertheless inspections determined the continuation of grants to schools and therefore of salaries to teachers. Tensions in contemporary Victorian culture concerning this regime are easily documented. The Church of England in particular strenuously opposed it and forced key compromises, despite the fact that inspectors were manifestly selected with "safety" in mind. They were reportedly all men of respectable origins and university training, many of them clergymen (Lawson and Silver, 269, 272).

Credentialization via inspection, public examination, or both was becoming indispensable in the furtherance of a professional career. From 1846, in an enhancement of elementary education, pupil-teachers of both sexes could obtain certification after annual inspection and examination for five years, training at a college for a further two years, and an eventual final examination (Evans, 20–21). Being predominantly working class, such trainees of course could not claim the same social standing as the professional middle class (Lawson and Silver, 287–288), which relied on pretensions to gentlemanly status quite as much as on education (Collini, 31). Anxieties about the possible permeability of barriers to more elevated status rapidly made themselves apparent. In complementation, at the higher social level, the Governesses' Benevolent Institution opened Queen's College in 1848, catering for girls over twelve years in age and attending to teacher training via a diverse and well-taught curriculum (Lawson and Silver, 306).

The ensuing decade saw a very marked proliferation of the examination system, to cover not just schools and colleges but the army and civil service as well. Even before it began, "more common and more searching" examinations could be foreseen by Thomas Arnold as inevitable (Lawson and Silver, 307) and were obviously part of the temper of Brontë's times. Nevertheless, the fact that in the 1860s the *Alexandra Magazine* still needed to advocate the participation of women in examinations, "because otherwise they would never be tested or qualified alongside men" (Beer, 174), suggests strong cultural resistance, and this we see attested in *Villette*.

The public examination to which Lucy is submitted by M. Paul, in the company of two colleagues from the Athénée, is a key moment in the novel's meditation on the subject position of the professional. Procedurally speaking, this examination has the potential to provide her with accreditation of her professional skills. But when Lucy recognizes the assessors Boissec and Rochemorte for her erstwhile harassers on her first arrival in Villette, the effect is to taint the idea of examination with implications of not merely harassment and prurience but also questionable social standing. These examiners are not fully gentlemen in the characteristically Victorian construction, which entailed a mix of social and moral worth (cf. Collini, 30): "Their dress implied pretensions to the rank of gentlemen, but, poor things! they were very plebeian in soul. They spoke with insolence" (125).

Moreover, the examination process amounts to cruel and unusual punishment. Academic examination of any kind is an anomaly in Mme. Beck's school (Gezari, 164), and when Lucy refuses to submit voluntarily, M. Paul makes the arrangements surreptitiously. In the high melodrama of the episode, there are overtones of a "show-trial" or medieval trial by ordeal (493) enacted in accordance with alien legal processes, using inquisition and torture to extract confessions from a suspected heretic (Helfield, 59–61). On the judicial front, M. Paul is vulnerable too, on an allegation of fraudulently signing Lucy's name to essays he has written himself (492). In the event, Lucy triumphs over her "judges" by composing a subversive satire on "Human Justice." She convicts the process of examination as confined to inadequate human justice and falling short of divine justice.

This judgment of the judges in turn implies a wider judgment. M. Paul is cast not simply as an educational professional. When he officiates at the charity concert or the Art Gallery, it seems to be as some kind of guardian of culture and morals. In this capacity he approximates to the Victorian moralists, described by Stefan Collini as well-connected intellectuals with a self-appointed "special duty to remind their more self-interested contemporaries of the strenuous commitments entailed by the moral values embedded in the public discourse of their society" (58). Later Matthew Arnold was to speak in praise of such wardens of the public mind in *Culture and Anarchy* (1869). In the meantime, though, the characterization of M. Paul conveys unease about this type of guardianship. Although he stands as a staunch opponent of tyranny and injustice, confident that when he exerts his "terrible unerring penetration of instinct" he is doing justice, Lucy opines that "for my part I doubt whether man has a right to do such justice on man" (423–424). These suspicions against moral and philosophical wardens extend to readers (Larson, 335) and reviewers. The enshrinement of the sage is a distinctive aspect of the Victorian era, but *Villette* shows some of the countervailing suspicion of such reification of intellectual leadership.

CONCLUSIONS

In summary, professional men and women are constructed in this and other works of fiction as caught in a dilemma. They depend upon the public eye for authentication in their cultural role, yet simultaneously must cultivate reserve, even secrecy, as a protection against that eye—the eye being both Victorian information culture (see Welsh) and a deeper cultural skepticism. In cultivating the requisite reserve, the males amongst this new cohort of professionals must needs co-opt strategies traditionally associated with females. It would follow that Lucy, rather than speak exclusively for women, articulates some general Victorian anxieties and aspirations—and perhaps all the more urgently for speaking *in extremis*.

WORKS CITED AND SELECTED WORKS FOR FURTHER READING

Auerbach, Nina. "Charlotte Brontë: The Two Countries." *University of Toronto Quarterly* 42 (1973): 328–342.

Beer, Gillian. *George Eliot*. London: Harvester Wheatsheaf, 1986.

Bodenheimer, Rosemarie. "Ambition and Its Audiences: George Eliot's Performing Figures." *Victorian Studies* 34 (1990): 7–33.

Boumelha, Penny. *Charlotte Brontë*. London: Harvester Wheatsheaf, 1990.

Brontë, Charlotte. *Villette*. Ed. Mark Lilly. London: Penguin, 1979.

Carlisle, Janice. "A Prelude to *Villette*: Charlotte Brontë's Reading, 1850–52." *Bulletin of Research in the Humanities* 82 (1979): 403–423.

Cheng, Anne A. "Reading Lucy Snowe's Cryptology: Charlotte Brontë's *Villette* and Suspended Mourning." *Qui Parle: Literature, Philosophy, Visual Arts, History* 4.2 (1991): 75–90.

Collini, Stefan. *Public Moralists: Political Thought and Intellectual Life in Britain, 1850–1930*. Oxford: Clarendon, 1991.

Dames, Nicholas. "The Clinical Novel: Phrenology and *Villette*." *Novel: A Forum on Fiction* 29.3 (1996): 367–390.

Dent, Harold. *The Training of Teachers in England and Wales, 1800–1975*. London: Hodder and Stoughton, 1977.

Eagleton, Terry. "Class, Power, and Charlotte Brontë." *Critical Quarterly* 14.3 (1972): 225–235.

———. *Myths of Power: A Marxist Study of the Brontës*. London: Macmillan, 1975.

Edgecombe, Rodney Stenning. "Odic Elements in Charlotte Brontë's *Villette*." *Modern Language Review* 87.4 (1992): 817–826.

Evans, Keith. *The Development and Structure of the English Educational System*. London: U of London P, 1975.

Gates, Barbara. "Down Garden Paths: Charlotte Brontë's Haunts of Self and Other." *Victorian Newsletter* 83 (1993): 35–43.

Gezari, Janet. *Charlotte Brontë and Defensive Conduct: The Author and the Body at Risk*. Philadelphia: U of Pennsylvania P, 1992.

Gilbert, Sandra M., and Susan Gubar. *The Madwoman in the Attic: The Woman Writer and the Nineteenth-Century Literary Imagination*. New Haven: Yale UP, 1979.

Helfield, Randa. "Confession as Cover-Up in Brontë's *Villette*." *English Studies in Canada* 23.1 (1997): 59–72.

Heyck, Thomas William. "Educational." In *A Companion to Victorian Literature and Culture*, pp. 194–211. Ed. Herbert F. Tucker. Oxford: Blackwell, 1999.

Hoeveler, Diane Long. "The Obscured Eye: Visual Imagery as Theme and Structure in *Villette*." *Ball State University Forum* 19.1 (1978): 23–30.

Jacobus, Mary. "The Buried Letter: Feminism and Romanticism in *Villette*." In *Women Writing and Writing about Women*, pp. 42–60. Ed. Mary Jacobus. New York: Harper, 1979.

Kavaler-Adler, Susan. "Charlotte Brontë and the Feminine Self." *American Journal of Psychoanalysis* 50.1 (1990): 37–43.

Kazan, Francesca. "Heresy, the Image, and Description: Or, Picturing the Invisible: Charlotte Brontë's *Villette*." *Texas Studies in Literature and Language* 32.4 (1990): 543–566.

Kucich, John. "Passionate Reserve and Reserved Passion in the Works of Charlotte Brontë." *ELH* 52 (1985): 913–937.

Larson, Janet L. "'Who Is Speaking?': Charlotte Brontë's Voices of Prophecy." In *Victorian Sages and Cultural Discourse: Renegotiating Gender and Power*, pp. 66–86, 276–282. Ed. Thais E. Morgan. New Brunswick: Rutgers UP, 1990.

Lawson, John, and Harold Silver. *A Social History of Education in England*. London: Methuen, 1973.

Lawson, Kate. "Reading Desire: *Villette* as 'Heretic Narrative.'" *English Studies in Canada* 17.1 (1991): 53–71.

Litvak, Joseph. "Charlotte Brontë and the Scene of Instruction: Authority and Subversion in *Villette*." *Nineteenth-Century Literature* 42 (1988): 467–489.

Miller, D. A. *The Novel and the Police*. Berkeley: U of California P, 1988.

Neff, Wanda F. *Victorian Working Women: An Historical and Literary Study of Women in British Industries and Professions, 1832–1850*. London: Cass, 1966.

Nestor, Pauline. *Charlotte Brontë*. London: Macmillan, 1987.

O'Dea, Gregory S. "Narrator and Reader in Charlotte Brontë's *Villette*." *South Atlantic Review* 53.1 (1988): 41–57.

Preston, Elizabeth. "Relational Reconsiderations: Reliability, Heterosexuality, and Narrative Authority in *Villette*." *Style* 30.3 (1996): 386–408.

Shuttleworth, Sally. *Charlotte Brontë and Victorian Psychology*. Cambridge: Cambridge UP, 1996.

———. "The Dynamics of Cross-Culturalism in Charlotte Brontë's Fiction." In *Creditable Warriors, 1830–1876*. Ed. Michael Cotsell. 3 vols. London: Ashfield, 1990.

Silver, Brenda R. "The Reflecting Reader in *Villette*." In *The Voyage In: Fictions of Female Development*, pp. 90–111. Ed. Elizabeth Abel, Marianne Hirsch, and Elizabeth Langland. Hanover: UP of New England, 1983.

Stewart, Garrett. "A Valediction for Bidding Mourning: Death and the Narratee in Brontë's *Villette*." In *Death and Representation*, pp. 51–79. Ed. Sarah Webster Goodwin and Elisabeth Bronfen. Baltimore: Johns Hopkins UP, 1993.

Stoneman, P. M. "The Brontës and Death: Alternatives to Revolution." In *1848: The Sociology of Literature—Proceedings of the Essex Conference on the Sociology of Literature July 1977*, pp. 79–96. Ed. Francis Barker, et al. Colchester: U of Essex, 1978.

Surridge, Lisa. "Representing the 'Latent Vashti': Theatricality in Charlotte Brontë's *Villette*." *Victorian Newsletter* 87 (1995): 4–14.

Thomas, Syd. "'References to Persons not Named, or Circumstances not Defined' in *Villette*." *Texas Studies in Literature and Language* 32.4 (1990): 567–583.

Watkins, Susan. "Versions of the Feminine Subject in Charlotte Brontë's *Villette*." In *Ethics and the Subject*, pp. 217–25. Ed. Karl Simms. Amsterdam: Rodopi, 1997.

Welsh, Alexander. *George Eliot and the Art of Blackmail*. Cambridge: Harvard UP, 1985.

Wise, T. J., and J. A. Symington, eds. *The Brontës: Their Lives, Friendships and Correspondences*. 2 vols. Oxford: Oxford UP, 1932.

Charles Dickens

K. J. Fielding

Charles Dickens [John Huffam], the greatest Victorian novelist, was born on 12 February at Landport, Portsmouth, first son and second child of the seven children of John and Elizabeth Dickens. John Dickens's father was a clerk in the Navy Pay-Office who was always in financial difficulties. Family influence is a strong element in the action of Dickens's fiction: Wilkins Micawber of *David Copperfield* came from his father, Mrs. Nickleby from his mother. His father was posted to London in 1815, to Chatham in 1817, and to London again in 1822. Dickens's childhood was marked by a golden age in Chatham, where he began school before moving to London and suffering from his father's subsequent neglect, bankruptcy, and imprisonment in the Marshalsea debtor's prison, which was to be the scene of the opening of *Little Dorrit*. More dramatic for Dickens was being sent to work, age twelve, in a rat-ridden shoe blacking factory, while his elder sister went to the Royal Academy of Music. This is passionately told in his fragment of autobiography, used for *David Copperfield* and published for the first time in the biography by his friend John Forster. Though John Dickens was soon released, Charles was deeply wretched and depressed, all the more so because when there was the chance of his release from the factory, his mother opposed it. In fact, he went back to school and on to be a lawyer's clerk before continuing his self-education.

Like his father and uncle, John Henry Barrow, he became a reporter, at first in the law courts and then recording political speeches in and outside Parliament and the country, as "the fastest shorthand writer in the world." He was employed by various newspapers, such as the *Morning Chronicle*, and wrote his first literary journalism as essays to be collected in *Sketches by Boz* (1836). Dickens was always a journalist, topical, immediate, and sharply observant, a "special correspondent for posterity" (quoted in Collins, *Dickens: The Critical Heritage*, 384). In 1836 he married Catherine Hogarth (2 April), and published the first of twenty numbers of the *Pickwick Papers* (31 March). The first of their ten children was born in January 1837. *Pickwick* suddenly brought not just fame but immortality. Much more than journalism, it showed a breadth and brilliance of comedy, dramatic power, and a discriminating understanding of humanity in the scenes to which Pickwick descends in the chapters set in the Fleet debtors' prison.

Life and work intertwined. For a short time (from January 1837) he was editor of the monthly *Bentley's Magazine* in which *Oliver Twist* was serialized, striking out in a new direction. It has also been seen as journalistic, but if so, it was also an intensely dramatic and hostile study of Benthamism, or the view that everyone should be guided by self-interest. It exposed the life of the workhouse, the lower classes, petty criminals, and prostitutes. Respectable readers were alarmed, but the Artful Dodger, Fagin, and Sikes could not be ignored, nor the radical implications of what John Forster saw as their "school of practical ethics."

Serialization remained the form in which all Dickens's novels came out, either weekly or monthly, giving them certain characteristics, a close relationship with his readers in the need for him to hold their attention, multiple narrative lines and characters, and a greater concern with unifying themes and form, and devices to effect this. Chapman and Hall were Dickens's first and final publishers, followed by Richard Bentley, and then Bradbury and Evans (1845–59) as Dickens fought to repossess his copyrights and his independence. Though he could be overdemanding, Dickens's determination to stand up for an author's rights was part of a movement that changed and improved the position of the novelist in the nineteenth century.

Other early fiction followed fast, with *Nicholas Nickleby* (1838–39) and the weekly *Master Humphrey's Clock* (1840–41), including *The Old Curiosity Shop* and the historical novel *Barnaby Rudge*. From the first, all his fiction came as a revelation because of his keen insight into contemporary life. The leading former radical M. P., Sir Francis Burdett, wrote to his daughter, Angela Burdett Coutts, on reading *Oliver Twist*, "It is very interesting, very painful, very disgusting, and as the Old Woman at Edinburgh, on hearing of the suffering of Jesus Christ said, Oh dear I hope it isn't true. Whether anything like it exists or

no I mean to make inquiry for it is quite dreadful, and, to Society in this country, most disgraceful" (Fielding, *Charles Dickens*, 40). Yet the novels were not
only written to expose the abuses of the law, crime, the class system, education,
"Yorkshire schools," imprisonment for debt, and the whole money ethic, but
they were also a passionate declaration of the nature and rights of man.

Having erupted with five novels in five years, Dickens was determined not
to write himself out like Sir Walter Scott, and decided on a visit to the United
States. He and Catherine set out for six months in January 1842, enjoying an
enthusiastic reception in New England, and reaching as far south as Richmond. He had come expecting a utopian, classless republic, but was "sick and
sore at heart" after being strongly attacked when he questioned the piracy of his
works and absence of international copyright. None of this appeared in *American Notes* (1842), but anger and hurt show in the savage satire of some of the
American scenes in the next monthly serial, *Martin Chuzzlewit* (1843–44).
The novel stands out for its insights into the nature of society, its satiric thrust,
its brilliantly humorous Pecksniff and Mrs. Gamp, and for a new and not entirely successful attempt to structure his work around leading themes. It was
less popular than the earlier novels; its sales disappointed, some of its attacks
are still resented; but, like many minor figures Dickens met in America, it is always "remarkable."

The shorter Christmas books followed, *A Christmas Carol* (1843), *The
Chimes* (1844), *The Cricket on the Hearth* (1845), *The Battle of Life* (1846), and
The Haunted Man (1848). The first two are brilliant and avoid lapsing into the
oversentimentality that often disfigures the rest: Christmas came to be over-
played in the later Dickens. They overlapped *Dombey and Son* (1846–48),
characterized by Edmund Wilson as expressing Dickens's growing "indictment against a specific society: the self-important and moralizing middle-class." Dickens's central period is marked by *David Copperfield*, his further
incursion into journalism (from 1850), his enjoyment of amateur dramatics
and career as a public speaker. He allied himself with Angela Burdett Coutts in
her private charities and care for prostitutes or those likely to become so.
Copperfield is at the heart of Dickens, not just because of its closeness to Dickens's own career, but because it expresses the best in his writing and nature. "To
contemporary work so good," wrote Matthew Arnold, "we are in danger perhaps of not paying respect enough. . . . What treasures of gaiety, invention, life,
are in that book." At the same time, Dickens began his career as an independent editor, with *Household Words* (1850–59), continued in *All The Year Round*
(1859–70), full of his own contributions that were to be collected in his *Reprinted Pieces* (1858), the *Uncommercial Traveller* (1861, later enlarged), and in
other forms. To understand Dickens the novelist fully, we have to take into account the extraordinarily extended shelf-load of other works, including the

journalism, his speeches, and above all the twelve volumes of his completed *Collected Letters*: To see Dickens writing within their framework is an imaginative, theoretical, and even luxuriant route that drives into his work, vitally enriching any complete appreciation.

Bleak House, a monthly serial (1852–53), and *Hard Times,* a weekly (1854, first serialized in *Household Words*), have been seen as darker and more attuned to twentieth-century readers. The first is marked by its divided narrative, told half in the first person of a young heroine, half by an immediate, present tense, ironic narrator, and richly thematicized as a further study of society. *Hard Times* is less anti-Benthamite or anti-Utilitarian than an examination of the life of an industrial society, mostly without the industry. Both works, as Henry James was to say of *Our Mutual Friend,* were "intensely *written*" (quoted in Collins, *Dickens: The Critical Heritage,* 470), with greater concentration and less spontaneity. The novels themselves develop, rather than their characters. They were followed by the monthly serial, *Little Dorrit* (1855–57), which, like all Dickens's work, is distinctive but again develops his preoccupation with society and misgovernment, or "How Not to Do It," interwoven with his own autobiography and overshadowed by a concern with religion and self-examination. The same is true of *A Tale of Two Cities* (1859, serialized weekly in *All the Year Round*), a combination of a narrative experiment in melodramatic romance and a political study, retrospectively drawing on Carlyle's *The French Revolution,* but looking forward to a usually unnoticed consideration of contemporary continental nationalism and revolution, as in France and Italy. Dickens knew France, Italy, and Switzerland well, and had lived in all three countries: In 1846 he had written *Pictures from Italy* for the *Daily News,* when editor for a short time. He was an international figure even in his own day.

In 1857, Dickens met Ellen Ternan, a young actress who almost certainly became his mistress. In 1858, he publicly separated from Catherine Dickens, broke with his former publishers, started *All the Year Round* (1859), largely withdrew into private life, and took up public readings, which, by leaving him constantly playing a part, in some ways made him more remote. Yet, though outwardly he may have seemed unchanged, and remaining what Carlyle was to call "The good, the gentle, the high-gifted, honest, ever-friendly, noble Dickens—every inch of him an Honest man" (Forster, 11, 475), he showed an increasing reserve, which appears in the "secret prose" of *Great Expectations* (serialized in *All the Year Round*), as well as the monthly serial, *Our Mutual Friend* (1864–65). In fact, *Great Expectations* was written in response to a declining circulation for his periodical, when Dickens thought that "the one thing to be done" was for him "to strike in" by contributing himself. It is his most intricate, thoughtful, coherent, and deeply persuasive story, in which a blacksmith's boy grows up shadowed by his weird benefactors, Miss Havisham and the convict Magwitch. On another level, it is again a study of his times or those of his childhood and youth, their money ethic, snobbery, class system, and attitudes to sex and violence, seen with ironic humor and leaving many problems, which culminate in its ambiguous and alternative endings. It still calls for closer examination. The same may be true of *Our Mutual Friend*, in which design and plot attempt more and achieve less.

The final years saw Dickens relentlessly keeping up his public readings, including a triumphant return to the United States in 1867–68, followed, in spite of his health, by a commitment to a further hundred readings at home, which he could not sustain. An irreverent member of his staff wrote of him, "He had Westminster Abbey always before him" (MS, Dickens House, Doughty St., London). Dickens was buried there when he died on 9 June 1870, leaving unfinished *The Mystery of Edwin Drood*, which was to have been of twelve numbers, of which five were finished, stretched out on publication to six. In spite of a growing remoteness from most of his immediate circle, his death was felt by his public as a personal loss and a national calamity.

Any literary appreciation of Dickens needs to understand the intensity of his nature, his imaginative power, and the art of his writing. Above all there is the need to appreciate his humanity. He said of himself: "I hold my inventive capacity on the stern condition that it must master my whole life, often have complete possession of me, make its own demands on me, and, sometimes for months together, put everything else away from me. If I had not known long ago that my place could never be held, unless I were ready to devote myself to it entirely, I should have dropped out of it very soon" (to Mrs. Winter, 3 April 1855, Pilgrim *Letters*, vii, 583). He was not unintellectual, his reading was wide, his experience was extensive, but whatever the subject, scene, or story, his fiction dramatically displays human nature. Attempts to understand his writing have examined it in relation to gender, crime, education, politics, morality, society itself, the form and theory of the novel, and almost anything one can think of. Yet though following any one of these threads can bring us close to the heart of Dickens, his immensely comprehensive power is lost in restrictive analysis.

In a tribute to his rival Thackeray, Dickens declared that "every writer of fiction, though he may not adopt the dramatic form, writes in effect for the stage. He may write novels always and plays never, but the truth and wisdom that are in him must permeate the art of which truth and passion are the life, and must be more or less reflected in that great mirror which he holds up to nature" (Fielding, *Speeches*, 262). His essential truth and passion explain his continued survival and worldwide appeal—unaffected by troubled re-creation on screen and stage—and his place in the minds and speech of even those who have hardly read him. As Hazlitt said of Shakespeare, he was just like any other man, except that he was like every other man.

Criticism of Dickens has been affected as much by changing general approaches to literature as by individual research and insight. Yet both must be taken into account. His life by John Forster has an essential place. Forster knew Dickens intimately; he worked closely with him, fostered his career, was ready to stand up to him, and within limits, to speak openly about him. No one else who knew Dickens had written at length so frankly about him. His library and manuscript collection, at the Victoria and Albert Museum, is a central source in which discoveries remain to be made. Other biographers have written in the wake of successive editions of Dickens's letters. Studies of his childhood by Langton (1891) and Michael Allen (1988), memoirs by his children including Mamie Dickens (1897) and Henry Fielding Dickens (1928), and such associates as George Dolby (1885) have given more and more information about him. It is possible only to select landmarks in Dickens's biography: the work of Thomas Wright, who first raised the question of Ellen Ternan, followed by Gladys Storey's *Dickens and Daughter* (1939) and Ada Nisbet (1952), leading to Clare Tomalin's *The Invisible Woman* (1990). The Nonesuch Press *Letters,* in three volumes, edited by Walter Dexter (1938), appeared only in a limited edition but greatly extended knowledge that, combined with a flow of information in the *Dickensian,* have been used by successive biographers. These included Una Pope-Hennessy (1945), Edgar Johnson in his substantial work (1952), the Mackenzies (1979), K. J. Fielding, Angus Wilson, Fred Kaplan, and Peter Ackroyd (1990). The last word is never said, and the last two biographies are by no means final. Overlapping such lives have been often more important studies combining criticism and biography, including those by Edmund Wilson, George Orwell, Humphry House, and others.

Until lately, biography and criticism have merged, because Dickens's novels are so intimately related to his nature and experience. The term "Dickens scholarship" is sometimes dubiously applied, but such studies are part of its foundation. His narrative technique has also demanded attention, whether formally in the work of John Butt and Kathleen Tillotson, or by such writers as Harvey Peter Sucksmith, Sylvère Monod, and J. Hillis Miller and in many other studies diffused in recent criticism. Attention to Dickens's language has to be sought for, though it is found to some extent in criticism collected by George Ford, Philip Collins, Michael Hollington, and others. Such work offers ways into specialized understanding of Dickens's times, his publishing history, connection with the theater, his illustrators, his readers and own readings, his journalism, his interest in urban life and in the law, and in his connection with various other countries such as France and Italy, to all of which the novels can be closely related. *The Oxford Companion to Dickens* offers a useful guide to the novelist's life and work; the *Dickensian* and *Dickens Quarterly* provide on-going surveys and reviews.

WORKS CITED AND SELECTED WORKS FOR FURTHER READING

Ackroyd, Peter. *Dickens*. New York: HarperCollins, 1990.

Allen, Michael. *Charles Dickens's Childhood*. New York: St. Martin's, 1988.

Butt, John, and Kathleen Tillotson. *Dickens at Work*. London: Methuen, 1957.

Carey, John. *The Violent Effigy: A Study of Dickens's Imagination*. London: Faber and Faber, 1973.

Collins, Philip. *Dickens and Crime*. London: Macmillan, 1962.

———. *Dickens and Education*. London: Macmillan, 1963.

———, ed. *Dickens: The Critical Heritage*. New York: Barnes and Noble, 1971.

Dexter, Walter, ed. *Letters of Charles Dickens*. 3 vols. London: Nonesuch, 1938.

Dickens, Henry Fielding. *Memories of My Father*. London: Gollancz, 1928.

Dickens, Mamie. *My Father, as I Recall Him*. Westminster: Roxburghe, 1897.

Dolby, George. *Charles Dickens as I Knew Him: The Story of the Reading Tours in Great Britain and America (1866–1870)*. London: Unwin, 1885.

Fielding, Kenneth J. *Charles Dickens: A Critical Introduction*. London: Longmans, Green, 1958.

———, ed. *The Speeches of Charles Dickens: A Complete Edition*. 1960. Hempstead: Harvester, 1988.

Ford, G. H., and Lauriat Lane, eds. *The Dickens Critics*. Ithaca: Cornell UP, 1961.

Forster, John. *The Life of Charles Dickens*. 3 vols. London: Chapman and Hull, 1872–74.

Greene, Graham. "The Young Dickens." In *The Lost Childhood and Other Essays*. London: Eyre and Spottiswoode, 1951.

Gross, John, and Pearson Gabriel, eds. *Dickens and the Twentieth Century*. London: Routledge and Paul, 1962.

House, Humphry. *The Dickens World*. Oxford: Oxford UP, 1941.

Johnson, Edgar. *Charles Dickens: His Tragedy and Triumph*. 2 vols. New York: Simon and Schuster, 1952.

Kaplan, Fred. *Dickens: A Biography*. New York: William Morrow, 1988.

Langton Stephen. *The Childhood and Youth of Charles Dickens: With Retrospective Notes and Elucidations from His Books and Letters*. London: Hutchinson, 1891.

Leavis, F. R., and Q. D. Leavis. *Dickens, the Novelist*. New York: Pantheon, 1970.

Lohrli, Ann, ed. *Household Words: A Weekly Journal, 1850–1859*. Toronto: U of Toronto P, 1973.

MacKenzie, Norman, and Jeanne MacKenzie. *Dickens: A Life*. Oxford: Oxford UP, 1979.

Miller, J. Hillis. *Charles Dickens: The World of His Novels*. Cambridge: Harvard UP, 1958.

Monod, Sylvère. *Dickens: The Novelist*. Norman: U of Oklahoma P, 1968.

Orwell, George. "Charles Dickens." In *Inside the Whale and Other Essays*. London: Gollancz, 1940.

Patten, Robert L. *Charles Dickens and His Publishers*. Oxford: Oxford UP, 1978.

Rosenberg, Edgar, ed. *Great Expectations*, by Charles Dickens. New York: Norton, 1999.

Schlicke, Paul, ed. *Oxford Reader's Companion to Dickens*. Oxford: Oxford UP, 1999.

Slater, Michael. *Dickens and Women*. London: Dent, 1983.

————, ed. *Dickens's Journalism*. 4 vols. Columbus: Ohio State UP, 1994–99.

Stone, Harry, ed. *Uncollected Writings from Household Words, 1850–1859*. 2 vols. Bloomington: Indiana UP, 1968.

Storey, Gladys. *Dickens and Daughter*. London: Muller, 1939.

Storey, Graham, Madeline House, Kathleen Tillotson, et al., eds. The Pilgrim edition of *The Letters of Charles Dickens*. 12 vols. Oxford: Clarendon, 1965–2001.

Sucksmith, H. P. *The Narrative Art of Charles Dickens: The Rhetoric of Sympathy and Irony in His Novels*. Oxford: Clarendon, 1970.

Tomalin, Claire. *The Invisible Woman: The Story of Nelly Ternan and Charles Dickens*. New York: Viking, 1990.

Walder, Dennis. *Dickens and Religion*. London: Unwin, 1981.

Wall, Stephen, ed. *Charles Dickens: A Critical Anthology*. London: Penguin, 1970.

Wilson, Angus. *The World of Charles Dickens*. New York: Viking, 1970.

Wilson, Edmund. "Dickens the Two Scrooges." In *The Wound and the Bow: Seven Studies in Literature*. Boston: Houghton Mifflin, 1941.

George Eliot: Critical Responses *to* Daniel Deronda

Nancy Henry

Since the publication of F. R. Leavis's *The Great Tradition* (1948), George Eliot's last novel, *Daniel Deronda* (1876), has received a great deal of critical attention. Leavis initiated a controversy by claiming that the novel was divided into two halves—the English or good half, and the Jewish or bad half. The Jewish half, with its "Zionist inspirations" and aesthetic failings, should be "extricated," thereby liberating an encumbered masterpiece, which Leavis calls "Gwendolen Harleth." In recent years, critics of every ideological and methodological stripe—feminist, Marxist, new historicist, deconstructionist, psychoanalytic, postcolonial—have discussed the relationship between English and Jewish identities in this complex work. To survey recent readings of *Deronda* is to track successive and simultaneous approaches to Victorian literature in late-twentieth-century criticism. Why is *Deronda* so compelling and how does it sustain these various readings? Such questions direct us to the correspondences between a dislocated and cosmopolitan Victorian culture and our own multicultural, transnational society.

Interest in *Deronda* has been focused on an issue of as much contemporary as Victorian significance: identity. Race, gender, nationality, class, and sexuality were important aspects of nineteenth-century realist fiction and the world it sought to represent. George Eliot self-consciously placed the identity crises of both her male and female characters at the center of *Deronda*. Gwendolen

Harleth, the "spoiled child," searches for some foundation on which to make the decisions that affect her life, for a way to be "better" and to "live." She must reconcile her desire to be independent with the social expectation that she make a good marriage. As the narrator observes, "Of course marriage was social promotion; she could not look forward to a single life; but promotions have sometimes to be taken with bitter herbs—a peerage will not quite do instead of leadership to the man who meant to lead; and this delicate-limbed sylph of twenty meant to lead" (31). After making a profoundly bad marriage in order to win "social promotion" and to help her widowed mother and half-sisters, she comes to depend on Daniel Deronda. This dark and serious young man, raised by Sir Hugo Mallinger and educated at Eton and Cambridge, has the moral certainty she lacks. But he is in the process on the one hand of learning about Judaism from the visionary Mordecai Ezra Cohen, and on the other of uncovering his own mysterious parentage.

Daniel's discovery of his Jewish heritage enables him to marry Mordecai's sister Mirah and to devote his life to Jewish causes. This latter decision dictates that he leave England and part with Gwendolen, who is more dependent on him than ever after the traumatic death of her tyrannical husband, Henleigh Grandcourt. Their lives, which had intersected in the opening scene of the novel and come together over its course like "meeting streams," must continue separately. As the world seems getting "larger round poor Gwendolen" and she begins to realize the "wide-stretching purposes" in which she has no part (689), Daniel consoles her by saying that though they may never see each other again, their "minds may get nearer" (691). Many have interpreted the ending as Eliot's statement that Jewish and Christian cultures must remain separate. There is much in the novel to complicate this view, as there is to refute Leavis's argument that the "halves" of the novel are independent of each other.

Throughout the Victorian period, racial differences were categorized and discussed in the context of colonialism and imperialism—in terms of a non-white, non-English "other." With the initial lifting of Jewish disabilities in 1858, permitting Jews to sit in Parliament, and a trend toward religious toleration, English Jews were more likely to assimilate. They represented an "other" within; they were able increasingly to "pass" in a way that made many English Christians uneasy. At the time of its publication, *Deronda* was criticized by gentiles and praised by Jews for its detailed presentation of Jewish culture. Eliot studied Jewish history and religion as she had studied Renaissance Florentine culture in preparation for her historical romance, *Romola*. For an English author, her knowledge of Judaism was unprecedented, but she had a literary history on which to draw. Sir Walter Scott, one of her favorite novelists, contrasted Jewish and Anglo-Saxon identities through the characters Rebecca and Rowena in *Ivanhoe* (1819). Benjamin Disraeli, in works such as *Coningsby*

(1844), *Sybil* (1845), and *Tancred* (1847), introduced English readers to Hebrew tradition and the notion of Hebrew superiority. Matthew Arnold, in *Culture and Anarchy* (1869), analyzed the Hellenic and Hebraic components of
English culture. Closer to the publication of *Deronda*, Anthony Trollope's novels *The Eustace Diamonds* (1873), *The Way We Live Now* (1875), and *The Prime
Minister* (1876) explored the ambiguities of Jewish identity in English society
of the 1870s. Jewish identity became a way to interrogate English identity, and
the double plot of *Deronda* suggests that Eliot believed that the two were separate but interdependent.

MARIAN EVANS LEWES AND GEORGE ELIOT

Before turning to the criticism, it is important to remember some facts
about Eliot's life that show her ongoing effort to fashion her own identity. Born
in the English Midlands in 1819, Mary Ann Evans passed through an intensely
religious phase in her early years that marked the rest of her life. Her readings in
the Bible and Christian texts created an intellectual and cultural store of
knowledge on which she would draw when writing her novels. Her intense religious feelings also provided her with a sympathy for religious belief that many
of her contemporaries lacked. In her early twenties, however, she experienced a
crisis of faith, which in 1842 culminated in her refusal to attend church. This
provoked what she called a "holy war" with her conventionally religious father.
Her skepticism about Christianity and the church intensified when she translated David Strauss's *The Life of Jesus*, an important text of German Higher
Criticism, which insisted on the historicity and therefore the demystification
of Biblical narratives. This was the beginning of her literary career, and afterwards she moved increasingly in "free-thinking" circles in the city of Coventry,
where she now lived. In 1851, following her father's death, she moved by herself to London. She changed her name to Marian and assumed a position as editor of the influential journal, the *Westminster Review*. She supported herself by
making the most of her astonishing intellect and talent as a writer. She translated Ludwig Feuerbach's *Essence of Christianity* (1854), wrote book reviews,
and made herself invaluable to the *Westminster*. Her life was now strikingly different from her rural upbringing and her religious past.

As a single woman whose intellectual intensity attracted as many men as it
intimidated, she had several romantic affairs, a crucial part of her new freedom
and independence in London. Her first was with John Chapman (publisher of
the *Westminster*) in whose house she lived, along with his wife and mistress.
The situation was too volatile to continue and soon ended. She had become
friendly with the scientific thinker Herbert Spencer. She was devastated temporarily when Spencer informed her that she was not physically attractive

enough for him to consider as a mate. Soon, the notoriously ugly but brilliant woman of thirty-five fell in love with George Henry Lewes, an author, journalist, critic, and scientist. Lewes was estranged from his wife but still married when he and Evans traveled to Germany together in 1854, effectively announcing their scandalous relationship to the world. Lewes would never be able to obtain a divorce. When the two returned to England and set up house together, he was supporting his three sons, his wife Agnes, and Agnes's children by another man, his former friend Thornton Hunt. Marian had left behind her brother Isaac and sister Chrissey when she moved to London. When Isaac learned of her domestic arrangement, he ceased all communication with her. She insisted that people call her "Mrs. Lewes," but the fiction did not change the opinion of polite society, which, like her family, shunned her. Marian's life was again transformed; she had gone from the radical daughter whom many thought too brainy to catch a man, to a woman in a domestic partnership in which she performed the roles of wife and stepmother and believed in their moral legitimacy.

In 1857 she began writing fiction. Her first work, *Scenes of Clerical Life* (1858) consisted of three stories that had been serialized anonymously in *Blackwood's Edinburgh Magazine* the previous year. As a book, *Scenes* was published under the pseudonym George Eliot. Marian Evans Lewes now had a new vocation and an authoritative public voice, even if no one yet knew whose voice it was. Many thought that the author was a man who had clerical experience, but though the stories are full of clergymen, each has the life of a woman at its center. With the publication of her first novel, *Adam Bede* (1859), her identity was still unknown, even to her publisher, John Blackwood. It was not until an imposter named Liggins attempted to claim credit for the writings of George Eliot that Marian came out as the author of the two immensely successful works.

Her next novel, *The Mill on the Floss* (1860), is often thought to be her most biographical, the characters Maggie and Tom Tulliver assumed to be fictionalized versions of Mary Ann and Isaac Evans. Maggie's struggles as a misfit in her family and the conflict she experiences between her desire for intellectual and emotional independence and her duties to her family reflect the experiences of Mary Ann Evans. Next came *Silas Marner* (1861), a short, lyrical novel about love and redemption that she wrote as a relief from the strain of researching *Romola* (1863). Set in fifteenth-century Florence, *Romola* is her only novel set outside of nineteenth-century England. Influenced by Scott and scrupulously detailed, it also tells the story of a strong woman's conflict between self and her duties to her faithless husband and to Florence. Like Maggie, Romola experiences a religious conversion that shows her the path to selflessness and duty. *Romola* was Eliot's first and only work not published by Blackwood and Sons. In a special arrangement with publisher George Smith, it was serialized in the

Cornhill Magazine. It was also Eliot's first commercial failure. She returned to Blackwood for her next novel, *Felix Holt* (1866), set during the era of the first Reform Bill. Next, she wrote an epic poem, *The Spanish Gypsy* (1868), several shorter poems, and *Middlemarch* (1871–72), arguably her greatest work, certainly the one for which she is best known today. Its heroine, Dorothea Brooke, has an evangelical fervor reminiscent of the young Mary Ann Evans, and George Eliot takes an ironic look at the folly of Dorothea's denials of life's pleasures. The town of Middlemarch (which recalls Coventry in the early decades of the century) unifies the two main plot lines that intersect at various points in the narrative: that of Dorothea and her disastrous marriage to the pedant Casaubon and that of Tertius Lydgate, the young man whose aspirations to make a contribution to medical science are defeated by his entanglements in petty politics and his ill-fated romance with the local beauty, Rosamond Vincy.

This double plot device was one Eliot would use again in *Daniel Deronda*. That novel and the experimental fiction, *Impressions of Theophrastus Such* (1879), are her only two works with near-contemporary settings. Both began to depart from the realist aesthetic that had characterized her earlier fiction. Formally and thematically they manifest a self-consciousness, allusiveness, and disregard for popular audiences that make a break in her career as a writer of fiction. For example, the nonchronological narrative of *Deronda* and its use of interior monologue were new to her work. *Impressions of Theophrastus Such* defies categorization; it is a fiction unified by a single narrative voice—that of the author who is simultaneously one of his own characters. It has no plot but consists of character sketches (on the model of those by the ancient Greek philosopher Theophrastus) and essays on contemporary issues, such as the state of authorship and English national culture. Both *Deronda* and *Impressions of Theophrastus Such* take the relationship between Jewish and English Christian cultures as a subject.

Like her narrator Theophrastus, Eliot had moved from her rural Midlands home and become a citizen of the "nation of London." *Impressions of Theophrastus Such*, together with *Deronda*, asks where identity resides in such a mélange of cultures as London now represented. Critic Amanda Anderson writes that "Eliot's multivalent approach to the Jewish Question illuminates the complexity of her response to the challenges of modernity" (55). Some of those challenges were broadly social and political. As Catherine Gallagher writes in "George Eliot and *Daniel Deronda*: The Prostitute and the Jewish Question," an examination of the tropes of prostitution and usury in nineteenth-century discourse, "Imperial competition, the loss of London's power as the undisputed center of international finance, and various other difficulties in international relations were building toward a new mood of nostalgic nationalism." *Daniel Deronda*, she concludes, "connects with all this and takes the necessary step beyond Arnoldian internationalism" (59). Other "challenges of modernity" faced by Eliot were personal. Patrick Brantlinger writes that for Eliot, "Judaism represented a romantic cultural and political analogue for the difficulties she encountered throughout her career as a woman, an intellectual, one-half of a nontraditional (unmarried) couple, and a Positivist or at least secularist in an age of waning religious orthodoxy" (256).

In *Deronda*, Eliot resumed themes that had characterized her earlier fiction. She extends her treatment of women's struggle for self-identification, begun with characters such as Maggie Tulliver and Dorothea Brooke. And she develops her representation of the individual's relationship to the community—to racial, religious, and cultural inheritances—which she had examined in *Romola* and *The Spanish Gypsy*. With Gwendolen and Daniel, as well as the secondary characters Mirah, the Princess Halm-Eberstein, and Catherine Arrowpoint, she presents dilemmas and choices that are familiar to modern readers. The Princess chooses her career over motherhood, assimilation over Judaism; Mirah rejects the dishonest slavishness of her father in favor of her brother Mordecai's and her future husband Daniel's vision of a proud Jewishness. Catherine Arrowpoint, an heiress, chooses to marry the Jewish musician Klesmer at the risk of disinheritance by her newly arrived and newly landed parents. Deronda chooses authenticity, the ties of emotional, racial, and political inheritance over the comforts and privileges of his upbringing.

DANIEL DERONDA AND CIRCUMCISION

In terms of critical attention to *Deronda*, we can profitably focus on its theme of Jewish identity and more specifically on the "problem," posed as such by critic Steven Marcus, of circumcision, or the lack thereof, in the novel. Circumcision, as the physical sign of the Jewishness that Trollope found so threateningly elusive, has become the unlikely subject of aesthetic and thematic assessments of *Deronda*. By concentrating on this seemingly minute detail, we can see how diverse critical perspectives are unified by a single interest in the social constructions of identity.

It is not surprising that Marcus, author of *The Other Victorians* (1966), first raised the circumcision issue (via his graduate student Lennard Davis). In his article, "Literature and Social Theory: Starting in with George Eliot" (1974), he introduced circumcision in a footnote that seems barely related to his subject (the death of Milly Barton in "The Sad Fortunes of the Reverend Amos Barton"). The point is, if Deronda was circumcised, how could he not know that he was a Jew? How can the plot, which depends on his ignorance of his origins, work? He argues that "for the plot of *Daniel Deronda* to work, Deronda's circumcised penis must be invisible, or non-existent—which is one more demonstration in detail of why the plot does not in fact work" (212). Despite his emphasis on the formal question of whether the plot "works," his comments are representative of what would become a trend away from formal analysis and toward the interpretation of culture via the text. After Michel Foucault's *History of Sexuality* (Vol. I), the notion of Victorian "repression" has been immensely complicated; it cannot sufficiently explain Eliot's failure to acknowledge circumcision in the novel. And after Foucault, the methodology of new historicism has brought ways of looking at textual problems such as Eliot's silence about circumcision. Critics could look, for example, to all the Victorian discussion of circumcision that did take place in religious and medical discourses. Writing from a variety of perspectives, critics after Marcus took up the "problem" of why Daniel never "looked down" and attempted to solve it in ways that reveal fundamental methodological differences.

In her essay, "The Decomposition of the Elephants: Double-Reading *Daniel Deronda*"—a model of the critical practice known as deconstruction—Cynthia Chase claims that Eliot's novel does not merely explore identity, it "goes far toward undermining the authority of the notion of identity, as well as of origin and of cause" (204). Chase's approach clears away historical issues to focus on language. She has no interest, for example, in what "the decomposition of the elephants" might actually refer to. Rather, she lights on the circumcision question as a disruption of narrative coherence, which, in contrast to Marcus and earlier critics, is exactly what she hopes to find: "The text's insistent reference leads relentlessly to the referent—to *la chose*, in fact: the hero's phallus, which must have been circumcised given what we are told of his history" (208). Circumcision, she argues, "is a sign that stands for a story, told to account for the origin of Jewish identity" (212).

Whereas for Chase, circumcision is "a residue of the deconstructive process," for K. M. Newton, it is a matter of historical record, which when understood, can restore coherence to the plot. In "*Daniel Deronda* and Circumcision," Newton takes an historical approach by attempting to establish the place of circumcision in Victorian medical discourse and to suggest that it was practiced on gentile boys as well as Jews. He argues that Eliot intended circumcision to be present "though she cannot mention it directly" (316). He demonstrates that physicians prescribed circumcision for a variety of reasons—for example, to prevent masturbation. Circumcision, then, might have been associated in Deronda's young mind with "sexual excess and licence": "His anxiety about his identity is also more psychologically credible, given that this sign could mean both so much and so little" (321). By reading closely for coherence and supplying missing historical information, Newton concludes that the plot in fact does "work." Whereas Chases's reading was hermetically theoretical, Newton's is empirical and nontheoretical. Other critics writing on this subject have suggested new possibilities for combining theory and history.

In "'Bit of Her Flesh': Circumcision and 'The Signification of the Phallus in *Daniel Deronda*,'" Mary Wilson Carpenter combines historical and theoretical methods by looking at nineteenth-century Protestant discourse on circumcision. This historical discourse on circumcision "precedes and predicts" Jacques Lacan's theories, specifically "The Signification of the Phallus," because it "sought to repress the penis but to promote its symbolic significance" (10). Carpenter takes a feminist perspective to argue that circumcision is a sign that Eliot adapts and applies to her female characters, claiming that "the Victorian discourse on circumcision, that 'originary' rite formulated exclusively *between men* in conventional religion, constructs a bond between women in George Eliot's last novel" (3) and "marks a covenant between women" (16). She concludes that "the narrative constructs a subversive hermeneutics of circumcision that maps both its pain and its meaning on to the body of the daughter but that divests the Phallus of its status as 'privileged signifier'" (8). Her reading engages historical sources, as well as feminist and psychoanalytic theories.

In addition to looking at nineteenth-century texts and twentieth-century theory, Carpenter relies on close readings that show the language of cutting and pain throughout the novel. Jacob Press employs a similar technique in "Same-Sex Unions in Modern Europe: *Daniel Deronda, Altneuland,* and the Homoerotics of Jewish Nationalism." He focuses on the novel's imagery of circumcision (even when the act itself goes unmentioned). He deploys the methodologies of queer theorist Eve Sedgwick, and looks at turn of the century Zionist discourse, specifically the writings of Theodor Herzl. Where Carpenter sees bonding between women, Press finds a homosocial metaphor. He argues that Eliot represents Deronda's "decentered passivity as the consequence of his psychological and physical circumcision." She "thematizes *Deronda's* shame about his penis/parentage as a metaphor for what she reads as the nonphallic faux masculinity of the man whose consciousness and loyalties are European but who is nonetheless marked in his gender as a Jewish other" (303). For Press, Daniel's "marriage" to Mordecai is crucial to the reconciliation of Jewishness and manliness: "Mordecai initiates Deronda into a homosocial brotherhood that reconciles the identity categories of 'Jew' and 'man'" (306). He argues that the phallus should be "demystified as a subject of critique and not fetishized as an object of worship" (326). Writing in the late 1990s, Press's methodology is eclectic and promising for future combinations of critical approaches: historical, theoretical and political.

Coexisting in the 1990s with this synthetic trend is a steadfast adherence to new critical and empirical readings. John Sutherland, in one of his volumes of literary "puzzles," takes a determinedly rational and empirical approach, evaluating Marcus's and Newton's claims, and arriving at the last remaining conclusion, that Deronda was never circumcised. By limiting himself to evidence of Eliot's knowledge of Judaism and to Newton's empirical solution to the problem (i.e., that gentiles too were circumcised), Sutherland fails to take into account what Carpenter and Press identify as a subtext of circumcision in the pervasive language of "cutting" and its significance as a marker of identity. Press writes that Deronda's "crisis concerning the nature of his origins provokes a frenzy of circumcision imagery" (304). He points to language that justifies his identification of Daniel's "psychological circumcision" that "powerfully echoes the actual physical event" (305). As logical as Sutherland's answer to this literary puzzle may be, its exclusion of theoretical analyses reveals some interpretive limitations of a strictly literal approach. Those works that incorporate and adapt theoretical as well as historical approaches seem to point the way to future developments in literary studies.

Daniel Deronda is a novel that continues to provoke a multitude of critical investigations into matters of nineteenth-century identity. Circumcision, whether a matter of historical fact or metaphor, has been a preoccupation with critics and a sign of what late twentieth-century readers do not know about Victorian society or the intentions of Victorian authors. It remains a sign of the ambiguities and puzzles that Victorian literature continues to pose for today's readers. It is also revealing of a late-twentieth-century moment in which Deronda's confusion about and search for his identity came to seem startlingly modern, and the Victorian reticence in talking about sex, sexuality, and "la chose" gave twentieth-century critics an excuse for talking about it incessantly. The history of the criticism of *Daniel Deronda* shows Eliot to be an author who continues to speak to our most vital and pressing concerns.

WORKS CITED AND SELECTED WORKS FOR FURTHER READING

Anderson, Amanda. "George Eliot and the Jewish Question." *Yale Journal of Criticism* 10.1 (1997): 39–61.

Baker, William. *George Eliot and Judaism.* Salzburg: Universität Salzburg, 1975.

Bodenheimer, Rosemarie. *The Real Life of Mary Ann Evans. George Eliot, Her Letters and Her Fiction.* Ithaca: Cornell UP, 1994.

Brantlinger, Patrick. "Nations and Novels: Disraeli, George Eliot, and Orientalism." *Victorian Studies* 35.3 (Spring 1992): 255–275.

Carpenter, Mary Wilson. "'A Bit of Her Flesh': Circumcision and 'The Signification of the Phallus in *Daniel Deronda.*'" *Genders* (1988): 1–23.

Chase, Cynthia. "The Decomposition of the Elephants: Double-Reading *Daniel Deronda.*" In *George Eliot.* Ed. K. M. Newton. New York: Longman, 1991.

Eliot, George. *Daniel Deronda.* Ed. Graham Handley. New York: Oxford UP, 1988.

————. *The George Eliot Letters.* Ed. Gordon S. Haight. 9 vols. New Haven: Yale UP, 1954–78.

Gallagher, Catherine. "George Eliot and *Daniel Deronda*: The Prostitute and the Jewish Question." In *The New Historicism Reader.* Ed. H. Aram Veeser. New York: Routledge, 1994.

Henry, Nancy. "Ante-Anti-Semitism: George Eliot's *Impressions of Theophrastus Such.*" In *Victorian Identities: Social and Cultural Formations in Nineteenth-Century Literature.* Ed. Ruth Robbins and Julian Wolfreys. New York: St. Martin's, 1996.

Leavis, F. R. *The Great Tradition: George Eliot, Henry James, Joseph Conrad.* London: Chatto and Windus, 1960.

Marcus, Steven. *Representations: Essays on Literature and Society.* New York: Random House, 1976.

Newton, K. M. "*Daniel Deronda* and Circumcision." In *George Eliot.* Ed. K. M. Newton. New York: Longman, 1991.

Press, Jacob. "Same-Sex Unions in Modern Europe: *Daniel Deronda, Altneuland,* and the Homoerotics of Jewish Nationalism." In *Novel Gazing.* Ed. Eve Sedgwick. Durham: Duke UP, 1997.

Ragussis, Michael. *Figures of Conversion: 'The Jewish Question' and English National Identity.* Durham: Duke UP, 1995.

Sutherland, John. *Can Jane Eyre Be Happy?* Oxford: Oxford UP, 1997.

George Eliot's Reading Revolution and the Mythical School of Criticism

William R. McKelvy

For two decades—the 1860s and 1870s—the idea of novel writing as a high, serious, and refined art was most closely associated with one name, George Eliot. She was, like William Thackeray, renowned for her faithful descriptions of life, and like Charles Dickens, she repeatedly signaled to her audience that the novel and novel readers were participating in a redeeming social mission. Unlike Thackeray and Dickens, though, she acquired a reputation as a philosopher, a "serious" thinker as Henry James called her in 1866 (51). Her unique achievement combined the highest intellectual ambition with a frequently asserted attention to the quotidian. Whereas Dickens—by point of contrast—drew passionate caricatures and often distributed virtues, vices, or characteristics entire and unadulterated to individuals, Eliot depicted the world as a "mixed, entangled affair"; the novelist, as she wrote in *Adam Bede*, was "obliged to creep servilely after nature and fact" (176, 175).

Before her career as a fiction writer began, Eliot, as a book reviewer and journalist, praised other writers for their commitment to realism, and she briefly edited a distinguished journal that often counseled the reform of fiction along realist principles. Starting in 1853, she was also the companion of an extraordinary man of letters, George Henry Lewes, who was a sophisticated advocate of realism in modern English, German, and French literature. Later, the reputations of Eliot and Lewes would be somewhat undermined by the great success of their advocacy, for realism became a venerable Victorian literary institution; and like other earnest Victorian institutions, it fathered a generally resentful brood of critics. Some of the finest literature of the Victorian twilight of the 1880s and 1890s originated in antirealist rebellions. And the last half of the twentieth-century in particular, as Harry Shaw has recently argued, produced a variety of professional (or scholarly) attacks on realism. Some have found in literary realism a complacent confidence in knowing how the world works. Others have seen more ominous qualities in the power of realist narrative, a training program for the internalization of forms of surveillance. Still others credit Victorian authors with being aware of the complications or even perils of a realist project. George Eliot criticism, voluminous and various, includes versions of all these arguments, and the best studies have charted Eliot's shifting stance toward realism or directed attention to the ways in which her fiction features—rather than skirts—problems of knowing.

What has not been carefully considered is the extent to which Eliot's realism emerges from a more discrete transaction between Eliot the reader and Eliot the writer. This chapter first describes how Eliot's decision to model her writing career on realist principles was a reaction to her most significant and dramatic decision as a reader, her reading revolution of 1841. I then show how her fiction often featured the betrayal of realist principles precisely in those fictional spaces where the actions of writing and reading most closely shadow each other. Eliot's career, as others have shown, both manifests and betrays realist principles, and once this contradiction is admitted—rather than forced into some convenient resolution—what seems most characteristic of Eliot is a scene in which writing has a dual capacity to embody transparent truths and mysteriously hint at meanings. In some of her most interesting moments, the realist capacity of writing to record experience is balanced by a contrary view of writing as a cipher, a mysterious code needing some kind of hierophantic reader. In taking this approach to Eliot, I am thus interested in acknowledging the benefits accrued by attention to Eliot's practice and representation of reading (see Raven; Small; Tadmor).

PROVINCIAL LIFE AND THE HOLY WAR, 1819–42

The major publications on which Eliot's fame rests are *Scenes of Clerical Life* (1858), a collection of four stories, and seven novels: *Adam Bede* (1859), *The Mill on the Floss* (1860), *Silas Marner* (1861), *Romola* (1862), *Felix Holt* (1866), *Middlemarch* (1872), and *Daniel Deronda* (1876). With the exception of *Romola* and *Daniel Deronda*, all of Eliot's fiction is set in an inward looking English Midlands during the first third of the nineteenth century, and the story of Eliot's connection to and departure from that region suggests one great irony of her writing life. For the first half of her life, from 1819 until the death of her father in 1849, Eliot's world centered on a few square miles of Warwickshire—and she wrote no fiction. Six days after burying her father, Eliot left England for a long recuperative stay on the Continent followed by a generally deracinated interlude. A single woman with a small inheritance and no clear vocation, she was, figuratively and literally, searching for her place in the world. In 1851 she found it, and until her death in 1881, Eliot was a London-based, cosmopolitan writer, traveling widely and regularly across Europe—a writer who wrote almost exclusively and with an unprecedented fidelity about the provincial world she had left behind.

Closely surveying rural and small town life in the Midlands, Eliot carried on, after a fashion, the work of her father, Robert Evans, who was an estate manager renowned for his skillful handling of land and its resources. It was to Robert and Christiana Evans that Mary Anne Evans was born in 1819. (George Eliot was a pseudonym adopted in 1857.) Robert Evans had been apprenticed as a carpenter (the trade of his father), but he, a man on the rise, made himself indispensable to the local landowning gentry, became relatively wealthy, and was able to treat Mary Anne to the best formal education available to a young woman in the provinces in those days. From 1824 to 1835, mostly as a boarder, she attended several nearby schools where she acquired the skills and Christian piety that would prepare her to become a respectable man's accomplished wife or, failing that, perhaps a governess. With the death of her mother in 1836 and her older sister's marriage in 1837, Mary Ann (as she now signed her name) assumed another vocation open to women of her class, dutiful daughter presiding over her lone father's household. Then in 1841 Robert, at the age of sixty-seven, essentially retired, letting his son Isaac take his place as estate manager and occupant of Griff (the family home since 1820). Father and daughter moved five miles away to a home just outside Coventry, a town of some 30,000. Robert Evans would later claim that he had moved to give Mary Ann a greater opportunity to attract suitors. But instead of finding a husband in Coventry, she became deeply attached to some extraordinary neighbors, Charles and Caroline Bray, who assembled at their home Rosehill the region's intellectually progressive society.

Even before Mary Ann met the Brays in November of 1841, she had been making a classic Victorian mental journey: She moved from a devout, Bible-based Christianity to an increasingly confident skepticism, and like other converts, her change of heart was inspired by an intense reading experience that transformed her status as a Bible reader. Mary Ann in the late 1830s was, as she would remain all her life, a great reader. She took up with particular interest theological works ranging from Christian evidences to books and tracts focusing on individual doctrinal issues such as infant baptism or the credibility of the Church Fathers. She also began to read the writings of Thomas Carlyle, whose descriptions of the displacement of religious authority by literary culture reflected the extraordinary social agency then attributed to authorship. With the Anglo-Catholic Oxford Movement peaking in its promise and influence, a powerful Evangelical revival being sustained within the Church of England, an increasingly confident array of Dissenting communities articulating their theological and political claims, and influential secular prophets like Carlyle announcing the coming of an unprecedented posttheological age, the late 1830s was a great age of religious controversy. Most unlike our own times, everything from parliamentary representation, education (including the value of novel reading), and trade were discussed in a predominantly religious register. It was in this cultural context—a time obsessed with an anxious, incipient modernity, an aura of generalized cultural crisis, and solutions often extracted from a divinely inspired Bible—that we must imagine the young Mary Ann, sometime between August and November of 1841, reading a critique of the historical claims of Christianity, *An Inquiry Concerning the Origins of Christianity* (1841) by Charles Hennell.

Hennell provided a classic statement of a position best described as Christian theism. He concluded that the supernatural events of Christ's life—his miraculous birth, his working of miracles, and his resurrection—were stories that were attached to the authentic life of a mortal reformer. Some aspects of these legendary appendages to the real life of Jesus had their origin in universal patterns of cultural memory predominant in pre-modern societies; others arose to confirm specific literary traditions in the Hebrew Bible. This argument—considered blasphemous by many—was not new, but it was being aggressively reformulated in the 1830s and 1840s by liberal Christians, Unitarians, deists, and atheists, precisely the kind of freethinkers encountered in the Brays' society at Rosehill. Hennell, himself a Unitarian, was, as Mary Ann soon found out, Caroline Bray's brother.

Sometime late in 1841, at the age of twenty-two, Mary Ann Evans gave up her traditional belief in an inspired and historically accurate Bible, and in January 1842, she refused to attend church with her father, who was outraged at his daughter's double denial of his paternal authority and the authority of the Church. As a letter to her father made clear, the issue for Mary Ann was a matter of textual authority, her rejection of the divine authority of "the books comprising the Jewish and Christian Scriptures":

I regard these writings as histories consisting of mingled truth and fiction, and while I admire and cherish much of what I believe to have been the moral teaching of Jesus himself, I consider the system of doctrines built upon the facts of his life and drawn as to its materials from Jewish notions to be most dishonorable to God and most pernicious in its influence on individual and social happiness. (*Letters,* i, 128)

The immediate consequence of this episode (dubbed by Mary Ann her "Holy War" [*Letters,* i, 133]) was the threat of separation from her father and the society of the Brays, whose influence Mr. Evans suspected to be at the root of his daughter's heterodoxy. In March, Mary Ann was sent back to Griff and the "care" of her brother Isaac, but she soon returned to her place as her father's housekeeper and the neighborhood of the Brays. By mid-May, a compromise was reached in which Mary Ann agreed to resume attending church with her father, and she was allowed to maintain a certain independence of thought and association.

The tightly circumscribed domestic dimensions of the Holy War belie the universal proposition about human history and the status of all ancient writings that was the basis of Mary Ann's loss of faith. On the one hand, this was a question of her accompanying her father at certain times to their pew in the parish church. This was a conflict in which Mary Ann wrote long letters to her father while living under the same roof, a conflict in which the prodigal daughter was exiled to the nearby family farm. On the other hand, the Holy War was waged on behalf of the fundamental principle of historical criticism, the belief that Scripture had to be read in its historical context like any other book; it was a war waged to be at liberty to read Scripture as a product of mythic ages, those periods of human history defined by an inability to write true and natural accounts.

FROM TRANSLATING STRAUSS TO WRITING FICTION, 1844–56

Mary Ann's combination of learning, leisure, a new religious heterodoxy, and—after the truce of 1842—a certain liberty of thought and action allowed her to commence her first great literary labor in 1844 when she agreed, through opportunities opened up by the Brays, to translate David Friedrich Strauss's *Das Leben Jesu* (*The Life of Jesus* [1835]). The translation of this work, the most important and controversial nineteenth-century biography of Jesus, occupied Mary Ann for two years. She was paid the meager sum of £20, but the experience determined the course of her life.

In practical terms, the translation became her ticket out of her provincial circle of advanced thinkers and led to a more cosmopolitan, London-based society of similar types. The book's publisher was John Chapman, who also maintained a boarding house that was the first London home of Marian Evans (as she now signed herself) in 1851. That same year she published her first long article in the *Westminster Review*, Chapman himself bought the journal, she became its editor, and she met Herbert Spencer and George Henry Lewes. Marian probably had a physical relationship with Chapman, was involved with and eventually rebuffed by Spencer, but by 1853 she was fully engaged in one of the great intellectual marriages of the century to Lewes (who was legally married to another woman). After translating another naturalizing theological work to be published by Chapman in 1853, Feuerbach's *Essence of Christianity*, Marian Evans caused a great scandal by "eloping" with Lewes to the continent in 1854. They returned in 1855, devoted to each other and shunned by conventional society, and in 1856, Marian began writing what would appear as *Scenes of Clerical Life*, the act of authorship that called forth the name George Eliot.

The translation of Strauss was the threshold to the London of Chapman, Spencer, Lewes and the heady world of the *Westminster Review*. But Strauss's work also made it clearer how realist literary principles—at least for the novelist George Eliot—were affiliated with the principles of historical criticism and rationalism in general. Strauss's conclusions were substantially those featured in Hennell's work, and like Hennell, Strauss distanced his position from a more violently anti-Christian tradition that claimed Scripture was a false history forged by deceptive, self-serving priests. In the place of pernicious priestcraft, Strauss and other more "respectable" infidels situated the origin of Scripture in what they called mythic periods, times when miraculous narratives were composed because of ignorance about invariable physical laws, not intentional deception. "[N]o just notion of the true nature of history is possible," Strauss said, "without a perception of the inviolability of the chain of finite causes, and of the impossibility of miracles" (64). Strauss's entire argument was based on this materialist understanding of experience and its submission to consistent physical laws, a view of the world that was then defined as "rationalism."

Reviewing a popular history of the rise of rationalism in 1865, George Eliot—by then an established literary personality—chided the author for failing to provide a "careful preliminary definition." "[T]he development of physical science" and "the gradual reduction of all phenomena within the sphere of established law," Eliot impatiently made clear, carried with it a "rejection of the miraculous." This was the "supremely important fact" at the heart of rationalism. So when George Eliot, the realist novelist, embraced a vocation of creeping humbly after nature and fact, we should see a rationalist at work, the same person who saw "[t]he great conception of universal regular sequence" growing out of humble labor, "the patient watching of external fact" (*Essays*, 413). This rationalist was the mother of the realist, and standing behind both was the young Bible reader who decided to reject the historical credibility of Scripture, to read it as a text composed before historical verisimilitude was possible.

By becoming an active disseminator of heterodox Biblical criticism, Eliot did not simply reject the religion of her family and nation. She found significant sanction for the nobility and utility of her eventual vocation as a realist writer. She increasingly came to believe that her commitment to the verifiable put her in line with the culmination of intellectual evolution, a movement that united in the same cause historical critics of Biblical and classical texts, scientists, poets, novelists, art critics, and practitioners (like herself) of the higher journalism. Much of Eliot's best writing during her career as a working journalist (1851–56) had the same moral. Whether she was praising the "sacred" task of accurately portraying the working classes in "The Natural History of German Life" (*Essays,* 271) or attacking extravagant excursions from reality in "Silly Novels by Lady Novelists," she wrote from the same perspective, a worldview that inspired her to wound mortally the literary reputation of an eighteenth-century clerical poet with same poniard of the real: "In Young we have the type of that deficient human sympathy, that impiety towards the present and the visible, which flies for its motives, its sanctities, and its religion, to the remote, the vague, and the unknown" (*Essays,* 385). In nearly all that she wrote, she kept her eyes on what she called the supremely important fact, as in her 1855 praise of the art critic John Ruskin: "The truth of infinite value that he teaches is realism—the doctrine that all truth and beauty are to be obtained by a humble and faithful study of nature, and not by substituting vague forms, bred by imagination on the mists of feeling, in place of definite substantial reality" (*Selected Critical Writings,* 248).

REALISM AS A "PARCHMENT CODE": READING UNKNOWN CHARACTERS IN *MIDDLEMARCH*

Realist writing longs to inscribe the present and visible, the definite, substantial reality of life. But from today's perspective what most distinguishes Eliot's realist texts is their attention to a contradictory capacity for writing to signify what is both remote or unseen. *Middlemarch* in particular features attempts to convert vague signs into enlightened reality. The Reverend Edward Casaubon, a failed author and orthodox Bible reader, is the most obvious decoder in *Middlemarch*. Even though Eliot was a successful author and heterodox Biblical critic, she saw in Casaubon her true alter ego. Both authors staked their identity on a literary fame acquired in the illustration of Truth itself. And both discovered they were failing. Eliot's great achievement in *Middlemarch* is to sense and carefully construe the parallel dilemma shared by Casaubon, the doomed interpreter, and the realist narrator (Eliot herself). Eliot seems to have faced the conclusion that generalized truth—what Casaubon and the realist pursue—exists only in the form of a human desire. The idea that language can capture a verifiable external existence is just that—an idea—and Eliot recognizes in her own rationalism a creed, perhaps as much as any supernatural religion, against which experience may weigh.

As many critics have pointed out, Casaubon is repeatedly featured in the text as a text. He is described as a "sort of parchment code" (57); and when a drop of his blood was viewed under a magnifying glass, as one wit cracks, "it was all semicolons and parentheses" (58). The tragedy or wicked comedy of much of *Middlemarch* centers on the unequal match of this arid, inky grammarian to the young and florid Dorothea Brooke. What attracts Dorothea to Casaubon, though, is not his status as a text; he is not a book she wants to read. Rather, he is the author of a forthcoming book that will decode mysterious texts. Casaubon's life's labor has been the Key to all Mythologies, "a great work concerning religious history" that will show how "all the mythical systems or erratic mythical fragments in the world were corruptions of a tradition originally revealed" (10, 20). In Casaubon's project, Dorothea sees the potential reduction of a confusing Babel of past history—polylingual, polytheistic, and multicultural—into a single verified narrative. Casaubon's very words are like "the inscription on the door of a museum which might open on the treasures of past ages" (27). Many such keys—see Harcourt's *Doctrine of the Deluge*—were written in Georgian and Victorian England, and Eliot had earnestly studied several. In the eyes of most Victorian intellectual elites in the 1850s and after, though, these works appeared increasingly outdated (as Casaubon's work is often described) because they were based on the old view that Scripture was an inspired, accurate history of the ancient world and thus could be used to help decode various "heathen" mythologies, those dead religions that had at their origin some element of authentic revelation. Whereas the mythical method endorsed by historical critics used the broader category of primitive mythology to interpret Scripture, Casaubon follows the older, orthodox practice of seeing Scripture as a primary and privileged source for the interpretation of mythology. The error to which both Casaubon and Dorothea are wed is their belief in a single privileged key to antiquity and life in general.

But errors in the pursuit of truth—*Middlemarch* suggests—are not limited to Biblical critics who have failed to see the world bathed by the bright light of rationalism. We are presented with a host of other characters on doomed quests, a pattern of failure that extends to readers of the novel who witness a standoff in an ongoing debate about the value of two kinds of writing—the hieroglyphic and the transparent. By the end of the novel, Casaubon's attempt to use one kind of writing—clear revelation—to illuminate the other—the dimly lit relics of heathen antiquity—appears less like an extraordinary and absurd quest and more like the pattern of life for any seeker of truth.

Chapter 29, for example, features writing both as a reliable record and as a mysterious cipher. Newly conscious of the double failure of his marriage and literary ambition, Casaubon has decided to issue directly "a small monograph on some lately-traced indications concerning the Egyptian mysteries whereby certain assertions of Warburton's could be corrected. References were extensive even here, but not altogether shoreless; and sentences were actually to be written" (231). The capacity of Casaubon's monograph to embody meaning is promised on two levels: its ability to extract truth from the mysteries and its literal materialization of Casaubon's authorial ambition. This was a text "actually to be written" in the sense of both its actual production and its ability to translate occluded texts into their actual (true) significance. Casaubon is in the library at Lowick gamely pursuing this plan when Dorothea enters to join him for a morning's work, but instead of toiling over the remote past, they briefly quarrel over a newly arrived letter from Will Ladislaw, Casaubon's handsome young cousin and primary rival for the affection of his wife. Then in simmering silence, they both turn to their separate tables and begin to write. Casaubon, the ambitious decoder of mysterious texts, ends up writing indecipherable signs ("his hand trembled so much that the words seemed to be written in an unknown character" [233]), while Dorothea writes clearly and firmly and feels the significance of the Latin text she is copying being revealed to her:

> She did not in the least divine the subtle sources of her husband's bad temper about these letters: she only knew that they had caused him to offend her. She began to work at once, and her hand did not tremble; on the contrary, in writing out the quotations . . . she felt that she was forming her letters beautifully, and it seemed to her that she saw the construction of the Latin she was copying, and which she was beginning to understand, more clearly than usual. In her indignation there was a sense of superiority, but it went out for the present in firmness of stroke. (233)

After a half-hour of such firm, clear writing, the fall of a book and the near fall of Casaubon from the short library ladder break the silence.

There is here an artful, realistic portrayal of a bad marriage that is going to get worse. The scene illustrates the scholarly and physical limitations of Casaubon, whose jealousy turns him into a scribbler of dim signs. The climbing of three steps—not a Promethean height to scale—leaves him gasping for breath, nearly tottering to the floor and betraying the physical impotence inspiring his jealousy. In contrast to Casaubon's loss of faith in his larger project, his lowered ambition, illegible writing, and physical weakness, Dorothea enters the scene with her interpretive skills lauded ("she had learned to read the signs of her husband's mood" [231]), and like her judgment, her writing is firm. Just as her husband is losing his faith in his ability to read the mysteries of the past, Dorothea is developing hers. This new confidence recalls and reverses the moment when Dorothea wrote a letter accepting Casaubon's proposal, a letter she had to write three times "not because she wished to change the wording but because her hand was unusually uncertain, and she could not bear that Mr. Casaubon should think her handwriting bad and illegible" (37). And thus the old man and the project that attracted his wife are revealed as shams, and the novel's heroine begins to regain her autonomy and will eventually, with the total eclipse of Casaubon, win a suitably virile mate.

Such a reading follows closely the metaphoric value of language, which allows us to transfer (that's what "metaphor" literally means) Dorothea's chirographic firmness to her emotional state, or to transfer the fall of that book into a comment on the decline and fall of Casaubon's literary ambition. What our reading thus far has not paid attention to, however, is the potential status of writing as a code, a collection of characters that signify what they do not look like. We have had to ignore the fact that the unknown characters coming from Casaubon's shaky hand signify clearly his jealously. At the same time, the clearly writing, linguistically sensitive Dorothea is nowhere in the novel more self-deluded than when she pretends that her husband's jealousy is a mystery of obscure origins. Casaubon's gibberish in both cases—his shaky writing viewed by the narrator and his bad temper in the eyes of his wife—is ready to be decoded in a transaction between the other writer and reader in the fictional library at Lowick, Eliot and the novel reader. For this reader, Eliot has synchronized in Casaubon the emergence of accurate self-knowledge with his production of illegible text, and in Dorothea's case, self-deception is synchronized with the assumption of legibility. These meanings do not rely upon metaphor; they might be explained by irony, but to attribute them simply to generic irony is to forget that the central irony in *Middlemarch* is resolutely interpretive, an irony about the interpretation of a narrative that features interpretive folly. In *Middlemarch*, "key" is a keyword in a story that implies that any search for the Key to Anything is, like Casaubon's Key to all Mythologies, an exercise in futility. If *Middlemarch* offers a lesson in urbane skepticism, if it is a tract about the vanity of human knowledge, its skepticism itself is something that we are invited to decode in a way that relies infrequently on the realistic value of language. The dedicated reader of *Middlemarch*, working long and late, inspired by the errors of rival readers and by a solution about to break on the horizon is Casaubon himself: "With his taper stuck before him he forgot the absence of windows, and in bitter manuscript remarks on other men's notions about the solar deities, he had become indifferent to the sunlight" (162).

Casaubon's story is famously balanced by the parallel failure of Tertius Lydgate's search for the "common basis" of material life, "the primitive tissue" (122), but a more subtle complement to the story of Casaubon's shaky hand comes in the transformation of the handwriting of Fred Vincy, a young man whose father has planned for him to become, like Casaubon, a priest. Circumstances drive Fred to take up the less genteel pursuit of business under the tutelage of Mr. Garth, and to do this, Fred must exchange the purposefully illegible hand of a university educated gentleman for the clear hand of a clerk. As Fred strives to bring to his writing the same clarity and determinacy as a numerical account, Mr. Garth emphatically distances "business" from the world of books in which Casaubon was buried: "You can't learn it off as you learn things out of a book" (458). Fred is eventually the author of both an illegible and a clear hand. He writes in ciphers, and he writes clearly at different stages in his life. But in either mode, his hand remains both a clear sign and a cipher. His illegible hand, worthy of "any viscount or bishop," clearly indicates his social pretensions even though his "strokes had a blotty solidity and the letters disdained to keep the line" (462); and his clear handwriting is most significant as a cipher for his love of Mary Garth, a code in which this reader clearly sees the kind of love for another that can inspire self-transformation.

At any given moment—in the library at Lowick or at Fred's writing desk—and in surprising ways, Eliot's fiction might shine the bright light of full disclosure, or it might hint at shadowy meanings. At its best, it does what Eliot the rationalist knew to be frankly impossible: The black marks become magical (Hertz, 86–88). And for all this to happen, Eliot writes in a fashion that is realistic. But the definite substantial reality of the novel resides in ciphers as often as in clear accounts. In this way, Casaubon ceases to be a portrait of the author who has failed to embrace rationalism (and its attendant literary creed, realism). Instead, Casaubon is a participant in a narrative that subjects Casaubon and the realist author to a similar predicament. Casaubon's failure is attributed to his lack of insight into the relationship of Scripture, myth, and true history. His failure is based on his hope to divide clearly dark ciphers and clear revelation in precisely the same way the devout Mary Ann Evans did, as when she wrote in 1840, "How blessed that we are not left like the heathen to grope our way to a twilight of knowledge, but may be at once introduced to the clear sunshine of the full assurance of understanding of the study of Divine revelation" (*Letters,* i, 49–50). To the extent to which this statement identified Mary Ann's faith in the historical credibility of Scripture, the reading revolution of 1841 called for an unambiguous rejection of it, and that rejection was substantiated in George Eliot's realist fiction. To the extent to which this statement identifies ciphers and clear accounts with designs on each other, old Casaubon, the devout Mary Ann, and the realist novelist George Eliot were living in the same world of shadow and light.

WORKS CITED AND SELECTED WORKS FOR FURTHER READING

Ashton, Rosemary. *George Eliot: A Life*. London: Hamish Hamilton, 1996.

———. *The German Idea: Four English Writers and the Reception of German Thought, 1800–1860*. New York: Cambridge UP, 1980.

———. *G. H. Lewes: A Life*. New York: Oxford UP, 1991.

Bodenheimer, Rosemarie. *The Real Life of Mary Ann Evans: George Eliot, Her Letters and Fiction*. Ithaca: Cornell UP, 1994.

Carroll, David. *George Eliot: The Critical Heritage*. New York: Barnes and Noble, 1971.

Creeger, George R., ed. *George Eliot: A Collection of Critical Essays*. Englewood Cliffs: Prentice-Hall, 1970.

Eliot, George. *Adam Bede*. Ed. Valentine Cunningham. Oxford: Oxford UP, 1996.

———. *Essays*. Ed. Thomas Pinney. New York: Columbia UP, 1963.

———. *The George Eliot Letters*. 9 vols. Ed. Gordon S. Haight. New Haven: Yale UP, 1954–78.

———. *Middlemarch*. Ed. David Carroll. Oxford: Oxford UP, 1998.

———. *Selected Critical Writings*. Ed. Rosemary Ashton. Oxford: Oxford UP, 1992.

Haight, Gordon S., ed. *A Century of George Eliot Criticism*. Boston: Houghton Mifflin, 1965.

Haight, Gordon S., and Rosemary T. Van Arsdel, eds. *George Eliot: A Centenary Tribute*. London: Macmillan, 1982.

Harcourt, Leveson Vernon. *The Doctrine of the Deluge: Vindicating the Scriptural Account from the Doubts Which Have Recently Been Cast upon It by Geological Speculations*. 2 vols. London: Longmans, 1838.

Hertz, Neil. "Recognizing Casaubon." In *The End of the Line: Essays on Psychoanalysis and the Sublime*, pp. 75–96. New York: Columbia UP, 1985.

James, Henry. "The Novels of George Eliot." In *A Century of George Eliot Criticism*, pp. 43–54. Ed. Gordon S. Haight. Boston: Houghton Mifflin, 1965.

The Journals of George Eliot. Ed. Margaret Harris and Judith Johnston. Cambridge: Cambridge UP, 1998.

The Letters of George Henry Lewes. 3 vols. Ed. William Baker. Victoria: ELS, 1995–99.

Newton, K. M., ed. *George Eliot*. New York: Longman, 1991.

Perkin, J. Russell. *A Reception-History of George Eliot's Fiction*. Ann Arbor: UMI, 1990.

Raven, James, Helen Small, and Naomi Tadmor. *The Practice and Representation of Reading in England*. Cambridge: Cambridge UP, 1996.

Rignall, John. *Oxford Reader's Companion to George Eliot*. Oxford: Oxford UP, 2000. [For a brief but substantial review of materials essential for engaging with Eliot's reading, see William Baker's entry on Eliot's library (212).]

Shaffer, E. S. *"Kubla Khan" and the Fall of Jerusalem: The Mythological School in Biblical Criticism and Secular Literature, 1770–1880*. Cambridge: Cambridge UP, 1975.

Shaw, Harry E. *Narrating Reality: Austen, Scott, Eliot.* Ithaca: Cornell UP, 1999.
Strauss, David Friedrich. *The Life of Jesus Critically Examined.* 3 vols. Translated by George Eliot. London: Chapman, 1846.

Thomas Hardy

{ornament}

Edward Neill

"Thomas Hardy" was a man made out of words who was also particularly good at making women out of them. Indeed, Hardy may himself be figured as a Pygmalion of sorts who breathes fleshly life into female "phantoms of his own figuring." Hardy himself seems to have been well aware of this. His last novella, *The Well-Beloved* (1897), a virtually sidelined little opus, depicts the artist as a kind of Pygmalion reversed—in the form of the sculptor Jocelyn Pierston. Pierston turns (female) flesh to stone in achieving the Pyrrhic victory of art. This "victory" seems finally to prefigure the death of desire itself. In life, this was a consummation to be devoutly "unwished." As art, it made the perfect finish. Why, then, is *The Well-Beloved* such an unjustly neglected work? This is because Hardy made another attempt, and a much more speciously authoritative one, to "finish himself off" twenty-five years after. As a kind of "posthumous" novelist he made a rather bad decision to "write his life" in the form of an autobiography disguised as a biography by his second wife—the dull, depressed (and disloyal) Florence née Dugdale.

But the *Life*, an attempt to spike the guns of biographers, merely encouraged them in their wild goose chase after a real Thomas Hardy who had already not merely stood up to be counted, but, by his own account, "stood up to be shot at"—when he wrote *Tess of the d'Urbervilles* (1891). Biographers and their dupes will never realize, it seems, that, as Leo Bersani puts it, "the aesthetic effect depends on an absence, the absence of a subject as the authoritative source or origin of fantasies or ideas." Thus, The Death of Thomas Hardy may be said to have taken place after his "life of—and in—writing." This, paradoxically, took the form of various attempts (including, of course, his own) to write his life. And thus was born the "other" Thomas Hardy—- the defensive little "serial filler" who has wasted so much of our time—endlessly compliant, slightly cowed, vaguely complicit.

The "author of the *Life*" is surely something of a snob. The "author of *The Well-Beloved*" is a sardonically alienated analyst of High Society. We should not hesitate over which work to spend our time with (or on). Yet Hardy studies, like life, have their little ironies. The highly "anti-biographical" critic Peter Widdowson wants to make the *Life* into Hardy's last novel, a fiction of himself, as it were. This is a clever idea, but a most unfortunate one, as it must constitute a form of promotion for this dubious text. And in fact it is Hardy's scholarly but patronizing (and often quite philistine) biographer, Robert Gittings, who seems to have no trouble analyzing the *Life's* typically Pooterish, *Diary-of-a-Nobody* qualities.

Extrapolating from his *Life*, biographers unwittingly reproduce a figure in many respects the opposite of the one who made what was intended to be his creative debut with a work intent on "*miching mallecho*"—mischief-making—as his timid publisher noted. This led, apparently, to his being quashed on the spot. To be published at all, it seems, required the practice of sleights and stratagems. Fortunately, though, Hardy was quick to learn his lesson. Some of Hardy's ancestors may have been involved in smuggling, and in a sense he continued this tradition in textual form, with an illicit cargo of cultural disruption and dissent, in what would prove an impressively sustained "dance of the intellect among narratives." It might, then, be taken as a sort of allegory that, thanks to the efforts of officious and self-appointed custodians who crowded in to appropriate him, Hardy was ghoulishly dismembered in death. His heart was buried in "Wessex," the rest of his corpse, in the official ceremonies of interment, in Westminster Abbey. "He's the man we were in search of, that's true," claims Hardy's constable in his story, "The Three Strangers," "And yet he's not the man we were in search of. For the man we were in search of is not the man we wanted." Perhaps biography is similarly inclined to figure (and finger) the wrong suspect—to miss, as it were, the heart of the matter and mistake the corpse for the corpus. Lacan's seminar on Poe's "Purloined Letter" examined a tale in which the "letter" remained unexamined precisely from its being something of an open secret. As Poe's detective remarked, "the best clues" are "perhaps a little *too* self-evident." If one wishes to "revive" Hardy, one may find that "the letter giveth life," after all, while the spirit, in the sense of the ectoplasm pursued by biographers, is a treacherous phantom.

Hardy, in what we might suggestively describe as "propria persona," is reticent and actually inaccessible in his overtly decorous Victorian privacy. In his creative writings, though, as if by way of compensation, he openly conducts something of an inquisition into desire, language, and society. We might put this naughtily (if not inappropriately) by saying that he is never done with tweaking Mrs. Grundy's tail. Yet "Mrs. Grundy" is herself something of a comic misnomer, if not a "gender studies item," in being largely made out of what might be styled a collection of hysterical male editors. The traditional view of Hardy as a writer of rustic sincerity suggests someone of fairly unambitious intellectual gait. Yet on closer and more sophisticated inspection here, Hardy seems set on following unusual rubrics of representation, which might almost be described as "conceited" in a specific sense reserved for discussions of some kinds of poetry. To read "Hardy," we must realize that "realism" is an inadequate characterization of his mode, and those who attempt film adaptations may not have merely their work cut out, but also his. His feline, metamorphic approach to representation makes him well up to—or with—the sophistications of modernism, while there is much in Hardy that "modernism cannot reach." Hardy's intellectual brilliance proves to be a source of not-so-polite critical inquiry, spelling potential trouble for the author, not just innocuous, if pyrotechnic, entertainment for his audience. (It also cuts across the pleasantly geriatric image of the Older Hardy and recalls us to a sense of the younger man making his—in context—extremely experimental way.)

However, we are given to understand that "Wessex" is, among other things, rather chalky, and a certain "porosity" in acts of (re-)presentation will turn out to help Hardy in what we might almost call his running battle with the authorities. His silences are often rather eloquent, and, as the reader will see, the present study was particularly keen to hear from them. "Wessex" is an attractive fancy that becomes a menace only when used for the purpose of preemptive canon-creation, instantly producing a list of officially "major" works that, as it happens, serve to produce it. The insidiousness of this resides in the fact that the "helpful offer" of "rational" criteria actually favors a limiting set of conventions, attitudes and styles of representation.

"Wessex" is suspiciously twinned with nostalgia and conservatism, a strand in Hardy's work, and so a little too reassuring as a kind of shorthand indication of what Hardy is "about." If so, it is important to recognize that Hardy's creative intentions are not quite so easily assessed or characterized. For example, Hardy also gets a good deal of creative mileage out of a "sort-of Shelleyan" inquisition into metaphysics, mores, and social structures. His novels are what he himself might have called "retaliatory fictions"—a phrase annexed from words Grace Melbury uses to maximize discomfort in her erring husband in *The Woodlanders* (1887). The argument began here with reference to Hardy's last work of fiction but might be said to stem equally from his first—Hardy's "debut which was not one." What was intended to be an "inaugural" novel—*The Poor Man and the Lady* (1868)—was indeed quashed. But Hardy emphatically declined to become the "good little Thomas Hardy" (in the sadly patronizing phraseology of Henry James). Confident readers like George Meredith and John Morley advised perusal of the Wilkie Collins sensation-novel, which Hardy was indeed able to press into service as a kind of "stalking-horse." In fact, this excess of "well-meant" exhortation would certainly have killed off a lesser novelist.

No doubt it was as easy to dispense as it wasn't for the young "pharmacist" himself to dispense with. Accused of producing a disturbing text, Hardy ironically capitulates, "complies" with advice and exhortations to "cool it," and produces a rather more disturbing one—*Desperate Remedies* (1871), which achieves, among so much more, a kind of braiding of Virgil and the "sensation novel." The novel's *terminus ad quem* is the expunging and razing of the extremely impious Aeneas Manston, illegitimate son of the seduced and abandoned Cytherea I (Miss Aldcliffe), a darkly Byronic antihero "genetically modified" into a state of mysterious ethical dereliction understood to have resulted from the circumstances of his conception. He commits suicide in prison while awaiting trial for the murder of his first wife, Eunice. In his prison journal, however, which unties the knot instrinsicate of the vertigo-inducing plot, he is granted what might be called the Hardyean imagination—so much so, indeed, that the final restoration of Edward Springrove to Cytherea II and their attainment of the Knapwater estate may even strike the reader as slightly mawkish and insipid. The devils, it seems, finally have all the best artistic tunes, here, and literally: In a remarkable "sex scene" Manston, installed as new steward at Knapwater, plays the organ during a thunderstorm while an undeniably fascinated Cytherea II listens with "parted lips." This was rivaled by a "sort-of-lesbian" scene earlier in which the slightly deranged Cytherea I (Miss Aldcliffe) climbs into bed with the "Cythie" she has just been scolding—apparently, for Hardy, under the rubric "what naming has joined let no man put asunder," and the novel throughout is structured by just such abstract, "conceited" qualities.

Under the Greenwood Tree (1872) capitalizes on the idea of a pastoral world as it looks over its intertextual shoulder at *As You Like It*. But its characters, including Fancy Day and young Dick Dewy as romantic leads, and the doomed choir, do not "fleet the time carelessly," seem subject to the pressures of capitalism without quite capitulating to them. Dick and Fancy always seemed hymeneal, but this version of pastoral is so in a more "conceited" way, its very world a kind of permeable membrane as it at once enables and forbids alien intrusions: Notes of disharmony are heard as honey is threatened by money, the organic community by organs, men by women, use value by exchange value, and finally Dick himself by a Parson Maybold impressive enough to induce a fickle Fancy to temporarily succumb to what would complete an already well-advanced process of "bourgeoisification."

A Pair of Blue Eyes (1873) is commended but hardly read. Yet if one wished to proceed in the mode of recommendation, it would be perfectly possible to advance the claim for this to be considered as nothing less than the ultimate in "Victorian" novels, and that therefore if you could only read (or board the Titanic with) one, it should indeed be this one. Tennyson and Coventry Patmore adored the book and saw in it the work of a "natural born poet," a point that a still young but already much-abused Hardy must have found deeply gratifying. At the level of a kind of journalistic incitement to the reader that would still function as showing what a "cultural archive" it is, it might be described as being full of fogies, railway elopements, slender hypergamous Youths with Prospects, encrusted snobberies, misremembered Latin quotations, gout, rectories, broken-hearted peregrinations with a Baedeker, Family Vaults, geology, chess, church restoration, forelock-touching rusticity, heavy fathers pursuing flighty runaway daughters, and bitter widows muttering in the shades of the shrubbery, with the spirit of Samuel Smiles over all in the form of the "Every Man His Own Maker" Club of St. Launce deftly caricaturing the Victorian worship of pelf and property. And finally a wonderful post-Romantic sense of the world's body in the form of a wild Cornwall conscripted to underscore and orchestrate the human emotions, particularly feminine, which animate it.

Yet the fact remains that these emotions turn out to be, for the most part, extremely painful and unpleasant ones, and the novel acts as critique as well as ingratiation toward the Victorian world it projects and phallocentric imperatives and patriarchal propensities it propounds with such unflinching rigor. Seascapes compose a sense of that destructive psychological element, perhaps the feminine, in which imperious "linguistic mastery of the drives," a male and bourgeois prerogative, must founder, but it is Elfride who dies of a symbolic miscarriage at the end. She's cast off by Knight and borne to her final rest on a carriage attached to a train. This train carries rivals for her hand, Knight and young Stephen Smith, on deluded quests.

The better-known novel, which made him, *Far from the Madding Crowd* (1874) has been suspected of working too hard to give no offence to a highly "Grundian" Leslie Stephen at the *Cornhill* as Hardy becomes something of a purveyor of humorous rusticity to the gentry—but some rustic remarks, risqué Lawrentian moments with Troy, and the slightly overcrowded coffin of Fanny Robin fetched from the Casterbridge workhouse after her seduction and abandonment by Sergeant Troy make unmistakable mischief. On the whole though, Hardy gave Stephen what he wanted, ironically complied with his slightly hysterical "tone-down" requests. Brilliantly showing the world's fecundity at work and the work of desire, *Far from the Madding Crowd*'s extremely chastened (and chastening) ending again announces its erasure, and Bathsheba, with the death of husband Troy and a Boldwood confined at His Majesty's pleasure on her conscience, can hardly raise a smile on her own wedding day.

In *The Hand of Ethelberta* (1876) by contrast, the heroine Ethelberta, ruling family, husband, and several suitors with a rod of iron, passes over into a kind of masculinity that is not (quite) that, and her "gender troubling" is imbricated with class antagonisms and ambiguities. Her very name is interesting in this respect, as Ethelbert was the first (male) ruler of all the Anglo-Saxons, and her female appropriation of the name establishes her sex by the "little a" alone, the extra that signals a lack, the missing portion of maleness. As a young widow and protégée of Lady Petherwin, the early death of whose son sparks the incidents of the novel, Ethelberta's patronage is on the absolute condition of her not "owning" her poor "relations," a heist that makes her profession of storytelling (as themselves, perhaps, "poor relations," entailing "cancelled words," which "misrepresent" her relation to the economic base) a particularly apposite one. As we have seen, Hardy advances through conceits, allusions, or half-tones of "intertextuality."

This makes the novel an interesting tract as well as something of an essay on Hardy's sense of his own destiny. But Ethelberta's ambiguously "sacrificial" quest is deeply ironized: although she surrounds him always with regret and the idea of what he has to endure makes her tearful, her father, the butler Chickerel, does not want her help and is merely irritated by what Derrida would call the "useless pathos" with which she too quickly surrounds her sense of his fate, just as her angry, Republican brother Sol sets off on a vain quest to prevent the marriage to leering old Lord Mountclere of Lychworth, despite the fact that it will, in due course, "set him up." As previously, when Ethelberta broke down when she dropped her costume of fiction and invented incident and gave her audience the actuality in the form of the story of her life, Mountclere seemed to enter her story (a well-known prurient innuendo in Mallarmé) by suspending it. And this truth bartered as fiction by Etheleberta was a fiction bartered by Hardy that came close to the truth about his own life and motivation.

However, it would appear that Ethelberta has extirpated not only the corruption and extravagance of "estate mismanagement," but "the sexual relation" itself. She has, in a way, brought the puritan spirit of the lower orders, briefly victorious with Cromwell, to the hellraking debaucheries and corruptly parasitic mores of Lychworth (399), with the driving force that one should have been able to associate with Paula Power in *A Laodicean* (1881), a more "autonomous" Ethelberta. Finally, through her refusal to "have a heart" in the conventional sense, or to "be," or rather "become 'a woman'" in De Beauvoir's formula, according to the conventionally assigned roles, we may even conclude, with our inevitable hindsight, that Ethleberta has become something of a "cyborg" in the terms announced by Donna Haraway's "Cyborg Manifesto."

The Mayor of Casterbridge (1886) is nothing if not a somber-suited work. Set in the "dream-country" of Wessex (which came to be read as "shorthand" for the place, or space, of the "canonic" in Hardy), it also reassures the reader that s/he knows exactly where s/he is. Add the tone (if not the genre) of Tragedy, and an apparent rock-hard commitment to "character" as an absolute given prior to any social formation, what we have is nothing if not an "overdetermined" bid for literary respectability. Here in particular Hardy, himself reconstructed as a kind of literary master-mason by perceptive Proust, offers sound construction, well-knit members, almost, you might say, the intellectual equivalent of "having the builders in." "Henchard," it seems, was the name for an old building to be pulled down long before it became one for a rugged character to be pulled down. But the resulting study in insecurity—in a semantic and psychological instability that desolatingly demonstrates that there is no-"one" (and no-"where") to rely on—is in fact amusingly consistent with "stories of builders" (and builders' narratives).

Once again, then, we see Hardy playing dice(y) games that bring notions of the ludic, if not quite ludicrous, to shatter predictable notions of decorous literary genealogies. At once offering and suspending notions of the canny and the uncanny, Hardy seems to show how things may turn turtle, with each secreting "the other." Canny Scots may be the unwitting or even unwilling bearers of the latter, while the uncanny, Henchard's doom, is finally traced to its "canny" source in his "cursed pride and mortification at being poor," qualifying the text's own ruling idea of "character" as a stable signifier of playing-card fixity. *The Woodlanders* (1887) notes the early educational mortifications of Melbury, a timber merchant, in a novel finally more sociological than Sophoclean, that will lead him to an obsession with "bettering" his daughter. "Bettering" is a word Hardy hastens to surround with irony. With creaking social deference, Melbury will affiance Grace to a scion of the local aristocracy down on his luck, Edred Fitzpiers, rich in cultural capital, but louche and even salaud-like, with a snobbish contempt for the Melbury who sets him up in practice. "Bettered," Grace seems to be particularly good at not knowing her own mind—that Sherton "finishing school" might really have finished her off after all, and she is described as "caught between two storeys of society." The novel is, indeed, all about such liminalities.

Grace's heart should belong to Giles Winterborne, a kind of Keatsian wood-god, autumn's very brother, and he had previously been promised Grace.

Attractive but inhibited, Giles proves to have some of the "*délire de toucher,*" the fatal inhibition, of John Loveday in *The Trumpet-Major*, sublime but also sublimated in a rather bad Freudian sense. Losing his Grace no less than his grace and favored residence through a harsh decree of Mrs. Charmond, Giles bears too much for love, evicting himself from his shack to preserve the chastity that even Grace will finally beg him not to respect. In a desolating ending, the trap set by bitter Tim Tangs to avenge the former seduction of his wife Suke by Fitzpiers, the trap will catch only Grace's dress (she always was a little hard to get hold of), and its effect will merely be that of restoring Grace to a promiscuous husband while Marty South vows eternal fidelity to a Giles who, in life, had taken only perfunctory interest in her. This is an intolerable moment of ironized quasi-Wordsworthian pathos in which she is glimpsed by exhausted rustics forced by Melbury to traipse all the way from Little Hintock to Sherton only to find that Grace has shacked up with Edred yet again.

In *Tess of the d'Urbervilles* (1891), above all the other novels, the "semantic" is "somatic" and the "somatic" "semantic," with Tess's body as silent signifier. Hardy uses *Measure for Measure* adroitly here, cleverly splitting Angelo's priggishness and prurience between her lovers Alec d'Urberville and Angel Clare: "In her looks / there is a prone and speechless dialect / such as moves men" seems a particularly relevant citation, and might be used as a more telling epigraph or introductory quotation than the sentimental one he culled from *Two Gentlemen of Verona*. "Dialect" is particularly a word to seize on here as Shakespeare's linguistic metaphor for the sort of sexiness they find in Tess is specifically imaged as the "oppressed linguistic equivalent" of Tess's relatively unsophisticated but genealogically interesting rusticity.

Later, on Tess and Angel's "wedding night which was not one" at Wellbridge, Tess will identify herself and Angel as what we, if not she, might call "Shelleyan" counterparts ("doubles"). Matthew Arnold identified Shelley as an "Angel" in a famous description, and Angel is compared to Shelley and contrasted with Byron by Hardy here. But Tess forgot about gender differences and discriminations (and could hardly know that Angel was not merely a return of priggish, hortatory Clym in *The Return of the Native*, but also of the intellectual Henry Knight in *A Pair of Blue Eyes* [1873] with his bullying patriarchal passion for "untried lips"). Faced with all this evidence, one might feel that an alternative title for *Tess* might be *Habeas Corpus* ("You may have the body"), as the legal phrase will refer at once to Tess's claim to be spirit, her appropriation by Alec, her spiritual adoption of Angel, her specific doom of "hard, horrible work" with "stone-deaf taskmaster" Groby, and her hanging at Wintoncester after her discovery by Angel at Sandbourne and the dreamlike interludes of happiness at Bramshurst Court and Stonehenge—proving that, as Jane Austen might put it, "the whole affair was *in suspense*." Even poor Tess's story of her "out of body experiences" is describing a state of "suspended animation."

Some critics write of *Jude the Obscure* (1895) as if it represented a problem, others as if it problematized representation. Indeed, the novel does seem to be "making representations" of one sort or another, even if largely about how things are represented, and so about how literature and ideology are "meshed." "Interpellation" is the once-fashionable name for how one is ha(i)led into what John Bayley might describe as one's "ordained" place (in society), and this does seem to be what *Jude* is "about" (though a powerful faction might be on hand to inquire whether Althusser helps you with *Jude*, or *Jude* helps you with Althusser). Yet some people, it seems, can never quite be persuaded to notice that Hardy is a man used to "noticing such things" in addition to such phenomena as hedgehogs crossing lawns, "enchanting" as the poetic results of the latter process may be. Ultimately, too, there's a connection between these different forms of "noticing." The "thread" that links Jude to his fellow-creatures (for which, as an inadequately scary bird-scarer, he was promptly thrashed) may tacitly unite them as those "rightly (necessarily) excluded from consideration by the dominant social and political processes." Our sense of "Jude's rights" is sustained by his sense of "animal rights."

This is also, as it happens, a "thread" that will link Jude to cousin Sue. Sue is herself unhappily linked at this point to a connoisseur of Romano-British antiquities, and suggestively troubled by the rabbit caught in the gin (which Jude had gone out to "mercy-kill"), as herself caught in one, apparently. T. S. Eliot's idea of the "objective correlative" might be cited here. The formula of "the young man who could not go to Oxford: his struggles and ultimate failure" is an inadequate one because Christminster itself is finally "under erasure" thanks largely to Sue, but also because Hardy shows himself as a "real artist" here by developing Sue, or letting Sue develop, to the point where she becomes at least as "interesting" as Jude himself (challenging the adequacy of his own title, for example).

But perhaps the formula already offers a sort of "self-deconstructing" *Bildungsroman* through the attempt to "insert" what H. G. Wells calls "the educated proletarian" into a bourgeois genre, a novel of bourgeois formation and consequent, if temporarily thwarted, "upward mobility." We may say, then, that Hardy "perceives," as it were, that there is "something wrong with our literary formulas" no less than our "social" ones (to adapt Jude's crowd-hectoring phrasing on the occasion of his return to Christminster).

Jude himself will ultimately recognize "worldly ambition masquerading in a surplice," become quite ecclesiastical, painfully accuse Sue of being "quite Voltairean," then become "quite Voltairean" himself as Sue herself becomes quite laceratingly ecclesiastical. This was of course, as a result of Jude the Younger's becoming quite a (practicing) Malthusian, taking the problem of child overpopulation into his own hands. In its crisscross no-progress to emotional crucifixion, *Jude* is destroying, inter alia, the quite ideological idea that "character" is unformed or uninformed by ideology. *Jude* "makes representations" that challenge Victorian formation narratives ("*Bildungsroman*") no less than marital states. Those critics are clearly wrong to take at face value a reading that implies that Jude is merely an inveterate romantic whose "desire is too difficult to tell from despair." This plays into the hands of those privileged by society who, in Blake's idiom, "think they have done us no injury." There is no "exchange rate mechanism" for Jude's "cultural capital," but the point is that this is not his fault. Jude will die as Arabella steals off with Vilbert, himself a highly nomadic purveyor of quack medicines (*pharmaka*) that will not bear scrutiny (an interesting role, as the book is in a sense all about them on the social and spiritual level, a point not often remarked). Vilbert, teller of tall tales to innocents, finally filched Arabella, and his trickster role was suggestive from the outset.

When he failed to bring the grammars that would unlock Christminster's word-hoard for the schoolboy Jude, this seems a kind of anticipatory symbolism for his being traduced and excluded, just as Jude's verbal abuse by his terrible Aunt Drusilla and physical abuse by Farmer Troutham anticipated the rejecting college official Tetuphenay, whose letter was tellingly addressed to "Mr. J. Fawley, Stone-Mason," with thoughts from a dark and stony place of institutional power (un)helpfully suggesting a career set in stone. But even Tetuphenay would hardly have mattered tuppence-ha'penny if "crookedness, custom and fear" had not brought Sue and Jude low. Typically, Hardy succeeds here by presenting us with a *Bildungsroman* that fails (or stalls). He obviously enjoys his own "genre trouble," and does so here partly by impugning the social structures that will enable his novel to become a *Bildungsroman* in the first place. Certainly it did come to seem as if Jude's "estate" had been mysteriously "ordered," after all: he was "ha(i)led" into his "(no-) position," couldn't quite make it to a *déformation professionelle*. But it is, of course, entirely typical of Hardy that the reader may well feel, for quite long stretches, that this is, after all, not quite such a bad thing as the novel appears to commit itself to saying it is.

With fourteen novels to his credit, a thousand poems (originally in eight separate collections [1898–1928]), four collections of short stories, a new edition of the excluded and collaborative stories, and *The Dynasts* (1903–1908) to choose from, readers might well be looking for something one might bypass with a clear conscience. Hardy once described his work as a "trilithon," and with the fiction and poems as the uprights here, we might well envisage *The Dynasts* as the unhappy cross member that shortly after installation fell heavily to the ground. But this blank verse dramatization of the Napoleonic Wars certainly composes a kind of disenchanted "morning after" to the "night before" of Shelley's utopian hopes, in *Prometheus Unbound* in particular. Hardy wants to have a kind of "immediate" relation to history here, which cramps his style in the most literal sense imaginable, as it does also, in some degree *The Trumpet-Major* (1880), an earlier exercise in imagining the crisis period, intent on period charm but strongest in bodying forth the cruelties and obliquities of love in the rivalry of Bob and John Loveday for the hand of Anne Garland, with a particularly memorable vignette of the cowardly braggadocio figure of Festus Derriman (seemingly a kind of [*Mansfield Park*'s] Mr. Rushworth on viagra). "Thank God, I have seen my King!" exclaims nice Mrs. Garland of the man who lost us America, but elsewhere Hardy seems almost to parody Austen's *Persuasion*, itself "induced" by the Napoleonic war, in annexing charm and worthiness to the lower and middle orders as he locates chuckle-headedness and effeteness higher up the social scale. As it happens, not many would now trumpet *The Trumpet-Major* as "major" in any case, and one could easily end by selling it short.

We are not particularly amused, but Hardy, as always, has his moments here, as he also does in short stories, which rehearse the excellencies of the novels in a minor key, but have endured the deconstructions of J. Hillis Miller and the memorable outrage of T. S. Eliot in such a way as to suggest that they too "have something." The poetry itself, which unforgettably marries a larger music of alienated nostalgia to the more intimately elegiac work of mourning, is, of course, "indispensable."

WORKS CITED AND SELECTED WORKS FOR FURTHER READING

Bersani, Leo. *The Culture of Redemption.* Cambridge: Harvard UP, 1990.

Gittings, Robert. *Thomas Hardy's Later Years.* Boston: Little, Brown, 1978.

———. *Young Thomas Hardy.* Boston: Little, Brown, 1975.

Hardy, Thomas. *Desperate Remedies.* 1871. Ed. Mary Rimmer. London: Penguin, 1998.

———. *Far from the Madding Crowd.* 1874. Ed. Rosemarie Morgan. London: Penguin, 1998.

———. *The Hand of Ethelberta.* 1876. Ed. Tim Dolin. London: Penguin, 1996.

———. *Jude the Obscure.* 1895. Ed. Dennis Taylor. London: Penguin, 1998.

———. *A Laodicean.* 1881. Ed. J. H. Stape. London: Dent, 1997.

———. *The Life of Thomas Hardy.* Ed. Michael Millgate. London: Macmillan, 1984.

———. *The Mayor of Casterbridge.* 1886. Ed. Keith Wilson. London: Penguin, 1998.

———. *A Pair of Blue Eyes.* 1873. Ed. Pamela Dalziel. London: Penguin, 1998.

———. *Tess of the d'Urbervilles.* 1891. Ed. Tim Dolin. London: Penguin, 1998.

———. "The Three Strangers." In *Collected Short Stories*. Ed. Desmond Hawkins. London: Macmillan, 1988.

———. *The Trumpet-Major*. 1880. Ed. Linda M. Shires. London: Penguin, 1998.

———. *Under the Greenwood Tree*. 1872. Ed. Tim Dolin. London: Penguin, 1998.

———. *The Well-Beloved*. 1897. Ed. Patricia Ingham. London: Penguin, 1997.

———. *The Woodlanders*. 1887. Ed. Patricia Ingham. London: Penguin, 1998.

Widdowson, Peter. *Thomas Hardy*. Plymouth: Northcote, 1996.

The Vanities of William Makepeace Thackeray's Vanity Fair

Juliet McMaster

"I have (and for this gift I congratulate myself with a Deep and Abiding Thankfulness), an eye for a Snob" (*Snobs,* 261). So wrote William Makepeace Thackeray, with his customary irony, in the satirical series for *Punch* that he later published as *The Book of Snobs, by One of Themselves.* To know a snob, he conceded genially, you need to be one.

The writing of that timely analysis of British social relations overlapped with the early numbers of *Vanity Fair,* and in a sense it was a preparation for the great novel. Thackeray was developing a take on mid-Victorian society that was to become a vision for all seasons. The word "snob" as he inherited it was a contemptuous term for someone the speaker considers beneath him: In the town-gown disputes Thackeray was familiar with at Cambridge, the middle-class students would sneeringly refer to shoemakers and bargemen as "snobs." What Thackeray realized was that any such derogatory term reflects back on the user. It is not so much the "low" person who should be derided as a snob, as the one who considers himself superior. In this way Thackeray not only changed and extended the meaning of a popular term of abuse, he also put his finger on his culture's disastrous confusion of values. By Thackeray's definition, a snob is "*he who meanly admires mean things*" (269): someone who subordinates all issues of ethics, aesthetics, even simple bodily pleasure, to the single barren criterion of social status. Hence there are snobs in all classes and all sections of society. The quintessential snob is the English "gentleman" abroad:

A thousand delightful sights pass before his stupid eyes, and don't affect him. Countless brilliant scenes of life and manners are shown him, but never move him. He goes to church, and calls the practices there degrading and superstitious. . . . He goes to picture-galleries, and is more ignorant about art than a French shoeblack. Art, Nature pass, and leave no dot of admiration in his stupid eyes: nothing moves him, except when a very great man comes his way, and then the rigid, proud, self-confident British Snob can be as humble as a flunkey, and as supple as a harlequin. (388)

So searing a vision has its satirical uses, but "that brutal ignorant peevish bully of an Englishman" (383) has his limitations as a character to engage sympathy or interest in a satire that is also to be a realistic novel. The type is too crude to accommodate the vision of moral and psychological complexity that Thackeray had come to command. He needed some paradigm that would retain the satirical edge while allowing for characters of range and attractiveness.

The new vision came to Thackeray almost as a glorious revelation from heaven, when he had a midnight inspiration for his title. "I jumped out of bed," he told a friend, "and ran three times round the room, uttering as I went, "Vanity Fair, Vanity Fair, Vanity Fair'" (Ray, 385). The image was brilliantly evocative both of the sour vision of Ecclesiastes, according to which "all is vanity," and of Bunyan's more earnestly Christian evocation of the Fair where all vanities are for sale, from "trades, places, honors, preferments, titles" to "wives, husbands, children," and even truth.

Such a conception includes not only those brutal ignorant bullies who can think of nothing but sneering at those below them on the social ladder, and cringing to those above: It incorporates characters of brilliant talents and social flair like Becky Sharp, of lingering devotion like Amelia, of intelligent but misguided integrity like Dobbin. It likewise allows for evolution and change: Jos Sedley with his inflated ego and waistline, who becomes a pathetic victim; Rawdon Crawley, the thick-headed dragoon who learns loyalty and tenderness; George Osborne, a man of genuine courage and charm that are yet fatally flawed by his blind conceit. It is a vision that allows for ironies and contradiction. Even the moral (to the extent that there is one) is put in the mouth of the villain: "Everybody is striving for what is not worth the having!" says the unscrupulous cynic Lord Steyne (607). Still in the business of admiring mean things meanly, these characters are not dismissable as mere snobs and self-seekers. They give an echo to our own best intentions as well as our worst.

"There are far finer and more numerous shades of dignity in this country than in any other," wrote Thackeray's contemporary and literary rival, Bulwer-Lytton, in his book on *England and the English* (1831). No one paid

closer attention to these fine gradations than Thackeray, or more subtly satirized the snobbery involved in caring about them acutely. His characters are socially placed—with attention paid not only to birth, education, and financial
standing, but also to the markers of dress, accent, mannerism, occupation, and
the myriad other subtle signs of social status. In this chapter my procedure is to
turn snob myself, like Thackeray, in order to define the many rungs on the social ladder that Becky and her kind are always scaling, and in the process to
draw attention to Thackeray's searching commentary on his society's laborious
pursuit of what is not worth the having.

In the great crowded scene that is *Vanity Fair*, Thackeray provides a comprehensive sample, all the way from royalty itself to the little kitchen-maid on her
promotion. At the apex of Becky's career she is finally "admitted to the paradise
of a Court which she coveted" (599): She is presented to King George IV. With
mock reverence, the narrator refrains from providing an exact description of
this deity: "The dazzled eyes close before that Magnificent Idea," (604). But
Thackeray is more explicit elsewhere. "I try and take him to pieces," he wrote
in his lecture in *The Four Georges*, "and find silk stockings, padding, stays, . . . a
star and blue ribbon, . . . a huge black stock, under-waist-coats, more un-
der-waistcoats, and then nothing" (*Georges*, 783). So much for the primary deity of the Snobs' worship, Becky's "paradise," and "the very best company." The
god is no more than a stuffed shirt, in modern phrase: a mere aggregate of status symbols.

Becky's royal presentation is sponsored by Lord Steyne, Thackeray's representative of the great aristocrats who still owned a large proportion of the nation's land and capital, and were still highly influential in affairs of state too.
Steyne is one of the aristocrats of the old school, the kind that Carlyle designated as Dandies, who took their stand on privilege, and renounced moral responsibility. Steyne is fabulously rich and powerful, and highly intelligent. But
his is also a cynic, and totally unscrupulous.

As the middle class takes its stand on money, so the aristocracy is defined
and maintained by birth and heredity. It is appropriate, therefore, that
Thackeray should provide a genetic disorder—"a mysterious taint of the
blood"—hereditary madness, as the threat that overhangs the Gaunt family.
Steyne's son and heir is a confined lunatic, invested not with his father's star and
garter but "with the order of the Strait Waistcoat" (595).

Although the great aristocrats like Lord Steyne were still thriving, the lesser
aristocracy was feeling the pinch of the country's gradual shift from an agricultural to an industrial economy. The aptly named Bareacres family represents
the impoverished end of the aristocracy. Rather than put their energies into
stewardship and cultivate their estate, they have gambled and drunk away their
inheritance: The old earl borrows money from his former crony Steyne, and

marries his stuck-up daughter Lady Blanche into the Steyne family, where she fails to produce the desired heir. Thackeray's most memorable tableau of this outdated aristocracy is the image of Lady Bareacres sitting in her horseless carriage with her diamonds sewn into her stays. Wedded to her status symbols of carriage and jewels, she is going nowhere. Another degenerate aristocratic family is the Southdowns: Young Lord Southdown (named for a breed of sheep) frequents the Rawdon Crawley household, ripe for shearing by the "shepherd" Rawdon, the inveterate gambler. That estate will not last long.

The impoverished aristocracy notoriously needs infusion of ready cash. And since Hogarth's famous series "Marriage à la Mode," in which the earl's son marries the merchant's daughter, the union of old aristocratic blood with new industrial money was a bargain well understood in satire and in practice. "A comfortable thing it is to think that birth can be bought for money," comments the narrator of *The Book of Snobs* sarcastically (297). It is "this intermixture of the highest aristocracy with the more subaltern ranks of society," said Bulwer-Lytton, that produces the enviable range in gradations that he rejoiced in (Bulwer-Lytton, 31). Thackeray takes a savage delight in following through the ramifications of this sordid bargain. Lord Steyne, covering bases, marries his eldest son to "blood," Lady Blanche of the Bareacres family, and his second to "money," to the daughters of Jones—upgraded to "Jhones"—a banker. Neither marriage is a success.

Old Sir Pitt Crawley combines both connections in his own marital history: He first marries blood in the person of an offshoot of the noble Binkie family, and then when this Lady dies, he turns to new industrial money, and marries Rose, the daughter of a tradesman who has made his pile in ironmongery. Again, neither marriage could be called happy. When Sir Pitt finally decides to please himself instead of his progeny or his pocket, he proposes to the beautiful and artful governess, who has neither blood nor money. But he is too late.

The "money" side of the Crawley family is invested in a woman, Pitt's sister Matilda, whose £70,000 inherited from her mother gives her a power not usually available to women. Miss Crawley treats herself to the luxury of republican opinions, which she promptly renounces when her favorite nephew marries a nobody, Becky Sharp. But for all her wealth, and the family members constantly paying court to her, she is a lonely and haunted old woman, subject to the tyranny of a ruthless parson's wife, Mrs. Bute Crawley, who terrifies her with threats of hellfire. Miss Crawley with all her money is a grim reminder that you cannot take it with you.

The Crawley family are Thackeray's not-very-flattering representatives of the country gentry. They have a baronetcy (an inherited title), a country estate in Hampshire, a house in town, and a safe seat in an unreformed parliament. But old Sir Pitt has crippled his estate by ill-judged lawsuits. He belongs to the old school of the country squire, like Fielding's Squire Western of *Tom Jones*, who similarly speaks in dialect and enjoys "low" company. The Crawleys are a family of long standing, but they have survived by virtue of buttering up the reigning powers. The names they give their children demonstrate a history of time-serving and connection-mongering: for instance, "Charles Stuart Crawley," evidently born a monarchist, is "afterwards called Barebones Crawley," after the Parliament that voted to execute the sovereign.

The inheritance from the older to the younger Sir Pitt marks the advent of Victorian values of moral probity and do-goodism following the shamelessly self-seeking practices of the old land-owning classes. Whereas old Pitt counts farthings, talks dialect, takes his butler's daughter as his mistress, and does all he can to cheat the neighbors, young Pitt has a university education, a pious wife, a canting mother-in-law, and a fine flow of hypocritical discourse. With the notable assets of his pious wife and Miss Crawley's seventy thousand pounds, he can tidy up the estate, refurnish the house in town, and achieve presentation at court alongside his social-climbing sister-in-law Becky. His piety does not go very deep, however: It is merely a tool that avails in persuading his aunt to disinherit his brother in his own favor.

Younger sons of country gentry must shift for themselves, for the system of primogeniture, designed to maintain an estate intact through the generations, dictates that land and cash as well as title descend to the eldest son. Old Sir Pitt's younger brother Bute, though he has no calling to the ministry, becomes a parson *faute de mieux*. He continues to pursue his usual country pastimes of hunting and shooting, and his wife writes his sermons. Rawdon, the younger son of the next generation, takes to the army. Sisters, whether older or younger, are usually excluded from even a younger brother's meager inheritance. So it not surprising that a woman lucky enough to inherit her mother's money, like Miss Crawley, should favor a younger son. But Pitt's superior strategy secures that fortune to himself, as well as title and estate. It is among the laws of Vanity Fair that the haves get yet more, and the have-nots lose even what they have.

The middle classes define themselves not by birth but by property, and their ability to make more of it. In Vanity Fair, in the vain system of the pursuit of status, birth and money compete with each other in different contexts. Rawdon Crawley, without two half-crowns to rub together other than what he can borrow or win at play, patronizes George Osborne, the rich son of a City merchant, and wins money off him almost as a favor. Even the governess in a gentry family, if she is as resourceful as Becky, can turn the tables and make the patronizing George tremble before her. "We are not so wealthy in Hampshire as you lucky folks in the City. But then I am in a gentleman's family—good old English stock." And she scores off George by taunting him about his lack of "blood." "What was your grandpapa, Mr. Osborne?—Well . . . you can't help your pedigree" (173). With her royal "we" that identifies her with the family she works for, she adroitly lays claim to being of good old English stock.

The "money" side of society is largely represented by the City merchant, Osborne, and the old-style stockbroker, Sedley. Here again, as with the inheritance between the two Sir Pitts, Thackeray is registering change. Osborne's son George Sedley Osborne was named after this godfather Sedley, who at the time of the christening was "a better man than I was . . . I should say by ten thousand pound," as old Osborne admits, with a characteristic confusion between moral and cash value (773). However, when Sedley's fortunes plummet in the stock scare following Napoleon's return from Elba, Osborne's fortunes rise, and he decides to break the match between the two families that was arranged during Sedley's prosperity. The love match between Amelia and George, which to Amelia is exclusively absorbing, is thus part of the large picture of European politics and finance: All the small and personal doings in this spreading novel belong intensely to the large scene of history and social evolution.

Old Osborne is a magnificent psychological creation for his deep and ultimately destructive ambivalence. Just as he is both devoted to his son and enraged by him in corresponding measure, so his pride in being an independent British merchant who "could buy the beggarly hounds [earls, lords, and honorables] over and over" (538) coexists with a pathetic eagerness for recognition by those same "beggarly hounds." This "inflexible British snob" like all the others, can become as supple as a harlequin when he meets a man, however degenerate, with a title, as one chapter initial shows. "He groveled before him, and my-lorded him as only a free-born Briton can do" (154). There are multiple gradations among the money-makers, too. At school young Dobbin is called "Figs," because he is the son of a retailer, and is patronized by the younger George, whose father is a wholesaler and keeps a carriage (53).

Thackeray pays full attention to the professions, especially to the army, which has its own time-honored hierarchy. But commissions were normally purchased, not earned, so that here as elsewhere patronage and privilege pertain. A few dedicated soldiers, like Dobbin and O'Dowd, achieve promotion by merit, but they are exceptions. The best chance of rising by any other means than paying the substantial amount required for a commission is by the death in combat of a senior officer. Hence as the time for action at Waterloo draws near, Ensigns Stubble and Spooney "looked to get their companies without purchase"—that is, by stepping into dead men's shoes (220). It is one of Thackeray's many shots at the business of war, and his culture's disproportionate admiration of "military valour" (372). After their defeat at Waterloo, the French pant for revenge, as the English would if they had lost; and so war promotes war rather than ending it. "There is no end to the so-called glory and shame, and to the alternations of successful and unsuccessful murder, in which two high-spirited nations might engage," notes the narrator grimly (405). He requires the reader to re-examine the system of values that worships the successful killer, as well as that which worships the fatuous monarch or the blue-blooded lord.

"The jungle's the school for a general, mark me that," exclaims Jos Sedley enthusiastically, reminding Dobbin that Wellington gained his first successes in India (348). Bloated Joseph Sedley, the Collector of Boggley Wollah, with his terrorized native servant, his curries, and his hookah, is a representative of empire hardly calculated to make Britons rejoice in the imperial enterprise. Rather than bring morality and enlightenment to the benighted natives, as in the moralized Victorian conception of empire, his function is significantly only to "collect" taxes from them and to line his pockets (which he does fairly successfully). Himself born in India and the son of a colonial administrator, Thackeray was familiar with Anglo-Indian circles in London, and he characterizes them mercilessly. Jos's endless stories of tiger hunts and Mulligatawny are stiffeningly boring, and put even his own father to sleep (30).

The Church, very much a living rather than a calling, has its comparable representatives. Bute Crawley is succeeded as parish minister by his son James, who shares his father's love of blood sports and strong liquor, and shows no sign of spirituality. The changeover from the hard-riding, hard-drinking parson of the eighteenth century to the evangelically inclined churchman of the Victorian period is intimated in young Pitt Crawley's alliance with Lady Southdown and her tract-writing daughter, who sample the doctrines of a number of dissenting divines. The names of their passing favorites suggest their theology: "the Reverend Saunders McNitre, the Scotch divine; or the Reverend Luke Waters, the mild Wesleyan; or the Reverend Giles Jowls, the illuminated cobbler" (414–415). The fact that Lady Southdown insists on doctoring her parishioners' bodies as well as their souls suggests a daunting equivalence between quick-fix religion and quack medicine. Other clergymen in the novel are mainly notable for their sexual susceptibility rather than their spiritual elevation: Both Becky and Amelia have infatuated curates dangling after them at one stage of their careers (16, 556).

Other professions receive passing attention too, for Thackeray makes it his business to be inclusive. We see the mutual self-interest in the relation of Miss Crawley's doctor and apothecary. They concur that Miss Crawley should be removed from Mrs. Bute's care, not so much because of their concern for her health as because her death would deprive them of a lucrative patient. Lawyers, like doctors, make their money out of other people's troubles: Under old Sir Pitt, for instance, the revenues of Queen's Crawley are being eaten up by lawyer's fees. Both professions were on the rise in status and respectability during the nineteenth century, as Thackeray himself showed in his later novel *The Ad-*

ventures of Philip. And both use their skill in matters medical and legal to gain power. "Ye gods, what do not attorneys and attorneys' clerks know in London!" exclaims the narrator. "Nothing is hidden from their inquisition, and their familiars mutely rule our city" (323). Teaching is a career yet to achieve recognition and respectability—though Miss Pinkerton with her ostentatious refinement and her currying favor with rich parents is doing what she can to gain it. This is partly because it was a career open to women. Becky, our major character, is a governess—though she uses this job, as she uses everything and everybody, merely as a step on the ladder to higher things. She certainly does not take her pedagogic duties very seriously, and is happy to connive with her pupils in reading novels rather than history (106).

Thackeray is perhaps more sympathetic to the arts as a profession than to any other. He had been an art student and would-be artist himself, and he enjoyed the free-and-easy camaraderie of Bohemian life. Becky's father is an artist—"a dissolute, irregular, and unsuccessful man, but a man with great knowledge of his art" (540). This is hardly unqualified praise; but an artist who knows his art is surely greatly superior to the soldier, or parson, or merchant, or doctor who merely uses the profession for social advancement and financial gain. The sympathetic attribute of the artists and students and other frequenters of Bohemia is laughter. Whether creating dolls to mimic the Miss Pinkertons, or joking with the German students at the Elephant Inn in Pumpernickel, or imagining herself dancing in "spangles and trousers . . . before a booth at a fair" (638), Becky can laugh and enjoy herself. And when she is down on her luck after the fracas between Rawdon and Lord Steyne, and frequenting the circles of artists and students, "Becky liked the life. She was at home with everybody in the place, pedlars, punters, tumblers, students and all. She was of a wild, roving nature, inherited from her father and mother, who were both Bohemians, by taste and circumstance" (830). When Amelia and her family are down on their luck, the life is not so congenial. They become "shabby-genteel," the Victorian term for people who have fallen from a higher stratum of society to a lower: They spend their time reminding their landlady and surrounding tradesmen and tavern-frequenters of their former glories. But—ever sensitive to human perversity and ambivalence—Thackeray also focuses on the lugubrious pleasure of such a life, as you impress upon your present associates the fact that in the days of your prosperity they would have been beneath your notice. "The true pleasure in life," notes the narrator of Thackeray's later novel *The Newcomes*, "is to live with your inferiors."

There is a huge gulf separating the "respectable" classes from the working classes; but there are some human amphibians who manage to belong to both spheres. Becky Sharp, daughter of a painter and an opera girl, early acquired the "the dismal precocity of poverty" (17) and she has learned how to adapt.

Without parents or financial resources, she has had to earn even her schooling by her talents. Often a governess was of gentle birth but called on to work for a living: a combination that made her a figure of enormous interest in the Victorian era, as other novels such as *Jane Eyre*, *Agnes Grey*, and *Lady Audley's Secret* attest. She is socially and educationally above servants, but economically below them: Sambo the black footman sneers at Becky's light luggage (8), and Mrs. Blenkinsop, the Sedley housekeeper, confides to the maid, "I don't trust them governesses, Pinner. . . . They gives themselves the hairs and hupstarts of ladies, and their wages is no better than you nor me" (75). But Becky's nimble adaptability enables her to climb as high as presentation to the sovereign. True, she overreaches herself and has her fall. But by her resilience and resourcefulness, she manages to latch on to the next available male, and at last to achieve "a booth in Vanity Fair" (879).

The servants who sneer at the "hupstart" airs of Becky the governess are themselves engaged in the same struggle up the ladder as everyone else. The luxurious appointments and social arrangements of the Victorian society that Thackeray satirized were necessarily supported by an army of servants and servants' servants. Even the Sedleys of Russell Square, of a class very middling indeed, maintain a household of "Sambo and the coachman, and a groom, and a footboy, and a housekeeper with a regiment of female domestics" (485). Rather than make factory operatives his representatives of the working class, as in the "social novels" of the 1840s, such as Gaskell's *Mary Barton* and Disraeli's *Sybil*, Thackeray chose servants, who in their intimate relation to the members of the higher classes could maintain the unity of his vision. Upward mobility is their desire too: Raggles, the Crawleys' butler, uses his savings to buy a house in Mayfair and become a landlord; and he like Becky has his fall. Horrocks the butler's daughter hopes to become Lady Crawley by marrying the master, but settles for being his mistress. And the "little kitchen-maid on her promotion" flatters this would-be mistress shamelessly, until it comes time to betray her instead (505, 509). The lowest servant, that is, acts just like the "genteel sycophant in a real drawing-room" (505).

During the serial run of *Vanity Fair,* Thackeray wrote of his satiric purpose to present a whole population "living without God in the world . . . greedy pompous mean perfectly self-satisfied" (*Letters,* ii, 309). Their pursuit of vanity—of what is empty, and not worth the having—is relentless and on-going. Amelia, Dobbin, and Briggs were to be the partial exceptions, because, unlike Becky and George and Jos and the rest, they have love. But in the great denouement of Amelia's strand of the narrative, we learn that they too belong to Thackeray's theme, though not so fully as Becky. Amelia wastes her love on an undeserving object, devoting years of widowhood and pointless mourning to the falsified memory of the self-satisfied George. And Dobbin's pursuit of

Amelia is likewise his pursuit of vanity: "I knew all along that the prize I had set my heart on was not worth the winning: that I was a fool, with fond fancies, too, bartering away my all of truth and ardour against you little feeble remnant of love" (853). What makes a great difference is that Dobbin *knows*—has in fact known "all along"—of the unworthiness of the object of his desire. This is as close as any character comes to redemption: Dobbin does not escape the general delusion or give up his pursuit of what is not worth the having; but at least he is aware of his own human condition.

In his great crowded novel, Thackeray achieved not only the evocation of memorable and sparkling characters of extraordinary psychological complexity but also a coherent vision of a whole society in its pointless aspirations to empty triumphs.

WORKS CITED AND SELECTED WORKS FOR FURTHER READING

Bulwer-Lytton, Edward. *England and the English*. 1831. Ed. Standish Meachum. Chicago: U of Chicago P, 1970.

Ray, Gordon N. *Thackeray: The Uses of Adversity, 1811–1846*. New York: McGraw Hill, 1955.

Thackeray, William Makepeace. *The Book of Snobs, by One of Themselves*. 1846–47. Vol. 9. *The Oxford Thackeray*. Ed. George Saintsbury. Oxford: Oxford UP, 1908.

———. *The Four Georges*. 1860. Vol. 13. *The Oxford Thackeray*. Ed. George Saintsbury. Oxford: Oxford UP, 1908.

———. *The Letters and Private Papers of William Makepeace Thackeray*. Ed. Gordon N. Ray. 4 vols. Oxford: Oxford UP, 1945.

———. *Vanity Fair*. 1847–48. Ed. John Sutherland. Oxford: Oxford UP, 1983.

Anthony Trollope and "Classic Realism"

K. M. Newton

Most readers and critics of fiction would probably agree that of all the major nineteenth-century English novelists, Trollope is the most "realistic." This has clearly been a major factor in his great popularity with general readers, with the result that all of his forty-seven novels are now in print. Of course for certain critics, notably those influenced by Roland Barthes's view of realism, this would have the consequence of making his writing highly questionable and problematic. Barthes attacked nineteenth-century realism for being complicit with a conservative ideology that accepts the world as given. Although in *S/Z*, his major study of realism, he somewhat qualified his earlier negative view of realism in general by recognizing that in the realism of a novelist such as Balzac language achieves some plurality of meaning, he contended that even in Balzac meaning is largely controlled by codes that are rooted in ideology. Barthes's critical writings on realism generated the term "classic realist text," which critics such as Colin MacCabe and Catherine Belsey have popularized.

Surprisingly there is some common ground between critics who identify "classic realism" with a conservative ideology and a critic from the opposite end of the critical spectrum, namely David Cecil, whose study, *Early Victorian Novelists,* is still a useful and challenging book. What Cecil finds lacking in Trollope is any sense of style: "But it is in his style that Trollope's relative weakness of imagination shows itself most clearly. Style is the writer's power to incarnate his creative conceptions in a sensible form. . . . Now of style, in this sense, Trollope has none at all" (199). In addition to this, claims Cecil, Trollope accepts "unquestioningly the existing state of society" (187) and is committed to a form of realism that operates "simply by reproducing experience as exactly as possible" (188). But is even Trollope—generally seen as the most conventional and least artistically self-conscious of the major Victorian novelists—a straightforward or naïve realist committed to a conservative ideology? If not, then this would surely seriously undermine the concept of "classic realism." In considering this question, I focus mainly on *Barchester Towers*, perhaps the greatest of his early novels.

Though Cecil thinks Trollope has no style, it could be argued that this should not be seen as a lack but rather as an artistic choice. In a letter to George Eliot, Trollope remarked: "I have shorn my fiction of all romance" (Hall, *Letters*, i, 238). Trollope's comparative plainness of language, his avoidance of the kind of literary language that draws attention to itself, are best interpreted as stylistic choices on his part, not indications of an uninteresting or incompetent use of literary language. The less the reader is aware of language playing a mediating role and coming between the reader and the novel's representation of the world, the more the reader is likely to be convinced by that representation. But does this mean that Trollope believes that his language is a simple reflection of a pre-existing reality, thus justifying the critique directed against "classic realism?" An incident in *Barchester Towers* suggests that Trollope was aware that all forms of language are rhetorical, and the more persuasive and transparent language attempts to be, the greater must be the rhetorical control. Mr. Slope writes a letter to Tom Towers that suggests a parallel with Trollope's own practice as a novelist. Slope is aware that if his letter is to have a persuasive effect on Towers, it must seem artless and lacking in design, and he realizes that all of his rhetorical powers must be employed for this purpose:

This letter must, in appearance at least, be written without effort, and be fluent, unconstrained, and demonstrative of no doubt or fear on the part of the writer. Therefore the epistle to Mr. Towers was studied, and recopied, and elaborated at the cost of so many minutes, that Mr. Slope had hardly time to dress himself and reach Dr. Stanhope's that evening. (304)

It is legitimate, I think, to draw the implication that Trollope's realistic style, which also seems "fluent" and "unconstrained," is not naïve artlessness but is the outcome of an artistic control of rhetoric that is all the more powerful because it gives the appearance of being artless.

Does Trollope simply set out to reproduce experience as exactly as possible, as Cecil also asserts? *Barchester Towers* shows that this view is simplistic, because

Trollope suggests in that novel that fiction constructs the world into the form of a narrative, one that is designed to serve the purposes of fiction rather than to reflect reality in any isomorphic sense. He famously incurred the disapproval of Henry James, who objected to various comments by Trollope's narrator disclosing that he is writing a novel and is manipulating the narrative in order to achieve certain effects. Thus in Chapter 30 the narrator writes of Eleanor Bold: "How easily would she have forgiven and forgotten the archdeacon's suspicions had she heard the whole truth from Mr. Arabin. But then, where would have been my novel?" (281). For James, such comments undermined the credibility of the novel as a form: "It is impossible to imagine what a novelist takes himself to be unless he regard himself as an historian and his narrative as a history" (536). Trollope in *Barchester Towers*, however, continually emphasizes the fictionality of the narrative by such asides and by giving playful names to his characters, such as Dr. Fillgrave, Sir Omicron Pie, the Lookalofts. Another playful aside that draws the reader's attention to the novel's fictionality takes place in Chapter 4 when the narrator informs the reader of a rumor that Mr. Slope is descended from the doctor "who assisted at the birth of Mr. T. Shandy," Tristram Shandy being of course a fictional character in Sterne's novel of the same name, a work that satirizes the novel as a form.

Though omniscient narration is very much associated with the Victorian novel, Trollope's narrator is used not merely to narrate the story but to problematize the relationship between narration and the story that is being narrated. The intrusive narrator was criticized by critics such as Percy Lubbock for being an artistic weakness because the narrator forsook "showing" for "telling," (62, 87–88). But Trollope's narrator's intrusions in *Barchester Towers* go beyond "telling" for they disclose that the narrator is a constructor of the narrative. In particular the narrator draws the reader's attention to the role of suspense in the narrative while at the same time manipulating it for his own purposes. Suspense is of course one of the main elements in the novel as a form as it drives the plot and creates the desire in the reader to continue reading in order to find out what will happen. Trollope advertises suspense in titles of chapters, such as "Who will be the new Bishop?" or "Who shall be cock of the walk?" but the narrator raises questions in the reader's mind about the use of this device while still continuing to make use of it. The reader's sense of suspense in regard to who will be the new bishop is resolved quickly, but a more subtle suspenseful situation is created as it becomes clear that the new bishop is not strong enough to exert his own authority. We read on to discover who will dominate the bishop and exert power indirectly. Will Mr. Slope or Mrs. Proudie gain control of the bishop or will the bishop manage to outmaneuver them? The novel presents the reader with a series of such questions that create suspense and give the narrative onward movement.

But whereas in conventional realist fiction the narrative drive created by suspense tends to be projected onto and identified with the representation of reality in the novel, Trollope makes the reader aware that suspense is a device of fiction rather than a constituent of reality. The narrator also suggests that readers ought to be able to do without it and so find the lives of the characters interesting without the need for suspenseful situations. In Chapter 15 Trollope creates one of the most common plot devices in order to generate suspense in fiction, a device used in countless novels: Who will the heroine marry? Suspense is often accentuated when the heroine is vulnerable to the machinations of a villainous or morally dubious character who is interested in marrying her only for her money, and this is the case with *Barchester Towers*. Two characters in the novel are primarily interested in marrying Eleanor Bold for her money: Bertie Stanhope and Mr. Slope, the latter being a particular threat. The narrator, however, refuses to exploit this suspenseful situation and tells the reader that Eleanor will marry neither of them: "But let the gentle-hearted reader be under no apprehension whatsoever. It is not destined that Eleanor shall marry Mr. Slope or Bertie Stanhope" (126). The narrator then goes on to question suspense as a fictional device and "to reprobate that system which goes so far to violate all proper confidence between the author and his readers, by maintaining nearly to the end of the third volume a mystery as to the fate of their favourite personage," and declares, "Our doctrine is that the author and the reader should move along together in full confidence with each other" (127).

This of course is somewhat disingenuous on the narrator's part. Though we are told whom Eleanor will not marry, we are not told whom she will marry, so suspense remains in place at least partially though the reader may now have a good idea as to who will be her future husband. But it serves Trollope's fictional purposes better to shift the emphasis from the question, who will Eleanor marry, to the more interesting question of how other characters will be affected by the assumption that she intends to marry Mr. Slope. The reader, no longer being in suspense with regard to a possible marriage to Slope, will thus be in a better frame of mind to focus on what results from the mistaken interpretations of Eleanor's relationship to Slope by characters such as Mr. Harding and the Archdeacon, Dr. Grantly. Trollope also playfully pretends that he is acting for the reader's benefit in dispelling any apprehension that Eleanor might end up marrying a man like Slope. But of course to have such an apprehension is one of the pleasures of reading fiction, as Trollope is surely aware. But he is also aware that if readers' minds are dominated by the suspense of a situation, then they are less likely to be aware of more subtle considerations: "Have not often the profoundest efforts of genius been used to baffle the aspirations of the reader, to raise false hopes and false fears, and to give rise to expectations which are never to be realized?" (127). Freed from the grip of suspense, the reader is more likely to notice that Slope is not a conventional villain who wishes to get his hands on Eleanor's money to serve merely selfish ends. Slope's conscious intention is to use the money he would acquire by marrying a rich woman to promote the interests of his religion. He is thus not characterized as a cynical Tartuffe-like figure governed totally by greed; it is essential to his self-esteem to believe that he always acts from the best of motives. What the novel does suggest, however, is that this is a rationalization on his part that prevents him recognizing his own selfish motives. His religion masks any self-awareness on his part of a nature driven by a desire for power, and being wealthy will further that desire.

In *Barchester Towers*, therefore, suspense is handled ambiguously by Trollope. He draws attention to it, expresses disapproval of it as a plot device, but continues to use it. The three dominating suspense-creating elements in the plot—who will control the bishop, who will become warden of Hiram's hospital, and who will marry Eleanor—are still in place by Chapter 31, more than half-way through the novel. By this point, however, none of these has much force, and the reader can easily predict the outcome of all three. Again this downplaying of suspense puts the reader in a better position to respond to more subtle psychological aspects of the novel. But Trollope at this point introduces another suspenseful situation that gives renewed momentum to the plot in the latter part of the novel: Namely, who will be dean? As the death of the bishop at the beginning of the novel had created a sense of suspense that set the plot going, so this second imminent death provides sufficient suspense to drive the plot in the second half of the novel. Whereas previously Trollope had undercut suspense and assured the reader that Eleanor would not marry Slope, this time the reader is not informed that the Archdeacon's fear that Slope will become dean is groundless. So Trollope is quite prepared to use suspense straightforwardly if the narrative requires it. Before the death of the dean, Slope had seemed a defeated man, having lost the struggle for power with Mrs. Proudie in regard to control of the bishop and having failed in his plan to marry Eleanor, but the prospect of becoming dean allows him again to become a force to be reckoned with, and this would be dissipated if the narrator informed the reader that there was no prospect of his becoming dean. However, Trollope again only exploits suspense up to a point. After seven chapters, in Chapter 28 he breaks with suspense to inform the reader that Slope is not on the shortlist to succeed the dean. Again this allows the reader to observe Slope and his aspirations more objectively without being distracted by concern over whether or not he will succeed in becoming dean.

Critics who see Victorian fiction as exemplifying "classic realism" believe that it employs forms of representation designed to, as Colin MacCabe puts it, "transform the world into a self-evident reality where, in order to discover truth, we have only to use our eyes" (160). However, truth is hardly self-evident in Trollope. Though misinterpretation and self-deception are standard features of realist fiction, few novels explore the problem of interpretation to such a degree that epistemological questions about the nature, scope and reliability of our knowledge of reality are raised. Henry James's fiction is notable for its concern with such questions but ironically he fails to recognize in his essay on Trollope that *Barchester Towers* has a significant epistemological aspect though it is handled very differently from James.

Barchester Towers shows objectivity being undermined by the subjective interests that govern human perception. This is particularly clear in regard to Eleanor Bold in her relationships with the Archdeacon, Arabin, and her father, Mr. Harding. Preconceptions, interests, expectations, prejudices govern how the mind constructs reality. Eleanor's behavior in regard to Slope generates an ambiguous set of signs that interact with the preconceptions and fears of the Archdeacon, Mr. Harding, and Arabin to produce the interpretation that she has a romantic interest in Slope and wishes to marry him. She in turn misinterprets their behavior toward her as she has no conception that anyone could possibly suspect her of being willing to marry Slope. It might be thought that such misunderstandings can be resolved by asking questions designed to elicit the true state of affairs. But when Arabin attempts to do this and asks Eleanor directly what her feelings are toward Slope, she is so incensed at such a question and the assumption underlying it that she refuses to answer, leaving Arabin no wiser. It may be possible to arrive at the truth by inquiry and offering explanations, but such explanations are also motivated by interests and generate additional signs that are again open to interpretation. The question is raised in *Barchester Towers* as to whether misinterpretation can be completely overcome and full and reliable knowledge achieved, particularly of other people and perhaps even of oneself.

In conventional treatments of misinterpretation and misunderstanding, reliable knowledge is eventually achieved by the main characters. This is not true of *Barchester Towers*. For example, the Archdeacon and his wife, because the marriage between Eleanor and Arabin suits their purposes so well, assume that they must have been completely wrong in their earlier beliefs about relationships existing between Eleanor and Slope and Arabin and Madeline Neroni, but the reader knows otherwise. The marriage between Eleanor and Arabin is a traditionally happy one, but both do not have full knowledge of their earlier relationships with Slope and Madeline respectively. Even the closest relationships therefore are likely to be based on incomplete knowledge of the other.

Furthermore, full knowledge is inhibited by self-deception. In most novels, self-deception is treated as a moral failing, and to some extent this is true of *Barchester Towers* also as one sees in the characterization of Slope and the Archdeacon. But Trollope goes further and suggests that self-deception is virtually impossible to eradicate, and this raises doubts about whether one's knowledge of the world can ever be completely reliable. The reason for this, the novel suggests, is that for psychological reasons people need to possess and maintain self-esteem. Eleanor Bold particularly exemplifies this. Central to her self-esteem is the need to see herself as blameless in her actions. She cannot therefore admit that her actions were open to the interpretation of offering encouragement to Slope. Even when she finds out that her father had feared she had a romantic interest in Slope, she refuses to accept that anything in her behavior could be construed as encouraging Slope. When he actually proposes to her, a severe psychological blow to her because this would seem to prove that there was substance to the Archdeacon's and her father's fears, she still refuses to accept that there were any grounds for these fears. Her need to maintain self-esteem leads her to repress any knowledge that she might be culpable and shift the blame entirely onto Slope, whom she sees as "mad."

Eleanor represents an extreme, but her need for self-esteem exemplifies a general human situation, indicating insuperable barriers to reliable human knowledge. Not only is all knowledge inseparable from interpretation, but interpretation is governed by subjective needs that call into question its disinterestedness or impartiality. The novel does not deny that one should nevertheless strive to achieve knowledge of both oneself and others in as disinterested a spirit as possible even if this can never completely succeed, Mr. Harding exemplifying this moral commitment. It is also suggested that epistemological skepticism, even if justifiable at a philosophical level, is dangerous if applied to practical living because the realization that one's own motives will always be governed by egotistic interests and that one can never be sure of what is going on in the minds of other people could lead to moral inaction and a passiveness in the face of life. Arabin is subject to a disabling self-consciousness that promotes such passivity. Unsure of Eleanor's feelings and concerned that his motives in wishing to marry her could be construed as impure, he is incapable of any positive exertion in order to win her as his wife and has to rely on the matchmaking of Miss Thorne before the obstacles to their marriage are overcome.

It could be argued that the form of the novel is at odds with its concern with the problem of interpretation and the constitutive role of the ego in the relation between mind and world, because the narrator's knowledge of his characters and their world is not undermined or questioned; whereas, in contrast, other works that deal with such issues—Hogg's *Confessions of a Justified Sinner*, Emily Brontë's *Wuthering Heights,* James in works like *The Sacred Fount* and *The Turn of the Screw*—problematize narration itself in equating it with interpretation by having different narrators recounting the same events or, in the case of James, employing unreliable narrators. But though Trollope does not explicitly suggest that the narration may be unreliable by employing such devices, in showing the narrator as a constructor of the narrative, the novel implies that other constructions are possible and thus indirectly the question of the reliability of narration is raised.

Perhaps the aspect of *Barchester Towers* most obviously at odds with conventional realism is its use of allegory. Trollope had also used allegory in *The Warden*, the novel that preceded *Barchester Towers*, as James had noticed and disapproved of: "We are transported from the mellow atmosphere of an assimilated Barchester to the air of ponderous allegory" (James, 535). Allegory undermines the integrity and autonomy of dramatic situations by implying that they are the vehicle by which other issues are explored. In writing about a conflict within the Anglican church, it is obvious that Trollope is raising wider issues, notably the ideological struggle between the forces of conservatism and an opposing set of forces that threaten their power. The Archdeacon and his supporters are High Church and Tory in their political sympathies, and they are challenged by a grouping associated with the new bishop, Dr. Proudie, who are Low Church and Whig in their political outlook. This struggle for power within the Anglican community of Barchester exemplifies the wider political conflict between the established ruling class and a rising middle class that is seeking to displace it. The theological aspects of the conflict—which relate to the Anglican Church's difficulties in accommodating both Tractarianism and Evangelicalism within the one denomination—are played down in favor of the wider political issues that are raised, particularly the crisis that ensues when a long established structure of power is faced with a threat to its dominance. The death of the former bishop, the Archdeacon's father, and the appointment of Dr. Proudie in his place challenge the existing system by allowing forces opposed to High Anglicanism to gain a foothold within the hierarchy of the Anglican Church. Religious differences between the Grantly and Proudie parties are not highlighted as this would inevitably draw the reader into sympathizing on religious grounds with one party or the other; instead the narrator presents the conflict as a political struggle. People perceived to be neutral, such as the Stanhopes, are wooed by each side. The bishop himself has no desire for conflict, being in the latitudinarian tradition of the Low Church, but stronger characters, namely Mrs. Proudie and Mr. Slope, are strongly Evangelical in sympathy, and as long as they remain united, they are a force to be reckoned with and a serious threat to the Grantly party. But like many political parties, they are defeated not so much by their opponents but by internal divisions. The Grantly party is also affected by internal divisions but not as seriously.

The Thornes represent another political perspective, one that allows Trollope to develop the political allegory further. They embody a nostalgic conservatism that clearly belongs to a past age but still has its attractions in a modern world of complex social conditions that breed class conflict. They attempt to revive medieval social practices by organizing a *fête champetre*, a garden party that divides people into social groups in accordance with medieval notions of social hierarchy. However, the novel suggests that past social forms are no longer appropriate for modern conditions. For example, Harry Greenacre could have been seriously injured when he falls from his horse while engaging in jousting, and the attempt to impose medieval class separation on the guests by having different eating arrangements for "upper" and "lower" classes could have created serious social conflict if Mr. Greenacre had not been on hand to save the situation when the Lookalofts refuse to accept their appointed station.

Virginia Woolf criticized novelists who continued to use nineteenth-century conventions of realism in their approach to character for failing to penetrate below the surface and contrasted them with modernist novelists, who are concerned with "the dark places of psychology" (1925). David Cecil reflects this view when he writes of Trollope's characterization : "His great characters . . . are all simple and positive, absorbed in the avocations of average human beings, devoid alike of psychological complexities and abstruse spiritual yearnings" (206).Yet *Barchester Towers* shows that Trollope is not a mere "materialist," to use Woolf's term, uninterested in penetrating beyond the psychologically superficial. The novel suggests that neither at the individual nor at the wider social level is there any escape from the question of power. In representing character, Trollope's approach is only superficially mimetic; rather he anticipates the position taken by thinkers such as Nietzsche and Adler and more recently Foucault that the will to power is the fundamental human drive. *Barchester Towers* contains an assortment of power seekers, most notably the Archdeacon, Mr. Slope, Mrs. Proudie, and Madeline Neroni. Slope is the most significant of these as his desire for power manifests itself in a variety of ways: He desires in effect to be bishop by controlling Bishop Proudie; he seeks to have his favored candidate appointed warden; he plans to marry Eleanor Bold for her money; and finally he aspires to be dean. Though the novel is clearly critical of Slope's naked ambition, it does not merely condemn power-seeking. In the first chapter when the Archdeacon's father, the bishop, is on the point of death, the Archdeacon's desire to succeed his father is at odds with his role as grieving son as he knows that the sooner his father dies, the better chance he has of succeeding him. But the Archdeacon is not condemned for having unchristian thoughts: His dilemma is presented as a thoroughly human one, and we are encouraged to sympathize with his sense of guilt in this situation. Whereas the Archdeacon's, Slope's, and Mrs. Proudie's power drives take the form of a desire for control and authority; with Madeline Neroni it takes a more subtle psychological form because she gains gratification by making men her slaves. Though physically powerless as she is crippled, mentally she is able to master men such as Slope. Female power tends to be shown in a negative light in the novel through the characters of Madeline, Mrs. Proudie, and Charlotte Stanhope, but this negativity has to be seen in its social context as in this society women have little opportunity to channel the will to power more productively.

Trollope is particularly subtle in suggesting that characters who apparently have no desire for power or dominance are not devoid of this fundamental drive: It is merely displaced or sublimated. For example, Bishop Proudie is characterized by powerlessness: He is dominated by stronger personalities and fears confrontation and conflict. Because he is weak, he resorts to various devices to protect himself from being crushed by the likes of the Archdeacon, such as employing Slope as an intermediary so that he avoids being outfaced in any confrontation. He even thinks that he can play Slope off against his wife, but when this fails, he reverts to his previous strategy in his relationship with her; complete submission. Harding and Arabin are also characters free from ambition or any desire to dominate. With Harding, the power drive is sublimated into idealism and unselfishness, and all of his energies are directed to unselfish or idealistic ends. Though Harding is clearly to be preferred to Slope, the novel does suggest that unselfishness can have certain drawbacks: Harding is so intent on rising above self-interest and personal preference that he exerts no opposition to Slope as Eleanor's husband if that is her choice and thus makes no effort to protect her from what would have been a disastrous marital choice. Likewise, Arabin is a man who views himself in such an objective spirit that he finds it almost impossible to act in his own interest. The fact that he does finally marry Eleanor and become dean is due less to his own efforts than to the actions and support of other people.

Another indication that Trollope does not set up a simple dichotomy between selfishness or ambition and unselfishness can be seen in the character in the novel who on the surface is least motivated by ambition or narrowly selfish interests: Bertie Stanhope. He is revealed as a rootless dilettante and a man quite lacking in any sense of moral responsibility. He views the world in a spirit of lighthearted absurdity. His decision not to try to marry Eleanor for her money is motivated not by any moral repulsion to such behavior but by his sense that freedom is absolute and should never be compromised by prudential considerations. Is this unselfishness or merely a displaced form of egotism?

In the many novels that followed *The Warden* and *Barchester Towers,* Trollope appears to become a more conventional realist. Yet it is doubtful if the characteristics that I have drawn attention to in *Barchester Towers* entirely disappear; they are downplayed certainly but perhaps having foregrounded them in *Barchester Towers* and *The Warden,* he felt that there was no need continually to draw attention to them. To assume that it is ever safe to define Trollope as a "classic realist" would be unwise.

WORKS CITED AND SELECTED WORKS FOR FURTHER READING

Cecil, David. *Early Victorian Novelists: Essays in Revaluation.* London: Penguin, 1948.

Hall, N. John. *The Letters of Anthony Trollope.* 2 Vols. Stanford: Stanford UP, 1983.

James, Henry. "Anthony Trollope: *Partial Portraits.*" In *Trollope: The Critical Heritage*, pp. 525–545. Ed. Donald Smalley. London: Routledge and Kegan Paul, 1969.

Lubbock, Percy. *The Craft of Fiction.* London: Jonathan Cape, 1966.

MacCabe, Colin. "The End of a Metalanguage: From George Eliot to *Dubliners.*" In *George Eliot*, pp. 156–168. Ed. K. M. Newton. London: Longman, 1991.

Trollope, Anthony. *Barchester Towers.* Ed. Robin Gilmour. London: Penguin, 1984.

Woolf, Virginia. "Modern Fiction." In *The Norton Anthology of English Literature, Volume 2*, pp. 1921–26. Ed. M. H. Abrams. New York: Norton, 1993.

George Meredith at the Crossways

Margaret Harris

In the closing pages of George Meredith's first full-length novel, *The Ordeal of Richard Feverel* (1859), Lady Blandish laments over the damaged hero that "Richard will never be what he promised" (557). Whether ruefully or wrathfully, critics over time have delivered similar verdicts on Meredith: while he has been held to have promised many things, it is clear that what he always delivers is a challenge to social and literary orthodoxies. It was only after thirty years of authorship that he finally achieved a significant following. As John Lucas demonstrates, he was credited with "a radical reappraisal of lines of thought associated with Victorian England. Feminism, little England, paganism, advanced liberalism, skepticism, the Comic Spirit even: whatever marked a rejection of high-Victorianism could be attributed to Meredith" (7). Moreover, "His obscurity was a useful pointer to his integrity" (6). Writing in 1971, Lucas, a member of another rebellious generation, articulated the ambivalence that has characterized reactions to Meredith from the beginning: "Meredith is badly flawed, often infuriating, sometimes downright silly and vulgar" though "at his best he is probably a master" (12).

Lucas's essay led off the collection *Meredith Now*, edited by Ian Fletcher, part of a florescence of publications that might have resuscitated Meredith (the others were Beer, Cline, Pritchett, and Williams). Thirty years on, John Sutherland passed unequivocally the sentence implicit in Lucas's analysis. The champion of many unfashionable Victorians, from Bulwer-Lytton to Thackeray, pronounced "the brute commercial fact that Meredith doesn't sell" and declared him "to all intents and purposes a literary corpse." While the "brute commercial fact" is not to be disputed, Meredith's relationship with the marketplace was always tense, and frequently ambiguous: Witness the contradiction between his own mandarin fictional practices, and the advice he dispensed to aspiring authors as publisher's reader for Chapman and Hall. He was at once an insider and an outsider, fully cognizant of the going rate in fiction of his time, but determined to pursue his counteragenda. With all his taunting of convention and his idiosyncratic formulations of a vitalist ethic, however, he was at heart a liberal humanist: Gillian Beer reminds us that "Meredith's intensely experimental approach to the novel is always a part of his moral concern with human personality" (2). He certainly adhered to the classic realist assumption that character determines action, but his explorations of subjectivity tend to foreground the apparently irrational and random in human behavior, baffling concepts of character as coherent and predictable. For generations of readers, irremediably conditioned by the nineteenth-century classic realist text, the "intensely experimental approach" gets in the way. He flouts—at times denies—the basic realist assumption that a novel presents an illusion of an objective actuality in a narrative that moves to resolution and closure, observing a hierarchy of discourses (Belsey, 67–84).

Major modernists—Joyce especially—acknowledged and celebrated Meredith's experimentalism, but in the wake of postmodernism many of the perplexities of his texts are dissolved in a context where "Victorian" is no longer a self-evidently pejorative term synonymous with repressive morality. It is now possible, even obligatory, by focusing through contemporary formulations of identity, gender, race, or nationality to read the nineteenth century as being as conflicted as our own: so that Meredith's contestation of Victorian orthodoxies is not a Manichean struggle of dark and light but rather a perpetual interrogation of contemporary discourses, including the genres of Victorian fiction.

There is a scenario in which Meredith features as the complete Victorian man of letters. He published first as a poet, and comprehensively returned to verse when his career as a writer of fiction became established in the 1880s; he wrote journalism and one significant critical essay, on comedy; and for a long period he was a reader for an influential publisher. Such a narrative, however, edits out the instructive dialogues of this author with the literary institutions and conditions of production of his time. He knew, but was not of, the literary establishment. His first marriage, in 1849, to a widowed daughter of the Romantic who outlived his generation, Thomas Love Peacock, might have appeared to secure him an establishment place. By then, the twenty-one-year-old Meredith had already been through experiences that in particular and sometimes peculiar ways find their way into his fiction, and correlate with the concern with legitimacy and authority, the fascination with origin, to be found there: the early death of his mother, school in Germany, a degree of dissociation from his father (whose second wife was said to have been his cook, and who migrated to South Africa to follow the family trade of tailoring), a small legacy from an aunt.

By the late 1840s, Meredith was in London, articled to a lawyer and attempting to make his way in the world of letters. He began his literary career with a volume of *Poems* (1851), which would probably be quite forgotten were it not for Meredith's subsequent career in fiction. It included some vibrant nature poems, and some of a patriotic or political cast, many of them—such as "Love in the Valley"—displaying great technical virtuosity. A similar range of topics and treatments is to be found in his later poems, but his pretensions to full poetic presence in such poems as *Odes in Contribution to the Song of French History* (1898) are less durable than the drama and narrative energy of the extraordinary titular sequence of *Modern Love and Poems of the English Roadside, with Poems and Ballads* (1862).

His first volumes of fiction came later in the decade. *The Shaving of Shagpat: An Arabian Entertainment* (1856) tapped comically into a vogue for the Oriental; its successor, *Farina: A Legend of Cologne* (1857), was described by one reviewer as "grave yet facetious grotesque" in the style of Washington Irving (Williams, 50). Such emulation of fashions of the day is commonplace in a young writer, but Meredith characteristically critiques as he imitates. His ostentatious prose style—or styles—have always been at the epicenter of critical discussion, as the case of his first true novel demonstrates.

It has frequently been observed that *The Ordeal of Richard Feverel* appeared in an *annus mirabilis*, 1859, the year in which George Eliot brought out *Adam Bede* and Dickens *A Tale of Two Cities*, the year of the first of Tennyson's *Idylls of the King* and of Fitzgerald's *Rubáiyát of Omar Khayyám*, of Mill's *On Liberty*—and Darwin's *On the Origin of Species*. Meredith's is far and away the most original certainly of the prose fictions of the year, though not the best remembered. Though several of these works dealt with relation of present to past, *Richard Feverel* most tellingly shows strains in the present. Working at once flamboyantly and insidiously with various discourses, it speaks of many anxieties of its time. It pits nature against science, good against evil, masculine against feminine, comedy against tragedy, in fluctuating dialectics.

This novel provides a test case for the challenges of reading Meredith, to which Oscar Wilde memorably gestured in the exclamation that "his style is chaos illuminated by flashes of lightning" (Williams, 315; see Roberts, 1–12). Meredith's seemingly willful obscurity is in part due to the many competing voices in his texts, among which a dialogue is set in play in such a manner as to

refuse dominance or authority to any one of them. Various narratological ter-
minologies have been tested on Meredith according to the fashion of the day:
point of view, free indirect speech, and so on. The emergence of Bakhtin's concept of dialogism into critical discourse in English from the 1980s provides a
particularly effective framework for describing many effects of Meredith's texts
and cutting across complaints about failures of realism and formalism that are
the stock in trade of Meredith criticism. For Bakhtin, the novel is dialogic, "a
living mix of varied and opposing voices" (xxviii), not a monologic form in
which a single authorial voice or consciousness is dominant. Here is the essence
of the concept of heteroglossia that is central to Bakhtin's account of discourse
in the novel, extensively discussed and demonstrated by Neil Roberts in his important study. Roberts brings out that Meredith "is less a stylist than a stylizer":
that he is not concerned to impose his own stylistic personality on the text but
to register, represent, and organize a number of styles, genres, ideolects or languages (3). Moreover, language and discourse are constantly thematized in
Meredith's novels.

Thus proliferation of discourses in *Richard Feverel* is one isolable source of
bafflement among Meredith's contemporaries. There is a profusion of generic
models: novels of education, in French and German (Rousseau's *Emile* and
Goethe's *Wilhelm Meisters Lehrjahre*) as well as English (Richardson's influential *Sir Charles Grandison*, Sterne's *Tristram Shandy*, Fielding's *Tom Jones*, and
Hannah More's *Coelebs in Search of a Wife*). But the generic hybrid includes
New Comedy and chivalric romance: The assumptions upon which each proceeds, particularly that the narrative will close with reassurance and reconciliation, are deployed and unsettled throughout. In addition, there are many
voices in dialogue: some identified as emanating from particular characters or
positions, whether tacitly or explicitly—by inverted commas, in conversation
or quotation from Sir Austin's book of apothegms, *The Pilgrim's Scrip*, or Dia-
per Sandoe's poetry, or in letters, of which there are many.

For all its strangeness, *Richard Feverel* had a distinct critical success. By some
accounts, the making of Meredith as an author was due to his unmaking as a
man. He was before the world in a quite different way at this time. He had been
the model for the fraudulent poet-sensation Chatterton in Henry Wallis's most
famous painting, "The Death of Chatterton," exhibited at the Royal Academy
Exhibition of 1856. Allon White has argued brilliantly for "the painful symbolic importance of the double narrative in the portrait (Meredith-
as-Chatterton/Meredith-as-cuckold)" (80)—for Mary Ellen Meredith went
off with Wallis in 1857, leaving four-year-old Arthur Gryffydh Meredith with
his father. His wife's adultery and elopement dealt wounds to be cauterized cre-
atively, notably in *Richard Feverel* and the *Modern Love* poems. One reading of
Richard Feverel proceeds in terms of Meredith's own life, aligning him with Sir

Austin Feverel, also betrayed by his wife—in favor of a poet rather than a painter, however. The sonnet sequence *Modern Love,* which followed Mary's death in October 1861, confirms both the hurt and Meredith's need to heal it by reworking it from various points of view.

The personal displacement that has yielded so many illuminating readings of Meredith was not evident to readers in 1859; nor is knowledge of it essential for a recognition of the novel's extraordinariness. Some reviewers glanced sideways at its sexual frankness, picking up the term used in the novel and referring to "wild oats"; however the powerful Charles Mudie responded with censorious alarm, and in banning the novel from his circulating library dealt Meredith a severe blow. Richard's sexual education is central to Sir Austin's scientific System, intended to protect Richard from exposure to what is euphuistically and euphemistically called the Apple Disease (with coy reference both to Eve's transgression in the Garden of Eden, and to sexually transmitted diseases). The Ordeal is to test him as a bearer of original sin. This element of romance narrative in which the hero's identity is formed by tests of his fidelity in love and to the demands of the chivalric code is marked by stages in his sexual development. Sir Austin goes so far as to define the Ordeal in terms of the threats to men represented by women.

The aim of the System is to find fit stock to continue the Feverel line (which is in danger of being bred out—Richard is the only male Feverel of his generation; though his father had numerous brothers, none of whom has issue. One of them, Algernon, is symbolically castrated by the loss of a leg in a cricket accident). Some aspects of the System's conditioning are inescapably damaging: in particular, the demands of the chivalric code that several times over are interpreted to the letter rather than in the spirit. So in early adventures Ripton Thompson and Tom Bakewell, as well as Farmer Blaize whose hayrick is fired, suffer for Richard's idealism; and later, incorrigibly, this quality brings on the tragedy of Lucy's heartbreak and death. His cousin Clare also suffers and is destroyed. Yet the System, which depends on Richard's being quarantined from impurity, succeeds in spite of its inherent unnaturalness, when Richard, trusting his instincts, falls almost literally head over heels in love with Lucy Desborough. Each phase of Richard's ordeal involves a crisis of sexuality. My summary cannot do justice to the polyphony of Meredith's prose, which requires lengthy detailed analysis. He passes through the rapture of first love (Richard and Lucy meet at the very end of chapter 14, "An Attraction," in an extraordinary virtuoso passage where he saves her from slipping into the river. She is indulging her natural appetite by feasting on dewberries, and throughout the novel sexual appetite is coded in terms of eating, for instance in their gargantuan honeymoon breakfasts). He endures the trials of separation (in London to seek reconciliation with his father, Richard falls in with the significantly named Bella Mount, who in the tradition of disguise and shape-changing familiar from chivalric romance, cross-dresses as Sir Julius in order to seduce him). He proceeds through purgation to purification (in the Alps, scene of many epiphanies, he learns that he is a father. In one of the most audacious and triumphant passages in Meredith, stimulated by the sensory experience of a leveret licking his hand during a storm, and close to the figure of the Virgin Mother in a wayside chapel, he is cleansed). Meanwhile Sir Austin has accepted Lucy as the mother of the infant heir, assuming his entitlement to set up a regimen for the next generation of Feverels by manifesting an almost prurient obsession with Lucy's breastfeeding. The hero's homecoming does not complete a reconciliation. Richard sees his wife and son only briefly, holding back because he considers himself bound to fight a duel to avenge an insult to Lucy. He is wounded: This blow imposes an unbearable strain on Lucy, who succumbs to brain fever. It is she who dies, in a brutally tragic end to a work that has appeared essentially comic. It is profoundly disturbing that though both of them have suffered, neither Sir Austin nor Richard seems to have learned from his experience. The import of the subtitle, "A History of Father and Son," fully emerges in Richard left at the end with his motherless son. Can he re-author the script now, or will the story repeat itself?

In the excess of this novel, Meredith throws up a set of themes and situations on which he was to work variations to the end of his long career. Romantic idealism similar to Richard's is seen in other central characters in Meredith— Nevil Beauchamp is a case in point—and flaws their ability for effective action. And there are in *Richard Feverel* a number of characters who are to recur in various guises: Austin Wentworth, who has socially damaged himself by an inappropriate marriage, is the avatar of the staunch retainer, clear-sighted and imbued with both political sense and activism, and physically fit, sharing Meredith's passion for long walks (later versions of this figure include Vernon Whitford in *The Egoist* and Dartrey Fenellan in *One of Our Conquerors*, whose values are endorsed and rewarded by marriage to the heroine). Another is the cynical commentator Adrian Harley, who is malicious and mischievous in a way his successors such as Colney Durance are not. Sir Austin is a prototype of the full-blown egoist, of which Sir Willoughby provides the ultimate Patterne. A serious concern with exploration of the situation and consciousness of women is signaled in the representation of Lucy as female hero; and the widowed Lady Blandish is a version of the older women like Mrs. Mountstuart Jenkinson in *The Egoist*, who display a kind of wisdom and exercise a degree of power as social arbiters.

Meredith's next novel was *Evan Harrington* (1861), and in the decade following, he published four more three-deckers: *Emilia in England* (1864; retitled *Sandra Belloni* when included in Chapman and Hall's Collected Edi-

tion in 1886), and its curious sequel *Vittoria* (1867, which had the working title "Emilia in Italy"), *Rhoda Fleming, A Story* (1865), and *The Adventures of
Harry Richmond* (1871). Demonstrably, in each he is experimenting with contemporary concerns and fashions in fiction, at the same time pursuing his own
creative obsessions.

In *Evan Harrington or, he would be a gentleman* Meredith engages explicitly
with what it means to be a gentleman in mid-nineteenth-century England: a
preoccupation of much contemporary fiction, notably Dickens's *Great Expectations* (1860–61). The novel looks more to the comic and picaresque than its
predecessor, and in it Meredith again reworks family history, this time quite
transparently. The tailor Great Mel is his grandfather, and he also depicts his
aunts in Evan's sisters Caroline, Harriet, and the splendid comic creation,
Louisa, Countess de Saldar. This is a book that has had some good press in recent years: John Sutherland thinks it is "the novel which has worn best," and
Sophie Gilmartin opens a discriminating critical perspective emphasizing the
ways in which Meredith is working out through the text issues to do with his
family background in trade, and his ambitions in literature (Gilmartin, 132).

The latest written of this group, *Harry Richmond*, similarly takes its bearings
from eighteenth-century picaresque, from Dickens (*David Copperfield* in particular: Both are first person novels—this is Meredith's only venture in that mode),
and from Romance, archetypically the *Arabian Nights*. It has clear links both
with *Richard Feverel* (even to echoes of the hero's name in a pair of histories of father and son) and *Evan Harrington* (particularly in respect of parentage and social class). Questions of lineage, inheritance, and dynastic responsibility make up
a persistent refrain through Harry's exotic adventures, in which the action several
times moves to the Continent, but is concluded on home ground when Harry's
eventual choice of consort settles on the English Janet to whom his maternal
grandfather has willed his estate, Riversley. In a welcoming gesture gone wrong,
Harry's father, Richmond Roy, burns Riversley to the ground, and presumably
perishes. Roy is convinced that he is an illegitimate scion of the House of
Hanover. The novel relishes both the extravagance of Roy's conviction and the
damage caused by his obsession. Although his belief that he is a royal by-blow is
never conclusively disproved, a major element of his fantasy is shown to be a delusion when it emerges that his long-term anonymous benefactor has been his
sister-in-law rather than some royal personage. Roy has affinities with all
Meredith's male egoists, especially with Sir Austin's mission to bring his son
through his ordeal and to his majority (and hence into the property), and with
Victor Radnor's campaign in *One of Our Conquerors* to blot out the stain of illegitimacy on his daughter, which takes him into insanity. Once again, Meredith is
fictionalizing various modes of self-authoring as part of an ongoing interrogation both of discourses of authority and illegitimacy.

But there are also three novels whose eponymous heroes are female: *Emilia in England, Rhoda Fleming,* and *Vittoria.* As with the novels named for men, there are particular fictional negotiations conducted: with the genre of sentimental romance in *Emilia,* the political novel in *Vittoria,* and the seduction plot (Roberts comments that *Rhoda Fleming* is "a baleful version of *Adam Bede*" [73]). Though woman's lot is at issue throughout Meredith's fiction, these novels engage centrally with the difficulties of defining female identity, difficulties most fully acknowledged in a later novel (and the only other of Meredith's novels named for a woman), *Diana of the Crossways.* On one level, this concern is signaled in the many name changes of Emilia (to Sandra and Vittoria, and variants), but the issue goes beyond personal nomination, for women even more than men are constituted in discourse. In the "Emilia" novels, Meredith explicitly frames the question How to voice the female protagonist? One solution is to make her a singer, invoking the power of music to transcend the complications of language—but at least in this pair of novels, that transcendence is most effective outside England, and in a context (of Italian nationalism) where principles of loyalty and patriotism are in play and a symbolic register appropriate. Meredith's repertoire of representations of the Other in gender, race, or class terms (woman, the Celt, and the working class) are a study in themselves. For a male novelist, Meredith is unusually interested in friendships and relationships among women. Sisters give the readiest possibility of exploring such relationships: Evan Harrington has three sisters, a familial configuration repeated in the "Emilia" novels in the Pole family, three daughters and a son, where again contrast in the genetic sample is relished. In the characters of Rhoda and Dahlia Fleming, Meredith interestingly plays variations on the stock situation of the virtuous and the transgressing woman. Such reflections on bonds among and between women (evident already in Lucy, Mrs. Berry, and Lady Blandish, for example; or more painfully in Clare and her mother) occupy even more attention in later works.

In the 1870s, Meredith was less prolific. He found personal stability in his second marriage in 1864, followed by the birth of a son and a daughter, and the move in 1867 to Flint House, Box Hill, Dorking, where he lived for the rest of his life. In *Beauchamp's Career* (1876), he was still working with adventure romance, and engaged again with the political novel, this time in an English context. Meredith's close friend, Frederick Augustus Maxse, was a prototype for the central character, Nevil Beauchamp, and much detail of the novel can be traced to "real life" sources, especially Meredith's experiences in support of Maxse's campaign as a Radical candidate in Southampton in 1868. As is his wont, Meredith uses the "known" events to provide a context of expectation, but frustrates any desire for revelations in a *roman à clef.* The significance of topical details derives from their naturalization in the narrative in ways that bring out the Quixotic aspects of the behaviors of the hero in love and war. The politics of the novel are broader than party issues: England is shown to be a smugly insular country, whose institutions—particularly the dangerous anachronism of the aristocracy—need urgent reform. Once again, this hero's place in the world is insecure (he is a poor nephew of the Earl of Romney); and the narrative reflects on the role of women in supporting men, forming or deforming them. This is a novel in which the perpetuation of the line recurs as a paramount theme, with the capacity for self-destructiveness of men bent on heroism a dominant motif.

Moreover, *Beauchamp's Career* is a novel that supplies more examples of Meredith's characteristic narrative tactics. Frequently, major confrontations are not shown—like Everard Romfrey's horsewhipping Dr. Shrapnel—but reported, because their significance lies not in the action itself, but in its implications and effects. He is especially concerned to dramatize processes of thought, ways in which events come to be understood, and to explore the psychology behind apparently unmotivated or excessive actions (such as Beauchamp's hasty trip to France during the election campaign in response to Renée's summons). A related mannerism is the frequent occurrence in Meredith's texts of instances of "momentous effects produced by very minor causes," to abbreviate the title of Chapter 23 of *One of Our Conquerors,* where Victor Radnor's maiden aunts, who are devoted to their lapdog, are moved to invite Victor's daughter to stay after the dog disgraces himself by excreting inside the house. The implication is that the young woman is as innocent of offense as the dog, despite the ill odor that surrounds her unmarried parents. Such exaggerations—of which Victor's famous fall on London Bridge at the opening of the novel is another instance—are one of Meredith's favorite ways of developing a "fine flavor of analogy" (189), with disconcerting effects.

Meredith's experiments during the 1870s included short fiction: "The House on the Beach," "The Case of General Ople and Lady Camper," and "The Tale of Chloe" were all published in *New Quarterly Magazine* in 1877 and 1878, having in common elements of the comic, mannered, and grotesque of his earliest fiction. He also produced a scholarly essay on comedy, originally delivered as a lecture, "On the Idea of Comedy, and of the Uses of the Comic Spirit," in 1877. The theory of comedy articulated in this essay finds expression also in the novel on which Meredith was concurrently working, his masterpiece *The Egoist* (1879), dauntingly in its "Prelude," which opens with lucid poise ("Comedy is a game played to throw reflections upon social life, and it deals with human nature in the drawing-room of civilized men and women") but soon turns recalcitrant (the impenetrable opening chapter is something of a Meredithian trademark).

Here, Meredith engages less with fictional traditions than with dramatic
ones. The tough elegance of seventeenth-century stage comedy, both English
(Restoration comedy, with its brilliant sexual innuendo) and French (notably
Molière), braces this novel. Comic conventions and assumptions are mocked,
but the play of the Comic Spirit averts the sudden tragic deepening into bleak-
ness and waste that marks the end of *Richard Feverel, Beauchamp's Career,* and
even *Harry Richmond*. It is a text that is heavily overdetermined: as well as
adopting a structure that frequently references stage comedy, so providing cues
to the reader and assisting in determining the shape and pace of the narrative,
Meredith also alludes to the legend of the Willow Pattern plate in the name of
the central character, Sir Willoughby Patterne, and in the central situation in
which a young woman prefers a poor man, employed as a secretary, to the
suitor of her father's choice. The novel ends with two marriages, and possibly a
third if the alliance of Horace De Craye and Mrs. Mountstuart develops. For
all its "drawing-room" mode, and its demonstration of the civilizing capacities
of comedy, *The Egoist* is elemental: It is dominated by the need to secure the
line, to provide an heir. As the courtship rituals play out, the physical basis of
sexual conquest is dwelt on in the *doubles entendres* of the witty epigrams that
provide mannered conversational currency—notably the outrageous display
of "the leg," on one level alluding to Sir Willoughby's anachronistic re-creation
of the Cavalier court at Patterne Hall; at another, implying sexual exhibition-
ism. Willoughby's fantasizing about building up "the house" is generated in
part by a fear of invasion or contamination: Metaphorically, his fierce
territoriality is aligned with an imperialist ideology. Like Sir Austin Feverel, he
is self-authoring. When he is jilted he retreats to his domain and attempts to
regulate it completely, in the belief that the principles of his laboratory science
can be extended to ensure his control of all actions and reactions in his domain.
But his science is no match for the energies of the natural world, which are figured both in the familiar register of Home County rural beauty reinforced by
the sublimity of imagery drawn from Alpine heights, and also in Darwinian
terms (Meredith makes great play with monkeys who figuratively threaten de-
volution, or worse, revolution).

For all the insight with which women have been drawn in earlier novels, it is in
The Egoist that a significant shift in Meredith's address to women takes place. Because of the prevailing social mores, they are still defined in relation to
men—and the re-forming of couples that provides the action of this novel can be
interpreted as a transaction among men in which even so intelligent a woman as
Clara Middleton lacks agency. Nonetheless, it is significant that Clara, more
than any of the women who surround Harry Richmond or Nevil Beauchamp, is
allowed some independence in speech and action, and brings a positive energy to
her relationship with Vernon Whitford. She forms an alliance with Laetitia Dale,

who becomes the next Lady Patterne—though as she is unlikely to produce the desired heir, the estate will probably pass to young Crossjay, whose prepubescent natural vigor marks out a different Patterne. *The Egoist* acknowledges the conventions of comedy but works anarchically within them.

The 1880s were a period of consolidation for Meredith. Chapman and Hall began to issue a Collected Edition in 1885, following his great success, *Diana of the Crossways* (1885), the second of his two novels in this decade. The subtitle of *The Tragic Comedians: A Study in a Well-Known Story* (1880) indicates an affinity between the two. Both rework "given" stories, respectively incidents based on the love affair of Helene von Racowitza and the radical German socialist politician Ferdinand Lassalle, and on a rumor about the poet and novelist Caroline Norton, confidante of English statesmen. Neither text is overly concerned with what happened in fact, but with what "really" happened: The opening chapter of *Diana* declares a commitment to being "veraciously historical, honestly transcriptive" by "reading the inner as well as exhibiting the outer." The fullest understanding precludes simple acceptance of any single viewpoint, and involves exposure to and evaluation of competing texts, discourses, or registers.

The titular heroine of *Diana of the Crossways* is a novelist who makes fiction and capital out of her own experience, and the experience of people known to her—as Meredith did. But any affinity so suggested between Diana Merrion and George Meredith is only one of many elements contributing to her identity. Diana is curiously elusive: Her iridescence is both an indication of her brilliance and of her uncertainties. She is known by various names (Diana, Tony, her authorial pseudonym, her married name) and partakes of various of the roles of Diana, goddess of the hunt, the moon, childbirth—and crossways. The question "Who is she?" is posed in a barrage of texts in the opening chapter, where memoirs and other reports and recollections provide a series of impressions dramatizing the circulation of gossip and the pressures society brings to bear on women. Having been subjected to sexual overtures from several men including the husband of her best friend, Diana marries for protection: a bad decision, one consequence of which is that she seeks to make her own way in the world, as a novelist and as a society hostess. She is reliant on relationships with women, her maid Danvers, for one, but more important, her sentimental friendship with the invalid Emma Dunstane. She strikes out a feminist line, demanding rights for women (her Irishness reinforces presentation of the oppressiveness of the English patriarchy). A would-be independent woman is especially vulnerable. In particular, Diana suffers from rumors that she has sold to a newspaper a state secret communicated to her by a lover. She runs the gauntlet of a number of compromising or sexually threatening situations, her honor upheld through all her trials by the stalwart Thomas Redworth, a kind of New Man to Diana's New Woman, his manly attributes and practical strengths enhanced by developing insight and appreciation of culture. After Diana has rejected or evaded other relationships, their union becomes possible because both have learned and matured.

Meredith persisted in his challenges to orthodoxy in each of his extraordinary late novels, *One of Our Conquerors* (1891), *Lord Ormont and His Aminta* (1894), and *The Amazing Marriage* (1895, but at least begun in the late 1870s). All of them center on socially unsanctioned sexual situations and rework with unflagging inventiveness such Meredithian preoccupations as England, the Empire, fanaticism, education, the power of nature, gender differences, and debate about the art of fiction. Like the rest of Meredith's novels, they demand effort of their readers, effort rewarded by exhilaration as well as exasperation. Meredith's compact with his readers, enunciated over and over in his novels, was to provoke, to effect re-vision, and he still delivers.

WORKS CITED AND SELECTED WORKS FOR FURTHER READING

Bakhtin, M. M. *The Dialogic Imagination: Four Essays*. Ed. Michael Holquist. Trans. Caryl Emerson and Michael Holquist. Austin: U of Texas P, 1981.

Beer, Gillian. *Meredith: A Change of Masks*. London: Athlone, 1970.

Belsey, Catherine. *Critical Practice*. London and New York: Methuen, 1980.

Cline, C. L., ed. *The Letters of George Meredith*. 3 vols. Oxford: Clarendon, 1970.

Gilmartin, Sophie. *Ancestry and Narrative in Nineteenth-Century British Literature: Blood Relations from Edgeworth to Hardy*. Cambridge: Cambridge UP, 1998.

Johnson, Diane. *Lesser Lives: The True History of the First Mrs. Meredith and Other Lesser Lives*. London: Heinemann, 1973.

Lucas, John. "Meredith's Reputation." In *Meredith Now: Some Critical Essays*, pp. 1–13. Ed. Ian Fletcher. London: Routledge and Kegan Paul, 1971.

Meredith, George. *Works*. 27 vols. London: Constable, 1909–11.

Pritchett, V. S. *George Meredith and English Comedy*. London: Chatto and Windus, 1970.

Roberts, Neil. *Meredith and the Novel*. London: Macmillan, 1997.

Stevenson, Lionel. *The Ordeal of George Meredith*. New York: Scribner's, 1953.

Stone, Donald D. "Meredith and Bakhtin: Polyphony and Bildung." *Studies in English Literature* 28 (1988): 693–712.

Sutherland, John. "A Revered Corpse: The Peculiar Unreadability of George Meredith." *Times Literary Supplement*, 5 September 1997, 5.

White, Allon. *The Uses of Obscurity: The Fiction of Early Modernism*. London: Routledge and Kegan Paul, 1981.

Williams, Ioan, ed. *George Meredith: The Critical Heritage*. London: Routledge and Kegan Paul, 1971.

Wilt, Judith. *The Readable People of George Meredith*. Princeton: Princeton UP, 1975.

"Not Burying the One Talent": Mrs. Gaskell's Life of Duty

Barbara Quinn Schmidt

Increased appreciation of Elizabeth Gaskell (1810–65) since the centennial of her death includes a growing awareness of her as a socially active wife of a minister and mother of four daughters, who had a successful career in a period considered incompatible to such achievement by women. Shortly after Mrs. Gaskell's death, E. Thurstan Holland, fiancé of her eldest daughter Marianne, wrote to her friend, Charles Eliot Norton, on 18 November 1865, "I feel her loss deeply for all who knew her well must have loved that kind sympathetic heart which shared every one's joys or griefs, that fresh intellect, that powerful imagination, that kindly interest that she took in every one about her" (Chapple and Pollard, 971).

Because she sought, and nearly achieved, a seamless weave of the duties and desires in her personal and professional lives, her writings were based on her realistic depiction of her own experiences and observations, minutely described. She strove to inspire and educate readers, especially women and girls, to remain steadfast in what they knew was right, even when counter to society's dictates or confronted by those in authority. In the midst of the vast social change in Victorian England, Mrs. Gaskell aspired to live an exemplary life within a community not wholly congenial to dissent.

Although born in London, Elizabeth Cleghorn Stevenson grew up in rural Cheshire—the geographical setting for *Cranford, Ruth, Wives and Daughters,* and several shorter works—attended school in Warwickshire like George Eliot, and lived her entire married life in Manchester, the burgeoning center of the industrial North—the setting for *Mary Barton, North and South,* and "Lizzie Leigh." Her loss of her mother and her only brother, a distant relationship with her father's second family, and the love of her maternal extended family—all make their appearance in her realistic fiction.

To escape the city's pollution, the constant demands on a minister's wife, and the adverse criticism for untactful remarks in her published writings, she balanced her active life with rest and contemplation. Her travels improved her health and spirit and often resulted in fresh ideas for her writing in harmony with her sense of duty. She wrote Eliza Fox, "I do believe we have all some appointed work to do, why no one else can do so well; first we must find out what we are sent into the world to do, and define it and make it clear to ourselves, (that's *the* hard part) and then forget ourselves in our work" (Chapple and Pollard, 106–107). Mrs. Gaskell found her work to be in the family, the parish, and the literary world. As a Unitarian she was well-educated and felt the greatest gifts she could bestow on her daughters were moral development and education. She wished they would "avoid competition by developing different and complementary parts of themselves" (Levin, 55).

Her first known writing was for her six-month-old daughter Marianne, begun in March 1835. Because her mother died during Elizabeth's infancy and her own first infant daughter died, she feared for Marianne (who outlived her parents and siblings) and for her own life, lest she leave Marianne half-orphaned. Having nothing to remember her own mother by, Elizabeth Gaskell began a diary to remember her infant better or for her infant to remember her and be safeguarded in her faith. "She perceived her maternal role as a sacred trust and a solemn duty" and worried about her own "inadequacies and spiritual shortcomings" (Wilson, 23).

She and her husband sought to teach Marianne self-governance and to help her find her own work in the world. To do that, Mrs. Gaskell observed details of behavior and individuation. She wrote in the diary, "I try always to let her look at anything which attracts her notice as long as she will, and when I see her looking very intently at anything, I take her to it, and let her exercise all her senses upon it—even to tasting, if I am sure it can do her no harm. My object is to give her a habit of fixing her attention" (Chapple and Wilson, 51).

She later advised an aspiring writer to live "an active and sympathetic life" (Wilson, 26), only possible through focusing on the details. Her keen sense of observation, sympathy, curiosity, and humor became the strengths of her writing. Despite her own fears expressed in her letters, in the diary she dutifully focused more on shaping "Marianne's future attitude toward herself and toward the idea of motherhood" (28).

Encouraged by her husband to write in order to forget her grief after the death of their nine-month-old son Willy from scarlet fever in 1844, she wrote in her preface that her first novel, *Mary Barton*, would recount

the lives of some of those who elbowed me daily in the busy streets of the town in which I resided. I had always felt a deep sympathy with the care-worn men, who looked as if doomed to struggle through their lives in strange alternations between work and want; tossed to and fro by circumstances, apparently in even a greater degree than other men. . . . Whether the bitter complaints made by them, of the neglect which they experienced from the prosperous—especially from the masters whose fortunes they helped to build up—were well-founded or no, it is not for me to judge. It is enough to say, that this belief of the injustice and unkindness which they endure from their fellow-creatures, taints what might be resignation to God's will, and turns it to revenge in too many of the poor uneducated factory-workers of Manchester. (1)

Believing that making readers aware of a deplorable situation would right the wrong through a general interest in communal harmony and mutual understanding, Mrs. Gaskell focused on the strengths and weaknesses of individuals, primarily workers, in specifically detailed surroundings, both geographical and spiritual, providing a contemporary resonance with readers. But readers needed closer personal identification before they moved beyond sympathy to seek change; therefore many, shocked that John Barton was a murderer, only made the book a best-seller.

Ruth, her first three-volume novel, is more directly moral propaganda promoting charity in confronting the plight of the unwed but good mother, based on Gaskell's concern for one of her own former servants (see Chapple and Shelston). Here, Ruth gave her life, contracting typhus fever while nursing the man who wronged her. She had been rescued by a nonconformist minister whose lie provided her with employment as a governess to an evangelical family until her secret was revealed. Gaskell consciously offended with her challenge to social attitudes but hoped the goodness and vulnerability of her main character would embolden readers. Arguing for the dignity of nursing even before she met Florence Nightingale, Mrs. Gaskell considered encouraging her daughter Meta "to prepare herself for entering upon a nurse's life of devotion when she is thirty or so, by going about among sick now" (Chapple and Pollard, 320) to see if she was sufficiently interested.

In response to the outcry against a perceived pro-worker bias to *Mary Barton*—despite her efforts throughout her novels to balance opposites—and the unsatisfactory response to *Ruth*, Mrs. Gaskell examined in *North and South* more of the middle-class perspective represented by Margaret Hale, who lived in both the North and the South—rural and urban—and befriended both the self-made owner's and the workers' families. Margaret accepted an individual's right to question and resist authority, whether it was her father uprooting his family when he gave up his clerical position because of religious doubt or the worker who sought to resist perceived oppression by greedy mill owners. Margaret mastered her own desires, did what was right, and nurtured individuals including her mother who failed to adapt to the city where her father had found employment. And after insisting he go out and talk to the mob, she physically shielded John Thornton, the mill owner, from them when they turned violent. Her actions inspired both worker and owner to seek a more workable balance. Although her parents' deaths provided the opportunity to return to the self-serving, upper-class society of her London youth, Margaret sought instead the rustic delight of her former home, the vicarage in Helstone. When she found that it no longer existed for her, she returned to the challenges of Milton Northern and marriage to Thornton, who had learned from the labor leader of Margaret's selfless devotion to her brother. Appreciating both abstract and practical knowledge, Thornton visited his beloved Margaret's family home where he plucked a flower as a remembrance prior to her return. Mrs. Gaskell was satisfied with her creation of Thornton: "I want to keep his character consistent with itself, and large and strong and tender, and *yet a master*" (Chapple and Pollard, 321). Together Margaret and John will endeavor to bridge the two nations of England.

Elizabeth Gaskell applied equal vigor to all aspects of her life. After her reputation as an important writer was established by the publication of *Mary Barton* in 1848, she was introduced to Charlotte Brontë, who became her closest literary colleague, and was invited by Charles Dickens to submit to his new magazine, for which she was to write nearly forty contributions including *North and South*. She entertained extensively as befitted her position as a minister's wife, especially in 1857 during the Manchester Art Treasures Exhibition, "a cultural triumph for the industrial north" which brought "a perpetual stream of visitors" during the time she was revising *The Life of Charlotte Brontë* (Uglow, 436); she taught Sunday school; she visited the poor and set "up a sewing machine for poor needlewomen during the American Civil War when the blockade of the southern ports had stopped the flow of cotton causing the terrible cotton famine of 1862–63" (497, 498). Her trips for her health and the educational and social development of her daughters were paid for by her writing.

Mrs. Gaskell successfully managed time and elicited loyalty from people, writing while visiting friends or absorbing ideas for writing while traveling with her daughters. "Gaskell's effective and energetic management of household, children, finances, and social obligations made her an excellent Victorian housewife while simultaneously undermining conventional domesticity" (Wilson, 31). Her husband was coauthor of their first publication, read her manuscripts, helped with research, checked out library books, and provided invaluable help with her characters' dialects. Their daughters, especially the two oldest, provided secretarial assistance. From 1842, when they moved to their second of three homes, Ann Hearn, a country girl, served the Gaskells, only later to become a most valued friend and chief support for Mrs. Gaskell and her growing family. Hearn, who remained with the family for fifty years (Uglow, 150), served as a model for many faithful fictional companions.

Mrs. Gaskell traveled and corresponded in her thorough researching for *Sylvia's Lovers* and *The Life of Charlotte Brontë*, the two works that were least directly connected with her own experience. In her quest for realism, she called upon friends, acquaintances, her publisher, and anyone who knew Charlotte Brontë to acquire detailed knowledge of her subject's personal and professional lives.

James Kay-Shuttleworth, whose wife invited Mrs. Gaskell to her first meeting with Charlotte Brontë at their home in Windermere, later accompanied Mrs. Gaskell to Haworth and served as intermediary between author and widower who preferred privacy for his wife's memory. Through Sir James's tenacity, Mrs. Gaskell "came away with the manuscript of *The Professor* [the unpublished first novel], the beginning of the new novel *Emma*, and a collection of Charlotte's extraordinary juvenilia" (Selleck, 300). Although Mrs. Gaskell remained critical of Kay-Shuttleworth's motives and methods, she used what they acquired in her biography. However, abiding by the wishes of the deceased, she saw to it that Arthur Bell Nicholls, her widower, not Sir James, made the necessary changes to *The Professor* before publication by Smith, Elder.

Despite the demands on her time and attention, Mrs. Gaskell produced numerous short pieces, usually stories—often more controversial because less likely to receive critical attention—and a few novellas as well as six novels and the biography. In the nearly two decades of her career, she published in ten periodicals, sometimes two at a time once her daughters were in school, and her works were translated into several languages.

Asserting authorial control over her work, she sparred with her publishers when she felt ill-treated and ill-paid compared with male writers. Therefore she sought various publishing opportunities. When angry with Charles Dickens about his editing, especially of *North and South*—a long novel not suited to a weekly—and his uncredited use of her ideas in his own work, she began to write for George Smith's new *Cornhill Magazine* in 1860. Yet she published in Dickens's *Household Words* and *All the Year Round* from 1850 to 1863. And in writing the biography for Smith, Elder, Charlotte Brontë's publisher, Mrs. Gaskell ceased writing for Chapman and Hall.

In response to Dickens's initial request, she surprisingly contributed "Lizzie Leigh" about a self-sacrificing fallen woman, driven away by her father, who brought harmony to her family before her death. Subsequent writings focused on ordinary rural life and the difference altruism makes in everyday events.

Her Christmas book *The Moorland Cottage*, whose heroine Maggie conquered her own desires in her attempts to do good for others and to rescue her disgraced brother who drowns, provided inspiration for George Eliot's *The Mill on the Floss*. In the same month *Cranford* (1851–53) began in *Household Words*. Originally thinking "Our Society at Cranford" to be a single tale set in the Knutsford area where she grew up, Mrs. Gaskell provided an heroic death for Captain Brown and a wedding for his surviving, dutiful daughter. Its popularity required a series, written at her convenience, which developed into a narrative by a young woman, Mary Smith, visiting from the nearby city of Drumble (Manchester), possibly Gaskell herself given the similarities to Knutsford events and people with whom she was familiar (see Levin), Amazons in a patriarchy quietly facing everyday challenges without male guidance yet ever fearful of outside interference whether from the city or foreigners. A self-effacing, aging woman, Matty Jenkyns, becomes the unlikely heroine who, through her gentle, loving actions in response to circumstances, slowly ceases to follow blindly the authority of her deceased sister who had emulated their father. The failure of the Town and Country bank, where Miss Jenkyns had entrusted their financial future, afforded the first opportunity for Miss Matty to become the moral center of her social circle through her refusal to seek financial benefit at the expense of others. Mary's summation in the last sentence of *Cranford* refers both to her fellow characters and to readers as well: "We all love Miss Matty, and I somehow think we are all of us better when she is near us" (278).

This novel best reveals the author's versatility in altering genre, direction, and character, bringing her the most pleasure in creative achievement. In February 1865, she wrote John Ruskin, "It is the only one of my own books that I can read again; but sometimes when I am ailing or ill, I take "Cranford" and—I was going to say, *enjoy* it! (but that would not be pretty!), laugh over it afresh" (Chapple and Pollard, 747)! In her thoughtful "Introduction" to the novel, Anne Thackeray Ritchie wrote, "At Cranford love is a memory rather than a present emotion; [it] . . . is everywhere, where people have individuality and kindliness and where oddities are . . . greatly loved for the sake of the individuals" (x–xi). And Mrs. Ritchie succinctly encapsulates Mrs. Gaskell: "She . . . always kept her cow, even in Manchester; she understood the practical facts of life as well as its feelings" (xxiii).

In *My Lady Ludlow*'s fourteen weekly parts (1858) that followed *North and South* (1855) in *Household Words*, Gaskell combined the English fear of possible revolution with the need for community building and social change. The Ludlow name suggests Luddite or laid low by life's circumstances, a reminder that individuals can either rise or fall financially. Lady Ludlow outlived her entire family of nine children and nearly lost her own inherited estate Hanbury Court because her last son left no heir or will and her husband borrowed against Hanbury for his family estates in Scotland. However, she hired her son's friend, who through employing new farming methods introduced by a Birmingham former baker, now owner of the neighboring estate, effectively paid off the debt.

Like Miss Matty, my Lady's good heart was ruled unquestioningly by tradition that stifled progress. The danger of not accepting change might have resulted in the disaster that occurred in France when the aristocracy too long suppressed the poor. A young French boy, in not respecting privilege, revealed the contents of a note he carried and thoughtlessly read, thereby causing the capture and ultimate beheading of the son of Lady Ludlow's friend and his beloved. This tragedy convinced my Lady that education for the lower classes caused disaster. The irony was obvious to the readership of *Household Words*, many of whom had begun their social climb and were more interested in imitating the aristocracy.

They could empathize with my Lady's confusion and loneliness as presented by Margaret Dawson, the narrator, who provided a partisan ethnography of the democratization of Lady Ludlow through her experiences. Margaret, an impoverished distant relative and the eldest of nine children, had gone to live with Lady Ludlow in her effort to assist the family. After a debilitating accident, Margaret reclined in the public room where she overheard conversations that she recalled with delicate emotional nuances. The accident of declining social position for friendless women brings poignancy and urgency to the necessity of all joining together. Society must include the foolish, the innocent, the repentant, the children of fallen women, even the talents of prodigal sons and daughters.

Whereas *Cranford* focused on middle-class ladies, here the focus was on the power and limitations of privilege. Lady Ludlow's earlier strong resistance gave way through her sense of loyalty and fairness toward her neighbors and dependents. The lower-class clergyman Mr. Gray, finally had his school to educate and improve the deserving poor. As a result the son of a poacher became a clergyman eventually succeeding Mr. Gray, who had been his mentor and father-in-law. As in *Cranford*, clerical influence, individual worth, a moral center, an outsider narrator, a genteel atmosphere with rigid rules for women resulting in unrequited love once again led to greater openness. A woman who lost her opportunity for a happy marriage made a home for his orphaned daughter. Both novels furnished *Household Words* readers with an achievable ideal to strive for. Virtuous living can yield fairness, peace, and joy. Women with education and good breeding can perform capably as clerks, shopkeepers, or countesses as well as nurture in times of need. The loss of family and wealth tests such women's generosity and courage in crossing social boundaries with genuine kindness. The ideal comes close to wish fulfillment in a fairy tale, yet remains separated by the minutely described behavior and detail of daily living that root it in reality.

Mrs. Gaskell's writings—whether overtly exposing broad social problems in *Mary Barton*, *Ruth*, or *North and South*, subtly seeking to alter women's lives in numerous works, or affirming the importance of moral strength for women in the face of seemingly harmless social pressure—continue to reveal her realistic assessment of conditions in the everyday lives of the working and the middle classes, and how those without power—women, children, and work-ers—achieved their moral stature instead of society's expectation that they simply be docile and pliable.

Mrs. Gaskell set high standards for herself as well as her characters, chafed at personal limits, overextended and undervalued herself. Later she worried that she relied too heavily on the assistance of Marianne and Meta, her oldest daughters, and vowed to spare the younger girls. She was demoralized while writing *Sylvia's Lovers* by the realization that despite her own emphasis on living a moral life, she lacked the genius of George Eliot, whom Gaskell wished more moral to validate her worldview. Having read Eliot's *Romola* in the *Cornhill Magazine*, Gaskell complained to Edward Hale, "I feel as if nothing of mine would be worth reading ever-more and that takes the pith out of one. Then Meta says 'But Mama remember the burying the one talent'—& I cheer up. I mean to get strong and do the best I *can*" (quoted in Uglow, 497) to finish *Sylvia's Lovers* for Smith. Following her colleague Charlotte Brontë's death, Mrs. Gaskell looked to Eliot's work for inspiration, modeling Sylvia's parents on Eliot's Poysers, for example. Mrs. Gaskell would have appreciated Eliot's praise for this novel and her use of the declaration of love between Sylvia and Kinraid for Lydgate and Rosamond in *Middlemarch* (1872) (Lerner, 16), which also echoes the broad scope of *Wives and Daughters*, in its Darwinian influence and altruistic heroine, who experiences great loss and emotional pain.

When her first novel *Mary Barton*, although praised by Eliot, was widely criticized by members of the Unitarian chapel, several of whom owned cotton mills, she was surprised and upset. Engaged in so many activities, she mis-judged the effect of her words and relied on her good intentions. She fre-quently worked at a feverish pace and dashed off letters to friends deploring her ill health while asking indulgence for too many subjects or a jumble of ideas. (Uglow extensively chronicles her activities.) During the writing of the biogra-phy, she lamented, "Miss Brontë . . . puts all her naughtiness into her books, and I put all my goodness . . . my books are so far better than I am that I often feel ashamed of having written them and as if I were a hypocrite" (quoted in Lerner, 25) in the face of great social need.

When *The Life of Charlotte Brontë* appeared in 1857, Mrs. Gaskell fled to the Continent expecting negative reactions from a few people mentioned unfavorably. Her husband and Smith handled the outcry by suppressing the first edition, and requiring revisions of the offending parts when she returned. Even before she had been invited to write the biography by Rev. Brontë, Mrs. Gaskell intended to write a short piece about her colleague. She accomplished her goal of rescuing the reputation of her friend, damaged by gossipy and critical obituary notices and articles, through writing one of the best biographies of the century.

According to Linda Hughes and Michael Lund, Elizabeth Gaskell also established herself therein as like Charlotte Brontë in being both a private Victorian woman married to a clergyman and a gifted writer (see Hughes and Lund, Chapter 5). Her empathy with Brontë was strengthened by her growing awareness of the many blessings she experienced in her own life through the support of family and friends unlike the secluded life of the Brontë sisters. Both women needed to write and to feel loved and accomplished. Both set high personal standards of behavior as civic and moral duties and fuller expression of individuality in keeping with God's plan. Both experienced frequent bouts of ill health partially because they pushed themselves beyond the socially sanctioned role for women. In their writings they worked through the problems women faced in the changing world of the early and mid-Victorian periods. Although Brontë was more of a romantic, both understood the value of fairy tales to inspire hope. And both were quite aware of the terrors of nightmares and the value of gothic horror based on guilt. They incorporated both into their stories to empower female readers with hope or to put on the armor of light as protection against evil. For example, Gaskell's "The Old Nurse's Story" (*Household Words*, December 1852) dispensed a warning against harboring jealousy and self-righteous ill-will, which returned to haunt the guilty and threatened subsequent generations. Both authors taught the importance of acting according to a well-developed conscience in the face of nearly overwhelming challenges and rewarded their heroines for their fidelity to truth and loyalty to loved ones, often marrying them to worthy husbands.

Gaskell honed her writing skill through constant practice, seeking criticism from her husband and friends, closely observing her surroundings and the people who occupied them, and reading, although not as extensively as George Eliot and George Henry Lewes, who also worked more judiciously with publishers, possibly because they were less distracted. Mrs. Gaskell's busy life and hurried communications led editors to believe that her writing, with its careless inattention to names of characters and places, required intervention, which she found disruptive. She frequently chafed at the editorial demands and changes. However when *Sylvia's Lovers* took three years to write during the American

Civil War, she received only an occasional gentle reminder from Smith. Because she was not writing it for a periodical, she had the freedom to postpone writing and do her social duty.

When Smith wanted a serial novel for *Cornhill Magazine* and she wished to purchase a retirement home for her husband, which would also provide her more quiet and a healthier environment, Mrs. Gaskell flung herself into writing *Wives and Daughters*, successfully meeting deadlines. With the assistance of her children and her publisher, she purchased and furnished her dream home, similar to the Manchester home, but in Hampshire, with plenty of bedrooms, a spacious drawing room, expansive grounds with a stream running through the property, located near Jane Austen's home and the Alton railway station with easy access to London. Frederick Greenwood, the editor, followed her ideas for posthumous completion of the last part. Laurence Lerner proclaimed it in 1969 as "surely the most neglected novel of its century" (7).

Charles Darwin's assertion of the importance of environment in natural selection confirmed Mrs. Gaskell's experience and inspired her to show more fully the influences of the environment on her heroine Molly Gibson. Like other Knutsford-based works, the apparently static community is affected by change brought in from the outside, in the person of Cynthia Kirkpatrick and science through Mr. Gibson, Roger Hamley, and Lord Hollingford decried by the traditionalist Squire Hamley, Roger's father. Appropriately, Molly falls in love with Roger, whose practical scientific mind and experience parallels Darwin's. Because Molly is motherless, her father, the well-respected doctor, surrounds her with role models and even sends her to live under the protection of Mrs. Hamley after his young assistant shows too much interest in his daughter. Therefore, the girl is supported by women of all classes, including Lady Harriet, Mrs. Hamley, middle-class spinsters, and servants. These women, plus her father and the Hamleys create a nurturing environment for Molly, whose developing qualities sustain her through the darkest trials. Mr. Gibson never considers that Molly might be susceptible to the younger Hamley son. Roger wins her trust when advising forbearance in her distress over her father's marriage to Mrs. Kirkpatrick, who proved to be neither the wife nor the mother he had hoped for. Although Molly ultimately saved Mrs. Kirkpatrick's daughter Cynthia's reputation, her character had been set by her mother's transparent selfishness.

Because the end was incomplete, readers can only surmise if Mrs. Gibson dies, if Roger's instruction of Molly leads to joint scientific discovery, or if they become the moral center for London scientists. (The BBC television version [1999] sends them off to Africa to further scientific work.) But it seems certain that Roger and Molly are strong enough to survive in whatever environment they find themselves. Darwin validated Mrs. Gaskell's sense that her writing was a valuable ministry showing the powerful effect of heredity, environment, and free will. Mrs. Gaskell's corrections to the manuscript of this novel provided minute differentiations, which firmly delineated her characters and their actions.

That she had received little attention earlier in this century was due to the attitude exemplified by David Cecil in *Victorian Novelists* (first published in 1935), a standard critical text for a quarter of a century. Cecil thought her feminine: "gentle, domestic, tactful, unintellectual, prone to tears, easily shocked" and serenely satisfied, "wholly lacking in the virile qualities," mired in specifics. He denigrated her as "the typical Victorian woman" with unsophisticated ordinariness or "a minister's wife in her drawing-room" (184, 185).

We have learned to appreciate Elizabeth Gaskell's daring efforts to strengthen the typical Victorian woman both in her fiction and her life and decry her overtaxing herself. In ignoring the signals of her body and her many bouts with ill health, she died suddenly of a heart attack—a death she often spoke of preferring—having finished her first cup of tea with her daughters and future son-in-law in her new house, prior to completing *Wives and Daughters*. She did not live to see her grandchildren. Except for being buried next to his wife in Knutsford, her husband remained in Manchester, which he loved, ministering to his devoted flock for two more decades, cared for by his two unmarried daughters who continued to live in the family home, 84 Plymouth Grove, until their deaths in the new century.

WORKS CITED AND SELECTED WORKS FOR FURTHER READING

Cecil, David. *Victorian Novelists*. Chicago: U of Chicago P, 1958.

Chapple, J.A.V., and Arthur Pollard, eds. *The Letters of Mrs. Gaskell*. Manchester, New York: Mandolin, 1997.

Chapple, J.A.V., and Alan Shelston, eds. *The Further Letters of Mrs. Gaskell*. Manchester: Manchester UP, 2000.

Chapple, J.A.V., and Anita Wilson, eds. *Private Voices: The Diaries of Elizabeth Gaskell and Sophia Holland*. New York: St. Martin's, 1996.

Gaskell, Mrs. *Cranford*. New York: A. L. Burt, n.d.

———. *Mary Barton*. Oxford: Oxford UP, 1987.

———. *My Lady Ludlow*. Chicago: Academy, 1995.

———. *North and South*. London: Penguin, 1970.

———. *Wives and Daughters*. MS, The John Rylands University Library of Manchester.

Hughes, Linda K., and Michael Lund. *Victorian Publishing and Mrs. Gaskell's Work*. Charlottesville: UP of Virginia, 1999.

Lerner, Laurence. Introduction. In *Wives and Daughters*, pp. 7–27, by Mrs. Gaskell. London: Penguin, 1969.

Levin, Amy K. *The Suppressed Sister*. Lewisburg: Bucknell UP, 1992.

Ritchie, Anne Thackeray. Preface. In *Cranford*, pp. ix–xxiv, by Mrs. Gaskell. New York: A. L. Burt, n.d.

Selleck, R.J.W. *James Kay-Shuttleworth: Journey of an Outsider*. Ilford: Woburn, 1994.

Uglow, Jenny. *Elizabeth Gaskell: A Habit of Stories*. New York: Farrar, Straus, and Giroux, 1993.

Wilson, Anita. Critical Introduction. In *Private Voices: The Diaries of Elizabeth Gaskell and Sophia Holland*, pp. 11–49. Ed. J.A.V. Chapple and Anita Wilson. New York: St. Martin's, 1996.

Wilkie Collins's Challenges to Pre-Raphaelite Gender Constructs

Sophia Andres

From the very beginning, Pre-Raphaelite art involved the intersection of poetry and painting. The short-lived Pre-Raphaelite publication, *The Germ*, which after the first two numbers was called *Art-Poetry*, contained the Pre-Raphaelite poet-painters' compositions that attempted to achieve a fusion of poetry and painting, of temporal and spatial dimensions. Inspired by poems, vibrant and sensuous paintings such as John Everett Millais's *Mariana* and *Lorenzo and Isabella*, Arthur Hughes's *April Love*, Dante Gabriel Rossetti's *The Blessed Damozel* may be seen as attempts to make palpable and visible impalpable and verbal poetic expressions.

But the fusion of the verbal and the visual, achieved by the Pre-Raphaelites, extended beyond poetry into another genre—the Victorian novel. Novelists as diverse as Elizabeth Gaskell, Wilkie Collins, George Eliot, and Thomas Hardy, whose philosophical and literary perspectives differed considerably, were all fascinated by the Pre-Raphaelites, corresponded with them, visited their studios, and quite often transformed Pre-Raphaelite paintings into narratives (Byerly, Frick, Nicholes, Schor). It is quite possible, as Alison Byerly contends, that, by alluding to Pre-Raphaelite paintings, Victorian novelists attempted to establish "an imaginative space where the fictional world and the real world came together" (121).

Elsewhere I have demonstrated that the intersection of painting and the Victorian novel at times emanated cultural conflicts or underscored ideological contradictions (Andres, "Gendered Incongruities"). Here, I wish to explore Wilkie Collins's debate with the Pre-Raphaelites over their representations of gender, a debate subtly and obliquely articulated in his sensational and popular novel, *The Woman in White*. Recently critics have focused on Wilkie Collins's subversion of Victorian stereotypes but have overlooked the Pre-Raphaelites' influence on Collins's challenges to conventional gender constructs (Balee, Bernstein, Elam, Langbauer, Williams). An understanding of Wilkie Collins's transformations of Pre-Raphaelite paintings into literary images of masculinity, femininity, and feminism necessitates an awareness of the means by which these artists attempted to revise stereotypical representations of gender.

THE PRE-RAPHAELITE REVOLT

Three young talented artists in their early twenties, John Everett Millais, Dante Gabriel Rossetti, and William Holman Hunt, banded together in 1848 to form the Pre-Raphaelite Brotherhood that was opposed to the principles of British art, beginning with Raphael's achievement and established by the eighteenth-century renowned artist and President of the Royal Academy, Sir Joshua Reynolds. The Brotherhood lasted only until 1853, but the Pre-Raphaelite influence on British art persisted throughout the remainder of the century and extended as late as the 1920s. Hundreds of books have been published on these artists assessing their contribution to art, thoroughly interpreting individual paintings. Here I wish to briefly discuss those aspects of their art that are related to their representations of gender. From the very beginning Pre-Raphaelite artists rebelled against Sir Joshua Reynolds's idealism that he discussed in his acclaimed Discourses on Art. In the third discourse Reynolds encouraged prospective artists to idealize, universalize, and generalize when painting portraits or landscapes. It was an artist's responsibility, according to Reynolds, to depict "Ideal Beauty," that is, to remove the perceived flaws of a composition and to "correct" nature's blemishes by replacing the imperfect with the "more perfect" (95–105).

To this concept of ideal beauty the Pre-Raphaelites countered their aim "to sympathize with what is direct and serious and heartfelt in previous art, to the exclusion of what is conventional and self-parading and learned by rote" (W. M. Rossetti, i, 135). Instead of "ideal beauty," the Pre-Raphaelites sought to express the idiosyncratic uniqueness of their subjects; instead of idealized permanence, they attempted to capture realistic change. For this reason instead of excluding "particularities," they accurately displayed minute details—even "blemishes." In an attempt to capture realistic change, they often painted their subjects in awkward poses to the dismay and outrage of conservative reviewers. Indeed their subversion of conventional beauty became the target of censure. Referring to the Pre-Raphaelite paintings exhibited at the Royal Academy at the time, a critic of *Athenaeum*, for instance, wrote on June 1, 1850: "Abruptness, singularity, uncouthness are the counters with which they play for fame. Their trick is to defy the principles of beauty and the recognized axioms of taste" ("Royal Academy," 590). Two weeks later an outraged Charles Dickens in his notorious review of John Everett Millais's *Christ in the House of His Parents* (*The Carpenter's Shop*), published in his journal *Household Words* in 1850, vilified the painting for the unconventional representation of the holy family, particularly for its lack of "ideal beauty." The Virgin Mary, Dickens objects, is "a kneeling woman, so horrible in her ugliness, that . . . she would stand out from the rest of the company as a Monster . . . in the lowest gin-shop in England" (265). As Tim Barringer observes, "gender and class are the chosen terms of Dickens's attack: the Christ child is not sufficiently manly; the Virgin is too vulgar in her physiognomy, too coarse in comparison with the sweet features of the Raphaelesque Madonna. Her hardened face appears working class" (40). The Pre-Raphaelites' defiance of established concepts of beauty remained through the century the focus of hostile reviewers. Yet such defiance, as David Masson pointed out in *British Quarterly Review* in August 1852, was consistent with the Pre-Raphaelites' goal to accurately represent reality: "But what we desire specially to note at present is, that this tendency towards forms not conventionally agreeable, which has been found fault with in the Pre-Raphaelites was . . . inevitable on their part; and was, in fact, a necessary consequence of their zeal in carrying out their favourite principle of attention to actual truth" (204). The same reviewer observed what hostile critics of Pre-Raphaelite representations of gender failed to notice: "in painting the human figure, their notion was that they should not follow any conventional idea of corporeal beauty, but should take some actual man or woman, and reproduce his or her features with the smallest possible deviation consistent with the purpose of the picture" (200).

Yet critics disregarded such justifications; instead, established notions of beauty dictated their responses to Pre-Raphaelite representations of gender. In reading such reviews, we may surmise the means by which Pre-Raphaelite painters undermined conventional gender constructs. John Eagles's "The Fine Arts and the Public Taste in 1853," published in *Blackwood's Edinburgh Magazine* in July 1853, may serve as a typical example of reviewers who upbraided Pre-Raphaelites for their transgressions of conventional gender boundaries. Of particular interest is Eagles's review of John Everett Millais's *The Order of Release* depicting a woman rescuing her imprisoned husband by compromising her virtue. "Her face, instead of being lovely," the critic contends, "is plain to a degree. . . . Far from pale, is blotched with red, and the shadows stippled in with bilious brownish green" (100). Essentially the critic here objects to the representation of a woman who exhibits traditionally masculine qualities: a defiant gaze, a shapeless body. But above all the critic berates the artist for a flagrant reversal of gender roles—a woman rescuing a man. Precisely for such a reversal, the same critic scoffs at Millais's *The Proscribed Royalist, 1651*, representing a woman rescuing a cavalier from persecution by hiding him in an oak tree (101).

These reviews are but a few examples of contemporary responses to the Pre-Raphaelite representations of gender, often seen as subversive to conventional gender constructs. As Susan Casteras persuasively argues in "Pre-Raphaelite Challenges to Victorian Canons of Beauty," "Hunt, Millais, and Rossetti all engineered their own self-conscious transformations of conventional norms of beauty, in the process stripping art of what they saw as its pretensions and substituting a new vocabulary of face and figure" (32). Yet as Jan Marsh and Joseph Kestner have already demonstrated, the Pre-Raphaelites also inscribed at times conventional gender constructs, representing, for instance, man as "the gallant knight" or "the valiant soldier"; women as "fallen Magdalens," "stunners," or "sorceresses," to mention but a few (Kestner, *Masculinities*, 92, 189; Marsh, 77, 17, 109).

WILKIE COLLINS AND THE PRE-RAPHAELITES

Through his brother, Charles, himself a Pre-Raphaelite, Wilkie Collins came to know Dante Gabriel Rossetti and became intimate friends with John Everett Millais and William Holman Hunt. His close friendship with these Pre-Raphaelites is evident in his correspondence with them (Baker and Clarke). William Clarke points out that Collins, Millais, Hunt, and Rossetti, "all these friends were inextricably linked with each other, through art or literary endeavors" (57). In his *Pre-Raphaelitism and the Pre-Raphaelite Brotherhood*, William Holman Hunt mentions Wilkie Collins's intention to write an article on the Pre-Raphaelite principles (i, 304). In a long review of the 1851 Royal Academy Summer Exhibition, Collins claimed that he admired the Pre-Raphaelites' "earnestness of purpose, their originality of thought, their close and reverent study of nature" (624–625). Specifically, he pointed out "[Charles] Collins was the superior in refinement, Mr. Millais in brilliancy, and Hunt in dramatic power" (625).

Elsewhere I have shown the impact of the Pre-Raphaelite artists on possible themes Collins explores and on some of the narrative techniques he uses (Andres, "Pre-Raphaelite"). Here, I wish to demonstrate that in crucial phases of his most successful novel, *The Woman in White*, Collins evokes well-known

Pre-Raphaelite paintings and subtly undermines their representations of gender moving away from rigid Victorian stereotypes towards an ambivalent definition of gender. It is curious that a novel supposedly about a woman is actually the story of a man's quest for psychic fulfillment that becomes possible by his encounters with women. Thus Wilkie Collins anticipates postmodern theorists in demonstrating that masculinity "does not exist in isolation from femininity—it will always be an expression of the current images that men have of themselves in relation to women. And these images are often contradictory and ambivalent" (Brittan, 2–3).

Hartright's initial encounter with Anne Catherick becomes the origin and the center of his journey toward selfhood and identity. By placing Anne Catherick, the illegitimate daughter of a fallen woman, in the center on which the novel pivots, Collins, like his Pre-Raphaelite friends, aroused and allayed the fear of the Other. Initially presenting the illegitimate figure of Anne Catherick as the threat of the Other to Walter Hartright, Collins eventually transforms her into a part of the protagonist's own self. Even before the woman in white first appears at the beginning of the novel, we are aware of a landscape suffused in Pre-Raphaelite interplays of light with shadow. That summer evening, oppressed by humidity, Walter decides to "stroll home in the purer air . . . to follow the white winding paths across the lonely heath," eerily illuminated by the moonlight: "The moon was full and broad in the dark blue starless sky, and the broken ground of the heath looked wild enough in the mysterious light to be hundreds of miles away from the great city that lay beneath it" (46). As he is enjoying "the divine stillness of the scene," he is startled by the sudden appearance of the solitary figure of Anne Catherick, the woman in white: "There, as if it had that moment sprung out of the earth or dropped from the heaven—stood the figure of a solitary Woman, dressed from head to foot in white garments, her face bent in grave inquiry on mine, her hand pointing to the dark cloud over London as I faced her" (47). The description of this "extraordinary apparition" draws attention to the moonlight mentioned earlier but perhaps forgotten by the reader at this point. The woman in white pointing toward London, her figure silhouetted in the moonlight, cast in an interplay of light and shadow, could very well serve as a dramatic description of William Holman Hunt's celebrated *The Light of the World*, "the most famous of all Victorian religious images" (Wood, 43).

In this painting, Christ with his hand raised, knocking on the sinner's door, is captured in the moonlight, the moon in the background serving as his halo. It is entirely possible that Wilkie Collins had this painting in mind when he drew its literary transformation in *The Woman in White*. After all, he had seen the first version of this painting when he spent time with his brother Charley, John Everett Millais, and William Holman Hunt at Rectory Farm in Ewell in

1851 (Hunt, i, 304). Collins must have been struck by the extraordinary circumstances of Hunt's work on the painting. True to the Pre-Raphaelite principle of representing nature accurately, Hunt worked from 9 P.M. to 5 A.M. when the moon was full, in the light of a lantern suspended from a tree (Parris, 118–119). Collins must have also known that "the character of the head was a composite taken from several male sitters . . . while Lizzie Siddal and Christina Rossetti sat for its coloring" (Parris, 119). In the hands of a Pre-Raphaelite artist, then, the creation of the image of the ultimate patriarchal figure became possible through the fusion of opposite genders.

It is not surprising, then, that Collins would transform this representation of Christ into the image of a destitute woman (the illegitimate daughter of a fallen woman)—the Other. In an attempt to contain his bewilderment, Hartright resorts to conventional standards of respectability and gender constructs: "All I could discern distinctly by the moonlight was a colorless, youthful face, meagre and sharp to look at about the cheeks and chin; large, grave, wistfully attentive eyes; nervous, uncertain lips; and light hair of a pale, brownish-yellow hue. There was nothing wild, nothing immodest in her manner: it was quiet and self-controlled, a little melancholy" (48). Indeed the details relating to Anne Catherick's appearance could be the ones describing Christ's face in *The Light of the World*. Eventually, Anne becomes a Christ figure, an integral part of Hartright's conscience and later of Sir Percival's and Count Fosco's.

Hartright's intriguing encounter initiates an identity crisis that is not resolved until the end of the novel. "Was I Walter Hartright?" he asks himself (50). His bewilderment may be partly explained by Anne Catherick's transgression of conventional gender and class boundaries. When he consents to help her, he is astonished by her defiance of conventional feminine behavior: "'You are very kind.' . . . The first touch of womanly tenderness that I had heard from her trembled in her voice as she said the words: but no tears glistened in those large, wistfully attentive eyes of hers, which were fixed on me" (49). Thus Anne undermines the traditional dynamics of the gaze that dictate the male/female, spectator/spectacle, subject/object hierarchical gender ideology. Whereas the meeting creates a conventional situation, a woman in distress, a man coming to her rescue, Collins, like his Pre-Raphaelite friends, opts for the unconventional, depriving Hartright the opportunity to affirm his masculinity by acting out the traditional role of the rescuer. Collins then intimates that in a way Hartright's identity crisis is bound to this suspension of gender constructs during his extraordinary meeting with the woman in white. As the novel progresses, a series of destabilizations of gender constructs constitute the most important phases of Hartright's journey toward psychic integration.

Unable to explain his extraordinary encounter in terms of conventional gender constructs, Hartright attempts to repress its memory, hoping to start a new life at Limmeridge, secured within traditional gender boundaries: teaching Laura Fairlie and her half-sister, Marian Halcombe, drawing and painting. But his first encounter with Marian is yet another test to his conventional gender notions. As Marian is standing by a window gazing outside with her back turned on Hartright, he is unable to see her, yet he indulges in the spectator/spectacle, masculine/feminine, superior/inferior, subject/object gender binaries. From a distance, before even meeting her, Hartright turns Marian into an object of desire: "The easy elegance of every movement of her limbs and body as soon as she began to advance from the far end of the room, set me in a flutter of expectation to see her face clearly." But his anticipation is thwarted as she moves closer: "She left the window—and I said to myself, The lady is dark. She moved forward a few steps—and I said to myself, The lady is young. She approached nearer—and I said to myself (with a sense of surprise which words fail me to express), The lady is ugly!" (58). Hartright's response echoes contemporary reviewers to the Pre-Raphaelites' unconventional representations of gender. In this case his conventional expectation of femininity is unsettled by the disjunction of femininity with masculinity, and in this respect Collins's portrait is consciously Pre-Raphaelite: "The lady's complexion was almost swarthy, and the dark down on her upper lip was almost a moustache. She had a large, firm, masculine mouth and jaw; prominent, piercing, resolute brown eyes; and thick, coal-black hair, growing unusually low down on her forehead" (58). Indeed, Marian becomes a composite Pre-Raphaelite figure resembling Rossetti's "dark Venuses" with an "Amazonian body (often with enlarged hands)" and Hunt's "exotic," "swarthy models" that were the targets of the reviewers' racial slurs in the 1850s (Casteras, 29, 31).

Certainly, Marian gazing outside a window is reminiscent of John Everett Millais's *Mariana* also capturing Mariana turned toward a window, anxiously waiting for her lover who never returns. The choice of the name itself, Marian, seems a deliberate allusion to that painting. But unlike Mariana who pines away for her lover and remains imprisoned, Marian's fierce independence from any romantic attachment enables her to become both Laura's and Hartright's rescuer. Initially unable to see beyond gender boundaries, Hartright eventually recognizes Marian's beauty, which is defined beyond conventional constructs: "She caught me by both hands—she pressed them with the strong, steady grasp of a man—her dark eyes glittered—her brown complexion flushed deep—*the force and energy of her face glowed and grew beautiful with the pure inner light of her generosity and her pity*" (148; emphasis added). But most importantly, though Hartright is ultimately responsible for Laura's reinstatement of identity, he realizes that his accomplishment would not have been possible without Marian's rescue of Laura from the asylum and her protection from Sir

Percival's and Count Fosco's schemes: "I was indebted to Marian's courage and Marian's love" (565).

Yet Walter's idealistic depiction of Laura involves mainstream art principles that dictate that "the most beautiful soul must have the most beautiful body" (Wornum, 271). Considering Laura's conventional role in the novel as the angel in the house, we can see why Collins's Reynolds-like portrait here is deliberate: "Lovely eyes in color, lovely eyes in form—large and tender and quietly thoughtful—but beautiful above all things in the clear truthfulness of look that dwells in their inmost depths, and shines through all their changes of expression with the light of a purer and better world" (75). Such idealization lacking in Hartright's response to Anne Catherick's sister, who strikingly resembles her, underscores the fact that gender is a relational construct. Set in the luxurious surroundings of the aristocratic Limmeridge House, Laura is seen as the ideal woman. Seemingly destitute, Anne Catherick, Laura's double, alone in the street in the dark lacks conventional beauty. Yet their figures become interchangeable by the machinations of Laura's husband, Sir Percival, and his ally Count Fosco. By transposing the illegitimate Anne Catherick with her respectable half-sister Laura Fairlie-Glyde, the outcast with the privileged, Collins further undermines contemporary gender ideology, demonstrating that women, as long as they are deprived of social and legal rights, run the same risks whether they be outcasts or honored members of the upper classes.

As the novel progresses, Collins demonstrates that Laura Fairlie is representative of an outdated ideal of femininity—a fair lie—vulnerable to abuse and exploitation. This is why Collins chooses Reynolds's principle of ideal beauty when drawing Laura's portrait. Such construct of femininity, Collins implies, is but a vanishing ideal. Laura's fate has been sealed in the past through her promise to her dying father to marry Sir Percival Glyde, representative of corrupt and degenerate aristocracy. It is precisely the qualities that society mostly values—truthfulness, honesty, innocence, and trust—that her husband thoroughly exploits, incarcerates her in an asylum as Anne Catherick, depriving of her identity in order to inherit her property.

Through his representations of Sir Percival and Walter Hartright, Collins also criticizes outdated constructs of masculinity. Sir Percival's name evokes the Arthurian eponymous knight distinguished for his innocence and chivalry, glorified by Tennyson. The cynical aspect of the allusion is underscored in a scene in the novel that takes place in Rome when Laura and Sir Percival visit the tomb of Cecilia Metella, a memorial of her husband's love. "Would you build such a tomb for *me*, Percival?" Laura asks. "If I do build you a tomb," Percival sarcastically responds, "it will be done with your own money" (281). The scene itself, husband and wife, leaning over a woman's tomb, evokes an early Rossetti watercolor with the rather laborious title, *How Sir Galahad, Sir Bors and Sir*

Percival Were Fed with the Sanc Grael; but Sir Percival's Sister Died by the Way, depicting Sir Percival with a woman leaning over a woman's body. Collins further draws the connection between King Arthur's knight and Sir Percival in his novel when the villagers, gathered around the burning church in which Percival perishes, question his identity: "'Who was he? A lord, they say.' 'No, not a lord. *Sir* Something; Sir means Knight'" (540). Rossetti planned this work for an Oxford mural, and it is entirely possible that Collins had seen it (Faxon, 109). Thus Collins evokes a chivalric construct of masculinity only to cynically deconstruct it.

Similarly Hartright's encounters with Anne Catherick evoke Pre-Raphaelite representations of rescue destabilized by isomorphic scenes in the novel. When Hartright, for instance, meets Anne Catherick in the cemetery where she is cleaning the cross on Mrs. Fairlie's tomb, the narrator emphasizes her posture, her kneeling by the cross several times (121, 126). At this point in his conversation with her, Hartright, in an attempt to garner information against Sir Percival, presents himself as Anne's rescuer: "'You remember me?' I said. 'We met very late, and I helped you to find the way to London'" (119). When she refuses to cooperate, Hartright informs her that he knows she is the author of the anonymous letter she sent Laura, incriminating Sir Percival. Anne's shocked reaction could very well describe details in Rossetti's painting *Found*: "She had been down on her knees for some little time past. . . . The first sentence of the words I had just addressed to her made her pause in her occupation, and turn slowly without rising from her knees, so as to face me. The second sentence literally petrified her" (126). *Found* depicts the plight of the fallen woman; in this case she kneels with her petrified face turned to the wall as her former fiancée tries to reclaim her. Even her response, "Leave me—I do not know you—go away" echoes Anne Catherick's reaction to Hartright's intrusion (Faxon, 64). But unlike the fiancée in *Found*, Hartright, instead of a rescuer, unwittingly becomes a pursuer, for Anne springs to her feet and disappears from his sight. Thus Collins once again undermines a stereotypical representation of masculinity by defusing the power that traditional gender relations ascribe to men.

The final rescue scene, when Hartright futilely attempts to rescue Sir Percival from the burning church, also underscores Hartright's helplessness and powerlessness:

I crouched on the roof as the smoke poured out above me with the flame. The gleams and flashes of the light showed me the servant's face staring vacantly under the wall . . . the scanty population of the village, haggard men and terrified women, clustered beyond the churchyard—all appearing and disappearing in the red of the dreadful glare, in the black of the choking smoke. And the man beneath my feet!—the man, suffocating, burning, dying so near us all, so utterly beyond our reach! (536)

The description of this scene evokes yet another painting, Millais's *Rescue,* that depicts a fireman rescuing two children from fire and delivering them to their anguished mother. The red glare of the fire permeates the entire painting, illuminating the faces of the subjects. Millais feverishly worked on this painting to meet the deadline for the exhibition, and it was with the help of Wilkie Collins's brother, Charles, who painted the fire-hose, that he was able to complete it in time (Parris, 132). Unlike Millais's painting that celebrates heroic masculinity and iconographically delineates gender power relations, Collins's isomorphic equivalent defuses masculine power.

These are but a few of the Pre-Raphaelite paintings Collins evokes and redraws in *The Woman in White*. Like his Pre-Raphaelite friends, Collins provoked his "audiences to reconsider what was decorous or "correct" in art as well as private life" (Casteras, 32). In a letter addressed to a friend on November 26, 1887, he explained that the central idea of *The Woman in White* was the destruction and the recovery of a woman's identity (Baker and Clarke, ii, 545). But, as the novel discloses, gender identity was also his central preoccupation, particularly gender defined beyond the stereotypical Victorian boundaries. As Susan Balee recently argues, "*The Woman in White* subverts Victorian sexual stereotypes (the angel in the house, the manly man) in order to promote new icons" (201). Some of these icons are carefully chosen images, isomorphic equivalents of Pre-Raphaelite paintings. Wilkie Collins's transformations of these paintings give us insights not only into his novel but also into literary history and nineteenth-century gender conflicts. If we are to fully appreciate Wilkie Collins's disguised criticism of his culture's ideology, we must then take into consideration the Pre-Raphaelite dimension of his narratives. Indeed, *The Woman in White* seems to orient us toward a new perspective on Wilkie Collins's challenge to gender ideology not only in this novel but in his other works as well.

WORKS CITED AND SELECTED WORKS FOR FURTHER READING

Amor, Anne Clark. *William Holman Hunt: The True Pre-Raphaelite.* London: Constable, 1989.

Andres, Sophia. "Gendered Incongruities in George Eliot's Pre-Raphaelite Paintings." *The Journal of Pre-Raphaelite Studies* 5 (1996): 45–60.

———. "Pre-Raphaelite Paintings and Jungian Images in Wilkie Collins's *The Woman in White.*" *Victorian Newsletter* 88 (1995): 26–31.

Auerbach, Nina. *Woman and the Demon.* Cambridge: Harvard UP, 1982.

Baker, William, and William M. Clarke. *The Letters of Wilkie Collins, 1838–1889.* 2 vols. New York: St. Martin's, 1999.

Balee, Susan. "Wilkie Collins and Surplus Women: The Case of Marian Halcombe." *Victorian Literature and Culture* 20 (1992): 197–215.

Barringer, Tim. *Reading the Pre-Raphaelites*. New Haven: Yale UP, 1998.

Bernstein, Stephen. "Reading in Blackwater Park: Gothicism, Narrative, and Ideology in *The Woman in White*." *Studies in the Novel* 25 (1993): 291–305.

Brittan, Arthur. *Masculinity and Power*. Oxford: Blackwell, 1989.

Bullen, J. B., ed. *The Sun Is God: Painting, Literature, and Mythology in the Nineteenth Century*. Oxford: Clarendon, 1989.

Byerly, Alison. "Art Works: Thomas Hardy and the Labor of Creation." In *Realism, Representation, and the Arts in Nineteenth-Century Literature*, pp. 149–183. Cambridge: Cambridge UP, 1997.

Casteras, Susan. "Pre-Raphaelite Challenges to Victorian Canons of Beauty." *The Huntington Library Quarterly* 55 (1992): 13–35.

Clarke, William M. *The Secret Life of Wilkie Collins*. Chicago: Ivan R. Dee, 1991.

Collins, Wilkie. "The Exhibition of the Royal Academy." *Bentley's Miscellany* 29 (1851): 617–27.

———. *The Woman in White*. New York: Penguin, 1985.

Dickens, Charles. "Old Lamps for New Ones." *Household Words* 1 (1850): 265–267.

Eagles, John. "The Fine Arts and the Public Taste in 1853." *Blackwood's Edinburgh Magazine* 74 (July 1853): 89–104.

Elam, Diane. "White Narratology: Gender and Reference in Wilkie Collins's *The Woman in White*." In *Virginal Sexuality and Textuality in Victorian Literature*, pp. 49–63. Ed. Diane Elam. Albany: State U of New York P, 1993.

Faxon, Alicia Craig. *Dante Gabriel Rossetti*. New York: Abbeville, 1989.

Flaxman, Rhoda L. *Victorian Word-Painting and Narrative: Toward the Blending of Genres*. Ann Arbor: U of Michigan P, 1987.

Fleming, Gordon H. *That Ne'er Shall Meet Again: Rossetti, Millais, Hunt*. London: Michael Joseph, 1971.

Frick, Patricia. "Wilkie Collins and John Ruskin." *Victorians Institute Journal* 13 (1985): 11–22.

Grundy, Jane. *Hardy and the Sister Arts*. New York: Barnes and Noble, 1979.

Harding, Ellen, ed. *Re-framing the Pre-Raphaelites: Historical and Theoretical Essays*. Brookfield, Vermont: Ashgate, 1996.

Hilton, Timothy. *The Pre-Raphaelites*. London: Thames and Hudson, 1970.

Hunt, William Holman. *Pre-Raphaelitism and the Pre-Raphaelite Brotherhood*. 2 vols. London: Macmillan, 1905.

Kestner, Joseph A. *Masculinities in Victorian Painting*. Brookfield, Vermont: Ashgate, 1995.

———. *Mythology and Misogyny: The Social Discourse of Nineteenth-Century British Classical-Subject Painting*. Madison: U of Wisconsin P, 1989.

Lambourne, Lionel. *Victorian Painting*. London: Phaidon, 1999.

Landow, George P. *Victorian Types, Victorian Shadows: Biblical Typology in Victorian Literature, Art, and Thought*. Boston: Routledge, 1980.

Langbauer, Laurie. "Women in White, Men in Feminism." *Yale Journal of Criticism* 2 (1989): 219–243.

Marsh, Jan. *Pre-Raphaelite Women: Images of Femininity in Pre-Raphaelite Art.* London: Artus Books, 1987.

Marsh, Jan, and Pamela Nunn. *Women Artists and the Pre-Raphaelite Movement.* London: Virago, 1989.

Masson, David. "Pre-Raphaelitism in Art and Literature." *British Quarterly Review* 16 (August 1852): 197–220.

Meisel, Martin. *Realizations: Narrative, Pictorial, and Theatrical Arts in Nineteenth-Century England.* Princeton: Princeton UP, 1983.

Mitchell, W.J.T. *Iconology: Image, Text, Ideology.* Chicago: U of Chicago P, 1986.

———. *Picture Theory: Essays on Verbal and Visual Representation.* Chicago: U of Chicago P, 1994.

Nicholes, Joseph. "Dorothea in the Moated Grange: Millais's *Mariana* and the *Middlemarch* Window Scenes." *Victorians Institute Journal* 20 (1992): 93–124.

Parris, Leslie, ed. *The Pre-Raphaelites.* Exhibition Catalogue. London: Tate, 1994.

Regan, Stephen, ed. *The Politics of Pleasure: Aesthetics and Cultural Theory.* Buckingham: Open UP, 1992.

Reynolds, Joshua. *Discourses on Art.* Ed. Stephen O Mitchell. Indianapolis: Bobbs-Merrill, 1965.

Rossetti, William Michael, ed. *Dante Gabriel Rossetti: His Family Letters, with a Memoir.* 2 vols. 1895. New York: AMS, 1970.

Roston, Murray. *Victorian Contexts: Literature and the Visual Arts.* New York: New York UP, 1996.

"Royal Academy." *Athenaeum* (1 June 1850): 590–591.

Schor, Hilary. "The Plot of the Beautiful Ignoramus: *Ruth* and the Tradition of the Fallen Woman." In *Sex and Death in Victorian Literature*, pp. 158–177. Ed. Regina Barreca. Bloomington: Indiana UP, 1990.

Starzyk, Lawrence J. *"If Mine Had Been the Painter's Hand": The Indeterminate in Nineteenth-Century Poetry and Painting.* New York: Peter Lang, 1999.

Stein, Richard L. "The Pre-Raphaelite Tennyson." *Victorian Studies* 24 (1981): 279–301.

Sussman, Herbert. *Victorian Masculinities: Manhood and Masculine Poetics in Early Victorian Literature and Art.* Cambridge: Cambridge UP, 1995.

Williams, M. Kellen. "'Traced and Captured by the Men in the Chaise': Pursuing Sexual Difference in Wilkie Collins's *The Woman in White*." *Journal of Narrative Technique* 28 (1998): 91–110.

Witemeyer, Hugh. *George Eliot and the Visual Arts.* New Haven: Yale UP, 1979.

Wood, Christopher. *The Pre-Raphaelites.* New York: Crescent Books, 1981.

Wornum, R. M. "Modern Moves in Art." *Art Journal* 12 (1850): 269–271.

V
Contemporary Critical Approaches to the Victorian Novel

Postcolonial Readings

❦

Roslyn Jolly

"The novels with which our fortunate generation is so abundantly supplied," wrote Alfred Lyall in 1894, "may be divided broadly into two classes, overlapping and interlaced with each other, yet on the whole distinguishable as separate species—the Novel of Adventure and the Novel of Manners" (532). The former class was masculine in orientation, more concerned with action than character, often set in "rough societies or remote places" (537); the second class was feminine, concerned with "analysis of character within the range of ordinary experience" and "the play of civilized emotion" in familiar settings (545). To Lyall, as to most contemporary and subsequent commentators, it was apparent that the domestic fiction of manners and morals dominated the Victorian novel. "Clearly English literature had organized itself into a system, of which the central seriousness was hostile to the material of adventure and therewith of empire and frontier" (Martin Green, 65). The critical process of canon-formation in the twentieth century confirmed this hierarchy of fictional genres, so that almost all canonical Victorian novels—including those brought into the canon by feminist criticism in the later twentieth century—belong to the class of domestic rather than adventure fiction. The task of postcolonial criticism with regard to the Victorian novel has been twofold: to retrieve from interpretative and pedagogical neglect the fiction of the overseas empire; and to expose and analyze the imperial subtext of the domestic novel, largely obscured by, but often crucial to, its concerns with individual identity and social relations at home.

In 1985 Gayatri Spivak wrote, "It should not be possible to read nine-teenth-century British literature without remembering that imperialism, un-derstood as England's social mission, was a crucial part of the cultural representation of England to the English" (243). Yet, as Edward Said has ob-served, although characters in canonical Victorian fiction often display a "nor-mal and secure connection with the empire," "it is only in recent years that these connections have taken on interpretative importance" (xvi). Said's *Cul-ture and Imperialism* (1993) analyzes the imaginative interdependence of do-mestic and colonial regimes within the nineteenth-century British imperium. Other critical studies from the 1990s also address the co-implication of domes-ticity and imperialism in nineteenth-century literature, showing that colonial relations were often closely linked to the domestic management of class and gender relations (Azim, Meyer, Perera). All these studies show that at the levels of plot, imagery, and the organization of social space, canonical nine-teenth-century fiction drew upon the realm of empire, as well as of home.

The most famous Victorian novel in which the colonial irrupts into the do-mestic is *Jane Eyre* (1847). In *Wide Sargasso Sea* (1966), Dominican-born Jean Rhys rewrote *Jane Eyre* by using the perspective of Bertha Mason to expose the gender and imperial politics of Rochester's first marriage, and to show how Brontë's novel demonizes the colonial woman in order to plot the English her-oine's path to personal happiness. Rhys's insights are elaborated by Spivak, who claims that Jane is "moved from the place of the counter-family to the fam-ily-in-law" through "the active ideology of imperialism" (247). She argues that the erotic relation between Jane and Rochester is legitimized, and Jane's place in family and social networks is therefore consolidated, through the sacrifice of Bertha's subjecthood. Furthermore, Rochester's release from the imperialist so-cial mission ("Go . . . and live again in Europe" [Brontë, 336]) is balanced by St. John Rivers's dedication to that mission ("he labours for his race" [Brontë, 477]), so that St. John's assumption of the burden of "soul making" through imperialist missionary work frees Jane and Rochester to remain in the domestic sphere of subject formation through "childbearing" (244). Brontë's deploy-ment of the colonial/imperial characters, Bertha and St. John, enables the hap-piness of the domestic characters, Jane and Rochester. But Susan Meyer finds the novel's relation to imperialism more "shifting and conflicted" (25) than this. Unlike Rhys and Spivak, who identify Bertha Mason as white, Meyer notes the colonial woman's racial indeterminacy as a "creole"; this ambiguous term, in nineteenth-century usage, suggested a range of modifications of white identity, from transculturation to miscegenation. Bertha's unstable position in the novel's imagination of imperialist power relations, Jane's complex figurative strategy of imaging both victims and agents of oppression as nonwhites, and the text's suggestions that British imperialists were doubly corrupted by their tyrannous power over and contaminating proximity to other races, all contribute to a deep anxiety about the colonial world from which Jane tries to distance herself but with which her story is intimately connected: "The critique of imperialism that the novel promises to make through its metaphorical yoking of forms of oppression finally collapses into uneasiness about the effects of empire on domestic social relations in England" (95). Similar uneasiness is evident in Wilkie Collins's *The Moonstone* (1868): In the words of the novel's first narrator, "Here was our quiet English house suddenly invaded by a devilish Indian Diamond—bringing after it a conspiracy of living rogues" (36). The domestic mysteries of sensation fiction are grounded here in imperial history; the security of the English country house is threatened by three Indians looking for a sacred jewel looted from their people at the storming of Seringapatam in 1799. In this multiperspectival narrative, anxiety about invasion by alien people with whom the English have become entangled through imperial conquest is set against a larger historical perspective in which the Indians are not criminals but victims seeking justice, for, as John Reed has argued, "imperial depredation is the true crime of *The Moonstone*" (289).

In stories of emigration and return, such as Dickens's *Great Expectations* (1861) and Braddon's *Lady Audley's Secret* (1862), key characters are temporarily exported to colonial space, then brought back to resume and complicate domestic relationships. For the emigrants, colonial experience has no intrinsic meaning; Abel Magwitch makes money in Australia not to transform himself but to fashion a transformed metropolitan life for another, and George Talboys interprets his Australian stay teleologically: "I toiled on steadily to the end; and in the end I conquered" (Braddon, 21). Fortunes made in Australia give both men imaginary control over relationships at home, but the return to England leads to disillusion. Meanwhile, metropolitan fantasies are also shattered. *Great Expectations* and *Lady Audley's Secret* are novels about the desire to become someone else, an illusion destroyed by the return of the Australian exiles to reclaim intimate relationships (quasi-filial in the case of Pip, marital in the case of Lady Audley) that are profoundly disturbing to the protagonists' achieved identities. Patrick Brantlinger writes that the figure of the returned convict in Dickens suggests "a sociological 'return of the repressed'" (120–121), but the trope may also be applied in its original, psychological usage to both novels where the colony, like the unconscious, stores and finally yields up the secrets of the conscious self.

In these novels, colonial wealth cannot solve domestic problems, which are aggravated by the emigrant's return. In many other Victorian novels, however, colonial emigration is a proposed solution to various social problems. Elizabeth Gaskell's *Mary Barton* (1848) ends with a colonial idyll, which allows the novel to sidestep the problems of English industrial society by relocating its central characters in Canadian pastoral. Dickens also uses colonial settings to imagine flexible social spaces that could accommodate characters for whom no place could be found in the domestic ideological structure. At the end of *David Copperfield* (1850), he sends Micawber, Peggotty, Emily, and a host of minor characters to Australia, which functions as a realm of second chances, a place where the improvident can find respectability, the poor can find economic opportunity, the fallen woman can find a home—in short, a place governed by an antipodean logic that allows futures to be imagined for characters with no imaginable futures in England. The redemptive qualities of the colonial space are limited, though: The prostitute, Martha, marries in Australia, but the seduced and rescued Emily can play only supplementary roles in domestic structures that do not fully integrate her. This may be compared with the even more punitive plotting of *Adam Bede* (1859), where the fallen woman and convicted infanticide Hetty Sorrel is transported to Australia; having served her sentence, she dies before returning to England, thus relieving George Eliot of the need to imagine her reintegration in domestic society. Another character who cannot be absorbed into the domestic sphere and therefore must be expelled to colonial space is St. John Rivers in *Jane Eyre*. Where Hetty Sorrel falls below the standard of domestic morality, St. John overreaches it; an unhomely character, he despises "domestic endearments and household joys" (Brontë, 416) and, as Jane realizes, "this parlor is not his sphere . . . the Himalayan ridge, or Caffre bush, even the plague-cursed Guinea Coast swamp, would suit him better. Well may he eschew the calm of domestic life. . . . It is in scenes of strife and danger—where courage is proved, and energy exercised, and fortitude tasked—that he will speak and move, the leader and superior" (419). Effectively, St. John is in the wrong novel, for he has no place in the ideological and generic structures of domesticity within which Jane's and Rochester's happiness is achieved. In 1847, when *Jane Eyre* was published, such scenes and settings as Jane imagines for St. John belonged almost exclusively to children's fiction.

Eighteenth-century juvenile literature had been a didactic literature of piety and improvement, designed to interpellate the child in systems of authority. Yet children enjoyed reading adult works of travel and adventure, such as *Robinson Crusoe*, and in the mid-nineteenth century this kind of reading was harnessed to such ideological projects as the task of Christian instruction and the popularization of England's imperial mission. In the 1840s, adventure fiction became one of the dominant forms of children's—especially boys'—literature, just as (with the rise of realism) the genre passed out of serious adult literature. Mid-century children's adventure fiction typically promoted informal colonization through trade and missionary influence rather than through annexation of territory and direct rule. Frederick Marryat's *Masterman Ready* (1841) proselytized a liberal, free-trade colonialism, and R. M. Ballantyne's *The Coral Island* (1858) was more forcefully interventionist but still imagined missionary-led rather than state-led forms of colonization. The stories of Marryat, Ballantyne, and W. G. Kingston promoted the export to the non-European world of Christianity, commerce, and civilization, and used colonial settings to present their boy-protagonists with challenges (surviving shipwrecks, fighting with "savages" or pirates) through which they would learn an Anglo-Saxon masculinity imagined as adventurous, chivalrous, and pious. Such lessons about gender and race could be applied by readers when they grew up and entered the real world of imperial action. The colonial adventure story was thus an ideal vehicle for both entertaining and instructing children, but it was not considered an appropriate form for adult fiction; at mid-century, Victorian children had adventure to themselves.

In the 1880s, two novels changed that. Robert Louis Stevenson's *Treasure Island* (1883) and Henry Rider Haggard's *King Solomon's Mines* (1885) were adventure stories that bridged the gap between children's and adult's fiction, revitalizing the romance form and challenging the dominance of the domestic novel. Both narratives take the form of a quest, using the device of a treasure map. Haggard doubled Stevenson's quest for buried treasure with a search for a lost brother: In the adventure-romance, masculine relationships (filial, fraternal, comradely) displace the traditionally central love-relations of the domestic novel—as Haggard's narrator Allan Quatermain says of *King Solomon's Mines*, "There is not a *petticoat* in the whole history" (9). "Danger is the matter with which this class of novel deals; fear, the passion with which it idly trifles," wrote Stevenson ("A Humble Remonstrance," 176), and *Treasure Island* revels in physical risk. *King Solomon's Mines* is still more violent; even the "timid" (7) Allan Quatermain finds that in battle he is seized with "a savage desire to kill and spare not" (224), bearing out Andrew Lang's claim that romance appeals to "the ancestral barbarism of our natures": "Not for nothing did Nature leave us all savages under our white skins; she has wrought thus that we might have many delights, among others 'the joy of adventurous living,' and of reading about adventurous living" (689). In *King Solomon's Mines,* romance operates as rejuvenative regression, with the English aristocrat Sir Henry Curtis and the African prince Umbopa/Ignosi paired as noble barbarian warriors. More subtly, *Treasure Island* in its prefatory poem also makes an appeal to readers' "ancient appetites" for the sensuous pleasures of physical action.

Postcolonial critics of Victorian fiction have linked the romance revival of the 1880s and 1890s to the conscious and unconscious energies of imperialism. Elaine Showalter sees the romance-adventure as both a vehicle of imperialist propaganda—"boys' fiction was the primer of empire. Little boys who read will become big boys who rule, and adventure fiction is thus important training" (80)—and a response to female dominance in domestic culture, as these "stories about men told to men" (82) imagined places of primitive freedom where men could "explore their secret selves" (81). Patrick Brantlinger finds within imperial romance the subgenre of "imperial gothic" in which atavism, including social and psychological regression and embrace of the occult, is a key topic (229–230), and he argues that in works of this kind "Africa, India, and the other dark places of the earth become a terrain upon which the political unconscious of imperialism maps its own desires, its own fantastic longitudes and latitudes" (246).

Haggard's fiction aligns easily with this theory. The fantasies of barbarian brotherhood in *King Solomon's Mines*, the story's sexual topography (see McClintock, 1–5), and its romantic allegorization of colonial mining wealth (Chrisman, 49–56) all work to reinforce masculine imperialist ideology. However, even in this exemplary imperial romance, not everything fits with British colonial policy; the African prince, Ignosi, finally promises to adopt British ideas of the rule of law but declares: "I will see no traders with their guns and rum. My people shall fight with the spear, and drink water, like their forefathers before them. I will have no praying-men to put fear of death into men's hearts, to stir them up against the king, and make a path for the white men who follow to run on" (306). Ignosi's astute analysis of how unofficial forms of colonialism often precede the official forms of invasion and conquest underwrites a power of resistance to the imperial will unavailable to an earlier generation of fictional natives, such as those of Ballantyne's *The Coral Island*, who are depicted gratefully receiving the benefits of missions and trade. *Treasure Island*, with its eighteenth-century setting and its lack of interaction with native people (the "others" are the pirates), is harder to see as a specifically imperial romance, although a contemporary pro-imperialist critic argued that it tapped "the race-instinct for adventure," was "one prolonged incitement to mental courage and energetic action," and was therefore part of the "revival of the national spirit" that stimulated the new imperialism in England from the mid-1880s (Mullin, 86–87).

Although Haggard and Stevenson were constantly paired by reviewers in the 1880s and are still linked by postcolonial critics, their paths as authors diverged after *Treasure Island* and *King Solomon's Mines*. In 1887 Haggard published the most notorious imperial romance, *She*, and remained a prolific producer of novels with colonial settings and imperial themes. As well as his imperial romances, with their occult elements, lost races, and hidden kingdoms—fantasies that mapped the dreamscape of imperialism—he wrote novels interpreting the historical reality of imperialist expansion, such as the annexation of the Transvaal (*The Witch's Head*, 1884). His fictions embodied the values of the "new" imperialism that had its roots in the Indian Mutiny (1857), was impelled by Disraeli's Crystal Palace speech (1872), and emerged fully with public outrage at the death of General Gordon (1885). Where the old imperialism had imagined itself as a beneficent partnership of planted settlements and newly evangelized nations under the umbrella of free trade, the "new" imperialism was aggressively expansionist and demanded a more militaristic ethos, which was celebrated in the work of the most successful boys' writer of the late Victorian period, G. A. Henty. Henty's novels such as *With Clive in India* (1896) and *With Kitchener in the Soudan* (1903) were plotted to bring the ordinary boy protagonist into personal, or at least historical, relation to the great military heroes of the empire; where for an earlier generation of readers moral and colonial authority was embodied in figures of peaceful influence such as the gentlemanly missionary of Ballantyne's *The Coral Island*, in Henty's stories, moral and military power merge in the professional soldiers of the British empire. Haggard's work is more polyvalent and expresses at times a deep ambivalence about the effects of imperial expansion on native cultures; yet he was a self-declared apologist for empire, as he wrote to *The Times* in 1920: "All my life, so far as opportunity was open to me, by means of fictional and other writings, and as a humble servant of the country, I have done my best to spread knowledge of the Empire and all it means or should mean to us" (Katz, 153).

Stevenson's career was very different. Through the 1880s he produced a series of historical and contemporary romances with largely European settings; *The Master of Ballantrae* (1889), with its exotic Indian character Secundra Dass, was his last work to imagine Britain's overseas empire from a metropolitan perspective. When Stevenson finished this novel, he was in the Pacific, experiencing non-European cultures and witnessing colonialism for himself; henceforth he produced no imperial romances and certainly no apologies for empire. "The Beach of Falesá" (1892) used the story of a mixed-race marriage and family to disrupt established oppositions on which Victorian theories of both romance and imperialism depended: romance and realism, adventure and domesticity, masculinity and femininity, white skin and brown (Jolly). In *The Ebb-Tide* (1894) he rewrote *Treasure Island* as an anti-imperialist anti-romance, challenging contemporary conceptions of "adventure" with its naturalistic manner, degraded white men, and refiguring of the gentleman-missionary as the brutal Attwater. Stevenson did not abandon romance altogether—the fables "The Bottle Imp" (1891), "The Isle of Voices" (1893), and "Something in It" (1895) use their Pacific settings and characters to question Western secular, sacred, and epistemological authority—but the keynote of his treatment of Pacific subjects was a shift towards realism. This meant that in the 1890s critics

increasingly linked Stevenson's name with that of another writer of realistic colonial stories, Rudyard Kipling. In a review of Stevenson's *The Wrecker* in 1892,
Lionel Johnson noted the global reach of both writers' work: "Mr. Stevenson
makes us interested in such things as a 'deep-water tramp, lime-juicing around
between big ports, Calcutta and Rangoon and 'Frisco and the Canton River':
Mr. Kipling in such experience as 'loafing from Lima to Auckland in a big, old,
condemned passenger-ship turned into a cargo-boat and owned by a sec-
ond-hand Italian firm'" (Maixner, 406). In 1894 Stephen Gwynn claimed that
the two novelists were performing similar work in imaginatively realizing, for
domestic readers, the conditions of modern life in the non-European world:
"What Mr. Kipling has done for British India, Mr. Stevenson is doing for the
Southern Seas. He is peopling a definite field in our imaginations" (778). But
the Pacific islands of which Stevenson wrote were not officially part of the British empire, and although his fictions attest to the quasi-colonizing effects of
British trading, missionary work, and consular interventions in the region, and
explore the workings of colonial power outside the imperial polity, his sub-
ject-matter seemed marginal to domestic readers, compared with Kipling's India, the "jewel in the crown" of the British empire.

Having published stories in India for some years, Kipling burst onto the
British literary scene in 1888 with *Plain Tales from the Hills*, a series of snap-
shots of colonial life that generated considerable critical and popular excitement. Kipling's stories came as "revelations" to reviewers (R. L. Green, 74, 139,
140, 206), who used the (sexualized) image of the lifted veil (51, 137) to convey their sense of the new imaginative possession he offered. As Francis Adams
wrote in 1891 of the early response to Kipling: "England has awakened at last
to the astonishing fact of her world-wide Empire. . . . The writer who can 'explain,' in a vivid and plausible manner, the social conditions of India, Australia,
Canada, and South Africa . . . is assured of at least a remarkable vogue" (R. L.
Green, 143). More cynically, Henry James observed that "India has not been
'done'" (R. L. Green, 162); Kipling was therefore able to stamp his name on
the subject, so that for many British people, India was Kipling's India.

Conservative critics saw the political significance of Kipling's work in representing India to the English. "The vastness of the empire, the imperial character of British rule in India, the unflinching courage and rectitude which
soldiers and civilians displayed in the silent discharge of their duties abroad
were first brought home to the man in the street by Kipling" (Mullin, 89). As
Gleeson White wrote of Kipling's achievement in 1892, "To have made India a
real place to dwellers in Great Britain is in itself an imperial conquest" (R. L.
Green, 169–170). The veteran novelist and critic, Mrs. Oliphant, suggested
that Kipling's achievements deserved official recognition: "What Mr. Rudyard
Kipling has done is an imperial work, and worthy of an imperial reward. The

Star of India!" (R. L. Green 142). Indeed, as an imperial author Kipling took on a quasi-official status, hailed by his supporters as a "laureate" of England and her empire. Yet as the 1890s progressed, his status as the "apostle of muscle and aggressive Imperialism" (R. L. Green, 232) was increasingly attacked by liberal critics, and eventually caused his fall from critical, if not popular, favor. Robert Buchanan's 1899 article, "The Voice of the Hooligan" (R. L. Green, 233–249), typified the growing hostility to Kipling's work on political grounds, which was intensified by his support for the Boer War and his association with Cecil Rhodes.

Contemporary readers, whether supporters or detractors of his work, tended to view "Kipling" as a monologic discourse of empire; more recently, critics have drawn attention to the multivocal and ideologically fractured nature of his fiction. Kipling's fiction was generically diverse, and although the slice-of-life realism of his tales of native and expatriate manners first captured the attention of English readers, postcolonial critics have explored the psychological and ideological anxieties impelling the frequent appearance of gothic elements in his stories of cross-cultural encounter. Zohreh Sullivan discusses a dialogic fiction, in which the voice of the "daytime Kipling, who staunchly defends Imperial values and institutions" (129) is subverted by other voices betraying a fascination with and terror of the various forms of regression, abjection and otherness embodied in "nighttime India" (133). This analysis of "colonial fear of boundary loss in India" (131) may be contrasted with Edward Said's reading of *Kim* (1901) as a celebration of "the pleasures of imperialism" in which British dominion is imagined as an expansive, inclusive field of freedom and belonging (132–162). Kipling also explored the psychological strain of coordinating imperial and domestic lives: In "Mrs. Bathurst" (1904), a cinematographic glimpse of "Home and Friends" precipitates an ordinary soldier's descent into the abyss; in the autobiographical "Baa Baa, Black Sheep" (1890) the psychological torments of a child of the empire sent "home" to the care of strangers are recounted with a grim realism that contrasts with Henry James's gothic treatment of the same subject in "The Turn of the Screw" (1898).

In the second half of the 1890s a new writer of empire emerged, the Polish-born Joseph Conrad. His early fictions drew upon his experiences with the British merchant navy in the Malay archipelago; a visit to the Belgian Congo inspired one of postcolonial literature's key reference points, *Heart of Darkness* (1899). Conrad experienced neither Kipling's spectacular rise nor his equally meteoric fall from critical favor; indeed, while appreciation of his fiction grew slowly, he came to be accorded the very highest position in the literary canon, but only at the price of effacing the historical conditions to which his work responded. The modernists adopted Conrad where they despised Kipling, precisely because it was possible to abstract and universalize his fiction, so that it could be seen as an exploration of the human condition rather than of nineteenth-century imperialism. In 1919 T. S. Eliot, explicitly contrasting Conrad with Kipling, wrote: "He is, for one thing, the antithesis of Empire (as well as of democracy); his characters are the denial of Empire, of Nation, of Race almost, they are fearfully alone with the Wilderness" (298). F. R. Leavis absorbed Conrad into the "great tradition" of English fiction only by setting aside all his Victorian fictions of empire. He disparaged *Almayer's Folly* (1895) and *An Outcast of the Islands* (1896) as "those excessively adjectival studies in the Malayan exotic of Conrad's earliest vein" (190), listed *Lord Jim* (1900) and *Heart of Darkness* as "minor works," and of *Youth* (1902) wrote that "the prose laureate of the British seaman does sometimes degenerate into a 'Kipling of the South Seas'" (189). Fortunately, from Leavis's point of view, this ignominious fate was avoided because he believed that Conrad's later fictions had a moral significance that transcended their specific situation in place and time.

A major impetus to rethinking Conrad's relation to imperialism (or even remembering that he had one) came from the Nigerian novelist Chinua Achebe, who attacked *Heart of Darkness* for racism in its representation of Africans. Although marred by its conflation of the views of narrator and author, Achebe's essay provoked new critical discussion of the politics of *Heart of Darkness*, part of a larger postcolonial movement to resituate Conrad's novels in Victorian systems of historical and geographical meaning. Overturning Eliot's pronouncement, late twentieth-century Conrad criticism has explored the ways in which his fiction not only reflected but helped to construct and contest ideas of empire, nation, and race. In the 1980s and 1990s, postcolonial critics analyzed the degrees of complicity and criticism, blindness and insight, with which Conrad's fictions address imperialist ideology (Parry, Said), the Victorian adventure tradition (White), and the modern notion of "the West" (GoGwilt).

At the turn of the twentieth century, when Conrad's formal experimentation led the Victorian novel of adventure into modernist territory, Henry James was similarly extending the boundaries of the Victorian novel of manners. James's *The Golden Bowl* (1904) pushed domestic fiction's concern with "the play of civilized emotion" (Lyall, 545) to new extremes of introspection and aestheticism. Yet this most metropolitan of novels opens with a startling acknowledgment that cultural forms like itself are underwritten by military, economic, and imaginative manifestations of imperial power. In "the City to which the world paid tribute," the Roman-born Amerigo sees tokens of wealth "tumbled together as if, in the insolence of the Empire, they had been the loot of far-off victories": "If it was a question of an *Imperium*, he said to himself, and if one wished, as a Roman, to recover a little the sense of that, the place to do so was on London Bridge, or even, on a fine afternoon in May, at Hyde Park Corner" (43). Amerigo is aware that the meanings of social space at the imperial center have been determined by acts of violence and conquest at the "far-off" margins. Perhaps James's position as a postcolonial American gave him the insight that the far-reaching power networks of the British empire provided the enabling material and discursive conditions for his stories of individual consciousness and personal relationship. And it is to the "question of an *Imperium*"—a total system of meanings and relations connecting metropolis and colony, the arts of peace and the arts of war, the emotions of individuals and the power of the state—that postcolonial criticism of the Victorian novel must also attend.

WORKS CITED AND SELECTED WORKS FOR FURTHER READING

Achebe, Chinua. "An Image of Africa: Racism in Conrad's *Heart of Darkness*." In *Hopes and Impediments: Selected Essays, 1965–1987*, pp. 1–13. London: Heinemann, 1988.

Azim, Firdous. *The Colonial Rise of the Novel*. London: Routledge, 1993.

Braddon, Mary Elizabeth. *Lady Audley's Secret*. 1862. Oxford: Oxford UP, 1987.

Brantlinger, Patrick. *Rule of Darkness: British Literature and Imperialism, 1830–1914*. Ithaca: Cornell UP, 1988.

Bratton, J. S. *The Impact of Victorian Children's Fiction*. London: Croom Helm, 1981.

Bristow, Joseph. *Empire Boys: Adventures in a Man's World*. London: HarperCollins, 1991.

Brontë, Charlotte. *Jane Eyre*. 1847. London: Penguin, 1985.

Chrisman, Laura. "The Imperial Unconscious? Representations of Imperial Discourse." *Critical Quarterly* 32 (1990): 38–58.

Collins, Wilkie. *The Moonstone*. 1868. Oxford: Oxford UP, 1982.

Dixon, Robert. *Writing the Colonial Adventure: Race, Gender and Nation in Anglo-Australian Popular Fiction, 1875–1914*. Cambridge: Cambridge UP, 1995.

Edmond, Rod. *Representing the South Pacific: Colonial Discourse from Cook to Gauguin*. Cambridge: Cambridge UP, 1997.

Eliot, T. S. "Kipling Redivivus." *Athenaeum*, 9 May 1919, 297–298.

GoGwilt, Christopher. *The Invention of the West: Joseph Conrad and the Double-Mapping of Europe and Empire*. Stanford: Stanford UP, 1995.

Green, Martin. *Dreams of Adventure, Deeds of Empire*. London: Routledge and Kegan Paul, 1980.

Green, Roger Lancelyn, ed. *Kipling: The Critical Heritage*. London: Routledge and Kegan Paul, 1971.

Gwynn, Stephen. "Mr. Robert Louis Stevenson: A Critical Study." *Fortnightly Review* 56 (1894): 776–792.

Haggard, H. Rider. *King Solomon's Mines*. 1885. Oxford: Oxford UP, 1989.

James, Henry. *The Golden Bowl*. 1904. London: Penguin, 1985.

Jolly, Roslyn, "Stevenson's 'Sterling Domestic Fiction': 'The Beach of Falesá.'" *Review of English Studies* 50 (1999): 463–482.

Katz, Wendy R. *Rider Haggard and the Fiction of Empire: A Critical Study of British Imperial Fiction*. Cambridge: Cambridge UP, 1987.

Lang, Andrew. "Realism and Romance." *Contemporary Review* 52 (1887): 683–693.

Leavis, F. R. *The Great Tradition: George Eliot, Henry James, Joseph Conrad*. London: Chatto and Windus, 1955.

[Lyall, Alfred C.] "Novels of Adventure and Manners." *Quarterly Review* 179 (1894): 530–552.

Maixner, Paul, ed. *Robert Louis Stevenson: The Critical Heritage*. London: Routledge and Kegan Paul, 1981.

McClintock, Anne. *Imperial Leather: Race, Gender and Sexuality in the Colonial Contest*. New York: Routledge, 1995.

Meyer, Susan. *Imperialism at Home: Race and Victorian Women's Fiction*. Ithaca: Cornell UP, 1996.

Mullin, E. H. "Stevenson, Kipling, and Anglo-Saxon Imperialism." *The Book Buyer* 18 (1899): 85–90.

Parry, Benita. *Conrad and Imperialism: Ideological Boundaries and Visionary Frontiers*. London: Macmillan, 1983.

Perera, Suvendrini. *Reaches of Empire: The English Novel from Edgeworth to Dickens*. New York: Columbia UP, 1991.

Reed, John R. "English Imperialism and the Unacknowledged Crime of *The Moonstone*." *Clio* 2 (1973): 281–290.

Richards, Jeffrey, ed. *Imperialism and Juvenile Literature*. Manchester: Manchester UP, 1989.

Richards, Thomas. *The Imperial Archive: Knowledge and the Fantasy of Empire*. London: Verso, 1993.

Said, Edward W. *Culture and Imperialism*. New York: Knopf, 1993.

Showalter, Elaine. *Sexual Anarchy: Gender and Culture at the Fin de Siècle*. London: Bloomsbury, 1990.

Spivak, Gayatri Chakravorty. "Three Women's Texts and a Critique of Imperialism." *Critical Inquiry* 12 (1985): 243–261.

Stevenson, Robert Louis. "A Humble Remonstrance." In *Memories and Portraits*, pp. 168–182. 1887. London: Chatto and Windus, 1925.

———. *Treasure Island*. 1883. Oxford: Oxford UP, 1985.

Sullivan, Zohreh. "Kipling in India." *English Literature and the Wider World*. Vol. 4. *The Ends of the Earth*, pp. 125–139. Ed. Simon Gatrell. London: Ashfield, 1992.

White, Andrea. *Joseph Conrad and the Adventure Tradition: Constructing and Deconstructing the Imperial Subject*. Cambridge: Cambridge UP, 1993.

Feminist Criticism and the Nineteenth-Century Novel

Eileen Gillooly

Regardless of its parentage (which is most frequently traceable on the paternal side to Marxist or psychoanalytic theory, and on the distaff, to frustration with the lot of women in a patriarchal world), late twentieth-century feminist literary criticism came into being largely through the midwifery of the nineteenth-century novel. At least three of the earliest and most influential books of feminist criticism—Ellen Moers's *Literary Women* (1977), Elaine Showalter's *A Literature of Their Own* (1977), and Sandra Gilbert and Susan Gubar's *The Madwoman in the Attic* (1979)—concentrate almost exclusively on the work of the best-known British women novelists of the century. All three discover in various ways that behind Jane Austen's perfectly balanced, understated prose and George Eliot's earnest, authoritative address lies the same sort of anger and anxiety about the cultural disabilities nineteenth-century women suffered as Charlotte Brontë more loudly—and Mary Shelley more eerily—expressed. One might even argue that despite the rapid spread of feminist critical interest to other times and places and the important work produced on the ancient to postmodern periods that has thereby resulted, the nineteenth century has remained particularly fertile in the generation of feminist literary scholarship. One reason for this fertility (besides, of course, the sheer quantity of literary material with which critics have had to work) is the frequent marriage in Victorian studies between interests in feminism and related forms of "otherness"—like race, class, ethnicity, and sexuality—just as these concepts were beginning to accrue their current meaning. Another reason is the expanded scope of feminist interest not only to include the work of male as well as female novelists but also, and perhaps most importantly, to consider how both masculinity and femininity were produced and coded in the nineteenth century and how such gender constructions participated in even larger transactions of cultural power (see, for example, Poovey). The effect of feminist criticism upon the study of the Victorian novel, indeed, has been so widespread and potent that there is scarcely a book on the period now written in which the issue of gender does not receive at least preemptive mention.

Yet "feminist" interest in the nineteenth-century novel was present long before feminist literary criticism entered the academy almost thirty years ago. To locate early manifestations of such interest requires that we broaden our definition of the concept somewhat beyond that currently in vogue, however. That is, although we might argue, along with Theresa Mangum, that the "woman question" was not articulated with any notable force or consistency until the emergence in the 1880s of the "New Woman" novel (whose female characters, transgressing "the boundaries of late-Victorian feminine proprieties" introduced "what we would now call feminist issues and feminist characters into the realm of popular fiction"), many (predominantly female) nineteenth-century literary critics nevertheless found in the work of a number of (predominantly female) nineteenth-century novelists a quiet preoccupation with what it meant to be a woman in a culture that politically, economically, and educationally privileged men (1). Margaret Oliphant is exemplary in this regard—indeed, the model of a Victorian feminist critic. For though undoubtedly Victorian—opposing female suffrage, disapproving of George Eliot's unmarried union with George Henry Lewes from "the point of view of morality" (though "nothing could have been better for literature than the union thus formed"), and looking with abhorrence upon the emancipative fantasies of the New Woman novelists ("imps of evil meaning, polluting and profaning the domestic hearth")—she nevertheless seizes every apparent opportunity to praise what she considers the peculiarly womanly virtues of her middle-class female subjects (their sympathy and "pretty humor," for example), cheering their achievements and reminding us of the unfavorable ideological conditions under which they wrote (*Victorian Age,* 463; *Women Novelists,* 50; *Literary History,* 221). Oliphant maintains, for example, that George Eliot, contrary to popular opinion at the time, did not transcend her gender to win a large, admiring male readership but rather did so, remarkably, by writing as a woman: "a woman who was to be kept out by no barriers, who sat down quietly from the beginning of her career in the highest place, and if she did not absolutely excel all her contemporaries in the revelation of the human mind and the creation of new human beings, at least was second to none" (*Victorian Age,* 461). Although she took exception to what she considered Charlotte Brontë's ruthless, undisguised portrayal of real acquaintances and to her implying that "jealousy, spite, and rancor" were "native" to women, Oliphant nonetheless applauds *Jane Eyre* for having "for the moment," at any rate, given "the *coup de grace*" to that "empty," irritating, and "primitive ideal" of "the heroine in white muslin, the immaculate creature who was of sweetness and goodness all compact" (*Women Novelists,* 17–18). She also credits Brontë with first giving voice not just to female sexual desire but to "the longing, the discontent, the universal contradiction . . . to which so many grey and undeveloped lives are condemned" in a society where—for "her class" at any rate—"everything depended upon" a woman's marrying (*Women Novelists,* 49). And Oliphant understood, with painful clarity, the longing and discontent of married life, too—as, she insisted, did Jane Austen, despite the latter's sanguine connubial closures: "Nobody knew better that Anne Elliot would have lived and made herself a worthy life anyhow, even if Captain Wentworth had not been faithful" (*Literary History,* 234).

More than simply a promoter of women's efforts to write fiction, Oliphant actually strives in her *Literary History of England* (1882) to articulate a "feminine" aesthetic that complements and contends with the dominant (masculine) nineteenth-century theory of literary value.

[A]s we mark the growth and rise of the new flood of noble poetry at the meeting-point of the two centuries, we should be negligent of one of the first duties of a historian if we did not note likewise the sudden development of purely feminine genius at the same great era. Female writers have never been wanting. . . . How it is that these have never risen to the higher notes and led the strain, as the feminine voice does in music, we need not inquire. . . . But the opening of an entirely feminine strain of the highest character and importance—a branch of art worthy and noble, and in no way inferior, yet quite characteristically feminine, must, we think, be dated here [in the novels of Maria Edgeworth, Jane Austen, and Susan Ferrier]. (206)

Almost a century later, in *A Literature of Their Own* (itself an attempt to discern an alternative literary tradition in the writing of nineteenth-century women), Elaine Showalter describes the earliest "phase" of that writing as "feminine," characterized by "*imitation* of the prevailing modes of the dominant tradition, and *internalization* of its standards of art and its views on social roles" (13). Yet for a number of prominent Victorian reviewers besides Oliphant, as we shall see momentarily, the most valuable feature of nineteenth-century female-authored fiction was neither its imitative success nor its internalization of cultural norms but rather its demonstration that traditionally feminine traits—such as delicacy, tenderness, sympathy, careful observation, and attention to the ordinary and familiar—could be the source of so much literary excellence. Rather, that is, than simply accept femininity as a culturally inferior construction, these early (proto)feminist critics reassess the traits associated with the stereotype in an effort to conceptualize an idea of literariness that might accommodate female novelists more comfortably than did the industry standard—that might recast masculine weaknesses (delicacy and tenderness, for example) as feminine strengths.

As a matter of common practice, Victorian reviewers considered both literary and behavioral traits to be gender-marked. Men, for example, were—or should be, at any rate—good at plot, imagination, originality, and humor; women, at finely delineating commonplace character, making it seem "solid, living and true" (Oliphant, *Victorian Age,* 468), and at rendering "life in its everyday aspect" (Kavanagh, *English Women,* ii, 235). Daring flights of imagination and corrosive irony were equally unladylike: Julia Kavanagh, otherwise a fan of Austen's, disapproved of her irony, "though gentle," considering it to be "a fault, and the parent of much coldness" (ii, 193). Women's humor, if one could call it that—and only a few (female) reviewers were confident that one could (humor having been so often "asserted" to be a trait in which "the whole female sex was deficient")—was gentle and good-natured, a "keen and smiling derision," an "amiable contempt" (*Victorian Age,* 461; *Literary History,* 232). Although individual authors might with impunity exhibit traits of the opposite gender, men were still widely expected to write like men (women like women), which accounts in large degree for contemporary reviewers' rather anxious speculation as to the gender of their authors (Casey, 154) and for the discomfort they felt when individuals transgressed gender boundaries too blatantly or on too many fronts. Trollope, for instance, excited severe gender uneasiness not only because his weaknesses—or lacks—were perceived to be feminine ones (lack of imagination, plot, irony, idealism, and originality) but because his "fertility" was as Henry James put it "gross, importunate" (quoted in Gillooly, 52). For critics like Oliphant and Anna Jameson, however, reporting the view from the traditionally under-represented feminine position was vastly more important than determining the gender of the viewer. Oliphant applauds the "effeminate art" of those novels written by men with a woman as "the subject and inspiration" (*Women Novelists,* 19), admiring Anthony Trollope most for his "delicately drawn" characters (*Victorian Age,* 473). And Jameson, like Oliphant (467), credits Shakespeare above all others of his gender with having understood that women were no less womanly—and were far more interesting—when displaying "wit, energy, intellect" (*Characteristics,* 40) than they were otherwise—knowledge that eluded most of her contemporary audience:

Many women have possessed many of those qualities which render Portia so delightful. She is in herself a piece of reality, in whose possible existence we have no doubt: and yet

a human being, in whom the moral, intellectual, and sentient faculties should be so ex-
quisitely blended and proportioned to each other—and these again, in harmony with
all outward aspects and influences—probably never existed; certainly could not now
exist. A woman constituted like Portia, and placed in this age and in the actual state of
society, would find society armed against her; and instead of being like Portia, a gra-
cious, happy, beloved, and loving creature, would be a victim, immolated in fire to that
multitudinous Moloch termed Opinion. (58)

Jameson's *Characteristics of Women: Moral, Poetical, and Historical,* first published in 1832 and reprinted frequently over the next fifty years, qualifies as the
earliest feminist critical study of Shakespeare (the book sometimes appeared
under the title *Shakespeare's Heroines* and was even more often referred to as
such). It undoubtedly influenced Mary Cowden Clarke, the author of the
three-volume study entitled *The Girlhood of Shakespeare's Heroines* (1850), and
her observations in "Shakespeare as the Girl's Friend" (1887) that the play-
wright's heroines present cautionary tales to the wise young female reader.
Desdemona and "her ill-fated career," for example, constitute for Clarke a
quasi-feminist "lesson on the danger of allowing gentleness to merge into timidity, and timidity into untruthfulness" (quoted in Lootens, 197). Jameson
herself seems to have been of two minds as to whether femininity was a natural
or cultural phenomenon: On the one hand, "a woman is no woman" without
"modesty, grace, and tenderness" (*Characteristics,* 154); on the other, she questions whether there really are "essential masculine and feminine virtues and
vices" or whether, "as civilization advances, those qualities which are now admired as essentially *feminine* will be considered as essentially *human,* such as
gentleness, purity, the more unselfish and spiritual sense of duty, and the dominance of the affections over the passions" (*Commonplace Book,* 78). In either
state of mind, however, Jameson consistently underscores the importance of
gender to interpretation, insisting that gender relations "as at present constituted" (in 1832) are "false" in themselves and "injurious" to women and that
they tend "to increase fearfully the sum of misery and error in both sexes"
(*Characteristics,* 5).

In her two-volume study of eighteenth- and nineteenth-century *English
Women of Letters* (1863), Julia Kavanagh similarly stresses not only the adverse
conditions under which women usually labor (their education has been "neglected, as a general rule," which results in "disadvantages which natural powers, though great, rarely conquer" [i, 253]) but also the "thoroughly feminine"
qualities of their writing: "that of teaching," for example, particularly evident
in Edgeworth, or of "minuteness" in Burney—minuteness being "one of the
modern characteristics of fiction," which, "if did not come in with women, is
assuredly the offspring of domestic life" (ii, 12; i, 144). Like Oliphant,
Kavanagh discerns in the novels she considers the beginnings of an alternative,

feminine literary tradition that softly voices the "longing of woman," the protest against a lifetime of "forced inaction" in which "the sufferer feels how
strong is the current of life in her own veins, and how capable she is of all the active duties of existence" (*Women Novelists*, 45–46). Anne Elliott pines for the
same reasons as Jane Eyre, Kavanagh notes, albeit in a more subdued manner:
"Here we see the first genuine picture of that silent torture of an unloved
woman, condemned to suffer thus because she is a woman and must not speak,
and which, many years later, was wakened into such passionate eloquence" by
Charlotte Brontë (ii, 231).

More than twenty-five years after the publication of *English Women of Letters*, the critical anthology entitled *Women Novelists of Queen Victoria's Reign: A
Book of Appreciations* (1897) appeared. Nine Victorian novelists, including
Oliphant, Eliza Lynn Linton, and Charlotte Yonge, discuss the merits and (despite the subtitle) the shortcomings of their subjects: fifteen other Victorian
novelists, then deceased. Although the quality of the writing appreciated varies
greatly (as the contributors acknowledge), the anthology itself demonstrates a
remarkable consistency as to the literary traits of the authors worth valuing.
Charm, delicacy, instructiveness, "deep and earnest feeling" and "intensely
real" characters are singled out for praise time and again, as are—with particular emphasis—humor and sympathy (112, 135). Thus, the fervid, reactionary
Eliza Lynn Linton, best remembered perhaps for her highly disapproving *Saturday Review* essay "The Girl of the Period" (1868), maintains that George
Eliot's "three most noteworthy qualities" are her "lofty principles, lifelike delin-
eation of character, and fine humor, both broad and subtle" (66). From the
other side of the political spectrum, Edna Lyall—author of *Doreen* (1894) and
Wayfaring Men (1897), advocating Irish Home Rule and divorce law reform,
respectively—dwells affectionately on Elizabeth Gaskell's "delightful humor"
and "wonderful sense of sympathy" (124, 119). Indeed, for all these Victorian
women critics, sympathy is the single most literarily significant of feminine attributes. Kavanagh goes so far as to doubt the existence of "a novel of any merit
written by a woman" that fails in sympathy (ii, 188). And Oliphant suggests
that the sense of "gentle fun" (229) these women particularly appreciate in each
other—their "genial humor, satirical yet kind" (238)—is achieved by adding a
liberal dose of sympathy to an otherwise caustic (masculine) perspective. The
result is "a laughing assault" full of "tender ridicule," rather than unforgiving
irony or punishing political satire *(Literary History*, 229, 238).

Eliot herself imagines sympathy, in a series of *Westminster Review* essays, as
the *sine qua non* of a truly feminine writing—an intriguing anticipation of
what French feminists like Hélène Cixous and Luce Irigaray were to theorize a
century later as *ecriture feminine*. "In art and literature," Eliot contends,
"woman has something specific to contribute." She has "sensations and emo-

tions—the maternal ones" that work a "wondrous chemistry of the affections and sentiments, which inevitably give rise to distinctive forms and combinations," and that produce "a precious speciality, lying quite apart from masculine aptitudes and experience" ("Woman in France," 53; "Silly Novels by Lady Novelists," 324). Elsewhere in these essays, she refers to such "maternal sensations" simply as "sympathetic emotions," though she continues to assume that women are in a unique position to employ them as "a mode of amplifying experience and extending our contact with our fellow-men beyond the bounds of our personal lot" ("German Wit," 67; "Natural History," 184). For Eliot, then, sympathy is not just a quintessentially feminine trait and an aesthetic virtue but the means by which her ethical goal—"wide feeling with all that is human"—is achieved (*The Mill on the Floss,* 498).

It is certainly more than coincidental that these first stirrings of feminist interest in the novel should have come into being at precisely the historical moment when the doctrine of "separate spheres" of action for men and women was most fully in vogue. Although values, behaviors, character traits, and duties have since the advent of recorded history in the West been subject to classification by gender (by what is, at any given moment, culturally considered to be descriptive of men or women—but not of both), the Victorians are justly famous for having indulged their impulse to gender rather more obsessively than most. One need only recall the taxonomies of Darwin and Freud to comprehend the sobering significance of gender distinctions to the Victorian production of knowledge. John Ruskin, in his lecture of 1865 entitled "Of Queens' Gardens," indeed, argues more confidently than did Freud that anatomy is destiny: that the biological state of being female endows one with the capacity "for sweet ordering, arrangement, and decision" and, more importantly, with the "power" for moral rule (59). Incumbent upon those so empowered is the duty to "heal, to redeem, to guide, and to guard," though Ruskin chastises the sex wholesale for its failure to do so (72):

There is not a war in the world . . . but you women are answerable for it. . . . There is no suffering, no injustice, no misery in the earth, but the guilt of it lies lastly with you. Men can bear the sight of it, but you should not be able to bear it. Men may tread it down without sympathy in their own struggle; but men are feeble in sympathy, and contracted in hope; it is you only who can feel the depths of pain; and conceive the way of its healing. Instead of trying to do this, you turn away from it. (75)

As the public sphere became increasingly identified as exclusively masculine space—an arena unfit for women, overrun by industrial giants and other Philistines, with their crass commercialism and questionable ethics—domesticity came more visibly under feminine management. From her privileged if confining position at the center of the household, the Angel in the House (otherwise known as the wife and mother) was expected to radiate sympathy and moral influence throughout the domestic sphere—and sometimes, as Ruskin would have it, beyond. And as the spheres themselves were gendered, so too were the philosophies that governed them. J. B. Schneewind reminds us that the arguments of Intuitionists like James Martineau and William Whewall (who held that "the good" was self-evident and intuited by the mature, reflective individual) vied energetically for attention throughout most of the nineteenth century with those of Utilitarians like John Stuart Mill and Henry Sidgwick (who held that "the good" was what increased the happiness of the many). In the end, Utilitarianism suited the market-driven economy better, encouraging, at least in Mill, enlightened self-interest and protection of individual liberties along with the promotion of the least pain for the greatest number. Conversely, Intuitionism—which considered the difficulty of individual moral action to lie in a weak will or a failure of sympathy rather than in the unpredictability of its results—seemed more at home ultimately in feminine areas of endeavor: like mothering and novel writing, where personal rather than contractual relationships, emotional rather than economic investments, were of paramount interest. Although now almost completely forgotten by students of Victorian culture as a rival philosophy to Utilitarianism, Intuitionism had a much greater impact upon novelists of the day who, like Gaskell and Eliot, were dedicated to presenting moral dilemmas in the complex social circumstances in which they occurred. A sense of "wide fellow feeling with all that is human," Eliot insisted, serves better than even the most broadly construed self-interest in gauging the moral worth of one's actions. According to Intuitionism, "calculations and rules come in only as personal relations resting on sympathetic understanding break down" (Schneewind, 35).

If, indeed, as the Intuitionists claimed, morality required the exercise of sympathy, then what more likely candidate for the center of moral and narrative consciousness than a woman, whose most cherished generic virtue was her capacity to sympathize? Oliphant notes that a "new reign of fiction" began the day that the "individual womanhood" of Elizabeth Bennet became the focus of readerly interest (*Literary History*, 249). Unlike male characters, whose activities in the marketplace might put their moral integrity at risk, female characters were ideally situated (in the home) to dramatize the moral questions raised by their novels, to portray the everyday decisions of ordinary people within their highly particularized set of social and domestic relations. Not the epic hero, but the domestic heroine was suddenly in popular demand. To paraphrase Eliot's famous observation in the "Prelude" to *Middlemarch*, the "many Theresas" of the world born to a "life of mistakes" of varying severity, alternating between "a vague ideal and the common yearning of women," had at last come into their own (xiii).

And once the heroine was discovered to be of abiding interest, so too were the peculiarly feminine difficulties of her moral negotiations. Social problem novels like Gaskell's *Ruth*, which addresses the plight of the unwed mother, constituted an obvious site of nineteenth-century feminist concern, as did Charlotte Brontë's novels of gender-marked discontent. But so also, in its odd way, did *Cranford*—an amusing, if almost plotless, tale of a village governed by its middle-aged spinsters and widows. Eliot's novels from *Scenes of Clerical Life* to *Daniel Deronda* abound in moral predicaments commonly faced by women: from whether to leave an alcoholic and abusive husband ("Janet's Remembrance" in *Scenes*), or to betray friendship for sexual passion (*The Mill on the Floss*), to how best to bear the hopelessness and torment of a failed marriage in an age without divorce (*Middlemarch*, *Romola*, and *Daniel Deronda*). Nor are such problems and perspectives confined to fiction written by women. Dozens of novels—like Charles Dickens's *Dombey and Son*; Thomas Hardy's *Tess of the d'Urbervilles*; George Meredith's *Diana of the Crossways*; George Gissing's *The Odd Women*; and any number from Anthony Trollope's prodigious output—have convincingly imagined the disabilities and frustrations their heroines endure as a cultural consequence of their gender.

In the latter half of the nineteenth century, the political and social conditions of Victorian women's lives began to change dramatically. Landmark legislation such as the Married Women's Property Acts of 1870 and 1882 (which granted married women the right to their own property) and the series of Matrimonial Causes and Child Custody Acts (which, by degrees, extended the rights of women to divorce and to petition for custody of their legitimate children, respectively) signified that women were slowly being recognized as independent legal entities, rights-bearing British subjects separate from their husbands or fathers. Complete recognition was long in coming (one might argue that, culturally speaking, it has still not quite arrived); but agitation for rights theretofore restricted to men—the right to university education and professional training, the right to a full range of paid employment, the right to vote—noticeably increased in both volume and frequency in the final two decades of the nineteenth century.

The "New Woman" novel added to the clamor. Coined by Sarah Grand—author of *The Heavenly Twins* (1892) and *The Beth Book* (1897), two of the most famous examples of the genre—the term covers a wide sweep of novels published largely in the 1880s and 1890s that address, through one of its main characters, new ideas about female political and personal independence. Although the issues the New Woman novel raises may be broadly construed as feminist, not all the authors advocate reform: Grant Allen, for example, in *The Woman Who Did* (1895), about a woman who rejects marriage, warns against deviating from existing moral codes. And although Hardy's sympathies were undoubtedly more feminist than Allen's, Sue Bridehead in *Jude the Obscure* (1895) nonetheless presents something of a cautionary tale to the would-be New Woman. Others—declared feminists like Grand, Olive Schreiner (*Story of an African Farm* [1883]), and Mona Caird (*Daughters of Danaus* [1894])—search for an alternative to the marriage plot, struggling to imagine a heroine's life freed from the stranglehold of domesticity. If, as Oliphant claimed, "Charlotte Brontë was the first to overthrow" the "superstition" that women were naturally passionless, then these New Woman novelists were the first to "debunk conventional femininity" in concert, by "redirecting" "female desire" away "from romance to education, occupation, and community" (*Women Novelists,* 24; Mangum, 9).

Oliphant and her contemporaries—the earliest generation of nineteenth-century critics to address "the woman question"—objected strenuously to the New Woman novelists (Linton referred to them as "the mud-born ephemeridae of literature" [*Women Novelists,* 64]). Oliphant considered them, perhaps unfairly, to be single-mindedly preoccupied with "'Passion' (as if there was but one passion in the world!)" and perceived their political attack on the institution of marriage as fatally threatening not only to home life but to the personal happiness of women as well (*Victorian Age,* 500). Women were no Angels, she understood, but their greater demonstrated willingness to sympathize, to place duties above rights, made them—or at least made the heroines they respected—models of conduct for both genders in a culture ideologically invested in advancing civilization. Yet, despite her quarrel with New Woman solutions to gender inequities, Oliphant readily acknowledged that the points of inequity they raised were essentially the same as those to which earlier writers like Brontë more decorously called attention:

We have traveled through many years and many gradations of sentiment: and we have arrived at a standard of opinion by which the "sex-problem" has become the most interesting of questions, the chief occupation of fiction, to be discussed by men and women alike with growing warmth and openness, the immodest and the indelicate being equally and scornfully dismissed as barriers with which Art has nothing to do. My impression is that Charlotte Brontë was the pioneer and founder of this school of romance, though it would probably have shocked and distressed her as much as any other woman of her age. (*Women Novelists,* 26–27)

Like Oliphant, a number of mostly female critics of the last twenty-five years have been intent upon distinguishing the gender concerns of their subjects. Indeed, a casual search of Library of Congress holdings under the rubric "women and literature—Great Britain—history—nineteenth century" reveals more than 170 books published on the topic since 1975. Although we now commonly acknowledge a nineteenth-century literary tradition characterized by such concerns, we have almost completely overlooked the efforts of Oliphant, Jameson, Kavanagh, and their kind in conceptualizing it. For despite what we might consider their antifeminist stance on particular issues, these critics pioneered the enterprise of feminist criticism as we know it today, discerning among their contemporaries a common preoccupation with what it meant to be classified as a woman in Victorian culture—and still, to a surprising extent, in ours.

WORKS CITED AND SELECTED WORKS FOR FURTHER READING

Casey, Ellen Miller. "Edging Women Out?: Reviews of Women Novelists in the *Athenaeum*, 1860–1900." *Victorian Studies* (Winter 1996): 151–171.

Cixous, Hélène. "The Laugh of the Medusa." In *New French Feminisms: An Anthology*, pp. 245–263. Ed. Elaine Marks and Isabelle de Courtivron. New York: Schocken, 1980.

Easley, Alexis. "Gendered Observations: Harriet Martineau and the Woman Question." In *Victorian Woman Writers and the Woman Question*, pp. 80–98. Ed. Nicola Diane Thompson. Cambridge: Cambridge UP, 1999.

Eliot, George. "German Wit: Heinrich Heine." In *Essays and Leaves from a Notebook*, pp. 64–114. New York: Harper, 1884.

———. *Middlemarch*. 1872. New York: Norton, 1977.

———. *The Mill on the Floss*. 1860. Oxford: Oxford UP, 1980.

———. "The Natural History of German Life: Riehl." In *Essays and Leaves from a Notebook*, pp. 170–225. New York: Harper, 1884.

———. "Silly Novels by Lady Novelists." In *Essays of George Eliot*, pp. 300–324. Ed. Thomas Pinney. London: Routledge and Kegan Paul, 1963.

———. "Woman in France." In *Essays of George Eliot*, pp. 52–81. Ed. Thomas Pinney. London: Routledge and Kegan Paul, 1963.

Ferris, Ina. "From Trope to Code: The Novel and the Rhetoric of Gender in Nineteenth-Century Critical Discourse." In *Rewriting the Victorians: Theory, History, and the Politics of Gender*, pp. 18–30. Ed. Linda M. Shires. New York: Routledge, 1992.

Fulmer, Constance M. "Edith Simcox: Feminist Critic and Reformer." *Victorian Periodicals Review* 31.1 (Spring 1998): 105–221.

Gilbert, Sandra M., and Susan Gubar. *The Madwoman in the Attic: The Woman Writer and the Nineteenth-Century Imagination*. New Haven: Yale UP, 1979.

Gillooly, Eileen. *Smile of Discontent: Humor, Gender, and Nineteenth-Century British Fiction*. Chicago: U of Chicago P, 1999.

Irigaray, Luce. *Speculum of the Other Woman*. Trans. Gillian C. Gill. Ithaca: Cornell UP, 1985.

Jameson, Anna. *Characteristics of Woman, Moral, Poetical, and Historical* [*Shakspeare's Heroines*]. 1889. New York: AMS, 1967.

———. *A Commonplace Book of Thoughts, Memories, and Fancies, Original and Selected.* New York: Appleton, 1856.

Jay, Elisabeth. *Mrs. Oliphant, "A Fiction to Herself": A Literary Life.* Oxford: Clarendon, 1995.

Johnston, Judith. *Anna Jameson: Victorian, Feminist, Woman of Letters.* Aldershot: Scolar, 1997.

Kavanagh, Julia. *English Women of Letters: Biographical Sketches.* 2 vols. London: Hurst and Blackett, 1863.

Lootens, Tricia. *Lost Saints: Silence, Gender, and Victorian Literary Canonization.* Charlottesville: UP of Virginia, 1996.

Mangum, Theresa. *Married, Middlebrow, and Militant: Sarah Grand the New Woman Novel.* Ann Arbor: U of Michigan P, 1998.

Moers, Ellen. *Literary Women.* Garden City: Doubleday, 1977.

Oliphant, Margaret. *The Literary History of England in the End of the Eighteenth and Beginning of the Nineteenth Century.* Vol. 3. London: Macmillan, 1882.

———. *The Victorian Age of English Literature.* Vol. 2. New York: Tait, 1892.

Poovey, Mary. *Making a Social Body: British Cultural Formation, 1830–1864.* Chicago: U of Chicago P, 1995.

———. *Uneven Developments: The Ideological Work of Gender in Mid-Victorian England.* Chicago: U of Chicago P, 1988.

Robinson, Solveig C. "'Amazed at Our Success': The Langham Place Editors and the Emergence of a Feminist Critical Tradition." *Victorian Periodicals Review* 29.2 (1996 Summer): 159–172.

Ruskin, John. "Of Queens' Gardens." In *Sesame and Lilies, The Two Paths and The King of the Golden River.* 1865. London: Dent, 1960.

Schneewind, J. B. "Moral Problems and Moral Philosophy in the Victorian Period." *Victorian Studies* (September 1965): 29–46.

Showalter, Elaine. *A Literature of Their Own: British Women Novelists from Brontë to Lessing.* Princeton: Princeton UP, 1977.

Sutton-Rampseck, Beth. "Shot Out of the Canon: Mary Ward and the Claims of Conflicting Feminisms." In *Victorian Women Writers and the Woman Question.* Ed. Nicola Diane Thompson. Cambridge: Cambridge UP, 1999.

Thompson, Nicola Diane. *Reviewing Sex: Gender and the Reception of Victorian Novels.* New York: New York UP, 1995.

Tillotson, Geoffrey. *Criticism and the Nineteenth Century.* London: Athlone, 1951.

Women Novelists of Queen Victoria's Reign: A Book of Appreciations. By Mrs. Oliphant, Mrs. Lynn Linton, Mrs. Alexander, Mrs. Macquoid, Mrs. Parr, Mrs. Marshall, Charlotte M. Yonge, Adeline Sergeant, and Edna Lyall. 1897. London: Folcroft, 1969.

Otherness and Identity in the Victorian Novel

Michael Galchinsky

Much recent journalism to the contrary, migrations, diasporas, and even glob-alization are not phenomena originating in the postcolonial, postindustrial, post–Cold War period of our own day (Crossette). Population transfer, at least, was already a prominent feature of the post-Enlightenment, post–French Rev-olution era of national consolidation and imperial expansion that we call the Victorian period. The increased mobility of populations and their concentra-tion in cities were distinctive signs of this period, driven by the Industrial Revo-lution's vast production of wealth, by the slave trade and colonial expansion, and by new technologies like the train, the canal, and the steamship. Such mo-bility inevitably compelled the Victorians to experience greater regional, reli-gious, racial, and national diversity.

Yet until relatively recently literary critics paid little attention to the way Victorians represented such experiences. To be sure, since the 1960s, Victorian critics have been aware that the Victorian writers and readers did not comprise a unified body. Histories like E. P. Thompson's *The Making of the English Working Class* (1966) helped to nuance critics' awareness of Victorian class di-visions. Steven Marcus's *The Other Victorians* (1966) helped to dispel our sense that Victorians were unified by sexual prudishness. During the 1970s, Gilbert and Gubar's *Madwoman in the Attic* (1979) and other early feminist texts helped inspire the production of an increasingly sophisticated analysis in the way critics understood Victorian women writers and the period's representation of gender.

Historically, the equally complex representations of racial, ethnic, religious, and regional Others took somewhat longer to come in for critical consideration. "Others" were members of marginalized groups whose collective identity was perceived to differ in fundamental ways from the Victorian mainstream. Majority writers often perceived a group's Otherness as an ineradicable barrier to its acceptance into the full rights and privileges of citizenship. This perceptual barrier reinforced and was reinforced by immigration policies, economic and political restrictions, newspaper articles, social scientific reports, Darwinian racial rankings, and, not least, the representations of Others in novels, poems, and plays. These texts gave voice to the suspicion (growing, at various heated moments, into a widespread conviction) that members of nonwhite, non–Protestant, non–English-speaking groups were unalterably alien, unassimilable, and inferior. The texts frequently posed questions about how England's marginal groups might be brought into relation with the emerging nation-state and empire. Victorians debated the social and political status of Jews, of freed slaves, of immigrants from the colonies, of migrants from annexed domestic regions, and of nonconforming Christian groups.

The earliest critical consideration of these "Other Victorians," from the first two-thirds of the twentieth century, tended to treat such representations as "stereotypes," collections of exaggerated or false traits ascribed to a group and assumed to remain fixed through time (cf. Modder). For example, a critic might consider the question of whether Dickens's Jewish criminal, Fagin, was a forerunner to the anti-Semitic types propounded by the Nazis (cf. Stone). Though this kind of approach paid close attention to the elements of a given representation, it lacked attention to the particular historical and biographical contexts in which the representation emerged. More recently critics interested in cultural history have tried to demonstrate that such representations were for the most part not fixed stereotypes but were constantly shifting in form and meaning throughout the period. Indeed, the peculiar and sometimes horrifying power of images of the Other resided in their very mutability, in the way they could become transformed to express diverse, even opposed, cultural anxieties. The earliest of these critical considerations was probably Said's controversial *Orientalism* (1978), a work that aimed to explain representations of "the Oriental" using an early version of what has come to be known since the late 1980s as a postcolonial approach. His *Culture and Imperialism* (1993) made this methodology even more explicit. The two works have inspired a cottage industry of studies of the literatures of colonialism and imperialism.

A more hidden and therefore more troubling lack in the earlier criticism was its neglect of literary texts published by Victorian writers of Indian, African,

Scottish, or Jewish descent. Critics paid almost exclusive attention to the appearances of the Other in the "great" texts, which (incidentally) had been written by those whose own race, religion, ethnicity, or region was hegemonic. Yet by attending only to texts in the received canon, such criticism neglected what could be called Victorian counterliteratures, for all of the marginalized groups produced literatures of their own that engaged in provocative and productive encounters with the hegemonic literature. Since the late 1980s, critics of colonial, Anglo-Jewish, and Irish and Scottish literatures have begun to reintroduce readers to writing by those deemed Other, in order to provide what Edward Said calls a "contrapuntal" reading of the period's literary history (Said, *Culture*, 18). Such a reading, these critics argue, not only brings to light previously forgotten or neglected writing, it also gives a fuller, more accurate account of the "uneven development" of Victorian literary history (Poovey).

Victorians had numerous ways—literary and otherwise—of articulating their ideology concerning English national and British imperial identity in light of their experiences of diversity. Two of the most important nonliterary venues were scientific tracts and polemics. Victorian scientists developed a number of distinct "sciences of race"—craniometry, phrenology, eugenics, statistics, anthropology, and social Darwinism, just to name a few—devoted to demarcating and prioritizing all the imagined shades of color the scientists called races. In the realm of politics, polemicists engaged in pamphlet wars over the question of Jews' and Catholics' emancipation, and Indian education in the 1830s and 1840s. For example, the liberal Member of Parliament and historian Thomas Babington Macaulay gave both a "Speech on Jewish Civil Disabilities" (1831) and later, as President of the Committee on Public Instruction in India, a "Minute on Indian Education" (1835). The question of Africans' rights was addressed as early as Edmund Burke's *Sketch of a Negro Code* (1780) and, although still a burning issue a century later, was treated quite differently in Thomas Carlyle's essay on liberal democracy, "Shooting Niagara: And After?" (1867).

Literary representations of the Other appeared in every genre, but especially in the novel, which more than any other literary form of the period attempted to analyze and represent Victorian sociopolitical stratification. Critics have usefully examined the novelistic representations of each form of Otherness, considering, for instance, representations of the "Oriental," the "African," the "Indian," the "Irish," the "Jew," or the "Scot." Recently, by relating the characteristics of these representations to one another, critics have begun to develop what might be called "a unified field theory" of Otherness, describing how each such representation functions in a larger Victorian project: the project of disciplining the conceptual borders of the nation-state. At the same time, such criticism has sought to avoid the assumption that, for the Victorians, all forms of

Otherness could be reduced to a fixed collection of stereotyped traits. As we will see, while Victorians attempted to relate different kinds of Otherness to one another, they made both great and subtle distinctions between different marginalized groups.

The literary representation of Jews and Jewishness can serve as an excellent starting point, both a test case and yardstick for comparisons, in our attempt to understand Victorian discourses of Otherness. Throughout the period, representations of Jews appeared in novels pervasively and disproportionately. Jews and the idea of Jewishness made regular appearances in all areas of cultural production, but they were particularly noticeable in the novel. Every major Victorian novelist, and most minor novelists, included Jewish figures in some of their fictions. The sheer quantity of Jewish representations might strike a historian as surprising, given that, demographically speaking, Jews were not the single, or even the central, figures of Victorian marginalization: The effort spent maintaining perceived British interests in India or Ireland far outweighed what was put toward the English encounter with its small Jewish population. Yet Jews figured more prominently in literary and social-scientific literature than did Indians or Irish, at least until the latter part of the century. The disproportionate prominence of Jewish figures was due to their malleability. Victorian writers were concerned less with actual Jews than with what Jews and Jewishness could be made to represent—which was almost anything.

At various times, a Jewish figure was represented as the type of the liberal, the capitalist, the criminal, the parvenu, the socialist, the revolutionary, the degenerate, the conspirator, the immigrant, the monarchist, the repressor of natural drives, or the journalist. Moreover, the term "Jewish" was available for a variety of readings due to Jews' "category indeterminacy"—their capacity to be understood in diasporic, religious, national, or racial terms. By projecting Victorian social tensions onto Jewish figures, a writer could gain the distance necessary to explore and exploit these tensions. That is to say, when gentile Victorian writers wrote about Jews, they were in fact almost always writing about themselves. What were at stake in such depictions were the nature and limits of English national identity. Victorian writers abstracted Jewishness and figuratively identified it with almost every aspect of the nation.

Although such abstraction and identification routinely occurred in novels, the most famous example probably comes from *Culture and Anarchy* (1869), Matthew Arnold's seminal work of social criticism. Arnold defined "Hebraism" as a type of energy, specifically an "energy driving at practice, this paramount sense of the obligation of duty, self-control, and work" (Arnold, 129). Arnold sees this abstract characteristic, Hebraism, as one of two rival energies (the other being Hellenism) struggling for predominance within the English national character. Thus, Arnold's Hebraism has nothing to do with Jews. Rather, Arnold uses Hebraism to define an aspect of the essence of Englishness.

As in Arnold's case, what Jews or Jewishness might mean in any given instance seemed to depend largely on whom a given writer compared them to. This is because national and marginal identities alike are both relational: Their constructed meaning depends in large part on the definitions they gain through juxtaposition. When a writer compared the legal standing of Jews in England to that of Africans in slavery, for example, the figure of the Jew helped the writer reflect on the racial limits of citizenship. When a writer compared the Jewish "colony" in London's East End to native enclaves in British India, the writer reflected on the contrasts between the administration of Empire at home and abroad. For this reason, the Victorians' perception of "Jewishness" was constantly shifting. Like every other form of Otherness, Jewishness was not (despite the claims of German Romantic philosophers like Herder and his English counterparts, Scott and Arnold) an essence, a collection of fixed traits or stereotypes that remained stable throughout the period; rather, Jewishness was an overdetermined collection of Victorian projections, fears, hopes, and ideologies, its value in any local instance depending upon the writer's historical context, ideological predispositions, and comparative framework.

From the standpoint of literary history, understanding a discourse of Otherness like that of Jewishness can help us trace the formation and historical evolution of the novel's various subgenres. The representation of Others puts pressure not only on a writer's political ideology but even on the very form in which the writer writes. As discussed later, Jewish characters not only figure prominently in such novelistic subgenres as the historical romance, domestic fiction, the realist novel, and the Condition of England novel, their presence frequently compelled writers to transform their genres into something new. Moreover, these subgenres were themselves transformed by those Victorian novelists who claimed Jewishness as an important part of their identity. Anglo-Jewish writers engaged in a fascinating and complex encounter with the prevailing representations, both assimilating and resisting the ideologies and generic forms produced by the majority culture. Once we understand how these dynamics of assimilation and resistance work for British Jewish writers, we can begin to compare them to analogous (though in many ways dissimilar) dynamics present in the work of writers from other marginalized groups.

By paying close attention to the way the discourse of Jewishness and other forms of Otherness were interrelated, then, we will be able to raise questions that are at the heart of Victorian studies: To what extent did aesthetic representations, especially in novels, take part in contemporary debates regarding the boundaries of English and British identity? To what extent did political, social, economic, legal, and ideological boundaries constrain the development of literary genres? And to what extent were members of groups classed as Other able to develop "literatures of their own?"

Taking the discourse of Jewishness as my test case, then, I wish first to demonstrate that it cannot fully be comprehended apart from discourses on Africans, Indians, Muslims, and Scots. For that reason, I now turn to examine writers who brought their texts to bear on several different Others. If identity is relational, then Victorians' shifting concept of Jewish identity can best be perceived if we adopt a comparative mode of analysis. Many novelists represented both colonials and Jews. For example, in *Vanity Fair* Thackeray examined the limits of Britishness primarily through two figures: Jos Sedley, an English son gone to make his fortune in India, and Miss Swartz, an heiress who seems be the progeny of a Jewish entrepreneur and a West Indian slave. In both cases, Thackeray hints that English wealth and pretension have their source in exploitation and brutality. In a moment I will draw a more extended series of comparisons between the novelistic uses of Jewish and other marginalized discourses in order to tease out the complex relation between the ideology of Englishness at play in a given literary text and its use of genre. But first, because the ideological issues at stake are much more explicit in nonfiction polemics than in narrative, let me begin by comparing two political speeches, Macaulay's "Speech on Jewish Civil Disabilities" (1831) and his "Minute on Indian Education" (1835).

As an orator on explicitly ideological issues, Macaulay was compelled to articulate clearly his sense of the relationship between Jews, Indians, and the limits of Englishness. In his speeches on Jewish civil disabilities and Indian education, Macaulay laid out a liberal paradigm for how the British empire ought to deal with religious and racial differences at home and abroad. Two contexts seem important here. Most significantly, his speeches took place during and just after the debate over the First Reform Bill, a bill that, once enacted, transformed the experience of English citizenship by extending the franchise and increasing the numbers of Englishmen who could participate in the political process. It may also be relevant that Macaulay spoke in the wake of the Catholic Emancipation Act of 1829, which for the first time permitted Catholics to sit in Parliament. The backdrop to both speeches, then, was how far the English concept of citizenship—and the English political and social system—might expand to tolerate and contain religious and racial Otherness.

Presented during the debate over the first of many bills for Jewish Emancipation, Macaulay's speech on Jewish civil disabilities self-consciously placed the issue in the context of religious emancipation and reform. Macaulay compares Jews to Catholics directly, and also to Hindus, Muslims, Parsees, and Huguenots (Macaulay, "Civil Disabilities," 44, 50, 55–56). Mimicking the voice of an MP resistant to including Jews in the polity, Macaulay says, "But where are we to stop, if once you admit into the House of Commons people who deny the authority of the Gospels? Will you let in a Mussulman? Will you let in a Parsee? Will you let in a Hindoo who worships a lump of stone with seven heads?" (44). In his own voice he responds to the resisting "honorable friend" as follows: "I will answer my honourable friend's question by another. Where does he mean to stop? Is he ready to roast unbelievers at slow fires?" (44). A liberal nation ought not be a brutal one, but rather should learn to tolerate religious differences. In fact, liberal nations have already learned this lesson with other groups, as he reminds the House when he asks, "Why not try what effect would be produced on the Jews by that tolerant policy which has made the English Roman Catholic a good Englishman and the French Calvinist a good Frenchman?" (56).

Nor does Macaulay admit a distinction between an otherness based on religious belief and one based on divinely appointed race. He several times compares Jews to African slaves, saying in one instance, "We treat [Jews] as slaves, and wonder that they do not regard us as brethren" (57). This would seem to suggest that toleration might be applied to Africans as well. True, he maintains a distinction between the civilized and the savage, but he reminds his audience that "in the infancy of civilization, when our island was as savage as New Guinea, this contemned people [the Jews] had their fenced cities and cedar palaces, their splendid Temple, their fleets of merchant ships, their schools of sacred learning" (58). That is, he shows how the opposition between civilization and savagery might easily be reversed. It is the British who have the history of savagery—and in the fashion of good Whig history these savages have been able to develop and progress. As for the Jews, there is "nothing in their national character which unfits them for the highest duties of civilization" (58). They, too, might participate in the Whig paradigm of progress and development.

Thus, the liberal politician articulates a standard of toleration for religious and racial others when it comes to the rights of citizenship in the nation. We should not imagine, however, that toleration means full participation in the nation. Although Macaulay says, "Let us do justice to them," he does not suggest that *they* should or will have the same status as *us*. Doing justice does not mean dissolving the Christian power structure. Christianity will indeed triumph, but through toleration rather than bigotry, just as it has already "triumphed over the superstitions of the most refined and of the most savage nations" (59). Macaulay adopts a stance that was characteristic of the English discourse of Jewishness from the time of the Readmission of Jews to England by Cromwell in the seventeenth century. Known (somewhat confusingly) as "philo-semitism," the term did not mean loving Jews, but rather using love to persuade Jews to convert to Christianity. Macaulay's logic: We will succeed better at converting Jews to Englishness (and Christianity) if instead of brutalizing them we show them how tolerant we can be.

It is remarkable to see how precisely this program of Anglicization and philo-semitic conversionism are transferred to the program Macaulay set forth in his Minute on Indian Education four years later. As President of the Committee on Public Instruction in India, he is asked to comment on whether he thinks the Indian school curriculum should focus on traditional Arabic and Sanskrit texts or on English texts. In casting his vote for English, he employs the same rhetoric of tolerant Anglicization that he had employed in the speech on Jewish civil disabilities. Just as he believed that Jews would benefit by exposure to Christianity in a tolerant context, he believed that Indians would benefit by exposure to English history, philosophy, religion, and literature in their schools. For Macaulay (who admits to having no fluency in any of the languages of India [Macaulay, "Minute," 722]), it is a given that "the dialects commonly spoken among the natives contain neither literary nor scientific information" (721). He is also certain that "a single shelf of a good European library was worth the whole native literature of India and Arabia" (722). Yet if these lines sounds like nothing more than the arrogant self-justifications of a member of the hegemonic elite, we should consider that by 1835 the East India Company was beginning to be nationalized and to become an official arm of the British government. The Empire was beginning to be formalized. In the Company's employ were hundreds of thousands of native functionaries, whose chance of upward mobility would depend on their capacity to mimic their English higher-ups in learning, fashions, and religion (Bhabha). Although it was clearly informed by cultural bias, Macaulay's program was designed to help these functionaries attain a measure of success within the imperial system. In both his "Minute" and his speech on Jewish disabilities, then, Macaulay tried to ameliorate the marginalized group's suffering while simultaneously ensuring the maintenance of English Christian power.

If there is a difference in Macaulay's programs for Jews and Indians, it is that Jews (perhaps because of their small unthreatening population or their European acculturation) are not conceived to be as great a threat to the power structure as Indians. Macaulay even complains against the existence of a political glass ceiling for Jewish citizens, lamenting that "the Jew may be a juryman, but not a judge. . . . He may rule the money-market but he must not be a Privy Councilor" (Macaulay, "Civil Disabilities," 47). Indian schoolchildren, on the other hand, might learn all of Locke and Milton and Newton, but until Independence they would never rise above secondary administrators, and they were not meant to. The realization on the part of anglicized Indians that their glass ceiling was intended to be permanent helped fuel the Mutiny of 1857 (Brantlinger, Chapter 7).

This is but one example of the ways polemicists might use Jews and other Others as limit cases to test the borders of Englishness. Turning now to novels, we notice immediately that their "literariness" does not prevent them from likewise engaging in the constant conceptualization of national and imperial identity. Novels represented Jews as comparable not only to Africans and Indians, but also to Irish, Scots, and Arab Muslims. As we will see, in these comparisons two kinds of shifts in meaning take place: The meaning of both Englishness and Jewishness alters depending on to which group the writer compares the Jews.

In the comparison between Jews and Scots or Irish, the diasporic aspect of Jewishness is paramount. By 1794, when William Godwin wrote his revolutionary novel *Caleb Williams*, he was already linking Jewishness to England's oppression of its regional Other, the Irish. When Caleb Williams takes on a series of disguises to escape his oppressor, he ends up donning the clothing of both an Irishman and a Jew (Godwin, 240, 264). Like his contemporaries the Irish novelist Maria Edgeworth and, over a century later, James Joyce, Godwin correlates Irish and Jewish territorial dispossession. By 1819, Walter Scott was making a similar comparison between Jews' diaspora and the Scots' lack of regional autonomy. In the *Waverley* series of historical romances, Scott contemplated the past and future of Scottish regional identity in the wake of the 1707 Act of Union that merged Scotland into Great Britain. By ending the series with a Jewish historical romance, *Ivanhoe*, Scott seemed to imply a parallel between Scottishness and Jewishness, between regional and diasporic identity—a parallel based, perhaps, on both groups' dispossession of territory and sovereignty. Rebecca of *Ivanhoe* is essentially the Flora MacIvor of the Jews. When in *Waverley* Flora sings in her hidden bower of the Scots' former national glory and the theft (by the English) of their territory and sovereignty, the narrator calls her the Scots' "Celtic muse" (Scott, *Waverley*, 106), as though she were the Scottish spirit incarnate. Her song contains the essence of the Scottish "national character" (Trumpener, Chapter 3). So, too, in *Ivanhoe*, Rebecca functions as the essence of the Jewish national character, the echo of the Jews' former national glory. During the Battle of Torquilstone, Rebecca actually becomes the text's narrator briefly (Scott, *Ivanhoe*, 314ff.), her voice merged with that of Scott the Scot. It is as if the Scottish and Jewish voices become merged in a sympathy of suffering.

Yet there is one area of discord in Scott's perceptions of the two oppressed groups. In the *Waverley* series, Scott recognizes the costs to Scotland of the Act of Union with England, but he nevertheless uniformly defends the union. For example, at the end of *Waverley*, the Act of Union is reinforced by the marriage of Edward Waverley (the Englishman) and Rose Bradwardine (the Scot). The personal act of union concretizes and celebrates the political act of union (cf.

Trumpener, Chapter 3). In *Ivanhoe*, however, Scott ultimately rejects any such act of union between Rebecca and Wilfred, between Jewish and English identity. Rather, despite his love for her, Wilfred tells Rebecca that she quenches chivalry and is "no Christian" (318), even though she is "of England" (299ff.). In the end, Scott has Rebecca go into exile in Granada. Scott claimed in a preface that the marriage of Wilfred and Rebecca would have been ahistorical, but many of his readers thought that Scott was writing, not about the relationship between medieval Jews and Christians, but about the contemporary relationship. His banishment of Rebecca from the English political union seemed to many to contain a statement regarding the prospects of Jews' emancipation in Scott's own time. As discussed later, a number of readers responded by writing romances of their own in which the union of Christian and Jew was made possible by the Jewish woman's conversion.

Scott was not the only writer to perceive a limited relation between the two groups. Although the Victorian Jewish writer Grace Aguilar had her difficulties with Scott, she nonetheless absorbed his lesson of the parallel between regional and diasporic identity. She herself wrote, not only a Jewish historical romance patterned after *Ivanhoe*, but also a Scottish historical romance, *The Days of Bruce* (1852). She also published her groundbreaking essay, "The History of the Jews of England" (1847), in the radical Edinburgh journal *Chambers's Miscellany*. Thus, in the comparison between Jews and a regional Other, the aspect of Jewish identity that emphasized their statelessness became paramount. At issue was the territorial and ethnic borderline that constituted the nation-state.

When comparing Jews and Arabs, what became paramount was the two groups' common history of wandering, their supposed oriental natures, and increasingly, the pseudoscientific "evidence" of their shared racial inheritance. Here what separates the English "race" from other races is at issue. Early in the nineteenth century, Jews and Arab Muslims were both seen as romantic, nomadic, oriental peoples (Said, *Orientalism*, 102). Cain, Byron's brooding wandering Jew, holds an equivalent place in Byron's worldview to the Giaour, his brooding wandering Muslim (cf. Byron 207–246, 881–938). Like gypsies, both Jews and Muslims partook of the spirit of wandering (although the myth of the "wandering Jew" did have its own separate history and significance). By the 1840s, the young Benjamin Disraeli had absorbed Byron's romanticization of Jewishness and turned it in a nationalistic and racist direction, both in his early historical romance *Alroy* and in the later novel *Tancred*. But in the latter he also claims that an Arab is "but a Jew on horseback" (quoted in Said, 102). Here he gives voice to an understanding of Semitism, later justified by social Darwinian science, as a racial inheritance shared by Jews and Arabs.

George Eliot's *Daniel Deronda* most self-consciously invokes the idea of Jews as oriental when she has her hero, Daniel, choose to wander away from

England to found a Jewish nation in the East. But she also sees in Daniel a figure she can use to meditate on colonialism, nationalism, and race. The figure Mordecai, a consumptive prophet who speaks in Biblically inflected prose, seems to step out of ancient Israelite history in order to exert a converting influence on Daniel's mind and awake him to the deterritorialized plight of Jews. Mordecai argues that Jews need to "revive the organic center"—that is, to re-create a Jewish homeland on the model of a modern nation-state. Such a suggestion—that predated the foundation of political Zionism, or Jewish nationalism, in the 1890s—was imaginable only in the context of colonial expansion, in which new colonies and nations were being added to the map with increasing speed starting in the 1870s. Yet although Daniel undergoes a spiritual marriage of sorts to Mordecai, his conversion is not merely a turning of the mind or heart toward a proto-Zionist nationalism, for after he decides to become Jewish, Daniel finds out that he was in fact a Jew all along. He discovers that he was born to a Jewish mother, the Princess Halm-Eberstein. He does not need to convert once he has discovered the biological truth of his inherited Jewishness. Eliot seems here to accept, at least in part, a racial and somewhat mystical explanation of Jewish inheritance. This racial understanding perhaps explains the most perplexing feature of the text, Daniel's and Mirah's self-exile to the East in the end. Even though in correspondence Eliot explained that she deliberately set out to use her final novel to raise the level of liberal toleration of Jews, the novel itself seems to suggest quite a different conclusion—namely, that Jews ought to leave England to set up their own nation-state rather than remain as English citizens. In this, Eliot copied the ending of her friend Harriet Beecher Stowe's sentimental blockbuster, *Uncle Tom's Cabin*, which she much admired. There, the archetypal liberated blacks set out to found their own colony in Canada. Thus Eliot borrows a plot element to express a racial understanding of Jewishness. (This is an excellent example of how representations of the Other could cross-fertilize one another). So in an unexpected way, a novel by a liberal writer that set out to question the racial divisions of English society ends up reconfirming those divisions.

From this brief survey, we can see that what I have called Jews' category indeterminacy opens up the possibility of endless varieties of representation. One important means of determining which category is being invoked at any given time is to ask which group Jews were being compared to and for which ideological purposes. By using a comparative lens, we can inquire in a sophisticated way how Jews were used in the larger discursive endeavor of shaping English and British identity. Better still, if we assume with Benedict Anderson that national identity itself is never a fixed quantity but is rather a never-realized, ever-shifting set of imaginary blueprints, then perhaps we can ask how each instance of Jewishness functions to help a particular writer articulate a particular national blueprint at a particular moment (Anderson, "Introduction").

Such representations teach us about more than writers' perceptions of English national identity; they also teach us about the limits of literary genre. There are numerous examples to choose from—the impact of the Jewish parvenu on Trollope's novelistic practice in *The Way We Live Now* (1875); the introduction of romantic racism into the political novel in Disraeli's *Tancred*; the formative role of the wandering Jew in Du Maurier's late Victorian novel of degeneration, *Trilby* (1895); the relation between Jewish folklore and the development of the gothic novel in Shelley's *Frankenstein* (1818), or the impact of the anti-Semitic association of Jews with vermin on the development of Stoker's *Dracula* (1895). But for simplicity's sake, let me expand on two of the examples—*Ivanhoe* and *Daniel Deronda*—to suggest how the introduction of marginalized figures into a text can compel a writer to abandon or transform a genre to which he or she is committed.

As a matter of form, Scott's historical romance should end with the marriage of its hero, Wilfred, and its heroine, Rebecca, the Jewess. The genre typically includes a marriage between a male figure from the dominant group and the female figure from the oppressed group. Their union is symbolic: It represents the transcendence of seemingly immovable barriers to bind the stratified social order into a unified whole. Yet the romance ends with Rebecca's voluntary departure from England. As Michael Ragussis has demonstrated, Rebecca's departure is a sign that English national identity, strong enough to convert Normans and Saxons into one nation of Englishmen, is not, for Scott, capacious enough to include Jews (Ragussis, Chapter 3). But this result violates the generic conventions of Scott's own historical romance form, as numerous contemporaries complained. Thus Scott's ideological commitment to Jews' unassimilability compels him to violate his own literary form.

In consequence, a number of Scott's contemporaries wrote romances set, not in the past, but in contemporary England, in which a spiritual Jewish woman leaves her materialistic father's house to convert to Christianity and wed a charismatic Christian suitor (Galchinsky, Chapter 1). Examples include Edward Bulwer-Lytton's *Leila, or the Siege of Granada* and Thackeray's "Romance Upon Romance," *Rebecca and Rowena*, among others. These conversionist novels were themselves seen, by British Jews, as troubling. Victorian Jews disliked the conversionists' implication that the Jewish woman was easily convertible, and that Jewish men were materialists. In consequence, Anglo-Jewish writers like Grace Aguilar in *The Vale of Cedars* (1850) and Marion and Celia Moss in *The Romance of Jewish History* (1842) wrote historical romances in which a Jewish woman resists the suit of the charismatic Christian and marries a charismatic Jew. Walter Scott's perceived violation of genre thus provoked the publication of a series of countertexts that took the romance subgenre in new directions. When Scott introduced a Jewish figure into his text, he unwittingly gave rise to a major transformation in one subgenre of narrative.

George Eliot's *Daniel Deronda* (1876) is likewise a case in which the introduction of Jewishness propels the novelist in generically unforeseen ways. Eliot's novels are usually called "realist" because they depict plot as a series of probable, everyday sequences of events, they depict characters with believable psychological depth and inner conflict, and they exhibit "organic form," in which all events tell on all the other events. Yet in the depiction of Jews, Eliot's realism seems to break down, both in terms of plot and character. Even before the utopian ending, the plot is filled with numerous coincidences, mysteries, and other violations of the probable. For example, when Daniel decides by chance to attend services in a synagogue in Frankfurt, he meets an old man, Joseph Kalonymos, who turns out to have been his grandfather's best friend, who has a chest of his grandfather's papers for him, and who immediately recognizes him. Eliot's messianic figure, Mordecai, seems to be able to foretell future events, which the narrator refers to as his "second sight."

At the level of character, Eliot's typical realism is more apparent in some characters than others. She carefully delineates what she calls the "unmapped territory within" Gwendolyn's mind (235), demonstrating step by step that Gwendolyn is herself a kind of Wandering Jew, a moral nomad, because she did not grow up "rooted in some spot of a native land" (16). So, too, Eliot's insight into the psychology of Daniel's mother is quite penetrating. But when it comes to Mirah, the Jewish singer who is Gwendolyn's rival for Daniel's interest and affection, Eliot relies much more on melodrama than realism. And although Mirah's brother, Mordecai, may have been based on an actual Jewish scholar, Emmanuel Deutsch, his pronouncements sound not like everyday speech but like speeches either from the Bible or from James Fenimore Cooper romances depicting "noble savages." He is a Romantic figure of the primitive, an ancient prophet reborn to speak the truth momentarily, only the next moment to die.

Finally, the majestic organic form of a realist novel like Eliot's *Middlemarch* seems compromised in the seemingly split structure of this text. *Deronda* meanders back and forth from what the critic F. R. Leavis called the "Jewish part"—the sections dealing with Daniel's discovery of his mission to bring Jews back from their wandering into a re-created homeland—to the sections centering on the moral wanderings of Gwendolyn Harleth, the Christian heroine. Leavis was so bothered by the seeming bifurcation of the text that he published an edition with the "Jewish part" cut out, calling it *Gwendolyn Harleth* (Leavis, 79–87, 122–124). In my view, Leavis's perception of the text's lack of unity was overstated: The sections of the text are more unified than they at first appear, both thematically and structurally. But his criticism serves to make us aware that Eliot's laudable political aim—to increase Victorians' awareness and toleration of Jews—had literary consequences for the shape of her text.

We can see, then, that paying attention to representations of the Other has much to teach us regarding both the construction of English national identity and the historical evolution of literary forms like the novel. Yet if we stop here, our work will still be insufficient to account for the complex interplay of images of Others in nineteenth-century England. For what we have said so far has mostly been limited to the anxieties and genres reflected in depictions of the Other by writers in the majority. We have asked little about the anxieties and genres of writers who are members of groups classed as Other. An approach asking only the first kind of question cannot generate a comprehensive contrapuntal knowledge of nationalism, marginalized identities, or the literary attempts to represent them.

To fill in the picture, students of the nineteenth century must also compare the ways in which Jews and other marginalized subjects of the British Empire wrote back in relation to the images of them produced by others. Against the images produced by English Christian writers scholars can juxtapose the products of marginalized subjectivity—Olaudah Equiano's slave narrative from 1789 or Mary Prince's slave narrative from 1831, narratives of Indian identity like Hasan Shah's *The Dancing Girl* from 1790 or Rabindranath Tagore's short stories from the 1890s, Julia Frankau's novel of internalized anti-Semitism, *Dr. Phillips: A Maida Vale Idyll* from 1887, for example—in order better to conceive of the imagined nation as a series of encounters between major and minor writers. Through such juxtapositions literary and cultural critics can find out to what extent members of marginalized groups identified their own Otherness with the regional, colonial, diasporic, racial, or religious differences of the multiple aliens living in the British dominions. We can find out to what extent Jews, for example, attempted to form political or literary alliances with other marginalized groups. Literary critics and historians can elucidate how minority writers grappled with genres and ideas they inherited from mainstream culture or from other marginalized communities, and to what degree they were able to alter what they had assimilated in order to create new hybridized forms.

Two brief examples of Anglo-Jewish writers' development of new or hybrid forms will serve to illustrate. The first is Israel Zangwill's novel *Children of the Ghetto* (1892), recently reissued. In this sprawling novel about the late Victorian Jewish ghetto in the East End of London, Zangwill draws from the sentimental tradition of Dickens. He does so, however, not merely to pay homage to the great novelist, but in order to depict the rich, multifaceted life of the ghetto. He gives us the ghetto's pious paupers and wealthy hypocrites, its multiple languages and profusion of civic and religious organizations, its sweatshop owners and tailor-socialists, its religious reformers and entrenched traditionalists, its skeptics, atheists, Zionists, narcissists, self-haters, and messiahs of every stripe. In short, he puts the Dickensian form and tone to the task of imagining a London far different from the one Dickens described. The depth and texture of Zangwill's knowledge of Jews and Jewishness far outstrips what Dickens is able to achieve in his portraits of Jewish figures in *Oliver Twist* (1837–38) and *Our Mutual Friend* (1864–65). Thus Zangwill puts the sentimental novel to a use for which it was not originally conceived. The desire to depict what he calls a "peculiar people" (Zangwill) compels him to expand and alter the permissible content of the genre.

The second example is *Reuben Sachs* (1887), a novel of Jewish identity by Amy Levy, a late Victorian Jewish novelist and poet who wrote back against George Eliot's *Daniel Deronda*. In the text, Bertie Lee-Harrison, a Christian, visits a Jewish family. After his departure, one of the family remarks that Lee-Harrison was probably "shocked at finding us so little like the people in *Daniel Deronda*" (Levy, 238). Ridiculing the ending of Eliot's novel, another member of the family then replies, "Did he expect . . . to see our boxes in the hall, ready packed and labeled *Palestine?*" (Levy, 238). Here Levy uses her characters to respond directly to (and resist) the major novelist's ideological program. But Levy responds to Eliot at a more indirect and subtle level as well—at the level of form. For while Levy adopts a number of elements of the realism for which Eliot is noted, she also moves in a more experimental direction. This is most apparent during the novel's crisis, when Levy gives us the heroine's experience not in a connected, probable, realist narrative, but in a series of brief, disconnected impressions separated by blank space. This technique of rendering the heroine's psyche anticipates Modernist experiments. In this way, Levy both assimilated and altered the form she inherited from Eliot.

The rich potential of this sort of comparative analysis has only begun to be realized. By employing a relational and contrapuntal methodology, students of Victorian literature can continue the task of tracing continuous, parallel shifts in imperial, national, and marginalized identities, as well as in literary form, throughout the period. Through this process, we can also succeed in putting the discussion of Jews and other Others back where it came from: the messy, complex, multicultural fray that was Victorian England.

WORKS CITED AND SELECTED WORKS FOR FURTHER READING

Aguilar, Grace. *The Days of Bruce*. New York: Appleton, 1903.
———. "History of the Jews in England." *Chambers's Miscellany* 18 (1847): 1–32.
———. *The Vale of Cedars; or, The Martyr*. New York: Appleton, 1850.

Anderson, Benedict. *Imagined Communities: Reflections on the Origin and Spread of Nationalism*. Rev. ed. New York: Verso, 1991.

Arnold, Matthew. *Culture and Anarchy*. Ed. J. Dover Wilson. New York: Cambridge UP, 1971.

Baker, William. *George Eliot and Judaism*. Salzburg: Universität Salzburg, 1975.

Bhabha, Homi. "Of Mimicry and Men: The Ambivalence of Colonial Discourse." *October* 28 (1994): 125–133.

Biale, David. *Gershom Scholem: Kabbalah and Counter-History*. 2nd ed. Cambridge: Harvard UP, 1982.

Brantlinger, Patrick. *Rule of Darkness: British Literature and Imperialism, 1830–1914*. Ithaca: Cornell UP, 1988.

Burke, Edmund. *Reflections on the Revolution in France*. Ed. Thomas H. D. Mahoney. New York: Liberal Arts, 1955.

———. *The Writings and Speeches of Edmund Burke*. Vol. 3. Ed. W. M. Elofson and John A. Woods. Oxford: Clarendon, 1996.

Byron, George Gordon. *Byron*. Ed. Jerome J. McGann. New York: Oxford UP, 1986.

Carlyle, Thomas. *Shooting Niagara: And After?* London: Chapman and Hall, 1867.

Chatterji, Bankim Chandra. *The Poison Tree*. New York: South Asia, 1996.

Cheyette, Bryan. *Constructions of "the Jew" in English Literature and Society: Racial Representations, 1875–1945*. Cambridge: Cambridge UP, 1996.

Cohen, Robin. *Global Diasporas: An Introduction*. Seattle: U of Washington P, 1997.

Crossette, Barbara. "Europe Stares at a Future Built by Immigrants." *New York Times* (2 January 2000): sec. 4, p. 1.

Dabydeen, David, and Paul Edwards, eds. *Black Writers in Britain, 1760–1890*. Edinburgh: Edinburgh UP, 1991.

Davis, Leith. *Acts of Union: Scotland and the Literary Negotiation of the British Nation, 1707–1830*. Stanford: Stanford UP, 1998.

Disraeli, Benjamin. *Alroy and Ixion*. London: Longmans, Green, 1846.

———. *Tancred, or, the New Crusade*. London: Longmans, Green, 1880.

Du Maurier, George. *Trilby*. London: Osgood, McIlvaine, 1895.

Eliot, George. *Daniel Deronda*. Oxford: Oxford UP, 1984.

Endelman, Todd. *Radical Assimilation in English Jewish History, 1656–1945*. Bloomington: Indiana UP, 1990.

Equiano, Olaudah. *Equiano's Travels*. Ed. Paul Edwards. Portsmouth: Heinemann, 1967.

Feldman, David. *Englishmen and Jews: Social Relations and Political Culture, 1840–1914*. New Haven: Yale UP, 1994.

Frankau, Julia. *Dr. Phillips: A Maida Vale Idyll*. London: Vizetelly, 1887.

Galchinsky, Michael. *The Origin of the Modern Jewish Woman Writer: Romance and Reform in Victorian England*. Detroit: Wayne State UP, 1996.

Geertz, Clifford. *Interpretation of Cultures*. New York: Basic, 2000.

Gilbert, Sandra M., and Susan Gubar. *The Madwoman in the Attic: The Woman Writer and the Nineteenth-Century Literary Imagination*. New Haven: Yale UP, 1979.

Gilroy, Paul. *The Black Atlantic: Modernity and Double Consciousness*. Cambridge: Harvard UP, 1993.

Godwin, William. *Caleb Williams*. New York: Norton, 1977.

Gould, Stephen Jay. *The Mismeasure of Man*. New York: Norton, 1996.

Katz, David. *Philo-Semitism and the Readmission of the Jews to England, 1603–1655*. Oxford: Clarendon, 1982.

Leavis, F. R. *The Great Tradition: George Eliot, Henry James, Joseph Conrad*. London: Chatto and Windus, 1955.

Lessing, Gotthold Ephraim. *Nathan the Wise*. Trans. Bayard Quincy Morgan. New York: Continuum, 1988.

Levy, Amy. *The Complete Novels and Selected Writings of Amy Levy*. Ed. Melvyn New. Gainesville: UP of Florida, 1993.

Lipman, V. D. *Social History of the Jews in England, 1850–1950*. London: Watts, 1954.

Macaulay, Thomas Babington. "Civil Disabilities of the Jews." *Edinburgh Review* 52 (January 1831): 40–60.

———. "Minute on Indian Education." In *Macaulay: Prose and Poetry*. Ed. G. M. Young. Cambridge: Harvard UP, 1967.

Marcus, Steven. *The Other Victorians: A Study of Sexuality and Pornography in Mid-Nineteenth-Century England*. New York: Basic, 1966.

McClintock, Anne. *Imperial Leather: Race, Gender, and Sexuality in the Colonial Contest*. New York: Routledge, 1995.

Melman, Billie. *Women's Orients: English Women and the Middle East, 1718–1918*. Ann Arbor: U of Michigan P, 1992.

Modder, Montagu Frank. *The Jew in the Literature of England to the End of the Nineteenth Century*. 1939. New York: Meridian, 1960.

Moss, Celia, and Marion Moss. *The Romance of Jewish History*. London, 1842.

Poovey, Mary. *Uneven Developments: The Ideological Work of Gender in Mid-Victorian England*. Chicago: U of Chicago P, 1988.

Prince, Mary. *The History of Mary Prince: A West Indian Slave/Related by Herself*. Ed. Moira Ferguson. Ann Arbor: U of Michigan P, 1997.

Ragussis, Michael. *Figures of Conversions: "The Jewish Question" and English National Identity*. Durham: Duke UP, 1995.

Said, Edward. *Culture and Imperialism*. New York: Vintage, 1993.

———. *Orientalism*. New York: Vintage, 1978.

Scott, Walter. *Ivanhoe*. New York: Penguin, 1983.

———. *Waverley*. New York: Oxford UP, 1986.

Scheinberg, Cynthia, ed. "Editor's Topic on Anglo-Jewish Literature." *Victorian Literature and Culture* (1999).

Shah, Hasan. *The Dancing Girl*. Trans. Qurratulain Hyder. New York: New Directions, 1993.

Showalter, Elaine. *A Literature of Their Own: British Women Novelists from Brontë to Lessing*. Princeton: Princeton UP, 1999.

Smith, Woodruff D. *European Imperialism in the Nineteenth and Twentieth Centuries*. Chicago: Nelson-Hall, 1982.

Spivak, Gayatri Chakravorty. *In Other Worlds: Essays in Cultural Politics*. New York: Routledge, 1988.

Stoker, Bram. *Dracula*. Ed. Glennis Byron. Peterborough: Broadview, 1997.

Stone, Harry, "Dickens and the Jews." *Victorian Studies* (March 1959): 223–253.

Tagore, Rabindranath. *Selected Short Stories*. New York: South Asia, 1994.

Thompson, E. P. *The Making of the English Working Class*. New York: Vintage, 1966.

Trollope, Anthony. *The Way We Live Now*. London: Chapman and Hall, 1875.

Trumpener, Katie. *Bardic Nationalism: The Romantic Novel and the British Empire*. Princeton: Princeton UP, 1997.

Zangwill, Israel. *Children of the Ghetto*. Ed. Meri-Jane Rochelson. Detroit: Wayne State UP, 1998.

Selected Bibliography

Abel-Smith, Brian, and Robert Stevens. *Lawyers and the Courts: A Sociological Study of the English Legal System, 1750–1965*. Cambridge: Harvard UP, 1967.

Ackroyd, Peter. *Dickens*. New York: HarperCollins, 1990.

Allen, Michael. *Charles Dickens's Childhood*. New York: St. Martin's, 1988.

Altick, Richard D. *Deadly Encounters: Two Victorian Sensations*. Philadelphia: U of Pennsylvania P, 1986.

———. *The English Common Reader: A Social History of the Mass Reading Public, 1800–1900*. Chicago: U of Chicago P, 1957.

Anderson, Benedict. *Imagined Communities: Reflections on the Origin and Spread of Nationalism*. Rev. ed. New York: Verso, 1991.

Arata, Stephen. *Fictions of Loss in the Victorian Fin de Siècle*. Cambridge: Cambridge UP, 1996.

Armstrong, Nancy. *Desire and Domestic Fiction: A Political History of the Novel*. New York: Oxford UP, 1987.

Ashton, Rosemary. *George Eliot: A Life*. London: Hamish Hamilton, 1996.

Auerbach, Nina. *Woman and the Demon*. Cambridge: Harvard UP, 1982.

Aycock, Wendell, and Michael Schoenecke. *Film and Literature: A Comparative Approach to Adaptation*. Lubbock: Texas Tech UP, 1998.

Azim, Firdous. *The Colonial Rise of the Novel*. London: Routledge, 1993.

Baker, William. *George Eliot and Judaism*. Salzburg: Universität Salzburg, 1975.

Barker, Juliet. *The Brontës*. London: Weidenfeld and Nicolson, 1994.

Barreca, Regina, ed. *Sex and Death in Victorian Literature*. London: Macmillan, 1990.

Beer, Gillian. *Meredith: A Change of Masks*. London: Athlone, 1970.

Bersani, Leo. *The Culture of Redemption*. Cambridge: Harvard UP, 1990.

Bloom, Harold. *The Western Canon: The Books and School of the Ages*. New York: Harcourt Brace, 1994.

Bodenheimer, Rosemarie. *The Politics of Story in Victorian Social Fiction*. Ithaca: Cornell UP, 1988.

———. *The Real Life of Mary Ann Evans. George Eliot, Her Letters and Her Fiction*. Ithaca: Cornell UP, 1994.

Botting, Fred. *Gothic*. London: Routledge, 1996.

Boumelha, Penny. *Charlotte Brontë*. London: Harvester Wheatsheaf, 1990.

Boyle, Thomas. *Black Swine in the Sewers of Hampstead: Beneath the Surface of Victorian Sensationalism*. New York: Viking, 1989.

Brantlinger, Patrick. *The Reading Lesson: The Threat of Mass Literacy in the Nineteenth-Century British Fiction*. Bloomington: Indiana UP, 1998.

———. *Rule of Darkness: British Literature and Imperialism, 1830–1914*. Ithaca: Cornell UP, 1988.

Bratton, J. S. *The Impact of Victorian Children's Fiction*. London: Croom Helm, 1981.

Briggs, Julia. *Night Visitors: The Rise and Fall of the English Ghost Story*. London: Faber and Faber, 1977.

Byron, Glennis, and David Punter, eds. *Spectral Readings: Towards a Gothic Geography*. London: Macmillan, 1999.

Cartmell, Deborah. *Adaptations: From Text to Screen, Screen to Text*. London: Routledge, 1999.

Cazamian, Louis. *The Social Novel in England, 1830–1850*. 1903. London: Routledge and Kegan Paul, 1973.

Cecil, David. *Early Victorian Novelists: Essays in Revaluation*. London: Penguin, 1948.

Cheyette, Bryan. *Constructions of "the Jew" in English Literature and Society: Racial Representations, 1875–1945*. Cambridge: Cambridge UP, 1996.

Childers, Joseph W. *Novel Possibilities: Fiction and the Formation of Early Victorian Culture*. Philadelphia: U of Pennsylvania P, 1995.

Colby, Robert A. *Fiction with a Purpose: Major and Minor Nineteenth-Century Novels*. Bloomington: Indiana UP, 1967.

Colby, Vineta. *The Singular Anomaly: Women Novelists of the Nineteenth Century*. New York: New York UP, 1970.

Craft, Christopher. *Another Kind of Love: Male Homosexual Desire in English Discourse, 1850–1920*. Berkeley: U of California P, 1994.

Craig, Patricia, and Mary Cadogan. *The Lady Investigates: Women Detectives and Spies in Fiction*. New York: St. Martin's, 1981.

Cunningham, Valentine. *Everywhere Spoken Against: Dissent in the Victorian Novel*. Oxford: Clarendon, 1975.

Cvetkovich, Ann. *Mixed Feelings: Feminism, Mass Culture, and Victorian Sensationalism*. New Brunswick: Rutgers UP, 1992.

Dabydeen, David, and Paul Edwards, eds. *Black Writers in Britain, 1760–1890*. Edinburgh: Edinburgh UP, 1991.

Dale, Peter Allan. *In Pursuit of a Scientific Culture: Science, Art, and Society in the Victorian Age*. Madison: U of Wisconsin P, 1989.

Dalziel, Margaret. *Popular Fiction 100 Years Ago: An Unexplored Tract of Literary History*. London: Cohen and West, 1957.

Dentith, Simon. *Society and Cultural Forms in Nineteenth-Century England*. London: Macmillan, 1998.

Dijkstra, Bram. *Idols of Perversity: Fantasies of Feminine Evil in Fin-de-Siècle Culture*. Oxford: Oxford UP, 1986.

Dixon, Robert. *Writing the Colonial Adventure: Race, Gender and Nation in Anglo-Australian Popular Fiction, 1875–1914*. Cambridge: Cambridge UP, 1995.

Dolin, Kieran. *Fiction and the Law: Legal Discourse in Victorian and Modernist Literature*. Cambridge: Cambridge UP, 1999.

Donaldson, William. *Popular Literature in Victorian Scotland: Language, Fiction, and the Press*. Aberdeen: Aberdeen UP, 1986.

Edwards, Peter. *Some Mid-Victorian Thrillers: The Sensation Novel, Its Friends and Foes*. Queensland: U of Queensland P, 1971.

Emsley, Clive. *Crime and Society in England, 1750–1900*. 2nd ed. London: Longman, 1996.

Endelman, Todd. *Radical Assimilation in English Jewish History, 1656–1945*. Bloomington: Indiana UP, 1990.

Erickson, Lee. *The Economy of Literary Form: English Literature and the Industrialization of Publishing, 1800–1850*. Baltimore: Johns Hopkins UP, 1996.

Ermath, Elizabeth Deeds. *The English Novel in History, 1840–1895*. London: Routledge, 1997.

Feldman, David. *Englishmen and Jews: Social Relations and Political Culture, 1840–1914*. New Haven: Yale UP, 1994.

Feltes, N. N. *Modes of Production of Victorian Novels*. Chicago: U of Chicago P, 1986.

Fielding, Kenneth J. *Charles Dickens: A Critical Introduction*. London: Longmans, Green, 1958.

Flint, Kate. *The Victorian Novelist: Social Problems and Social Change*. London: Croom Helm, 1987.

———. *The Woman Reader, 1837–1914*. Oxford: Oxford UP, 1993.

Galchinsky, Michael. *The Origin of the Modern Jewish Woman Writer: Romance and Reform in Victorian England*. Detroit: Wayne State UP, 1996.

Gallagher, Catherine. *The Industrial Reformation of English Fiction: Social Discourse and Narrative Form, 1832–1867*. Chicago: U of Chicago P, 1985.

Gilbert, Pamela K. *Disease, Desire, and the Body in Victorian Women's Popular Novels*. Cambridge: Cambridge UP, 1997.

Gilbert, Sandra M., and Susan Gubar. *The Madwoman in the Attic: The Woman Writer and the Nineteenth-Century Literary Imagination*. New Haven: Yale UP, 1979.

Gillooly, Eileen. *Smile of Discontent: Humor, Gender, and Nineteenth-Century British Fiction*. Chicago: U of Chicago P, 1999.

Goodwin, Sarah Webster, and Elisabeth Bronfen, eds. *Death and Representation*. Baltimore: Johns Hopkins UP, 1993.

Greenslade, William M. *Degeneration, Culture, and the Novel, 1880–1940*. Cambridge: Cambridge UP, 1994.

Guy, Josephine M. *The Victorian Social-Problem Novel: The Market, the Individual, and Communal Life*. London: Macmillan, 1996.

Hall, Donald E., ed. *Muscular Christianity: Embodying the Victorian Age*. Cambridge: Cambridge UP, 1994.

Harrison, Brian. *Drink and the Victorians: The Temperance Question in England, 1815–1872*. Pittsburgh: U of Pittsburgh P, 1971.

Harvey, John R. *Victorian Novelists and Their Illustrations*. New York: New York UP, 1971.

Helmstadter, Richard J., and Bernard Lightman. *Victorian Faith in Crisis: Essays on Continuity and Change in Nineteenth-Century Religious Belief*. Stanford: Stanford UP, 1990.

Herdman, John. *The Double in Nineteenth-Century Fiction*. London: Macmillan, 1990.

Hilton, Boyd. *The Age of Atonement: The Influence of Evangelicalism on Social and Economic Thought, 1795–1865*. Oxford: Clarendon, 1988.

Hughes, Linda K., and Michael Lund. *The Victorian Serial*. Charlottesville: UP of Virginia, 1991.

Hughes, Winifred. *The Maniac in the Cellar: Sensation Novels in the 1860s*. Princeton: Princeton UP, 1980.

Ingham, Patricia. *The Language of Gender and Class: Transformation in the Victorian Novel*. London: Routledge, 1996.

James, Louis. *Fiction for the Working Man, 1830–1850*. Oxford: Oxford UP, 1963.

Jordan, Thomas E. *Victorian Childhood: Themes and Variations*. Albany: State U of New York P, 1987.

Kaplan, Fred. *Dickens: A Biography*. New York: William Morrow, 1988.

Keating, P. J. *The Haunted Study: A Social History of the English Novel, 1875–1914*. London: Secker and Warburg, 1989.

Landow, George P. *Victorian Types, Victorian Shadows: Biblical Typology in Victorian Literature, Art, and Thought*. Boston: Routledge, 1980.

Langbauer, Laurie. *Women and Romance: The Consolations of Gender in the English Novel*. Ithaca: Cornell UP, 1990.

Leavis, F. R. *The Great Tradition: George Eliot, Henry James, Joseph Conrad*. London: Chatto and Windus, 1955.

Ledger, Sally. *The New Woman: Fiction and Feminism at the Fin de Siècle*. Manchester: Manchester UP, 1997.

Levinson, Sanford, and Steven Mailloux, ed. *Interpreting Law and Literature: A Hermeneutic Reader*. Evanston: Northwestern UP, 1988.

Lootens, Tricia. *Lost Saints: Silence, Gender, and Victorian Literary Canonization*. Charlottesville: UP of Virginia, 1996.

Lynch, Deidre Shauna. *The Economy of Character: Novels, Market Culture, and the Business of Inner Meaning.* Chicago: U of Chicago P, 1998.

Malchow, H. L. *Gothic Images of Race in Nineteenth-Century Britain.* Stanford: Stanford UP, 1996.

McClintock, Anne. *Imperial Leather: Race, Gender, and Sexuality in the Colonial Contest.* New York: Routledge, 1995.

Meisel, Martin. *Realizations: Narrative, Pictorial, and Theatrical Arts in Nineteenth-Century England.* Princeton: Princeton UP, 1983.

Meyer, Susan. *Imperialism at Home: Race and Victorian Women's Fiction.* Ithaca: Cornell UP, 1996.

Miller, J. Hillis. *Victorian Subjects.* Hemel Hempstead: Harvester Wheatsheaf, 1990.

Morgan, Susan. *Sisters in Time: Imagining Gender in Nineteenth-Century British Fiction.* Oxford: Oxford UP, 1989.

Poovey, Mary. *Making a Social Body: British Cultural Formation, 1830–1864.* Chicago: U of Chicago P, 1995.

———. *Uneven Developments: The Ideological Work of Gender in Mid-Victorian England.* Chicago: U of Chicago P, 1988.

Porter, Dennis. *The Pursuit of Crime: Art and Ideology in Detective Fiction.* New Haven: Yale UP, 1981.

Punter, David, ed. *A Companion to the Gothic.* Oxford: Blackwell, 2000.

Ragussis, Michael. *Figures of Conversion: "The Jewish Question" and English National Identity.* Durham: Duke UP, 1995.

Roston, Murray. *Victorian Contexts: Literature and the Visual Arts.* New York: New York UP, 1996.

Showalter, Elaine. *The Female Malady: Women, Madness and English Culture, 1830–1980.* London: Virago, 1987.

———. *A Literature of Their Own: British Women Novelists from Brontë to Lessing.* Revised ed. Princeton: Princeton UP, 1999.

———. *Sexual Anarchy: Gender and Culture at the Fin de Siècle.* London: Bloomsbury, 1990.

Smith, Sheila M. *The Other Nation: The Poor in English Novels of the 1840s and 1850s.* Oxford: Clarendon, 1980.

Sussman, Herbert. *Victorian Masculinities: Manhood and Masculine Poetics in Early Victorian Literature and Art.* Cambridge: Cambridge UP, 1995.

Sutherland, J. A. *Victorian Fiction: Writers, Publishers, Readers.* London: Macmillan, 1995.

Thompson, Nicola Diane. *Reviewing Sex: Gender and the Reception of Victorian Novels.* New York: New York UP, 1995.

Trodd, Anthea. *Domestic Crime in the Victorian Novel.* New York: St. Martin's, 1989.

Welsh, Alexander. *Strong Representations: Narrative and Circumstantial Evidence in England.* Baltimore: Johns Hopkins UP, 1992.

Widdowson, Peter. *Thomas Hardy.* Plymouth: Northcote, 1996.

Williams, Raymond. *Culture and Society, 1780–1950.* London: Chatto and Windus, 1958.

————. *The English Novel from Dickens to Lawrence.* London: Hogarth, 1984.

Wolff, Robert Lee. *Gains and Losses: Novels of Faith and Doubt in Victorian England.* London: John Murray, 1977.

Wolfreys, Julian. *Being English: Narratives, Idioms, and Performances of National Identity from Coleridge to Trollope.* Albany: State U of New York P, 1994.

Wright, T. R. *The Religion of Humanity: The Impact of Comtean Positivism on Victorian Britain.* Cambridge: Cambridge UP, 1986.

Index

About the Contributors

Christine Alexander is Professor of English at the University of New South Wales, Australia. Her books include the British Academy prize-winning *Early Writings of Charlotte Brontë*, several editions of Brontë juvenilia, and the coauthored *Art of the Brontës*. She is completing an edition of Jane Austen's juvenilia and coediting (with Juliet McMaster) *The Child Writer from Jane Austen to Virginia Woolf*.

Lynn Alexander is Professor of English at the University of Tennessee at Martin where she teaches courses in the British Novel, Literary Theory, and Women's Literature. Coeditor of *The Slaughter-House of Mammon: An Anthology of Victorian Social Protest Literature* (1992), she has published several essays on Victorian social protest literature and art. She has recently completed a manuscript on iconology of the seamstress in Victorian art and literature.

Sophia Andres is Associate Professor of English at the University of Texas, Permian Basin. Her work has appeared in *ELH, Journal of Narrative Technique, Victorians Institute Journal, Victorian Newsletter, CLIO,* and the *Journal of Pre-Raphaelite Studies*. She is writing a book on the Pre-Raphaelites and the Victorian Novel.

Lucie J. Armitt is a Lecturer in English at the University College of Wales, Bangor. She is the author of *Contemporary Women's Fiction and the Fantastic* and *Theorizing the Fantastic*. She is editor of the *Reader's Guide to George Eliot* and *Where No Man Has Gone Before: Women and Science Fiction*. Her current research concentrates on nineteenth-century women's writing and ghost narratives.

William Baker is Professor, Department of English, and Professor, University Libraries, at Northern Illinois University. He is the editor of *George Eliot–George Henry Lewes Studies*, as well as the author or editor of such volumes as *Harold Pinter, George Eliot and Judaism, The Libraries of George Eliot and G. H. Lewes, The Early History of the London Library, F. R. Leavis and Q. D. Leavis: An Annotated Bibliography*, and *The Letters of George Henry Lewes, Literary Theories: A Case Study in Critical Performance*. His two-volume edition of *The Letters of Wilkie Collins* was recently honored by *Choice* as one of 2000's most outstanding academic books. His *George Eliot: A Bibliographical History* will be published in 2002. He is editor (with Kenneth Womack) of *The Year's Work in English Studies*.

Martin Bidney is Professor of English and Comparative Literature at State University of New York at Binghamton. He is the author of *Blake and Goethe: Psychology, Ontology, Imagination* and *Patterns of Epiphany: From Wordsworth to Tolstoy, Pater, and Elizabeth Barrett Browning*.

Nancy Cervetti is Associate Professor of English and Chair of Humanities at Avila College in Kansas City. In addition to publishing widely in such journals as *Women's Studies* and the *Journal of Modern Literature*, she is the author of *Scenes of Reading*. Currently, she is completing an edition of the selected letters of Silas Weir Mitchell, nineteenth-century neurologist and novelist.

Todd F. Davis is Associate Professor of English at Goshen College. The author of numerous articles and reviews in such journals as *Critique, Studies in Short Fiction, Mississippi Quarterly, Style*, and *Literature/Film Quarterly*, Davis is the coeditor (with Kenneth Womack) of *Mapping the Ethical Turn: A Reader in Ethics, Culture, and Literary Theory*.

Helen Debenham is a Senior Lecturer in the Department of English at the University of Canterbury, Christchurch, New Zealand, where she teaches eighteenth- and nineteenth-century British fiction. She has published on various Victorian writers, most recently on Rhoda Broughton and Anne Thackeray Ritchie.

Ian Duncan is Professor of English at the University of California, Berkeley. His publications include *Modern Romance and Transformations of the Novel: The Gothic, Scott, Dickens*; editions of Scott's *Ivanhoe* and *Rob Roy*, as well as imperial romances by Conan Doyle, Hudson, and Buchan for Oxford World's Classics series; and essays on James Hogg, George Borrow, Adam Smith, John Ruskin, and others. He is completing a book entitled *Scott's Shadow: Fiction, Politics, and Culture in Post-Enlightenment Edinburgh* and an edition of James Hogg's *Winter Evening Tales*.

K. J. Fielding is Emeritus Professor of English Literature at the University of Edinburgh. In addition to serving as joint-editor of two volumes of the Pilgrim edition of the *Letters of Charles Dickens*, he has edited the *Speeches of Charles Dickens* and was senior editor of *The Collected Letters of Thomas and Jane Welsh Carlyle*. He has written numerous other books and shorter pieces on Dickens, Carlyle, and other Victorians.

Michael Galchinsky teaches courses in British Literature, Cultural Studies, and Narrative Theory at Georgia State University in Atlanta. He is the author of *The Origin of the Modern Jewish Woman Writer: Romance and Reform in Victorian England*, the coeditor of *Insider/Outsider: American Jews and Multiculturalism*, and the editor of a forthcoming volume of writings by the Anglo-Jewish poet, novelist, and essayist Grace Aguilar.

Eileen Gillooly teaches nineteenth-century literature and culture at Columbia University, where she is Director of the Core Curriculum. The author of essays and reviews in a variety of publications, including *Feminist Studies, ELH, Victorian Studies*, and *The New York Times Book Review*, she is currently at work on *Parental Affects in Nineteenth-Century Fiction and Culture*. Her book *Smile of Discontent: Humor, Gender, and Nineteenth-Century British Fiction* was recently awarded the Perkins Prize by the Society for the Study of Narrative Literature.

Margaret Harris is Professor in English Literature and Director of the Research Institute for Humanities and Social Sciences at the University of Sydney. Her publications on the Victorian period include *The Notebooks of George Meredith* (with Gillian Beer) and editions of several of Meredith's novels. After publishing *The Journals of George Eliot* (with Judith Johnston), she is working on George Eliot and sculpture.

Nancy Henry is Associate Professor of English at the State University of New York at Binghamton. She is the editor of an edition of George Eliot's *Impres-*

sions of Theophrastus Such (1994) and the author of numerous articles about George Eliot.

Roslyn Jolly is a Senior Lecturer in the School of English at the University of New South Wales. She is the author of *Henry James: History, Narrative, Fiction* and the editor of *South Sea Tales* by Robert Louis Stevenson. She has contributed articles on Victorian and postcolonial literature and culture to the *Journal of Commonwealth Literature* and the *Review of English Studies*, and has coedited (with Christine Alexander) a special issue of the *Australasian Victorian Studies Journal* on the Victorians and childhood.

Elizabeth F. Judge is a member of the Faculty of Law at the University of Ottawa. Her law and literature research includes the areas of law and technology, particularly intellectual property, privacy, and the property of personal information, as well as eighteenth- and nineteenth-century British novels and evidence, legal history, law and literature, and jurisprudence.

Peter J. Kitson is Professor of English at the University of Dundee and has taught at the University of Exeter and the University of Wales, Bangor. His most recent publications include *Coleridge, Keats, and Shelley: Contemporary Critical Essays*; *Romanticism and Colonialism: Writing and Empire, 1780–1830* (with Tim Fulford); *Slavery, Abolition, and Emancipation* (with Debbie J. Lee); and *Travels, Explorations, and Empires* (with Fulford). He was the editor of *The Year's Work in English Studies* from 1994 to 2000.

Graham Law is Professor of English Studies at Waseda University, Tokyo. The author of *Serializing Fiction in the Victorian Press*, he has produced editions of Victorian novels including Dickens's *Hard Times* and *Great Expectations*. He also acts as coeditor of the *Wilkie Collins Society Journal*.

M. Clare Loughlin-Chow recently completed her dissertation at Oxford University on the relationship between Dickens's fiction and journalism. She recently served as Research Editor for the *New Dictionary of National Biography*. In addition to working as a Senior Research Fellow at Worcester College, Oxford, she acts as director of the college's visiting student program.

Kathleen McCormack, Associate Professor of English in the State University System of Florida, has written widely on Victorian literature. She is the author of *George Eliot and Intoxication: Dangerous Drugs for the Condition of England* and is currently working on a book-length biographical/critical project on George Eliot's travel within Britain.

William R. McKelvy is Assistant Professor of English at Washington University in St. Louis and has published essays on Tennyson, Macaulay, and the Victorian politician William Ewart Gladstone. He is currently working on *Priestcraft and the Cult of Literature*, a book about secularization and the literary imagination in Georgian and Victorian times.

Juliet McMaster is Professor of English at the University of Alberta, where she specializes in the eighteenth- and nineteenth-century English novel. She has published books on Thackeray, Trollope, Dickens, and Austen. In addition to coediting *The Cambridge Companion to Jane Austen*, she is the general editor of the Juvenilia Press, which involves students in the editing, annotating, illustrating, and publishing of early works by well-known authors.

Lillian Nayder is Associate Professor of English at Bates College, where she teaches courses on Victorian fiction and the English novel. In addition to authoring *Wilkie Collins*, she has published essays in various journals and collections. She is currently working on *Bleak House*, a biography of Catherine Dickens.

Edward Neill teaches literature at Middlesex University in London. His areas of research include modern poetry, literary theory, and eighteenth- and nineteenth-century literature. His books include *The Politics of Jane Austen*, *Trial by Ordeal: Hardy and the Critics*, and *The Secret Life of Thomas Hardy*. He has published widely in such journals as *Essays in Criticism*, *Cambridge Quarterly*, *Critical Quarterly*, and *English*.

James G. Nelson is Emeritus Professor of English at the University of Wisconsin, Madison. His trilogy of books on the literary publishers of the 1890s includes *The Early Nineties: A View from the Bodley Head*; *Elkin Mathews: Publisher to Yeats, Joyce, Pound*; and *Publisher to the Decadents: Leonard Smithers in the Careers of Beardsley, Wilde, Dowson*. He has published widely on Victorian poetry, prose, and the novel and has taught courses in the intellectual backgrounds of Victorian literature. He is the recipient of many research awards and grants including a Guggenheim fellowship and a Bibliographical Society of America fellowship.

K. M. Newton is Professor of English at the University of Dundee, Scotland. His publications include *George Eliot: Romantic Humanist*, *In Defense of Literary Interpretation: Theory and Practice*, and *Interpreting the Text*.

Russell Poole holds an M.A. in English from the University of Otago and a Ph.D. in Medieval Studies from the University of Toronto. He is a member of the faculty at Massey University, New Zealand. He is the author of *Viking Poems on War and Peace* and numerous other publications on medieval literature and Victorian fiction.

Barbara Quinn Schmidt is Emeritus Professor of English at Southern Illinois University at Edwardsville. She formerly served as editor of *Victorian Periodicals Review*, for which she recently edited special issues on the *Cornhill Magazine*, the subject of her dissertation and several articles.

Peter L. Shillingsburg is Professor of English at the University of North Texas. He is the author of *Pegasus in Harness: Victorian Publishing and W. M. Thackeray* and *W. M. Thackeray: A Literary Life*. He serves as general editor of the *Works of Thackeray*, a scholarly edition in progress from the University of Michigan Press.

Marianne Thormählen is Professor of English Literature at Lund University, Sweden. Her publications on T. S. Eliot include *The Waste Land: A Fragmentary Wholeness*, *Eliot's Animals*, and (as editor) *Eliot at the Turn of the Century*. She has also published on Restoration poetry, including *Rochester: The Poems in Context*. In addition to recently publishing *The Brontës and Religion*, she is currently editing a volume of papers entitled *Elusive Modernism*.

Michael H. Whitworth teaches Victorian and modernist literature at the University of Wales, Bangor. Articles by him on the relations of literature and science have appeared in *English Literature in Transition*, *Publishing History*, *Review of English Studies*, and the *Selected Papers* of the Eighth- and Ninth-Annual Virginia Woolf Conferences. He is currently completing a book on modernism and the new physics, and compiling a descriptive bibliography of Herbert Read.

Julian Wolfreys is Associate Professor of Victorian Literary and Cultural Studies at the University of Florida. He is the author and editor of numerous books, including *Writing London: The Trace of the Urban Text from Blake to Dickens*, *Deconstruction/Derrida*, *Peter Ackroyd: The Ludic and Labyrinthine Text* (with Jeremy Gibson), and *Readings: Acts of Close Reading in Literary Theory*. He is general editor of Palgrave's Transitions series.

Kenneth Womack is Assistant Professor of English at Penn State, Altoona. In addition to coauthoring *Recent Work in Critical Theory, 1989–1995: An Anno-

tated Bibliography and coediting the *Dictionary of Literary Biography*'s three-volume *British Book-Collectors and Bibliographers* series, he has published numerous articles on twentieth-century British and American literature and film, as well as on bibliography and textual criticism. He is editor of *Interdisciplinary Literary Studies: A Journal of Criticism and Theory*, correspondent for the *World Shakespeare Bibliography*, and associate editor of *George Eliot-George Henry Lewes Studies*.